Jerome
Charyn

**Once
upon a
droshky**

A NOVEL

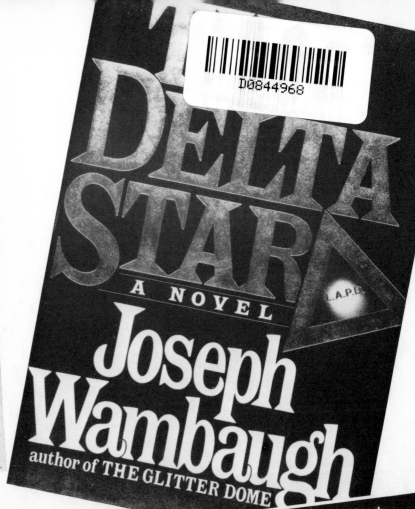

THE
**DELTA
STAR**

A NOVEL

L.A.P.D.

**Joseph
Wambaugh**

author of THE GLITTER DOME

D0844968

John Jakes

THE NEW NOVEL BY THE AUTHOR OF

The Kent Family Chronicles

NORTH
AND
SOUTH

CHRONICLE·OF·A
DEATH·FORETOLD
GABRIEL·GARCÍA·MÁRQUEZ

DICTIONARY OF LITERARY BIOGRAPHY YEARBOOK: 1983

Dictionary of Literary Biography

DICTIONARY OF LITERARY BIOGRAPHY YEARBOOK: 1983

Edited by
Mary Bruccoli
and
Jean W. Ross

Associate Editor
Richard Ziegfeld

A Bruccoli Clark Book
Gale Research Company • Book Tower • Detroit, Michigan 48226

Manufactured by Edwards Brothers, Inc.
Ann Arbor, Michigan
Printed in the United States of America

Library of Congress Catalog Card Number 82-645185
ISBN 0-8103-1627-7
ISSN 0731-7867

Contents

Plan of the Series

. . . Almost the most prodigious asset of a country, and perhaps its most precious possession, is its native literary product—when that product is fine and noble and enduring.

Mark Twain*

The advisory board, the editors, and the publisher of the *Dictionary of Literary Biography* are joined in endorsing Mark Twain's declaration. The literature of a nation provides an inexhaustible resource of permanent worth. It is our expectation that this endeavor will make literature and its creators better understood and more accessible to students and the literate public, while satisfying the standards of teachers and scholars.

To meet these requirements, *literary biography* has been construed in terms of the author's achievement. The most important thing about a writer is his writing. Accordingly, the entries in *DLB* are career biographies, tracing the development of the author's canon and the evolution of his reputation.

The publication plan for *DLB* resulted from two years of preparation. The project was proposed to Bruccoli Clark by Frederick G. Ruffner, president of the Gale Research Company, in November 1975. After specimen entries were prepared and typeset, an advisory board was formed to refine the entry format and develop the series rationale. In meetings held during 1976, the publisher, series editors, and advisory board approved the scheme for a comprehensive biographical dictionary of persons who contributed to North American literature. Editorial work on the first volume began in January 1977, and it was published in 1978.

In order to make *DLB* more than a reference tool and to compile volumes that individually have claim to status as literary history, it was decided to organize volumes by topic or period or genre. Each of these freestanding volumes provides a biographical-bibliographical guide and overview for a particular area of literature. We are convinced that this organization—as opposed to a single alphabet method—constitutes a valuable innovation in the presentation of reference material. The volume plan necessarily requires many decisions for the placement and treatment of authors who might properly be included in two or three volumes. In some instances a major figure will be included in separate volumes, but with different entries emphasizing the aspect of his career appropriate to each volume. Ernest Hemingway, for example, is represented in *American Writers in Paris, 1920-1939* by an entry focusing on his expatriate apprenticeship; he is also in *American Novelists, 1910-1945* with an entry surveying his entire career. Each volume includes a cumulative index of subject authors. The final *DLB* volume will be a comprehensive index to the entire series.

With volume ten in 1982 it was decided to enlarge the scope of *DLB* beyond the literature of the United States. By the end of 1983 twelve volumes treating British literature had been published, and volumes for Commonwealth and Modern European literature were in progress. The series has been further augmented by the *DLB Yearbooks* (since 1981) which update published entries and add new entries to keep the *DLB* current with contemporary activity. There have also been occasional *DLB Documentary Series* volumes which provide biographical and critical background source materials for figures whose work is judged to have particular interest for students. One of these companion volumes is entirely devoted to Tennessee Williams.

The purpose of *DLB* is not only to provide reliable information in a convenient format but also to place the figures in the larger perspective of literary history and to offer appraisals of their accomplishments by qualified scholars.

We define literature as the *intellectual commerce of a nation*: not merely as belles lettres, but as that ample and complex process by which ideas are generated, shaped, and transmitted. *DLB* entries are not limited to "creative writers" but extend to other figures who in this time and in this way influenced the mind of a people. Thus there will be volumes for historians, journalists, publishers, and screenwriters. By this means readers of *DLB* may be aided to perceive literature not as cult scripture in the keeping of cultural high priests, but as at the center of a nation's life.

DLB includes the major writers appropriate to each volume and those standing in the ranks immediately behind them. Scholarly and critical counsel has been sought in deciding which minor figures to include and how full their entries should be.

*From an unpublished section of Mark Twain's autobiography, copyright © by the Mark Twain Company.

Wherever possible, useful references will be made to figures who do not warrant separate entries.

Each *DLB* volume has a volume editor responsible for planning the volume, selecting the figures for inclusion, and assigning the entries. Volume editors are also responsible for preparing, where appropriate, appendices surveying the major periodicals and literary and intellectual movements for their volumes, as well as lists of further readings. Work on the series as a whole is coordinated at the Bruccoli Clark editorial center in Columbia, South Carolina, where the editorial staff is responsible for the accuracy of the published volumes.

One feature that distinguishes *DLB* is the illustration policy—its concern with the iconography of literature. Just as an author is influenced by his surroundings, so is the reader's understanding of the author enhanced by a knowledge of his environment. Therefore *DLB* volumes include not only drawings, paintings, and photographs of authors, often depicting them at various stages in their careers, but also illustrations of their families and places where they lived. Title pages are regularly reproduced in facsimile along with dust jackets for modern authors. The dust jackets are a special feature of *DLB* because they often document better than anything else the way in which an author's work was launched in its own time. Specimens of the writers' manuscripts are included when feasible.

A supplement to *DLB*—tentatively titled *A Guide, Chronology, and Glossary for American Literature*—will outline the history of literature in North America and trace the influences that shaped it. This volume will provide a framework for the study of American literature by means of chronological tables, literary affiliation charts, glossarial entries, and concise surveys of the major movements. It has been planned to stand on its own as a vade mecum, providing a ready-reference guide to the study of American literature as well as a companion to the *DLB* volumes for American literature.

Samuel Johnson rightly decreed that "The chief glory of every people arises from its authors." The purpose of the *Dictionary of Literary Biography* is to compile literary history in the surest way available to us—by accurate and comprehensive treatment of the lives and work of those who contributed to it.

The *DLB* Advisory Board

Foreword

The *Dictionary of Literary Biography Yearbook* is guided by the same principles that have provided the basic rationale for the entire *DLB* series: 1) the literature of a nation represents an inexhaustible resource of permanent worth; 2) the surest way to trace the outlines of literary history is by a comprehensive treatment of the lives and works of those who contributed to it; and 3) the greatest service the series can provide is to make literary achievement better understood and more accessible to students and the literate public, while serving the needs of scholars. In keeping with those principles, the *Yearbook* has been planned to augment *DLB* by reflecting the vitality of contemporary literature and summarizing current literary activity. The librarian, scholar, or student attempting to stay informed of literary developments is faced with an endless task. The purpose of *DLB Yearbook* is to serve these readers while at the same time enlarging the scope of *DLB*.

DLB Yearbook is divided into four sections: articles about the past year's literary events or topics; obituaries and tributes; updates of published *DLB* entries; and new author entries. The articles section features essays which discuss the year's work in literary biography, fiction, poetry, and drama. The *Yearbook* also endeavors to cover major prizes and conferences; this volume covers the 1983 Nobel Prize in Literature (including the Swedish Academy's announcement, William Golding's acceptance speech, and appreciations of his work), the Strauss Livings awards (including interviews with recipients Cynthia Ozick and Raymond Carver), and the Vladimir Nabokov Festival at Cornell University. Each year a literary research archive will be described; the 1983 *Yearbook* includes an account of the Berg Collection in the New York Public Library by its curator. Literary topics of current interest will also be explored: in this *Yearbook* there is a report on the Public Lending Right system in the United Kingdom and comments by American writers on a proposed PLR for the United States. In addition, there is a report on the Center for the Book of the Library of Congress by its director. A special feature of the first section is an interview with a distinguished practicing biographer.

The death of a literary figure prompts an as-

sessment of his achievement and reputation. The obituaries and tributes section marks the passing of seven authors in 1983. Comments from the authors' contemporaries have been solicited, as in the cases of William Goyen, Kenneth Millar (Ross Macdonald), and Tennessee Williams.

Updated Entries in the third section are designed to supplement the *DLB* series with current information about the literary activities of authors who have entries in previously published *DLB* volumes. Each Updated Entry takes as its point of departure an already published *DLB* entry, augmenting primary and secondary bibliographical information, providing descriptions and assessments of new works, and, when necessary, reassessing an author's reputation. Exclusive interviews are included in the Updated Entries section: George Garrett is interviewed for the 1983 *Yearbook*. The form of entry is similar to that in the standard *DLB* series, and each Updated Entry is preceded by a reference to the *DLB* volume in which the basic entry on the subject appears. Readers seeking information about an author's entire career should consult the basic entry along with the Updated Entry for complete biographical and bibliographical information.

The fourth section is devoted to New Entries on figures not previously included in *DLB*. These entries follow the established format for the series: emphasis is placed on biography and summaries of the critical reception of the authors' works; primary bibliographies precede each entry, and a list of references follows the entry. As with Updated Entries, New Entries may be followed by exclusive *Yearbook* interviews. The 1983 volume includes interviews with David Bottoms, Kelly Cherry, John Jakes, Alfred Coppel, and Jonathan Penner.

Each *Yearbook* includes a list of literary prizes and awards, a necrology, and a checklist of books about literary history and biography published during the year.

From the outset, the *DLB* series has undertaken to compile literary history as it is revealed in the lives and works of authors. The *Yearbook* supports that commitment, providing a useful and necessary current record. The march of literature does not halt.

Acknowledgments

This book was produced by BC Research. Karen L. Rood is senior editor for the *Dictionary of Literary Biography* series.

The production manager is Lynne C. Zeigler. Art supervisor is Claudia Ericson. The production staff included Mary Betts, Rowena Betts, Patricia Coate, Lynn Felder, Kathleen M. Flanagan, Joyce Fowler, Laura Ingram, Patricia C. Sharpe, Joycelyn R. Smith, and Meredith Walker. Jean W. Ross is permissions editor. Joseph Caldwell, photography editor, did the photographic copy work for the volume.

Walter W. Ross did the library research with the assistance of the staff at the Thomas Cooper Library of the University of South Carolina: Lynn Barron, Sue Collins, Michael Freeman, Gary Geer, Alexander M. Gilchrist, Jens Holley, David Lincove, Marcia Martin, Jean Rhyne, Karen Rissling, Paula Swope, and Ellen Tillett. Valuable help was given also by the South Caroliniana Library at the University of South Carolina, and by staff members of the Richland County Public Library in Columbia, South Carolina: Information Services staff Sarah Linder, Sarah Shaw, Helen Young, Dot Wilson, Jennifer Walker, Maryann Fowler, and Tine Culler; and Periodicals staff Janice Yelton and Cathy Barber.

The following publishers kindly provided photographs for the volume: Atheneum; Black Sparrow Press; Harper and Row; Alfred A. Knopf; Little, Brown and Company; New Directions; Pantheon; Clarkson N. Potter; and the University of Pittsburgh Press.

Special thanks are due to the Swedish Embassy in Washington, D.C., and the Swedish Academy; to the Center for the Book in the Library of Congress; to the office of Sen. Charles McC. Mathias, Jr.; and to the Berg Collection, New York Public Library.

DICTIONARY OF LITERARY BIOGRAPHY YEARBOOK: 1983

Dictionary of Literary Biography

The 1983 Nobel Prize in Literature

ANNOUNCEMENT BY THE SWEDISH ACADEMY

William Golding's first novel—*Lord of the Flies* (1954)—rapidly became a world success and has so remained. It has reached readers who can be numbered in tens of millions. In other words, the book was a bestseller, in a way that is usually granted only to adventure stories, light reading and children's books. The same goes for several of his later novels, including *Rites of Passage*, 1980.

The reason is simple. These books *are* very entertaining and exciting. They can be read with pleasure and profit without the need to make much effort with learning or acumen. But they have also aroused an unusually great interest in professional literary critics, scholars, writers, and other interpreters, who have sought and found deep strata of ambiguity and complication in Golding's work. In those who use the tools of narration and linguistic art they have incited to thinking, discovery, and creation of their own, in order to explore the world we live in and to settle down in it. In this respect William Golding can perhaps be compared to another Englishman, Jonathan Swift, who has also become a writer for the learned and the unlearned, or to the American Herman Melville, whose works are full of equivocal profundity as well as fascinating adventure. In fact the resemblance extends farther than that. Golding has a very keen sight and sharp pen when it comes to the power of evil and baseness in human beings—just like Jonathan Swift. And like Herman Melville he often chooses his themes and the framework for his stories from the world of the sea or from other challenging situations in which odd people are tempted to reach beyond their limits, thereby being bared to the very marrow. His stories usually have a fairly schematic

drama, almost an anecdote, as skeleton. He then covers this with a richly varied and spicy flesh of colorful characters and surprising events.

William Golding can be said to be a writer of myths. It is the pattern of myth that we find in his manner of writing.

A very few basic experiences and basic conflicts of a deeply general nature underlie all his work as motive power. In one of his essays he describes how as a young man he took an optimistic view of existence. He believed that man would be able to perfect himself by improving society and eventually doing away with all social evil. His optimism was akin to that of other utopians, for instance H. G. Wells.

The Second World War changed his outlook. He discovered what one human being is really able to do to another. And it was not a question of headhunters in New Guinea or primitive tribes in the Amazon region. They were atrocities committed with cold professional skill by well-educated and cultured people—doctors, lawyers, and those with a long tradition of high civilization behind them. They carried out their crimes against their own equals. He writes:

"I must say that anyone who moved through those years without understanding that man produces evil as a bee produces honey, must have been blind or wrong in the head."

Golding inveighs against those who think that it is the political or other systems that create evil. Evil springs from the depths of man himself—it is the wickedness in human beings that creates the evil systems or that changes what from the beginning is, or could be, good into something iniquitous and destructive.

There is a mighty religious dimension in Wil-

3

The Bookseller, *15 October 1983*

liam Golding's conception of the world, though hardly Christian in the ordinary sense. He seems to believe in a kind of Fall. Perhaps rather one should say that he works with the myth of a Fall. In some of his stories, chiefly the novel *The Inheritors* (1955), we find a dream of an original state of innocence in the history of mankind—a prehistoric race or breed of animals, poor in words but rich in pictures and wordless communication, a peaceful existence with the women or female qualities in the lead. The Fall came with the motive power of a new species. The aggressive intelligence, the power-hungry self-assertion, and the overweening individualism are the source of evil and violence—individual as well as social violence. But these qualities and incentives are also innate in man's nature, in man as a created being. They are therefore inseparably a part of his character and make themselves felt when he gives full expression to himself and forms his societies and his private destiny.

We come across this tragic drama in many different ways in William Golding's novels. In *Lord of the Flies* a group of young boys are isolated on a desert island. Soon a kind of primitive society takes shape and is split into warring factions, one marked by decency and willingness to cooperate, the other by worship of force, lust for power, and violence. In *The Pyramid* (1967) we find similar tensions in a more everyday setting—an English country town. The social class differences exercise an insidious but equally ruthless violence in an existence full of lovelessness and prejudiced hypocrisy. The novel *Pincher Martin* (1956) depicts how the main character, the narrator, is drowning. Actually he is already dead or dying as he tells his story. In his passionate absorption in himself he seems for a time to get the better of death. He does so by recounting his life to himself, a life full of ruthless egoism and cruelty to others, a miserable life, yet it was *his* and on no account does he want to lose it. He, the dead man, tries to make the rock to which he is clinging into a picture of himself. It is a weird ghost story, a fable of a will to live without shame or moderation.

In the novel *Rites of Passage*, the drama is enacted in the microcosm that the author arranges on a ship of the line at the beginning of the nineteenth century. The book gives a cruel and drastic description of social barriers and aggressions on this ship, with an underlying black comedy and a masterly command of the characters' various linguistic roles. The scapegoat—one of many in Golding's works—is a priest who, naively trusting in the authority of his office, tries to assert his own dignity. He is subjected to outrages, each worse than

the last, himself taking part in them, and ends up in such a desperate situation that he dies of shame.

The title of the previous novel, *Darkness Visible* (1979), alludes to Milton's depiction of hell. It is a complicated book which in many ways sums up the author's view of mankind and the world, such as one can fancy it to be in his work. The novel can be regarded as a description of hell or of purgatory here on earth. The advocates of evil appear with almost diabolical traits in the form of two beautiful young girls, who are driven by a liking for evil for its own sake. Opposed to them is yet another of Golding's scapegoats—a young man born out of a blazing inferno in London during the Blitz and on a pilgrimage in a world without mercy towards his own destruction, again through fire. He is both human being, pitiful and weak as such, and something more, in league with powers of another kind, whether they belong to a superhuman region or to an all too human world of fancies and illusions. *Darkness Visible* is a dualistic book—one is tempted to say an illustration in myth form of a Manichean philosophy with good and evil as two independent forces in life.

All is not evil in the world of mankind, and all is not black in William Golding's imagined world. According to him, man has two characteristics—the ability to murder is one, belief in God the other. Innocence is not entirely lost. The new race, which defeated its predecessors in *The Inheritors*, became mixed with features from the conquered. There is a striving away from evil. This striving often goes astray in self-assertion and illusionism. But it is there nevertheless and is allied with something that is not merely human. In the novel *The Spire* (1964), this striving is embodied in a story about the building of a medieval cathedral. The builder is a priest who believes he has been ordered by God to build a spire that defies all reasonable calculations and measurements. His striving is both good and bad, containing the most complex reasons—humility and conviction but also arrogance, wilfulness, and furtive sexual motives. Despite its taut and composite form the novel is one of Golding's most diversified and significant works.

William Golding's novels and stories are, however, not only sombre moralities and dark myths about evil and about treacherous, destructive forces. As already mentioned, they are also colorful tales of adventure which can be read as such, full of narrative joy, inventiveness, and excitement. In addition there are plentiful streaks of humor, biting irony, comedy and drastic jesting. There is a vitality which breaks through what is tragic and misanthropic, frightening in fact. A vitality, a vigor, which is infectious owing to its strength and intractability and to the paradoxical freedom it possesses as against what is related. In this too Golding reminds us of the predecessors mentioned at the beginning. His fabled world is tragic and pathetic, yet not overwhelming and depressing. There is a life which is mightier than life's conditions.

BOOKS: *Poems* (London: Macmillan, 1934; New York: Macmillan, 1935);

Lord of the Flies (London: Faber & Faber, 1954; New York: Coward-McCann, 1955);

The Inheritors (London: Faber & Faber, 1955; New York: Harcourt, Brace & World, 1962);

Pincher Martin (London: Faber & Faber, 1956); republished as *The Two Deaths of Christopher Martin* (New York: Harcourt, Brace & World, 1957);

Sometime, Never: Three Tales of Imagination (London: Eyre & Spottiswoode, 1956; New York: Ballantine, 1962);

Free Fall (London: Faber & Faber, 1959; New York: Harcourt, Brace & World, 1960);

The Spire (London: Faber & Faber, 1964; New York: Harcourt, Brace & World, 1964);

The Hot Gates and Other Occasional Pieces (London: Faber & Faber, 1965; New York: Harcourt, Brace & World, 1967);

The Pyramid (London: Faber & Faber, 1967; New York: Harcourt, Brace & World, 1967);

The Scorpion God: Three Short Novels (London: Faber & Faber, 1971; New York: Harcourt Brace Jovanovich, 1972);

Darkness Visible (London: Faber & Faber, 1979; New York: Farrar, Straus & Giroux, 1979);

Rites of Passage (London: Faber & Faber, 1980; New York: Farrar, Straus & Giroux, 1980).

NOBEL LECTURE 1983
by
William Golding

Those of you who have some knowledge of your present speaker as revealed by the loftier-minded section of the British Press will be resigning yourselves to a half hour of unrelieved gloom. Indeed, your first view of me, white bearded and ancient, may have turned that gloom into profound dark; dark, dark, dark, amid the blaze of noon, irrecoverably dark, total eclipse. But the case is not as hard as that. I am among the older of the Nobel Laureates and therefore might well be excused a touch of—let me whisper the word—frivolity. Pray do not misunderstand me. I have no dancing girls, alas. I shall not sing to you or juggle or clown—or shall I juggle? I wonder! How can a man who has been defined as a pessimist indulge in anything as frivolous as juggling?

You see it is hard enough at any age to address so learned a gathering as this. The very thought induces a certain solemnity. Then again, what about the dignity of age? There is, they say, no fool like an old fool.

Well, there is no fool like a middle-aged fool either. Twenty-five years ago I accepted the label "pessimist" thoughtlessly without realising that it was going to be tied to my tail, as it were, in something the way that, to take an example from another art, Rachmaninoff's famous Prelude in C sharp minor was tied to him. No audience would allow him off the concert platform until he played it. Similarly critics have dug into my books until they could come up with something that looked hopeless. I can't think why. I don't feel hopeless myself. Indeed I tried to reverse the process by explaining myself. Under some critical interrogation I named myself a universal pessimist but a cosmic optimist. I should have thought that anyone with an ear for language would understand that I was allowing more connotation than denotation to the word "cosmic" though in derivation universal and cosmic mean the same thing. I meant, of course, that when I consider a universe which the scientist constructs by a set of rules which stipulate that his constructs must be repeatable and identical, then I am a pessimist and bow down before the great god Entropy. I am optimistic when I consider the spiritual dimension which the scientist's discipline forces him to ignore. So world wide is the fame of the Nobel Prize that people have taken to quoting from my works and I do not see why I should not join in this fashionable pastime. Twenty years ago I tried to put the difference between the two kinds of experience in the mind of one of my characters, and made a mess of it.

He was in prison. "All day long the trains run on rails. Eclipses are predictable. Penicillin cures pneumonia and the atom splits to order. All day long year in year out the daylight explanation drives back the mystery and reveals a reality usable, understandable and detached. The scalpel and the microscope fail. The oscilloscope moves closer to behaviour.

"But then, all day long action is weighed in the balance and found not opportune nor fortunate nor ill-advised but good or evil. For this mode which we call the spirit breathes through the universe and does not touch it: touches only the dark things held prisoner, incommunicado touches, judges, sentences and passes on. Both worlds are real. There is no bridge."

What amuses me is the thought that of course there is a bridge and that if anything it has been thrust out from the side that least expected it, and thrust out since those words were written. For we know now, that the universe had a beginning. (Indeed, as an aside I might say we always *did* know. I offer you a simple proof and forbid you to examine it. If there was no beginning then infinite time had already passed and we could never have got to the moment where we are.) We also know or it is at least scientifically respectable to postulate that at the centre of a black hole the laws of nature no longer apply. Since most scientists are just a bit religious and most religious are seldom wholly unscientific we find humanity in a comical position. His scientific intellect believes in the possibility of miracles inside a black hole while his religious intellect believes in them outside it. Both, in fact, now believe in miracles, credimus quia absurdum est. Glory be to God in the highest. You will get no reductive pessimism from me.

A greater danger facing you is that an ancient schoolmaster may be carried away and forget he is not addressing a class of pupils. A man in his seventies may be tempted to think he has seen it all and knows it all. He may think that mere length of years is a guarantee of wisdom and a permit for the issuing of admonition and advice. Poor young Shakespeare and Beethoven, he thinks, dead in their youth at a mere fifty-two or three! What could young fellows such as that know about anything? But at midnight perhaps, when the clock strikes and another year has passed he may occasionally brood on the disadvantages of age rather than the advantages. He may regard more thoughtfully a sentence which has been called the poetry of the fact, a sentence that one of those young fellows stumbled across accidentally, as it were, since he was never old enough to have worked the thing out through living. "Men," he wrote, "must endure their going hence, even as their coming hither." Such a consideration may modify the essential jollity of an old man's nature. Is the old man right to be happy? Is there not something unbecoming in his cheerful view of his own end? The words of another English poet seem to rebuke him.

King David and King Solomon
Led merry, merry lives,
With many, many lady friends
And many, many wives;
But when old age crept over them,
With many, many qualms,
King Solomon wrote the Proverbs
And King David wrote the Psalms.

Powerful stuff that, there's no doubt about it. But there are two views of the matter; and since I have quoted to you some of my prose which is generally regarded as poetic I will now quote to you some of my Goon or McGonagall poetry which may well be regarded as prosaic.

Sophocles the eminent Athenian
Gave as his final opinion
That death of love in the breast
Was like escape from a wild beast.
What better word could you get?

He was eighty when he said that,
But Ninon de L'Enclos
When asked the same question said, no
She was uncommonly matey
At eighty.

Evidently age need not wither us nor custom stale our infinite variety. Let us be, for a while, not serious but considerate. I myself face another danger. I do not speak in a small tribal language as it might be one of the six hundred languages of Nigeria. Of course the value of any language is incalculable. Your Laureate of 1979 the Greek poet Elytis made quite clear that the relative value of works of literature is not to be decided by counting heads. It is, I think, the greatest tribute one can pay your committees that they have consistently sought for value in a work without heeding how many people can or cannot read it. The young John Keats spoke of Greek poets who "died content on pleasant sward, leaving great verse unto a little clan." Indeed and indeed, small can be beautiful. To quote yet another poet—prose writer though I am—you will have begun to realise where my heart is—Ben Jonson said:

It is not growing like a tree
In bulk, doth make man better be,
Or standing long an oak, three hundred year,
To fall a log at last, dry, bald and sere:
A lily of a day,
Is fairer far in May,
Although it fall and die that night;

It was the plant and flower of light.
In small proportions we just beauties see,
And in short measures, life may perfect be.

My own language, English, I believe to have a store of poets, of writers that need not fear comparison with those of any other language, ancient or modern. But today that language may suffer from too wide a use rather than too narrow a one—may be an oak rather than a lily. It spreads right round the world as the medium of advertisement, navigation, science, negotiation, conference. A hundred political parties have it daily in their mouths. Perhaps a language subjected to such strains as that may become, here and there, just a little thin. In English a man may think he is addressing a small, distinguished audience, or his family or his friends, perhaps; he is brooding aloud or talking in his sleep. Later he finds that without meaning to he has been addressing a large segment of the world. That is a daunting thought. It is true that this year, surrounded and outnumbered as I am by American laureates, I take a quiet pleasure in the consideration that though variants of my mother tongue may be spoken by a greater number of people than are to be found in an island off the West coast of Europe nevertheless they are speaking dialects of what is still centrally English. Personally I cannot tell whether those many dialects are being rendered mutually incomprehensible by distance faster than they are being unified by television and satellites; but at the moment the English writer faces immediate comprehension or partial comprehension by a good part of a billion people. His critics are limited in number only by the number of the people who can read his work. Nor can he escape from knowing the worst. No matter how obscure the publication that has disembowelled him, some kind correspondent—let us call him "X"—will send the article along together with an indignant assurance that he, "X," does not agree with a word of it. I think apprehensively of the mark I present, once A Moving Target but now, surely a fixed one, before the serried ranks of those who can shoot at me if they choose. Even my most famous and distinguished fellow laureate and fellow countryman Winston Churchill did not escape. A critic remarked with acid wit of his getting the award, "Was it for his poetry or his prose?" Indeed it was considerations such as these which have given me, I suppose, more difficulty in conceiving, let alone writing this lecture than any piece of comparable length since those distant days when I wrote essays on set subjects at school. The only difference I can find is that today I write at a larger desk and the marks I shall get for my performance will be more widely reported.

Now when, you may say, is the man going to say something about the subject which is alleged to be his own? He should be talking about the novel! Well, I will for a while, but only for a while, and as it were, tangentially. The truth is that though each of the subjects for which the prizes are awarded has its own and unique importance, none can exist wholly to itself. Even the novel, if it climbs into an ivory tower will find no audience except those with ivory towers of their own. I used to think that the outlook for the novel was poor. Let me quote myself again. I speak of boys growing up—not exceptional boy, but average boy.

Boys do not evaluate a book. They divide books into categories. There are sexy books, war books, westerns, travel books, science fiction. A boy will accept anything from a section he knows rather than risk another sort. He has to have the label on the bottle to know it is the mixture as before. You must put his detective story in a green paperback or he may suffer the hardship of reading a book in which nobody is murdered at all;—I am thinking of the plodders, the amiable majority of us, not particularly intelligent or gifted; well-disposed, but left high and dry among a mass of undigested facts with their scraps of saleable technology. What chance has literature of competing with the defined categories of entertainment which are laid on for them at every hour of the day? I do not see how literature is to be for them anything but simple, repetitive and a stop-gap for when there are no westerns on the telly. They will have a far less brutish life than their nineteenth century ancestors, no doubt. They will believe less and fear less. But just as bad money drives out good, so inferior culture drives out superior. With any capacity to make value judgements vitiated or undeveloped, what mass future is there, then, for poetry, for belles-lettres, for real fearlessness in the theatre, for the novel which tries to look at life anew—in a word, for intransigence?

I wrote that some twenty years ago I believe and the process as far as the novel is concerned has developed but not improved. The categories are more and more defined. Competition from other media is fiercer still. Well, after all the novel has no built-in claims on immortality.

"Story" of course is a different matter. We like to hear of succession of events and as an inspection of our press will demonstrate have only a marginal interest in whether the succession of events is minutely true or not. Like the late Mr. Sam Goldwyn who wanted a story which began with an earthquake and worked up to a climax, we like a good lead in but have most pleasure in a succession of events with a satisfactory end-point. Most simply and directly—when children holler and yell because of some infant tragedy or tedium, at once when we take them on our knee and begin shouting if necessary—"once upon a time" they fall silent and attentive. Story will always be with us. But story in a physical book, in a sentence what the West means by "a novel"—what of that? Certainly, if the form fails let it go. We have enough complications in life, in art, in literature without preserving dead forms fossilised, without cluttering ourselves with Byzantine sterilities. Yes, in that case, let the novel go. But what goes with it? Surely something of profound importance to the human spirit! A novel ensures that we can look before and after, take action at whatever pace we choose, read again and again, skip and go back. The story in a book is humble and serviceable, available, friendly, is not switched on and off but taken up and put down, lasts a lifetime.

Put simply the novel stands between us and the hardening concept of statistical man. There is no other medium in which we can live for so long and so intimately with a character. That is the service a novel renders. It performs no less an act than the rescue and the preservation of the individuality and dignity of the single being, be it man, woman or child. No other art, I claim, can so thread in and out of a single mind and body, so live another life. It does ensure that at the very least a human being shall be seen to be more than just one billionth of one billion.

I spoke of the ivory tower and the unique importance of each of our studies. Now I must add, having said my bit about the novel—that those studies converge, literature with the rest. Put bluntly, we face two problems—either we blow ourselves off the face of the earth or we degrade the fertility of the earth bit by bit until we have ruined it. Does it take a writer of fiction to bring you the cold comfort of pointing out that the problems are mutually exclusive? The one problem, the instant catastrophe, is not to be dealt with here. It would be irresponsible of me to turn this platform into a stage for acting out some anti-atomic harangue and equally irresponsible at this juncture in history for me to ignore our perils. You know them as well as I do. As so often, when the unspeakable is to be spoken, the unthinkable thought, it is Shakespeare we

must turn to; and I can only quote Hamlet with the skull:

> Not one now, to mock your own grinning? Quite chop-fallen? Now get you to my lady's chamber and tell her, let her paint an inch thick, to this favour she must come; make her laugh at that.

I am being rather unfair to the lady, perhaps, for there will be skulls of all shapes and sizes and sexes. I speak tangentially. No other quotation gives the dirt of it all, another kind of poetry of the fact. I must say something of this danger and I have said it for I could do no less. Now as far as this matter is concerned, I have done.

The other danger is the more difficult to combat. To quote another laureate, our race may end not with a bang but a whimper. It must be nearer seventy years ago than sixty that I first discovered and engaged myself to a magic place. This was on the west coast of our country. It was on the seashore among rocks. I early became acquainted with the wonderful interplay of earth and moon and sun, enjoying them at the same time as I was assured that scientifically you could not have action influenced at a distance. There was a particular phase of the moon at which the tide sank more than usually far down and revealed to me a small recess which I remember as a cavern. There was plenty of life of one sort or another round all the rocks and in the pools among them. But this pool, farthest down and revealed, it seemed, by an influence from the sky only once or twice during the times when I had the holiday privilege of living near it—this last recess before the even more mysterious deep sea had strange inhabitants which I had found nowhere else. I can now remember and even feel but alas not describe the peculiar engagement, excitement, and, no, not sympathy or empathy, but passionate recognition of a living thing in all its secrecy and strangeness. It was or rather they were real as I was. It was as if the centre of our universe was there for my eyes to reach at like hands, to seize on by sight. Only a hand's breadth away in the last few inches of still water they flowered, grey, green and purple, palpably alive, a discovery, a meeting, more than an interest or pleasure. They were life, we together were delight itself; until the first ripples of returning water blurred and hid them. When the summer holidays were over and I went back again about as far from the sea as you can get in England I carried with me like a private treasure the memory of that cave—no, in some strange way I took the cave with me and its creatures that flowered so strangely. In nights of sleeplessness and fear of the supernatural I would work out the phase of the moon, returning in thought to the slither and clamber among the weeds of the rocks. There were times when, though I was far away, I found myself before the cavern watching the moon-dazzle as the water sank and was comforted somehow by the magical beauty of our common world.

I have been back, since. The recess—for now it seems no more than that—is still there, and at low water springs if you can bend down far enough you can still look inside. Nothing lives there any more. It is all very clean now, ironically so, clean sand, clean water, clean rock. Where the living creatures once clung they have worn two holes like the orbits of eyes, so that you might well sentimentalize yourself into the fancy that you are looking at a skull. No life.

Was it a natural process? Was it fuel oil? Was it sewage or chemicals more deadly that killed my childhood's bit of magic and mystery? I cannot tell and it does not matter. What matters is that this is only one tiny example among millions of how we are impoverishing the only planet we have to live on.

Well now, what has literature to say to that? We have computers and satellites, we have ingenuities of craft that can land a complex machine on a distant planet and get reports back. And so on. You know it all as well and better than I. Literature has words only, surely a tool as primitive as the flint axe or even the soft copper chisel with which man first carved his own likeness in stone. That tool makes a poor showing one would think among the products of the silicon chip. But remember Churchill. For despite the cynical critic, he got the Nobel Prize neither for poetry nor prose. He got it for about a single page of simple sentences which are neither poetry nor prose but for what, I repeat, has been called finely the poetry of the fact. He got it for those passionate utterances which were the very stuff of human courage and defiance. Those of us who lived through those times know that Churchill's poetry of the fact changed history.

Perhaps then the soft copper chisel is not so poor a tool after all. Words may, through the devotion, the skill, the passion and the luck of writers prove to be the most powerful thing in the world. They may move men to speak to each other because some of those words somewhere express not just what the writer is thinking but what a huge segment of the world is thinking. They may allow man to speak to man, the man in the street to speak to his fellow until a ripple becomes a tide running through every nation—of commonsense, of simple

healthy caution, a tide that rulers and negotiators cannot ignore so that nation does truly speak unto nation. Then there is hope that we may learn to be temperate, provident, taking no more from nature's treasury than is our due. It may be by books, stories, poetry, lectures we who have the ear of mankind can move man a little nearer the perilous safety of a warless and provident world. It cannot be done by the mechanical constructs of overt propaganda. I cannot do it myself, cannot now create stories which would help to make man aware of what he is doing; but there are others who can, many others. There always have been. We need more humanity, more care, more love. There are those who expect a political system to produce that; and others who expect the love to produce the system. My own faith is that the truth of the future lies between the two and we shall behave humanly and a bit humanely, stumbling along, haphazardly generous and gallant, foolishly and meanly wise until the rape of our planet is seen to be the preposterous folly that it is.

For we are a marvel of creation. I think in particular of one of the most extraordinary women, dead now these five hundred years, Juliana of Norwich. She was caught up in the spirit and shown a thing that might lie in the palm of her hand and in the bigness of a nut. She was told it was the world. She was told of the strange and wonderful and awful things that would happen there. At the last, a voice told her that all things should be well and all manner of things should be well and all things should be very well.

Now we, if not in the spirit, have been caught up to see our earth, our mother, Gaia Mater, set like a jewel in space. We have no excuse now for supposing her riches inexhaustible nor the area we have to live on limitless because unbounded. We are the children of that great blue white jewel. Through our mother we are part of the solar system and part through that of the whole universe. In the blazing poetry of the fact we are children of the stars.

I had better come down, I think. Churchill, Juliana of Norwich, let alone Ben Jonson and Shakespeare—Lord, what company we keep! Reputations grow and dwindle and the brightest of laurels fade. That very practical man, Julius Caesar—whom I always think of for a reason you may guess at, as Field Marshal Lord Caesar—Julius Caesar is said to have worn a laurel wreath to conceal his baldness. While it may be proper to praise the idea of a laureate the man himself may very well remember what his laurels will hide and that not only baldness. In a sentence he must remember not to take himself with unbecoming seriousness. Fortunately some spirit or other—I do not presume to put a name to it—ensured that I should remember my smallness in the scheme of things. The very day after I learned that I was the laureate for literature for 1983 I drove into a country town and parked my car where I should not. I only left the car for a few minutes but when I came back there was a ticket taped to the window. A traffic warden, a lady of minatory aspect, stood by the car. She pointed to a notice on the wall. "Can't you read?" she said. Sheepishly I got into my car and drove very slowly round the corner. There on the pavement I saw two county policemen. I stopped opposite them and took my parking ticket out of its plastic envelope. They crossed the road to me. I asked if, as I had pressing business, I could go straight to the Town Hall and pay my fine on the spot. "No, sir," said the senior policeman, "I'm afraid you can't do that." He smiled the fond smile that such policemen reserve for those people who are clearly harmless if a bit silly. He indicated a rectangle on the ticket that had the words 'name and address of sender' printed above it. "You should write your name and address in that place," he said. "You make out a cheque for ten pounds, making it payable to the Clerk to the Justices at *this* address written here. Then you write the same address on the outside of the envelope, stick a sixteen penny stamp in the top right hand corner of the envelope then post it. And may we congratulate you on winning the Nobel Prize for Literature."

THE STATURE OF WILLIAM GOLDING

Mark Dolan
University of South Carolina

The television cameras catch William Golding riding his horse across the Wiltshire countryside and relay his image for a moment to millions of living rooms. A white beard softens the seventy-two years chiseled in his face, and his thin hair floats in the wind as he rides. Yet the British novelist who wrote *Lord of the Flies*, the book that became required adolescent fiction in the 1960s, still exudes a kind of kid toughness, an irrepressible spunk that suggests Golding's life and works are all an affirmation of our potential, a reminder of our limitations, a chronicle of our birth, growth, and death.

When William Golding was awarded the

Roger and Ralph moved on, this time leaving Jack in the rear, for all his brave words. They came to the flat top where the rock was hard to hands and knees.

A creature that bulged.

Ralph put his hand in the cold, soft ashes of the fire and smothered a cry. His hand and shoulder were twitching from the unlooked-for contact. Green lights of nausea appeared for a moment and ate into the darkness. Roger lay behind him and Jack's mouth was at his ear.

"Over there, where there used to be a gap in the rock. A sort of hump—see?"

Ashes blew into Ralph's face from the dead fire. He could not see the gap or anything else, because the green lights were opening again and growing, and the top of the mountain was sliding sideways.

Once more, from a distance, he heard Jack's whisper.

"Scared?"

Not scared so much as paralyzed; hung up here immovable on the top of a diminishing, moving mountain. Jack slid away from him, Roger bumped, fumbled with a hiss of breath, and passed onwards. He heard them whispering.

"Can you see anything?"

"There—"

In front of them, only three or four yards away, was a rock-like hump where no rock should be. Ralph could hear a tiny chattering noise coming from somewhere—perhaps from his own mouth. He bound himself together with his will, fused his fear and loathing into a hatred, and stood up. He took two leaden steps forward.

Behind them the sliver of moon had drawn clear of the horizon. Before them, something like a great ape was sitting asleep with its head between its knees. Then the wind roared in the forest, there was confusion in the darkness and the creature lifted its head, holding toward them the ruin of a face.

Ralph found himself taking giant strides among the ashes, heard other creatures crying out and leaping and dared the impossible on the dark slope; presently the mountain was deserted, save for the three abandoned sticks and the thing that bowed.

—from Lord of the Flies

Nobel Prize this year, he told the newspapers he was awed, overwhelmed, delighted with disbelief. And as a writer whose works have dealt with the nastiness of man's ego, the brutality of his will and folly of his intellect, Golding will not now seek cocktail parties where literary cant and shoulder pats are sliced and served like little sandwiches.

The enduring popularity of *Lord of the Flies*, the 1954 novel about English schoolboys marooned on a desert island, appears to have been the primary consideration by the Swedish Academy, who for the first time, spilled a private spat beyond its chamber doors to the ears of journalists eager to understand the selection process that has neglected Proust, James, Tolstoy, Joyce, Conrad, Ibsen, and Strindberg.

When first published in the United States, *Lord of the Flies* sold 3,000 copies. Since then, the book has been bought over seven million times after 106 printings. So Golding may have been the safe choice, a writer whose plot-building prose is traditional enough to be linked with Thomas Hardy, yet whose restrained experimentation and subject matter are more closely tied to Joyce and Conrad.

But the Academy needed something more to issue a Nobel for Golding, more than a novel about lost boys who fight gamely to establish a peaceful society and fail, more than a fable-like document of savagery in the face of English education, more than the fall of man. The six novels that followed *Lord of the Flies* were lambasted by those groping only for a good read, and were routinely dissected by academics everywhere.

After *Lord of the Flies* Golding published a flow of stories, novels, and plays. *The Inheritors* (1955) was followed by *Pincher Martin* (1956), *Free Fall* (1959), *The Spire* (1964), and *The Pyramid*, which appeared in 1967 and was the last major work Golding produced for twelve years. Little overall assessment was made until 1979 when *Darkness Visible*, Golding's comeback novel after a twelve-year hiatus, appeared. The story, about an abused waif named Matty and terrorist twin sisters, is a panoramic showcase of characters and a grand extension of Golding's core themes. And when the sea novel *Rites of Passage* was published in 1980, Golding found himself firmly rooted in the kind of critical loam that invites future reappraisal.

This was not enough, however, for Artur Lundkvist, the seventy-seven-year-old senior Academy member who protested the award. Lundkvist, who was appointed in 1968, is an authority on Spanish, French, and Italian writing. In the past he

has tried to direct the Academy toward bold experimental writers, chiefly those of Latin America. Lundkvist has made his modernist presence felt before. Last year's Gabriel García Márquez was a probable Lundkvist choice, as was surrealist poet Vicente Aleixandre in 1977. And while the man on the street grows hoarse shouting Graham Greene, Lundkvist remains opposed to novelists like Greene for their listless experimentation and simple failure to reside in the right hemisphere. This year, Lundkvist favored French philosopher Claude Simon because of the influence he has exerted over the Latin American writers, who by popular reports represent the last unmined literary ore in the waning twentieth century.

The official Academy citation hailed William Golding "for his novels which, with the perspicuity of realistic narrative art and the diversity and universality of myth, illuminate the human condition in the world of today." According to Lundkvist, though, Golding has written some good books but lacks the essential Nobel nutrients. Himself a poet and essayist, the durable surrealist has published collections entitled *Life as Grass* and *Dartuanga, or the She Wolfe's Milk*. When the prize was announced, Academy secretary Lars Gyllensten told reporters the selection process was tranquil and that Golding won without a ripple. Lundkvist later told the same reporters the decision amounted to a coup against him (*New York Times*, 7 October 1983).

The reasoning behind the exclusion of Greene, or for that matter Jorge Luis Borges or Günter Grass, was not revealed. But the decision does prove that one novel translated into twenty-two different languages assumes a universality appealing to the Academy. Yet the novels following *Lord of the Flies* are vital in assessing Golding's worth. Call them fables, myths, or dark doses of humanity, each is part of a prose pyramid yet unfinished, an effort to crystallize on the page the forces that make us what we are.

In *Pincher Martin*, Golding combs the blackest depths of consciousness while providing a detailed account of Christopher Hadley Martin, a sailor who clings to a rock in mid-Atlantic after his British destroyer is torpedoed during World War II. In what is perhaps his finest and certainly most effulgent narrative, Golding manages to wrap his reader in Martin's ego while teasing any verisimilic expectations of just how a novel ought to be written. With every sentence more of Martin's shortcomings surface and, despite ample hints, only in the final chapter does Golding reveal that his protagonist is

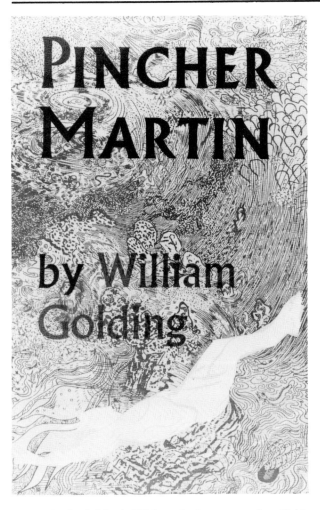

*Dust jacket for Golding's 1956 novel, about a man whom Gold-
ing later described as having "no belief in anything but the
importance of his own life"*

reader experiences newfound sympathy and can
accommodate Martin's most loathsome defects,
even cheer him for grappling so with the universe.
In the final chapter, however, Golding hammers
home Martin's biggest mistake. Only in death can
the temporal be made eternal, the confounding
clear. Martin's life and, most importantly, his death
amount to a colossal folly and blind failure to bow in
the light of human limitation.

The same is the case in *The Spire*, Golding's
fifth and possibly most flawed novel. Ostensibly, the
book is about the psychological battles of a
thirteenth-century priest who sacrifices all to erect a
religious monument on a foundation of mud and
slime. Dean Jocelin pompously believes his plan to
be the direct will of God when, in actuality, the
project is being funded through a king who has just
had an affair with Jocelin's cousin. Like Christopher
Martin, the priest is able by the end of the novel to
confront these qualities within himself and at least
partially accept them. Acceptance, Golding asserts
with vigor, is the first step to a sort of imperfect
salvation.

The main problem with *The Spire*, as in much
of Golding's fiction, is that thematically and struc-
turally narrative serves symbol, and not symbol narrative. For Jocelin, the spire represents everything
from a buried sex drive to the failure of humanity to
construct an eternal monument to itself. In some
chapters, the spire stands for Jocelin's weakening
faith, while in others it becomes a tribute to the
priest's most sterling efforts. Most of the time, however, the spire serves as a symbolic mirror in which
the other characters are reflected—a fallen woman,
an aging priest, and a simian master builder. Golding evaluates his characters by their relationship to
the spire, which can change at any given point in the
novel.

Yet for its weaknesses, *The Spire* contains some
of Golding's most immediate and compelling prose.
When Jocelin peers into the slime pit that hampers
the completion of his stone folly, faith , intellect, and
will merge to become "Some form of life; that which
ought not to be seen or touched, the darkness under
the earth, turning, seething, coming to a boil." Later
Jocelin confesses, "I thought it would be simple. I
thought the spire would complete a stone bible, be
the apocalypse in stone. I never guessed in my folly
that there would be a new lesson at every level, and a
new power." Like so many Golding characters,
Jocelin is forced finally to see the duplicity of an
impure world. And what makes Golding's work important and enduring is that he makes the reader

already dead—and that his struggle is a desperate
projection from the mind and body of a corpse that
refuses to accept its demise.

Christopher Hadley Martin is nothing more
than a faint vapor in a vaguely deterministic order.
Golding requires his reader to both condemn and
applaud Martin's rejection of that order. Martin
muses, "If this rock tries to adapt me to its ways I will
refuse and adapt it to mine. I will impose my routine
on it, my geography. I will tie it down with names."
Elsewhere Martin relies upon "Intelligence. Will
like a last ditch. Will like a monolith. Survival. Education, a key to all patterns, itself able to impose
them, to create."

Golding's use of nicknames implies that a
Pincher is greedier than Martin's Christian name
suggests. Yet by the close of *Pincher Martin*, the

deal with this duplicity long before the characters, who often die with only a dim, nascent realization of moral relativity. Humanity careens forward, though the characters have no more print.

In a shining salute, *Newsweek* book critic Peter Prescott wrote that even when Golding's "fables are not firmly structured, they remain remarkable for their excellence of individual scenes, for their dark and unified vision of the incorrigible beast in man." *Time*'s Paul Grey was less praising, and asked, "Can those charged with making the awards tell quality when they see it? Golding is fine to be sure, but not before Gordimer, Grass and Greene."

As the news made its way through the Swedish literary circles, the Golding decision was greeted as a soft compromise. Arne Ruth, editor of *Dagens Nyheter*, a Stockholm daily, said the Academy would probably never award the Nobel Prize to Greene now and said, "I don't think it's one of the really bad choices. There have been worse. There is no consensus that he [Golding] is a terrible writer." In the United States, Richard Straus, president of Farrar, Straus and Giroux, fifteen of whose authors have won the Nobel Prize, including four of the last six, said, "It's one of the most closely guarded secrets there is. They [the Academy] have their own screening committees and one never knows how names get on there."

But why Golding, and why now? In past years the selection process may have been fueled with Academy politics or hemispheric snubbery, but an explanation of the Golding decision can perhaps be found with the man himself, with the old face that flashed across the television sets, and the words which fall with terrible brilliance upon the page. His novels look deep into a bleak catacomb so that humanity may emerge strong, whole, and wiser for the peering.

At seventy-two, Golding is content to share his country home with his wife Ann, giving his days to the novels, his mind sated with images stored since childhood, through Oxford, and a teaching career that delayed his first novel until age forty-five. The years spent serving in the Royal Navy, from enlistment in 1940 through witnessing the sinking of the *Bismarck* off the coast of France, still provide him with the characters, the places, the searing glances at man's capacity to embrace darkness. As Golding said in 1970, referring to *Lord of the Flies*, "I said to Ann, wouldn't it be a good idea to write a book about real boys on an island, showing what a mess they'd

Slowly his mind came back to its own life. If David could not build the temple because he had blood on his hands, what is to be said of us, and of me? Then the terrible christening leapt into his eye and he cried out; and then, just when he had put it away again, a host of memories flew together. He watched, powerless to stop as they added to each other. They were like sentences from a story, which though they left great gaps, still told enough. It was a story of her and Roger and Rachel and Pangall and the men. He was staring down—down past the ladders, the floors of wood, the vaulting, down to a pit dug at the crossways like a grave made ready for some notable. The disregarded bale fires shuddered round the horizon, but there was ice on his skin. He was remembering himself watching the floor down there, where among the dust and rubble a twig with a brown, obscene berry lay against his foot.

He whispered the word, in the high, dark air.

'Mistletoe!'

So at last, he tried to pray again; but she came, treading the golden maze with bowed head and billowing dress, and the bale fires shuddered round them both. He groaned, out of his terror.

'I am bewitched.'

He went halting down the ladders, without seeing them; and the story, with the disjunct sentences, burned before his mind; and at the crossways, the replaced paving stones were hot to his feet with all the fires of hell.

—from The Spire

make? After that it was 2,000 words a day. One lot of 2,000 words was scribbled in the choir stalls of Salisbury cathedral during a rehearsal for the school Founder's Day concert."

As William Golding gallops his horse across the land, the images multiply, and the words are stored. For the living novelist there is no rest, retirement, or pension. Each sentence is a harder look at man, a deeper etching of his failures and fears, all his hopes for greatness. With the Nobel Prize behind him, Golding's task looms larger than ever. He must put away his saddle and complete another piece in an unfinished puzzle of humanity.

The Public Lending Right in the United Kingdom

Brigid Brophy

CRISIS

Lending libraries are a development of that sensible and social age, the eighteenth century. The device now known as "multiple use" created clubs, whereby a gentleman could enjoy the amenities of a home in the middle of town for the price merely of his subscription. On the same principle, his subscription to a circulating library enabled him and his family to read many more books than they could afford to buy.

The fly in this sensible, social ointment was the author's pay. A library volume had scores of readers in succession. The author was paid only for the one sale. The eighteenth century opened, in Britain, with the Queen Anne Act of 1709, the prototype of copyright statutes, which protected authors from piracy with the express purpose of "the Encouragement of Learned Men to compose and write useful Books." By the end of the century an institution was proliferating that contained the potential to defeat that purpose.

In most Western countries, the spread of literacy during the nineteenth century produced yet more commercial libraries and also prompted the state to enter the book-lending business, establishing "free" libraries that were in fact paid for out of taxes and that were aimed at borrowers too poor to pay even a subscription. Yet the crisis for authors was staved off. Improved technology brought down the cost and the price of books, with the result that book-buying increased as well as book-borrowing; and the total number of copies bought for library use remained tolerably high so long as the commercial libraries were in competition with one another and so long as the state-supported libraries were *not* in competition with the commercial ones. It was not indeed until after World War II that the crisis truly bit the profession of authorship.

What then happened in Britain set the pattern for Western experience of the crisis, though it happened in Britain on a larger scale than anywhere else and though in several countries the main crisis for authors was compounded by an extra crisis in which a native language and literature were in danger of the encroachment of numerically more powerful neighbours.

Brigid Brophy (© Jerry Bauer)

A speaker of one Scandinavian language has little difficulty in reading the other Scandinavian languages or even German. The Antipodes have their own idioms of the English language, but Antipodean readerships are vulnerable to the large publishing industries that produce books in the North American and the British idioms.

Perhaps it was these extra, specialised crises that made Denmark the first country to introduce, in 1946, a remedy for the main crisis, in which it was followed by Sweden (1957) and Iceland (1963) and, presently, New Zealand (1973) and Australia (1974).

In Britain, a remedy for the crisis libraries had brought on authorship was first proposed in 1951 (by my father, John Brophy, who was, like myself, a professional writer), but it was not until the next generation that it was implemented. In the interim, proposals were put up and shot down until, in 1972, a pressure group was formed under the name WAG or Writers Action Group. WAG, of which I was the coorganiser, put together and advanced a technically feasible plan and led an eventually united campaign, which issued in government legislation in 1979.

World War II brought crisis on authors thanks, ironically, to one of its few beneficial results. It demolished the snobbery that had kept out of the "free" libraries all those who would have been ashamed to be thought poor, including some who truly were poor. The "free" or public libraries in Britain are administered at local level but overseen (since 1964) by central government, and they are financed in roughly equal proportions from the rates (local taxes on house property) and central taxes. The postwar middle class discovered that public library books neither harboured infectious diseases nor induced proletarian accents. Given that the middle class was obliged to contribute to them in any case, through taxes, the only postwar shame associated with them in middle-class eyes was to be silly enough not to use them.

This was the signal for the public libraries to set out on a huge expansion of their service to borrowers for all classes. They quickly penetrated not only every social nook but every geographical cranny. If a rural population could not reach its local public library, the library went to it in a "mobile library" van. Sporadic vestiges apart, the once numerous and rich commercial libraries in Britain had been, by the 1960s, destroyed by the public libraries. Since the late 1960s the public libraries in Britain have been lending books at a rate of between 600 and 700 million a year, a rate that is, relatively, to the population of 56 million without equal anywhere.

Whereas book-buying by the commercial libraries was maximised by the rivalry between libraries, the public libraries are not rivals to one another. Each is a monopoly in its own area. Its relation to other public libraries is cooperative. A library that lacks a copy of a rare title requested by a reader does not buy one but borrows one from another library in the network. Moreover, public library spending on books is the first and softest target for spending cuts.

For these reasons the postwar expansion of the public libraries was a disaster to authors, and doubly so in that it destroyed not only the commer-cial libraries but many of the bookshops. There is no area of Britain without access to a public library but several, including densely populated areas, without a bookshop. West Germany makes, from libraries of all kinds taken together, only about a third of the number of loans made by the public libraries alone (educational and institutional libraries excluded) in Britain. As a consequence, West Germany has at least twice as many stock-holding bookshops as Britain, and as a consequence of *that* it has a publishing trade that produces more titles and has a larger turnover.

Some 70 percent of the loans made by the public libraries in Britain are loans of fiction. "Literary" fiction (fiction either pretentious or with aspirations, according to taste) is the chief of several categories for which, in hardback, the publisher can now expect virtually no sale beyond the sale to public libraries, which does not produce royalties enough to keep the author alive were the book written by a flea. Authors of many kinds took other jobs, turning themselves into amateur writers, until even that possibility was virtually closed by the massive unemployment that followed the general election of 1979. The public libraries in Britain give employment to 25,000 librarians and library assistants. It is virtually certain that the royalties on works sold to public libraries do not yield a living for anything approaching the same number of writers. It is increasingly doubtful whether professional authorship will survive to keep up the supply of the books that Britons borrow so insatiably.

REMEDY
The remedy now adopted by seven countries consists of paying the author for the service his books render the public by means of libraries.

In Australia, the payment is officially described as a recompense to the author for the fact that he "may lose income when readers do not have to buy books they want to read because those books can be borrowed freely from a library." But while the author undoubtedly may, it can nowhere be asserted that he definitely does "lose income." After all, even such gluttonous borrowers as Britons might, if they were suddenly deprived of the opportunity to borrow without charge, stop reading altogether.

In Britain there is considerable evidence that the ubiquity of the public libraries has inculcated the habit of borrowing rather than buying books and has made it difficult in many cases for even a person who wants to buy to do so. WAG was careful to campaign, however, only for payment for the service done by library books, whether or not that involved a loss of potential income to the author. This was largely a matter of tact or tactics. Before WAG came into existence the governing circles of the professional librarians had declared against the payment of authors, had denied that the public libraries harmed authors and had, perhaps rashly, claimed that, on the contrary, they were a boon to authors. The fierce opposition of the librarians to the authors' claim for payment was unique to Britain, and many of the actions of the campaigners and of the government that eventually introduced the payment for authors were dictated by the need to avoid seeming to slap the librarians' faces in public.

STATUS
In Danish and in German, the payment to authors is called the "library royalty," in Icelandic "author's right," in Swedish "author's pence." The three English-speaking countries that recognise the author's entitlement call it "public lending right" (PLR), a name meaningless to people who do not know its history and misleading to those who do. It derives from a now anonymous proposal, that was in fact shot down, to introduce the right by adding "lending the work to the public" to the list, in British copyright law, of actions "restricted by the copyright" in a literary work. The name thus coined stuck indelibly in the official mind, though in none of the countries where the right bears the official name of PLR has it in fact any connexion whatever with copyright law.

The only country where PLR is implemented through copyright is the Federal Republic of Germany (West Germany). The German copyright statute of 1965 is both in substance and in its German name a creator's right statute. It makes the creator invariably the first owner of the copyright in his own work, and the copyright is inalienable from him during his lifetime. Consequently, the amendment that was added to the statute in 1972, which entitles the copyright owner to payment when the work is lent from a library accessible to the public, is bound to benefit creators and, principally among creators, writers, since books are the objects chiefly lent by libraries.

By contrast, the British Copyright Act of 1956, like copyright acts in several countries, especially those that historically derive their concept of copyright from the British concept, does not invariably make the creator even the first owner of the copyright in his own creation and, even where he is the first owner, leaves him vulnerable to dispossession. Authors of books, who are endemically short

of money, are particularly vulnerable.

If it is introduced as an addition to a copyright law of this type, PLR benefits not authors as such but copyright owners. In Germany, at least during the author's lifetime, the two are identical, but in Britain, where they are not, the proposal to make PLR a branch of copyright had to be discountenanced, as any such proposal would have to be in any country with a copyright statute less exemplary than the West German. In Britain, WAG's campaign resulted eventually, after the government had had two shots at getting the legislation through, in the Public Lending Right Act of 1979, which creates PLR as an independent right, unconnected with copyright and conferred specifically on authors.

It is possible, however, for a country to introduce PLR without legislation. In Britain the librarians preferred, ultimately, to be compelled by law to cooperate with the PLR system rather than be asked to give their voluntary assistance. In New Zealand and in Australia PLR operates by virtue only of a ministerial decision. This method creates the danger that what one minister has instituted another minister might revoke, which is easier to do than repealing a statute, but PLR has now existed in Australasia for an unbroken decade, successfully surviving all changes of government.

What is not possible is to introduce PLR without exercising political persuasion. This need not be, and probably for preference should not be, party-political. WAG secured first the support of the Labour Party and, almost immediately afterwards, of the Conservative Party. The PLR bill was introduced by, and passed under, a Labour government, with the support of the Conservative opposition and of most of the smaller parties. (This did not prevent the first attempt at legislation from falling foul of a tiny filibuster that was equally an all-party affair.) The 1979 Act, though it created the right, stipulated that it should not become effective until Parliament should approve a PLR Scheme laying down the details of its operation. No sooner was the Act passed than there was a general election, in which power changed hands. The PLR Scheme of 1982 was introduced by, and passed under, a Conservative government, with the support of the Labour opposition.

In whatever way it does so, a PLR campaign must persuade the legislators of the need for PLR, for the simple reason that the legislature controls the public purse. It is vital that the payments to authors be funded from a source independent of the funds with which the libraries buy books.

Otherwise, their liability to pay or to suffer through the payment of PLR would merely cause the libraries to reduce their book purchasing, and authors would lose on the swings anything they gained on the roundabouts.

This principle is recognised in every country that operates PLR. In Germany, the creators in theory exert a claim under copyright directly on the libraries themselves, but that is no more than a legal fiction. In practice, the money to pay PLR in West Germany comes from a combination of central (federal) and regional government, and in every other PLR-operating country it comes from central government.

Because it is unique in having introduced PLR as an aspect of copyright, West Germany is the exception to most generalisations about PLR. Six of the seven countries that have PLR make PLR payments only on books (which, in British public libraries, account for some 98 percent of the loans made, cassettes and gramophone records being a very small sideline in the library business). In Germany PLR is theoretically payable on works of every kind in which copyright subsists, but since books remain the chief subject of library business PLR on printed words absorbs 91 percent of the total sum allocated to PLR.

Again, authors and librarians are everywhere anxious to avoid the time-wasting and costly anarchy that would be the result if each author had to write to each library asking for an account of the library's dealings with his works. Six of the seven countries concerned have, therefore, either set up a new body or, as in New Zealand and Australia, pressed an already existing body into new service and have given it exclusive responsibility for administering PLR throughout the country. By contrast with these countries, the PLR amendment to the German copyright statute sets up no administrative machinery. By way of limiting anarchy, all it does is decree that a creator may not exercise his claim to PLR individually but only through membership of a government-recognised (but not government-run) collecting society—that is, a copyright utilisation society run on behalf of creators. The legislation does not limit the number of such societies that might administer PLR. There were originally four in operation, a number that amalgamation has now reduced to three, which deal with PLR on, respectively, printed words, music, and works of visual art. Since the choice is left by the legislation to the societies, each society administers PLR on a different system—or, in the case of one society, operates two different systems.

In Sweden, Iceland, Australia, and Britain, PLR is paid in relation to books in public libraries only. Denmark and New Zealand include some educational libraries. Only the German collecting society that at present deals with PLR on books purports to take account of libraries of all kinds, though in fact the statistics it gathers, by spot-check, from a few libraries of assorted kinds are cursory in the extreme. The German collecting societies have no legislation to rely on except copyright, which is notoriously difficult to enforce. One of the advantages of special PLR legislation, as in Britain, or of PLR legislation tacked on to library legislation, as in Denmark, or even of PLR by ministerial arrangement, as in Australasia, is that it gives the PLR administration the power to require the libraries to supply thoroughgoing annual data on which the annual (in all cases) payments to the authors are based.

PLR SYSTEMS
PLR operates on one of two mutually exclusive systems.

In both systems the initial impetus comes from the author, who supplies the PLR administration with a list of his published titles on which he wants to claim PLR. Rules vary from country to country about whether he has to apply formally for registration and about the conditions that make an author or a title eligible for PLR.

Once the author has supplied the impetus, the two systems diverge—in principle as well as detail.

The shelf-fee or stock-census method operates in Denmark, Iceland, New Zealand, and Australia. The authors' lists are compared with a list, obtained from the libraries, of the titles (and the number of copies of each) stocked by the libraries. The census of titles is complete and annual in Denmark and Iceland; in the Australasian countries it is based on a sporadic sample-census.

The author then receives an annual payment consisting of a fee for each copy, above a certain minimum, stocked by the libraries during the year.

The stock-census system is an "unfair" one, inasmuch as it pays for the availability of the titles in the libraries, not for the public's decision to take advantage of that availability. The same fee is paid to the author whether his work remains untouched on the library shelf throughout the year or whether thirty borrowers queue up and take it out. It is a system that makes librarians the arbiters of PLR. The author's pay depends on whether the library stocks his work in the first place and then on whether it keeps it in stock long enough for it to incur repeated annual fees. The borrowing habits of the readers influence the matter only insofar as they influence the librarians' decisions.

Most countries that operate PLR confine payment to their own nationals, though in some cases residents are included as well. The stock-census system is particularly appropriate to countries that place a high priority on bolstering the very existence, irrespective of the popularity, of a native literature. Australia evidently accords a similar priority to a native publishing industry. Australia and one of the West German collecting societies operate the only two PLR systems that make PLR payments to (native) publishers as well as to authors.

In the other PLR system, the decisions of the borrowing public to take certain titles out of the library are directly responsible for the amount of PLR each author earns. This system, which is based on loans sampling, operates in Sweden and in Britain, each of which has an exceptionally large public-library network. A sketchy version of it, based on a cursory spot-check of some loans, is one of two systems operated by the German collecting society that deals with PLR on books.

In Britain a record of every loan made to the public is kept perpetually in a representative sample of sixteen libraries, so sited throughout the country as to give a fair geographical and social picture of the lending activity of the public-library service as a whole. To iron out any idiosyncrasies, four of the sixteen libraries are "rotated" at the end of each year's sample. The PLR administration compares the lists of eligible and registered titles, supplied by eligible and registered authors, with the record of a year's total loans, supplied by the libraries in the sample, and works out the annual payment due to each registered author in proportion to the showing of his works in the loans record.

When WAG took on the task of convincing a sceptical government and civil service that loans sampling was feasible even in the colossal British library service, a system was designed, to what WAG writers considered fair criteria, by generous statisticians and computer consultants. It is in essence their design, a small statistical marvel, which attains very high accuracy on the basis of a comparatively small and therefore administratively comparatively cheap sample, that is now in operation in Britain. Registration of eligible applicant authors by the PLR administration, which is headed by a registrar appointed by the government, began in September 1982. Recording loans in the libraries began in January 1983. The first payments to authors are expected in February 1984.

The recording of the loans is done electronically, without disturbance to the public and at minimum pain to the library assistant, who has only to pass a rod over a coded mark in the volume when he issues it to the borrower. The code marks, which identify the title by its International Standard Book Number (or, in the small percentage of cases where the ISBN is lacking from a library volume, by another unique number), are recorded on magnetic tape. The libraries in the sample pass the tapes to the PLR administration and are reimbursed for any and all money they spend on operating PLR. The PLR administration grosses up the loans in the sample proportionately to the total loans made in the area which the sample library in question represents.

A sophisticated loans-sampling system of this kind gives, for a comparatively low expenditure, an accurate representation of the choices of the borrowing public and thus the fairest basis for calculating the payment of the authors. In itself it can pay only for loans over the counter, since those are all that the sample records. About 12 percent of volumes in British public libraries are not, however, permitted to leave the library premises but are held there, in reference libraries or sections, where they may be consulted by the public *in situ*. Sweden has dealt satisfactorily with this problem. Having instituted payments on loans, it added, three years later, another payment consisting of an annual fee per title held in reference stock and not available for lending. WAG pleaded for the extra payment in Britain and persuaded the government to prepare a sample of reference stock, but the government declined, in the end, to include the extra payment in the legislation. Having achieved its main objective of loans payments on lending volumes, WAG dissolved in 1982 but has left behind two trade unions, the Writers' Guild of Great Britain and the Society of Authors, which continue to press in concert for payment on reference stock as well as for the considerable number of improvements needed in the rules of the British PLR system.

In addition to the stock-based and the loans-based systems of PLR, there is a substitute for PLR which should be mentioned if only by way of warning. It is operated by one of the German collecting societies and also in Holland, where the writers' organisations have been trying in vain for a decade to persuade the government to replace it by PLR proper on the loans-sampling system. The substitute for PLR makes a once-only payment to the author when a volume is bought by a library. This inevitably condemns all the volumes already in libraries to serve out the rest of their library lives, which may be long, being lent to the public but bringing no payment to their authors. The patent injustice of this, especially to older authors unlikely to produce new titles, did much, when the substitute was proposed in Britain, to unite professional writers behind WAG's opposition to it. Usually known as the purchase scheme, the substitute for PLR has the further disadvantages that its once-only payment, being made in advance of any public use of the volume, cannot reflect the amount of use the borrowers choose to make of it, and that it is very much less socially useful to authors than the annual payments made by PLR which, so long as the work continues in demand in the libraries, continue to be made even in years when the author is ill, old, tired, or writing a long new book. The substitute seems to crop up on some international network wherever there are bureaucrats opposed to the payment of PLR to authors. The claim is usually advanced that it would be cheaper to administer than PLR, but the experiments and costings done for the British government in 1975 prove that it lacks even that merit.

INTERNATIONAL STATUS

With one exception, all the countries that operate PLR confine payment to some combination of their own nationals and/or residents. In Britain, an author is eligible for PLR only if he is both a citizen of some country belonging to the European Economic Community and a resident of the United Kingdom.

By rules of this kind countries justifiably protect themselves from outflows of their PLR funds to authors in foreign countries from which no PLR can be expected in return, whether because the foreign country has, like the USA and France, no PLR or because it has a PLR system confined to its own nationals.

The exception to this rule is, of course, Germany, whose PLR-under-copyright is in theory not subject to restrictions of nationality. In practice, however, the collecting societies that administer German PLR can take a certain amount of cover behind the legislative stipulation that PLR must be claimed through a collecting society. The German collecting societies, being free to make their own rules, refuse to admit non-German authors as members. On the whole, they pay PLR to foreign authors only if there is a collecting society in the foreign country with which the German collecting society can make an agreement.

British authors here benefit from another legacy of WAG, which formed a literary collecting society, open to all writers, called the Authors' Lending and Copyright Society (ALCS). British members of the ALCS have been receiving their PLR from West Germany annually since 1980 (four years before any British PLR was scheduled to be paid).

The British writers' unions have naturally asked the British government, in the interests of fairness, to make British PLR payable to German authors. Talks began in 1983 towards that end. So far, British-German reciprocity is the only arrangement of the kind under active and formal discussion, but writers have long envisaged an ideal world in which every country that has libraries should have PLR, and every country that has PLR should have a reciprocal agreement with every other.

There are, however, many obstacles to be hurdled. Even between existing systems, agreement has to be sought between organisations of fundamentally different status. In six countries the PLR administration is a national monopoly, controlled by the parliament concerned, whereas in Germany the administrations are private and self-governing, explicitly without monopoly powers. Funding, unlike administration, is everywhere central, but, since no government would want to be a net loser in any reciprocal agreement, difficulties are bound to arise from disparities of funding and from differences in borrowing pattern. In relation to the total number of loans, German PLR, for example, is much more generously funded than British, and the problem is compounded by the fact that German borrowers take out more books of British origin than British borrowers do books of German origin.

Indeed, in some cases the PLR allocation is so generous that it is required by the parliament that votes it to fulfil two purposes. Both in Sweden and in Iceland, only part of the allocation is used to pay PLR. The other part is put into solidarity funds for the benefit of the profession of authorship. The solidarity funds pay grants and pensions to authors according to financial need or awards and scholarships according to literary merit. In other words they are required by law to fill in gaps in the provisions of the welfare state for artists, who, insofar as they count technically as "self-employed," often have difficulty in claiming sickness or unemployment benefit, and to fill in gaps in state subsidy for the arts. In West Germany the law does not require part of the PLR allocation to be paid into solidarity funds, but the collecting society that administers PLR on books chooses to pay only 45 percent of his PLR earnings to the individual author, 55 percent going into collective funds. This creates a further problem for a German-British reciprocal agreement, since 55 percent is removed, willy-nilly, from the German PLR of a British author, who is not, however, eligible to benefit from the solidarity funds into which it has been paid.

DIVERSITY

Besides the fundamental division between stock-census systems and loans-sampling systems, there are innumerable differences in the rules that govern the various national (or, in Germany, the various private) PLR systems. Denmark pays only one author per title; he may be the original writer or the translator. Britain is prepared to divide the PLR earnings of one edition of one title, in proportions designated by themselves in agreement, between a maximum of three authors; they may be writers or illustrators, in any combination, but not translators or editors. The varieties or, as it may be, vagaries of the world's PLR systems, no two of which fully coincide even on such matters as the posthumous duration (if any) of PLR, its assignability, and whether a slim volume qualifies equally with a ten-volume encyclopaedia are exhaustively described in my book *A Guide to Public Lending Right* (Aldershot: Gower, 1983).

Some submission to political control is the price a PLR system pays for its public funding. Political control is smallest in Germany, but then so are the advantages of it; the state provides neither an administrative apparatus nor criteria to which PLR administrations must conform. An author who is dissatisfied with a collecting society has little resort except to form an alternative collecting society.

Swedish PLR is controlled by a body on which representatives of authors outnumber those of government. By contrast, British authors are the ones who have been obliged to submit to the highest degree of political control in exchange for the most miserly PLR allocation (£2 million a year, from which all expenses, estimated at between 15 and 20 percent, are taken first, before the remainder is distributed in PLR). British authors had a statutory right to be "consulted" in the framing of the PLR Scheme of 1982 and in any alterations to it. This does not, however, amount to a right to be heeded. In practice, the authors were and are frequently disregarded. The rules are in effect devised by the civil service and obediently passed by Parliament. As a result, the rules constitute a bureaucratic maze, with several anomalies and injustices. An author who wants his PLR is obliged to thread the maze for himself, since it is on the applicant author that the

rules place the responsibility for declaring that he and his works are eligible under the rules. This he has to affirm in a "statutory declaration" witnessed by a lawyer, for which most lawyers charge him £2. Since one of the rules ordains that each new edition is to count as a new work, an author who has already paid to declare the eligibility of a title in hardback has to pay again when it goes into paperback, and then again when he publishes a new title. The purpose of the declaration he pays for is to make it easier to prosecute him should he make a false statement. PLR in Britain will certainly not make any author rich, since there is a limit of £5,000 on what any single author may earn from it in a year, but it looks like doing wonders for the legal profession. The number of writers and illustrators who had applied for registration by June 1983 (in time, that is, for the first payout) was, at not quite 8,000, well below expectation. Cynics suspect that the rules and application procedure were made deliberately deterrent.

Any group, in any country, that is contemplating a campaign for the introduction of PLR would be foolish not to insist on loans sampling as the basic system. It should insist also on the Swedish supplement to deal with books held in reference sections, but for a basic model of a cheap and accurate loans sample it could not find a better exemplar than the British sample. For the rules of administration, however, it would do well to copy the relaxed and rational Swedish system. In that department, Britain can offer only the most ferocious model of what to avoid.

PUBLIC LENDING RIGHT: THE FIRST YEAR IN THE UNITED KINGDOM

Two million pounds were allocated for 1983, of which £412,000 was required for setup and operational costs.

A total of 66,850 books were registered by 7,750 authors. The 6,086 payments averaged £261 (approximately $390): 46 payments of £5000; 81 payments between £2500-£4999; 247 payments between £1000-£2499; 318 payments between £500-999; 1,516 payments between £100-£499; and 3,878 payments between £1-£99.

Payments were based on a sampling of 2,997,000 loans at sixteen libraries, and the payment per loan was calculated at 1.02 pence.

The Public Lending Right in America

The 29 September 1983 Library of Congress Center for the Book symposium on PLR marked the commencement of serious investigation of the granting of royalties to American authors for library circulation of their books. Among the participants were Robert Caro (former president of the Authors Guild), Thomas Stave (University of Oregon Library), Dorothy Shrader (Copyright Office), Dennis Hyatt (University of Oregon), William B. Goodman (Godine Publishers), Anne Edwards (president of the Authors Guild), John W. Sumsion (PLR registrar, Great Britain), George Piternick (University of British Columbia), and Robert Wedgeworth (American Library Association).

As a result of the Center for the Book symposium, Senator Charles McC. Mathias, Jr., of Maryland (chairman of the Subcommittee on Patents, Copyrights and Trademarks of the Senate Committee on the Judiciary) introduced a bill (S.2192) in November 1983 to establish a commission for the study of an American PLR. Under S.2192 this commission would consist of the Librarian of Congress and ten other members appointed by the President: two authors, two publishers, three librarians, and three public members. The commission would enter a preliminary report after one year and a final report after two years.

Senator Charles McC. Mathias, Jr.

STATEMENT BY
SEN. CHARLES McC. MATHIAS, JR.

On the last day of the first session of the 98th Congress, I introduced a bill, S.2192, to establish a commission to study both the desirability and feasibility of compensating authors whenever their books are borrowed from public libraries.

Congress, by protecting the rights of authors through our copyright laws, achieved two valuable goals—the continued creation of works of high literary merit, and the widest possible dissemination of these works to the reading public. I think the public lending right idea is ripe for a review on the basis of these two goals.

The Commission would examine the great questions that are raised by the idea: Would a public lending right system be in the public interest? Would it encourage authors to write? Could it be financed without burdening our libraries or discouraging reading?

The Commission would be made up of librarians, authors, publishers, and representatives of the general reading public. It would take care to study the examples set forward by the ten nations that already have public lending right systems. These include the Federal Republic of Germany and the United Kingdom.

The Commission's final report would be submitted to the Congress within two years of its first meeting. The report will give Congress expert guidance to help it carry out its constitutional mandate "to promote the Progress of Science and the useful Arts, by securing for limited Times to Authors and Inventors the exclusive Right to their respective Writings and Discoveries."

In a position paper prepared for *DLB Yearbook* William Goodman examined the copyright aspects of the problem. Mr. Goodman is editorial director

II

98TH CONGRESS
1ST SESSION   **S. 2192**

To establish a commission to study and make recommendations on the desirability
    and feasibility of compensating authors for the lending of their books by
    lending institutions.

IN THE SENATE OF THE UNITED STATES

NOVEMBER 8 (legislative day, NOVEMBER 14), 1983

Mr. MATHIAS introduced the following bill; which was read twice and referred to
the Committee on Rules and Administration

A BILL

To establish a commission to study and make recommendations
    on the desirability and feasibility of compensating authors
    for the lending of their books by lending institutions.

1   *Be it enacted by the Senate and House of Representa-*

2 *tives of the United States of America in Congress assembled,*

3

4   FINDINGS, ESTABLISHMENT AND PURPOSES OF THE

5   COMMISSION

6   SECTION 1. Congress hereby finds and declares that—

7   (a) authors' works enrich and shape our national

8   and cultural identity;

Senator Mathias's bill proposing a study "to determine whether specific compensation to authors for the public lending of their works could promote authorship without adversely affecting the activities of the lending institutions or the reading public"

at David R. Godine, Publisher, in Boston, and a lecturer at Harvard.

PLR AND THE MEANING OF LITERARY PROPERTY

William B. Goodman

If PLR is to become public law in the United States, the case for it cannot succeed unless there's wide recognition of the meaning of literary property, the meaning of what the fact of copyright signifies. In the ten countries where PLR exists, it is based on such recognition. Copyright secures a property right. It means that the text of a book in copyright belongs to the person or persons who wrote it and belongs to them as long as they live and as property may be passed on to their heirs and assigns for fifty additional years. Wherever PLR obtains, the laws that define it turn on the recognition that property is involved. While the proprietary issue at the heart of PLR is clear enough to its advocates and claimants, it is not as clear to others as it will be once there's wide general discussion of PLR. That discussion may be expected as a result of the hearings to be held in the Senate on Senator Charles McC. Mathias, Jr.'s bill (S. 2192) "to establish a commission to study and make recommendations on the desirability and feasibility of compensating authors for the lending of their books by lending institutions"—hearings expected sometime in 1984.

In understanding PLR it is essential to see that it is neither charity nor patronage but payment for services rendered—the reading of a book in copyright borrowed from a public library—a fee for service that long custom has sanctioned but which is actually legalized theft. Library patrons without knowing it are freeloaders. Moreover, they haven't the slightest idea that they are and doubtless would be surprised if they knew it. PLR, while it remedies unacknowledged theft, is not a threat to local libraries. Its full cost in the ten nations where it is in force is paid by the central governments involved. It is seen as a proper national expense, an expression of a national interest like national highways, the national defense, or agricultural price supports. In this country the arguments before the Congress some years ago that supported the establishment of the National Endowments for the Arts and the Humanities may also be brought to the support of PLR. While that contention is true in spirit, it is not the central issue at stake in PLR

because PLR is not in any sense a patronage scheme. That central issue has nothing to do with the Arts, with literature whether capital or lowercase *l*. The issue is property and the rights of those who have created and own it. In America the meaning of such rights is as clear as midsummer daylight. They have absolute Constitutional force and overwhelming practical effect.

Whatever the truth of PLR's claim, or the public interest rationale for it as a Federal undertaking, however good such may be, still, to suggest in 1983 that borrowing a book in copyright from a public library is theft—the use of someone else's property without payment for such use—is incomprehensible to most Americans. It seems to violate the very idea of free public libraries because the right to borrow a book from a public library is hallowed by long custom, by deeply held notions of education and public enlightenment and of free access to its materials. Books in libraries are there, after all, because libraries paid good public money for them. Librarians have long been taught to assume that to make them available without charge to the public is a contribution to the "general welfare." Such usage is good public policy and has implicit Constitutional warrant. The term "general welfare" is not in the Constitution by accident. From its implications over time have come legislation as different as that which established our land grant colleges and that which produced the Social Security Act. Given such experience and the depth of a feeling of rightness it engenders, to suggest to librarians and those they serve that repeated borrowings of books in copyright is theft seems no more than a clever hustle. If that initial negative response is to be changed into positive support for PLR, American writers and their allies will have to convince the public and the Congress, our only institution capable of a redress of their grievance, that the case for PLR is justified, a proper object of legislative remedy, and *not* a threat to public libraries.

The first thing needed is a scrutiny of what kind of transaction borrowing a book in copyright from a public library is and thus disclose the kind of property use involved. When a publisher sells a book to a library, or when a library jobber does, both know that the result will be repeated borrowings of that book without limit. The author as copyright owner receives one royalty payment for each such copy so sold. He is rueful at best about it. The pleasure of the recognition involved doesn't mean too much and soon becomes resentment. His publisher shares the resentment but like the author suppresses it because to suggest that borrowing a book from a public library somehow picks his or his author's pocket would be taken to mean opposition to public libraries. And, of course, no one near his right mind is against libraries. It would violate a tenet of our civic religion to express such opposition, but more to the point, it misses the nature of the borrowing transaction to think that acknowledging it as *also an act of theft* must threaten libraries.

It is vital that it be understood that to sell one or more copies of a book in copyright to a public library for repeated use by the public is an act with inherently different consequences than the purchase of a book by an individual from a bookshop or a book club, a book that may or may not be borrowed by a friend. When a library buys a book it does so in order to make it available for repeated borrowings by its patrons. Implicit in its purchase, therefore, is what amounts to a license to distribute the book as many times as borrowers call for it and to do so *without* further payment of any kind to the actual owner of the copyrighted text involved, that is, to the writer of the book. I'm confident that once this fact is widely perceived, acknowledgment and remedy will follow in decent due course.

PLR is good public policy. It will not overburden or destroy our public libraries. The essential technology needed for it—"light pencil" or similar recording of each book borrowing that can be duplicated on tape for PLR—is in place in a sufficient number of libraries nationwide to enable whatever PLR institution the Congress may devise to get on with its job without jeopardy to the continued smooth operation of our libraries.

PLR is good public policy because it is good for writers. And whatever is good for writers, to paraphrase the late "Engine Charlie" Wilson of General Motors, is good for the country.

STATEMENTS ON PLR BY AMERICAN WRITERS

From HORTENSE CALISHER

Since I'm a longtime friend of Brigid Brophy and Maureen Duffy, who together both initiated the idea of the Public Lending Act and worked toward and with the organisation which carried it through, I some years ago brought this to the attention of the Authors League, which at the time was not interested. Or so their executive secretary then wrote. I believe that now that it is a fait accompli in

Britain their interest may have changed. (I am not a member of the AL.)

Certainly I am in favor of PLR—as what author would not be? My guess is that the campaign for it will be even more difficult than it was in Parliament. For one thing, people here tend to confuse it with the assumption that libraries will somehow be abrogated. For another, if authors' organisations are lackadaisical, then who will work for it? Individual writers can do little more than adhere to the principle, or give over their working lives to it, as both Brophy and Duffy did—and I assume others.

Most writers like to write. In addition it is said to be good for society, rather than not, and possibly good for our character. Therefore we will be rewarded in heaven—and must not mind if a library buys two copies of a book and dispenses it to hundreds. ASCAP and the Dramatist's Guild regulate performance royalties very strictly. Actors get residuals on one performed commercial—sometimes for years. But a book for free is everybody's inalienable right—I have even heard the PLR confused with censorship. Librarians, too, are often against it—as so many were against restricting the Xerox privileges by which libraries infringe copyright.

From FRED CHAPPELL

In countries where reading is regarded as pleasure and privilege, the Public Lending Right law will be found attractive and feasible. In the United States, where reading is regarded as a distasteful and perhaps politically subversive activity, the law is a useless and onerous possibility.

And whatever income accrued to the writer from it would be more than offset by the tax complications involved.

I think it would be much more trouble that it could possibly be worth.

From JOHN CIARDI

On principle, I am in favor of pouring all sorts of money in the direction of all sorts of authors. I am also generally in favor of virtue, so long as it does not interfere with vice.

In practical terms, I think I would as soon lobby Congress to give the country back to the Indians. As a former library trustee, I am terrified by the possible record keeping that might be involved.

If, however, Key West were hit by a July snowstorm, I'd be willing to dream of a white Christmas.

From MALCOLM COWLEY

I have mixed feelings about the possibility of our having a PLR in the United States. It would be marvelous for authors whose books are widely circulated in libraries but have only modest sales in bookstores. In simple justice they ought to receive a little more money for books that have proved generally useful.

It happens that I am one of those authors. Many years ago I needed a copy of one of my own books and couldn't find it in any bookstore. It had gone out of print after selling fewer than 1,000 copies and yielding me a total royalty of $350. When I looked for it in the public library, their copy was literally read to pieces.

Of course I have had better luck with my other books, but still I belong to a wide category of authors who might be helped by PLR. I would support such a measure enthusiastically except for the fact that it would create an enormous lot of paperwork. Already we have so much paperwork in this country, where we are in danger of being buried under mountains of papers. We may soon be so busy filing them away that we will have no time for anything else. The wheels in our heads will stop turning like all the factory wheels.

From PETER DE VRIES

Yes, I certainly feel deprived by the lack of PLR in America. Writers are entitled to more than a single-copy royalty on books issued to scores and maybe hundreds of readers, in some cases rented over and over for a fee. Cut us in!

From ANNIE DILLARD

I wholeheartedly oppose the notion of writers' receiving royalties from the circulation of library books—if the libraries have to pay.

Our poor public libraries are already horribly imperiled by slashed funds. They can't keep up with *existing* paperwork. Many, if not most, have cut back on hours, on acquisitions, on maintenance. I wouldn't be a writer if it weren't for public libraries. All I want as a writer is to have my books available to readers; whatever is good for public libraries is good for me. (It's good for the country, too.)

I'm sorry if this seems righteous or pious; I acknowledge that I've been fortunate to have a liv-ing from my writing without socking library users. The Carnegie Library in Pittsburgh—the library I used—has chiseled over the broad door: FREE TO ALL THE PEOPLE. This principle must outweigh others. The interests of the many must not be sacrificed to the few. Surely nothing is more precious than our free flow of information? Nothing is more precious, then, than open library doors.

From WILLIAM GADDIS

Since it would seem likely that the books in demand at the libraries must also be those in demand at the bookstores, I would feel that in order for PLR not to become simply another avenue opened for the rich to get richer it would be only fair and supportable if developed along some such lines as ASCAP, wherein the "writers of literature would benefit as well as the writers of books" but even here, frankly, I should have reservations since our free public libraries do constitute one of the few great American institutions not yet submerged by commercialism; and any complications, however well intended, which might place them in further jeopardy than they are already would merit close examination in just those terms.

From WILLIAM H. GASS

I was in England when this campaign began, some years ago, and then it was clear that the commercial hacks were miffed that a few people were reading their books without paying for them.

I shall only mention one factor which leads me to oppose this act of greed, although it is enough, namely, that the proposal is a direct attack upon the American ideal of a free (and therefore really public) library system. The poor should not be punished, not even a penny, for their interest in books—on the contrary.

The serious and dedicated writer wants readers first, and other rewards can follow after as they may. Politically, free libraries are essential. This is a reactionary step.

From HERBERT GOLD

I wish there were a Public Lending Law in the U.S. to help me with kith & kin. I also wish people reading over the shoulders of others would pay a fee. I would like a penalty, like a parking ticket, to go into a fund for my benefit every time someone says, "I'd like to read your book, when does it come out in paperback?" Ten dollar fine for this; fifty dollars for: "I hear you're an interesting writer, would you lend me one of your books?" I don't want to bankrupt libraries, but being an optimist, I suspect funds from the Dept. of Defense would flow into the depositories of cultural power if they were besieged by my fellow famished writers.

From SHIRLEY ANN GRAU

Britain's experience with PLR will undoubtedly be watched with great interest by writers in the United States. Even a partial success will change a great many minds, mine included. Right now, however, I am opposed to PLR.

First, a matter of feeling. I find very distasteful the idea of a tariff imposed on readers. I consider my royalties quite adequate compensation.

Second, PLR would inevitably create another whole level of bureaucracy with its predictable inefficiency and stupidity.

Third, PLR would increase the expenses of a library system that is already underfinanced. I feel that the survival and health of the public library system is in the long run more important to me than any small increase in royalties.

From SHIRLEY HAZZARD

Indeed I do feel the absence of this civilised acknowledgment in the United States—not simply for myself but as a principle and as a rightful benefit to all authors. The lack of public lending right can be seen, I think, in context—not merely as a vacuum but as indicative of an attitude of government, and by extension of society, towards the articulate independence of literature. Conversely, the adoption of such a law as that operating in Britain and elsewhere would be expressive of a degree of maturity and enlightenment in this nation's processes, immeasurably outweighing the small public expense incurred.

From JULIAN MOYNAHAN

Of course the concept of royalty should be extended to include Public Lending Right. A book,

unlike other articles of manufacture, is a unique creation. How many of these can a writer, even a very successful one, come up with in a lifetime—twenty? fifty? how about five or six? That is why the opportunity for some limited reward should follow the book past the point where it is first disposed of—usually in a shop—at least as far as the public collections of the American library system. How many writers have heard, always from some very well-off acquaintance, "I see your book got wonderful reviews—can't wait until it turns up at the library!" But I doubt Congress will do anything. With IRS recently ending the special rules exempting publishers' back list inventories in the calculation of Federal taxes, the trend seems to be all the other way. Let the author beware—or go into some other line of work.

From MAY SARTON

There is no doubt in my mind that PLR would be of real service to writers of distinction who are not best-sellers. My books sell only about 20,000 but are in constant use in the public libraries. In Detroit, for instance, I was told that they have to rebind every six months. So it would indeed help to even things out if I could get a small royalty from borrowers.

From ARTHUR SCHLESINGER, JR.

I strongly favor the Public Lending Right principle as a matter of simple justice to authors; and I very much hope that Congress will study the British and Scandinavian legislation and devise an equivalent legislation in the United States.

From IRWIN SHAW

Naturally, I am in favor of the law which gives even a small revenue to authors whose books are taken out again and again from our public libraries. A limit of $5,000 that any author can make in one year out of this fund ensures that the authors of big best-sellers do not profit too much from the plan but may make the difference between keeping on working and surrendering to many of the writers whose books are on the library shelves. However, I have small hope that this law will be passed in the U.S.

From LEWIS TURCO

No, I do not "feel deprived by the lack of PLR in America," for the following reasons:

First, I believe that such a law would create a bureaucratic quagmire. Perhaps small countries like the United Kingdom will find that they can handle it, but I cannot imagine what the system would be like in the United States, with the thousands of titles and editions published here each year. I have no doubt that such a system would cost the taxpayers, of whom I am one, far more than the profits most authors would earn from fees charged by libraries for the circulation of their books. It would create, I am sure, a large new category of civil servants and require an incredible computer system to keep track of book borrowings and bookkeeping.

Further, it appears to me that the law would be as unenforceable as the present laws regarding photocopying of texts in libraries, and as laws to prevent the audio- or video-taping of publicly broadcast radio and television programs, let alone the copying of computer programs. The law would run contrary to the current thrust of technology, which is making all sorts of information accessible to the masses. The thought of what it would take to enforce a PLR in the U.S. is a nightmare. Privacy would have to be suppressed along with the public right to access of information.

Finally, I remember that it was my hometown library that lent me the books which helped turn me into a reader and, eventually, a writer myself. A PLR would, I believe, be the straw that breaks the back of many a local, small-town public library. These institutions are having a rough go of it anyway at the present time, and they are among the first institutions to be cut or underfunded when local taxes become burdensome for the citizens. It would be counterproductive to the writers, it seems to me, to have generations of potential readers from small town America kept ignorant of books and authors because they were no longer available on Main Street.

Most of us who are writers in the United States do not make our livings from royalties anyway. The small sums that would be forthcoming from a PLR would do little to change the situation. Quite the contrary, it would hurt us in the pocketbook in the long run, because many of us make more money from talks and lectures in the hinterlands than we do from royalties. If the hinterlands don't know about us, they will not ask us to come and read or lecture to them. The more freely our work circulates in the libraries and schools, the better off we are. Reputations are not made by restricting access to books, or handicapping the institutions that circulate books.

From GORE VIDAL

Since all civilized countries of the West have a Public Lending Right Law, it is only natural that the United States does not—and will not, ever. Our national bibliophobia is about as old as Dutch elm disease; and as lethal.

A New Voice: The Center for the Book's First Five Years

John Y. Cole, Executive Director

In "A Design for an Anytime, Do-It-Yourself, Energy-Free Communication Device," published in *Harper's Magazine* in 1974, historian Daniel J. Boorstin analyzed the "wonderful, the uncanny, the mystic simplicity" of the book. Three years later, after he had become Librarian of Congress, Boorstin's concern that in the fast-paced world of instant information the book was in danger of "being stifled, drowned, buried, obscured, mislaid, misunderstood, and unread" led to the creation of the Center for the Book in the Library of Congress.

Established by Public Law 95-129, approved in October 1977, the Center for the Book's goal is to serve as a catalyst that will "keep the book flourishing" by focusing national attention on books, reading, and the printed word. With help from national organizations and individual members of its National Advisory Board, the Center for the Book reminds the public of the vitality and importance of books, promotes reading, and encourages the study of books. The Center functions by bringing together members of the book, educational, and business communities for projects and symposia. It also sponsors lectures, exhibits, research, publications, a visiting-scholar program, and other events that enhance the role of the book in our society.

The Center for the Book's goals and organizational structure were determined after a series of planning meetings held with advisors from around the nation. Most of the forty-three individuals who participated in these meetings became part of the Center's first National Advisory Board, led by Ambassador George C. McGhee. Summarizing the results of the planning meetings, Librarian Boorstin explained that the Center for the Book would be:

An informal, voluntary organization funded primarily by contributions from individuals, corporations, and foundations.

Nonpartisan and without any official connection to the publishing community and without any official government policy role.

Project-oriented and dependent on other organizations to carry out projects and ideas generated by the Center's activities.

Wide-ranging and interdisciplinary in its interests, drawing on the resources of the Library of Congress and other organizations for a varied program of activities aimed at both general and scholarly audiences.

Today the Center for the Book's National Advisory Board, chaired by publisher Simon Michael Bessie, has approximately a hundred members. They include authors, editors, book and newspaper publishers, booksellers, librarians, broadcasters, scholars, educators, and readers. Board members serve a three-year term and are expected to contribute ideas, participate in projects and symposia of

Ambassador George C. McGhee, Daniel J. Boorstin, and Simon Michael Bessie (Library of Congress)

particular interest to them, and, occasionally, to represent the Center for the Book at events outside of Washington, D.C.

The Center for the Book is a cooperative endeavor between the public and private sectors of American society. Administrative support is provided by the Library of Congress, but most of the Center's annual operating budget must come from tax-deductible contributions from individuals, corporations, and foundations. The Center was started in 1977 with a generous contribution from McGraw-Hill, Inc.; its annual fund-raising goal since then has been $100,000. During its first five years, other major contributors have been Mrs. Charles W. Engelhard; Time, Inc.; the Exxon Educational Foundation; the Xerox Publishing Group; Franklin Book Programs, Inc.; Prentice-Hall International; Doubleday, Inc.; the Hearst Corporation; and Datus C. Smith, Jr. Among U.S. government agencies, the Center for the Book has received support for specific projects from the U.S. Information Agency (USIA), the National Institute of Education, and the U.S. Office of Education.

Its founding act, Public Law 95-129, called upon the Center for the Book "to provide a program for the investigation of the transmission of human knowledge" and to "heighten public interest" in the role of books and reading in our society. After five years one can review the Center's work in promoting books and reading with some satisfaction, although it is difficult to gauge the effectiveness of its efforts. The shaping of the Center's various activities into a coherent, well-balanced program for exploring the role of books, reading, and the printed word "in the transmission of human knowledge" is a challenge and a goal for its second five years.

THE BOOK IN CONTEMPORARY SOCIETY

With the assistance of its National Advisory Board and other organizations, the Center for the Book has held several national symposia concerned with books, reading, and education. "Television, the Book, and the Classroom"* (1978), which featured Board members Mortimer Adler and Frank Stanton, dealt with the possible uses of television in the classroom and television's effects on culture and learning. "Reading in America 1978,"* (1979) was a

---

*For information about the availability of these publications, write the Center for the Book in the Library of Congress, Washington, D.C. 20540.

forum to discuss the findings of a study of American reading and book-buying habits sponsored by the Book Industry Study Group, Inc. Textbook authorship, adoption, and current issues in textbook publishing were central topics at the symposium on "The Textbook in American Society"* (1981). A 1980 program titled "The State of the Book World"* featured talks by critic Alfred Kazin, publisher Dan Lacy, and former U.S. Commissioner of Education Ernest L. Boyer. Board member Barbara Tuchman's lecture, "The Book," in which she described books as "humanity in print," was cosponsored with the Authors League of America.

Four symposia took place in 1983. The fortieth anniversary of the Armed Services Editions was celebrated in February. "Radio and Reading" brought broadcasters and reading specialists together to discuss new ways of using radio to promote books and reading, particularly at the national level. "U.S. Books Abroad" examined the diminished role, in the past decade, of the U.S. book abroad. In September, at a symposium on "The Public Lending Right," authors, librarians, and government officials discussed the notion of reimbursing authors for multiple uses of their books in public libraries. "In Celebration of Biography" presented a program of biographers and publishers in November.

Publishing and book production are quite naturally topics of prime concern to the Center for the Book. *Responsibilities of the American Book Community,** published in 1981, brings together papers presented by publishers, booksellers, and scholars at two Library of Congress seminars, along with statements by authors and others at the 1980 U.S. Senate hearings on corporate concentration in American publishing and bookselling. The Center works with the Library of Congress Preservation Office to alert and educate members of the book community about the serious problem of book paper and binding deterioration. *In Celebration: The National Union Catalog, Pre-1956 Imprints** (1981) marks the completion of the 754-volume *NUC* publishing project. *In Celebration* emphasizes the editing, publishing, and scholarly uses of the National Union Catalog.

The future of the book in the information age and electronic publishing are the principal subjects of two publications. In *Gresham's Law: Knowledge or Information?** (1980), presented at the 1979 White House Conference on Library and Information Services, Daniel J. Boorstin discussed "the distinction between knowledge and information, the importance of the distinction, and the dangers of failing to recognize it." *Books, Libraries, and Electronics: Essays on the Future of Written Communication** (White Plains, N.Y.: Knowledge Industry Publications, Inc., 1982), contains essays by people associated with the Center for the Book. Thanks to the generosity of the publisher, Eliot Minsker, a Center for the Book Board member, the Center receives the royalties from the book's sale.

Children's literature is a lively, vital sector of the book world. In cooperation with the Children's Literature Center in the Library of Congress, the Center for the Book has sponsored programs on "The Audience for Children's Books"* (1980) and "Scandinavian Children's Books Today," and continues to sponsor annual lectures on writing children's books. Since 1978, Jill Paton Walsh, Elaine Konigsburg, Peter Dickinson, Natalie Babbitt, Astrid Lindgren, and Madeleine L'Engle have presented Children's Book Week lectures.

In November 1981 the Center hosted a major meeting on "Reading and Successful Living: the Family-School Partnership." Speakers included Robert Andringa, executive director of the Education Commission of the States; Mrs. George Bush; and representatives from four sponsoring organizations: the National PTA, the International Reading Association, the American Association of School Administrators, and the American Association of School Librarians. Each sponsoring organization is incorporating recommendations from the symposium into its own national and regional programs. The recommendations for each organization and the symposium papers were published in 1983 as *Reading and Successful Living* (Shoe String Press).

International aspects of the Center's program are carried out in the spirit of the Charter of the Book, set forth in 1972 during UNESCO's International Book Year. The charter stresses the importance of the two-way flow of books and other printed material across national borders and the essential role of books in promoting international understanding. In 1979, with the Asian Division of the Library of Congress, the Center sponsored an international symposium on Japanese Literature in Translation. *The International Flow of Information: A Trans-Pacific Perspective** (1981) presents papers and discussion from a symposium and study tour sponsored by the Center for the Book and the U.S. International Communication Agency (now USIA). A project that surveyed book programs sponsored by U.S. government agencies and U.S. private organizations resulted in the 61-page book *U.S. International Book Programs 1981** (1982).

The Center's Executive Director and three members of its National Advisory Board participated in UNESCO's 1982 World Congress on Books. The Congress, held in London in the spring of 1982 and attended by 315 delegates from 92 countries, attempted to assess progress made in book promotion since 1972 and to identify new goals and objectives for the 1980s. The Center is now planning projects relating to recommendations made at the Congress.

In cooperation with organizations represented on its National Advisory Board, the Center occasionally hosts forums, ceremonies, and receptions at the Library of Congress. Examples include a 1981 forum on paper and book longevity (Council on Library Resources, Inc.), a ceremony in 1982 observing UNESCO's International Literacy Day (International Reading Association), and a reception for participants in a symposium on library preservation (American Library Association).

READING AND BOOK PROMOTION

Using television and radio to encourage people to read has been one of the Center for the Book's major motifs. The cue came from a 1977 speech made by Librarian Boorstin in which he emphasized his belief that radio, television, and other new technologies were *not* enemies of the book; moreover, he noted, "we must find ways to make television our ally, to make it the trailer and the appetizer for the library and for the whole world of books." One purpose of the Center's 1978 symposium on "Television, the Book, and the Classroom" was to establish partnerships that would stimulate television viewers to draw on the world of books for additional enjoyment and information. The Library of Congress/CBS Television "Read More About It" book project, inaugurated in 1979-1980 television season, was a direct and beneficial result of the symposium.

Planning is now under way for the fifth season of "Read More About It," which uses well-known stars of major, prime-time CBS Television specials to promote books and reading. In thirty-second messages following their programs, performers mention books about the program's theme recommended by the Library of Congress and urge viewers to go to their local libraries and bookstores for these and other books on the subject. Since 1979 over forty CBS specials have included "Read More About It" messages. Each program has been seen by millions of viewers; for example, the first of the

1982-83 programs, "Charles and Diana: A Royal Romance," had an estimated audience of twenty-five million. Gregory Peck, Christopher Reeve, Helen Hayes, Cicely Tyson, Mickey Rooney, Jean Stapleton, Henry Fonda, and even Mickey Mouse and Charlie Brown are among the performers who have presented messages.

The books mentioned in "Read More About It" messages are selected from lists prepared by Library of Congress subject specialists. These lists are published in library and book trade publications prior to the telecasts, enabling libraries and bookstores to plan exhibits and distribute their own materials with the telecasts. CBS promotes the project nationally through film clips, posters, bookmarks, and a traveling exhibit. The Center for the Book coordinates the project, which has as its slogan: "Linking the Pleasure, Power, and Excitement of Books and Television."

"Read More About It" is a book awareness project that attempts to stimulate people to "think books" after viewing a television program. Another Center for the Book national reading promotion project, "Books Make a Difference," also encourages the book connection, but on a personal, more introspective level. "Books Make a Difference" began in 1980 under the guidance of the Center's Board member Ann Heidbreder Eastman. More than 300 citizens in over 50 communities throughout the United States were interviewed about books that had helped shape their lives. The two questions asked were: "What book made a difference in your life?" and "What was that difference?" The thought-provoking and entertaining responses provide ample evidence of the importance of books and reading to citizens at every level of society.

The Center for the Book is now encouraging libraries and schools to incorporate the "Books Make a Difference" idea into their own activities. "Books Make a Difference" was the theme of several 1981 segments of National Public Radio's "All Things Considered" program and of the 1981 American Book Awards promotion and awards ceremony. In 1982 Xerox Educational Publications received a gratifying response from schools around the country when it sponsored, in cooperation with the Center for the Book, a national "Books Make a Difference" essay contest for grade-school students. In 1983 the Shoe String Press published *Books That Made a Difference: What People Told Us* by project interviewers Gordon and Patricia Sabine.

Friends of Libraries U.S.A., an organization consisting of friends' groups for public and academic libraries throughout the country, is one of the Center for the Book's principal partners in promoting books and reading. A forum on "Good Ideas for Friends' groups," held in 1981, featured many of the Center's promotion ideas; an expanded version of the program that will result in a publication is being planned in 1984.

HISTORY OF BOOKS

The interdisciplinary study of books, focusing on the relationship of the history of books, reading, and the printed word to society, is another of the Center's major interests. The Center encourages the historical study of books and reading through a visiting-scholar program, as well as through various lectures, publications, projects, and symposia. Elizabeth Eisenstein, professor of history at the University of Michigan, was the Center's first visiting scholar; the second is Marianna Tax Choldin of the University of Illinois, whose major interests are Russian censorship, translation, and bibliography.

The Engelhard Lecture Series on the Book, a commissioned series of public lectures by prominent scholars, is aimed at a general, nonspecialist audience. Lecturers have been Dan H. Laurence, Nicolas Barker, Philip Hofer, Elizabeth Eisenstein, Edwin Wolf II, Ian Willison, and Robert Darnton. Most of the lectures have been published in the *Quarterly Journal of the Library of Congress*. Laurence's lecture, *A Portrait of the Author as a Bibliography** (1983), has been published separately. Other Center for the Book publications include *On the History of Libraries and Scholarship** (1980), by Ian Willison, head of the Rare Book Collections, The British Library; *A Nation of Readers** (1982), delivered by Daniel J. Boorstin at the opening of a Library of Congress exhibition illustrating the significance of books and reading in American life; and *The 1812 Catalog of the Library of Congress: A Facsimile** (1982), featuring an essay by historian Robert A. Rutland about the importance of books to our first congressmen.

An important scholarly publication based on a Center for the Book symposium appeared in 1982. *The Early Illustrated Book: Essays in Honor of Lessing J. Rosenwald**, edited by art historian Sandra Hindman, focuses on three different subjects that are well represented in the Library's Rosenwald collection: 15th- and 16th-century Dutch and Flemish books, landscape works, and the illustration of Vergil. Containing eleven essays accompanied by 175 black-and-white illustrations and eight full-color plates, this volume was cited by the

Front cover for Daniel J. Boorstin's 21 April 1982 address at the opening of a Library of Congress exhibition that drew on the library's collections to illustrate "the significance of reading in American life"

American Institute of Graphic Arts in 1982 as one of the year's best-designed books. Another scholarly symposium that will result in a major illustrated book is "To Show the World: the Atlas in History," which will be sponsored with the Library's Geography and Map Division and convened in October 1984.

Literacy in Historical Perspective,* another collection of papers from a Center for the Book symposium, was published in 1983. Edited by historian Daniel Resnick, the volume contains historical essays about literacy in England, China, Russia, and the United States. Finally, the Center for the Book has commissioned a publication by Paul Needham of the Morgan Library about his exciting discovery, in the Library's Rosenwald collection, of an unrecorded Indulgence printed by William Caxton, England's first printer.

Members of the Center's National Advisory Board are helping develop three projects of potential significance to the study of the history of books. The first is a guide to the resources in the Library of Congress for the study of the history of books; it is being prepared by consultant Alice Schreyer. A proposed guide to book trade and publishing archives in the United States is still in the planning stages. The final project, a complicated and long-range bibliographical endeavor, is the indexing and publication of the 1790-1870 U.S. copyright records now in the Rare Book and Special Collections Division of the Library of Congress.

PUBLICATIONS SPONSORED BY THE CENTER FOR THE BOOK

Reading

Reading in America 1978. 1979. $4.95.
A Nation of Readers. 1982.
Reading and Successful Living–The Family-School Partnership. (Hamden, Conn.: Shoe String Press, 1983). $11.50.
Books That Made a Difference: What People Told Us. (Hamden, Conn.: Shoe String Press, 1983). $13.50.

The International Role of Books

The International Flow of Information: A Trans-Pacific Perspective. 1981.
U.S. International Book Programs 1981. 1982.
U.S. Books Abroad: Neglected Ambassadors. 1983.

The Book in Contemporary Society

Television, the Book, and the Classroom. 1978. $4.95.
The Textbook in American Society. 1981. $5.95.
Responsibilities of the American Book Community. 1981. $7.95.
The Book. 1980.
The Audience for Children's Books. 1980.
Gresham's Law: Knowledge or Information? 1980.
The State of the Book World 1980. 1981.
The World Encompassed. 1981.
The Book Enchained. 1984.

The History of Books

The Circle of Knowledge. 1979.
On the History of Libraries and Scholarship. 1980.
In Celebration: The National Union Catalog, Pre-1956

Imprints. 1981. $5.95.
The 1812 Catalog of the Library of Congress: A Facsimile. 1982. $15.
The Early Illustrated Book: Essays in Honor of Lessing J. Rosenwald. 1982. $50.

A Portrait of the Author as a Bibliography. 1983.
Literacy in Historical Perspective. 1983. $8.
Books in Action: The Armed Services Editions. 1984.
A Rounceval Indulgence: Unrecorded Printing by William Caxton. 1984.

First Strauss "Livings" Awarded to Cynthia Ozick and Raymond Carver

Cynthia Ozick and Raymond Carver have been selected as the first recipients of "The Mildred and Harold Strauss Livings" by the American Academy and Institute of Arts and Letters.

These major grants, amounting to $350,000 over a five-year period, are the result of a bequest from Mildred and Harold Strauss to provide writers of demonstrated ability and productivity with an annual stipend to cover their living expenses so that they can devote their time exclusively to writing. The grants are among the largest available to writers, amounting to $35,000 annually, and are given for a minimum period of five years, tax free.

The recipients were chosen by a jury of writers who are members of the Academy: Donald Barthelme, Irving Howe, Philip Roth, and Elizabeth Hardwick, who served as chairman. Nominations were made by members of the Academy who themselves are not eligible.

Harold Strauss, who died in 1975, was a former editor-in-chief of Alfred A. Knopf, Inc. He identified strongly with writers and the financial problems they face. Together with his wife, Mildred, who died in 1980, he gave a bequest to the Academy-Institute to provide funds for "Livings" to free deserving writers from the need to devote their time to outside employment.

CYNTHIA OZICK specializes in the short story and has published three collections of stories and a novel. She has written more than a hundred essays, as well as criticism, translations of fiction and poetry. She received an Academy-Institute Award in 1973, a Guggenheim Fellowship in 1982 and numerous other awards. Two of her short stories were awarded O. Henry First Prizes.

Cynthia Ozick was born in New York City in 1928 and is a graduate of New York University and Ohio State University. She taught at both institutions and was, most recently, Distinguished Artist-in-Residence at City College of the City University of New York. Her first novel, *Trust*, was published in 1966, followed in 1971 by *The Pagan Rabbi and Other Stories*, *Bloodshed and Three Novellas* in 1976, and *Levitation: Five Fictions* in 1982. A collection of her essays, *Art and Ardor*, and a novel, *The Cannibal Gallaxy*, were published in 1983. Ms. Ozick is married to Bernard Hallote and has a daughter, Rachel.

RAYMOND CARVER gained recognition first as a poet with three published collections: *Near Klamath* (1968); *Winter Insomnia* (1970); and *At Night the Salmon Move* (1976). He was named a National Endowment for the Arts Fellow in Poetry in 1971, an honor which he received again in 1980 for Fiction. Since 1974 he has published five collections of critically acclaimed short stories: *Put Yourself in My Shoes* (1974); *Will You Please Be Quiet, Please?* (1976); *Furious Seasons* (1977); *What We Talk About When We Talk About Love* (1981); and *Cathedral* (1983). *Fires: Essays, Poems, Stories* was also published in 1983.

Mr. Carver has taught creative writing at several universities, including the University of California at Santa Cruz and Berkeley, University of Iowa, Goddard College, University of Texas at El Paso, and Syracuse University. He was awarded a Guggenheim Fellowship in 1979 and an O. Henry First Prize for a short story in 1983.

Raymond Carver was born in Glatskanie, Oregon, in 1938. He attended Chico State College, where he studied writing with the late John Gardner. He is a graduate of Humboldt State University in California and the Writers' Workshop at the University of Iowa. Mr. Carver divides his time between Port Angeles, Washington, and Syracuse, New York.

Winners of Strauss "Livings" who are

employed must resign their positions before receiving "Livings" funds.—*Announcement from the American Academy and Institute of Arts and Letters.*

AN INTERVIEW
with CYNTHIA OZICK

DLB: "Even at age 6—no, as soon as I was conscious of being alive—I knew I was a writer," you told Eve Ottenberg for the *New York Times*, 10 April 1983. How did you know you wanted to write, and where do you think the desire came from?

OZICK: It really is just as I said; I always knew it. It was a very strong and genuine feeling. Maybe the idea of becoming a writer was not distant because my mother's brother, my uncle, was a poet. But I certainly was never consciously aware of him as a model in the sense that people nowadays speak of models.

   I think the desire to write came from that absolute shudder of ecstasy one gets reading fairy tales. You want to dream stories and live in them, too. But it really preceded literacy, because I remember being five or so and feeling overcome by wanting to make up a moon poem. "O Moon," it began. I hadn't yet been taught to read or write, so my mother set it down for me. That's my earliest memory of composing anything.

DLB: You write a great deal about the burdens and the isolation of being Jewish. Were you aware early in your writing—or in your thinking about writing—that this would be a theme, or did it evolve out of the writing itself?

OZICK: Let me say first that I would quarrel with the sense of "burden" or "isolation." There is an ocean of Jewish intellectual history, extraordinary texts and ideas, some of them unique on the planet; the subject is extremely interesting to me intrinsically. Jewish experience isn't just a very long history of externally applied unpleasantness—it is, more essentially, a very long history of ideas. I am attracted to Jewish ideas for their own sake. To narrow it to a simple question of a people singled out for oppression is to tell less than half the story.

   But to answer the question, I never dreamed that I was going to go so far in this direction. My imagination belonged at the start to English and American literature; in important ways it still does. My Jewish passion, though rooted in childhood, evolved, to use your word—and very, very gradu-

Cynthia Ozick (©Ricki Rosen)

ally, as a matter of fact, through years of historical and critical reading. When I collected these essays recently for *Art and Ardor*, I was amazed that I had done so many on Jewish themes. This wasn't altogether an independent event; several were in response to book review, lecture, or conference invitations. And in terms of the course of my writing, this thematic material developed late. In *Trust*, my first novel, there was only one Jewish character. I went into that book dazzled by Fitzgerald, and came out attached to Akiva. In the end I chose idiosyncrasy. Instead of parroting America, I thought I would try to complicate it.

DLB: Has your brief teaching experience affected your own writing in any way?

OZICK: No, it didn't affect my work. It affected my life, because I met some gifted young writers who impressed me very much. I think I relived my own anxieties and ambitions through watching them, and I felt deep empathy with them.

DLB: Your work has had good critical reception. Do you hope for more readers?

OZICK: I consider myself a generally obscure writer who has now and then had some good reviews. Yet those good reviews appear to have made almost no difference at all in my fate as a writer, which remains privately obsessed. I have a tiny readership, if "readership" means numbers. When the article about my work came out in the *New York Times Magazine*, it was somehow humiliating, because what people said was, "I never heard of you. What are you doing in the *Times*?" Like the protagonist of James's comical story "The Next Time," I will never be a popular writer or household name. I recognize that I'm not easy to read. I write demanding sentences.

DLB: Then how do you feel about writing for what you regard as an almost nonexistent readership?

OZICK: I think, as a writer, all you need is consummation of the work. And I know when the point of consummation comes for me: that's when the thing, whatever it is, is published. When the work is in manuscript, no matter how polished it may seem, no matter how joyful the victory of editorial approbation may be, it is not really finished, fulfilled, or, again, *consummated*, until it reaches print. And when that moment comes, I feel ultimately satisfied. That is the end of the process. The rest is wholly out of my hands. I never do think of what happens afterwards. And I'm always surprised, really essentially, from-scratch surprised, when I meet somebody who says he or she has read something of mine. It took me so many years to get published that I think I will probably never get over that surprise.

DLB: How will your life and work be affected by receiving one of the first two Mildred and Harold Strauss Livings?

OZICK: The timing is quite wonderful because my daughter is going off to college and you know what a burden tuition is.

I'm just beginning to be able to answer the question in a deeper way. I've had a kind of evolution in my feelings that's been very striking. Usually one doesn't pay much attention to gradualism in one's own sensibility—it's very difficult to do that. But I've really felt the difference internally.

I was away—in Italy—when the letter came. My husband opened it, thinking it might be of some moment. So when I got home, he already knew its contents. I was not prepared for it, and it took me a very long session, sitting at the kitchen table, to absorb what it said. I simply couldn't assimilate such news. When it did enter my mind, about the money and what this meant, I was distressed. My first

thought was, I cannot possibly accept this. There was a very, very profound sense of guilt. Why did I deserve this any more than a hundred other writers with the same, what's the expression, track record? When in the course of events I got truly courteous expressions of goodwill and congratulations from other writers, the sense of guilt and indebtedness to them deepened.

That feeling is unabated. But something else has been growing parallel to it: a sense of moral support. I feel, not confident—I'm just as paralyzed at beginning a page as before, if not more so, because now I have to live up to something—but less isolated.

Now, on top of the guilt and the mysterious business of feeling less isolated (this will wane, I'm certain—isolation will surely return), it is dawning on me—late; all my feelings seem to come late—that I'm in a state of high jubilation and that what has happened to me is extraordinary. How could I not feel gratitude? My sense of gratitude to the Academy is permanent—and will in some way outlive me.

DLB: Has writing become any easier for you?

OZICK: Writing is always hard and nothing makes it any easier. It's always, it seems to me, at least, an act of supreme courage against very powerful forces of paralysis and silence. I don't bubble out. Writing, for me, is a series of masks and disguises and discoveries. It seems to be about truth-telling, the desire to say something very straightforwardly despite the fact that fiction is a maze of schemes and strategies. There is no glory in it, and no hope of glory. There is a shyness and a huge anxiety. I think that's the best way I can summarize at this late point what writing means.

–Jean W. Ross (May 1983)

AN INTERVIEW
with RAYMOND CARVER

DLB: In the title essay in *Fires*, you described the bleak early years of odd jobs, being confined by the demands of parenthood, hoping for an hour or two a day to write, being forced by these circumstances to write short fiction and poetry rather than longer fiction. Then there was a quieter period. Now that you're one of the first two recipients of the Mildred and Harold Strauss Livings, what further changes do you anticipate in your writing patterns and your life?

Raymond Carver (©Kelly Wise)

CARVER: Well, for sure I won't have to teach anymore; I've resigned my teaching position at Syracuse University. So this fall, instead of preparing for classes and the literature course, I can commence writing a novel. It's going to give me what seems to be limitless freedom to do what I want to do, a long span of uninterrupted time not having to worry about teaching, meeting classes, student conferencing and paperwork, all the duties of a university professor.

DLB: The urge to write must have been very strong to get you through those difficult years. How far back does it go?

CARVER: I'd wanted to write since I was a kid twelve or thirteen years old. I had grown up listening to my dad's stories; he was from the South, and he liked to tell stories about himself and my great-grandfather and other friends and relatives of his. I always liked to listen to those stories, and I liked to read. I had no guidance or instruction about what to read and there were no books in the house, so I'd mosey down to the library and grab anything that came to hand.

I hoped I'd grow up being able to write. *What I'd write about didn't matter to me; I just wanted to* write. But I didn't really begin until my first or second year of college. It occurred to me then that if I was going to be a writer, I'd have to write something! I wasn't just going to wake up thirty years old and find myself a writer. So I began writing seriously when I was nineteen or twenty. And I began sending my efforts out in the mail. Unfortunately, or maybe fortunately, everything came back to me.

DLB: Did you start with one or the other, or were you writing short stories and poems at the same time?

CARVER: I was doing both at the same time. I was as attracted to poems as I was to short stories and novels. Now I write fiction nearly exclusively. But I hope this situation won't pertain forever. I like writing poetry, and I want to write more.

DLB: Do you think short fiction is coming into a more successful time commercially?

CARVER: Without question. There are so many good and exciting short-story writers today. Far more serious attention is being paid to short-story writers today than, say, ten years ago—or even five years ago. Collections of short stories are becoming more attractive to publishers, and the university presses are publishing more short stories. Most importantly, perhaps, people are *reading* short-story collections today—perhaps because more collections are being taken more seriously by the critics and reviewers.

DLB: Is there work in progress that you'd like to talk about?

CARVER: There's work in progress, but nothing to talk about yet. In fact, I never talk about work or show it to anyone until it's well along. I want to commence something long, call it a novel, when I go back to Syracuse in September.

DLB: Will you miss teaching?

CARVER: I don't think so. I did it, and I think I did a good job with it. Some people need that position, that structure, that place in the sun. But I don't think I will. I have too many things to do now. I'll certainly miss some of the students, but I consider myself fortunate to have gotten the award so that I can be free now to write full-time, to turn all the attention and energy I'm capable of to that end.

–Jean W. Ross (May 1983)

The Practice of Biography II

with B. L. REID

B. L. Reid is emeritus professor of English at Mt. Holyoke College. He received the Pulitzer Prize for biography for *The Man from New York: John Quinn and his Friends* (1968). Professor Reid's other volumes are *Art by Subtraction: A Dissenting Opinion of Gertrude Stein* (1958); *William Butler Yeats: The Lyric of Tragedy* (1961); *The Long Boy and Others: Eighteenth-Century Studies* (1969); *Tragic Occasions: Essays on Several Forms* (1971); and *The Lives of Roger Casement* (1976).

DLB: You have written critical essays as well as biography. How are these forms of scholarship related?

REID: They are related in the sense that there is a literary, critical, historical base for all of them. The essays are essentially literary criticism, but they all have bits of biography. The biographies themselves are things I was led into by interests in literature and art history, so that you might say they have common subject matter fundamentally but there are different emphases, different lengths. They are all somehow rooted in literature.

But your question is really two questions: Why do I do both things; and, Do I see a relationship between them?

DLB: Yes; is one an adjunct of the other?

REID: I think so—that is, in terms of my own tastes and my own principles as a reader, as a writer, and as a teacher. I've always been interested in the way these things work together. I suppose to some people these ideas would seem heretical, but they don't seem odd to me.

As a critic, insofar as I can call myself such an animal, I guess my training was really in the so-called New Criticism. I was trained in the art of close reading—looking at a work of literature as free-standing. A thing to be read, understood, enjoyed, but as a whole object around which you can draw a line and say, That's a work of art. But I found I was, at the same time, equally interested in the lives of the artists. And it seemed to me, though I tried to be the hardworking new critic, I kept finding myself being instructed by things I learned about the lives. Particularly through other people's biographies of

B. L. Reid

them, their own autobiographies, and letters too. I'm fascinated with the letters, the journals. These seem to me ways of enriching one's reading of the work of art without violating it. I don't see any crime in learning from fact. To read more humanely, more copiously, perhaps, more expansively, so long as you don't go off your head and lose sight of the fact that the work of art *is* a work of art.

I've always enjoyed trying to put them together—trying to enrich the reading of the work of art by what I can pick up in the way of fact. And of utterance by the writers that was not designed to be specifically literary, such as letters. I'm thinking particularly of cases like Keats or Yeats where it seems to me you learn many, many things from the letters that help you read the poems they wrote.

The Roger Casement biography is a different kind of thing. It was a hangover from a problem with the life of John Quinn. When I got through with Quinn, I had enjoyed writing a biography and

I had learned not only a lot about Quinn, but about his associations with artists and writers, and I was interested in both those sides of his life. I was also interested in his Irishness. For some reason I have accumulated a fascination with the Irish writers. That was one of the things that led me to him. His being Irish-American and a patron and follower and general helper-out of writers I was interested in, as well as painters and sculptors. Many writers, many of whom were Irish (though by no means all). His Irish side interested me as well as his side as the helpful fan of the arts. He struck me as the kind of guy who really wants to be an artist but has no particular talent, so he goes and does the next best thing—he steeps himself in original works and says, Now how can they help me, and, on the other hand, how can I help the artists? That was his way of working it.

When I got through with Quinn, the next obvious subject, it seemed to me, was George Russell, who was one of Quinn's beneficiaries, friends, and a prime mover in the Irish Literary Renaissance. He seemed to me in some ways the most interesting figure across the board, in that whole pattern. He's nowhere near as good a writer as Yeats, and he doesn't have Yeats's history as a man of the theater, but he did a great many things very well, and he's an especially interesting and useful kind of person. So I thought maybe I'd tackle a biography of Russell, and I looked into that a little bit. I talked to Russell's son and quickly learned that there was another man, up in Canada, writing a rather long biography. Whereas I could have pursued it, that took the edge off of it and I let Russell go.

Then I had a notion of doing a biography of John Crowe Ransom, who interested me from many points of view. I had met Ransom and liked him. He had been at Mount Holyoke doing a reading and acting as a judge in the Glascock contest. He came to our house for lunch. I was charmed by him; I was already a fan of his because of his poetry particularly (which was what I mainly knew—at that time I hadn't read a whole lot of his independent criticism), and I knew of his work as editor of the *Kenyon Review*. Ransom again struck me as a good subject: interesting man, fine poet, good critic, great editor—all of these things as well as a hardworking academic person. He interested me as a Southern gent. He seemed to me a kind of classic type of persona.

So I wrote to Ransom about the idea and, somewhat to my surprise, he seemed interested—sort of gave me a go-ahead, try it and see how you come out. I was teaching all the time, of course; in my spare time, I began doing some work on Ransom. I wrote him another letter in which I said, I want to come down and see you. I want to talk with you about your life. The idea seemed to scare him. I think at that point it hadn't really dawned on him that a biography might be a kind of invasion. That turned him off, though he didn't say absolutely no. But he still wouldn't give me any time, wouldn't name a date. I thought, well I can always try again. But the next time I tried him he was very off-putting, very cool; in fact, you might even say cold. And I decided he really wanted me to give it up. I didn't understand why.

Later I learned that a fellow at Vanderbilt, Thomas Daniel Young, was working on *Gentleman in a Dustcoat*. Pretty good book. I think Ransom chose Young because of the Vanderbilt connection. I didn't resent it. I thought Ransom, who was a cranky fellow, had behaved in ways I respected, though I was disappointed.

Well, this left me sort of hanging and it was at that point that I thought of doing something with Casement, who like Russell had interested me as a spin-off from the Quinn biography. Casement had been a major figure in a short period of Quinn's life and had an extremely interesting life of his own. So Casement was actually my third choice. That turned into a very complicated operation, but I was glad, finally, I had done it. I ended up thinking Casement was a second-rate person, but his life was fascinating.

DLB: How do you decide which subjects you will write criticism of and which warrant a full-scale biography?

REID: It's a combination of whim and taste, and quite often it will be something I hadn't necessarily a passion to do, but was asked. I'm thinking mostly of the essays here. They were along my lines of interest and so someone would say, How about an essay on "X"? And I would say, I'll see. I'd think it over, and if I found I was really interested, I'd do it.

I got started doing biographies partly out of revulsion against my own critical style, if that makes any sense. I felt in some of the critical essays that I was writing, I was overwriting—getting too fancy—and that sometimes style was essentially masking vacancy. This began to turn my stomach, this feeling about my own writing. I decided that I wanted to straighten out my style, simplify it, make it less pretentious, less fancy; and maybe one way to do it would be to try biography, where I'd be dealing not so much with opinion as with evidence, with

*Dust jacket for Reid's most recent book, a biography of a man
whom he finally considered "a second-rate person,"
but "fascinating"*

facts. I was interested in those things too; I was
interested in the subjects and the form and I was
reading the stuff, so I thought maybe I could put all
these things together: I could talk about some
people whom I was genuinely interested in, and at
the same time do sort of a cross rough between
literature and biography, which I see as a branch of
history.

I had always been interested not only in literature but in art. That was the thing that got me
going on Quinn, because he overlapped so many
people and so many different fields that I had a
funny feeling: This is an interesting guy and nobody knows anything about him. Who the heck was
he? What can I find out about him and say about
him? That's what really started me.

DLB: Are you working on a biography now?

REID: I had a notion of tackling Frank O'Connor,

yet another Irishman, but I haven't done anything
about that really except feel it out a little bit. This
takes a lot of time, you know, a lot of consecutive
time to concentrate; and you've always got to go
where the papers are. In the last ten years or so I
haven't been able to do that. I haven't felt free to do
the necessary research for a book on that kind of
man. Now I see somebody else has done the book.

DLB: What do you find is the most interesting part
of writing a biography?

REID: There are two most interesting parts. One is
finding the stuff—finding it and reading it and
evaluating, sorting it out, deciding what's worth
keeping and what isn't, what really matters. The
other thing is writing it. Just plain putting it into
language. The hardest part of it all, it seems to me, is
the structure, the organization. There's no great
fun in that most of the time. It tends to be pure hard
work. I've tended to take the easiest way out in
writing biography, which is straight chronology.
That gives you a ready-made structure. And I think
it's defensible. In fact, I've written articles defending it, but it's obviously not the only way to do it.

The things that I've taken the most pleasure
from in doing biography? Well, you can start with
conceiving the idea, because that means choosing
from a variety of possible things in terms of your
own tastes in art. Beyond that point the things that
interest me most are finding the stuff, studying
it—and writing it is fun. Again it goes back for me to
that question of style. It has got to be straight and
clear. It can't be dull.

DLB: You've done a lot of teaching. Do you think it
is possible to teach someone else to write biography?

REID: I often wonder about that. I think it's a very
tricky question. I certainly think I can improve the
writing of students. But I can't put my finger on a
single person whom I can say I've taught to write.
We used to call our freshman English courses
Reading and Writing. And it used to seem to me
that I could teach reading; I really could show students how to read better. But when it comes to the
matter of their writing, I think the main thing you
can show them is what's wrong with it. Whether they
choose to do anything about it remains their problem. I was thinking about this just the other day.
Here we are at the end of another semester of
freshman English, and it seems to me that all of my
students are writing better than they did in February. But I ask myself, Have I taught that? And I

don't think I can say yes. All I do is sort of pick at their papers, and do in effect what amounts to an editorial process. I try to read papers carefully and 1) show what is wrong, and 2) show ways of improving. But it really rests with the student to decide whether she wishes to learn to write—and then I think she can learn something from the teacher. In the long run, though, she's got to do most of the teaching herself, or so I feel. Then, too, the students write better at the end of the semester simply because they're older—not much, half a year, but that matters a lot at their age. And furthermore, they're reading and writing all over the place, not only in English class. One of the big problems about trying to teach writing is that so much published writing is so bad. So much of what is handed to the student in print is bad writing, particularly in textbooks. The well-written textbook is rather rare. It happens mostly in English and history.

DLB: Can you name some biographies that you think are particularly fine?

REID: This is the sort of thing that takes some thinking. I shouldn't do this off the cuff because names go out of the head. I think Walter Jackson Bate is a very fine biographer and a fine writer. I've admired greatly his books on Keats and on Johnson. Another good recent biography is Frederick Pottle's biography of Boswell, which is still in progress—the first volume is first-rate. That'll go on, undoubtedly, down through the years. There's a good new life of Matthew Arnold, I'm told. Lionel Trilling's *Life of Arnold* I like a lot. I like this James Mellow. I liked his book on Hawthorne. I liked Justin Kaplan's books—the one on Mark Twain and the new one on Whitman.

Boswell's *Life of Johnson* still seems to me a great book, but it's not a well-made book. It's well written—Boswell is a good stylist—but there's a slapdash sort of structure. What makes that book great, clearly, is not Boswell but Johnson. Boswell stumbled on the world's best subject, and one who certainly must have been the greatest talker in the history of the English language. When you've got that kind of subject, and when you have recorded it as successfully as Boswell did, you've got a ready-made book—it's hard to go wrong. Johnson's own *Lives of the Poets* are very spotty, very uneven, but among them is some great biographical and critical writing.

Keats's letters strike me as great biography, great autobiography, though they weren't designed as such. Another collection of letters that is almost

equally striking is Ezra Pound's. They're great. Very uneven, very hectic, hurried kinds of things, but full of brilliance. Very funny. High comedy there.

Henry James is great all over the place, but his autobiographical things are especially interesting. I wish he had done more formal biography. I think he would have been a master, but he was so busy writing those great novels that he didn't have time. We need a better life of Melville than we have.

That's a very spotty set of recollections. I like the new book of Humphrey Carpenter. It's a better book than one would have thought could be written so soon about Auden's life. It's a fine book. T. S. Eliot, of course, needs a great biography, and I don't know who's going to produce that. We need a new biography of Yeats. That's another one I would have loved to do, but it's being done by a man named F. S. L. Lyons, an academic at Trinity College, Dublin. I imagine that's going to be slow in coming, but again it's a great subject.

DLB: What do you see as a biographer's responsibility to the reader?

REID: 1) Find a good subject; 2) Find out as much fact as you can about it; 3) Try to interpret it both sensibly and sensitively. Don't bore the reader, but don't cajole him. Don't chuck him under the chin. Don't put yourself in the way of the story. Keep out of it as much as you can.

DLB: Is there such a thing as a perfect reader?

REID: A perfect reader? I don't think there is a perfect reader. No. There's a very wide range in the quality in readers, and there are some who are superlative. Bate would be a case in point. I don't know any perfect readers. Ransom was a great reader. Eliot was a great reader. Pound was a great reader. Yeats was a very cranky kind of reader but nonetheless good. Often, I think, the best readers are artists, though sometimes their vanity, or their envy, gets in the way.

DLB: As a rule, how is the criticism of contemporary biography?

REID: It's another thing I don't follow in any systematic way. I read what falls under my eyes. I think it's pretty good. I tend to trust criticism of biography more than I trust criticism of fiction. That's partly because I think the quality of biography nowadays is better than the quality of fiction, and this elicits from the critic a better performance, as it should

Page from the manuscript for Reid's unpublished autobiography (the author)

and I think does. I think critics of biography tend to be a little saner and a little less vainglorious than the critics of fiction or poetry. If you're going to ask me who are the great critics of biography, I haven't tried to study it in those terms.

DLB: It has been fifteen years since *The Man from New York.* Do you look back and wish you could change the book in any way? Anything you would have done differently? Anything you would add?

REID: I'm pretty satisfied with that book. I didn't waste a lot of time on it. I worked very hard on it within concentrated spurts of time. I had really one full writing year after I had got all my stuff together, and I wrote it very carefully.

I originally had a very different concluding chapter—very critical of Quinn because he made me angry, and I was disgusted in a certain way with things about him as a person that were impossible to like. Particularly what seemed to me a vulgar strain in him, an overbearing strain, a tendency to bully people. That got under my skin. I wrote a long concluding chapter in which I sort of took him apart as a human being. And then I showed the manuscript to various people and they didn't like that last chapter. They said it felt dirty to them, nasty, like a cheap shot, hitting him when he couldn't hit back. Furthermore, I had had the run of his archive, and people had been so generous in letting me get at the evidence that they persuaded me that was the wrong way to end the book. So I just wiped that chapter out completely and wrote a new conclusion, which was straight fact. I'm glad I did it that way. I have no particular regrets about it.

As far as I can see, not a whole lot has emerged since the book came out. I don't feel I missed a lot that mattered. There's a big correspondence between Quinn and Lady Gregory that's in the works, and I could have made fuller use of that if I'd

spotted it. The whole story about Quinn and his possession of *The Waste Land* manuscript—it's too long and complicated to go into there—I felt I had to skimp in the book because ownership, copyright, of the manuscript was under dispute. That would have been fascinating if I could have worked it into the book, but I didn't feel that I had the right. I may have been wrong or timorous about that. Maybe if I'd pushed harder and been belligerent I could have got a simple permission to do my work. But I didn't feel free at that time to exploit the manuscript. In fact, I didn't learn until my book was practically complete where the manuscript really was. And then I learned about it in such circumstances, such hush-hush terms, that my feeling was that I couldn't talk about it at all.

DLB: Have you ever considered autobiography?

REID: I've already written a manuscript of about 350 pages on my early life. It's fun to read. But that's all I intend to write and I can't find anybody who's willing to publish that. They all say it hasn't any shape. It's straight narrative, straight chronology, pure fact. But I resolved to write it that way from the beginning, not to jazz it up, not to try to give it fancy emphases, and let it run its own risk. It carries me down to where I start teaching, and that's as far as I want to go. I don't want to write about my academic career. I think it's going to end up in the family archives.

DLB: What is your current project?

REID: I've got a new idea of a very different kind. I'm not even going to tell you about it. I think it's such a good idea, I'm afraid somebody will steal it. It's in some sense a biographical idea, but it's more dramatic. That's all I'm going to tell.

–Mary Bruccoli

Literary Research Archives II:
Berg Collection of English and American Literature of The New York Public Library

Lola L. Szladits, Curator

lbert Ashton Berg (1872-1950), prominent New York surgeon, erected a memorial to his brother, Henry Woolfe Berg (1858-1938), who was also a physician, by donating their joint collection of some 3000 items to The New York Public Library in 1939. Although the collection was not confined to any one century, its strength lay in nineteenth-century authors, and it consisted mostly of first editions and some manuscript letters. While the doctors practiced medicine, their avocation was literature, and their collection aimed less for completeness in any one author than for a broad range of works by those writers whom they preferred to read themselves: Dryden, Defoe, Coleridge, Dickens, and Thackeray, among the English; and Hawthorne, Longfellow, Poe, and Whitman, among the Americans. Dr. Berg manifested his generosity further by equipping a room to house the collection and endowing a sufficiently large sum for a librarian's salary and for further additions "similar in character."

The way the room was set up in 1940 reflected the original wishes of a living donor who, from 1944, was also a member of the library's board of trustees. Certain objets d'art were installed from Dr. Berg's town house at 10 East 73rd Street. Most prominent among them is a ceramic statue of Moses representing the Old Testament, from a fifteenth-century triptych by Giovanni della Robbia, which decorates the doorway to the reading room. Two portraits of the Berg brothers flank a memorial inscription, beneath which, according to Dr. Berg's wish, some of his jewelry is on permanent display.

In 1940 the original collection was enriched by adding that of W. T. H. Howe (1874-1939), which was purchased by Dr. Berg from Mr. Howe's estate. It had long been recognized as one of the outstanding collections of English and American literature in private hands. Mr. Howe of Cincinnati, president of American Book Company, spent forty

years assembling his 16,000-volume library of books, autograph letters, drawings, and objects (many Dickens memorabilia, including one of the novelist's desks and his gas lamp) by purchases made in auction rooms and through gifts of contemporary authors who had been his friends. Among their number were John Galsworthy, James Stephens, W. B. Yeats, AE (G. W. Russell), and many others. Like many other collectors of refinement and bibliophilic acumen, Mr. Howe was fond of association copies, but he possessed other treasures such as Poe's *Tamerlane* (1827), a first edition of Gray's *Elegy Wrote In A Country Church Yard* (1751) in original wrappers, the Rosebery copy of Keats's *Endymion* (1818), and a whole list of unique items. The Howe Collection's chief attraction to Dr. Berg, however, was its Dickens and Thackeray holdings, in which he found eleven annotated prompt copies Dickens the actor carried with him when he gave his readings. The strength of the collection in source material for research suddenly increased, and Dr. Berg asked for a second room.

The extraordinary acquisitiveness of Dr. Berg was reinforced by the library's director, Harry Miller Lydenberg (1874-1960), and the first curator, John D. Gordan (1907-1968). In 1941 the internationally renowned collection of rare books and manuscripts assembled by Owen D. Young (1874-1962), chairman of the board of the General Electric Company, was presented to the library by Dr. Berg and Mr. Young. At the time of the gift it was described as "the largest and most important single collection ever presented to the Library." In terms of sudden accrual of great resources for literary research, it certainly still is. With the Young library, the Berg Collection acquired its important Burney Papers; a second copy of Poe's *Tamerlane*; such incunabula as *De Imitatio Christi* (circa 1473), Homer's first collected works published in the West (Florence, 1488), a Caxton printing of *The Chronicles Of England* (1482), and Pynson's printing of *The Canterbury Tales* (circa 1491); printed and manuscript items by New England authors as well as Mark

Giovanni della Robbia's Moses, *over the door to the Berg Collection Reading Room (Bob Serating)*

Twain; association copies; extraordinary fine copies of William Blake's hand-colored works of art; and other literary treasures far too voluminous to enumerate. The Berg Collection also grew in duplicate volumes, many of which are unique because of inscriptions and personal associations. According to Dr. Berg's instructions, nothing once acquired can be resold or exchanged; and it became necessary for him to ask for a third room.

The public spirit which triggered the initial extraordinary growth of what had been a private collector's passion manifested itself in public only once: on 11 October 1940, during the formal presentation of the collection, Dr. Berg spoke the following words:

> These books, manuscripts, and letters, together with the appointments in this room, were the dear friends of my late brother and myself. In presenting them to you and the Trustees of The New York Public Library of our City, and through you to the Public, it is with the pleasant anticipation that their new friends will use them and love them as we did.

After Dr. Berg's death in 1950, when in his will he generously endowed his collection further, the use and love of his books and manuscripts were encouraged by curator John D. Gordan, Conrad scholar and meticulous public guardian of literary research. One of the three rooms, according to an instruction in Dr. Berg's will, was enlarged into air-conditioned stack and office space (construction was completed in 1962). The exhibition room, one of the largest in the nation, was distinguished by Dr. Gordan's exhibitions, most of which were accompanied by printed catalogues funded by an endowment presented by Dr. Berg's sister. Gordan's catalogues of author exhibits such as Bernard Shaw, George Gissing, and John Masefield became major milestones in bio-bibliographical education. Gordan also embarked on a relentless search for new research materials, because he believed scholarship would best be served by adding to the collection's archival holdings. It was during his twenty-eight-year tenure that such papers as Sir Edward Marsh's correspondence with Georgian poets; Lady Gregory's papers, which provide a vast background to the Irish Liter-

Inscription in the dedication copy of Mark Twain's The Prince and the Pauper *(Berg Collection of English and American Literature, New York Public Library)*

ary Revival; and Virginia Woolf's manuscripts of her novels and her diaries were acquired. It was Gordan who drew up procedures under which a collection of ever-increasing value can be fairly administered. As testimony to Gordan's leadership Richard Altick wrote in *The Art Of Literary Research* (1963): "The [New York Public] Library's jewel, as far as literary research is concerned, is the Berg Collection."

From Joyce Hemlow's biography *The History of Fanny Burney* (1958) to Quentin Bell's equally celebrated biography of his aunt, *Virginia Woolf* (1972), and from Gay Wilson Allen's *The Solitary Singer: A Critical Biography Of Walt Whitman* (1955) to James

Mellow's *Nathaniel Hawthorne* (1980), a whole pageant of writers and stacks of published works testify to the enduring value of the Berg Collection as a research center and a shrine for scholars. Nothing in the history of a public collection can match the sudden excitement of a decade in which the emergence of Virginia Woolf as a major twentieth-century writer kept a small curatorial staff constantly on the go. A large body of literary publications speaks volumes of praise for a small but dedicated staff, the size of which may not increase even under growing demands for its services.

No literary collection is an island. No archive—personal or public—can be considered complete and whole in itself. It is impossible to collect in one place all the written traces of a writing and reading man or woman. It is when all the pieces of a life and oeuvre are conflated, often from two or three continents, resting in private or, as is often the case since World War II, public hands; relocated and recollected, often by two generations of scholar-writers, that biographical and critical studies of lasting value emerge. Successive generations of collectors and curatorial staff at the Berg Collection of English and American Literature are among those without whom, as the cliché dedication pages say, a great deal could not have happened.

APPENDIX I: Exhibitions at the Berg Collection, with Attendance Figures

New in the Berg Collection; 1962-1964. 10 March 1969-1 October 1969. 17,575.

Pen and Brush; the Author as Artist. 10 October 1969-15 May 1970. 19,699.

Charles Dickens; 1812-1870. 9 June 1970-9 January 1971. 17,375.

New in the Berg Collection; 1965-1969. 19 January 1971-20 August 1971. 20,448.

1922; a Vintage Year. 9 February 1972-31 October 1972. 19,681.

Documents; Famous and Infamous. 15 November 1972-31 May 1973. 15,089.

New in the Berg Collection; 1970-1972. 11 June 1973-6 January 1974. 15,977.

Other People's Mail; Letters of Men and Women of Letters. 15 January 1974-18 May 1974. 10,569.

Washington Irving; Man of Many Worlds. 3 June-12 October 1974. 13,146.

Owen D. Young; Book Collector. 29 October-12 April 1975. 14,692.

Joint Lives: Elizabeth Barrett Browning and Robert Browning. 1 May-1 November 1975. 13,480.

Independence; a Literary Panorama 1770-1850. 18 November 1975-17 September 1976. 21,526.

Arrivals in the Berg Collection; 1973-1975. 27 September 1976-16 April 1977. 14,378.

Self-Explorations: Diarists in England and America. 2 May 1977-22 October 1977. 11,744.

Literature in Exile. 1 November 1977-13 May 1978. 12,486.

Patrons and Publishers: the Economics of English Literature. 3 June 1978-13 January 1979. 16,224.

The Awkward Age: American Writers in the 1890's. 29 January-13 October 1979. 24,075.

The Thirties in England. 31 October 1979-30 April 1980. 16,113.

25 Years - 25 Additions. 19 May-31 October 1980. 15,131.

W. H. Auden. 21 November 1980-30 May 1981. 18,848.

Mirror the World: A Survey of Satire. 15 June 1981-15 January 1982. 23,453.

Two Centenarians: Virginia Woolf and James Joyce. 25 January 1982-30 June 1982. 20,100.

James Stephens: 1882-1950. 19 July 1982-19 March 1983. 23,926.

Ramblers: Literary Travels at Home and Abroad. 1 April 1983-30 September 1983.

APPENDIX II: New York Public Library Publications
Based on Materials in the Berg Collection

Richard Aldington. *A Passionate Prodigality. Letters to Alan Bird*, edited by Miriam J. Benkovitz. 1975.

William Blake. *Book of Thel*, edited by Nancy Bogan. 1971.

Charles Dickens. *A Christmas Carol*, the reading copy with editorial notes by Philip Collins. 1971.

Sean O'Casey. *The Harvest Festival*, with a foreword by Eileen O'Casey and an introduction by John O'Riordan. 1979.

Virginia Woolf. *The Pargiters; The Novel-Essay Portion of The Years*, edited with an introduction by Mitchell A. Leaska. 1977.

Charles Dickens. *Memorandum Book*, edited by Fred Kaplan. 1981.

APPENDIX III: Major acquisitions since July 1968

1968/1969: Sean O'Casey's literary estate; the papers of Humbert Wolfe; a portion of the papers of William Sansom; some 8,500 letters from the archive of A. P. Watt, literary agents.

1969/1970: The William Rees-Mogg collection of 614 eighteenth-century books and ballad sheets; more than 200 letters from Virginia Woolf to Vanessa Bell; the late work of Randall Jarrell; W. H. Auden's notebooks containing drafts of *New Year Letter*. Upon the death of Leonard Woolf in the summer of 1969, Virginia Woolf's diaries, on which Berg had an option, became the property of the collection.

1971/1972: 80 titles by or about Evelyn Waugh; Harper's file on Edna St. Vincent Millay; Lytton Strachey's 380 letters to Roger Senhouse and 237 letters from Senhouse to Strachey; Faulkner's *Soldier's Pay* and manuscripts of early stories; Ezra Pound's 94 letters to his son-in-law, Prince Rachewiltz; D. H. Lawrence's corrected typescript for *Kangaroo*; Wilkie Collins's dramatization of *The Moonstone*.

1972/1973: Copies of William Faulkner's *The Marble Faun* and W. H. Auden's *Poems* (1928); Siegfried Sassoon's *Picture Show* in manuscript; Walt Whitman's English circle; May Sarton's papers; Henry Miller's typescript for *The Tropic of Capricorn*; two journals by Arnold Bennett and the manuscript for *Those United States*; the papers of Edna St. Vincent Millay's sister Kathleen; Doubleday's Joseph Conrad papers with typescripts for *Victory* and *The Rescue*.

1973/1974: Corrected page proofs for *The Waste Land*; a collection of 129 Beckett titles and the manuscript for *The Lost Ones*; the manuscript for James M. Barrie's *The Wheel*, an unpublished play; Washington Irving's manuscript fragments for *Sleepy Hollow*; 37 Rupert Brooke letters; Aldous Huxley's typescript and correspondence for *The Genius and the Goddess*; manuscript poetry sheets by Cid Corman and letters to him from Lorine Niedecker; the "makings" of Tillie Olsen's *Yonnondio*.

1974/1975: Virginia Woolf's rarest Hogarth Press publication, *Two Stories*, and the second Hogarth Press title, Katherine Mansfield's *Prelude*; papers relating to Glenway Wescott's early works and published essays from his middle years; Jack Kerouac's notebooks; Ezra Pound letters and his operatic composition from the 1920s, "Père Nöe." The Auden collection added 42 letters to Hedvig Petzold, a few manuscripts, including his earliest known notebook, and his letters to Robert Lederer and Michael Newman. The Auden manuscripts left upon his death in 1973 to Chester Kallman were received in October 1974 as a gift. The Gotham Book Mart presented its correspondence and ledgers kept for the Joyce Society.

1975/1976: Archival purchases included papers of Elinor Wylie; 131 letters from Robert Graves to Siegfried Sassoon; numbered and signed Faulkner titles; numerous titles by or relating to Auden, including the dedication copy of *Another Time*; further Auden manuscripts from many private sources.

1976/1977: Howard Griffin's Auden papers; a further notebook with drafts of *New Year Letter*; the original manuscript of *The Chase*; letters of Michael Roberts in connection with his editing the *Faber Book of Modern Verse*; Lewis Carroll's corrected proofs for *Sylvie and Bruno*.

1977/1978: W. C. Bryant's manuscript of the translation of *The Odyssey*; the papers of Muriel Rukeyser; Robert Graves's annotated copy of *Good-Bye To All That*; 260 letters from Arnold Bennett to his wife; Henry Miller letters and a notebook; two lines of John Keats on a John Clare letter to John Taylor; Conrad Aiken notebooks; and family correspondence and papers of Hall Caine.

1978/1979: Max Beerbohm's earliest letters to his family; H. G. Wells's letters to Lord Beaverbrook; 276 Frank Swinnerton letters to Martin Secker; 42 letters from Robert Nichols to Siegfried Sassoon; letters written to Anne Fremantle; the archival file of authors who contributed to *Authors Take Sides on Vietnam*; the manuscript for a story by A. E. Housman; Washington Irving's "Don Fernando."

1979/1980: 16 poems and 57 letters by Edward Thomas; Robert Graves poems and letters to Selwyn Jepson; Elizabeth Bishop's letters to Howard Moss; James Stephens's typescript for *Irish Fairy Tales*.

1980/1981: Collection of galley proofs and manuscripts of Edna St. Vincent Millay; Rupert Brooke letters to Dudley Ward; Norman Douglas's "Beetroots"; the 200 typescripts S. J. Perelman left at his death; a notebook of Edward Thomas; Robinson Jeffers manuscripts and letters; the papers and correspondence of Jean Garrigue.

Nabokov Festival at Cornell University

George Gibian
Cornell University

The life and works of Vladimir Nabokov were the subject of a multimedia festival at Cornell University during the spring semester of 1983. American and European writers and scholars came throughout the semester "to consider various aspects of Nabokov—the writer, the translator, the critic, the teacher, and the friend." Nabokov, who died in 1977, was a professor of Russian and world literature at Cornell from 1948 to 1958. While on the faculty, he wrote his best-known novel, *Lolita* (1955), as well as his autobiography, *Conclusive Evidence* (1951; later revised as *Speak, Memory*, 1966), the novel *Pnin* (1957), and commentaries on and translations of *The Song of Igor's Campaign* and Pushkin's *Eugene Onegin*. Hundreds of former students remember his unusual, unforgettable emphases in teaching and examining. The Nabokov Festival celebrated him for his achievements and continuing influence on creative writers and on literature and film. The five-month festival featured an exhibition that included items such as Nabokov's butterfly collection and correspondence, a series of films that are associated with or adaptations of Nabokov novels, and a recital by his son, Dmitri Nabokov, of Russian songs important to Nabokov's work.

The exhibition, organized by the curator of the Slavic Collection in the Cornell University Libraries, Marilyn Kann, was contained in twenty-seven cases on two floors of the Olin Library and concentrated on his Ithaca years. Featuring photographs, letters, first editions, magazine and book publications, Nabokov's butterfly collection, and other items associated with Nabokov, the exhibit, held from January through March, aroused the interest of students, faculty, the Ithaca community, many other Nabokov fans and scholars, and the press. Especially interesting were Nabokov's butterfly collection (donated to Cornell in the keeping of Professor Franclemont) and his correspondence with Cornell colleague Morris Bishop (on loan from the late professor's wife, Alison Bishop) which contained interesting references to *Lolita*'s alleged risqué character and the advisability and possibility of publishing it. Also of interest were early editions of Nabokov's books, his translation of *Alice in Wonder-* land into Russian, class notes, a handwritten final exam, and records of his years in Ithaca. The exhibition materials, which have been photographed and, with their informative captions, are available for study in the Cornell Olin Library Slavic section, constitute a documentary source book on Nabokov's life and works.

The film series included three films based on Nabokov's works—*Lolita*, directed by Stanley Kubrick; *Laughter in the Dark*, directed by Tony Richardson; and *Despair*, directed by R. W. Fassbinder, script by Tom Stoppard—as well as *Scarlet Street*, directed by Fritz Lang, who described his Americanization in words close to Nabokov's own history, and *Vladimir Nabokov*, a BBC documentary-interview with Nabokov, made in Montreux, Switzerland.

Among the lecturers were prominent writers who spoke on what Nabokov meant to them—three Americans, Edmund White, Herbert Gold, and James McConkey; a Russian émigré, Nina Berberova; and an Argentinian, Jorge Luis Borges. The series opened with an elegant, warm lecture by White, whose first novel, *Forgetting Elena* (1973), Nabokov once cited as the American novel he most admired.

White described Nabokov as "the most passionate novelist of the twentieth century, the high priest of sensuality and desire, the magus, who knows everything about what is at once the most solemn and elusive of all our painful joys, the stab of erotic pleasure, that emblem of transitory happiness on earth. . . ." and asserted that all his intelligence was at the service of the emotions. Delighted with the notion of parallel lives impossibly converging with the concept of two worlds, of two histories "slightly out of synch," Nabokov employed wit and parody as a way of rescuing romance because, said White, he found the vocabulary of religion, fairy tales, and myths to be the only one adequate to his sense of the beauty and mystery of the sensual, of love, of childhood, of nature, of art, and of human nobility. White called Nabokov "the supreme Alpinist of the art of scaling those new heights" and added, "Whereas Horace and Pushkin could well consider their verse a monument they

49

had erected to their own eternal glory, Nabokov, writing in exile for a tiny, Russian-speaking audience that would soon be dying out, imagined a fantastic, garrulous visitor coming to his room at night. 'Your poor books,' he breezily said, 'will finish by hopelessly fading in exile. Alas, those 2,000 leaves of frivolous fiction will be scattered.' As we know now, and know with gratitude, the prophecy was not fulfilled. More glorious and surprising in his own metamorphosis than any of his butterflies, Nabokov turned himself into a writer in English, in fact, the best of the century. . . . I think it's most appropriate that Cornell should now be adding yet another volute to the Corinthian capital that tops that mighty monument."

The second writer to speak was Nina Berberova, Russian scholar, novelist, and poet. Berberova, born in 1901 and part of the most advanced literary circles of Russia during the Revolution of 1917, married Vladislav Khodasevich (1886-1939), whom many Russians consider the best poet of the twentieth century, and emigrated with him in 1922. Well known among fellow émigrés for her poetry, stories, three novels, and various biographies, she is best known to the non-Russian reading public in America for her autobiography, *The Italics Are Mine*, in which she describes her meetings with Nabokov, whom she knew in Europe.

She gave her first lecture, "The Poetic Devices and Structural Themes in Nabokov's *The Gift*," in Russian. Her second lecture, in English, was "Nabokov's British Ancestry: Nabokov's Readings 1910-1930." A member of Nabokov's generation and possessing a similar social heritage, Berberova could speak knowledgeably of the sort of British works in English and in translation that the Nabokovs' social circle read. She recalled that upper-class Russians read popular English works rather than the classical ones that are now studied by readers of English literature. Berberova's thesis is that as a boy, under the supervision of his father, Nabokov read and was influenced in various ways by nine writers of his father's generation or older: Lewis Carroll, Rudyard Kipling, Robert Louis Stevenson, Joseph Conrad, G. K. Chesterton, H. G. Wells, Somerset Maugham, Norman Douglas, and Compton Mackenzie.

The next speaker, Herbert Gold, novelist, short-story writer, and editor, had come to Cornell as visiting professor in 1958 to teach the retiring Nabokov's courses—including the famous European-novel course. Gold's stylistic dexterity had appealed to Nabokov, who listed Gold's *Death in Miami Beach* as one of his "half dozen particular

favorites." (Other writers on Nabokov's list were John Cheever, John Updike, J. D. Salinger, and Delmore Schwartz.) Gold's contribution to the festival was twofold, a reading and a speech. First he read a story, about his stay at Cornell, that he wrote for the festival as his tribute to Vladimir Nabokov. Gold's speech consisted of recollections. Having interviewed Nabokov for the *Saturday Evening Post* and the *Paris Review* and having written reviews and articles about Nabokov, Gold spoke of him from the viewpoint of "an informed friend, connecting his personality and person with the books, rather than as a formal critic."

James McConkey, novelist and teacher of creative writing at Cornell, prefaced his reading with remarks about Nabokov as a colleague and fellow artist and then read a section of his book *Court of Memory*, because he felt that a fictional piece best expressed his artistic relationship with Nabokov.

Jorge Luis Borges, widely considered one of the masters of twentieth-century literature, drew the largest audiences of the entire festival. Nabokov was an avid reader of Borges, and in 1964 he praised Borges's work for its "lucidity of thought, the purity and poetry, the mirage in the mirror." When he was asked what he thought of George Steiner's linking him with Samuel Beckett and Jorge Luis Borges as the three figures of genius in contemporary literature, Nabokov replied that "in the triptych you mention, I would feel like a robber between two Christs. Quite a cheerful robber, though." Borges gave a short statement on the nature of literature, as something which others considered a game but which to him was a thing of fantasy, and then answered questions. He came out vehemently on the side of literature as art, not political engagement, while showing himself to be a man steeped in history and poetry. He repeated that students should not be forced to read what they did not enjoy; only what was enjoyable would be meaningful to them. He spoke as a scholar of Old Germanic and Icelandic literature who, although he has been without sight for almost twenty years, carries within his memory thousands of lines of poetry in many languages. In answer to a question about the passage in his "Averroes' Search," in which Averroes "condemned the ambition to innovate as both illiterate and vainglorious," Borges exclaimed that the story was one of his favorites; and he asserted that Averroes's opinion reflects his own.

Also featured at the festival were reminiscences by Nabokov's Ithaca colleagues and friends. Morris Bishop, author of many poems published in

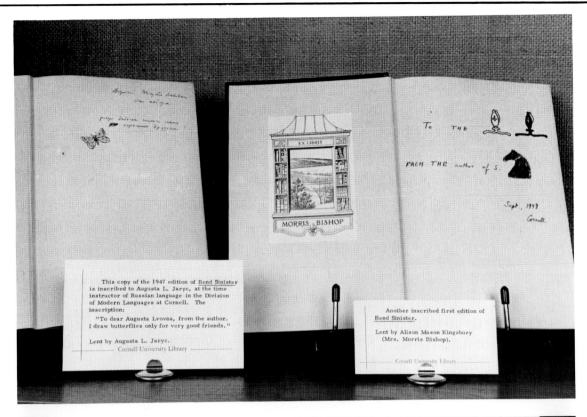

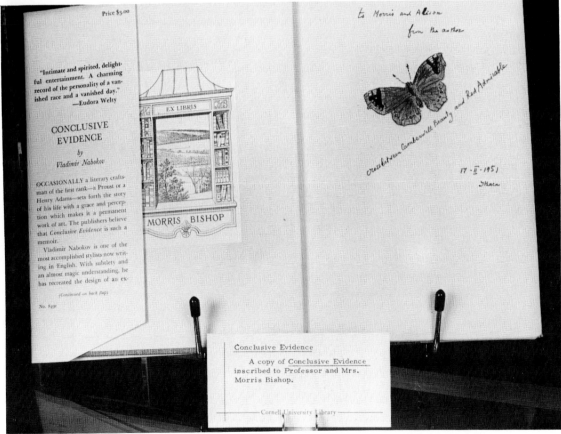

Inscribed copies of Nabokov's books (©Jon Crispin, 1983)

the *New Yorker*, translator, historian of French literature and culture, and Nabokov's best friend in Ithaca, was represented by his widow, Alison Bishop, who opened the session devoted to personal recollections. Meyer Abrams, professor of English literature, spoke of Nabokov as a teacher; and Milton Cowan, in Nabokov's days head of the Division of Modern Languages, remembered that, as a tennis player, Nabokov preferred playing from the baseline rather than rushing to the net. John Franclemont and William Brown, two entomologists who were colleagues of Nabokov's, summarized his place as lepidopterist and entomologist. Parallels between Nabokov's interest in identifying particular species and subspecies and his approach to literary scholarship, criticism, and creation became apparent.

The formally prepared reminiscences of the afternoon were followed by impromptu recollections after dinner. Peter Kahn, painter and teacher of fine arts at Cornell, recalled plans he and Nabokov had made to write and conduct a puppet play. They also shared a passion for gathering edible mushrooms. Professor Franclemont said of Nabokov, "He collected butterflies, I collected moths. . . . As a collector, I'd say he was right near the top."

Professor Ephim Fogel, native of Odessa, translator of Russian poetry, professor of Elizabethan literature at Cornell, and the only Russian-speaking colleague of Nabokov's still on the Cornell faculty, recalled their many conversations about Pushkin, American professors, and university practices. Mrs. Augusta Lyovna Jaryc, former teacher of Russian language at Cornell, spoke of her acquaintance with Nabokov and their common Russian background.

On 22 April Dmitri Nabokov, Vladimir and Vera Nabokov's son, gave a recital. An opera singer who has performed in Italy, France, Germany, Spain, Belgium, Colombia, Venezuela, and the United States, Dmitri Nabokov began his program with songs associated in various ways with his father's works and interests: Pushkin's poem "For the Shores of Your Far Country," with music by Borodin; the popular song "Stenka Razin"; songs by Glinka; another poem by Pushkin, "The Nocturnal Zephyr," with music by Dargomyzhsky; and Lermontov's "I Come Out Alone Upon the Highroad." The songs were performed in Russian and English. After an intermission, he sang four German songs, to texts by Heine, and then the same songs in Vladimir Nabokov's Russian translations. The program concluded with the "Death of Boris" from

Mussorgsky's *Boris Godunov*, which Nabokov performed with Caryl Emerson, mezzo-soprano, and the Cornell University Russian Chorus.

A two-day program of scholarly papers was presented on 22 April and 23 April, Vladimir Nabokov's birthday. It consisted, first of all, of surveys of scholarship on the work of Nabokov. The most comprehensive paper presented was by Professor Stephen Jan Parker, who had been an undergraduate student of Nabokov's and went on to receive his Cornell Ph.D. in Russian literature. A professor of Slavic literature at the University of Kansas and editor of the *Nabokov Newsletter*, Parker, in "Nabokov Studies: The State of the Art," gave a thorough survey of Nabokov scholarship, finding more than thirty books, scores of essays and articles, and more than forty doctoral dissertations that had been written about Nabokov. He noted that contemporary Russian émigré critics, contrary to their predecessors, believe that Nabokov's art, far from "betraying" his heritage, continues an important Russian tradition which runs from Pushkin to Chekhov. A recent study worthy of special note, according to Parker, is Ellen Pifer's *Nabokov and the Novel*, which demonstrates that Nabokov is neither an aesthete nor a sterile puppeteer, but rather a writer "ardently concerned with and committed to moral truth." Parker considers a 1967 two-part essay by Alfred Appel, Jr., in the *New Republic* seminal in the development of Nabokov criticism because Appel identified the major Nabokovian themes: confrontation with death; exile; the importance of consciousness; the transcendence of solipsism; the concern with time and timelessness; and the central roles of games and of the devices of involution—parody, coincidence, patterning, the work-within-the-work, staging, and authorial voice. Parker concluded by listing and describing the lacunae in work on Nabokov done so far.

Vjaceslav Paperno, linguist, literary scholar, novelist, former resident of Leningrad, at present graduate student and teacher of Russian language at Cornell University, spoke on the references to Nabokov in the Soviet press from earliest days to the present, concluding that the day when Nabokov's work may be openly read in the USSR is still far away.

John V. Hagopian, professor of comparative literature at SUNY Binghamton, who has spent a semester in the USSR doing literary research, spoke about the Russian reception of Nabokov in the underground literary world. In this unofficial literary Russia, there exists a veritable Nabokov cult limited in size but unexcelled in intensity.

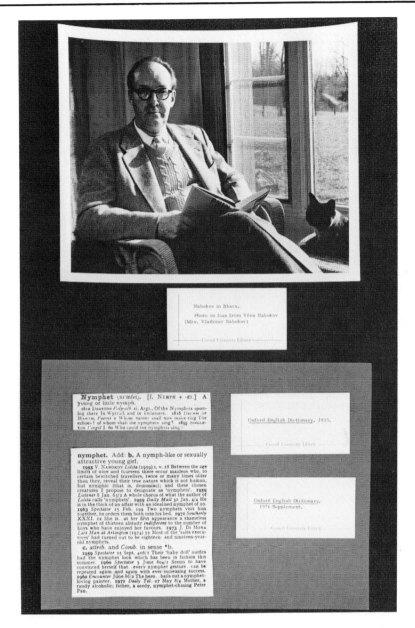

Photograph of Nabokov and definitions from the OED *demonstrating the impact of* Lolita *(©Jon Crispin, 1983)*

Alfred Appel, Jr., also a student of Nabokov's at Cornell, now a professor at Northwestern University and author of essays and books about Nabokov, used photographs taken of Berlin and other European cities at the time Nabokov wrote the story "A Guide to Berlin" to argue that Nabokov was a modernist whose formal and thematic preoccupations are analogous to those of painters and photographers of the time. Technology, the urban scene, the use of trivia, were among the points of similarity between the visual arts and Nabokov's modernism.

Priscilla Meyer, professor of Russian at Wesleyan University, gave a lively and provocative paper arguing that in many ways *Lolita* can be read as a parody on Pushkin's *Eugene Onegin*. She developed the thesis that *Lolita* represents Nabokov's translation of a Russian literary monument of the 1820s, through space and time, into an American one of the 1950s, a parody of "paraphrastic" translation of *Eugene Onegin* at its most extreme, which Nabokov wrote concomitantly with his literal translation of that work.

Ephim Fogel of the Cornell University English

department analyzed Nabokov's story "Signs and Symbols," refuting the thesis that the ending is unresolved and the story enigmatic. Professor Fogel assembled evidence to show that there could be only one interpretation of how the story ends. In the process of throwing light on the construction of one story, Fogel illuminated Nabokov's literary technique in general.

The two culminating lectures were by the writer's son and Brian Boyd, a member of the English department at the University of Auckland, who is working on a biography of Nabokov. Dmitri Nabokov started with an account of how, after his graduation from Harvard, he worked with his father on a translation of Lermontov's *Hero of Our Time* and of how he later translated various of his father's Russian works into English. He then gave an extended explanation of his father's "unflinching literality" in translating *Eugene Onegin* and other poetry, defending it against critics and detractors, citing the exchange of letters on the subject in the London *Times Literary Supplement* and the *New York Times* and passages from an essay he is now completing. He spoke also of the difficulties of translating his father's Russian into Italian and gave several samples of his translations of Nabokov's poetry into English. The lecture was a moving combination of filial tribute and critical exegesis and analysis.

Brian Boyd's lecture, "Nabokov at Cornell," provided much specific information and gave promise that the biography of Nabokov he is writing will be a thorough, rich work. Boyd drew parallels among Nabokov's "passion and patience" as a scholar, as a lepidopterist counting and mapping the scales on butterfly wings, and as a student of metrical patterns in Russian verse. He then gave an account of Nabokov's concept of the workings of Fate—in love, in history, in his life.

Nabokov's view of literature, according to Boyd, was reflected in the structure he gave his courses at Cornell: he emphasized a writer's finest performances, the "one or two great games, not a high lifetime average"; individual genius which transcends its circumstances; internationalism of literature; evolution of literature toward perfection, subtlety, precision. Nabokov liked "to emphasize the formality and the finish of his lectures,

in keeping with his ideal of the finality of a work of art and his distaste for the limitation of the moment."

The conclusion of Boyd's paper expresses the purpose of the entire Nabokov Festival. First Boyd cited Nabokov's exhortation to his students:

> The more things we know the better equipped we are to understand any one thing and it is a burning pity that our lives are not long enough and not sufficiently free of annoying obstacles, to study all things with the same care and depth as the one we now devote to some favorite subject or period. And yet there is a semblance of consolation within this dismal state of affairs: in the same way as the whole universe may be completely reciprocated in the structure of an atom, in the same way may an intelligent and assiduous student find a small replica of all knowledge in a subject he has chosen for his special research and if, upon choosing your subject, you try diligently to find out about it, if you *allow* yourself to be lured into the shaded lanes that lead from the main road you have chosen to the lovely and little known nooks of special knowledge, if you lovingly finger the links of the many chains that connect your subject to the past and the future and if by luck you hit upon some scrap of knowledge referring to your subject that has not yet become common knowledge, then you will know the true felicity of the great adventure of learning, and your years in this college will become a valuable start on a road of inestimable happiness.

Boyd commented: "Those lines I think provide one of the best clues possible to the generosity and the power to inspire that are everywhere in Nabokov's art. His novels are designed to invite their readers into adventures of personal discovery and acts of individual attention and imagination that disclose what a surprise and a treasure-trove the world can be. That was exactly his attitude as a teacher: if you see the world with your own eyes, if you palpate it with your own imagination, you can tap the happiness lurking in life."

Rites of Passage

Aram Saroyan

I got the telephone call on a morning in late June. It was from a law office somewhere—it sounded like a long-distance call, but I never made certain of that—and the man who spoke to me was making an inquiry on behalf of a lawyer, who no doubt had more pressing, first-person business somewhere else. It was an inquiry about a play of my late father's—the sort of call I get from time to time now. I referred him to the attorney for the William Saroyan Foundation. As the call was concluding, the man, whose vocal inflection sounded possibly Armenian, mentioned that he had just read my piece on my father in the July issue of *California* magazine. My interest picked up considerably. I hadn't seen the magazine yet; he had gotten an early copy by subscription.

"It's very interesting," he told me. Did I imagine he was hedging on a straightforward compliment here?

"Yes," I said. I knew it was interesting myself.

He laughed, perhaps uneasily.

Then he added: "The title is 'Daddy Dearest.'"

My breathing did a sort of somersault that made me grateful I was on the phone and not facing the man. It took me a moment to restore a breathing pattern that would allow me to speak again.

"'Daddy Dearest?'" I asked, as levelly as possible.

"Yes," he said. "It's very interesting."

"I'll bet," I said, emboldened by the shock.

He laughed again. We never got beyond that word—interesting. Now that I think about it, though, he wasn't the worst sort of person in the world to break the news that you have added a tiny item to the luggage of that swiftest and most indefatigable traveler of our time, mass media. "Daddy Dearest" . . . I see.

Sorry about that, Pop.

Not altogether unexpectedly, Fresno, wherein reside apparently a number of *California* readers and where there are certainly more than a number of William Saroyan fans, took the article personally. There was an editorial in the *Fresno Bee* denouncing me. The local columnist hit the ceiling. There were several Armenians on the television evening news talking about the bad boy I was for writing the piece. There were also many distraught letters to the editor in the *Bee*.

First a Fresno TV news team was going to fly up to the San Francisco Bay Area to interview me on camera. On second thought, they decided to do it over the phone. We had a preliminary interview during which I detected more than an edge of hostility in the female reporter's line of questioning. My father's name is on a very large building in the downtown Arts Center in Fresno. The article, excerpted from my book *Last Rites: The Death of William Saroyan* [New York: Morrow, 1982] portrayed my father as a person of mortal failings. However, at the same time all of this was happening, other people were phoning and writing me that they found the article compassionate and moving. (The title aside, I thought the editors of *California* had done an excellent job of excerpting the book.)

By the time I did the interview that was taped for broadcast, I had decided to take a gentle tack. I would tread softly and even apologetically. I realized, after all, that these people loved my father and, upset by the unfortunate title *California* had given my piece, they were rallying to his defense.

The reporter who conducted the taped interview, a man, went about it less fiercely than the woman had—but there was still an edge to his voice. He told me that a lot of people were accusing me of capitalizing on my father's famous name, of writing the book for money. Had I?

I said a few things about the book that were meant to be indirect replies to that question. I had written it in a white heat. I had never before had a book happen like this one. It had been as close to being an involuntary reflex as I could imagine writing a book ever could be. It had been written in three weeks.

Had I written it for money, the reporter wanted to know again. I sensed that he was under a certain pressure to ask that question a second time; that the force of community sentiment was looming behind him. It was his final question.

"No," I answered. I didn't say anything more.

The truth, of course, was less simple. For the first ten years of the twenty I've been a published

William and Aram Saroyan, San Francisco, 1964 (Archie Minasian)

writer, I wrote mostly poetry. Then, after marrying and starting a family, I branched out into prose. I wrote an autobiographical novel about the 1960s which I imagined was going to make a financial killing. My father had told me again and again over the years that if I wrote a novel, it would establish me. So, at last, I took his advice and wrote one. Then, for the following eight months, I tried to get either an agent or a publisher for it. Though many who read the book seemed to genuinely like it, I was told repeatedly that publishers just weren't interested in the 1960s anymore. It was the spring of 1973. I had a wife and a two-and-a-half-year-old daughter. And that fall we had our second daughter. And still there was nobody who wanted my book.

I fell back on my poetry and little-press background—"Don't kick down the ladder you stepped up," wrote the poet Louis Zukofsky—and the book was eventually brought out by a small outfit in the Berkshires [*The Street,* 1974]. A nice job;

but no money. However, my father now read the book, and liked it.

"It's their fault," he told me over the phone, referring to the publishers who had turned the manuscript down. Then he gave me what still strikes me—for the thoughtful room it leaves for future aspiration—as the best spot-review a young writer could get from an older writer: "It comes close to being great," he said of my book.

"Thanks, Pop," I replied, delighted.

Next I did a biography of a Beat poet, Lew Welch, and helped along by the revival of interest in the Beat Generation, this one was published by a major New York house. I was given a modest advance, but it was still the most money I'd seen for a piece of writing. Then the book came out. And the critics hated it.

I had written the book as a kind of stylistic tribute to Beat writing at the same time that it told the story of the Beat Generation. Unexpectedly, however, it was reviewed the way Kerouac's own books had been reviewed when they appeared in the late 1950s—with one exception. I didn't get the review in the daily *New York Times* that said this book was my generation's *The Sun Also Rises*. I really missed that one. But I got all of the others—the ones that were less reviews than they were character assassinations.

I developed a cough. I told my wife that the reviews didn't really affect me at all. But the cough wouldn't go away. I read about John Keats. He had gotten such a roasting from the critics on his first book that Shelley said it had killed him. My wife told me it was an honor to get such bad reviews—that only very good artists got them. We talked about the way the Impressionists had been received at the beginning in France. It was me and Kerouac, me and Keats, me and Renoir. But my cough still wouldn't go away. It occurred to me that I might have the initial symptoms of throat cancer. Perhaps I did. But thanks to the support of my wife, my family and friends, and of those readers who liked the book and wrote or told me so, after several months, I seemed to recover my balance—and the cough gradually went away.

However, I made the decision not to do another book. I'd learned my lesson. I didn't want to die. All I wanted was to make a living. I took up screenwriting. It was a new ball game. Let my friends scoff and accuse me of selling out; I'd cry all the way to the bank. I would stay young while they grew prematurely crotchety, guarding their dignity and integrity, yet committed to nothing so much as dispiriting poverty. But I was going to have a *life*. The first script was written in a breezy two months. One draft.

And only one problem. It wasn't, in the end, a very commercial script.

The next script—was different. It was a good idea, but it wasn't an easy script to write. At times, in fact, it seemed impossible. I did one draft. Then another. And then another after that. It's now in its eighth draft. And it's been optioned, but not yet bought. I've made a discovery. Screenwriting can be gruesomely hard work, and until a movie that one has written is made, one is not likely to be paid a lot of money for the work.

It was shortly after I'd finished the fifth draft of the screenplay that I got a call from my sister, Lucy, telling me that my father, from whom I'd been estranged for the previous three and a half years, was dying of cancer. And the next day I got another call from Lucy, now in Fresno, reporting through her tears that my father didn't want to see her—or me.

Around ten days before, after finishing the fifth draft of the script, I happened to have started a diary—more or less to take up the slack each day now that I was off any writing assignment. With Lucy's second call, the diary turned into a marathon journal which I wrote eight, ten, and twelve hours a day as my father was dying. Since I had been told in no uncertain terms that he didn't want to see me, writing the journal became the means by which I tried to deal with the fact that he was dying without being able to know that reality at firsthand.

The initial entries after Lucy's call were written in anger. Suddenly, for the first time in my life, I was allowing myself to feel the depths of my own frustration as the son of a famous man whom I knew to be quite different from his public legend. As I wrote these first entries, I won't deny that visions of a six-figure book contract danced in my head (over toward the side, as it were). After all, I was telling a story that the world didn't know about a celebrity; indeed it even crossed my mind that this might be another *Mommie Dearest*.

But as the days went by, my mood changed, and so did the book. It became clear to me, once I had vented my anger, that there were good and deep reasons why my father was the man that he was. It also became clear that the way for me to deal with my frustration at being kept at a distance from him during his final days was to go to see him—whatever the consequences.

The heart of *Last Rites* is the meeting I had with my father in his hospital room. The emotional culmination of the book was also the emotional culmination of our relationship, which had now spanned thirty-seven years. Had I not been writing the journal, I can't be sure I would have gone to see him at all. It was the deepening frustration in what I wrote that enabled me to see the necessity of my visiting him. My life and my journal interacted and, in conjunction, brought me to an entirely unexpected moment of healing with my father.

I never got the six-figure contract. There weren't, after all, any wire hangers in my story. It's true, *California* called the excerpt they ran "Daddy Dearest," but almost all of the readers I heard from said they thought the title had misrepresented the piece they read.

Then the book itself came out, and I steeled myself for another onslaught from reviewers. Remember, I had intended to give up writing books forever—to protectively gild myself with the big money in Hollywood. But then *Last Rites* happened, and once it happened, I knew from the outset that I wanted to publish it. This was so important, perhaps, because when one is born into a celebrity's family, one hears so often from other people what kind of person the celebrity is. Since I was now reporting something quite different from what had been reported *to* me all my life, an essential part of completing the arc the book began was to have it end up, not on a shelf somewhere, but in that larger world which for so long had been telling me my father was another man than the one I knew.

But the reviews worried me. For if my biography of the Beats had provoked such malevolent attacks, who dared imagine what might happen with a book that debunked my father's image as a sort of boisterous Santa Claus of American letters? It was worth it to me to suffer whatever slings and arrows might loom over the horizon in order to finally have my private truth made public, but it certainly made me uneasy.

But then the reviews began to come in and they turned out to be wonderful: the *New York Times Book Review*, the *San Francisco Chronicle*, the *Los Angeles Times*, the *Washington Post*, the *Philadelphia Inquirer*, the *Chicago Sun-Times*, the *Alabama Journal*, the *Dallas Morning News*, and many more—the reviews of a lifetime, certainly of my lifetime. And the letters that came from readers were, if anything, even more wonderful: lovely, deep and caring letters that told me what was true of my father and me was true, too, of the relationships many others struggled with in their own families. In fact, the book seemed to reach both critics and general readers less on the level of a celebrity exposé than as the story of a father and a son, and of a passage in both their lives when, at the very eleventh hour, the two had finally broken through to one another.

Will the book ultimately diminish my father's name and reputation? In my opinion, no. It's true, he doesn't emerge from my pages as the bigger-than-life folk hero of his later persona, but it might be remembered that the public was never very drawn to that mustachioed legend in any case, as the neglect my father suffered during the last thirty years of his career testifies. Whereas the man in *Last Rites*, though both troubled and difficult, seems to me a deeper, more complex, and more compellingly *human* figure than his public image had ever allowed. I don't see how this could do him harm.

Likewise, the anger I released in the first part of *Last Rites* now seems to me to have been only the necessary, initial step in an extended and ultimately healing emotional trajectory. For if, at the beginning, I myself entertained sly notions of "Daddy Dearest," in the end, knowing more of both myself

and my father, I discovered I held him dear indeed.

*   *   *

It wasn't very long after I'd completed the manuscript of *Last Rites* that I received a letter from Matthew J. Bruccoli proposing I write a literary biography of my father. My first reaction was that the book I'd just completed fulfilled the assignment, or as much of it as I, specifically, might fulfill. On second thought, however, a new book seemed to offer a whole range of possibilities that *Last Rites*, with its very personal emphasis, had largely skirted.

Then, too, I sensed that in the first book there were a number of ideas I had given only broad, glancing outline to—as I went about the main, very different mission of the first book—that a literary biography would provide an opportunity to explore in fuller detail. In addition to this, as a poet I'd long been aware that the literary biography, per se, was something of a tradition of poet's prose. *Genesis Angels*, my book about Lew Welch and the Beat Generation, might, of course, be taken as my own essay at the form: but, in truth, that book, written quickly and, like *Last Rites*, in a kind of accelerated swoop of inspiration, seemed to me closer to a prose poem than the more conventional exercise of the medium I had in mind. The models that occurred to me for the new book were John Berryman's biography, *Stephen Crane*, and Freud's monograph, *Leonardo da Vinci*.

Over the years, I've been aware of an ongoing debate among literary professionals who work primarily in the medium of biography about the validity of using Freud's theories as a resource of their study of any given life. My sense has been that there is a certain amount of professional reticence with regard to using Freud too schematically. One hears of the "vulgar Freudianism" of a particular study, presumably meaning its author has applied Freud's principles with cookie-cutter imperviousness, in the process lopping off too much of the raw matter at hand in the interest of a neat, tidy "explanation." Anyone who is fascinated by Freud, as I have been, is certainly liable to run that risk.

Nevertheless, it seemed to me it might still prove to be a worthwhile approach. For although there is undoubtedly such a thing as "vulgar Freudianism," I, for one, would be hard put to find an example of it in the writings of the master himself. On the contrary, the exhilaration to be found in his work seems to me to issue precisely out of his respect for, and his attention to, the exactness and specificity of nature itself. At his best, Freud is perhaps the supreme biographer of our age for his unique ability first to recognize the presence of a whole range of facts which we had previously either considered irrelevant or had remained entirely oblivious to, and then to extract a coherent general pattern out of his study of those facts. In *Leonardo da Vinci*, a remote figure is brought vividly to life by this process; and one is given, in the end, not a sense of the small, inconsequential nature of even the greatest of human lives, but rather a heartening sense of how such lives are subject to the same general forces as our own. In this way, Freud speaks very vividly to the oneness underlying all human beings: the artist and the criminal, the tyrant and the mother, the child and the psychotic are all shown to be individual experiments with the same basic laws of nature. As such, too, all of his subjects, from the most dismal to the most exalted, are almost equally fascinating. For by the fineness of Freud's attention, each becomes a window through which we gaze at something larger: at the fundamental laws of nature itself.

John Berryman scrupulously presented the facts of Stephen Crane's life and writing, and only in his final chapter essayed a Freudian interpretation of those facts. The book is wonderful—and yet, reading this last, extraordinary chapter, one might wish he had integrated his interpretation from the beginning.

In my biography of my father, *William Saroyan* [San Diego and New York: Harcourt Brace Jovanovich, 1983], I tried to identify the primary, operative forces of his life from its beginning, through its middle, to its end. In writing the book, I was aware I ran the risk of both vulgar Freudianism and vulgar post-Freudianism, and even so there are very likely places where I fail to overcome those risks. On the other hand, in aspiring to come to terms with my father's life and work as a whole, the value of Freud's approach, as well as specific insights of his, seemed to me to be beyond serious question.

The Year in Literary Biography

Ira B. Nadel
University of British Columbia

In *Parallel Lives* (Knopf), her unusual account of five Victorian marriages, Phyllis Rose remarks that "art has a more powerful hold on the imagination than experience." This comment summarizes a principle that unites many of the literary biographies discussed in this survey. In these sixteen biographies, written by critics, academics, journalists, and professional writers, one repeatedly sees greater attention to form than to mere fact gathering, more awareness of the presentation as well as the record of the subject. Victoria Glendinning in her comprehensive *Vita: The Life of Vita Sackville-West* (Knopf) expresses this concern in her opening paragraph: "This is Vita Sackville-West's story. One of the 'lies' of all biography is in that fact. (Another is that any story can ever be the whole story.)" Every biography must include the lives of others—arranged along narrative lines that in their shaping and expression involve fictive elements. Phyllis Rose shares this emphasis on story in *Parallel Lives*, emphasizing more strongly the "imaginative patterns" that "determine the shape of a writer's life as well as his or her work." Every marriage, she continues, is "a subjectivist fiction with two points of view." The unraveling of individual or group fictions and the telling of such stories are the keynotes of the literary biographies of the past year.

Biographies in 1983 focusing on English authors are preponderantly nineteenth-century lives, partly because of the continued interest in the Victorians and partly because of the availability of new materials. Literary lives before the nineteenth century have been few in the last twelve months, with A. N. Wilson's *The Life of John Milton* (Oxford University Press) an erudite and polished example. In his account of the poet-statesman, Wilson, the author of six novels and former literary editor of the *Spectator*, brings not only imagination but scholarship to his narrative. Beginning with a colorful description of Bread Street and the young Milton reading late into the night, Wilson then initiates a swiftly paced account of Milton's career—as student, teacher, courtier, poet, traveler, husband, and polemicist. The shape of the life, however, is controlled by Wilson's sense of the contradictions in Milton and a sustained understanding and criticism of his writing. Describing Milton's tribulations in 1652, Wilson emphasizes the conflicting forces, explaining that he was "a blind man who had been punished unnecessarily by God. He was an independent republican, increasingly disenchanted by Cromwell, but devoting almost all of his time and energy to his various appointments as Latin Secretary." Furthermore, the personal quality of Milton's prose and poetry ("*Paradise Lost* is really no more than one man's reading of the Bible.") results in a close reading by Wilson of the life as a text for the work, but always with stylistic flair, an awareness of language, and a sense of the contemporary.

Only one of the five biographies devoted to nineteenth-century figures published in 1983 is a first biography of the subject: James A. Davies's *John Forster, A Literary Life* (Barnes and Noble). Drawing on many unpublished documents, Davies provides a full account of the man who was drama critic, editor of the *Examiner*, literary associate and confidant of Dickens, and biographer of Goldsmith, Landor, Dickens, and Swift. Because of Forster's multifaceted career, Davies employs a structure that reflects this variety and emphasizes his most striking characteristic, his friendships. Part one deals with Forster's early life and influential friends, notably Leigh Hunt, Lamb, Bulwer-Lytton, and Macready. Part two discusses Forster's literary life and the sometimes volatile nature of his literary friendships; part three focuses intensively on four associations: with Browning, Landor, Dickens, and Carlyle. The final part of the biography considers three professional concerns—journalism, history, and biography.

Davies's decision to alter the narrative from a chronology to analysis of Forster's personal relations is appropriate for the nature of his subject, a man who defined his success through the success of others. Such a treatment, however, often seems at the expense of fuller details of the private life. Concentrating on Forster's literary ideas and criticism, rather than the development of his personality, alters the biography from a treatment of the individual to a discussion of his ideas. Only ten pages, for example, cover the first twenty-one years of his life. The details of Forster's literary friendships are revealing for a fuller understanding of Victorian literary life in both its artistic and commercial form,

but further analysis of why Forster became literary adviser to so many and what rewards it provided might have conveyed a more complete understanding of the man rather than his accomplishments. Forster's rooms at no. 58 Lincoln's Inn Fields became "private club, library, consulting rooms and tourist attraction," but he persists as Maclise represented him in his drawing of Dickens's reading of "The Chimes": an outsider. Although he organized the evening and helped Dickens in the writing of the story, Forster remains at the edge of the central circle of listeners.

Another adviser and man of letters is the subject of Sarah Bradford's lively biography, *Disraeli* (Stein and Day). The focus of preceding and distinguished biographies (Moneypenny and Buckle, revised 1929, and Blake, 1966), Disraeli, in Bradford's presentation of him, is seen intimately, not politically. Drawing on formerly unavailable sources such as letters and an unpublished novel Disraeli wrote with his sister ("A Year at Hartlebury or The Election"), Bradford writes a personal life of Disraeli expressed in a highly readable style. Well-paced and comprehensive without being ponderous, the book is an entertaining account of a Victorian hero, recognized equally for his literary as well as political successes. Beginning with recognition of the problematic but central role of Disraeli's Jewishness, Bradford then narrates the story of Disraeli's private hopes, personal defeats, and public desires.

"In England, personal distinction is the only passport to the society of the great," Disraeli wrote in *Vivian Grey*, published when he was twenty-one. This theme unites Bradford's life, which repeatedly stresses the uniqueness of Disraeli, his ambition, intellect, and political acumen—fashioning a man of distinction who was twice Prime Minister, appointed a Knight of the Garter, and celebrated throughout Europe. He was recognized as a young man of great promise; Bradford illustrates rather than documents the application of that promise to the literary, social, and political worlds of the nineteenth century. Whether it is Disraeli's peacocklike appearance parading down Regent Street in a blue coat, light blue trousers, and bright red shoes or his luxurious reception in Constantinople by Sir Robert Gordon, Byron's first cousin, or the opening of Parliament on 20 November 1837 (the first under the authority of the young Victoria), Bradford reveals the personality of the man with remarkable literary skill. Never does she sacrifice substance for style, but neither does she mistreat fact for narrative emphasis. Literary works are blended with the personal life so that a clearer context for understanding both emerges. Although Bradford underrates *Sybil* and provides insufficient details of the 1874 election which gave Disraeli his greatest political victory, she nonetheless has written an engaging, absorbing life of a man once described as being "satirical, contemptuous, pathetic, humorous, everything in a moment" but who also possessed "the most intellectual face in England — pale, regular, and overshadowed in the most luxuriant masses of raven-black hair."

Three other biographies of nineteenth-century figures appeared in the past year. The first is *Robert Browning, A Life Within* (Viking) by Donald Thomas. This book again studies the psychological dimension of Browning's life (see Betty Miller's earlier 1953 treatment) but uses not letters or private documents but the poetry to interpret the life. No explicit psychoanalytic approach is applied, although Alfred Adler's notion of the "life within life" that characterizes the refuge of the supremely ambitious — criminals, neurotics, artists — is mentioned and casually cited. Thomas, who writes in a clear although somewhat flat manner, provides an account that emphasizes the continuity of Browning's life as seen in the poetry. The influence of Browning's parents, especially his father, the importance of his education, the romantic impact of Camberwell and Shelley all introduce themes that Thomas elaborates and buttresses (excessively) with passages from the poetry. There is in this biography no new material nor any new insights, only unique but often questionable comparisons; for example, according to Thomas, Browning's diagnosis of the corruption of human conduct puts him more in league with the Marquis de Sade than Wordsworth. Throughout the biography there is a tension between discussing the life and analyzing the poetry. The pull toward literary criticism undermines his commitment to biography. Despite his wish to use the poetry as a guide to the inner life and darker side of Browning, Thomas writes a public rather than private biography of the poet.

Unlike Thomas, Fred Kaplan provides a comprehensive, scholarly, and complete life of his subject, Thomas Carlyle. Presenting the first detailed, major one-volume life of Carlyle — Froude's encyclopedic four-volume life appeared between 1882-1884 and David Alec Wilson's excessive six-volume account in 1923-1934 — Kaplan has turned to primary and formerly unpublished materials in an effort to concentrate on the man and not the reputation. *Thomas Carlyle, A Biography* (Cornell University Press) is a work of major scholarship and research, which at the same time offers an impor-

tant evaluation of its subject and his age. Furthermore, its treatment of historical detail enhances its authority.

In writing a modern life of Carlyle, Kaplan felt compelled to reexamine original documents while drawing on new materials not available to earlier biographers. Most important for his research has been the publication of Carlyle's letters, an ongoing project of Duke and Edinburgh universities. But clearly not every element of the life could be included and, as Kaplan wisely decided, he has discussed Carlyle's writings only in relation to their usefulness for "central biographical issues. This, then, is no life *and* works," he states. Nonetheless, *Thomas Carlyle* is a big biography with 649 pages and 49 photographs, although it consistently concentrates on the main subject, a focus at the expense of fully analyzing the character of Jane Carlyle, the most important influence on Carlyle's personal life. But as one reads of Carlyle's early struggles, of his courtship of Jane Welsh, of his efforts with *Frederick the Great*, one directly experiences his difficulties because Kaplan conveys a sense of immediacy through his use of historical materials. His reading of Carlyle and his career provides a fresh sense of the emergence of Carlyle as a social prophet, moralist, historian, and biographer. Through his direct style, Kaplan analyzes relationships in a way that clarifies the reader's understanding of the complex self that was Carlyle's, as these brief passages show — on his association with Francis Jeffrey, editor of the *Edinburgh Review*: "Though Jeffrey had not yet gauged the extent of Carlyle's stubbornness or appreciated his idiosyncratic radicalism, he had correctly anticipated Carlyle's strong commitment to tradition and continuity"; on Goethe: "For a crucial ten year period, during which he struggled to find a vocation, an identity, a livelihood and a mate, Carlyle obsessively read, wrote about and championed German literature and its most famous writer"; on Carlyle himself: "Despite his cultivation of a stoic exterior, Carlyle was a man who hated partings, mourned change, and created a melancholy inner poetry. . . ."

The value of Kaplan's formidable *Thomas Carlyle* is not only in its accuracy, research, or facts, all of which are carefully handled, but in its boldness of judgment. The details do not stand alone, unanalyzed. The completeness of the life derives not from the fullness of its record, broad and comprehensive as that is, but in the use of its detail to provide a critical view of its subject. Carlyle is not idolized but neither is he reviled; he is seen closely and perceptively from the perspective of a scholar and the distance of time. Kaplan presents a balanced, historical view of his subject, convincing his readers of Carlyle's ambitions and drives, epitomized in his determination to write a masterpiece and in his belief that "in general, except when writing, I never feel myself that I am *alive*." Such a commitment created tension, of course, and conflict in Carlyle's life, such as in his attachment to Jane but involvement with Lady Harriet Ashburton or in his love-hate relation with London. However, the accomplishment of Kaplan's biography is our feeling both Carlyle's ambitions and his paradoxes through his life as moralist, writer, and visionary.

Another work that establishes various themes among the Victorians but also merges biography with social history is *Parallel Lives* by Phyllis Rose. A study of five Victorian marriages or love affairs—those of Thomas and Jane Carlyle, John Ruskin and Effie Gray, John Stuart Mill and Harriet Taylor, Charles Dickens and Catherine Hogarth, and George Eliot and G. H. Lewes—*Parallel Lives* is equally about sexuality, marriage, power, and politics in all relationships. Rose argues that every life has a narrative structure and that important fictions exist in our daily lives. She then analyzes each Victorian relationship in these terms, providing a provocative approach to nineteenth-century marriage and twentieth-century issues. Her subject is as much cultural and social history as it is an account of individual lives. Written in a lively style, conscious of its tone and narrative progression, *Parallel Lives*, although it uncovers no new material, is a stimulating work. Documents are dramatically used, literary concepts are applied in original ways, and marriage is freshly redefined. As a form of group biography, the volume displays a uniqueness rarely seen in the treatment of Victorian lives.

Additional literary biographies include Noel Riley Fitch's *Sylvia Beach and the Lost Generation* (Norton), Victoria Glendinning's life of Vita Sackville-West, *Vanessa Bell* (Ticknor and Fields) by Frances Spalding, and James Matthews's narrative of the Irish writer Frank O'Connor, *Voices, A Life of Frank O'Connor* (Atheneum). Fitch presents a contextual group biography placing the American Beach in the vortex of activities that surrounded her bookshop and lending library, Shakespeare and Company, established in 1919 in Paris. The coterie of English, American, and French writers that used the shop as post office, lecture room, cafe, and social center sustains this fascinating, often-told (but never so comprehensively told) tale. Threading Beach's personal history through such literary events as the publication of *Ulysses*, the development

of Hemingway, the habits of Gertrude Stein, or the importance of Thornton Wilder creates a work that constantly maintains the reader's interest. Indeed, certain sections totally obscure Beach as Fitch concentrates on the activities of Ezra Pound in aiding Joyce, or Joyce's difficulties in looking after his family *and* in trying to write. The use of formerly suppressed passages from Beach's memoirs, interviews with writers and others who were familiar with Shakespeare and Company, and the evocation of the atmosphere of the bookshop, aided by a number of captivating photographs, make this an absorbing biography that successfully unites literary history with individual lives.

Vita: The Life of Vita Sackville-West by Victoria Glendinning does not focus on an age or group but on an individual. The wife of Sir Harold Nicolson, intimate friend of Virginia Woolf, and author of almost fifty books, Vita Sackville-West was witness to literary and cultural developments in England for roughly the first sixty years of this century. Glendinning's account, the first full life of her subject, is compelling in its attention to Sackville-West's vibrant personality, her ambivalent sexual attitudes, her unsure relationship with her husband, and her demanding creative drives. Providing accurate knowledge of Sackville-West's affair with Violet Trefusis, her involvement with Virginia Woolf, as well as her continuous dialogue with her husband over the nature of *their* relationship creates an intriguing but never disreputable story. The use of letters, private diaries, and journals enhances the life account which reveals openly and honestly the romantic character of the woman whose mother was the illegitimate daughter of a Spanish dancer and whose husband was an important member of Parliament and a distinguished writer. "Sex," she wrote her eldest son Ben in 1933, "is probably the most exciting but not the most important thing in life." *Vita* explains how the subject came to understand that statement fully. But as Glendinning ironically remarks late in the biography, Sackville-West and her family could often write to one another what they could not say.

Frances Spalding's life of Vanessa Bell lacks some of the spirit of *Vita*, but then the subject is quite different. Leonard Woolf called Bell "monumental, monolithic, granitic"; Roger Fry, in love with her, stressed her natural but intense ability to live and admired her reserve and quietude. The sister of Virginia Woolf, however, is shown by Spalding to be a woman of tension buttressed by reserve. The elder of the two sisters, she assumed a dignity befitting her responsibilities at eigh-

VANESSA
BELL

FRANCES SPALDING

Dust jacket for Frances Spalding's biography of the woman at the center of the Bloomsbury circle

teen—the head of a household of three younger children, two half brothers and an elderly father, Sir Leslie Stephen. His death freed the family for a new liberality, marked initially by a move to Bloomsbury, which initiated a new social and intellectual life well-documented by literary and art historians. Painting became Vanessa Stephen's passion and eventually led to her marriage at twenty-seven to the art critic Clive Bell, possibly, Spalding suggests, on the rebound from the sudden death of her brother Thoby.

However, the difficulties with her marriage, the affair with Roger Fry, and her later involvement with Duncan Grant are not distinctly nor clearly told, largely because of Bell's reticence and lack of any adequate primary material. Spalding nonetheless provides appropriate details of how Clive Bell, Roger Fry, and Duncan Grant oriented their lives around Vanessa, especially after 1912 when she and Clive moved to the country. Angelica, the daughter

of Vanessa and Duncan born in 1917, was genially accepted by Clive, but the death of his eldest son, Julian, in the Spanish Civil War was a tragedy he and Vanessa never overcame. Through all, Vanessa painted, and Spalding's expertise as an art historian enhances this narrative of intellect and creativity, of uniqueness and unorthodoxy.

A figure the very opposite of Vanessa Bell in his outgoing, spontaneous, and controversial nature is the Irish short-story writer and critic Frank O'Connor. This active, polemical individual, actually named Michael O'Donovan, is the subject of James Matthews's energetic, amusing, and sympathetic biography *Voices, A Life of Frank O'Connor*. In his account of the writer who was also a poet, translator, lecturer, and journalist, Matthews conveys O'Connor's audaciousness, from his struggling life in Cork to his magnetism as a lecturer at Harvard, Northwestern, and Stanford. His abrasive behavior and strong use of language are dramatically present in the biography, which is about writing and the value of literature as much as it is a record of O'Connor's life. Although he spent a number of years in the United States, O'Connor once remarked that he "couldn't write outside Ireland because nowhere else in the world was his presence as a writer resented so much as it was at home." Matthews creates a singularly absorbing life that is both entertaining and informative.

American literary biographers have also been productive in 1983 with a broad range of works from a life of Willa Cather to accounts of Dashiell Hammett and James Gould Cozzens. Phyllis C. Robinson's *Willa: The Life of Willa Cather* (Doubleday) furnishes a detailed history of the woman who spent her youth in Red Cloud, Nebraska, but spent more than forty years in New York City. Robinson's Cather is a woman of immense vitality rather than austerity who in her relationship to literature as well as to Edith Lewis displayed commitment and sincerity. Written informally but not casually, *Willa* is immensely readable. Robinson's sympathy for her subject is everywhere apparent.

Gilbert A. Harrison, former editor of the *New Republic*, narrates the life of Thornton Wilder in *The Enthusiast* (Ticknor and Fields). His theme is the conflict between Wilder's wish to be a creative performer and a writer: the first suggesting a social and even artificial persona; the second implying an honest effort to be an artist. Concisely presenting Wilder's childhood in Wisconsin, California, and China, his education at Oberlin and Yale, his activities in Rome and later in New York and Hollywood, Harrison conveys a sparkling sense of Wil-

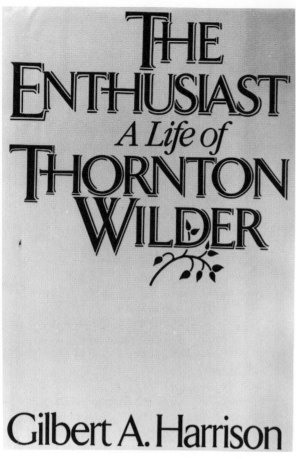

Dust jacket for the biography that Leon Edel praised for its "great biographical skill, exemplary concision, and a liveliness akin to Wilder's own leaping and gyrating imagination"

der's liveliness. Wilder's enthusiasms for the stage, Lope de Vega, *Finnegans Wake*, and travel are all vividly presented in prose that expresses what Lillian Gish called Wilder's "healthy spirit." His friendships with Gene Tunney and Gertrude Stein; his acquaintanceships with Freud, Max Reinhardt, and Lady Ottoline Morrell are all colorfully recorded. Of *Our Town*, which brought him his second Pulitzer Prize, Wilder said it was an attempt "to find a value above all price for the smallest events of our daily life." Harrison succeeds in giving us the value of Wilder's daily life, which he records with verve and understanding.

The career of another American writer was not as sustained nor successful as that of Thornton Wilder. Dashiell Hammett, whose reputation rests on a slim but outstanding set of detective novels, spent the years between 1934 and his death in 1961 without finishing another work. In 1951 he was sentenced to six months in jail for failing to answer questions at a Communist witch-hunt trial. At his funeral, even Lillian Hellman was surprised at the large turnout. But to Diane Johnson, author of *Dashiell Hammett, A Life* (Random House), this very period of decline confirms Hammett's heroism. "It is the long blank years that prove the spirit," she declares.

The style of Johnson's *Dashiell Hammett* is novelistic, not at all surprising since she has written works of fiction. The scenes of Hammett working in dingy surroundings in San Francisco on his first novel, *Red Harvest*, or locking himself in the Sutton Hotel (run by Nathanael West) in New York to finish *The Thin Man* are told with a writer's sense of pacing, setting, action, and detail. The facts are meshed with the image of Hammett as a no-nonsense man determined to write, educate himself, and, when possible, live well. There were times, however, when this was difficult, as in 1932 when he had to sneak out of the Hotel Pierre wearing layers of clothes because he could not afford to pay his $1,000 bill. The drama in the biography often comes from Hammett's own words, notably the many letters Johnson quotes, although occasionally incorrectly. Johnson's own style fuses with Hammett's, at times becoming laconic, tight, and exact. "The needlessly involved sentence, the clouded image, are not literary," Hammett wrote, and Johnson strives to follow this principle. The biography, critical and interpretative, also benefits from the cooperation of Hellman and Hammett's daughter and reflects Johnson's clear sense of his life as a tragedy with the protagonist falling from popular hero to political villain and, finally, alienated man. It is the plight of the American writer, summarized by Hellman in her eulogy of Hammett as a man who "respected words in books and suspected them in life."

A figure who respected words in books as well as in life was Wallace Stevens, and in his unusual volume *Parts of a World, Wallace Stevens Remembered* (Random House), Peter Brazeau presents an oral biography of the distinguished poet. Devoting five years to interviewing those who knew Stevens, Brazeau supplies a detailed, verbatim set of edited transcripts that furnish an intimate yet varied portrait of Stevens—as insurance executive, man of letters, husband, and father. Concentrating on the 1916-1965 period, essentially while Stevens lived in Hartford, Connecticut, Brazeau renders narrative links for the excerpts, often setting the scene or providing background. But, of course, the details, anecdotes, and reminiscences by Richard Eberhart, Harry Levin, Samuel French Morse, Elder Olson,

Dust jacket for the book that Marjorie Perloff called "an important first step in setting Stevens in his REAL setting"

Richard Wilbur, and others give the book its special quality. The result for readers is a sense of Stevens as a presence, not as an abstraction. Although there are critical passages in the interviews, the book is essentially an appreciation of Stevens from a variety of personal perspectives.

Two other, and opposite, American writers have also been the subjects of new biographies: Langston Hughes and James Gould Cozzens. In Faith Berry's account of the rise and struggle of the black American poet, novelist, essayist, dramatist, and traveler, *Langston Hughes, Before and Beyond Harlem* (Lawrence Hill), the difficulty of Hughes's determination to live as a writer is made extraordinarily clear. His early youth separated from his father, who ran off to Mexico to gain his fortune (surprisingly, he succeeded), his adolescence and young manhood spent in Mexico, Africa, and Europe, his identification with and enthusiasm for Harlem—all blend together in this account to give perhaps the most detailed narrative of the life of a

major American black poet yet available.

Berry begins by emphasizing the youthful successes of Hughes, who had his first important poem published at nineteen. At twenty he had no less than thirteen poems printed in the *Crisis*, the NAACP periodical, including such well-known works as "Negro" and "The South." But dislocation and disappointment characterized Hughes's life, qualities exacerbated by his Communist sympathies and travels in Russia in 1932 and 1933. In Russia he found the absence of prejudice and for the first time the ability to earn a living from his writing alone. Berry writes sympathetically but critically of Hughes, focusing continuously on his unstable personal life and problematic literary career. The biography furthermore gives a strong sense of the social and political circumstances that surrounded Hughes's movements in America and Europe in the 1920s and 1930s. His activities during these years led to his later investigation by the FBI and an appearance before the McCarthy Sub-Committee in 1953. Berry ends her biography at the beginning of Hughes's twenty-six-year residence in Harlem (1941-1967), although she provides an overview of those later years and his growing reputation. Excluding this period has the value of reforming Hughes's image from the stereotype of the Harlem poet, but at the expense of telling little of his activities at that vital and fertile time for his writing.

The theme of isolation, although represented more as seclusion, organizes Matthew J. Bruccoli's *James Gould Cozzens: A Life Apart* (Harcourt Brace Jovanovich). Using the materials Cozzens himself amassed and presented to Princeton University, Bruccoli writes an engaging life of an essentially reclusive individual. The source of the biography's success is, in part, Bruccoli's decision to allow Cozzens's work to tell as much of the story as possible. The record of his private thought and life resists paraphrase, Bruccoli argues: "the force of his mind is conveyed by the force of his expression." Bruccoli also skillfully uses Cozzens's fiction to aid in describing the life, beginning with the problem that the novels resist categorization. The works are, curiously, social novels written by an antisocial man. Cozzens, Bruccoli makes clear, was not a critical success, although his themes and characters involved the problems and responsibilities of successful men. The ethics of duty, the limitations of the will, the conflicts within lives are his themes.

What emerges most distinctly in this well-written and considered biography is Cozzens's devotion to writing. The biography, while giving us the details of Cozzens's life at Harvard, in Cuba, or on his farm in Lambertville, New Jersey, is finally a testament to literature. Cozzens, who had written seven novels and published four of them by his twenty-sixth year, was not only precocious but talented. He was also, however, worried by success. Bruccoli shows in detail how Cozzens handled that concern and went on to write such important but undervalued works as *Guard of Honor* and *By Love Possessed*, although at his death in 1978 he was "the least read and the least regarded major American novelist." For Cozzens his work was his life. However, Cozzens's privacy and his indifference to fame

meant not a fear of society but a withdrawal to a stronger force, literature. He was the opposite of Langston Hughes, who in 1923 on the S. S. *Malone* shipping out to Africa threw overboard all the books he had till then accumulated. The act symbolically stood for his belief in people and experience rather than in texts and commentaries. Cozzens would have found such an action abhorrent. But to compare these two lives is to understand something of the compelling and often opposite drives that create American writers of authority and conviction.

The Year in Drama

Howard Kissel

One way of viewing the history of literature is as a series of encounters between texts and readers. Occasionally a long-forgotten or underrated writer will be "rediscovered" by an especially alert or sensitive reader. One such instance occurred shortly after World War I, when a descendant of Herman Melville, quite indifferent to her ancestor's admittedly dim literary reputation, showed a young scholar some manuscripts that had been waiting patiently in a family trunk. One of them was *Billy Budd*, whose publication in the 1920s reawakened interest in Melville and created the first wide readership for *Moby-Dick*, seventy years after it was first published and thirty years after the author's death.

Imagine if Melville's "comeback" had depended not upon the diligence and sympathies of an eager scholar but upon the intelligence and talent of an actor, and you see why the history of dramatic literature is inevitably a quirky one. Certain texts—Shakespeare and Molière are obvious examples—can transcend the ineptness of actors or the conceits of directors. Others—particularly those of the last century, whose dialogue is deliberately nonliterary—can make sharply different impressions depending on the quality of performance they receive. It sometimes happens, of course, that a play receives acclaim because a charismatic actor has lent the text nuances it may not possess, but more often the reverse is true.

The dependence of dramatic literature on performance, sometimes even on the mood of an

audience, introduces variables that make judgment more precarious than it is in a solitary encounter with a literary work. Sometimes it is easy to see why certain plays that had enormous impact in their own time have virtually none in ours. We may, for example, find Alfred Jarry's *Ubu Roi* amusing and historically significant, but we can never enter the theater with enough rigidity, smugness and self-importance—which is to say we can never be sufficiently bourgeois to be "shocked" by the play, as its first audience was. Nor can we bring to the theater the bewilderment, the despair and the fortifying ideological certainties that made audiences of the Group Theater respond with such fervor to the early plays of Clifford Odets.

Because they abound in witty literary allusions, the plays of Jarry still make pleasurable reading. Those of Odets now strike us as agitprop or hackwork. (Yet for decades after their initial productions, Odets's plays were considered important plays, in no small part because they remained dear to the eminent drama critic Harold Clurman, who had been one of the three founders of the Group Theater.)

These examples seem useful in any assessment of a year in the theater because they make clear the extent to which we inevitably pass judgment "through a glass darkly." If, for example, Tennessee Williams's *The Glass Menagerie* were to be judged by the revival mounted in December 1983, a production that adamantly refused to grant the play the sentimentality it unabashedly demands, we might find the work an abrasive one. Even Jessica Tandy, one of America's most beloved actresses, plays Amanda Wingfield in so astringent a manner it is impossible to understand any response to her except her son's intense desire to get as far away as possible. But Williams's early play is so familiar, so solidly embedded in the repertoire that we are almost painfully aware of the disparity between the text and director John Dexter's Brechtian approach to it. If this were our first exposure to the play, could we sense the poetry, the pathos beneath the deliberately grating tone of this production?

Similarly, if we had never heard of Noel Coward and had to judge him by the Elizabeth Taylor-Richard Burton revival of *Private Lives,* we might imagine he was merely a precursor of television sitcom, since almost none of his wit survived the savage onslaught of Taylor and Burton.

No one has suffered more at the hands of actors and directors than Chekhov, who was not even pleased by the landmark production of *The Seagull* directed by Stanislavski, which restored his confidence in himself as a playwright after the disastrous premiere of the play some time earlier in St. Petersburg. How much more would he have been disturbed by a recent production of *Uncle Vanya* directed by Andrei Serban, in which his work was treated as if its major significance was in foreshadowing the absurdists. Actors engaging in "intimate" conversation were placed dozens of feet from one another—as if there were no other way to make their alienation from one another clear to the audience. Again, we know the characters in *Uncle Vanya* before we enter the theater. We see what is pretentious and wrongheaded about Serban's approach. If the play were unfamiliar, would we attribute our boredom to the production or to the author?

Sam Shepard has long been regarded as one of the major voices of contemporary American drama, but the importation of a production of *Fool for Love,* with a cast directed by Shepard himself, indicated we may not have heard Shepard's voice accurately. Productions over the last ten years have tended to focus on Shepard the Angry Young Man of the 1960s, Shepard the caricaturist, Shepard the connoisseur of the grotesque in American life. It frequently happened that somewhere in the middle of these productions one's ear would suddenly be caught by undeniably authentic poetry.

Shepard's astringency was stressed, making him seem merely a playwright for the disaffected, one whose smart-aleck vision of American life provided easy catharsis for Madison Avenue ad-

men wearing boots, cowboy hats, and fringed leather—by laughing raucously, they were able to recover the anger and purity of their rebellious youth.

Several of Shepard's recent plays have been portraits of bizarre families. Works such as *Buried Child* (which won the Pulitzer Prize in 1979) and *Curse of the Starving Class* have generally been performed so broadly that one could only regard them as, in popular parlance, "goofs." But the way his last two plays were performed suggests Shepard sees the family as more than a gag. In both *True West* and *Fool for Love,* he focuses on siblings—two brothers in one case, a half brother and half sister in the other. Both are structured as a series of fights, those in *True West* purely comic, those in *Fool for Love* comic with poignant, darkly romantic overtones. Despite a sharp sense of place, of social class, of the nuances of certain kinds of American speech, these plays seem to have little of Shepard's earlier concern with social criticism. Here the family is not an object of sociological or political interest but a place where one confronts—and wrangles with—one's destiny.

The two brothers in *True West* at first seem total opposites. One is a deliberate boor, the other a fastidious, upwardly mobile Hollywood screenwriter. But the readiness with which, in the course of the play, they reverse roles implies that each senses the extent to which his character contains the other. (Their sparring continues even as the lights dim on the concluding act, and one wonders if Shepard is suggesting that the two elements in his own psyche, the earthy and the poetic, are similarly engaged in an unresolved battle for supremacy.)

True West was first presented in New York several years ago by Joseph Papp at the New York Shakespeare Festival Public Theater in a production so misguided Shepard disavowed it. The critics dismissed the play as a lesser effort. In the fall of 1982 it was given an entirely new Off-Broadway production; the critics reversed their judgment, and several succeeding casts have captured the play's wild humor without ever reducing the characters to cartoons.

In *Fool for Love,* one of Shepard's most tightly written plays, the "contenders" are linked by a common father. As they vent their rage and jealousy on one another—an intense, graphic way of depicting their love—their father, boozy, half senile, muses at the side of the stage. His presence—an odd kind of "chorus"—tempers with gentle irony and melancholy, remorseful poetry what might otherwise have been an unfashionably romantic work. Even with the raucous tone their relationship often takes and despite the sometimes vulgar, roughhouse comedy, *Fool for Love*, with its evocation of lonely lovers, their union shadowed by taboo, fleeing and seeking one another across the pungently drawn bleak Southwest desert, takes on the air of an American *Wuthering Heights*.

A less skillful production than the one that arrived from San Francisco's Magic Theatre, where Shepard is playwright-in-residence, might have emphasized the play's shock value, as local productions of other Shepard work have. Instead, this one focused on the characters' surprising vulnerability, so that even the men's preoccupation with their masculinity seemed touching, not, as often happens, adolescent. The poetry that has, in earlier works, popped up unexpectedly, here broods over the whole play. It was always easy to understand the hold Shepard's plays had on actors—he is a master of stage metaphor and action, and the fact that his plays are frequently structured as a series of physical encounters makes them appealing to actors, who want to make use of their whole bodies, not just their voices. It has not always been so easy to see them as works having more than two dimensions—it would be interesting to see whether the earlier plays seemed deeper if approached as character studies rather than social commentary.

Performance played an even more telling role in one of the more controversial works to reach New York in 1983—Peter Brook's *la tragedie de Carmen*, a *Reader's Digest* condensation of Bizet's opera intended to return the character to the earthiness and brutality of its first incarnation, Prosper Mérimée's 1845 novella. Because *Carmen* is a work that excites the admiration of the unmusical as well as the connoisseur (the eminent English musicologist Ernest Newman, best known for his four-volume biography of Wagner, went so far as to say of Bizet's opera that "the world would obviously be incomplete without it"), not everyone was convinced that it required any help from Peter Brook.

Brook, along with the French screenwriter and playwright Jean-Claude Carrière, reduced the four-act work to eighty-two minutes, employing a simple narrative probably comprehensible only to those already familiar with the full opera. His intent was clearly to strip *Carmen* of all the diversions created in 1875 to protect bourgeois Parisian audiences from the full force of the erotic, death-obsessed plot. Brook's streamlined version eliminated the children's chorus, the singing gypsies, the bullfight fans—all the "local color"—and concentrated on the four major characters. The set con-

sisted merely of three tons of dirt—a mixture intended to evoke both the bullfight ring and the earth of Carmen's native Andalusia. An orchestra of fourteen accompanied the performers, and even in the treatment of the score there was a chipping away at the familiar edifice. The first chorus of the "Habanera," for example, was performed with only timpani accompaniment, throwing into sharp relief its exotic rhythm and sensuous lines. A few phrases of the "Toreador Song" were sung with no instrumental accompaniment and in a tremulous, hushed voice, reminding us that bullfighting is about more than just "the roar of the crowd."

There was a minimum of spoken dialogue and a maximum of stage business, to tell the story "visually" (though it is doubtful anyone unfamiliar with the full work—admittedly a small minority—would really understand the plot in this truncated version). Some of Brook's "bits" seemed ingenious. At one point he has Don José hovering over Carmen like a master offering a dog a bone—José cuts an orange and squeezes its juice into her upturned mouth, a striking, sensuous gesture. In another scene the only light is provided by three balsa-wood campfires, which send a fragrant, earthy aroma through the theater. Some of the business is less inspired and frankly gimmicky—like having tuxedoed members of the orchestra step out from the wings to play in Lillas Pastia's café, presumably the lowest of dives, from which no one in evening dress would escape alive. In such a moment and often in the better ones, one questions whether *la tragedie de Carmen* really prompts one to think about the nature of the tragic heroine or simply the cleverness of Brook. In any case, Brook's most important collaborators were the performers. The principals, who were trained singers with strong acting skills, rotated performances. Depending on the singers one saw, one could come away either admiring the work's inventiveness and playfulness or finding it entirely superficial.

Brook, of course, has been one of the most influential directors of the past two decades. As far back as 1958, when he directed the Lunts in Friedrich Durenmatt's *The Visit*, he began to move away from conventional psychological realism. In such productions as his *King Lear, A Midsummer Night's Dream*, and the pivotal *Marat/Sade*, he has tried to bring to Western theater some of the potent ritual gestures of the Orient, some of the experimentalism of Eastern Europe. One of the consequences of Brook's influence has been the increasing tendency to regard actors as pawns in some schematization of a play by directors more interested in theater as a form of cerebration than as a psychological experience.

The notion of the director as the "star" of the production, imposing some intellectual grid on a play, has been in vogue for some time. In the past few years it has become more common because more directors find employment in university-oriented or regional theaters, away from commercial pressures. Not all of their ideas have necessarily benefited the theater, but one of the side effects of their work has been a growing necessity for the actors to take a broader view of their task than they did in the postwar era, the heyday of "The Method."

The Method, of course, has been much discussed and much misunderstood. In its simplest form, it seemed to be an invitation to the actor to recreate emotional high points in his life. Method actors had a reputation as being hostile to literary texts, preferring to rearrange words to suit their taste or lack thereof. Interestingly, Lee Strasberg, the leading exponent of this school, did not tolerate this attitude, especially in dealing with classical texts. Moreover, he was fond of relating an incident that took place in one of his classes, indicating his interest in actors as literate rather than merely emotive beings. A young actor playing the balcony scene in *Romeo and Juliet* was climbing toward Juliet. When she said the line, "If that thy bent of love be honorable, / Thy purpose marriage . . . ," the young man fell down, stunned, making it clear that matrimony was not the object of his climb, a witty response to a line generally ignored.

The new generation of American actors no longer sees nurturing emotional memories as their major training. There is a new interest in building the voice, inarticulateness no longer being held proof of emotional genuineness. A symptom of the fresh mood was Kevin Kline's interpretation of *Richard III*, produced by Joseph Papp in Central Park and directed by an Englishwoman, Jane Howell, who had her actors stress the play's complex, fascinating narrative line. The last two Richards New York had seen were Michael Moriarty and Al Pacino, both closely identified with the Method approach, both of whom treated the character not as a historical figure but rather as a pretext for self-exploration. Kline, on the other hand, brought to the role considerable vocal and technical prowess and a fresh conception—normally Richards do everything but twirl their mustaches to demonstrate the depths of their capacities for evil; Kline showed one may smile and smile and smile and be a villain.

Equally heartening winds are blowing from across the Atlantic. The Royal Shakespeare Company exported Trevor Nunn's production of Shakespeare's most astringent play *All's Well That Ends Well*. Nunn set his production in the autumnal glow of Europe before World War I. The muted, understated tone he set beautifully captured the bittersweet mood of the play. The acting was quiet and entirely natural, a refreshing modulation of the larynx-oriented British style that used to be the norm.

The weaknesses of "the norm," alas, were apparent in *Edmund Kean*, a one-man show based on the career of the nineteenth-century actor. One-person plays about historical figures tend to be didactic, and we generally sense a discomfort as the actor veers between his two roles, first as narrator, filling us in on biographical details that help us understand emotional moments, then as performer, living those moments. For one act, author Raymond Fitzsimmons managed to avoid this problem by showing us Kean as an underdog, fighting to keep his family from starving, determined to force managers to stop typecasting him as Harlequin and to let him play Shakespeare. The first act ends in triumph as he stuns London with his interpretation of Shylock.

But in the second act Fitzsimmons does something worse than make Kean a narrator. He has him confide in the audience what a bastard he has become now that he's a success, a position that lacks both dramatic irony and any real plausibility—it seems unlikely that an actor so intent on winning our applause would blacken himself so relentlessly in our eyes. Ben Kingsley, who was so beguiling as Gandhi and so subtle in the film of Harold Pinter's *Betrayal*, gave a conventional performance. His strongest scene came at the end of the first act, when he both narrated the circumstances of his triumph as Shylock and played the role in a style we could sense as of another era but nevertheless affecting. Throughout much of the evening, however, Kingsley hoped to gain his effects merely through the counterpoint of different voices, which only heightened the feeling of artificiality one-man shows inevitably carry with them. As a tour de force for an actor, the play may be richer than Kingsley made it seem, since many of his acting choices seemed superficial and easy.

A consideration of the influence of the actor has seemed useful because so much New York theater now consists of revivals. During the 1950s the British director Tyrone Guthrie observed that

Broadway was the world's greatest "experimental theater," since virtually everything produced there was new (as opposed to London, where a great percentage of productions were of classics). The situation has changed rapidly, largely for economic reasons: it is safer to produce a revival or to import a revival from a regional theater than to invest in a totally unknown commodity. The success of these revivals hinges on the actors. In many cases the prime consideration was not actors but "stars." In some cases the two categories overlapped. Rex Harrison was an example—he was at his most charming as Capt. Shotover in a competent revival of Shaw's *Heartbreak House.* Jason Robards, Colleen Dewhurst, and Elizabeth Wilson, along with a marvelous company of character actors, created an endearing revival of *You Can't Take It With You*, a play that has held up better than Odets's *Paradise Lost*, which was presented with Geraldine Page Off-Off-Broadway under the skilled direction of John Strasberg. Tony Lo Bianco, best known as a television actor, gave a moving performance as the anguished stool pigeon in a revival of Arthur Miller's *A View from the Bridge.* Michael Moriarty and John Rubinstein led an unusually strong cast in a successful production of *The Caine Mutiny Court Martial*, which, apart from its epilogue, has held up surprisingly well. And Al Pacino, as he did two years ago, revived what still seems the richest play of the last decade, David Mamet's *American Buffalo.*

In all these cases it was the actors who determined the continued viability of the plays. In the case of Samuel Beckett, the author's vision is so total, so rigid that the actor and director know they can only succeed if they place themselves completely under his control. On the printed page Beckett's plays often seem elusive, but if the productions follow his very precise instructions they invariably have a deep theatrical and emotional impact.

Three short Beckett works (with two ten-minute intermissions the evening runs less than ninety minutes) were presented at the Harold Clurman Theater, on a block of Forty-second Street known as Theater Row, consisting of a series of tiny, heavily subsidized companies devoted to presenting noncommercial work. The Beckett plays proved surprisingly commercial—they opened in June and were still drawing nearly full houses in January.

Each of the three pieces was written for a special occasion—*Ohio Impromptu* in 1981 for an international symposium at Ohio State University on the author's seventy-fifth birthday, *What Where* in 1983 for the Graz Festival in Austria, and *Catastrophe* in

1982 for an evening in tribute to Czech playwright Vaclav Havel, who had been imprisoned because of his writing.

In *Ohio Impromptu*, two men clothed entirely in black sit at one end of a long table. One reads from a large book. The other, whose face is covered by his hands and whose head is lowered in apparent concentration, knocks on the table—hard when he wants a passage repeated, softly when he is ready to proceed. The text itself is about a man who has disregarded the admonition of "the dear name" to "stay where we were so long alone together . . . my shade will comfort you." In the text a "shade" sent by "the dear face" comes to spend the night reading to the old man, a seeming parallel to the situation onstage. "With never a word exchanged they grew to be as one till one night, having closed the book . . . when the dawn appeared . . . did he disappear."

An enormous tension builds as the reader approaches the end of the book. Without ever addressing each other, the two figures onstage have made us aware of the intensity of their relationship. The relationship derives from their mutual commitment to the text, and the approach of the last page seems to presage an enigmatic but deep sense of closure and loss.

Seeing a Beckett play is like becoming fluent in a foreign language. The fluency occurs when one ceases to translate, when one begins to see the "foreign" words as having meaning in their own right. Similarly Beckett is baffling when one tries to see his plays as explicit references to the outside world. When one enters into their self-contained images, rhythms, and moods, one finds them moving. This was especially true of the third play, *What Where*, in which a dominant figure asks a series of underlings if they have given a victim "the works" and if he has confessed. When they admit failure, each in turn becomes the victim, is given "the works" until only the dominant figure is left and he has to order himself to receive "the works."

The term *the works* suggests a grade-B movie, and the author's irony, even if it does imply some kind of torture, is compounded by the characters' names—Bam, Bom, Bim, and Bem—which sound like the imaginary playmates of a precocious, lonely child. These elements of humor undercut the tones of the actors' voices, which are somber, and their movements on the dark stage, which resemble the mechanized initiation rites of some fraternal order. Nevertheless the repetition in the words, the odd dialogue established between the dominant figure's actual voice and his prerecorded voice as it issues from a megaphone suspended in the air beside him,

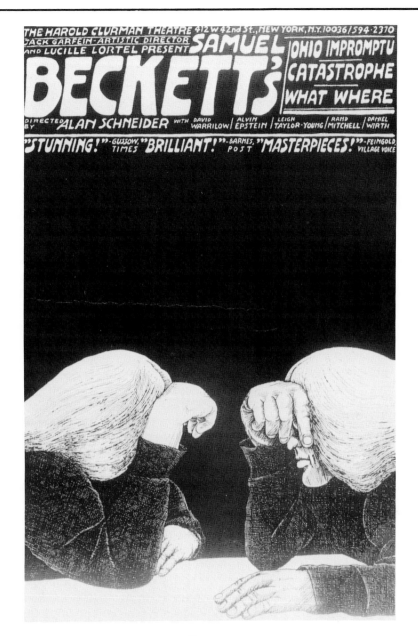

Lobby poster

and the carefully stylized movements all contribute a powerful sense of ritual.

Of the three plays *Catastrophe* is the only one whose references to the outside world are clear. In it a brutal, dictatorial stage director gives his cowering assistant explicit instructions about how to treat an actor (he is so disciplined and compliant that at first he seems a statue, not a living actor) who is supposed to represent catastrophe. However buffoonish and self-caricatured the director may be, at the conclusion of the piece, when the actor has been set according to his specifications and his face properly

lit, the image is absolutely haunting.

Though it never reduces itself to easy commentary on the plight of Eastern European artists, *Catastrophe*, in its suggestion that art can arise out of the most untoward circumstances, does indeed seem a tribute to those artists whose vision must establish itself against the odds of censorship, bureaucratic tampering, and malignant stupidity.

Havel, in whose honor the play was written, was himself represented in New York by three works under the heading *A Private View*, produced by Joseph Papp and directed by the film actress Lee

Anne Pitoniak and Kathy Bates in 'night, Mother

Grant. Havel's one-acts are about the ways in which a dissenter is forced to act in a Soviet society. In each play a dissident just out of prison encounters people who have accommodated themselves very nicely to "the system." They make clear their resentment of his "purity" (though there is nothing "holier than thou" about his behavior). They have no desire to emulate him, but their consciences trouble them and, as a result, they demand from him some sort of "endorsement" of their position. In each case the dissident, rather than humiliate these people, responds to their pleas for acceptance—each of his gestures of "absolution" takes on an aura of poignancy and irony.

The performances were self-conscious and overly satiric, but Havel's plays showed their strength nevertheless. In the case of the Beckett, the actors, under the knowing direction of Alan Schneider, submitted themselves to the precise demands of the text, and the result was an evening that added up to more than its ostensible parts, a demonstration of why Beckett is the great theater imagination of our period.

The Pulitzer Prize in 1983 went to Marsha Norman's *'night, Mother*, in which a young woman determined to commit suicide spends her last hour and a half briefing her mother on the reasons for

her decision and counseling her on how to behave afterward.

Norman's writing is skillful, and the play offers moments of deep poignancy, as when the mother, horrified at her daughter's coolheadedness about her self-destruction, exclaims, "You are my child." Her daughter responds grimly, "I am what became of your child." Only a few moments earlier her mother made the valid point "If you've got the guts to kill yourself, Jessie, you've got the guts to stay alive." Again, quite coolly, her daughter tells her, "I know that. So it's really just a matter of where I'd rather be." Perhaps the play's weakness is in making the daughter's choice so simple—all the cards are stacked against her: Her father mistreated her; her husband has left her; her son is a drug addict who returns home only to steal things he can sell to support his habit. Understandably she is overweight. On top of all this she is an epileptic. She lives with her mother, a pleasant if inane woman whose company is admittedly no inducement for hanging on.

Despite the fact the young woman is in total control of her emotions throughout the play; despite the fact she has reasoned out everything about her suicide with steely precision; it has never occurred to her to begin a new life by moving someplace else—the extreme nihilism of her decision seems at odds with the strength of her mind and her resolve. (What seems more probable in the lower-middle-class milieu in which the play is set is that such a woman, recognizing the hopelessness of her situation, would simply become an alcoholic and make everyone around her miserable.)

The lack of anything to complicate her decision makes the play seem too easy. If she were even slightly attractive, for example, or if she had a single close friend, the choice she makes would be harder. It would seem the decision of a woman too profoundly troubled for her to change course. Here she seems really to be giving up nothing. There seems to be no real choice for her to make. Because there seems little doubt she will make good on her promise, the ninety minutes of the play (which we see ticking away on several onstage clocks on Heidi Landesmann's remarkable, photorealist set) seem a way of marking time, almost a way of teasing the audience before the shocking moment we know will take place.

The above is, of course, a minority view, since 'night, Mother, in addition to the Pulitzer, received generally excellent notices. Its success with audiences may stem from a speech Jessie makes shortly before the end: "It's somebody I lost, all right. Only it's not anybody out there . . . it's my own self. Who I never was. Or who I tried to be and never got there. Somebody I waited for who never came. And never will . . . I'm what was worth waiting for and I didn't make it. Me . . . who might have made a difference to me. I'm not going to show up, so there's no reason to stay. . . ."

As simple, eloquent, and moving as these lines are, as directly as they address themselves to unfulfilled women (and men) in the audience, they do not convey any sense of inevitability. They do not reflect a malaise so intense only suicide is the answer. If the conclusion of the play does not seem convincing on a deep level, the play is nevertheless affecting, and unquestionably the acting of Kathy Bates as the young woman and Anne Pitoniak as her mother gives it as persuasive a reading as it could have.

Death made its presence felt in another two-character play that, by chance, opened the same week, Patrick Meyers's K2, about two men on their way back down after having scaled the world's second-highest mountain. One of them has injured a leg very badly, and it becomes obvious he will never make it down. During the course of the play the two men, in effect, explain their lives to one another, sometimes ironically, sometimes vulgarly and, for a few moments, poetically. The final mo-

ments of the play find the stranded climber describing the Japanese albino glacier fox, whose retinas are burned by the glare of the spring sun off the glacier snow. The blind creatures live in their burrows for a while, tended by their fellow foxes. But at a certain point they move down from the heights to the beach. "And they sit there and curl their plume white tail around their feet and wait, staring blindly at the rolling Japanese sea . . . and they never move a muscle—not a muscle—once they face the sea . . . they sit . . . and let the waves rise around them . . . till they're gone. . . ." "I want to be calm like the little fox," the man awaiting death cries to his friend, now far out of reach, as the lights dim. The fox, he says, remains still "because he knows he'll be back . . . and he'll have eyes next time," an exquisite ending for an often coarse and aimless play.

Though there were beautiful performances by Jeffrey De Munn and Jay Patterson, their work (and much of the dialogue itself) was overshadowed by the play's third character, the mountain. Ming Cho Lee's design filled all but a fraction of the stage with the massive flank of the mountain. The set was actually constructed of styrofoam and extended both above and below the proscenium opening. At one point De Munn scaled the set using a pickaxe, fell below the level of the stage, then slowly climbed back into view. A breathtakingly executed "avalanche" and the mesmerizing way the icy surface gleamed under the changing lights created an aura of poetry seldom present in the text.

The New York Drama Critics Circle gave its best play award to Neil Simon's Brighton Beach Memoirs, a seemingly autobiographical work about growing up in Brooklyn at the end of the Depression. The play is narrated by a fifteen-year-old would-be writer, an engaging portrait of the artist as a young cynic. Simon gives this character typically funny lines. Of a dinner where half the family wants to bring up problems for the stolid father to solve, the boy says, "The tension was so thick you could cut it with a knife. Which is more than you could say for the liver." Later he says of his mother, "She's angry at the whole world—that's why she's making lima beans." Without his customary sledgehammer technique Simon made the poignancy and gentle comedy of this unhappy household convincing for most of the first act, though the tone was broken by the two sons' discussion of masturbation, a pretext for cheap, easy laughs. In the second act, when most of the crises had already been resolved, Simon hardened his attitude toward the characters. The humor was replaced by shrieking as the drama descended to conventional kitchen-sink material, too ordinary, too shrill to be moving.

A more sustained effort at depicting the comedy and pathos of family life was Tina Howe's *Painting Churches*, a beautiful play in which the daughter of a long-established Beacon Hill family returns home to paint her doddering parents before they leave the house in which they have been living apparently since The Flood. The play's five scenes show her trying to get their cooperation, to cope with their eccentricities, to keep them from hurting one another, and to understand them from the hurried, often touching glimpses they give her of their past. The skill with which Howe depicts these people, their comic charm, the malice beneath their sometimes dotty, oddly gracious behavior, seems that of someone who has learned some fine technique of etching that has long fallen into disuse. The writing has a fineness, a delicacy not always realized in the performances.

In examining the vanishing world of the Haute WASP, Howe is trespassing on A. R. Gurney territory, not as movingly as his 1982 *The Dining Room* but more effectively than Gurney's two entries this year, *What I Did Last Summer* and *The Middle Ages*. The former is set in the summer of 1945 in an Upstate New York summer community where a fourteen-year-old boy has to choose between following the conventional path of his parents or striking out on his own under the influence of an old Bohemian woman. In *The Middle Ages* the action, as in *The Dining Room*, is set in a single room fraught with sociocultural implications, in this case the trophy room of the country club in some small American city. As the play moves from the late 1940s to the near present, we see a bastion of old American values besieged by the trends of recent times.

Both these plays are examples of Gurney's great economy and wit. The fact that their affectionate view of derriere-garde America has been received so warmly may indicate a new maturity on the part of audiences. Most native playwrights have been rebels, suspicious of the past and angry about the present. That we can now regard Gurney's world with as much irony and dispassion and bemusement as he does implies a healthy broadening of our sympathies.

A greatly sophisticated view of the American past was offered in Michael Weller's *The Ballad of Soapy Smith*, which opened the magnificent new Seattle Repertory Theater. *The Ballad of Soapy Smith* stands in marked contrast to most of the plays that opened in New York last year for a number of reasons, the controlling one being simply the size of the cast. Even in subsidized theaters, plays that require thirty actors have become all but impossible to mount. Of all the new plays discussed so far, only *Brighton Beach Memoirs* had a cast of more than six (it had seven). Most had only two or three, which accounts for a certain purposefulness and intensity but which limits the writer's palette.

For Weller to write a play on an epic scale set at the turn of the century was a significant departure for several reasons. In such works as *Moonchildren* and *Loose Ends*, Weller has been the only playwright to capture the language, the concerns, the mood of the generation that came of age in the turbulent 1960s. In view of the preponderance of books and journalism, even films, about these people, it seems extremely odd that there should be no record of them in the theater—except for Weller's plays, which treat them in even measures of humor and sympathy. (Other playwrights have written about them, but generally satirically, not capturing their special voice.)

Both in its language and its characters *The Ballad of Soapy Smith* was far removed from contemporary concerns, except perhaps for its preoccupation with American history as a source of moral ambiguities rather than merely a record of material progress. Though it had the trappings of a pageant—Eugene Lee's enveloping set gave the theater the boisterous, festive feel we associate with frontier life, an appropriate way to open a theater in the Pacific Northwest—*The Ballad of Soapy Smith* was essentially a study of two men, both concerned with codes of justice in a climate where only expediency and force have mattered.

Smith himself, a historical figure, was a con man at the turn of the century. At the close of his career he arrived in the Gold Rush town of Skagway, Alaska, where he imagined he could set his past behind him, make a quick fortune, and establish himself as a public benefactor. "Show me a man of reputation, and I'll show you a man whose grandfather was a horse thief," he reasons, as valid a theory of American upward mobility (European too, if you go back far enough) as any.

In Skagway (what fictional name could convey the sleaziness of this actual one?) he finds a rival in a man named Frank Reid. Reid lacks Smith's openness and cynicism. He too has a past he wants to forget. He too wants a reputation for civic virtue. He is torn between his liking for Smith, an unscrupulous politician with his heart in the right place, and a prior allegiance to a band of vigilantes, ostensibly upright citizens trying to establish a code of justice that will serve their own interests.

Clayton Corzatte, Denis Arndt, and Michael Santo in The Ballad of Soapy Smith *(© Chris Bennion, 1983)*

As the play progresses, Reid is drawn first toward Smith, then toward the vigilantes. Clearly he wants to do the right thing. Neither side offers him a chance to do so with a clear conscience. While Reid's hesitancy keeps him in a state of moral tentativeness, Smith's desire for self-justification leads him to increasing self-righteousness and ultimately demagoguery.

Weller presents these crises of public morality in a manner consistent with contemporary styles—constantly offering fresh provocations, never affording comfortable resolutions. Nor does he allow the audience the satisfaction of identifying with one man or the other—we are alternately attracted to and repelled by both. At times the play seems con-sciously Brechtian in its epic sweep and its harsh ironies (though Weller never hits us over the head with these, as Brecht might). At other times we are aware of Weller's effort to contain his prickly dramas of conscience within the contours of a "festival play," a "piece d'occasion." In its panoramic flourishes, *The Ballad of Soapy Smith* has comic scenes that bear too close a resemblance to the staples of Hollywood Westerns, but these are a kind of mortar (doubtless pleasing to much of the audience not particularly interested in moral dilemmas) that holds the bricks together. The first historical play of consequence in many years, *The Ballad of Soapy Smith* is a major achievement, injecting new seriousness and vitality into a long-ignored and difficult genre.

The production, evidence of Seattle's significance as a theater city, was directed with vigor and great sensitivity by Robert Egan.

As is customary, New York was the recipient of several British plays that broke no new ground but reminded us how satisfying a well-made evening of theater can be. Simon Gray's *Quartermaine's Terms* seemed a significant advance over *Butley* and *Otherwise Engaged*, both of which are structured rather rudimentarily—a man sits alone in a room and has a succession of visitors, all of whom complicate his already difficult existence, never, though, more than one at a time. In *Quartermaine's Terms* we follow seven characters—teachers in a school devoted to introducing foreigners to English culture—over a period of about three years. We see their frustrations, their ambitions, the ploys they use to keep one another at arm's length. They are a petty, unsuccessful lot, but Gray invests each with vulnerability, with an admirable resilience that makes us care deeply about them.

In some plays we meet characters facing problems and feel they are "settled" when the evening is over. Here the characters seem to have a Chekhovian permanence—like the sisters fretting about how their lives have escaped them, we can imagine these pedagogues stumbling through the same paces long after the curtain falls.

C. P. Taylor's *And A Nightingale Sang . . .* is a lovely portrait of a lower-middle-class family in Newcastle-on-Tyne muddling through World War II. We watch the anxieties of two daughters whose love lives are made alternately sweet and anxious by the abrupt, patternless comings and goings of their soldier lovers. In this family, where everything is made difficult by the shadow of war, generational battles "go onward the same, though Dynasties pass." Taylor's juxtaposition of homely, comic, poignant people and the awfulness of war makes beautiful theater out of what might have been soap opera.

It seems worth noting that both these plays were given splendid "ensemble" performances. Not surprisingly, both productions originated out of town, *Quartermaine's Terms* in New Haven, *And A Nightingale Sang . . .* in Chicago, where the main concern remains serving the play, not the box office.

The most adventurous British play of 1983 was Steve Berkoff's *Greek*, which had enjoyed both critical and popular success in Los Angeles and San Francisco but lasted only a week in New York (perhaps due to the shortsightedness of the pro-

ducers, but perhaps because New York may be, as one of the embittered, departing actors put it, "a bourgeois toilet"). *Greek* is a comic updating of the Oedipus myth in the vulgar language of contemporary lower-class England.

Berkoff's stream-of-consciousness dialogue is delivered in a high-pitched whine, the shrill, coarse tones to which all the events of the world are reduced in grimy backyards and pubs. The deliberate vulgarity seems a way of conveying the cynicism that now pervades our lives—Oedipus lived in a world in which profound shock was possible; Eddie, his latter-day counterpart, does not. When, for example, he learns that the woman he has been sleeping with is his mother, he uses Freud to rationalize it, rather than going berserk. In both the writing and the style of performance, a desire to outrage reminds one of the 1960s theater; but what would have been done in humorless, earnest rage two decades ago is now delivered with intense, sardonic humor.

Edward Albee's latest attempt at epatisme, *The Man Who Had Three Arms*, is a parable about a man who becomes a celebrity when he mysteriously grows a third arm, then becomes a nonentity again when the arm just as mysteriously disappears. It was hard to see the play as anything but an attempt by Albee to berate his audience for treating him as a freak—embracing him when his plays were a novelty, then deserting him. As an autobiographical metaphor, the third arm does not work. Unlike his title character, Albee owes his acclaim and subsequent lack thereof not to a trick of nature but to his own writing. The tone of the play was snotty in the extreme.

David Henry Hwang wrote two promising one-acts produced by Joseph Papp under the title *Sound and Beauty*. Neither seemed entirely fleshed out, but the first, based on some images of the Japanese novelist Yasunari Kawabata, was both provocative and poetic in its exploration of two old people whose relationship is both erotic and death obsessed. Another young writer, Kathleen Tolan, showed comic gifts in *A Weekend Near Madison*, a play about old friends of the 1960s at a reunion years later. Her comic sense was, alas, swamped by a plot that resolved itself into soap opera. Whatever its faults, Tolan's treatment of this material was more affecting than that in the film *The Big Chill*. Playwrights Horizon continued to produce writers who capture the comic hysteria of urban life—Christopher Durang in *Baby with the Bathwater*, Harry Kondoleon in *Christmas on Mars*, and Wendy

Wasserstein in *Isn't It Romantic* all created funny characters and situations that never really jelled into plays.

It would be unfair to leave the impression that actors are adversaries of literary texts. One of the most hopeful trends in the past year was a new interest and aptitude on the part of actors toward stylized comedy. Lee Kalcheim's comedy about a husband-and-wife radio team on the order of Dorothy Kilgallen and Richard Kollmar, *Breakfast With Les and Bess*, was quite synthetic as a play, but Holland Taylor and Keith Charles played the couple with such finesse, such an understanding of how to make brittle humor work, that the play gave an illusion of substance. Even more remarkable, an all-American cast achieved both critical and commercial success with a British farce, *Noises Off*. Michael Frayn's play is about a troupe of hack actors, touring a pointless sex comedy through the British provinces. Farce is invariably about nothing, but this one, as the brief plot outline indicates, is about Nothing Twice Removed. In the first act we see the actors rehearse the farce; we learn about their professional and personal idiosyncrasies. In the second, a month later, we are behind the scenes as the same material is performed—the shifting backstage romantic entanglements create vendettas so intense the onstage comedy pales by comparison. By the third act, a month later, the backstage dramas have totally obliterated the play. We watch what was initially a precarious structure degenerate into a total shambles.

To cover the same idiotic material no less than three times is clearly an act of reckless courage, but Frayn does so ingeniously. That the audience cares about what happens (only a madman would describe in any detail a play many of whose crises hinge on the appearance and disappearance of plates of sardines) is indeed a miracle. But it is proof that farce is the purest form of theater because it elicits an audience response without addressing any moral, emotional, or social issues. It demonstrates conclusively that Something can come of Nothing.

Of all comedies, farce is the hardest to perform. To mask the lack of discernible content, the actors must perform with precision and deadly seriousness. If they treat the play as a joke, it falls flat. If they regard their inane tasks as reverently and ominously as people tiptoeing around the kitchen when there is a soufflé in the oven—miraculously, it works. In the case of *Noises Off*, a cast of nine under the direction of Michael Blakemore performed their outrageous tasks with consummate skill.

If farce can be served with the same dedication traditionally reserved only for O'Neill, Williams, and Inge, the American theater has reason for hope.

The Year in Poetry

Lewis Turco
State University of New York at Oswego

One keeps hearing these days rumors and siftings of a return to formalism in American poetry. The Australian poet A. D. Hope delivered the obsequy for "free verse"—that is, prose—in an essay, "Free Verse: A Post Mortem," which was published in his book *The Cave and the Spring* more than ten years ago (University of Chicago Press, 1970). In this very cogent essay, Hope says that many of us confuse the terms "rhythm" and "metre." He points out that "verse employs another set of rhythmic devices in addition to the natural rhythms already described. We call this metre, or measure." Thus, the essential difference between prose and verse is that prose is unmeasured language, and verse is measured language. If one is counting syllables or stresses, or both, one is writing in verse; if one is not, one is writing in prose. If one breaks prose into lines according to phrasing or punctuation or one of the other "natural" kinds of rhythm, then one is writing in prose still, even if one wishes to justify such writing according to the tradition in English culture that poetry (a genre) is written in verse (one of the two modes) by calling it "free verse," which is clearly a contradiction in terms. If language is "measured" in verse, it is not "free" (though it may be "variable"). But one strays from

Hope's point. "The essence of metre," he says, "is that it is an organization of rhythm on a basis of recurrence or expectation."

One cannot tell from reading most of these books under review that the hegemony of "free verse," that is, *prose*, has been broken in American poetry, though perhaps it has been in Australian. Recent generations of American poets have been "trained" in the writing of prose poems, and that metrical competence which marked many of the writers of the 1950s has now been entirely lost except by a few of the elder generation who continue to write formally; who, as it were, still have the *ear* for blending and counterpointing the various kinds of rhythms of the English language.

The result is that there has grown up an unwritten protocol or convention having to do with how one ought to write prose poems, so that many of the poems appearing in a number of these books might easily be mistaken for the work of a single author, if we did not have the various authors' names printed on the title pages. Here are some examples:

> When I tell you I've waked as if in a basement,
> and the windows are open, I can
>   smell roots—
> *don't do anything*, you say, *just stand there*.
>
> Because I said I did and because I never did
> I am now someone who has only to imagine
> the evenings where the boats dock
> and men drink,
>
> to live the lie again.
>
> Absurd to sit here chained. They mean
> to kill me, to draw their life from mine.
> My eyes bulge huge and placid and intent.
> My mouth grows wider, deeper, wears a grin.
> The circle narrows and I take them in.

The first four lines are from "Learning a New Language" by Margaret Gibson in her book *Long Walks in the Afternoon* (Louisiana State University Press), which is the Lamont Poetry Selection for 1982; the next five lines are from "Anonymous Meditation" by Jane Miller in *The Greater Leisures* (Doubleday), published in the National Poetry Series and selected by Stanley Plumly; and the last five lines are from "Vortex" by Rika Lesser in *Etruscan Things* (Braziller). In order to make up this "found poem" one had to do nothing more than leaf through a few books to find a first-person "I" narrator and select two first strophes and a final one.

The "poem" has a certain feeling of completeness about it, and this is due in part to the Lesser strophe, which illustrates what Hope was talking about. All these lines except the last three are written in prose made to look like verse by disposing the lines according to phrasing—what W. C. Williams used to call the "breath pause." But the third-to-last line is written in iambic tetrameter verse—the two kinds of rhythm, prose, and verse are thus harmonized. The last two lines are an iambic pentameter ("heroic") couplet rhymed *aa*. Thus, the tetrameter line serves as a bridge to the heroic couplet, in which the expectation of completion set by the meter is juxtaposed with the preceding prose. This expectation is fulfilled, giving a good deal of pleasure, a feeling of climax (which it also did in the original poem). But this hardly indicates a return to formalism in American poetry. Furthermore, the "poem" has a feeling that it has been built by jury-rigging, which indeed it was. The same feeling is in the originals. Here is another poem built in much the same way:

> Through rain I see huge moonless spaces,
> intricate scars in the earth,
> a fine thread of water.
> Two voices in the clouded space name
>   the planets,
> the moon, the earth.
>
> Body upon body
> flattened by wave-press,
> the purple and brown stars
> cling to each other in heaps:
> the opposite of a Japanese garden,
> where a few enduring stones
> suggest the significance
> of time and distance.
>
> I won't wake you. I am staring
> into the dark, making the storm happen.
> But if it never breaks? If all things
> must hang in violent equilibrium?
>
> I never thought we'd end up
> this far north, love.
> Cold blue tinge in lieu of heavens.
> Quarter moon like chalk on a slate.

All of these lines are nearly plain prose, rhythmless except for some accidental approaches to meter, as in strophe three. The tradition is the backwash of Imagism. If anything has changed here in the last decade, it is that "deep image surrealism" appears to have been abandoned by nearly everyone, and people are again writing poems that make sense.

There is, however, very little sense of *line* — "the moon, the earth" has no reason for being a line other than length, perhaps: if it had been appended to the line above, that line would have *seemed* too long, but this seeming would have been owing entirely to typography, not rhythm. (Perhaps Charles Olson would have justified it on the basis of "eye-rhythm.") The same is true for "Body upon body," "suggest the significance," "this far north, love."

There is very little sense of the poem's architecture, either of overall plan or movement. No doubt the apologists for "free verse" will be delighted with this state of things, because poetry has now become so democratic that anyone can do it. The danger in writing poetry in verse is simple: The reader can tell almost instantly if the poem is badly written—one can check the meters—do they jingle? Do they grate? Are the sounds of the poem trite or inventive? Is something said poorly or superbly? But there is little danger in writing prose poems. Who is going to say whether one of them is badly written? There are no counterpointing rhythms to bother the ear, not even much punctuation, probably. Conrad Aiken, late in life, said contemporary poetry is so much "sawdust cornflakes." Some of these volumes have won prizes; but, truly, how does a "judge" tell that one is better or worse than the other? How does one go about telling them apart?

The first strophe of the second found "poem" is from "Photograph" by Anthony Petrosky in *Jurgis Petraskas* (Louisiana State University Press), winner of the 1982 Walt Whitman Award. If read for story value, this book has some excellent character sketches and scene evocation. The second is from "Not Stars, Not Fish" by Erika Funkhouser in *Natural Affinities* (Alice James Books); the third is from "Storm Watch" by Celia Gilbert in *Bonfire* (Alice James Books), and the last is from "Rural Delivery" by Charles Simic in *Austerities* (Braziller). Celia Gilbert in her poem "The Constellation" has a last line, "hymned by flies," that we can compare with its unattributed source, Richard Wilbur's "The Pardon," in which a dead dog is "clothed in a hymn of flies"; but there is no comparison—not in image, not in rhythm.

Irving Feldman is a member of that generation which was the last to be trained in the craft of writing rather than in the trick of imitation. He learned how to do all the hard things with language before he was encouraged to find a "voice"; being unique thus came easier to him than to subsequent waves of poets who, told from the start to "be themselves," in desperation learned, by osmosis, how to survive by writing what they were expected to write—to imitate their teachers, to follow the latest guru or the fashionable style.

The result is that Feldman built on a solid foundation and achieved a voice that is truly his own. He is praised by Richard Howard on the dust jacket of *Teach Me, Dear Sister* (Viking/Penguin) as a poet who "invokes and invades the entire resource of his art." This is true, but the thing that catches one's attention first, perhaps, is Feldman's wonderful sense of humor that invests his compassion and ability to empathize with an edge of mockery that undercuts our tendency to make too sententious a thing of the human condition.

Feldman writes whole poems. He writes very often—though not always—on a solid metrical base, his usual line being either iambic tetrameter or pentameter unrhymed. Very often the two are mixed; but he has straight prose poems here, and some made of the Biblical grammatic parallels. There are few better storytellers around, and none who have a better insight into our secret places. Feldman is one of our best poets, a whole man of parts. He is one of the sane among us.

Carol Frost is one of the few younger poets who has been working toward a sense of complex rhythm during the past few years. In her new collection, *The Fearful Child* (Ithaca House), her former strengths—nuance, image, sensitivity—are blended now with a solid feel for the movement of language, and the result is a strong book of poems. Donald Petersen has characterized them as "loosely formal poems with lots of good sense grounded in strong images," which is a good way to characterize them in general; but in particular there are some stunningly beautiful poems here, very sensitive in terms of emotion and language. "Death in Winter" is very effective, and the title poem, "The Fearful Child," is poignantly evocative. "Country Marriage" conjures up a whole life, a kind of experience I have not before seen put into such fine distinctions of words.

The State University of New York Press launches its "invited poetry" series with C. D. Wright's *Translations of the Gospel Back into Tongues*—the "inviter" is Paul Zweig. This collection is straight out of Robert Bly's now dated "deep image" surrealism. Wright's work is full of strange tropes and arcane non sequiturs. W. S. Merwin claims that the poems are in the "tradition of the blues," but Langston Hughes would likely raise his eyebrows at that characterization; there is no sense of rhythm at all in these poems, either traditional or modern. Now and then Wright invents a word—"transbluent," "well-witcher"; the latter one understands as an unfortunate pun in context (what other reason can she have for not using the standard "water-witch"?), and the former is opaque. The book is beautifully produced.

Mary Oliver does sensitive work. Her poems, like some of the others here, can be read for the narratives they contain, and there are some wonderful stories that she tells in *American Primitive* (Atlantic-Little, Brown). These are, strictly speaking, prose poems, but there is a subtle beat lying beneath the lines, though many of these lines end arbitrarily, and the sense of thought-unit is weak in the line if not in the strophe. Oliver's feeling for nature and the mythology of America's past is very strong. There are many poems here that are well worth reading and rereading. The nostalgia she evokes is for what we might have been rather than for what we are; thus, though she conjures isolation and loneliness in her poems, what arises out of them is hope couched in mystery.

Two quotations next:

> Though the view from my door
> was still more contracted,
> I did not feel crowded
> or confined in the least.
> There was pasture enough
> for my imagination.
> The low shrub-oak plateau
> to which the opposite shore arose,
> stretched away toward
> the prairies of the West
> and the steppes of Tartary,
> affording ample room for all
> the roving families of men.

> Snowstorms high-traveling, furry clouds
> blur over our zero air: wind streams (or
> smokes) fine snow off the eaves, settled ghosts
> trailing up and away: the pheasant, too cold
> to peck, stands on one foot like a stiff weed.

The "Poem" above is a few lines of H. D. Thoreau's *Walden* broken into lines according to phrasing. The paragraph below it is a poem, "Down Low," from A. R. Ammons's book *Lake Effect Country* (Norton) written out as a prose paragraph. Ammons has won every prize in sight not, perhaps, because he is a poet, but because he is a fine nature writer, like Thoreau.

Exactly the same thing might be done with the pieces in Frederick Feirstein's chapbook *Fathering*

(Apple-wood Books), but the results would be much less well written and insightful. This is a sequence about being a father written very fondly by "a practicing psychotherapist."

For years John Fandel, one of our better unsung poets, has been getting up little pamphlets of poems, sometimes in odd shapes, and sending them to his friends. The latest of these fetching publications, privately printed, are *Inside/Outside*, *Four Friskans*, *Views*, and *A Window on K-2 and Other Views*. Fandel is at once the most unassuming of poets, and one of the purest. He has never ceased to be interesting, inventive, simultaneously traditional and experimental; and he has never ceased to write. One hopes he never does.

William Stafford's *Roving Across Fields* (Barnwood Press Cooperative) is edited by Thom Tammaro and subtitled "A Conversation and [nineteen] Uncollected Poems, 1942-1982." Many people think of Stafford as an "open-form" poet, but in fact his practice may best be described, like Carol Frost's, as "loosely formal." The gentle iambics lie there beneath the lines, and the rhymes, too, which are often internal. Stafford is one of the good people of this world. He believes that "anyone who can talk can write," so he is democratic to a fault; he is a fine nature writer, like Ammons; his method most nearly resembles that of Emily Dickinson, however, rather than Thoreau. If his self-critical faculty is nearly nonexistent—he has said in an interview, "I never met a poem of mine I didn't like" (and this little volume proves it)—he has nevertheless written some of our best contemporary poems. Unfortunately, none of them is in this volume.

Of all the books so far the one this reviewer has most *enjoyed* is Frank Polite's chapbook *The Pool of Midnight* (Pangborn Books) in the Youngstown Area Writers Collector Series. It is a sustained work of the imagination—unlike the others—a coherent series based partly on "certain phrases included in . . . the films *Sudan*, *Bagdad*, *Ali Baba & the Forty Thieves*, and Abu Sidhuli's unpublished *Oral Histories of the Lost Tribes of the Ara'mak*." This is a fine, consistently well-written work. It glitters!

In Larry Eigner's *Waters/Places/A Time* (Black Sparrow Press) we have ". . . this pitiable dot and dash splinter poetry, or sawdust cornflakes which we usually get" that Aiken deplored toward the end of his life—words (sometimes soulful) scattered down the page without syntax. Now and then a short, haikuish piece contains a good image and overtone.

Kodachromes in Rhyme by Ernesto Galarza (University of Notre Dame Press) is a sleeper by an unknown, at least in the field of poetry. None of these straightforwardly formal (for the most part) pieces appears to have been published in periodicals before their collection here; they meter and rhyme in an unstrained, conversational way, and some of them are better than competent.

They do not measure up, however, to the standard set in John Woods's *The Valley of Minor Animals* (Dragon Gate). Woods is an old master formalist, of the generation of Feldman. Although his practice has loosened up over the years (there are even some prose poems here), these pieces have a strong sense of rhythm and language, of story and sound. This is one of the strong collections of the year, wide-ranging in topic and effect. Woods has had very little attention over the years, but as James Wright says on the jacket, "John Woods is one of the best writers we have, and I don't know whether or not it is any consolation to him to know (how could a person write that well and not know?) that his labors mean something and that his work is fine." Agreed. It's time he was considered for some of the major prizes.

There are, next, four books from New Directions. The first, Denise Levertov's *Poems 1960-1967*, is a gathering and reprinting in one volume of three earlier collections—*The Jacob's Ladder, O Taste and See*, and *The Sorrow Dance*—all published in the 1960s originally. Jerome Rothenberg's *That Dada Strain* is comprised of three series of poems. The first, the title series, assumedly attempts to do for poetry what Dadaism did for art sixty years ago; the second continues in the same vein, but the word *Dada* is not repeated over and over again. The third is a bit more intelligible, but not much. *Think a Bored Angel* by Samuel Hazo is an occasionally interesting collection, but by far the most interesting of the four is *Fragments of Perseus* by the Beat poet Michael McClure. McClure has been developing an idiosyncratic style for many years; he has a lyric ear and a fine sense of the mad. Many of these poems have the quality of Amerindian chants.

Baron Wormser's *The White Words* (Houghton Mifflin) is a first book, and a very good one. Here is a younger poet who is a formalist in fact, but a catholic formalist—that is to say, his range of technique is so broad that he can do anything he pleases, whether traditionally or more adventurously. With the range there is also depth—of thought, of emotion, of observation. The combination is irresistible. Wormser knows how to *write*; he has the talent and capacity to use the language to illuminate the human experience.

Lewis Warsh's *Methods of Birth Control* (Sun and

Moon) is a great contrast. This book is comprised of four sets of "poems"; each set is made up, in turn, of aphoristic statements and remarks in short prose lines, many of them of a scientific cast, bearing often vague connections with one another. This sort of performance passes for experimental poetry in some circles, but there is little language interest here. A fair sample of the method and style is "LIV" from the title set: "There may be enough sperm / in the pre-ejaculatory fluids / to result in pregnancy."

Another book from the same press is Jonas Wine's *Longwalks*. The first part of the collection is a sequence that bears some resemblance in layout to the Warsh pieces, but the resemblance is superficial. Wine's work has a good deal more language interest, particularly on the sonic level. The later poems are longer-lined and textured; therefore, they are capable of sustaining more complex patterns on the ideational level.

In Cathy Song's first book, *Picture Bride* (Yale Series of Younger Poets, introduced by the late Richard Hugo), we return to poems that have a strong story line. The poems are phrased prose written well and intelligently. They have a sensitive sensory level in particular.

Another first book is *The Hands in Exile* by Susan Tichy (Random House), published in the National Poetry Series. These, too, are story-line, phrased prose pieces, most of them of the "kibbutzim experience" genre. They therefore have a topical interest as well.

The same sort of interest attaches to *Shadow Country* by Paula Gann Allen (University of California/Los Angeles), published in the Native American Series of the American Indian Studies Center. Here, again, the narrative line is important. On the sonic level the Amerindian chant and refrain are prominent; the sensory level is crisp and clear, creating solitary moods and a pervasive sadness that rises like dust off the plains and pages.

The work of Stephen Todd Booker in *Waves & license* (Greenfield Review Press) was written by a prisoner on death row, but this topical interest is not the most fetching aspect of the pieces. What is most remarkable is the humor of the situations and observations. Written in a sort of neo-Beat style, the best poems contain some very good jazzy rhythms. Poor editing has left quite a number of typos and misspellings that tend at times to take the attention off what the poet is saying.

It is always a pleasure to run across a poet who takes the language seriously and handles it with love, whether in verse mode or prose. Such a writer is Ellen Bryant Voigt in *The Forces of Plenty* (Norton).

Her poems, though written in phrased prose, are rhythmic and sensuous. The ideational level is intelligent and reflective. The book is altogether a true literary experience given to us by someone who knows how to compose in words.

Clayton Eshleman is discursive in his *Fracture* (Black Sparrow Press), but his involvement in classical mythology as it applies to building an archetype of the Self is often arcane, and the poems, as a consequence, can be quite obscure. Still, it is clear that Eshleman takes the language seriously. The only question, then, is does he take *himself* too seriously? Whitman was, in the view of some, the last (and the first) American poet to turn Himself successfully into a demigod. Not everyone agrees that he managed the feat. Most human beings fare poorly as Egyptian pharaohs or Roman emperors, descendants of the Powers. Eshleman fares no better.

Bill Knott, author of *Becos* (Vintage Books), has said elsewhere that his "major theme is avoidance of major themes." In this he succeeds very well. He has also said, "My usual verse form is iambic prose poems." One can agree with this at least in part. However, he has a taking sense of humor and a love for fooling around with the language that can be enjoyable.

David Citino's *The Appassionata Poems* (Cleveland State University Poetry Center) is a series of "Sister Mary Appassionata's" lectures to various "classes" of pupils. True to the title, these speeches concern the passions of humanity, but they resemble no lectures ever given by a Catholic nun on the face of this earth. It is impossible to imagine a real nun so intelligently open on the subject of passion, so wise and learned, so imaginative, lewd, and sacramentally secular; but parochial school principals should make this book required reading. Aside from all its virtues of textured thought and language, its compassion and wit, its amazing transformations of Christian mythology into the commonplace events of our everydays, this book is a whole thing: a story truer than true made of outrageous lies. Simply a wonderful book of poetry.

Another series is Paul Zimmer's *Family Reunion* (University of Pittsburgh Press). This is a fictive biography of a persona named Zimmer, to be confused, of course, with the author and thereby transformed into autobiography. The narrative line is varied and eventful, each poem readable and pleasurable, but the whole adds up to much more than the sum of its parts.

Many of the poems in Thylias Moss's *Hosiery Seams on a Bowlegged Woman* (Cleveland State University Poetry Center) are character sketches, all of them in phrased or straight prose. As stories, several are interesting and insightful. The people in them are ordinary, their tragedies common, and the author's stance is compassionate. Another book from the same press is *Exploded View* by Mark Kessinger. Here, it is the poems that are ordinary.

The pieces that comprise Lawrence Lieberman's *Eros at the World Kite Pageant* (Macmillan) start in Japan and end in Jamaica. Many of them are long and discursive, partaking as much of the travelogue as of the journal. Lieberman is a talented writer, but one confesses to a certain weariness reading through the book, the same sort of weariness one experiences during an evening of looking at other people's slides or home movies: The mind tends to wander, the eyes to unfocus, and the ears to muffle out. One begins to understand what Poe meant when he said that there is no such thing as a poem over a hundred lines long.

Home by Jim Simmerman (Dragon Gate) is a first book with many fine qualities: clean writing, good range of subject, varied approaches, wit, humor, intelligence, and sentiment. What more can one ask of a new poet?

Equally impressive, if more literary in tone, is *From the Abandoned Cities* by Donald Revell (Harper and Row), another first book, this one published in the National Poetry Series. A formal poet, Revell is at ease with structures as traditional as the sestina and the villanelle. He has already developed a strong voice which is to a degree dark and contemplative. His poems find the tension between language and subject, and they maintain it to strong resolutions. It is good to find a young poet who gives the lie to the prevalent notion that the old forms are "dead."

Another good collection from the same publisher is Dave Smith's *In the House of the Judge*. Smith is a stylist whose driving rhythms support imagery that borders on the hallucinatory, on surrealism, yet who finally does not lose touch with the particular: the event, character, or atmosphere. The strong symbolic level is supported at all times by an equally strong narrative.

Yet a third book from the same house is *Peru* by Herbert Morris. Whoever is the poetry editor at Harper and Row seems to have nearly infallible taste. This collection inhabits the middle ground between the Revell and the Smith books. On the one hand, this is a first collection; on the other, it is authored by a mature poet whose work has been appearing in some of our best journals for a quarter-century. Like Revell's poems, Morris's are

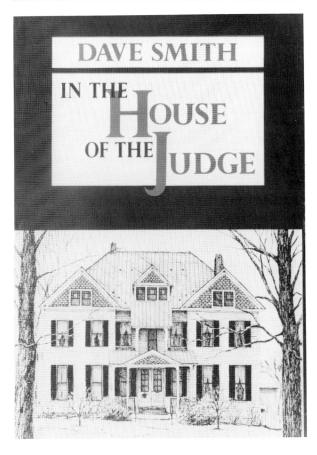

Dust jacket for Dave Smith's tenth poetry collection, which Robert Penn Warren calls "clearly his best"

classically controlled, though not so traditionally formal; like Smith's, the images border on the surrealistic, but the rhythms are incantatory rather than obsessive. One might write a longer review comparing these three excellent writers, all of whom deserve a wide and appreciative audience.

What to say of Gerard Malanga's *This Will Kill That* (Black Sparrow Press)? This collection of what look like fragments of language lying in the rubble after a blitz is the sort that Aiken deplored. The book concludes with the title piece, subtitled "An Experiment in Autobiography." It is really an essay on "experimental" poetics and aesthetics, and it is a good deal more readable than the work it attempts to justify.

The Attractions of Heavenly Bodies is a first book by Dennis Heinrichsen (Wesleyan University Press). It is deeply rooted in the American Midwest. The rhythms of his phrased prose poems often become iambic meters, and his tone is elegiac. His concerns are the simple tragedies and sorrows of the people he knows well—himself, his family, his

neighbors—but his sympathies never descend to truisms. These are sad and compassionate elegies and laments.

Sharon Bryan's *Salt Air* also is a first book from Wesleyan, and it shares many virtues with the Heinrichsen volume: the elegiac tone, the good, clean writing, the images rooted in the particular. There is a very high level of competence in much of our contemporary poetry, and Bryan is on the high edge of that competence.

Phenomena by Cathryn Hankla (University of Missouri Press) is remarkable in that the poems show a sense of rhetoric, an unusual quality in contemporary poetry; they are in the symbolist tradition also, though the tropes are often "deep images." She shares with Dave Smith something of a driving rhythm. The combination of these elements is both exciting and arresting.

Sarah Bernhardt's Leg (Cleveland State University Poetry Center) is a collection by a veteran, David Kirby, who has six other volumes to his credit.

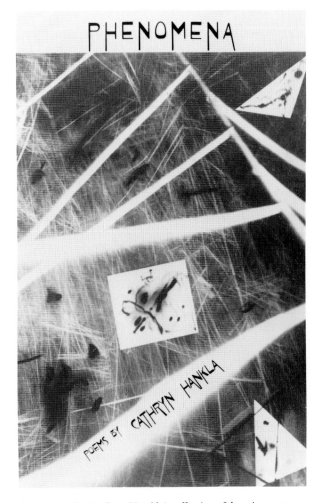

Front cover for Cathryn Hankla's collection of deep-image poems

Kirby's method is like that of Kafka: Take an ordinary situation, couch it in ordinary language, and then insert an element of hallucination to transform the commonplace into the bizarre. The effect can be either hysterically funny or chilling, or both. This is classic surrealism, but Kirby's poems are as American as apple pie containing a baked stuffed worm.

When she's not preaching, Wanda Coleman tells a good story now and then in *Imagoes* (Black Sparrow Press). Her language is jazzy prose; to make it even more hip, Coleman drops all terminal punctuation and capitals, plus most internal punctuation except for an occasional comma or slashmark. Although this practice impedes reading, it establishes her credentials as a bona fide West Coast poet out of Ferlinghetti by Ginsberg. The book is too long by at least half.

Quite a contrast is *Partita in Nothing Flat* by Judson Jerome (Barnwood Press). This chapbook is a set of twelve sonnets, variously flavored, in praise of the ménage à trois. There are quite a few linguistic Roman candles and aerial flares going off here, but not enough to take one's mind off the monotonous meters and, now and again, inept techniques, such as inverted diction for the sake of rhyme (or is it simply to be arch?). A rhymster memorizes a meter and works with it; a poet understands the meter and works against it to create counterpoint.

Marc Hudson's *Afterlight* (University of Massachusetts Press) is the winner of the 1983 Juniper Prize. Except for an earlier chapbook publication, this is a first collection. The poems are in the tradition of Northwest poets such as David Wagoner, Richard Hugo, and William Stafford, who have a feeling for both landscape and language. The poems are crisp and clear, the imagery evocative, the sensibility contemplative.

Add to these qualities a keen sense of narrative, a deep insight into character, a photographer's eye for composition, a painter's feeling for atmosphere, light, and color, and you have David Wagoner himself at his best in *First Light* (Atlantic-Little, Brown). Nor do these talents exhaust the abilities of one of the very best poets currently writing in English. Wagoner has an absolute sense of rhythm. His seemingly informal poems are expressions of a knowledge of pattern and sound so deep that one is unaware of the formalism of these pieces until one goes back to reread them with critical eyes. When this poet chooses to ignore punctuation, as in "The Bad Uncle," he does so for particular reasons—characterization, representation of situation and atmosphere, simulation of people's

thought processes—and not out of a programmatic adherence to an idiosyncratic style. The subjects treated in this book are as wide-ranging as the techniques. One might write a long essay on the broad theme of the possibilities of poetry, using David Wagoner as a paradigm, but it is more enjoyable just to read this master of the genre.

The tone of *Keeping Company* by Gibbons Ruark (Johns Hopkins University Press) is unrelievedly elegiac; the poems are uniformly contemplative, inhabited by a brooding mistiness. In nearly every poem, the point of view is egopoetic. Yet these are very well written pieces. Ruark's syntax and diction are as clear as new ice, and his formality is at once classic and at ease with itself.

Express by James Reiss, *Tunes for Bears to Dance To* by Ronald Wallace, *Only the World* by Constance Urdang, and *Shouting at No One* by Lawrence Joseph, winner of the Agnes Lynch Starrett Poetry Prize, are all from the Pitt Poetry Series of the University of Pittsburgh Press. Taken as a group, they reflect the sensibility of the poetry editor of that house as much as some earlier books reviewed here reflected the taste of the editor at Harper and Row. The latter wins hands down. All of these collections are written in good old democratic, colloquial prose, what Helen Vendler—quoted on the back cover of the Reiss book—calls "an accomplished plain style." The cover of the Urdang book claims that "she is incapable of writing a good, standard, mediocre poem," but that is what all four of these books are full of.

Antelope Light by Joanne Mahon (Pangborn Books) is a lovely little chapbook, full of sensitive prose poems with the feeling of verse. The author has a sure sense of line and rhythm. Every now and again, though, a typo or grammatic error brings one up short among these otherwise very well written pieces.

Mark Vinz in *Climbing the Stairs* (Spoon River Poetry Press) writes out of the same sensibility as Vern Rutsala: A sense of omen lurks within the straightforward diction, the ordinary scenes, the deliberately flat prose lines with their arresting images. The uneasiness that the poems inculcate in the reader is deliberate and effective. Now and then one looks up from reading and glances around the room to see who it is that is watching.

The pieces of *Glass Walker* by Imogene L. Bolls (Cleveland State University Poetry Center) are prose, written very largely on the sensory level. The images are sharp, and one feels that they are trying to say something beyond themselves, but at the point of overtone they verge over into statement rather than implication. The result is that the poems wind up coming down rather heavily on the thematic level, and they very often turn into small preachments or homilies at the last moment.

James Schevill's *The American Fantasies: Collected Poems 1945-1981* (Swallow Press) is a series on which the poet has been working, we are told, since the late 1940s. In a "Note," Schevill says that many of the poems "have been published in different books, some in different versions." They are "fantasies," often dramatic, intended to blend the subjective and the objective in a mirror of the United States over nearly forty years. Schevill is an excellent writer who is able to do many things technically; his approaches range from the traditionally formal to the "experimental," usually with a high degree of success.

Very similar in his ability to do many things, in his expertise with the dramatic voice, is David R. Slavitt in *Big Nose* (Louisiana State University Press); however, his manner is usually more biting and direct, his diction more colloquial; his rhythms drive harder. There is a strong sense of immediacy in the poems, a feeling of excitement.

Until now Wallace Fowlie has been known primarily as a critic and translator. With *Characters from Proust* (Louisiana State University Press) he intends to emerge as a poet; but his inspiration is still literary, as the jacket tells us, for these pieces form a series: Fowlie has taken "fifty moments from Proust's *Remembrance of Things Past* . . . and thoughtfully reordered them into verse." In a sense, then, these are "found" poems. The pieces are very definitely verse—not a prose line in the volume, though there are one or two that are iambic tetrameter rather than the pervasive, and in these hands quite deadly iambic pentameter blank verse. Fowlie has a metronome for an ear: very little of the sense of flow of language *against* the beat, no feeling for counterpoint. The result is that these verses come off very badly against Proust's dreamy prose, their source. It is the difference between a journeyman and a master.

The poems in James Applewhite's *Foreseeing the Journey* (Louisiana State University Press) probably have to be classified prosodically as phrased prose; but there is a strong iambic measure lying beneath the lines, and large sections of the longer-lined pieces are written in loose iambic pentameter blank verse. The genre of the poems is confessional; in fact, the first section, "Iron Age Flying," is an autobiographical sequence. The second section—

which is also the title of the book—is longer, but still thematically relevant to the autobiography. The poems are well written and interesting, though the tonal range is limited.

The mode of Alberta Turner in *A Belfry of Knees* (University of Alabama Press) is more straightforwardly prose, and its genre—as always in her work—is also confessional. The individual pieces operate very largely on the sensory level, and they are full of arresting images, whimsy that takes the form of self-mockery, and a surrealism of the ordinary. Nearly all the poems are short; the poet therefore leaves herself little space for depth of insight or epiphany. These are miniatures rather than murals, then, but delicacy and detail have their charm.

Lindon Stall's *Responsoria* is unusual. It is a pamphlet of sharp epigrams and flowing lyrics, some in French, some in English, some in both, all evidently composed by Stall. His subjects are religious: St. John, St. Augustine, Mary Magdalen, and others; but Stall's treatment is immediate and arresting.

Stall's publisher is R. L. Barth, who is the author of *Forced Marching to the Styx: Vietnam War Poems* (Percivale Press). This is a truly extraordinary volume. Barth is a pure formalist; his poems are composed in the old forms. The most experimental piece is "Letter from An Hoc (4), by a Seedbed," written in rhymed syllabics. The subject matter is both classic and contemporary: war in general, the Vietnam War specifically. Barth proves—if it ever needed proving—that the traditions are still viable if they are used by someone who understands and knows how to work them without being overwhelmed by the burden of all those who have preceded him. His language is modern, moving easily in the traces to discuss in depth or in flashes—whatever is called for—the desperation and degradation of combat, the human condition rising or falling in the eternal tides of destruction. It is a great shame that these marvelous poems will have a limited circulation in this chapbook from a small press, because they deserve the broadest audience possible.

Besides Stall's, four other chapbooks consisting exclusively of formal poetry have been published by Barth's press in 1983. *Measures* by James M. Young is aptly titled. These poems have a classical ring to them, reminiscent to a degree of J. V. Cunningham. If one has the impression that the meters of the poems are more regular than Barth's, scansion shows that there are many metrical variations of considerable subtlety. Young, too, is a fine writer.

Not only are the style and forms of David Middleton's *Reliquiae* classical and formal, but so is the subject matter: Narcissus, the Sirens, Hesiod, Plotinus. He too writes very well, but his themes remove the poems from the realm of the immediate. As a result, Middleton's work comes off as the academic exercises of a classical scholar. Middleton has not been able to get out from under the burden of tradition. Unfortunately, many people think all formal poetry is like this—or like John S. Anson's *A Family Album*, a sequence of domestic sonnets having many elements in common with, though less flamboyant than, the Judson Jerome chapbook discussed here. Anson's pieces are competently done, but they add little or nothing to the tradition.

The final chapbook from Barth is *Under Red Skies* by Charles Gullans, a collection of fine poems written by one of the elder generation schooled in the tradition of classic formalism. His patterns are iambic—blank verse, heroic and shorter couplets—each poem intelligently and elegantly written, yet with a surface clean as glass and a texture deep as a tarn. It is a sheer pleasure to read such poems as these. They make the word *literature* take on something of its old luster.

Gullans is also the author of *A Diatribe to Dr. Steele*, issued from his own press, Symposium. (The Dr. Steele in question is Timothy Steele, author of *The Prudent Heart*, also issued by Symposium this year.) *Diatribe* is a work in heroic couplets, an anachronism brought forward from the eighteenth century and fallen among us to discuss eloquently the state of the art in these times:

>   An editor wrote me the other day,
>   Who said he gives his magazine away
>   To the—now count them with me—
>   six hundred best
>   Poets in this America. The test?
>   What is a man to say. There aren't that many
>   In the *Oxford Book of English Verse*.
>   Did any,
>   Did all the greatest ages sport that number?

The answer is rhetorical. How many of our American "poets" believe, as Gullans does, that

>   Craft is the reproducible; but art
>   Measures the depth of all that you can bring
>   To the most difficult, discovering
>   The resonance of knowledge in your speech,

>   Or the failed heart and the failed mind
>   in each
>   And every line you write.

Not many. But Timothy Steele himself is one. He is that oddity in these antiformal times, a lyric poet. Coming across his chapbook, *The Prudent Heart*, is like stumbling through a desert and falling into a pool of cool, refreshing water. Jerome and Anson should read Steele's sonnet "Summer" to learn what the form is still capable of being. Steele's work gives hope that there *are* still poems to be written in the great tradition of formalism and people who can compose in it. This publisher produces beautiful volumes printed at the distinguished Stinehour Press, where format and typography present excellent work to its best advantage.

Richmond Lattimore's book *Continuing Conclusions* is subtitled *New Poems and Translations* (Louisiana State University Press). He is as well known for his classical scholarship as for his other writing, his translations of the Greek masterpieces being famous and widely read. He is capable of lyricism in his poems, and some of it appears, in these pages, well done; but there are other poems in various moods and prose mode as well, even translations of Wallace Stevens poems into Italian. Here is a book of wide range, but a vista, also, of peaks and valleys.

All That Autumn (Ithaca House) is by Eileen Silver-Lillywhite. Here again are the standard phrased prose lines of "free verse" written largely on the sensory level. The writer has a good sense of narrative, however, and the stories are leavened with a bit of surrealism, especially in the endings of the poems. The point of view is egopoetic. It is a first book, so there is room to grow.

Fields of Vision by Mariève Rugo (University of Alabama Press) is also a first book. The world has invaded this poet's sensibility, and she has surrounded it with textured tapestries of language. Everything is here, concretely, yet beneath the varied prose approaches there lies the ambiguity of existence, the darkness at the center. Rugo writes as though she had been born to words.

Barbara Howes is one of those 1950s formalists who abandoned formalism in the 1960s, but her essential training underlies all the poems of her volume *Moving* (Elysian Press). Most of the poems even appear to be formal, for Howes uses stanzas and indentations in the traditional way, and the effect of the major portion of these works is lyrical. Typography, sound, sensation, and sense—Howes knows how to use them all to sing her songs of affection and loss.

"*Le Fou*, [Robert] Creeley's first book, was published in 1952, and since then barely a year has passed without a new collection of poems," according to the release from New Directions accompanying this year's entry, which is titled *Mirrors*. The new collection has some tendencies toward concrete imagery, but Creeley's greatest fault has always been vagueness and abstraction. It is hard to understand Creeley's reputation as an innovative poet; even harder to imagine that his work lives up to the Black Mountain tenet—which he is supposed to have articulated—that "form is never more than an extension of content," for his poems are often written in couplet, triplet, and quatrain stanzas that break into and out of rhyme as whim or happenstance appear to dictate. The result is formally disconcerting, and the content of the poems often descends as low as the mundane or rises only as high

Front cover for Mariève Rugo's first collection of poetry, which surrounds the world "with textured tapestries of language"

as the obscure. When he uses imagery, Creeley can be interesting and effective. His *Collected Poems* (University of California Press), also published this year, covers the span from 1945 to 1975.

Josephine Miles this year has published her *Collected Poems, 1930-1983* (University of Illinois Press). In her earliest book, *Trial Balances* (1935), Miles established several things: first, a rather wide range of technical effects which she displayed in short poems, some of them traditional lyrics and others short-lined prose poems. Next, she found a voice—quiet, conversational—which she has never abandoned. Third, she wrote on a very wide range of topics. In all these things over the years Miles has been very consistent. It was not until 1955 that she began to write longer poems on occasion, and not until 1967 when she wrote poems in book-length series. Throughout, this poet has written quietly and well, composing many a poem as readable as anything in print, as intelligent and insightful as the most demanding reading could ask. This book is truly a pleasure to read, some pages over and over.

Wood–Birds–Water–Stones by Nick Bozanic (Barnwood Press Cooperative) is a chapbook, very nicely produced, containing four pieces titled "The Virtues of . . ." the things named in the title. They are little sermons or homilies, well written in prose poems.

From the same press comes a similar chapbook, *Four Ramages of Robert Bly*. Here again is the sentimental "deep image" in four pages of prose: "There is a gladness in the not-caring / of the bear's cabin; and in the gravity / that makes the stone laugh down the mountain." "Grackles stroll about on the black floor of sorrow." Bears do not have cabins, nor do cabins either care or not-care; stones do not laugh down mountains; grackles do not stroll on the black floor of sorrow—at least they don't without some context beyond non sequitur.

In *Constant Defender* (Ecco Press) James Tate does what Bly was attempting to do: write surrealism effectively. The important difference between the two collections is that Tate remembers to keep his eye on the concrete object, not on the abstraction, in order to conjure up the eerie emotion, the latent and largely inexpressible unease of the animal sunken in our minds. It is not unusual for the disciple to surpass the master.

A Book of Charms (Barnwood) is a double-author collection of poems on a single theme—charms. The authors have set out to write their own charms in the tradition of the genre. If those written by Angela Peckenpaugh seem closer in form to the chants of the old charms, the poems of Lois Beebe Hayna are equally well written. The book itself is well printed and produced.

Miller Williams in *The Boys on Their Bony Mules* (Louisiana State University Press) writes with a sense of story. His rhythms and tropes are so well grounded in meter and in the particular that we hardly notice the large issue, the thought, rising from its base. Williams is one of those who were trained in the basics of verse writing and who built from that solid foundation a style of writing and an angle of vision that enable the writer to range widely and plunge deeply into the world and the self. This is an excellent book.

W. S. Merwin is of similar background. His new book, *Opening the Hand* (Atheneum), is as good as anything he has written, and he has written extremely well. This present collection is remarkable as to technique: In many of the poems here Merwin has returned to Anglo-Saxon prosody and refined it so that it is a viable modern vehicle for poetry. Many poems are in series, each entry telling its own story, but the set tells a larger one that takes an overtone from its parts. This is a virtuoso performance by a first-rate poet.

Night Hurdling by James Dickey (Bruccoli Clark) is subtitled *Poems, Essays, Conversations, Commencements, and Afterwords.* There are only four poems here, written in the prosody that Dickey has called "split-line," which resembles in a way the Anglo-Saxon prosody discussed above. A much fuller survey of his poetry is to be found in *The Central Motion: Poems, 1968-1979* (Wesleyan University Press). This is a gathering together and reprinting of three previous collections, *The Eye-Beaters, Blood, Victory, Madness, Buckhead and Mercy* (1968), *The Zodiac* (1976), and *The Strength of Fields* (1979), to which is added a selection of more recent work.

Another reprint is the *Collected Poems* of John Wheelwright, one of America's strangest figures and a cult poet. New Directions, which published the hardcover edition in 1972, now reissues the book in paperback format. Wheelwright died in 1940, but his reputation is almost entirely contemporary.

The Author by Robert Wallace (Bits Press of Case Western Reserve University) is a chapbook produced in the format and the quality for which that press is well known. The booklet is a series of four parts. Each part examines a photograph of the author, each taken at a different stage of his adult life. The stanza form of each section is the rhyming iambic trimeter quatrain. Here, then, is part of an autobiography in verse. Written colloquially, the poignance of the set is leavened with self-mockery and wry humor. Very appealing, very well done.

Wallace is editor of Bits Press, which is the publisher of the anthology *Light Year '84.* It is a new annual edited by Wallace, who has done a wonderful job of bringing together recent humorous poems and light verse by many contemporary poets, including John Ciardi, Wesli Court, J. V. Cunningham, William Stafford, and Miller Williams. This volume is something desperately needed in a period when literature takes itself over seriously, even pompously.

Kenneth O. Hanson turns for the second time, in *Lighting the Night Sky* (Breitenbush Books), from his native American Northwest to write about Greece. The poems on their surface are utterly simple, but, like haikus, the individual pieces allow for considerable overtone, and the whole book "gathers," as William Matthews says, "the way good music gathers, like a fabric. . . ." These are not pseudo-Greek poems, but pieces that show Greece and her contemporary denizens through empathetic American eyes, and the narrator is no small character in the drama.

The initial effect of Roland Flint's *Resuming Green: Selected Poems 1965-1982* (Dial Press), at first also seems simple, though the style is considerably different from Hanson's. The poems move colloquially in a very wide range of approaches, from one formal lyric to straight prose "poems," though these latter seem more like lyric narrative episodes than poetry. No matter, for whatever one calls them they are very well done; they are intelligent, emotional, interesting, and capable of depth. Flint is a sophisticated writer. This is his first hardcover book, two paperback collections having preceded it.

David Ferry's statement on his own book, *Strangers* (University of Chicago), cannot be improved on: "My ambition has been to complete a book that is really a book, not just a collection of miscellaneous pieces. That is to say, the poems are intended to be highly resonant of one another, more and more so as you read consecutively, and all of them are intended to be responsive to the title and epigraph of the volume. At the same time I have tried for a persisting variety, so that I wouldn't ever seem to have written the same poem twice and so that there would be the least possible wasted motion." He has succeeded admirably in his intentions. The poems are cast in a wide variety of formal and informal patterns.

According to its "Introduction," David Kherdian's *Place of Birth* (Breitenbush) "is the third and last" of this poet's "volumes of autobiographical poems." It runs the risk of such poetry, always trembling on the brink of the chasm of sentimentality. Unfortunately, it often falls in. There is nothing so bathetic as feeling nostalgia about oneself.

In *Beside Herself: Pocahontas to Patty Hearst* (Knopf), Pamela White Hadas has written a large book, a sort of contemporary *Spoon River Anthology* of American women through history. The book is comprised of sets of monologues, soliloquies, epistles, and dialogues. Although not all the voices used by the personae are convincing—it is difficult to imagine Pocahontas speaking as she does here— these phrased prose poems are insightful and clever, usually interesting as to the narratives and the histories implicit in them. For authenticity of voice, one ought to compare these pieces with those by Judith Phillips in "The Taproot Diary," featured in the 1983 issue of the annual periodical *Escarpments*, published at S.U.N.Y. Buffalo. Phillips had her great-grandmother's diary from which to work, and the story she tells, of going west in a covered wagon, is eyewitness history.

The University of California Press has published a massive work, *The Maximus Poems of Charles Olson*, scrupulously edited by George F. Butterick. The three books here brought together are *The Maximus Poems*; *Maximus Poems IV, V, VI*; and *Maximus Poems: Volume Three*—all now out of print and collectors' items. Twenty-nine new poems, previously uncollected, are added and, according to the jacket copy, "Errors in the previous editions have been corrected . . . and the sequence of the final poems modified in light of the editor's research among the poet's papers." Butterick was a student of Olson; he is the author of the definitive *Guide to "The Maximus Poems" of Charles Olson* (University of California Press, 1978) and curator of Olson's papers at the University of Connecticut Library.

A Dandy Handy Pocket Anthology of Martian Literature (Pangborn Books) is farce masquerading as satire masquerading as science-fiction poetry. (There must be a better term for it than that—why not just "science-poetry"?) It isn't poetry, but it *is* funny. The name of its author, "Billy Knitehawke," is no doubt a pseudonym. Like this chapbook, *Noon Hour on Federal Plaza*, from the same publisher, is issued in The Youngstown Area Writers Collector Series. Its author is E. G. Hallaman, and his prose poems are embedded in the concrete particular. They have a wry and rueful humor. There must be an interesting poetry scene in Youngstown, Ohio.

Another chapbook is Julie Becker's *Sex Education* (Bieler Press). It is a single poem printed on six fold-out pages in a limited, signed edition, and it is a monologue spoken by a child who has been subjected to a sex-education course. Here is the first page:

> The man has teskles.
> The teskles have polliwogs
> in them.
> They have sperms too.
> The sperms and the polliwogs
> go swimming
> but I don't know where.
>
> The lady has floppian tubes.
> She has obums too.

The rest of this production is equally funny, but it has a serious point to make about sex education.

Patricia Hampl, in *Resort and Other Poems* (Houghton Mifflin), writes with the surest hand, and the most delicate sense of color, image, and nuance, a number of relatively short poems that lead up to the title poem, "Resort," a long poem or series of short poems—depending on how one looks at it—that shows she has not only a sense of the minute, but a sense also of the architecture of the whole. Though the poems are not "verse," they give a sense of verse, and the imagery reminds one quite often of Emily Dickinson's astonishing throwaway pictures in her letters: "July and the wild rose is the pink fact, repeated / like a rumor in every corner of the fresh season." This is very good work.

Equally well written, if more assertive and less lambent, is Amy Clampitt's *The Kingfisher* (Knopf). Some of the poems are laid out in stanzas rather than strophes, so that they appear to be verse, but they are not, unless they may be called variable accentuals, like some of W. C. Williams's work. These poems approach verse, however, inasmuch as there is a strong tendency toward iambics lying under the lines. Reading much of the work by contemporary poets, one wonders what would be produced if our bards spent as much time and effort cultivating the sonic level—rhythms, meters—as they do working the sensory. There is a sameness to much of the new work, even though it is often of a high caliber of competence. Clampitt gets so close sometimes—as in "The Local Genius," which flirts with becoming a sonnet—that one grits one's teeth in frustration.

Carol Jane Bangs's *The Bones of the Earth* (New Directions) is another entry in the field of well-written phrased-prose poetry with anchors in the descriptive. She has an unfailing sense of story line, and she evokes the Northwest very well. Her voice is strong, and she knows how to suggest as well as describe.

Ralph Burns's *Us* is from the Cleveland State University Poetry Center, which has published some outstanding work this year, including this book. Burns's poems bring the American Midwest—from Oklahoma to Indiana—so close one can smell it. This is, indeed, plainstyle with style. The poems about the narrator's father can make one shiver with their poignance, their *rightness*.

Like the authors of the three previous collections, Harry Humes in *Winter Weeds* (University of Missouri Press) is a concrete poet. Like them, he evokes a particular landscape, both of geography and of feeling. Like Burns's, his is a plainstyle; and like Clampitt, he flirts with traditional forms and meters. He too is an excellent writer. This is a first book, winner of the 1983 Devins Award.

Although Jenné Andrews's *Reunion* might also be called "plainstyle" poetry, most of the poems at first appear to be even more austere than that. On closer inspection, this austerity turns out to be merely a rather clipped, self-conscious syntax and diction wedded often enough to a brevity of line. The egopoetic narrator of the major portion of these pieces becomes annoying after a while, she is so deliberately "poetic" and soulful. Oddly enough, given the terseness of this work, what strikes the reader most irritatingly is the number and kind of adjectives the writer uses.

Though there is some very good work among these year's-end collections, there is still a disturbing tendency among them to sound more or less alike. It may be that the writing arts workshops have done their job too well and have produced poets whose competence is of so high a level that it is going to take a genius of the magnitude of Shakespeare to stand out from the musing horde.

Debra Bruce in *Pure Daughter* (University of Arkansas Press) does what others have done: good story line, phrased-prose mode, plainstyle, a bit more colloquial than some of the others, quite readable. Betty Adcock in *Nettles* (Louisiana State University Press) writes more of the same, if she is a bit more soulful than Bruce and less so than Andrews.

The blurb for *Living in Code* (University of Pittsburgh Press) reads, "John Ashbery, writing about Robert Louthan's first book, said '[his] poems are simple and strange. They speak the plain speech of dreams, and are quietly committed to that kind of order.'" Do dreams use plain speech? Is the unconscious orderly? This book is of an order with the other Pitt books, if it is a bit more surrealistic and

uses stronger language at times. The "father" poems here come off poorly when compared with those of Ralph Burns.

At last something different in Robert Kelly's *Under Words* (Black Sparrow Press). This is from the first poem, "Auguries":

Pleiades overhead   sisters

    I want
    more than

I want my hair ruffled by your hand
your fingertips pressing my eyebrows
            and cheekbones

we are braille to each other also

boy who collected maps the names
reaching for what he could of a real person

names are the tits of things
punk dictionaries
always selling out the language we invent

Not all of this book is "dot-and-dash splinter poetry," however. Some of it makes syntactic sense, as in "Five Precious Stones." The writing can be lively and interesting, the approaches are varied. Though he is an East Coast professor, one doubts that Kelly learned to write in a workshop, and it is clear his affinities are with the West Coast "experimental" schools.

It is a mystery why the Pacific Northwest seems to produce such a high percentage of excellent poets who, though nearly universally "plainstylists," nevertheless evoke nature and mood so well that one must stand back, applaud, and perhaps wish one inhabited such a region of heart and weather oneself. Here is another: Sam Hamill. His *Fatal Pleasure* (Breitenbush) is a vital pleasure to read.

Reading *The Courtesy* by Alan Shapiro (University of Chicago Press) is more like reading a book of stories than of poems. Even though many of these pieces are more formal than prose, their effect is prosaic, as Frost's poems were; and some approach Frost's power of narrative, though the subjects are worlds apart. These are straightforward tales of people and the human condition, very refreshing in their observations and points, sometimes ironically humorous, often touching.

Even more like stories are the pieces in Leonard Wallace Robinson's *In the Whale* (Barnwood), even to straight prose pieces that one can't tell from short-shorts. There are others, how-

*Dust jacket for the latest collection of poems by Sam Hamill, a
Pacific Northwest poet whom Thomas McGrath compares to
"Kenneth Rexroth at his peak"*

ever, that are quite jazzy—as, for instance, "Wonder," which is a poem: indeed, more of a poem than
many another in this landslide of volumes. Robinson is a fictioneer trying on a different pair of shoes.
Perhaps soon he will lace them up, get up, and run.
For now, he tells a good story.

If reading the Shapiro and Robinson books is
like reading stories, reading Albert Goldbarth's
Original Light: New & Selected Poems 1973-1983
(Ontario Review Press) is like sitting around listening to a garrulous and humorous uncle rattling
cleverly away about everything in the world. Maxine
Kumin says in her blurb, "Goldbarth's prodigious
output is matched only by his erudition. He seems to
have read everything and ingested centuries of
history, biology, religion." True, very true. Although we would be delighted to sit and listen to

such an uncle while he visits, we wouldn't want to
live with him. This book was edited by Raymond
Smith, who made all the selections—what a task!
Perhaps editing his own work is a foreign idea to
Goldbarth, who "writes like a one-man gang," ac-
cording to David Wagoner.

Alan Williamson's *Presence* (Knopf) is a
sophisticated, intellectual book. Its lines make one
think of polished garnets, but the poems to which
the lines build leave this reader with the feeling that
he is in the presence of a philosopher rather than a
poet. The concern with language is that of the poet,
but the concentration on exposition is that of the
essayist. These are thoughtful meditations in this
first book.

How to describe Robert Ronnow's *Janie Huzzie
Bows* (Barnwood)? It's impossible, but one must try.
Take a look at that title: How does one read it? What
does it mean? The poems are the same way—they
prance along the edge of making sense. One can
even follow them for a while, and then they drop off
the edge into the swivel-eyed where one stands before a mirror staring cross-eyed at one of two noses.
These are mad, enjoyable poems if one enjoys dis-
orientation, getting dizzy on language. Ronnow
puts some meaning back into the term "experimental," but he knows what he's doing, and he does
it terrifically well. This is certainly "catastrophe
theory" poetry. It is also a fascinating first book.

Tom Sleigh's *After One* (Houghton Mifflin) is a
first book, one that strikes a meticulous balance
between the formal and the open form, between
verse and prose—in the poems of the former there
is the spirit of the latter, and vice versa. Sleigh knows
what he wants to say, and he chooses the best way to
say it, blending craft and sensibility in the formula
proper to his expression.

The mainstream tradition of formal poetry in
English is still viable, as Sleigh proves, and there is
still room for the stylist, the inventor, as Ronnow
shows. Emily Dickinson said once to Thomas
Wentworth Higginson: "If I read a book and it
makes my whole body so cold no fire can ever warm
me, I know *that* is poetry. If I feel physically as if the
top of my head were taken off, I know *that* is poetry.
These are the only ways I know it. Is there any other
way?" Though one can criticize or admire, what one
looks for, really, is that shiver of recognition.
Perhaps one has not felt it often this year, or any
year; but it has happened, and it is a cause for
rejoicing.

The Year in Fiction: A Biased View

George Garrett
University of Michigan

This was a different kind of year, at least in a literary sense, for me. It was a year I would have to look at differently, from another standpoint and angle, than the years of the last decade. For now, finally, after years of working and a long time waiting (I had turned in the manuscript of *The Succession* to Doubleday in May of 1981), I had a book of my own coming out. It had been ten years since I had had a book commercially published. I guessed that I was pretty well out of touch with things, and I would learn soon enough that my guesswork was sound. You don't lose touch completely even in a decade and even though, as one editor has told me, "the American publishing industry, already famous for the brevity of its attention span, has a memory so short that it can't honestly be said to have any memory at all." For good or ill (it seemed to him) they don't remember you at all after a season or two unless you have somehow or other risen to a position of stardom in the fixed Ptolemaic firmament of . . . the Literary Establishment. In that case long silence can be an identifying characteristic, even a positive virtue. But below the salt, down in steerage, the day coaches, the back of the bus, in the trenches of American letters it is somewhat different. And there, in the trenches, far from any command posts, was where I had earned a little space and spent my time and was (and remain) proud of it.

I considered myself set free from the burden of illusions by the stressful experience of long service, an old-timer in the words of the (real) army I had once known well enough. Was not *completely* out of touch mind you. The proles of American letters have to keep working and moving, to keep on trucking or disappear. Fly or die. So, for a decade writing my book I had to earn the money to buy the time to do it. Had to hustle — give nickel-and-dime readings wherever they would have me, write nickel-and-dime pieces about anything for anyone who wanted one, work at conferences and part-time teaching jobs whenever I could with, occasionally, the good fortune of filling in, replacing some more desirable and distinguished writer who became ill or just cracked up or whacked out or bugged out. Coming off the splintery bench like George Blanda in his old Chicago Bears days.

Am I whining and complaining, you ask. You have a right to ask. The answer is . . . not exactly. Truth is, my experience is common, the lot of most American poets and novelists, the overwhelming majority. Basically they have a hard row to hoe. Anybody writing serious poetry or fiction, or, for that matter, serious nonfiction, in America today has to fight continually for survival as an artist, for the time (never mind the *conditions*) to practice the art. Except, of course, for a handful of the very rich. The very rich by birth whom no one can blame in the least or even envy very much. But about whom one must in all honesty point out that it is not necessarily an ideal situation for a democratic country, whose ideal has been for a very long time to have and to honor an aristocracy of achievement, to depend for the future of its arts upon the dedication and skill of the otherwise idle rich.

More enviable, and perhaps more culpable, are the lucky few who have (one way and the other) gained if not earned a measure of recognition, sometimes extraordinary in the lavishness of rewards, sometimes merely enough to move a body out of the hot sun of the cotton fields and into the cooler comfort of the living room and dining room of the big house. Where clothes are cleaner and sweat is a memory.

There is a very serious question as to whether these recognized American writers are, in fact, better than their anonymous brothers and sisters in the fields and trenches. My answer is that they are not; that there is far more talent and diversity and excitement out there than official histories and administrative endowments and councils and academies and institutes are even vaguely aware of; that, in fact, these aforementioned institutions of the arts are primarily engaged in maintaining the status quo, a status quo which they, themselves, have invented and imposed; that the main effort of maintaining any status quo in any society or enterprise is expended and demonstrated by denying not place or membership to the many but that the many exist at all; that is to say, the most exclusive institutions preserve exclusivity not by asserting it but rather by pretending to be at once representative and even inclusive.

The point of all this is simply to introduce the circumstances and prejudices of the witness. Not at all unbiased, I believed (still do) at the outset of 1983 that, having spent the greater part of my professional writing career, roughly thirty years, as a bona fide member of the American literary underworld and underclass, it had become for me both habit and badge of honor. Too late to change that. Certainly such ephemeral conditions as success or failure or any of the shades in between could not be expected to change either habit or pride.

Which is to say the witness, though biased, was curiously disinterested and, therefore, at least as reliable as any other. Maybe more so than many.

And it turned out to be, after all, a fairly lively and interesting year. . . .

Writing in praise of Nora Ephron's best-selling *Heartburn* (Knopf), in the "New Books" section of *Glamour* (May 1983), Nancy Evans inadvertently presented us with an accurate candid snapshot of the state of letters in America today. Recommending Ephron's artistry to her presumably young readers, Evans is at least confident that there is some general consensus as to what the average American reader wants in a book: "The writing is consistently snappy, the jokes nonstop, the book as easy to read as a copy of *People* magazine."

Let that be our epigraph celebrating the official values of the year gone by.

It was not an altogether bad year for the Establishment. Not only *Heartburn*, but also all kinds of books as easy to read (or skim) as the pages of *People*, many of these by reliable commercial old-timers, found their happy ways to self-sustaining niches on best-seller lists. James Michener was there twice, first with *Space* (Random House, 1982), then with *Poland* (Random House). So was the amazing and indomitable Stephen King with *Christine* (Viking)—"A car that kills is at large among a Pennsylvania town's high school set"—and his first book with a new publisher, Doubleday, which was in fourth place on the *New York Times Book Review* best-sellers list a month *before* publication date and number one as soon as officially published—*Pet Sematary* (Doubleday)—"The new family in town discovers the horrors that lie in a neighboring cemetery." Other solid sellers like John le Carré (*The Little Drummer Girl*, Knopf), Trevanian (*The Summer of Katya*, Crown), Andrew Greeley (*Ascent Into Hell*, Warner Books), Isaac Asimov (*The Robots of Dawn*, Doubleday), and Judith Rossner (*August*, Houghton Mifflin) proved that in fiction at least it helps most to have been there before, that the postman always rings twice and more for those known writers who can create a predictable product.

Interestingly enough all these people, and others with places on the lists, had glittery mass-market paperbacks available in airports and drugstores at the same time that their new hardcover books were thriving. There was, throughout the year, enough uniformity of this pattern so as to suggest that it was now systematic to support the one enterprise with the other, that hardcovers and mass paperbacks are at least believed to be as important to each other as ever before. To the skeptic witness it seemed possible that there was something defensive about this, that the careful coordination (whenever possible) of mass-market paperback activities with popular hardcover publication was indicative of an attempt by publishers to control and to regulate, if not manipulate, the market itself. As if, left to their own devices and choices, the reading public might go its merry way without regard to the plans of others.

I took this as a good sign. The Establishment was openly putting all its wagons in a circle.

It doesn't hurt, these days, to be a celebrity, either. Showbiz celebrity Bette Midler hit the fiction list with *The Saga of Baby Divine* (Crown). Literary celebrity Norman Mailer, of whom it can be safely said that nothing he makes is a predictable product, joined these others, and others, with his "historical" novel *Ancient Evenings* (Little, Brown)—"Ten centuries of rites and orgies in long-ago Egypt." Amid all these familiar things there were the (at an increasing rate) curiosities, books that seemed entirely unsuited for any best-seller list, books which were, in a relative sense at least, sleepers and surprises: Umberto Eco's *The Name of the Rose* (Harcourt Brace Jovanovich), a first novel and a translation from the Italian, a novel by a professor of semiotics ("Unraveling the mystery of a murder in a 14th-century Italian monastery") and the futurist fable *Winter's Tale* (Harcourt Brace Jovanovich), by Mark Helprin ("Heroic lives in Manhattan between the late 19th century and the year 2000"). The latter is somewhat less of a surprise than *The Name of the Rose*; for the Helprin book was supported by a huge advance and by a massive advertising campaign. Although the reviews nationally were, at best, mixed, Helprin profited from a very long and laudatory appreciation of the work in the *New York Times* by critic Benjamin DeMott; proof once again, if that is needed, that a national response in aggregate still cannot outweigh the commercial impact of the regional responses of New York City. It remains an undeniable fact that people in Georgia or Ohio or elsewhere are allowed to pick and choose the books they wish to read from among those preselected for them by folks in New York City. The significant

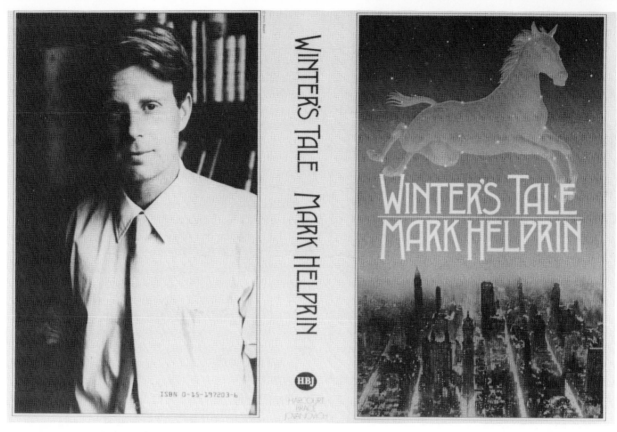

Dust jacket for Mark Helprin's second novel, which Publishers Weekly *called "a totally captivating reading experience"*

point here, however, is not that the commercial and critical Establishment does its work by strictly limiting the prospects and possibilities of . . . everybody else, but instead that it is deemed necessary for survival. Which means that the literary Establishment acutely fears that anything resembling a free market of books—or, thus, a free market of *ideas*—is dangerous and would inevitably tend toward the displacement of the Establishment. In other words, 1983, closely observed, gave every indication that the current American literary Establishment is fully aware that it is *not* representative of the energy, plurality, richness, and achievement of contemporary American literature. Like the courts of Louis XV and Louis XVI, the Establishment feels justly threatened. As long as the things published by small presses and little magazines were demonstrably minor league efforts, there could be no threat to the Establishment. But by 1983 the *Pushcart Prize* volume (Pushcart Press) had become commercially respected and, to an extent, commercially co-opted, but nevertheless a fact and a celebration of the quality of literature to be found in small, often unlikely places. Moveover the *Pushcart Prize* volumes,

together with other prize volumes, unintentionally testify to the extreme difficulty of keeping up with what is happening. For example, *The Best American Short Stories of 1983* (Houghton Mifflin), edited by Anne Tyler and Shannon Ravenel, has its full fair share of stories from the *New Yorker*, but also offers stories from little magazines such as *Ploughshares, Epoch,* the *Ohio Review,* and *Shenandoah*.

What we are talking about, of course, is not best sellers but "serious" literature. Which may or may not be to any degree commercial. And which may or may not be published by commercial publishers. The "official" history of the year, as evidenced by the not-so-surprising uniformity of all sorts of mid-year and year's end lists, most authoritatively the *New York Times Book Review* issues for 12 June 1983 ("Summer Reading") and 4 December 1983 ("Christmas Books"), included a goodly number of worthwhile books by recognized authors in good standing. Raymond Carver's latest collection of pared-down, minimal tales, *Cathedral* (Knopf), found its way onto everybody's best-books list (at least every one that I have found), widely and fully praised; though, as in the case of Mark Helprin, the critical response was not unmixed. A number of critics and reviewers had found fault with the book for its monotony of style and subject matter and for its routine condescension toward the very lower-class characters it professes concern for. *Ironweed* (Viking), third in a series of Albany novels by William Kennedy, was the "discovery" of the year. Joan Chase's *During the Reign of the Queen of Persia* (Harper & Row) was a much-celebrated first novel. Other well-noted first novels included Jim Shepard's *Flights* (Knopf), Gordon Lish's *Dear Mr. Capote* (Holt, Rinehart & Winston), and Jay Cantor's *The Death of Che Guevara* (Knopf). Both Cantor and Shepard were published by Knopf, where Lish, published by Holt, is an editor. Knopf was so active in 1983 with the publication of short stories and of serious fiction that one publisher (who prefers the safety of anonymity) called it "the year of creeping Knopfism."

Among the other widely praised books of the year, each of these with a solid pedestal on the *New York Times*'s strict and influential list, "Best Books of 1983," were Gabriel Marquez's *Chronicle of a Death Foretold* (Knopf); *The Moons of Jupiter* (Knopf), short stories by Alice Munro; and *The Anatomy Lesson* (Farrar, Straus & Giroux), Philip Roth's third and apparently final volume in the series of novels concerning the Roth-like Jewish-American novelist Nathan Zuckerman. Renata Adler's skinny and sophisticated autobiographical fiction, *Pitch Dark* (Random House), arrived on the scene too late to make the lists, but was nonetheless given the full set of flourishes and ruffles, all the serious critical attention accorded a major work of literary art. And in the waning days of the year the first full-fledged literary award for 1983 (*Los Angeles Times* Book Prizes) presented the prize for fiction to Australian writer Thomas Keneally for *Schindler's List* (Simon & Schuster). The National Book Critics Circle, on 15 December, announced its prize nominations, which included for fiction Roth, Carver, Joan Chase, and William Kennedy, together with Ron Loewinshon for *Magnetic Field(s)* (Knopf). There are 300 members of the National Book Critics Circle. That four out of five on the fiction list also appeared on the earlier Sunday *New York Times* list is . . . interesting.

Nineteen eighty-three witnessed the publication of works by many prominent fiction writers,

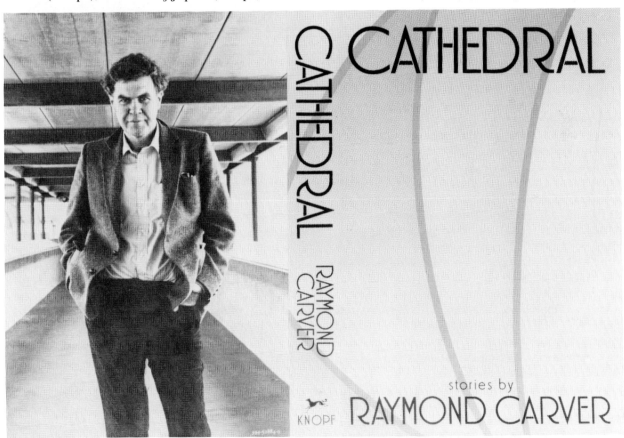

Dust jacket for Raymond Carver's second collection of short stories, in which, says Newsweek, *"he succeeds, seemingly without effort, in weaving the illusion that his characters are not only real but representative. . . ."*

"From the first page, the ride of Francis Phelan through the Albany cemetery where his immortal dead observe his passing with amusement and affection, through the whole rollicking, black wit of the rest of his progress, I relished Kennedy's awesome skill with his place and his people. His compassion for their automaton religion, their pragmatic politics, their warm and violent Irish lives...reaches a new height in *Ironweed*. His madcap, perfect-pitch prose has never been better."
—Doris Grumbach

"*Ironweed*, like Beckett's *Waiting for Godot*, gives an almost mythic dimension to the final wanderings of two completely down-and-out characters—in this case, a man and a woman. It is a remarkable and most original novel, which combines low comedy with high pathos; in my view, probably a modern classic."
—Alison Lurie

ISBN 0-670-40176-5

"These Albany novels will be memorable, a distinguished group of books"—Saul Bellow

Dust jacket for the third novel in William Kennedy's Albany cycle, which won the National Book Critics Circle award

works which, if not (yet) nominated for any prizes, still were widely reviewed and enjoyed varying degrees of success. Among these writers were (in chronological order of publication dates): Thomas Berger, Paul Theroux, Anthony Burgess, Cynthia Ozick, Julio Cortazar, Rita Mae Brown, Doris Lessing, Louis Auchincloss, Alberto Moravia, Barry Hannah, D. M. Thomas, Russell Hoban, John Knowles, James T. Farrell, Morris West, John Rechy, Jerome Charyn, Iris Murdoch, Barbara Pym, Larry McMurtry, Nelson Algren, Brian Moore, Ernest J. Gaines, Gail Godwin, Frederic Barthelme, Harry Mark Petrakis, Lynne Sharon Schwartz, Philip Caputo, William Trevor, Isaac Singer, Malcolm Bradbury, J. P. Donleavy, Hortense Calisher, V. S. Naipaul, Donald Barthelme, Richard Price, and Walter Tevis.

Not an inconsiderable list. By any means. And all that is fiction alone. Yet even that kind of listing, a few authors from among hundreds published in that single category, is unjustly brief and incomplete, patently unrepresentative. Which situation may be the best explanation for the way the official

record is invariably boiled down to a precious few examples. The explanation being that there is just too much; that the scene is too rich and diverse and energetic to be contained and managed by any single intelligence and imagination, no matter how well-informed; that thus critics and reviewers are forced to settle for the consensual crudities and oversimplifications of a collective point of view; that, thus, the existence and, indeed, the preservation of some sort of literary Establishment have a distinctly practical value. Without some sort of critical consensus, imposed or otherwise, there would be chaos and confusion.

Perhaps. . . .

From the realm of chaos and confusion I should like, here, to report very briefly on at least some of the new books of 1983 which especially pleased me. Some are by friends in the trade—one is obliged to read the books written by one's friends, though one is not obliged to admire them all without reservation. Some are by perfect strangers. Some were well and widely reviewed. Others were, in the words of a young writer whose work I admire, "published secretly." I will not make any distinction between the known and the unknown, because I can think of none. The better known are not, by any means, the better books.

If a part of bearing honest witness is open confession, then take this in that spirit—an appreciation; one man's favored reading from a year of watching and waiting to see what fate and what future, if any, waited for his own work.

Two books which, from my point of view and that of many others, I do believe, would be important in any given year and add considerable distinction to the year they happened to come along. The late William Goyen's lovely and original vision, at once as airy as a fable and as solidly earthy as a folksong for steel string guitar, is superbly realized in his tenth book—*Arcadio* (Clarkson Potter). Through the wonderfully realized voice of Arcadio, "half man, half woman, half Mexican, half Texan," Goyen created in the (for once accurate) words of the book jacket "a provocative, unforgettable parable about the loss of innocence and the gaining of wisdom and understanding." Who knows, really, what things, among all things, that 1983 will be remembered for? Surely, though, one of them, something truly memorable, will be Goyen's *Arcadio* and the imperishable genius of Goyen himself, whose death is a wound to so many of us.

It was a fine year (perhaps as much because of "creeping Knopfism" as in spite of it) for the American short story. Some collections that I found especially worthy were Bette Howland's *Things To Come and Go: Three Stories* (Knopf); Leon V. Driskell's *Passing Through: A Fiction*, nine related stories about Pearl Thirwell White of Owen County, Kentucky, and the first book published by Algonquin Books, a new and promising publisher located in Chapel Hill, North Carolina; *Wilderness Plots: Tales About the Settlement of the American Land*, by Scott R. Sanders, a small, elegant and elegantly illustrated book of some fifty brief tales of the Ohio Valley area in the years 1780-1850, a highly original concept resulting in (in the words of *Publishers Weekly*) "a strange and splendid little book," surprisingly published by a major commercial house—William Morrow; *An Amateur's Guide to the Night* (Knopf), which is Mary Robison's second collection of stories, half of them out of the *New Yorker* and which, despite the fact that neither the publisher nor many reviewers seem to have noticed it, is a very *funny* book, quite cheerfully far from the studied nihilism of Raymond Carver and of Ann Beattie; Nicholas Delbanco's *About My Table: And Other Stories* (Morrow), nine related stories, highly civilized and impeccably told by the

young author of ten novels and a recent work of nonfiction—*Group Portrait: Conrad, Crane, Ford, Wells, and James* (Morrow, 1982). Probably the most important gathering of short stories for 1983 and many a year on either side is *The Stories of Bernard Malamud* (Farrar, Straus & Giroux). Of which only this need be said—that he has strictly limited his choices, out of old work and new, to twenty-five stories, each of which is a gem. Already cited, *The Best American Short Stories 1983* deserves another mention, if only because in addition to work by veterans—Ursula K. Le Guin, Wright Morris, and John Updike—and by such soldiers of New Chic as Bobbie Ann Mason, Larry Woiwode, and Laurie Colwin, has plenty of new voices, at least two of whom, Carolyn Chute and James Bond, seem certain to be heard from again.

Novels are something else, another matter. In 1983, sweating out my own, I read fewer novels than usual, but enough (aside from a weight of the earlier mentioned works, many of which came with the full authority of an *assignment*) to find some favorites which I would recommend to anyone in any given year. Lee Smith's *Oral History* (Putnam Publishing Group) was a fine addition to her canon of first-rate fiction about new and old South. Kelly Cherry's *In the Wink of an Eye* (Harcourt Brace Jovanovich) is described on the jacket as "a modern fable in the form of a novel," also "a romantic satire," "a social burlesque," "an ironic fantasy," and "*all* of the above." Which means: (a) the publisher couldn't decide or define it on conventional terms, and (b) it is a most original piece of work. It *is* hard to describe, but it is a very funny book by a gifted and unconventional poet and novelist. Kelly Cherry is productive, too, despite an inexplicable hostility her work has sometimes aroused among reviewers; her new novel, *The Lost Traveller's Dream* (Harcourt Brace Jovanovich), which promises to be different from everything else she has created so far, is scheduled for spring 1984 publication. Leon Rooke's *Shakespeare's Dog* (Knopf) was highly original and very funny. Told by Shakespeare's dog, who convincingly imagines himself to be the brains and talent of the two, it is a tour de force engineered by a very skilled young writer best known for his short stories. The most outrageously original book among my list has to be Barry Hannah's latest. Which more or less describes itself—*Power and Light: A Nouvella for the Screen From an Idea By Robert Altman* (Stuart Wright). As long as "original and funny" are the chief criteria here, I cannot fail to mention R. H. W. Dillard's *The First Man on the Sun* (Louisiana State University Press), quite exactly de-

Dust jacket for Bernard Malamud's selection of short fiction. In his preface Malamud comments, "Working alone to create stories, despite serious inconveniences, is not a bad way to live our human loneliness."

scribed by its publisher as "an autobiographical novel in which a memoir of a year in the author's life is interwoven with the work of fiction that grows out of that period—a comic dream describing the Irish expedition to land a manned spaceship on the sun." Set precisely in 1977, "the time between Galileo Galilei's 413th and 414th birthdays," this is the most adventurously experimental novel I have read in many years, beginning, as it does, with seven full pages of pertinent epigraphs (remember *Moby-Dick?*) and midway offering a full-scale volume of poems, *Confessions of An Irish Solarnaut,* which even includes a sequence in semaphore.

Among the more serious novels (in tone, not necessarily in content), two have an historical framework. Leonard Tourney's *Low Treason* (Dutton) is an Elizabethan detective story, the second adventure of Matthew Stock, Village Constable, who was earlier introduced to us in *The Player's Boy Is Dead* (Harper & Row, 1980)—lively, authentic, and altogether unpretentious. *Kepler: A Novel* (Godine), itself a winner of the *Guardian* Prize in Great Britain, where it was published by Secker and Warburg

in 1981, and by a prizewinning Irish author, John Banville, is not always without affectation and pretentions; yet it is a wonderfully made work with more than a few breathtaking moments of simply superb writing.

Asked to name the best lyrical novel of 1983, I would without hesitation summon up Allen Wier's second novel, *Departing As Air* (Simon & Schuster). Wier has learned more than a little from both William Goyen and Wright Morris, has thoroughly assimilated these excellent influences and come to a lyrical voice entirely his own. There cannot have been many, if any, other works of fiction as *beautiful* as this one in 1983.

Another novel I pause to praise and to recommend is a first novel, *The Washington Square Ensemble* (Viking), by Madison Smartt Bell. A virtuoso technical performance, it is a solid and roundly dimensional realization of a group of major characters, all involved with dope dealing in a contemporary New York setting. Bell is a southern writer by birth, but he has done New York City more justice than many urban natives. The place is as real and as full as any place in Yoknapatawpha County.

What we have, then, is a list, a few books, among a great many sampled and sometimes slogged through, that I was pleased to read in 1983. That my list would not, probably, contain more than one or two of the same titles on the lists of others tells nothing except my point that, yawns and shrugs of critics aside, the world, even the literary world, is full of more than a number of wonderful things. For better or worse, next year will likely be much the same, come what may.

As for the books of 1984, well, the reviewers are already listing and naming the ones we should be waiting for. One of the books of 1984, J. M. Coetzee's *Life & Times of Michael K.* (Viking), has already been widely and prominently reviewed. Other things we are told to expect (with respect) are Gore Vidal's *Lincoln: A Novel* (Random House); Joan Didion's *Democracy: A Novel*; a collection of stories by Saul Bellow; and a new novel by Milan Kundera. Robert Ludlum's *The Aquitaine Progression* (Random House), with an announced first printing of 350,000 copies, is likely to find room on the best-seller list.

The Charles Wood Affair:
A Playwright Revived

Kimball King
University of North Carolina at Chapel Hill

Although in my recent biographical analysis of the English playwright Charles Wood I referred to him as a remarkably promising playwright who died in his prime, I must amend my premature evaluation and describe him more accurately as a remarkably promising playwright who may well have another half-century of distinguished participation in the world of theater, television, and films. It seems I was an unwitting participant in a hoax which attempted to promulgate exaggerated rumors, as Mark Twain would have said, of Wood's demise. As is my usual practice I sent my biographical entry for the *Dictionary of Literary Biography* to the playwright's agent in order to correct any errors that might have crept into the standard bibliographies or media releases. A wag returned my essay with an urgent plea to announce Wood's recent untimely death. In retrospect two elements should have alerted me to a practical joke in the making. First, the letter contained personal information that would only have been known by the author himself and, second, the letter was signed by a Geoffrey Endle, whose name should certainly have reminded me of a character in Wood's play *Veteran*, named Kendle. Believing that the letter had the authority of Wood's agent and faced with the prospect of a press deadline, I laboriously changed tenses throughout the original entry and added a poignant paragraph or two about the recent "tragedy."

The hullabaloo that erupted on both sides of the Atlantic when the dictionary entry was published was only slightly less vociferous than the reaction in 1983 to the alleged Hitler diaries. A smiling Charles Wood may have fantasized that the years from 1982 onward would be considered his "posthumous phase" by biographers of the twenty-first century. Despite the predictable emphasis which future scholars may place on the *morte manqué* theme in Charles Wood's later plays, I am delighted that the writer himself will continue to stimulate audiences with his keen social, political, and psychological perceptions. I regret contributing to misinformation in an encyclopedic series distinguished, I believe, by its overall accuracy, and I would like to propose a toast to the still vital author, one of my personal favorites in a generation of brilliant British playwrights, using the words of Goffer in Wood's *Has Washington Legs?*: "I shall see you bear a charmed life, no tripe to trip over."

OBITUARIES

John Fante

(8 April 1909-8 May 1983)

Michael Mullen
Indian Hills Community College

BOOKS: *Wait Until Spring, Bandini* (New York: Stackpole, 1938; London: Routledge, 1939);
Ask The Dust (New York: Stackpole, 1939);
Dago Red (New York: Viking, 1940);
Full of Life (Boston: Little, Brown, 1952; London: Panther, 1957);
Bravo, Burro!, by Fante and Rudolph Borchert, illustrated by Marilyn Hirsh (New York: Hawthorn Books, 1970);
The Brotherhood of the Grape (Boston: Houghton Mifflin, 1977);
Dreams from Bunker Hill (Santa Barbara: Black Sparrow Press, 1982).

SCREENPLAYS: *East of the River*, screen story by Fante and Ross B. Wills, Warner Bros., 1940;
The Golden Fleecing, story by Fante, Lynn Root, and Frank Fenton, M-G-M, 1940;
Youth Runs Wild, screenplay by Fante, screen story by Fante and Herbert Kline, RKO, 1944;
My Man and I, screenplay and screen story by Fante and Jack Leonard, M-G-M, 1952;
Full of Life, story and screenplay by Fante, Columbia, 1957;
Jeanne Eagels, screenplay by Fante, Daniel Fuchs, and Sonya Levien, Columbia, 1957;
Walk on the Wild Side, screenplay by Fante and Edmund Morris, Columbia, 1962;
The Reluctant Saint, screenplay and screen story by Fante and Joseph Petracca, Davis-Royal Films International, 1962;
My Six Loves, screenplay by Fante, Joseph Cavelli, and William Wood, Paramount, 1963;
Maya, M-G-M, 1966.

PERIODICAL PUBLICATIONS: "Altar Boy," *American Mercury*, 26 (August 1932): 395-404;
"Home Sweet Home," *American Mercury*, 27 (November 1932): 271-277;
"First Communion," *American Mercury*, 28 (February 1933): 171-175;
"Big Leaguer," *American Mercury*, 28 (March 1933): 281-286;
"The Odyssey of a Wop," *American Mercury*, 30 (September 1933): 89-97;

John Fante

"One of Us," *Atlantic Monthly*, 154 (October 1934): 432-439;
"Bricklayer in the Snow," *American Mercury*, 37 (January 1936): 50-55;
"Postman Rings and Rings," *American Mercury*, 40 (March 1937): 310-316;
"Charge It," *Scribner's*, 101 (April 1937): 28-31;
"Road to Hell," *American Mercury*, 42 (October 1937): 214-219;
"None So Blind," *Woman's Home Companion*, 65 (April 1938): 19-20;
"A Nun No More," *Virginia Quarterly Review*, 16 (Autumn 1940): 566-574;
"Helen, Thy Beauty Is to Me—," *Saturday Evening*

Post, 213 (1 March 1941): 14-15, 76, 78, 80;

"That Wonderful Bird," *Good Housekeeping*, 112 (May 1941): 24-25, 167-172;

"Mary Osaka, I Love You," *Good Housekeeping*, 115 (October 1942): 40-41, 167-178;

"Scoundrel," *Woman's Home Companion*, 72 (March 1945): 22-23;

"Papa Christmas Tree," *Woman's Home Companion*, 73 (December 1946): 18-19, 72-74;

"Dreamer," *Woman's Home Companion* 74 (June 1947): 22-23, 41-42, 44, 47;

"The Wine of Youth," *Woman's Home Companion*, 75 (December 1948): 24-25, 114, 122-125;

"One-Play Oscar," *Saturday Evening Post*, 223 (4 November 1950): 28, 109, 111-112, 114;

"In the Spring," *Collier's*, 129 (15 March 1952): 21, 34, 36, 38;

"Full of Life" [excerpt], *Reader's Digest*, 60 (May 1952): 131-156;

"The Big Hunger," *Collier's*, 130 (2 August 1952): 58, 60-61.

John Fante, who died on 8 May 1983 at the Motion Picture and Television Country House in Woodland Hills, California, was described by Will Balliett, in the August 1983 issue of *California*, as perhaps "the best chronicler of Los Angeles on record."

The son of Nicholas Peter and Mary Capolungo Fante, John Thomas Fante was born in Boulder, Colorado. After attending Catholic school there and Regis High School, a Jesuit boarding school, in Denver, he went on to the University of Colorado for a while but hated school and quit. Moving to California in 1930, Fante worked in a cannery, as a stevedore, as a hotel clerk, and as a grocery clerk, all without much interest or success, before enrolling at Long Beach Junior College, where, as he later said, he "was kicked out for general laxity and hell-raising."

During the early 1930s Fante started writing and began a lengthy correspondence with H. L. Mencken, who published Fante's first story, "Altar Boy," in the *American Mercury* in August 1932. While the *American Mercury* was the primary outlet for Fante's early work (during the years 1932-1937 eight of his stories appeared there), his stories were also published in the *Atlantic Monthly*, *Scribner's*, *Woman's Home Companion*, *Saturday Evening Post*, and other popular magazines.

Fante's first novel, written in 1934, was never published, but after he rewrote it, it was published by Stackpole as *Wait Until Spring, Bandini* in 1938, the year after his marriage to Joyce Smart. Al-

though it is the story of a poor family, the Bandinis, *Wait Until Spring, Bandini* is not a proletarian novel. The novel is finally more about the Bandini family, which is examined in detail, than it is about poverty. Set in a small Colorado town not far from Denver, the story is told from young Arturo Bandini's point of view (he is either twelve or fourteen; both ages are given for him). Arturo dislikes being poor, dislikes being Italian, dislikes his mother for losing her beauty because this loss led his father to desert the family for a rich and attractive widow, and wants to be a baseball player.

Though the book did not sell well, even for a first novel, the reviews were mostly favorable. James T. Farrell, in the *Atlantic Monthly*, called it "one of the most moving of recent first novels" and "a work rich in its humanness, a novel by a man of genuine talent." In a review for the *New York Herald Tribune Books*, Iris Barry said that *Wait Until Spring, Bandini* "is an impressive job"; and Eda Lou Walton in the *Nation* found that Fante's characters and style "bespeak more than the usual skillful novelist." Other reviewers agreed, crediting him with creating a convincing picture of an Italian-American family and finding his style simple but still "packed with meaning." Critics who disliked the novel found fault with some of the characters; however, Farrell, who otherwise liked the novel, felt that while the other characters were well drawn, the rich widow was not, and the critic of literature for the *Saturday Review* (identified by the initials W. S.) argued that Arturo was the only effective character in the novel. Some reviewers also criticized the novel's plot, which they claimed was too forced. W. S. opened by saying that Fante had "touched on a fresh theme," but it was "too bad that his book does not amount to more."

Fante was back the following year with another novel published by Stackpole, *Ask The Dust*, which continues the adventures of Arturo Bandini. In this second novel, Bandini, now a struggling author living in the Bunker Hill district of Los Angeles, unsuccessfully courts a Mexican waitress who is in love with a bartender who mistreats her. Mencken appears as J. C. Hackmuth, the editor who published Bandini's first story and who is the recipient of a string of letters from Bandini which he fashions into Bandini's first novel. The wry portrait of Bandini, who believes himself a great but undiscovered writer whose books will one day be found on library shelves, and the portrait of Los Angeles make the novel more than just another book about an aspiring writer. One reviewer wrote: "the California locale, so carefully particularized in every detail of street, beach and outlying desert, is very effective."

Ask The Dust is now usually regarded as Fante's best novel, but when it was published some reviewers compared it unfavorably to *Wait Until Spring, Bandini*. Though Iris Barry, reviewing *Ask The Dust* in *New York Herald Tribune Books*, liked the book, referring to its honesty, tension, and economical style, she felt it was "less effective and less entire" than Fante's first novel. The anonymous reviewer for the *New Yorker*, agreeing with Barry's appraisal of Fante's style, said the novel "doesn't add up to much" and was not as interesting as *Wait Until Spring, Bandini*. Fante was again compared, as he had been when his first novel was published, to William Saroyan—sometimes favorably and sometimes not. In the *Atlantic*, E. B. Garside wrote, "*Ask The Dust* realizes to the full the quizzical wonders inherent in Saroyan's fragmentary writings, and recognizes the cruelty of man's lot besides." Peter Monro Jack, in the *New York Times Book Review*, also referred to Saroyan, but did not think that Fante was quite as good, calling *Ask The Dust* "a clever little story by a second virtuoso—Saroyan being the first and better—who dramatizes the life of a young writer in all its brash young egotism." *Ask The Dust* sold more than twice as many copies as Fante's first novel, but total sales were fewer than five thousand copies.

Fante's third book in three years, *Dago Red*, a collection of short stories, was published in 1940 by Viking and continued the pattern established by his previous books: good reviews but poor sales. Marianne Hauser's review in the *New York Times Book Review* began: "Here is a book where the author's talent lies over each page bright as sunlight on a fresh green lawn." The book was also praised by reviewers in the *New Yorker*, the *Nation*, *Yale Review*, *New York Herald Tribune Books*, and *Time*, where it received enthusiastic support from a reviewer who stated that *Dago Red* "is perhaps 1940's best book of short stories: the sort many people wish that William Saroyan, with a grip on himself at last, would write."

It was not until almost twelve years later, in 1952, that Fante's next book, *Full of Life*, was published by Little, Brown, and in the first chapter of that novel he explained the gap: "Me, author, John Fante, composer of three books. First book sold 2300 copies. Second book sold 4800 copies. Third book sold 2100 copies. But they don't ask for royalty statements in the picture business. If you have what they want at the moment they pay you, and pay you well. At that moment I had what they wanted, and

every Thursday there came this big check."

Full of Life was not Fante's best book, but it was his most successful in terms of sales. *Reader's Digest*, in May of 1952, gave twenty-five of its pages to a condensed version of the book. It was translated into German and Italian, and in 1957 a movie version, for which Fante wrote the screenplay, was released, with Judy Holliday and Richard Conte in the starring roles. Unlike Fante's earlier books, *Full of Life* is openly autobiographical—instead of the fictional Bandini family of his first two novels, or the Toscana family featured in most of the stories in *Dago Red*, the Italian-American family in *Full of Life* is Fante's own—and the book, which tells the story of Joyce Fante's first pregnancy and her conversion to Catholicism, was marketed as nonfiction.

Reviews of the book were as favorable as any Fante had ever received. Jane Cobb, in the *New York Times Book Review*, called *Full of Life*, "touching as well as funny, neither wise-cracking nor ponderous." In the *Saturday Review*, P. M. Pasinetti praised Fante for his handling of the domestic-comedy material, stating that Fante "must have been so sure of his serious artistic purposes that he daringly liked to work in cliché-ridden territory to prove the freshness of his view. He is very successful in doing so."

Though Hollywood paid Fante well for his work, and his screen credits included *Walk on the Wild Side* (1962), *My Man and I* (1952), *The Reluctant Saint* (1962), and *My Six Loves* (1963), his Hollywood career was plagued by bad luck. He wrote "The Roses" for Harry Cohn and was with the director Richard Quine (who had also directed *Full of Life*) on location in Naples but was called back with the rest of the crew because of Quine's failure to report in regularly. In 1959 he wrote "The Fish Don't Bite" for Darryl F. Zanuck, who was then having an affair with Juliet Greco. At the same time Saroyan sent Zanuck a play that would star Greco. Zanuck took the play, and Fante's screenplay was never filmed.

Fante's next novel, *The Brotherhood of the Grape*, published by Houghton Mifflin in 1977, treats the death of Fante's father. Because Fante himself was battling diabetes at the time, Joyce Fante believes that he was confronting his own death as well. The novel was serialized in *City Magazine* in 1975, and Francis Ford Coppola planned to make a movie of the book, working with Robert Towne. Advertising for the book noted that it would be Coppola's next movie, but because of Coppola's production problems with *Apocalypse Now* and Fante's illness, the film was never made.

The Brotherhood of the Grape was not reviewed

widely, but the reception was favorable, not surprisingly, since the novel shares many of the traits of his previous books. The novel, which relates the last days of Nick Molise, a seventy-six-year-old stonemason, is narrated by Nick's oldest son, a writer who is called home to settle a dispute between his parents. *Publishers Weekly* called *The Brotherhood of the Grape* "outrageously funny yet sad," a description that could apply to nearly all of Fante's books, and said that the book "is a winner." David Bellamy, who reviewed the novel for the *New York Times Book Review*, was warmly receptive: "John Fante has an economical style, a measured confident gait, and a feel for one-liners and the unanticipated quintessential gesture. 'The Brotherhood of the Grape' is alternately full of cleansing laughter and as comical as a toothache."

In 1978 Fante went blind as a result of diabetes. Not long after, he developed gangrene, and both his legs had to be amputated. Still he continued to write, dictating his last novel to his wife. Originally titled "How to Write a Screenplay," it was published as *Dreams from Bunker Hill* in 1982 by the Black Sparrow Press.

Continuing the adventures of Arturo Bandini as he embarks on a career in Hollywood, *Dreams from Bunker Hill* is so loosely plotted that Elaine Kendall, one of the few reviewers of the book, described it in the *Los Angeles Times* as "informal recollections" and "separate stories, sidelights and reflections upon the events. . . ."

Ask The Dust has been most popular in California, and it is not surprising that the Fante revival—if it may truthfully be called that—started there. Ben Pleasants, a Los Angeles writer, introduced *Ask The Dust* to John Martin, owner of Black Sparrow Press, which republished *Ask The Dust* in 1980 (with a preface by Charles Bukowski), published *Dreams from Bunker Hill*, republished *Wait Until Spring, Bandini* in 1983, is planning to publish a complete collection of Fante's stories in 1984, and is considering publication of a recently discovered Fante manuscript about Arturo Bandini. A shortage of Fante's books can no longer be a cause for his neglect.

Ross B. Wills remembers showing Fante around the movie studios, where Wills worked and where Fante would soon be working, and asking, "So you're another one of these guys who's going to write The Great American Novel, are you?" Fante responded as Bandini might have: "Ten! Twenty! Why I've got *forty* great books in me! All I want is time, a typewriter, and a sandwich now and then!" Fante never found the time to write even ten, but those he did complete are well worth having.

References:

Olga Peragallo, "Fante, John Thomas," in *Italian American Authors and Their Contributions to American Literature* (New York: S. F. Vanni, 1949), pp. 93-96;

Ross B. Wills, "John Fante," *Common Ground*, 1 (Spring 1941): 84-90.

William Goyen
(24 April 1915-29 August 1983)

Thomas E. Dasher
Valdosta State College

See also the Goyen entry in *DLB 2, American Novelists Since World War II.*

NEW BOOKS: *Wonderful Plant* (Winston-Salem, N.C.: Stuart Wright, 1980);
Arcadio (New York: Clarkson Potter, 1983);
Leander (New York: Clarkson Potter, forthcoming);
The Precious Door (New York: Clarkson Potter, forthcoming).

PERIODICAL PUBLICATIONS: "The Texas Principessa," *TriQuarterly*, 56 (Winter 1983): 50-56;

"Margo," *TriQuarterly*, 56 (Winter 1983): 71-75;

"Tongues of Men and of Angels," *TriQuarterly*, 56 (Winter 1983): 76-90;

"Where's Esther?," *TriQuarterly*, 56 (Winter 1983): 91-96.

William Goyen (J. Gary Dontzig)

William Goyen died in Los Angeles on 29 August 1983. He had recently seen *Arcadio*, his first novel in nine years, readied for publication and had completed work on a collection of short stories, *The Precious Door*, which he hoped to see placed with a publisher. After a long, dry spell in the late 1960s, filled with frustration and desperation, he had once again experienced an extremely creative period which lasted for over a decade. In 1974, both *Come, the Restorer* and *Selected Writings of William Goyen* appeared; and in 1975, his collected stories and a twenty-fifth anniversary edition of *The House of Breath* were published to critical acclaim, a confirmation of the enthusiastic reception which he and his first novel had received in 1950. And yet during the last five or six years, he had been through another period of frustration and disappointment—not because he was not writing or could not write. Indeed, he was writing constantly—short stories, *Arcadio*, the forthcoming novella *Leander*, studies of St. Paul and St. Francis, and an autobiography/memoir of influential women in his life. However, he began to have some problems with his health and to experience, once again, the problems of finding a publisher. He always had a small audience in America, maintained largely through the efforts of several important journals such as the *Southwest Review* and *TriQuarterly*, which gladly published his stories and work-in-progress. In Europe, his audience was larger and often even more responsive; in 1979, the prestigious French journal *delta* devoted its entire ninth issue to Goyen, an honor earlier accorded to Flannery O'Connor, William Faulkner, Eudora Welty, and Herman Melville. In the United States, though, he had problems with both *Arcadio* and *The Precious Door*. After a distinguished career of over thirty years, he was forced to question whether some of his very best work would appear in book form. Fortunately, in the last year of his life, *Arcadio* was accepted by Clarkson Potter, its first venture into fiction, and prospects looked good for the short-story collection. He remained full of work and hope. As he told an interviewer in November 1982 about writing novels, "Of course it's an act of hope, and faith. Art is redeeming, and art is an affirmation. There's no other way. The creation, the result, may not be very wonderful in some cases, or even very good, but I'm given joy and faith again through watching people's impulse to make something, and their energy in making it, their willingness to make something."

Arcadio, published on 3 October 1983, is a triumphant culmination of Goyen's career. *Publishers Weekly* proclaimed that "this beautifully written book has the overwhelming power of myth brought to life," and Reginald Gibbons wrote in *The New York Times Book Review* that Arcadio's "song may be Goyen's finest achievement. The work of a master fabulist, it was one more courageous foray into fiction unlike anyone else's, haunting the reader with its tenderness and ferocity." *Arcadio* is a frame-story; the first-person narrator tells a story from his imagination which had been inspired by his uncle's telling of a story about a marvelously strange creature bathing in a stream. The narrator's story concerns Arcadio, the hermaphrodite who tells his own story and the stories of those with whom he has come into contact who, in turn, had told him their stories. The compulsion to tell, to find a listener, to create the connection between storyteller and listener has been a fundamental aspect of all of Goyen's fiction, and Arcadio emerges as one of Goyen's most fascinating speakers.

Arcadio spends his life in quest of unifying wholeness. Man and woman, brother and sister, son and daughter, religious believer and sexual profligate, sideshow freak and spiritual leader, he has wandered throughout the United States in search of his mother, his half brother, various individuals who have been lost to his traveling companions, and

Dust jacket for Goyen's first novel in nine years, which, according to Joyce Carol Oates, "ranks among his most powerful and original visionary works"

finally his father. He eventually finds all of them but loses each as the journey to self-knowledge and self-love continues. Fragmented and isolated, he yearns to be no longer alone. All the relationships which have been denied him draw him further toward himself as he continues to be pursued by some unknown, unseen posse.

"Used to sitting silent under the public gaze as a serene listener," Arcadio had enjoyed being a remarkable star in a seedy brothel before becoming a major attraction in a traveling show. There he sits within a glass jewel wagon upon his gilded chair behind the red velvet curtain and gazes out at those who stare back, one of whom gives him a white Bible and another of whom turns out to be his mother, Chupa. Thus he is handed a source of spiritual inspiration and discovers the long-desired object of filial need. The Bible stories are juxtaposed with the family stories; spirit and flesh, once again, plague both the singer and the listener. Chupa tries to explain why she long ago deserted Arcadio but

chooses to desert him again when he reveals himself to her, his dual nature, his conjoined genitals. Unable to accept that truth or resolve the divided self made manifest in her own child, she leaves Arcadio with only the desire to find her again and the knowledge that he has a half brother, also deserted years earlier in a jail in a place called Missoura.

Arcadio sets out on his own journey first to find his half brother, Tomasso. When he has found Tomasso, the brothers go together to search for their mother. However, Tomasso, still a child, mysteriously dies of hunger even though Arcadio has seen him regularly eat. Tomasso can exist now only in his brother's memory, his song being sung, along with others, within the strange, divided figure. Arcadio becomes a repository of all that he experiences, but he still searches for the spark which will bring the parts, the songs, together. "Sometimes I do not know if being found is being lost, if who I find is who I lose, I only wander, looking and singing, everything is taken from me 'cept the love of *Jesucristo*, soon I will not hunt and search no more, I will set down somewhere in love of God and seeing *Jesucristo* at my side. If people that I find do not run away from me they sink away from me cold upon my breast. I'm always left alone again. . . . *Jesucristo* will not go, he will not go."

Yet Arcadio meets one more member of his family, one more figure from his past—his father, Hombre, whose life has been determined entirely by his huge penis. He and the woman who now keeps him mock Arcadio and his quest; they tempt him to join them in sexual abandon, to forget the spiritual and become totally subsumed by flesh—a similar situation to the one in the brothel from which Arcadio had first begun his journey. They urge him to relinquish all the contradictions and turmoil and become one with them. Arcadio, though, finally must refuse and then watches as Hombre's penis whips its owner to death; Hombre's death relinquishes his song also to Arcadio, who seems no closer to an internal reconciliation of all the opposites which have swirled around and then within him.

Arcadio, however, has one last chance to find that wholeness; his listener, the first-person narrator, is still there. Also, of course, there are "God and *Jesucristo*, father and son, only thing that is the same today and yesterday and forever more. I'm on my way to them." Left alone in the night and unable to see his listener, Arcadio becomes a disembodied voice, a witness to the darkness which envelops and isolates one from another. And the singer and his song become one with the listener and his thoughts—fragile and vulnerable and, finally, unforgettable. The listener must remember, and in that memory lies a connection—perhaps *the* connection which man can know in flesh and which might approximate that which possibly exists in spirit.

Thus the reader is brought back by the frame to the narrator, to the initial storyteller who, like Arcadio, must face the aloneness of the singer. Goyen suggests that we are all singers, all brought back to the overwhelming questions which have no absolute answers and seldom disturb the universe. "Yet you, hearing me—who are you, where have you come from, why have you stayed so long to hear me? *Oyente!* who are we, what is life why are we all here where is God?" We are all doomed by the human condition to ask these questions again and again. Man's expulsion from Eden was not to be banished from paradise but to ask his listeners to hear his song, his version of the questions which the listener will in turn be forced to ask and to share. Yet man does not have to be overwhelmed by futility and despair. The essential unity in life, formed by man's songs and his willingness to listen to others' songs, links us to the wholeness of God which awaits us. Arcadio, Hondo, Sweet Janine, Hombre, Tomasso—Uncle Ben, the young narrator, his family—reach out to reader, listener, God-seeker yearning for reconciliation and wholeness.

It is a search which permeates all of Goyen's work and which underlies all he believed about the healing power of art. Not quite five months before his death, Goyen spoke at the Writer at Work Series sponsored by New York University. In that talk, he discussed at some length the story of the Biblical twins Jacob and Esau, who competed and fought from birth. Robbing his brother of his birthright, Jacob must struggle to regain his name and spirit, must come through the battle to be reconciled with his brother and himself. The artist for Goyen is a person who is involved in a similar struggle, seeking to be healed as did the Greek archer Philoctetes, poisoned by the snake, who forgets his wondrous gift, the bow. The writer is constantly being drawn into the darkness of modern civilization, of man's inhumanity to man, of his own human heart. And, of course, as Goyen recognized, many are trapped there or, worse, choose to stay there believing that darkness, isolation, alienation, and suffering are all. Goyen, though, refused to accept that dark vision as the only true view for the modern novelist. "Art and Spirit endure together. Art heals, puts the precious bow in our hands again; binds up and reconciles; recovers the dignity and the beauty in us that keep getting wounded by the wrestling with the angel in us, with the God in us, or—in the absence of angels or God—with the mystery in each of us, waiting in the night by the river that we shall surely come to, on our way home to meet our brother."

William Goyen's belief in the healing power of art never wavered; his work continues to challenge and to stimulate and, finally, to inspire man to overcome the contradictions and fragments and to make of ourselves whole beings within whose power lies the possibility of reconciliation with ourselves, with our fellow man, and with God.

Interviews:

Thomas E. Dasher and Jean W. Ross, "CA Interview," *Contemporary Authors*, New Revision Series, 6 (Detroit: Gale Research, 1982), pp. 194-196;

John F. Baker, "PW Interviews William Goyen," *Publishers Weekly*, (5 August 1983): 94-95;

Reginald Gibbons, with Molly McQuade, "An Interview with William Goyen," *TriQuarterly*, 56 (Winter 1983): 97-125.

TRIBUTES TO WILLIAM GOYEN

From GEORGE GARRETT

In fact and in flesh, *in person* as they say, we did not know each other much or well. We had worked together at a couple of writers' conferences and had met socially a few times. I remember once, to my surprise and delight, he showed up, just there, sitting in the small audience, at a poetry reading I gave one evening at Cooper Union in New York City. I didn't even know he was in town at the time. To show up at a poetry reading, even a friend's, when you don't have to and the friend won't be any the wiser, is way above and beyond the call of duty.

I remember what he looked like, of course, in photographs and in fact—tall, slender, but sturdy, well-formed, handsome, and by the time I actually met him, wonderfully weather-beaten—an honest and honorable East Texas face. I remember more acutely his tact and compassion, his good humor and his real skill with people. That last surprised me. I remember once seeing him act (skillfully) as toastmaster at a banquet in Houston. He was an adept, sophisticated, yes, *clever* toastmaster. I was much impressed. He told jokes, presented awards, and made everyone feel good.

Occasionally we did each other routine professional favors. For example, when I had to leave Princeton for a semester, I suggested and recommended Bill as my replacement. And he got the job. I recommended him also to the people at Hollins College (where he already had such dedicated fans as Richard Dillard and Allen Wier) as a writer-in-residence; and recommended to him that he should go. He went there and was wonderful and was much loved.

So, inevitably, we shared some students over the years—Madison Smartt Bell was one of them from Princeton days. And we shared some close friends. We even shared (as friend) an editor, Sam Vaughan at Doubleday, and sometimes communicated through him.

Near the end of his life—though I had no way to know how near the end was and, indeed, was under a kind of hearsay impression that his health was much improved—Bill did me an enormous favor. He agreed, without reluctance, to read all the way through the huge and unwieldy manuscript of my novel, *The Succession*, about which I was plagued with more than my usual quota of questions and doubts. He took precious time to read it with care and to write a response to me. Matter of fact he wrote me a couple of letters as he went along, letters which lifted my flagging spirits and greatly encouraged me. Later, as a practical matter, he called and dictated a blurb for the book to Sam Vaughan.

I am ashamed now, of course, to have stolen time and energy from him at that time. But, nevertheless, I am happy for his attention and shall always be grateful for it.

I shall always be grateful to him for more than that, far more—for his art and his example as an artist. I came to *The House of Breath* just about the time it came out, a time when, after fooling around with writing all my life, as long as I could remember, I was finally committed (without having a clue what that commitment might mean) to the art of writing as my vocation and my life. I can't even begin, not in a few words here and maybe not in many, to tell what that book meant to me. I had just returned from a job in East Texas, all over East Texas as a matter of fact, knew something about the "reality" of which he wrote, just as, with some blood kin there, I knew something about the people, too. But the book was a profound influence. Not an influence in the conventional sense. I never even imagined myself writing *like* William Goyen. From the first he was wholly admirable and wholly inimitable. But in an almost absolute sense both his achievement, then and there and in the other, later works as they came along one by one, and his example—the

example of his grace in survival as an artist of dedication and integrity, his *courage*, in good times and bad, courage which would be sorely tested and would finally triumph over fact and flesh, all these things were for me like trail signs blazed by a genuine and adventurous explorer. They were and are lights in and against the dark. In that deeper sense he dares (almost childishly, "I dare you," wonderfully so) anyone to try and follow after him—to aim to do the right thing with one's gifts and to try to do it well.

There is no dwindling or diminishment in his story. *Arcadio* has all the power and originality and the mystery that other works, early and late, make manifest. And these days I keep close by, and reckon I will do so while I live and I can, the printed version of his talk of 13 April 1983 at New York University—"Recovering: Writing and Healing." When I first read the words, I could hear him. When I read the words and heard him, he became, as I believe he intended to be, my brother. Not mine alone, but brother to anyone with ears to hear. A brother who will not permit the easy choices of despair and silence. At least not before the true time to embrace pure silence has arrived. He will not permit me (or you, either, if you listen) to succumb to the powerful temptation to deny the holy mystery of myself and thus of others.

From WILLIAM PEDEN

In Memoriam: William Goyen. A gentle man with a rare capacity for friendship and, like his work, unique. . . . I saw him last here in Boone County with death closing in upon him . . . and, I am sure, he knew it. A brave man, who will be remembered, who wrote his own coda . . . : "there's a world . . . where there's ghosts and a world where there's flesh, and I believe the real right way is to take our worlds . . . as they come and take what comes in em . . . and be what each . . . wants us to be."

From ROBERT PHILLIPS

Bill was, of course, a great storyteller, and often the stories he told were at his own expense. I remember his telling me about meeting with a group of students—I don't recall where, he had been lecturing on both coasts and in Texas, too. Anyhow, the subject turned to publishing. Bill immediately launched into a long diatribe against publishers. It was one of his favorite subjects, he could always rise to *that* occasion. He began to complain to the students that his new novel had not been taken by a publishing house. (This novel was, in fact, an earlier and shorter version of *Arcadio*, which in its final form will be published by Clarkson N. Potter in October. Already prepublication reviews are calling it a masterpiece.) Well, Bill told me that at that class he railed and railed against publishers and their concern only for the commercial.

Finally one of the students raised his hand and asked, "What's your novel about, Mister Goyen?"

"*About?*," Bill repeated, astonished. I can see him raising his great black brows in surprise. "Why, it's about a dying Tex-Mex hermaphrodite who ends up fornicating with his own father in a whore house."

"I *can't* imagine why they didn't take it," the student said.

At which Bill told me he broke into hysterical laughter, realizing how frightfully uncommercial such a book sounded, and how justified any publisher might have been in having second, or even third, thoughts.

But, of course, Bill Goyen's books were never "about" what they seemed to be about. Once the outrageous plots and the gorgeous language were assimilated, it became clear that his real subjects were ecstasy and anguish, becoming and being, the invincibility of the human spirit and the incorruptibility of the creative imagination. He spoke of exile and suppression of individuals and individuality, and often dealt with ecology, the diminished and lost things of this world. He spoke for the displaced in all of us. In his works the tension between the dark and the fair, the male and the female, the normal and the abnormal (whatever *that* is) is the balance between Jacob and the angel—a favorite image of Bill's—as they wrestle (or dance) with the heavenward impulse of the one correcting the earthbound impulse of the other. The result is poetry of the first order, and poetry will never be commercial.

A noted critic wrote me this week, expressing shock over Bill's obituary in the *New York Times*. Shock at the fact of his untimely death, of course; but shock too that the newspaper should think "fame," or rather the lack of it, mattered with a writer of Bill's genius. We know who the truly famous, or infamous, writers of today are. Part of this fame often rests on their ability to perform like trained seals on TV talk shows, something Bill refused to do. He also didn't play literary politics; indeed, he loathed them. Consequently he was

often overlooked. He didn't win a Pulitzer or any of the other major book awards. He was never inducted into the American Academy and Institute of Arts and Letters (as were his contemporaries Capote, Styron, et al.). It hurt, but it didn't matter. His job was to write.

In his introduction to his *Selected Writings* (Random House, 1974), Bill says: "What I intended was to make splendor. What I saw, felt, knew was real, was more than what I could make of it. That made it a lifetime task." It was a task he practiced to the very end. In addition to the five published novels, the four books of stories, the nonfictional account of the life of Jesus, the chapbook of poems, the selected writings, there is yet another novel to come—*Leander*, completed just before his death. There is also a book of thirteen new short stories, which he entitled *The Precious Door*; an autobiography created around the figures of six remarkable women his life touched—Frieda Lawrence, Margo Jones, Mabel Dodge Luhan, Dorothy Brett, Katherine Anne Porter, and an obscure landlady; the early, unpublished novel *Half a Look of Cain* (the manuscript of which is on deposit at the Woodson Research Center of Rice University); his unpublished plays *Christy, A Possibility of Oil, Aimee,* and *The Diamond Rattler*; and finally one should gather his lectures and speeches and book reviews, for he was a truly inspired critic, always finding perfect metaphors for his ideas, as he did last April at New York University, at what was his last public appearance here, knowing he had an illness usually fatal, yet speaking of recovery, writing, and healing. On that evening he spoke eloquently of the figure of Philoctetes, who was so concerned with his wound that he forgot his bow. For Bill, art and spirit endured together. They bound and reconciled, recovered the dignity and the beauty in us that keep getting wounded by wrestling with our interior angels.

A lot of the works I mentioned were written recently. Bill's late flowering is like Yeats's—a powerful, controlled rage. It is ironic that, in contrast to the six or seven years when he was trade editor at McGraw-Hill publishers and wrote not one word of his own, in the past several years, against time and in illness, he completed a great deal.

As I entered this building today, I passed a young man sitting on a fire hydrant, reading *The House of Breath*. It, and the other books, will continue to be read. Rainer Maria Rilke said, "Works of art are of an infinite loneliness and with nothing to be so little reached as with criticism. Only love can grasp and hold and fairly judge them." All of us gathered here have experienced that love which comes out of Bill's pages and which we bring to them time and again. For Bill Goyen's other great talent, besides writing, was loving. Toward the end, in the hospital, even off-duty nurses would return to work, just to sit by him and hold his hand, so great was his love. I often think his books can be thought of as prayers that he offered to those of us he loved.

In this sense, Bill's stories resurrect. They not only keep him alive as long as copies can be found. They also give new life to people and places he loved long gone, relics of himself which he offered as consolation to the living. His fictional land is a paradise—where the good are rewarded, the dove flies, the ark lands, the artist is saved. In his books the man who speaks is not a prophet clothed with thunder, but a seer who tries to understand. His rattlesnakes and oil wells, his tightrope walkers and flagpole sitters, his bearded women and hermaphrodites are haunting ambiguities. The essence of his poetic truth is that no final statement can be made of it. His books move forward on a chronology of emotions, not of dates. And emotions are timeless.

We have been blessed to have had William Goyen among us.

From CAROL SOUTHERN

Goyen's work, like the work of all the great writers, had always been concerned with the larger issues and ultimately with life and death. Because of Goyen's powerful spirituality as a person and as a writer, he was very much in touch with "the other side." Now, in death, those of us who knew him feel that he is very much in touch with us here in life. Perhaps this feeling is simply the power of his projection—in his books and in his personality. In any case, for those open to his unique style, his power will be ever present.

From SAMUEL S. VAUGHAN

Bill Goyen did not live long enough for those of us who loved him but he lived long enough to overcome the disadvantages of a precocious talent and early recognition. Whatever the twists and tortures of his young life, he became a mature writer of depths and dimensions—a person who found various voices for his fiction and a kind of joy that infuses the later work. Not only as an author but as an editor, a friend to writers and theater people,

and as a husband, Bill seemed finally to have found a way out of exile, a way home.

From STUART WRIGHT

Bill Goyen's death in August after a two-year fight with leukemia takes from the world of letters one of its finest postwar writers, and from many of us, a dear and cherished friend. I visited Bill and Doris in New York in April and in Los Angeles in June, and was moved on both occasions by his determination to live. Bill felt that he had been "allowed" at least two more years to finish his novel *Leander* and what might well have been his most important book, the autobiography. By the middle of June, however, Bill had suffered a serious setback; and he must have sensed at this time, or shortly after, that he would not recover. In his last letter to me he wrote: "I am now, after bleak feelings, ready to face it. . . . Think of Doris and me." I did think of Bill and Doris a great deal that summer, but I will always regret that I was not in closer touch with them then and at the end.

I published a sensitive and strange little novella of Bill's in 1980, *Wonderful Plant*. When Doris called to tell me that Bill had died, I turned to the final pages of this book, something I cannot explain but simply was moved to do:

> Many leaves were piled on the windowsill now. Time was short. Tony Sepulveda gazed at the plant. His tears ran down his cheeks so he could not stop them.
>
> "Mr. Purple!" he called. "Mrs. Purple! Baby Purple! Come back. Cool Cricket, Billy Ball, Ancient Order of Benevolent Insects, please come back!" But there was no sound, there was no answer.
>
> "Come back, Wonderful Plant," he whispered. "Don't leave me alone in the sad far West."
>
> The leaves began to fall.

Bill Goyen, unlike Tony Sepulveda, was not alone. I have been told that all of his doctors and nurses were there with him, many of whom had remained on even after their shifts were done that day. They wanted to be with Bill. And all of us, his friends, were there, too, in our thoughts, with our love and appreciation for this special person. Bill was not alone. We will miss him mightily.

Arthur Koestler

(5 September 1905-3 March 1983)

Sidney A. Pearson, Jr.
Radford University

BOOKS: *Von Weissen Nächten und Roten Tagen* (truncated version, Kharkov: Ukranian State Publishers for National Minorities, 1934);

Menschenopfer Unerhört (Paris: Editions du Carrefour, 1937); republished as *L'Espagne ensanglantée* (Paris: Editions du Carrefour, 1937); enlarged as *Spanish Testament* (London: Gollancz, 1937);

The Gladiators, translated by Edith Simon (London: Cape, 1939; New York: Macmillan, 1939);

Darkness at Noon, translated by Daphne Hardy (London: Cape, 1941; New York: Macmillan, 1941);

Scum of the Earth (London: Gollancz, 1941; New York: Macmillan, 1941);

Arrival and Departure (London: Cape, 1943; New York: Macmillan, 1943);

The Yogi and the Commissar (London: Cape, 1945; New York: Macmillan, 1945);

Twilight Bar: An Escapade in Four Acts (London: Cape, 1945; New York: Macmillan, 1945);

Thieves in the Night (London: Macmillan, 1946; New York: Macmillan, 1946);

Insight and Outlook (London: Macmillan, 1949; New York: Macmillan, 1949);

Promise and Fulfillment: Palestine 1917-1949 (London: Macmillan, 1949; New York: Macmillan, 1949);

The Age of Longing (London: Collins, 1951; New York: Macmillan, 1951);

Arrow in the Blue: An Autobiography (London: Collins/Hamilton, 1952; New York: Macmillan, 1952);

The Invisible Writing (London: Collins/Hamilton, 1954; New York: Macmillan, 1954);

The Trail of the Dinosaur, and Other Essays (London: Collins, 1955; New York: Macmillan, 1955);

Reflections on Hanging (London: Gollancz, 1956; New York: Macmillan, 1957);

The Sleepwalkers: A History of Man's Changing Vision of the Universe (London: Hutchinson, 1959; New York: Macmillan, 1959);

The Lotus and the Robot (London: Hutchinson, 1960; New York: Macmillan, 1961);

Hanged by the Neck: An Exposure of Capital Punishment,

Arthur Koestler (© Fay Godwin)

by Koestler and C. H. Rolph (Cecil Rolph Hewitt) (Harmondsworth: Penguin, 1961; Baltimore: Penguin, 1961);

The Act of Creation (London: Hutchinson, 1964; New York: Macmillan, 1964);

The Ghost in the Machine (London: Hutchinson, 1967; New York: Macmillan, 1968);

Drinkers of Infinity. Essays 1955-1967 (London: Hutchinson, 1968; New York: Macmillan, 1969);

The Case of the Midwife Toad (London: Hutchinson, 1971; New York: Random House, 1972);

The Roots of Coincidence (London: Hutchinson, 1972; New York: Random House, 1972);

The Call-Girls (London: Hutchinson, 1972; New York: Random House, 1972);

The Challenge of Chance, by Koestler, Sir Alister Hardy, and Robert Harvie (London: Hutchinson, 1973; New York: Random House, 1974);

The Heel of Achilles. Essays 1968-1973 (London: Hutchinson, 1974; New York: Random House, 1975);

The Thirteenth Tribe. The Khazar Empire and Its Heritage (London: Hutchinson, 1976; New York: Random House, 1976);

Janus: A Summing-Up (London: Hutchinson, 1978; New York: Random House, 1978);

Bricks to Babel: Selected Writings With Comments by the Author (London: Hutchinson, 1980; New York: Random House, 1981);

Kaleidoscope (London: Hutchinson, 1981);

The Stranger on the Square, by Koestler and Cynthia Koestler (London: Hutchinson, 1983).

COLLECTION: The Danube Edition of Koestler's works is being published in Great Britain by Hutchinson (1965-　) and in the United States by Macmillan (1967-1970) and Random House (1982-　).

OTHER: R. H. S. Crossman, ed., *The God That Failed*, includes an essay by Koestler (New York: Harper, 1950);

Alexander Weissberg, *The Accused*, foreword by Koestler (New York: Simon & Schuster, 1951);

Suicide of a Nation? An Inquiry Into the State of Britain Today, edited by Koestler (London: Hutchinson, 1963; New York: Macmillan, 1964);

Beyond Reductionism: New Perspectives in the Life Sciences, edited by Koestler and J. R. Smythies (New York: Macmillan, 1970);

"Humor and Wit," *Encyclopaedia Britannica*, 15th Edition (1974).

Whoever would undertake the formidable task of writing the intellectual history of the twentieth century would be well advised to include in it the works of Arthur Koestler and the controversies they helped to spawn. These controversies were both bitter and continuous throughout Koestler's career because with each of his books he peeled away another layer of twentieth-century consciousness. Many of these arguments, especially those centered on the political realities of communism, were among the most heated intellectual battles of the twentieth century. In his most powerful novel, *Darkness at Noon* (1941), Koestler explored the psychology of an individual Marxist so thoroughly that the novel itself has become inseparable from our general understanding of Marx and the Marxists. Koestler's portrait of the revolutionary personality is so sharply drawn that it must be counted among the indispensable pieces in the intellectual mosaic of modern Western man.

Arthur Koestler was born in 1905 in Budapest, Hungary, which was then part of the Hapsburg Empire. His parents, Henrik and Adela Jeiteles Koestler, were prosperous middle-class Jews, proud of their heritage yet fully assimilated into Germanic culture. When World War I broke out, Koestler's parents moved to Vienna, where he received his early education. His elementary education completed, he decided to study science and engineering. His parents enrolled him in a *Realschule*, a school that specialized in science and modern languages. In 1922 he enrolled at the University of Vienna, where the climate of postwar politics quickly pushed his scientific interests into the background. Attracted to Zionism, he became involved in Zionist activities, and in 1926 he left school, with his studies incomplete, for Palestine, where he lived and worked on an Israeli kibbutz. In 1927 he went to work for the Ullstein chain of German newspapers as a Middle East correspondent. By June 1929 he had left the Middle East and was sent to work for the Ullstein News Service in Paris. He returned to Berlin in September 1930 and became science editor for *Vossische Zeitung*, one of the Ullstein papers. In 1932, disillusioned with Zionism, he secretly joined the German Communist party, but within a few months he was found out and forced to resign his editorship. He went to work full time for the party, taking a series of assignments that eventually took him to the Soviet Union (1932-1933), back to Western Europe (1933-1936), and finally to the Spanish civil war (1936-1937) undercover as an English journalist. He gradually became disillusioned with the party and the fruits of the Russian revolution and made a formal break with the party during the Spanish civil war. When World War II broke out, he was in France, where he was captured after the country fell to the invading Germans. He eventually escaped to England, where he worked with the BBC during the remainder of the war. After the war he resumed his occupation as a journalist, covering the birth of Israel. He became a British citizen and from the security of his adopted country engaged in the political battles that helped to make him one of the most controversial figures of his day.

Koestler's fluency in foreign languages helped to make his transition to writing in English easier than for most writers similarly situated. His maternal language was Hungarian (Magyar), but he never wrote in it professionally. As a student in Vienna he pursued a course of study that emphasized modern languages along with science, and by the time he began to write professionally for the Ullsteins his first language was German. While living in France after the Spanish civil war and his apostasy from the party, Koestler wrote some articles in French, but German remained his literary language. His first two novels, *The Gladiators* (1939) and *Darkness at Noon*, were originally written in German and were translated into English by others. After *Darkness at Noon*, all of his professional writing was in English.

Koestler's domestic life is perhaps best described as "cosmopolitan." His first marriage was in 1935, during his active party days, to Dorothy Asher. At the time Koestler considered marriage a bourgeois institution that had been replaced by what was then called the "new proletarian morality." Nevertheless he did marry, not out of any sense of propriety but rather because they were living in Switzerland at the time, and Dorothy's passport was about to expire—it was either marriage or deportation for her. After a few months of marriage both parted company without bitterness or rancor. They

remained good friends afterward, and during the Spanish civil war Dorothy was instrumental in gaining Koestler's release from one of Franco's jails. After a series of affairs during the next decade, Koestler met and eventually married his secretary Mamaine Paget in 1950. Mamaine and her twin sister had been prominent debutantes in England during the 1930s, and the marriage seems to have been happy initially. But within a year Koestler and Mamaine separated, evidently with mixed emotions in both parties. Mamaine died after a prolonged period of ill health in 1954. In the meantime Koestler had begun an affair with his secretary Cynthia Jefferies Patterson, whom he married in 1965. Cynthia was twenty-two years Koestler's junior, but their marriage proved to be his most durable and apparently happiest partnership. Cynthia was absolutely devoted to her husband, even to the point of joining him in death through suicide in 1983.

In terms of subject matter Koestler's career may be divided into two distinct periods. The first period, from the mid-1930s until the mid-1950s, is marked not only by the dominance of political issues but also by the single-minded intensity of his work. He later wrote that the desire to understand the

Cynthia and Arthur Koestler (© Times Newspapers Limited)

nature of modern politics was the inspirational basis for all his most creative writing. The second period, from the mid-1950s until his death in 1983, stands in sharp relief with the first period because it seems apolitical and eclectic by comparison. In his later writing Koestler consciously eschewed political polemics in order to pursue his lifelong interest in modern science, especially with reference to the philosophical meaning of the post-Newtonian revolution. But this dichotomy is more apparent than real. The conceptual linkage between the two periods becomes more evident when we ask, as Koestler did, what accounts for the curious fascination so many intellectuals have had for Marxist totalitarianism? It was Koestler's conclusion, derived in large measure from the results of his early work, that this fundamental question could not be satisfactorily answered apart from an inquiry into the origins of modern science. Totalitarian political ideologies, he thought, were rooted in the inability of modern science to give a sufficiently rational and truthful account of the human condition to satisfy man's natural longing for spiritual meaning. It is a more correct reading of Koestler's writing to see the second period as a logical and deeper outgrowth of the first.

Koestler joined the Communist party, he later wrote in *The God That Failed* (1950), out of many of the same impulses that prompt a person to embrace a church and a religion: "I became converted because I was ripe for it and lived in a disintegrating society thirsting for faith." This initial experience colored his subsequent interpretations of Communist psychology, as it was more akin to an act of faith than an act of reason. He saw himself as engaged in a morally pure enterprise—a grand experiment in creating the City of God in the here and now—as devoted to a pure utopia and in revolt against a polluted society. "To the psychiatrist," he wrote, "both the craving for Utopia and the rebellion against the status quo are symptoms of social maladjustment. To the social reformer, both are symptoms of a healthy rational attitude." When he left the Communist party in 1937, it was with a sense the party had betrayed, had left him, rather than the other way around. His commitment to utopia was still intact, but he no longer saw the party as the vehicle to get from here to there. The problem with the revolution was that noble ends had become corrupted by ignoble means.

In Koestler's work the disparity between revolutionary ends and means is the modern version of the classic problem of the proper relationship between theory and practice. In one of his most in-

fluential essays he symbolized this dilemma as the problem of "The Yogi and the Commissar." These, he said, are the representative types of men who dominate all political debate, but from opposite ends of the political spectrum. At one end is the yogi, who represents the ethic of pure means. He believes that means alone count and will not compromise his moral integrity in pursuit of any end, no matter how noble, if that pursuit entails corrupt means. For all practical purposes then, the yogi is unable to act politically, but this scarcely seems important because his goal is not politics but rather communion with the Absolute. At the other end of this idealized spectrum stands the pure form of the commissar mentality. The mirror image of the yogi in every respect, he is the supreme political activist who conceives of all morality in terms of the ends sought. There are no "immoral" means, merely "ignoble" ends. In the final analysis, Koestler argues, all political choices are reduced to a choice between the yogi and the commissar. The tragedy of twentieth-century politics is not only that it is dominated by the commissar types—that is more or less inevitable in every era—but that we have forgotten altogether the morality of the yogi, and the yogi is the only brake on the commissar's actions. Attempts to find what Koestler calls ideological "halfway houses" between these extremes are doomed to failure at the outset because they are divorced from the real world of political action. Practical participation in politics necessarily means an initial commitment to the commissar mentality—the personality of the modern revolutionary who is the symbol of the contemporary political dilemma.

Given these dilemmas inherent in the yogi-commissar continuum, Koestler arrived at the conclusion that all revolutions are doomed to failure from the beginning. The yogi and the commissar define the limits of political possibilities. This fundamental fact of political life limits the ability of political action to solve permanently the problems of the human condition. But it does not thereby follow from this analysis that all attempts at revolution will fail for the same reasons. Some will fail because excessive concern with means will prevent them from reaching their goal. Others will fail because their fixation on the end will lead them to ignore means, and corrupted means will prevent them from ever reaching their end. In terms of politics, the common bond between the yogi and the commissar is the experience of failure. What remains for the student of modern politics therefore is an empirical analysis of the specific causes of revolutionary failure. Koestler explored this problem in a trilogy of novels on the nature of revolutionary ethics: *The Gladiators* (1939), *Darkness at Noon* (1941), and *Arrival and Departure* (1943). Each novel was intended to depict a separate aspect of revolutionary morality in terms of the yogi and the commissar.

Koestler's first novel, *The Gladiators*, is a fictionalized account of the revolt of Spartacus's army of slaves and gladiators against Rome during the first century B.C. The date of publication is significant. At that time European Communist parties were splitting into factions and debating the course of the Russian revolution. It was, for many, turning out far differently under Stalin than they had expected. But what if Trotsky had succeeded Lenin and not Stalin, would it have made any difference in the later course of the revolution? Koestler's answer is that it *might* have made a difference, but not in terms of the ultimate success or failure of the revolution. If Trotsky had been more scrupulous than Stalin in his choices of means, the revolution would have been crushed; and if he remained loyal to the ends of the revolution as defined by Marx, he would have to act precisely as Stalin had done. In *The Gladiators* Koestler portrayed the course of a revolution in which the means are allowed to dominate the end. The aim of Spartacus's revolt is to build a "Sun State," a gladiator-slave conception of utopia. So powerful is the dream that it inspires slaves and intellectuals throughout Italy to follow Spartacus. Along the way the dream runs afoul of the "Law of Detours," the hidden law of all revolutionary movements that decrees that the leader must be ruthless in pursuit of the goal, but Spartacus has seen too much suffering and is too solicitous of the feelings of his followers, who do not understand the political necessity of the Law of Detours, and at a critical moment he fails to do what he must to build the Sun State; he fails to kill one of his subordinate commanders who has wantonly destroyed a town. After this the people no longer flock to his banner and the Romans finally crush his revolt. Koestler's first lesson of revolutionary ethics is that to follow the morality of the yogi, the morality of means, is the surest road to defeat.

Koestler's second lesson of revolutionary ethics was the consequence of following the morality of the commissar. What would happen if the revolutionary leader were ruthless in pursuit of the final, eschatological end of human history, the perfect utopia that would abolish all human suffering and misery? Could the noblest end imaginable for a revolution justify the most savage means to bring it about? This course of political action was the subject of his most powerful work, *Darkness at Noon*.

The backdrop for *Darkness at Noon* is the Russian revolution and the infamous Moscow Purge Trials of the 1930s, although these historical events are never specifically mentioned by name. Stalin is a shadowy figure in the minds of the characters, referred to simply as "Number One." The physical action of the novel is slight. It consists of the arrest, interrogation, trial, and execution during the purges of one of the "Old Guard," Commissar N. S. Rubashov. The real heart of the novel is the intellectual unfolding of the revolutionary ethic in the mind of Rubashov. His personal problem is to understand where the revolution went wrong and reconcile his duty to the end of the revolution with his duty to the party that is the agent of that future. Rubashov has been singled out for public trial and execution, as opposed to a silent death in anonymity, precisely because of his lifelong dedication to the party and its goals. For reasons ordained by history, reasons that cannot be understood except through the eyes of the faithful, the revolution has reached a point at which it needs blood sacrifices to serve as examples to the still backward peasant and proletariat masses. Only the most dedicated party members, such as Rubashov, have been chosen for this special role because only they can be trusted not to betray the party in public trials—to confess to crimes they did not commit as a "last service to the Party."

At first Rubashov is reluctant to confess to these patently phony charges. He has come to doubt the truth that the party is supposed to embody and cannot render any last service. But his first interrogator, Comrade Ivanov, is confident that when Rubashov has time to think his thoughts out to their logical conclusion he will confess of his own free will and not as the result of physical torture. It is here, in the dialectic between Rubashov and his interrogators, first Ivanov and then Gletkin, that the full horror of the revolutionary mindset is revealed. In the end Ivanov is right—Rubashov works out in his mind the logic of the revolutionary ideal and comes to will what the party wills, even his own death. When Gletkin finally puts a bullet in the back of Rubashov's neck it comes as no surprise to the reader. But the intellectual agreement between Rubashov and Gletkin is a stunningly powerful and thought-provoking conclusion. It spawned a controversy over the nature of the Marxian revolutionary idea and its demonstrable appeal to many intellectuals that has never abated. Indeed, *Darkness at Noon* may be the prototype and paradigmatic novel explaining such appeals.

At this point in the development of Koestler's approach to revolution many of his friends and critics alike were left with certain problems of their own regarding his exact intentions. If the political morality of both the yogi and the commissar end in disaster, and there are no other alternatives, what then is the basis for political action? Here, it must be said, Koestler was far better at diagnosing the problems than at prescribing remedies. The closest he came to exploring the contemporary basis of political activism in the light of his yogi-commissar spectrum was in his third novel, *Arrival and Departure*.

Arrival and Departure is the story of Peter Slavek, a vaguely East European refugee literally washed ashore in the country of "Neutralia" (Portugal) during the opening months of World War II. Like Koestler, Peter is a former party member who is disillusioned by the course of the revolution. Though a former commissar-type, he is not a yogi-type either. He is trying to find some halfway position between these two extremes. His problem in terms of fighting the Fascists is that outside of the movement he can find no rationale for political action. How can he act without some goal that only the Party can provide? His answer is that he cannot act, and so he remains in Neutralia, where he is confronted with conflicting arguments as to what he ought to do. As with the case of Rubashov, the central drama of the novel is in the mind of Peter as he tries to think through what he must do: rejoin the party, join the Fascists, remain neutral, or flee to England and fight for a cause that is less than perfect? Each of these choices carries certain implications in terms of a choice between what Koestler calls "expediency" versus "morality." In the end Peter chooses England, as did Koestler, but it is out of a sense of "decency" rather than moral reasoning. This is because Peter sees reason run amok in the modern world, and reason can no longer be the measure of men's deeds. Peter's choice does not make him a hero, because there is neither God nor classical reason by which his actions can be judged. Living midway between the yogi and the commissar is Koestler's equivalent to modern man's intellectual purgatory.

The reception of and reaction to Koestler's dramatic indictment of revolutionary morality was partly delayed by World War II. After the war, however, the full fury of the intellectual storm over Koestler's work began to break. The reaction in France was especially strong. The Left newspaper, *Les Temps Moderne*, edited by Jean-Paul Sartre with Maurice Merleau-Ponty, two of the most influential French philosophers, was particularly outspoken in its criticisms. Merleau-Ponty collected his articles and published them as *Humanism and Terror* (1947), the most systematic Left critique of *Darkness at Noon* in the postwar years. There was, however, a certain irony in Merleau-Ponty's defense of Stalin's purges, for in defending revolutionary terror he affirmed the truth of Koestler's portrait of Rubashov more effectively than any work defending Koestler. These acrimonious intellectual debates in France were recorded in a fictional form by Simone de Beauvoir in her *The Mandarins* (1954). The reaction to Koestler in England was slightly different. The more skeptical British habits of mind had difficulty accepting his thesis that Rubashov would confess for reasons of ideological motivation. In George Orwell's *Nineteen Eighty-Four* (1949), the victim, Winston Smith, confesses to certain crimes, but only following psychological torture—Orwell would have none of the "last service to the Party" thesis. Everywhere the debates came more and more to ask the question, What were the political motivations of the Communists and "fellow travelers" of the 1930s? Was Rubashov *really* an accurate portrait of the "typical" party member?

The psychology and personal motivations of party members and fellow travellers led to a surge in what might be termed "confessional" writings during this period—autobiographical accounts by former party members on what attracted them to the Russian revolution in the first place. Were they duped by a clever Soviet propaganda, or did they know full well what was going on and what they were doing from the beginning? The most widely read of these books was a collection of confessional accounts appropriately entitled *The God That Failed*. In it Koestler had the lead essay, and his personal account immediately took on an authority of near biblical proportions; if there is an indispensable personal account of the "Pink Decade" by a former party member it is surely this essay by Koestler. The other contributors were Ignazio Silone, André Gide, Stephen Spender, Louis Fischer, and Richard Wright. Koestler followed up this brief memoir of his party days with an impressive two-volume autobiography that took his personal story up to the eve of his joining the party in 1932, *Arrow in the Blue* (1952), and *The Invisible Writing* (1954). Autobiographical writing about the years after he left the party may be found in his fiction, essays, and historical writings, and in *The Stranger on the Square* (1983). This incomplete final volume of Koestler's autobiography, written jointly with his wife Cynthia and described as "an experimental autobiography by two hands," often presents contrasting views of Koestler's private and public life.

Koestler's last political fiction for almost two decades was *The Age of Longing* (1951). It was intended to be his final statement on the nature of politics in the mold of the yogi and the commissar. The general mood of the novel is a pessimism that is unusual even for Koestler's generally pessimistic world view. Composed during the zenith of Stalin's postwar powers, it conveys to the reader the general impression that Koestler is expecting the imminent outbreak of World War III. The setting is Paris, Bastille Day in the late 1950s—in the near-enough in the future to have a necessary element of immediacy about it. As with most of Koestler's novels, the physical action is slight. The action is almost all intellectual, in this case debates among Parisian intellectuals over the *real* threat to peace in Europe: some blame the Americans, and others the Russians; some say the threat is more spiritual than political. All of the characters, in one way or another, long for a lost faith that none has known since his youth—faith in politics or faith in God. All are caught in some sort of political halfway position that prevents them from acting effectively in politics. Evidently for Koestler, postwar Paris lacked even that sense of decency that managed to move Peter in *Arrival and Departure*.

Most of the participants in these arguments are Left intellectuals who are unable to break out of their Marxist habits of thought in order to see the world aright. Only Julien, a disillusioned former party member, understands what is going on but is unable to convince anyone else that he is right. Julien is a Cassandra who tries to speak but is mute insofar as those around him are concerned. Julien no longer believes in "the West," and appears to be motivated by no other cause than an unrelenting hostility to the "Free Commonwealth" (Koestler's euphemism for the Soviet Union). In the end no one listens, and the novel closes with rumors of Russian paratroopers landing just outside Paris. A new French underground is being formed, but without even a glimmer of the hope and spirit that animated the World War II resistance.

By the mid-1950s the polemics over the true nature of Marxism and revolution had reached a dead end for Koestler. When he bid a formal farewell to these political battles in 1955, it was not because he thought the issues had been settled, but rather, as he said, because he had nothing more original to say. He had exhausted his creative energies on the subject. Yet it is also important to note that more was involved here than a simple decision

to abandon politics. It is apparent in some of Koestler's later work, fiction and nonfiction alike, that he was searching for a more rational mode of political knowledge than was being provided by the images of the yogi and the commissar. Koestler had always been impressed by the rupture between political theory and practice; all of his novels are predicated on that assumption. But he was still troubled by the inability of modern political theory to explain adequately the most salient features of modern politics. The reason for this gap, he thought, lay in a general failure of modern scientific thinking. The paradox was that most scientists were apolitical by nature and were only dimly aware, at most, of the impact science was having on the political world. The general result of this state of affairs was a profound misunderstanding both by scientists and the general public of the limits and possibilities of modern science. This was most conspicuous for those social and political theories, such as Marxism, that claimed to be "scientific." Koestler turned to the history and study of science because he was convinced that political theory could not advance beyond the sterility of debates between the Left and the Right until both sides had a better understanding of science itself.

The failure of modern political theory, so evident in the failed revolutions of the twentieth century, were linked, Koestler argued, to certain outmoded notions of science carried over from an earlier time. Marx and the Marxists are the very embodiment of that failure since they are the children of a now obsolete view of science. Marx had argued for a class structure of knowledge because he saw the human mind formed in a materialistic and deterministic world—such were the lessons of Newton applied to political thought. But, as Koestler understood it, twentieth-century science was nonmaterialistic, at least in the nineteenth-century meaning of the term, and probabilistic in its form. And, in any case, Koestler had always held that scientific truth, whatever it might be, was independent of any particular class structure in society. All of this added up to the notion that the first order of business in the restoration of reason to human affairs was the construction of a nonmaterial, probabilistic theory of the human mind. This task required an inquiry into the very origins of modern science and into its development until the twentieth century. It was this enterprise, a new science of the human mind suitable for the twentieth century, that occupied most of Koestler's work for the next quarter-century.

Koestler's major study of the science of the

mind was in the form of a nonfiction trilogy, *The Sleepwalkers* (1959), *The Act of Creation* (1964), and *The Ghost in the Machine* (1967). In addition to these larger studies, Koestler authored several interesting diversionary excursions into sidelight areas of modern science, *The Case of the Midwife Toad* (1971), *The Roots of Coincidence* (1972), and a book he wrote with Sir Alister Hardy and Robert Harvie, *The Challenge of Chance* (1973). These last two works were serious studies of extrasensory perception (ESP) and the various implications of probability theory in human psychology. (Koestler left $600,000 to promote university study of psychic phenomena.)

The most impressive, as well as the most controversial, of Koestler's trilogy was *The Sleepwalkers*. In broad outline, it is a survey of scientific thought from the early Greeks through the Newtonian revolution in physics. The primary emphasis, however, is on the period from Copernicus through Galileo, and Koestler deals with the issue of how the science of astronomy changed man's conception of himself. What helped to make Koestler's history both unique and controversial was his thesis on how science operates and develops. He challenged the widespread notion that there is a definite line between what scientists are wont to call "superstition" and science per se. Much of the inspiration for scientific discovery comes, he said, from an awe of the supernatural. Properly understood, religion and science are not polar-opposite ways of knowing, but rather are complementary to one another. In arguing for this view of science Koestler questioned the accepted notion that scientific knowledge can be traced along a linear notion of historical development, one in which science is the progressive accumulation of knowledge and the shrinking of superstition. His basic proposition is that science proper is not necessarily progressive in character; that there is no clearly definable boundary between science and superstition (the "science" of one epoch quickly dissolves into the "superstition" of the next); and that science, instead of following a straight line of progress into the twentieth century, follows "a wild zigzag which alternates between progress and disaster."

Koestler's emphasis in *The Sleepwalkers* was on the creativity of the scientific enterprise, and he steadily denied that the act of creativity was itself a scientific phenomenon. It was a mysterious working of the mind that could not be reduced to material causes. The flaw in scientific reasoning, however, was that in the contemporary world knowledge has outstripped man's ability to control science; science now threatens to control man. The evolution of the

human mind was too slow to cope with these changes, and the very future of the human species is in jeopardy. "Progress by definition can never go wrong; evolution constantly does; and so does the evolution of ideas, including those of the 'exact sciences.' " And since natural evolution had not equipped men to deal with the objects of their own creation, Koestler was prepared to suggest that man would somehow have to wrest from nature control over his own evolution. It was the only way man could regain control over science. Here, it must be said, Koestler may have been far more insightful in diagnosing a problem of modern science than prescribing a remedy, a fact he seems to have acknowledged later in his novel *The Call-Girls* (1972).

In *The Act of Creation* and *The Ghost in the Machine*, Koestler sought to diagnose the nature of human creativity analytically, not historically as he had done in *The Sleepwalkers*. The longest and most difficult of all of Koestler's books, *The Act of Creation* is almost an encyclopedia of knowledge and of his speculative thinking on the mystery we call "human creativity." He begins his study with an impressive inquiry into various forms of creativity—humor, wisdom, poetry, art, and creative writing. All of these acts of creation must be understood within a hierarchy of knowledge that tends to abolish any relevant distinctions between "wholes" and "parts" that is the way most scientists classify knowledge. It is a curious hierarchy without an apex because each apparent whole is in reality but a part of a larger whole; no whole or part can be understood as an end in and of itself. Wholes and parts present themselves to the mind with what Koestler calls a "Janus effect." "The members of a hierarchy, like the Roman god Janus, all have two faces looking in opposite directions." Wholes and parts are linked only through the mind in a mysterious joining of these wholes and parts that is the very essence of the act of scientific creation. The basic principles of this conception of hierarchy can be stated as follows:

> *The laws of the higher cannot be reduced to, nor predicted from the lower level; the phenomenon of the lower level and their laws are implied in the higher level, but the phenomenon of the higher order if manifest in the lower level appear as unexplainable and miraculous.*

These relationships between parts and wholes are the ultimate objects of science, but the linkage between them, through the workings of the human mind, is not itself a scientific act. It is one of the defects of the contemporary science of the mind, by which Koestler means primarily the behavioral psychology of B. F. Skinner and company, that it continues to operate not only from mechanistic assumptions but also as if wholes and parts of reality are in fact radically separate entities. Behavioral psychology, in brief, repeats all of the old, materialistic assumptions about the mind that have led Marxists into the abyss of Stalin's totalitarian politics. Unless the behaviorists alter their understanding of science they will inevitably be led into the same fatal errors of the commissar's ethos. In *The Ghost and the Machine* Koestler delivers his most devastating critique of behaviorism: "An age is drawing to a close in the history of psychology: the age of the dehumanization of man. Words like 'purpose,' 'volition,' 'introspection,' 'consciousness,' 'insight,' words which have been banned as obscene from the vocabulary of the so-called 'Behavioral Sciences,' are triumphantly reasserting themselves—not as abstract philosophical concepts, but as indispensable descriptive tools without which even a rat's actions in an experimental maze do not make sense."

Although Koestler thought that behaviorism would collapse of its own internal contradictions and the accumulated weight of scientific knowledge, he was not optimistic about the ultimate future of a rational science of the mind. His science had a certain quality of desperation about it that grew more pronounced with the passage of time—as if science were "the god that must not fail." He saw science in general as the last line of resistance against a chaotic, threatening, and perhaps even demonic universe. Since political revolution could not cure the dilemmas of the human condition, science was the only other alternative. But he did not really expect this to happen. Rationality and civility were a thin veneer over man as a species of animal that had not really evolved very much since genesis. In his essay on capital punishment, he wrote, "Deep inside every civilized being there lurks a tiny Stone Age man, dangling a club to rob and rape, and screaming an eye for an eye." The application of science to the ills of the human condition required at a minimum two preconditions. First, the *right* science had to be chosen for application. How could this be done when most working scientists still thought in terms of parts and wholes that are distinct from one another? Second, any application of science implied a conscious political act. How could the cure be applied without encountering the old nemesis of political action, the images of the yogi and the commissar? This problem of trying to bring modern science to bear on

politics was the subject of his last work of fiction, *The Call-Girls*.

The Call-Girls may be the least read of all Koestler's fiction. This is most unfortunate, because it may also be his best work after *Darkness at Noon*. Surely his wittiest and most playful book, it displays a strong sense of humor that readers of Koestler's other work might not have suspected. The setting is an academic conference, high in a remote Alpine village, where the greatest scientific minds of the age have been assembled for the express purpose of formulating a "plan" for the salvation of mankind through science. The pretentious title of the conference is "Approaches to Survival," and it has been hastily called by Nobel Prize-winning physicist Nikolai Solovief, one of the original members of the "Manhattan Project" team that built the first atomic bomb. The other almost equally distinguished participants represent a broad spectrum of scholarly, scientific opinion on the science of the human mind as it is currently understood. The tragedy of the conference is that each of these scientists has only a partial view of science qua science but fervently believes that their part is a whole. Naturally these various parts are logically incompatible and there is no agreement on what would constitute a viable synthesis between them. Furthermore, even if the participants could agree on a single course of action and proposal, there is considerable doubt that any government would pay any attention to them.

The various scientific ideas are presented in the form of academic papers, read and debated at the conference. Here Koestler is at his best in breathing life into the scientific controversies that are normally only matters of esoteric interest for specialists. As for the specific proposals, they range from the bizarre to the frightening to the oddly plausible. But while the reader may be intrigued by arguments that he has never heard before, the participants themselves are engaged in a sham debate. They know each other intimately, having delivered these same papers repeatedly at previous conferences, and they are even then preparing to leave for still more conferences where the same issues will be rehashed again. Each of these intellectual "call girls" resembles a modern Sisyphus, endlessly and impotently struggling against something inevitable. But Koestler also leaves the reader with the impression that much of what is produced by modern science may have much in common with the Augean stables without a Hercules to clean them out. In the end the conference breaks up with predictably nothing to show for the efforts. The participants depart for their next conference with the threat of World War

III in the background. "In view of the international situation, however, nobody could be sure whether they would reach their destination."

With *The Call-Girls* even science had apparently exhausted itself as a subject of interest for Koestler. In *The Thirteenth Tribe* (1976) he attempted to trace the origins of European Jewry to a non-Semitic people. His basic thesis was that the roots of European anti-Semitism were irrational because European Jews were not really Semitic people to begin with. Koestler's history was, to say the least, controversial. Most serious scholars of the subject dismissed the book rather curtly, and rightly so. It was an unfortunate epitaph for his scattered writings on Israel and Jewish affairs. His earlier novel on life in an Israeli kibbutz, *Thieves in the Night* (1946), and his reporting of the creation of Israel in *Promise and Fulfillment* (1949), were and remain interesting, though relatively minor, pieces of Koestler's work.

Even in death Arthur Koestler was characteristically controversial. He died in a double suicide with his wife—a suicide evidently prompted by the twin effects of leukemia and Parkinson's disease on his health. The Koestlers were members of the Voluntary Euthanasia Society, EXIT. Koestler became one of its vice-presidents in 1981, writing a preface to the group's *Guide to Self-Deliverance* on how to commit suicide. Humans, he wrote, unlike animals, do not die "peacefully and without fuss in old age." Koestler's death was apparently peaceful, unlike the demise of his fictional commissars.

References:

Jeni Calder, *Chronicles of Conscience. A Study of George Orwell and Arthur Koestler* (London: Secker & Warburg, 1968);

Pierre Debray-Ritzen, *Arthur Koestler* (Paris: Herne, 1975);

Iain Hamilton, *Koestler. A Biography* (New York: Macmillan, 1982);

Harold Harris, ed., *Astride the Two Cultures—Arthur Koestler at 70* (London: Hutchinson, 1975);

Sidney A. Pearson, Jr., *Arthur Koestler* (Boston: G. K. Hall, 1978).

A TRIBUTE

from J. M. FOX

Arthur Koestler's was one of the most important voices of our time, and Random House was honored to be his publisher. He was an enormously stimulating man, and one could see, through his conversations, an amazing mind at work. His works will endure as a testament to all that he saw, all that he suffered, all that he knew.

A TRIBUTE

from SIR FITZROY MACLEAN

In my view *Darkness at Noon* is one of the few really significant political novels of this century.

Kenneth Millar
(13 December 1915-11 July 1983)

Matthew J. Bruccoli

See also the Millar entry in *DLB 2, American Novelists Since World War II.*

Kenneth Millar/John Macdonald/John Ross Macdonald/Ross Macdonald/Lew Archer died in Santa Barbara, California, on 11 July 1983 after twenty-four novels. He had long been acknowledged as one of the big three—along with Hammett and Chandler—of the American hard-boiled detective novel. In the main he was comfortable in this category, which allowed him to reach the cross-section of the reading public he sought; and during

the last decade of his life he enjoyed the degree of recognition and sales that would gratify any writer.

Kenneth Millar expanded the private-eye genre and discovered its mythmaking capacities. Nonetheless, an attempt to assess his career properly must judge him as a novelist who wrote mysteries, not as a mystery writer—that is, against the whole field of American fiction. The seriousness of Millar's commitment to popular literature is documented by his introduction to *Great Stories of Suspense*, which he edited in 1974: suspense fiction "keeps the forms of the art alive for the writer to

Kenneth Millar, 1961 (Ray Borges,
Santa Barbara News-Press*)*

use. It trains his readers, endowing both writer and reader with a common vocabulary of structures and shapes and narrative possibilities. It becomes a part of the language in which we think and feel, reaching our whole society and helping to hold our civilization together."

It is too early to make such an assessment with a claim to finality; but it can be anticipated that time will be posthumously kind to Millar, as it was often unkind to him during his lifetime. *Time* is what he wrote about. Beginning with *The Galton Case* in 1959 he explored the consequences of the buried but unabsolved past. The twelve novels from *The Galton Case* to *The Blue Hammer* (1976) constitute a quest cycle; taken together, they form one of the splendid achievements in American fiction.

Kenneth Millar was born in Los Gatos, California, in 1915 to Canadian parents. When his father abandoned them in 1919, Kenneth and his mother went to Canada, where he suffered through a pauper childhood. He graduated from the University of Western Ontario in 1938, the year he married Margaret Sturm. As a graduate student at the University of Michigan, he wrote his first suspense novel, *The Dark Tunnel* (1944), after his wife

had commenced her highly successful writing career as Margaret Millar. He served in the U.S. Navy during World War II, and then settled in Santa Barbara as a full-time writer—with an interruption to complete his Ph.D. in English, for which he wrote a dissertation on Coleridge.

After four novels as Kenneth Millar, he published his first Lew Archer novel, *The Moving Target*, in 1949 under the John Macdonald by-line. After five novels as John Ross Macdonald, he fixed on Ross Macdonald in 1956 with *The Barbarous Coast*. During the 1960s—his most brilliant period—he published *The Ferguson Affair*, *The Wycherly Woman*, *The Zebra-Striped Hearse*, *The Chill*, *The Far Side of the Dollar*, *Black Money*, *The Instant Enemy*, and *The Goodbye Look*.

Since Ken honored me with his friendship, a personal note may be appropriate here. We had no common interests apart from literature, and Ken abandoned his attempts to share his strong ecological and ornithological concerns with me. When we talked books he was impressive; Ken was one of the two best-read authors I have known. But we spent as much time not talking as talking. He was a quiet man who could participate in a conversation by sitting in silence while smiling quizzically. I never penetrated his reserve, which seemed to result from a fundamental sadness. Not a bitterness or gloom or resignation, but a tranquil sadness—perhaps even a cheerful sadness. Only in his letters did he approach expansiveness:

> I sometimes regret the amount of writing and preparation that went into my graduate work. But the truth is I don't much regret anything. My life has been very interesting, the more so as I turn it over on fiction and retrospect. Perhaps one of these days the auto-critico-biographical bug will bite me hard where it hurts, and I'll have to write my way out of its clutches.

Ken was a generous man as well as a gentle man. His kindness to writers was remarkable, and he was a soft touch for a blurb or an interview or an encouraging letter. There is a rule that holds: If you like his books, avoid the author. This rule did not apply to Ken Millar.

The Foundation for Santa Barbara City College has established the Kenneth Millar Memorial Fund. Contributions may be sent to 310 West Padre Street, Santa Barbara, California, 93105.

First editions

References:

Matthew J. Bruccoli, *Kenneth Millar/Ross Macdonald: A Descriptive Bibliography* (Pittsburgh: University of Pittsburgh Press, 1983);

Bruccoli, *Ross Macdonald* (San Diego, New York, & London: Harcourt Brace Jovanovich, 1984).

A TRIBUTE

from MICHAEL AVALLONE

First, there was Dashiell Hammett, then Raymond Chandler, and Bad Boy Spillane came along to dominate the field of private detective writing. Sometime in the late 1940s, 1949 to be exact, *The Moving Target* entered the scene. The story was good, the prose clean and neat, and the eye named Lew Archer seemed to have something to say besides *"I had a shot of rye while I opened my mail."* So few critics really noticed. But real pros did—writing pros, that is.

So it was that the 1950s came and went and during the decade the John Ross Macdonald by-line was satisfying insurance of superior first-person narrator tales. The *milieu*, the mood, the clear thinking were first-rate. And all the critics were still talking about Hammett, Chandler, Spillane, and various upstarts named Spicer, Prather, Avallone, Carter Brown, and Halliday. Yet—and yet—John

Ross Macdonald, who dropped the "John" to please and no longer confuse his work with that of *the* John McDonald—was carving out a solid reputation. Hammett was genuinely hard-boiled and unfunny; Chandler was soft-boiled and funny. Ross Macdonald rose bloodlessly between the two styles of writing, more Chandler than Hammett but still with a sound of his own. That peculiar, individual *thing* which all really great writers strive for—and *have*. Other writers will *use* someone else's sound—imitate, plagiarize—but the Ross Macdonalds *own* it. And finally when Paul Newman, with his nonsense about the letter *H*, starred in *Harper*, the world discovered Ross Macdonald and the critics formally came out into the open and hailed a new conquering hero. The rest of us had known it all along.

I always called him Ross Mack to distinguish him from John Mack—though their prose, fortunately, is as far apart as the poles. When he acknowledged my title as the Fastest Typewriter In The East, he claimed *"the slowest ballpen in the West."* He wrote letters addressed to *Edwina Noone* sometimes and signed them *Louisa Archer*. When I twitted him once with "Do you Ken Millar with his prose so gray——?" he pealed back with a limerick that is a comic gem.

I always knew where I stood with him. When Alfred Knopf threw a prepublication party for him—and *The Blue Hammer*—I was the only writer present on the premises. The rest were publishers, newspapermen, and editors. The Mystery Writers of America had never understood him, and only got on the bandwagon when the rest of the literary world hailed him.

Being privy to the MWA scene, New York-headquarters-wise, since 1952 and on up through 1980, I was more than aware of all this. Ken, who was a pleasant cross between Gig Young and Robert Montgomery, was the gentlest and nicest of men. He ragged and rapped nobody. I never had his ability to suffer silently, but I was one up on him. He grew up reading Hammett and Chandler before he essayed our field. I had Hammett and Chandler *and* Ross Macdonald. . . .

My salute and acknowledgement to him is on the dedication of *Shoot It Again, Sam*, the definitive Ed Noon novel, as far as I am concerned. He thought so too—and that is good enough for me.

So—goodbye to a great one—he was my people, "One of Us," and if there is a pantheon for writers of the private detective story, he most certainly is there. I've said it before, many times, and I'll say it again. The three greatest executors of the form—Hammett (third person), Chandler (first person), and Macdonald (an amalgam of both formats)—there can be little argument about that. Many writers have had a fine single-shot at the field—Latimer, Prather, Michel, Spicer—but for a body of work, more than one, the Father, the Son, and the Holy Ghost—Dash, Ray, and Ken most certainly are the leaders of the pack.

The rest of us can fight for fourth place.

The private detective novel has been bastardized, parodized, butchered, slaughtered, and generally had to play second fiddle to the armchair boys and girls—thank God, there was a Ken Millar to give it the class it so richly deserves. Agatha Christie and Ellery Queen would talk to Ken.

He never wrote what he did not mean and feel and believe.

He never joined the trends, the fads, the commercial "musts."

He made a town his own staked-out property, the same way Fitzgerald, Faulkner, Derleth, Caldwell, and Cain did.

I honor him for all of that.

But most of all, I remember the gentle intellect that went with the territory. He was a gentleman in my era—one that held so few.

Thank God for the books.

Ken will live forever, now.

A TRIBUTE

from ROBERT EASTON

"Stay with it and it will stay with you," Ken Millar advised me gently but firmly as I entered my third year of work on a long book.

So, during thirty years of friendship, Ken stayed with me. We met first at an informal gathering of what later became known as the Santa Barbara Writers Luncheon. All five of us fitted into one booth at Harry's Cafe on lower State Street. I thought I'd never encountered anyone so taciturn, so prickly, as this sturdy baby-faced blue-eyed unsmiling unblinking Kenneth Millar.

At times he seemed downright rude. Hostility toward life apparently including me seemed to seethe just beneath his surface.

I learned later his manner concealed a sensitive, generous spirit of extraordinary perception and loyalty and was almost certainly the result of painful early experience.

His father abandoned Ken and his mother when Ken was four; they nearly starved, actually and emotionally.

So desperate did their condition become that

Ken's mother took him as far as the gates of an orphanage, resolved to give him up, but changed her mind at the last moment. Ken never forgot those gates. They remained in his mind like the gates of hell. Life became a chamber of horrors through which he passed at great peril.

"My father condemned me to a childhood of terrible deprivation," he once told me bitterly.

Yet Ken loved his father dearly. Much of his later writing was devoted to reconciling conflicting feelings about his father, controlling the keen resentments roused in him so young.

Thus Ken was early a victim of human error. His fictional alter ego Lew Archer, the detective hero of his novels, deals with similar victims. Archer himself is a victim who courageously struggles against the circumstances of his own difficult life and those of other people's.

Archer, the gallant victim, the helper of victims, the relentless foe of victimizers, is Ken's metaphor for himself and for most of us in the human condition. Understanding this I think we understand Ken and his work much more clearly. He saw life essentially as a struggle between victims and victim-makers.

Anyone, anything, being victimized reminded Ken of his own painful experience and was apt to rouse a fiercely personal response. Fresh out of college and traveling in Germany in 1937, he saw what Hitler was doing to the German people and might soon do to others. It helped make Ken an activist in political and social matters. As a volunteer naval officer during World War II he wholly—and characteristically—committed himself to the struggle against something which aroused his fierce anger: Hitler, the supreme example of victim-maker.

Here in Santa Barbara in the early '60s when the desperate plight of another endangered species, the California condor, became apparent, Ken again committed himself in typically forthright fashion. Again, it was human error which was responsible for the condor's decline. Ken saw the condor as a symbol for all of us. "The condor is like the canary in the coal mine. When the canary languishes the atmosphere is hostile to human life too!"

There were committee meetings, phone calls, hearings, media appearances, letters to editors, all the tedium of effort required to influence private and public opinion. Ken devoted time that he could ill afford to this struggle but gave gladly and became a leader in the ongoing effort to save the condor and its wilderness habitats.

Walking on Mountain Drive one day, looking out over Santa Barbara as we liked to do, we watched its beautiful waterfront being threatened by an ugly black oil slick from a blown-out offshore well. In indignation we asked ourselves: "How can we turn this catastrophe to some useful purpose?"

With thousands of others we'd already engaged in a variety of protests. Now we determined to make the oil spill the biggest symbol we could of man's victimization of his natural surroundings and those creatures who share them with us.

Ken wrote a powerful introduction to my factual book about the oil spill and its significance, *Black Tide* (1972). I helped with his fictional treatment of it in *Sleeping Beauty* (1972), perhaps the first environmental detective novel.

We collaborated more fully in an article, "Santa Barbarans Cite an 11th Commandment: Thou Shalt Not Abuse the Earth," about the oil spill for the *New York Times Magazine*. It may have been Ken's only published collaboration. For me it was like collaborating with a porcupine. Had I not known the quills were not as deadly as they seemed, our friendship might not have survived.

After a particularly irascible session, Ken would phone me and apologize, or I do likewise.

Ken valued his friendships deeply and had many—some with people he never knew except by correspondence, some with young writers who sought his advice and whom he felt needed encouraging, some with people in nearly every walk of life who perceived the true person beneath the often difficult exterior.

Environmental concerns by now had become part of Ken's feeling for the human condition as a whole. In his next novel, *The Blue Hammer* (1976), deadly air pollution threatens to obscure the reader's view of an imaginary city-society which is in fact Santa Barbara.

Ken thought it ironic Ronald Reagan should buy a ranch near here. During the height of the oil spill, when Reagan was governor, he never visited Santa Barbara, though President Nixon did, as did Democratic party leader Senator Muskie. Reagan seemed willing to let Santa Barbara be the victim of corporate oil's heedlessness. After enormous citizen effort prevented the area from becoming an oil field, Reagan settled in and waxed eloquent over its beauty.

As his fellow Santa Barbaran D. J. Palladino points out, Ken felt a particular concern for women as victims. He believed women in our society had been essentially victimized. He brought more women into the detective novel in more different ways than anyone before him. Even when his women are murderers they have been victims, and we sense his sympathy for them.

In the end as in the beginning the victim was Ken. He accepted the inevitable with the laconic wisdom of Lew Archer and a wry smile. For twenty years we'd been exchanging and criticizing each other's manuscripts before publication; as usual I asked if he would read my latest. "I'd better not," he said in his customary unblinking fashion. "I'm losing my memory."

He was in the grip of Alzheimer's disease. But he made no claim for sympathy, no protest against fate.

All of us who live on this earth are victims in the largest possible sense, he seemed to be saying. We must submit. But we need not surrender.

A TRIBUTE
from WILLIAM CAMPBELL GAULT

Two incidents I remember. At the Writers Lunch one day, Ken and I were discussing a writer we both admire, F. Scott Fitzgerald. A publisher got into what had been a dialogue by saying, "I have never been able to understand why he is so admired. I didn't like *The Great Gatsby*."

Ken gave him his nonconcerned stare and said, "Two writers have agreed on the man. It really doesn't matter what a publisher thinks of the book."

I agreed with him on that, and still do.

I proofread *The Blue Hammer* for him, and he gave me the script on the country club parking lot, as it was near his home. He also picked up the script there several weeks later. Both days were dark, gloomy, and windy. Margaret, who brought him there, thought it was quite a scene, like two foreign double-agents exchanging top secret documents. In *The Blue Hammer*, Ken wrote under the dedication to me: "Who knows that writing well is the best revenge, with admiration, Ken." Last offer I got for the book was seven hundred dollars; I said no.

Not all mystery writers are literate, so many of them didn't understand his prose. They grew up on the bang-bang, big-tit circuit in the pulps. But all of them admitted he was a solid and responsible professional who had helped many young writers.

A TRIBUTE
from JOE GORES

My relationship with Ken Millar's work—under his then-pseudonym of John Ross Macdonald—began when I ran across a two-bit Bantam paperback called *The Name Is Archer* while a graduate student at Stanford in 1955. It had a bilious green cover with a picture of a grey-faced gent wearing world-weary eyes and a revolver.

Inside were seven stories. Shocking stories to me, because they were exactly the kind of stories I wished I could write—and couldn't. I went back to find a copy of *The Moving Target*—the first Archer novel (1949)—and read my way forward through the oeuvre. His early work followed that of Hammett and Chandler in creating, shaping, and defining the American private detective novel, while at the same time lifting it from the pulps to a permanent place in American literature. Once I was current, it was hardcover purchase on the day his novels appeared in the bookstores, until there were no more books to purchase.

In *The Galton Case* (1959) Ken overcame what he called his "autobiographical embarrassment" and started to use fictionalized and transfigured elements of his own life in his novels. This was a watershed book, the one in which he shook free of the Chandler influence and began to speak in his own unique voice.

Unfortunately, it also carried the seeds of Ken's "father hunt"—his increasing obsession with detective novels in which some crime of the past was more important to his characters than their lives in the present. In these later books, his own lost father became the metaphor for lost people of the past—perhaps too literally, for quite often a long-dead or long-missing father was at the core of the story.

His novels moved further and further from the tradition out of which they had sprung, and more and more into sociology and psychology. Lew Archer became less a private eye and more an amateur psychiatrist. No longer personally involved, he became thinner than Hammett's thin man. This was done deliberately; Ken once told me that he wanted his detective hero to no longer cast a shadow.

This freed Ken of the genre restrictions but had an unforeseen limiting effect. He avoided these limitations himself by reducing Archer's personal involvement in his cases to the point where if he turned sideways he was invisible, but for those following him it became almost de rigueur for one's detective hero to be full of angst and to profess disgust at his own profession. They felt their protagonist had to be contemptuous of what he did for a living—a far cry from Hammett's professional manhunter who gloried in his ability to do a tough and sometimes dirty job better than anyone else.

Because of Ken's emancipation from his genre roots, the classic detective novel of the lone man going down those mean streets perhaps can no longer successfully be written. Not seriously. It can only be parodied, pastiched, or used to self-consciously evoke a time long dead. A final (and fine) echo of the form exists in the best of Robert Parker's Spenser novels, but they succeed only because they are novels of mores trying to answer the question: What is a man? They are hardly crime novels at all.

My relationship with Ken himself began over ten years after I had discovered his work. At that time I was in charge of the Northern California Chapter of Mystery Writers of America, and had to put together the monthly programs. I called Ken at his Santa Barbara home to ask him up to San Francisco as a guest speaker.

He responded by sending me bound galleys of Peter Dickinson's fine, enigmatic first novel, *The Glass-Sided Ant's Nest*, because he thought it singular. Letters and more phone calls followed, and a time finally was set. Our first meeting in person was in May 1968. He came to San Francisco alone; Margaret had to remain home because one of their dogs was blind and they were passionately attached to it.

Ken spoke on *"The Galton Case* and How It Grew." While being photographed under the brass plaque at the mouth of Burritt alley commemorating the death of Miles Archer in *The Maltese Falcon*, he remarked that he had named his detective hero after Archer as a conscious tribute to Hammett.

The next day he and I drove north across the Golden Gate Bridge for a day of bird-watching along the Marin headlands and coastline. Bird-watching was a positive passion of Ken's and a minor avocation of mine (since I have moved out of the city it has become a major passion for me as well).

He wanted to visit a bird-banding station off Mesa Road on the hunch-shouldered, wind-swept hills above Point Bolinas. Everyone there knew him, not as a writer but as a conservationist; we were allowed to tramp out to the gathering nets where the various species are trapped, banded, and released in the process of mapping their migration patterns and flyways.

His other "must" spot was an old white frame farmhouse set back from Shoreline Highway along the eastern edge of the Bolinas Lagoon. It looks like an ordinary farm from the road; but in the crowded hardwoods behind and above the house is a major rookery for the tree-nesting white egrets and blue herons which inhabit the lagoon. Five years later,

when I was working on the novel *Hammett*, I set a couple of key scenes at this lonely farmhouse now owned by the American Audubon Society.

Something else I got from the day: a rekindled interest in wildlife and the outdoors. I spent my youth along the Mississippi River, hunting, fishing, and observing nature. I also had spent three years in East Africa, much of it in game areas, the *bundu*, and in climbing mountains. But from 1965 until Ken's visit, I had been totally urban, either manhunting or at the typewriter. Ken reminded me of all those years outside the city limits, and of what they had meant to me.

Because Ken got the backgrounds for his novels from haunting the Santa Barbara courtrooms during criminal cases, he sometimes sought more firsthand material. He needed a sleazy repossessor-type character; I sketched one for him out of my own years in that business during our drive back to my apartment in the city. The grubby little fellow turned up in *The Goodbye Look* in 1969.

Ken felt there were patterns in people's lives by which they were brought together for a time, then the pattern changed and they drifted apart again. On Monday morning, he returned to Santa Barbara. We exchanged a few more letters, then the correspondence dropped. Our phone calls stopped. I saw him once more in San Francisco in 1971, once in New York, a time or two in Santa Barbara when I was passing through on my way to Los Angeles.

By the time of his death, we had not been in touch for nearly ten years. We never spoke to one another of birds, animals, or the outdoors again after that day in Bolinas.

A TRIBUTE

from ASHBEL GREEN

After the publication of *The Blue Hammer*, Ken Millar worked on a screenplay of *The Instant Enemy* for a couple of years. He didn't get back to writing novels. Concern over Margaret's cancer and her eyesight occupied him, and there were the beginnings of his own illness. On 3 September 1979 he wrote me: "I've been back at my desk for a short time, not making very much progress or very much noise. I seem to have been touched by the encroachments of age, which I suppose might naturally enough show themselves in the late months of my sixty-fourth year. The trouble seems to be lifting—even though no doctor could give it a name more searching than high blood pressure and the like—and while I can't certainly predict the future, it will surely allow me further writing." That fall, almost as a goad to himself, he decided to sign a contract for his next novel—in the past he would always deliver a manuscript and then make a contract.

In one of Ken's last letters to me, dated 3 February 1980, he wrote: "The less delightful people with whom I consort in fiction are slow to come to my bidding, but they're coming. I have some tentative ideas, and underlying them some new approaches, I think to the Archer story. You will forgive me if I say no more: my later books have been slow to bring in but I trust worth the carriage."

The knowledge that we will have no more books by Ross Macdonald leaves me inconsolably sad. Ken gave so much pleasure to his readers, and so much of his intelligence, that his death is irreparable. When the voice of a writer like Ross Macdonald is stilled, more than his family and friends are deprived. There are legions who have lost a companion, a soul mate, a source of enjoyment, a writer who reached into the hearts and minds of his readers.

A TRIBUTE

from HERBERT HARKER

On page one of *The Goodbye Look*, Lew Archer's way into his client's office is blocked by a pink-haired receptionist who bats her eyes at him and complains about her photographer husband. "His pictures never did me justice."

Archer reflects, "It was mercy she needed."

With one swift stroke, executed with such droll indirection that we almost miss it, Kenneth Millar (Ross Macdonald) establishes the matter of his book, and reminds us again that one of the great concerns of his life, and of his work, was the delicate motion of the winds that sift the chaff of justice.

His fiction is filled with characters who do cruel, or vicious, or destructive things. But with Millar the fundamental question is not who, but why. We cry out for justice, when often what we really need is mercy. And in the end his characters receive from divine justice, as he called it, punishment appropriate to the circumstances surrounding their crime. Thus, in Lew Archer's world, it is not obligatory that a murderer should die.

Millar was, of course, concerned with personal justice—the ways in which we humans strive to achieve it, both individually and through our institutions. On a larger scale, he was suspicious of power. He understood the way the world is held together by connections—"casual web" he called it—and he continually sought to strengthen or weaken some of the cords. During the Santa Barbara oil spill in 1969, I watched him destroy his Union Oil Credit Card. It was not an act he took pleasure in, nor did he express any malice. A snip of the shears tokened his separation from the despoilers. Then, not content to rest on his symbolic act (true symbols do not exist outside the reality they represent), he joined his friends and like-minded citizens in around-the-clock picketing of the oil activity at Stearn's Wharf. For the rest of his life he was involved in the effort to stop the drilling in Santa Barbara Channel.

In one sense he was an historian, giving us the authentic record of a time and place. But he also wrote prophecy, not as a man of God—the idea would have repelled him—but as a clear-eyed mortal warning us of the inevitable destination of our present course; telling us that it is not too late. He did more than write about it. He participated in meetings, organizations, picketing, and protests directed toward preserving our natural world.

He lived a simple life, each day very much like the one that preceded it. His time was spent writing, swimming, reading, writing letters, conversing, exercising his dogs, bird-watching. He rarely traveled. He cared little for possessions. He lived in an exclusive suburb because it gave him the privacy and quiet he needed for his work. He got his clothes at J. C. Penney. When he was about sixty he bought a BMW. It pleased him to believe that this was the last car he'd ever have to buy. He was wrong; he outlasted it.

Some people can view injustice with a measure of tolerance because they envision a balancing of the scales in the hereafter. Then the wicked will get their comeuppance, and the righteous their reward. This paliating thought, if such it be, was not available to Ken. He did not believe in an afterlife—if justice was ever to be done, it must be now. Men are vulnerable, he seemed to say, and dependent on each other for salvation, being wholly mortal.

Ken, too, was mortal. But whereas he was able to buy another car when the time came, where will we turn to find another Kenneth Millar? We won't. Kings and generals can be replaced, but a man like Ken Millar has not assumed an office—he has created it. Nobody can take it from him, and nobody can inherit it when he is gone. He holds it for life, and for as long afterward as his words endure. A hundred years from now, people will see in Lew Archer the representation of decent 20th Century Man, doggedly struggling to right the wrongs of a brutal and uncaring society. And if the world they sit and read in has any forests left, or birds, or wetlands, or clean oceans, or clear moral choices, those readers can do worse than tip a grateful hat in the direction of Kenneth Millar.

A TRIBUTE
from DENNIS LYNDS (MICHAEL COLLINS)

On 11 July 1983, five months and two days short of his sixty-eighth birthday and seven years after the publication of his final novel, at the end of a long illness that had left him unable to write, an American novelist died.

A novelist, not a mystery writer, because a novelist was what Ken Millar considered himself and what Ross Macdonald was. When, belatedly, he reached a wide audience in the early 1970s, people would ask Ken when he was going to write his "big" novel, his "real" novel. He would smile that small smile, say something neutral, but, later, say to me, "What do they think I've been writing all these years?"

What he had been writing were twenty-four novels trying to understand life in this universe and his place in it the same as any other artist. Eighteen of the twenty-four feature private investigator Lew Archer, and in the middle of these eighteen are at least a dozen of the best psychological novels of his or any other time. It is these novels, in which the very human voice of Lew Archer tells hot and dangerous stories from his own time and his own life, that Ross Macdonald leaves the world. What he left me and his other fellow writers was something else.

When I met Ken in 1965, I had published two novels and a number of stories, but I had not yet written my own suspense novels, had not read the novels of Ross Macdonald. I read them immediately—Ken was so obviously a man of exceptional literary commitment that I knew at once his books had to be exceptional. And they were. They were novels to admire, to respect, and, perhaps, to follow. Was it possible that the *roman noir* as Ken was using it was what I had been looking for to tell some stories I wanted to tell? We talked often back then—at the fortnightly Writers Lunch, during walks on the beach, at his swimming club,

strolling up and down State Street after the lunches—and it was these conversations, plus the example of his novels, that convinced me serious work could be done in the form of the American detective novel. Ken showed me what could be done, then helped me find a publisher, and I will always be grateful for both.

Why does a writer choose to spend his life working in what is considered a limited, secondary form rather than follow the mainstream to his own personal form? I expect there are as many answers as there are writers. I have my explanations and Ken had his, but explanations are really only reasons we give ourselves and the true answers may have to wait for our future critics. And do we need explanations? Conrad had no need to explain why he wrote "adventure" novels in "exotic" locales or used a narrator involved in the action, as Lew Archer is, but not at the center of the action, as Lew Archer is not. Conrad needed Marlowe for his purposes, and Ken needed Lew Archer for his. Ross Macdonald's novels are no more "just" mysteries than *Nostromo* is just a thriller or *Moby-Dick* just a whaling yarn.

Ken belonged not to the tradition of Christie and P. D. James, Van Dine and Gardner, Halliday and Spillane, but to the larger American line of Hawthorne and Melville, Dreiser and Crane, Hemingway and Faulkner, and he brought to the mystery/suspense/hard-boiled *roman noir* his own direction and his own voice. It was a unique voice. A voice to listen to and to savor. A voice and a direction that gave to me and his other fellow writers a liberation of what could be done with our form if we had the skill and the seriousness and the daring.

It is this expansion of what was possible in the form of the detective novel that is the true contribution of Ken Millar, the legacy of Ross Macdonald. He proved once again that an artist can do unique, serious, even important work in any form with any materials. He showed that there can be so much more to any genre than momentary amusement, parlor games, vicarious thrills, or voyeurism. He opened the way for the rest of us to take the form anywhere we have the need to take it.

Ken Millar, Ross Macdonald, forever expanded the range of his form, left the art in which he worked more than it had been when he came to it.

Mary Renault
(Eileen Mary Challans)

(4 September 1905-13 December 1983)

Joseph Cotter
Pennsylvania State University

BOOKS: *Purposes of Love* (London: Longmans, Green, 1939); republished as *Promise of Love* (New York: Morrow, 1939);

Kind Are Her Answers (London: Longmans, Green, 1940; New York: Morrow, 1940);

The Friendly Young Ladies (London: Longmans, Green, 1944); republished as *The Middle Mist* (New York: Morrow, 1945);

Return to Night (London: Longmans, Green, 1947; New York: Morrow, 1947);

North Face (New York: Morrow, 1948; London: Longmans, Green, 1949);

The Charioteer (London: Longmans, Green, 1953; New York: Pantheon, 1959);

The Last of the Wine (New York: Pantheon, 1956; London: Longmans, Green, 1956);

The King Must Die (New York: Pantheon, 1958; London: Longmans, Green, 1958);

The Bull from the Sea (New York: Pantheon, 1962; London: Longmans, 1962);

The Lion in the Gateway (London: Longmans, Green, 1964; New York: Harper & Row, 1964);

The Mask of Apollo (New York: Pantheon, 1966; London: Longmans, Green, 1966);

Fire from Heaven (New York: Pantheon, 1969; London: Harlow, Longman, 1970);

The Persian Boy (New York: Pantheon, 1972; London: Longman, 1972);

The Nature of Alexander (London: Allen Lane, 1975; New York: Pantheon, 1975);

The Praise Singer (New York: Pantheon, 1978; London: John Murray, 1979);

Funeral Games (New York: Pantheon, 1981; London: John Murray, 1981).

OTHER: Charles Kingsley, *Theseus; a Greek Legend Retold*, afterword by Renault (New York: Macmillan, 1964);

"Notes on *The King Must Die*," in *Afterwords: Novelists on their Novels*, edited by Thomas McCormack (New York & London: Harper & Row, 1969), pp. 80-87;

Mary Renault (Philip De Vos)

Arthur Conan Doyle, *Sir Nigel*, introduction by Renault (London: John Murray, 1975);

"According to Celsus," in *Women Writing, 3*, edited by Denys Val Baker (London: Sidgwick & Jackson, 1980), pp. 23-34.

PERIODICAL PUBLICATIONS: "Amazons," *Greek Heritage*, 1 (Spring 1964): 18-23;

"A Man Who Survived Transition," *New York Times Book Review*, 15 August 1965, pp. 1, 20;

"History in Fiction," *Times Literary Supplement*, 23 March 1973, pp. 315-316.

The books of Mary Renault, the pseudonym of Eileen Mary Challans, fall into two groups—the earlier, set in contemporary England; and the later, set in ancient Greece. Her first six novels were a series of psychologically charged love stories played out against the background of a sharply observed segment of English middle-class society: nurses, doctors, and patients; hospitals, dormitories, and Oxford; the wartime strains of 1939 and the early 1940s—all reflecting her years of experience as a practicing nurse. This early work was generally well received in both the English and the American press: to Charles Lee, writing in the *New York Times Book Review* (20 April 1947, p. 4), she was "an artist to her finger tips." *Return to Night* (1947), her fourth novel and the one which elicited Lee's compliment, won the M-G-M literary award, which brought her $125,000. This considerable sum permitted Renault to leave England and to move, with a friend whom she had met in her nursing days, to South Africa. She traveled widely in Mediterranean lands, and a visit to Greece, which she found "of all these places . . . the most moving and memorable," had both a profound and lasting effect on her career; all the books written after *The Charioteer* (1953) found their subjects in the world of ancient Greece. In this group of historical novels, legendary romances, and popular histories, Renault strove to set her fictional personae and her reimagined historical figures in a world as true to the social, psychological, and material realities of their period as historical and archaeological evidence would allow. In occasional public statements she was insistent upon this subservience of her craft to historical truth:

> The imaginative writer, unlike the historian, has to fill in gaps with invention, and express definite conclusions without definite proof. But if he tells lies on purpose, he has impoverished and warped the common store of truth, and everyone reached by his work will be that much the worse for it.

This is from her letter to *Encounter* (April 1969, p. 92) on Rolf Hochhuth's treatment of Churchill in his play *Soldiers*. For over twenty-five years she enjoyed both popular success and critical esteem as our foremost historical novelist.

Mary Renault was born in London, the elder daughter of a doctor, Frank Challans. She attended Clifton High School in Bristol, and there fell under the spell of a writer who was to exert a continuing influence on both her writing and her thought: "I

was riveted by Plato," she told Herbert Mitgang of the *New York Times*. She read English at St. Hugh's College, Oxford (1924-1927), and trained as a nurse at the Radcliffe Infirmary, Oxford (1933-1937). From 1938 until 1945 she worked as a nurse in a neurosurgical ward at the Radcliffe Infirmary. She did not return to England after moving to South Africa in 1948, and never visited the United States. Though a very popular writer, she chose to remain a very private person.

Renault's successful first novel, *Purposes of Love* (1939), took its title from the nurses' prayer for "wisdom, skill, sympathy and patience . . . to do Thy will and forward Thy purposes of love." The misleading American title, *Promise of Love*, forgets that for Renault love was not simply a matter of human relationships; it had its cosmic and mythic implications. With psychological acuity and sociological precision, the novel tells the story of nurse Vivian Lingard and her involved affair with an assistant pathologist, Mic Freeborn. The bisexual Mic has been in love with Vivian's cool, Hellenically handsome brother and look-alike, Jan. For Vivian to realize fully her nature and identity as Mic's lover, the plot requires a sacrifice—Jan's death in an automobile crash. Colonna Kimball, a lesbian, and the arrogant Dr. Scot-Hallard round out the cast of this complex novel, which sets off Platonic imagery and mythic role-playing against a realistic presentation of bisexuality, homosexuality, promiscuity, and the nurses' exhausting work schedules. The authoritative hospital scenes, careful character portrayals, and fluid style were praised by reviewers, but it was clear that some would have preferred "more reticence." Vivian's dogged acceptance of her identity as Mic's lover and the author's obvious concern for the moral strengths and weaknesses of her characters strike a note of didactic purpose, which is a hallmark of Renault's work.

Kind Are Her Answers (1940) centers on a ménage à trois: There is Kit Anderson, a young doctor who looks even younger; his wife Janet, who has just "borne their first and last child, dead, and had nearly died along with it"; and Christie Heath, a very theatrical actress who serves as nurse to the ailing Miss Amy Heath. Miss Heath's Victorian Gothic estate and the performances at the Brimpton Abby Theatre are deftly exploited by Renault for their picturesque and symbolic potentials. The satirical treatment of an Oxford religious group, called the Group, harmonizes with the censorious tone of the book as a whole. Renault's excellent characterizations, her "physical directness" in dealing with love, and her flowing style again won general praise; but, for some, it was a "trite" subject with "no depth to it."

The Middle Mist (1945) begins in Cornwall, where the likable, if mouselike, seventeen-year-old Elsie Lane is being driven from home by her parents' bitter and constant bickering. She goes off to stay with her sister Leonora, who had run away nine years earlier. Leo is living on a houseboat on the Thames. With her lives Helen Vaughan, a poised and relaxed contrast to the volatile and boylike Leo. At the heart of the novel lies a difficult "Platonic" love affair between Leo and Joe Flint, a gifted writer living on a nearby island. Leo's deeply felt need to find, and keep for herself, a friend, even more than a lover, is signaled at a crucial point in the book by her consideration of a demanding passage from Plato's *Lysis*:

> "For these things are called friends for the sake of a friend, but our true friend seems to be of a nature exactly the reverse of this; for it was found to be our friend for the sake of an enemy; but, if the enemy were removed, no longer, it seems, do we possess a friend.
>
> "Apparently not, said he, according at least to our present position.
>
> "But tell me this, said I. If evil be extinguished, will it be no longer possible to feel hunger or thirst, or any similar desire. . . ."

The "true friend" points toward a supreme and final love in which all lesser and intermediate affections terminate, and (unlike them) it will not be sought merely in satisfaction of physical pleasures and needs (the enemy) but for its own sake. Socrates is here suggesting to the young boy, Menexenus, a condition in which love and friendship might be congenial, mutual, and the same.

The rejection of easy solutions is seen in Renault's satirical treatment of Peter Brachnell, an attractive young doctor with an interest in psychology and smugly confident of the good that both he and it can do. This elusive and sensitive book was given a generally favorable reception, but some reviewers were puzzled as to the meaning of these "friendly young ladies."

Return to Night, winner of the M-G-M award, is, as might be expected, the most cinematic of her novels. The story is played out within continuously varied and often symbolic settings: a woodland grove, an operating room, a theater, a provincial country house, Hilary's rooms, a cave. Hilary Man-

sell, a doctor and a woman of thirty-four, manages to save the life of Julian Fleming, an inordinately good-looking actor of twenty-three. Hilary's struggle to free Julian from his mother's psychic clutches and to become for him not only mistress and lover, but mother and Madonna as well, is told in language and images of lyrical and mythical power. Birth and Death, Light and Dark, Beauty and Ugliness provide a scale of polarities within which Hilary and Julian try for a fruition of their own, one delicately foreshadowed in the birth of a baby girl to a lovely couple, the Clares, who are part of a carefully modulated subplot. In *North Face* (1948), a similar abundance of imagery and metaphor, this time from the language and procedures of mountain climbing, adds resonance to the moral tale. With two spinsters, Miss Searle, an Oxford don, and Miss Fisher, a more pragmatic nurse, serving as a sort of dualistic chorus, Neil Langton and Ellen Shoreland meet at a small resort in Devonshire, become lovers, and succeed in searching out and destroying psychological disorders rooted deep in their pasts. Renault's characters are not approached as if they were merely case studies; they are always free to choose.

Nowhere in her novels is moral choice a more dominating motif than in *The Charioteer*, her courageous and relentless study of Laurie Odell's tentatively successful effort to come to terms with his homosexual identity and to do so in a thoroughly decent way. In the fine opening chapters, the four-year-old Laurie sees his father, an Irish journalist too fond of drink and women, driven away from home, and at sixteen he witnesses an admired nineteen-year-old prefect, Ralph Lanyan, expelled from school because of a homosexual incident. Later in the novel Ralph and Laurie will become lovers, and Renault seems to be preparing a case study of the developing homosexual. Gradually, however, Plato—with his metaphor of the soul as a racing chariot, whose charioteer, Reason, must control its two horses: the one white, well-built, and chaste; the other black, warped, and oversexed—takes over from Freud. Laurie's dilemma—as he wavers between the attractive, chaste Andrew, a Quaker and pacifist, and the more sensual Ralph, a naval officer—is that he risks ending up as merely another of the boys in the band that is gathered together at a gay birthday party in chapter six. Renault is no admirer of collective mentalities, and her gay group is given the same sharp, satirical handling that the Group, the Oxford religious organization, was given in *Kind Are Her Answers*. William Morrow, the American publisher of her earlier books, rejected *The Charioteer* because of the subject matter, and the book had to wait six years for the first American edition, by Pantheon. While the reviews were generally favorable, the majority of reviewers were clearly troubled by her choice of subject.

In *The Last of the Wine* (1956), set in ancient Greece at the time of the Peloponnesian War (431-404 B.C.), Alexias writes an autobiography of the first four decades of his life: his own narrow escape from infanticide; his love for a slightly older boy, Lysis; the personalities he had met—Xenophon, Socrates, Plato, Critias; and the events that had shaped his life—the Isthmian Games, the Herm mutilations, the Sicilian Expedition, battles at the White Isles and at Goat's Creek, a reign of terror under the Oligarchs. The major themes of *The Charioteer*, homosexuality and a boy's growth into manhood and manliness (the literal translation of the Greek *arete*, Renault's "excellence" and some people's "virtue"), are being developed within a very different world. Reviewers responded favorably to Renault's detailed recreation of fifth-century Athens and to the tone of her Atticizing prose. The public, too, welcomed it, and not least for the reason given by Moses Hadas in the *New York Herald Tribune Book Review* (13 April 1958): "Books from which we learn so much so agreeably are rare."

In her best-selling *The King Must Die* (1958), she gives us a clever, undersized, and strictly heterosexual version of Athens's national hero, Theseus. This legendary romance is set—vaguely—in the fourteenth century B.C. and well before the Trojan War, and the chapter titles—Troizen, Eleusis, Athens, Crete, Naxos—testify as much to the impact of her visit to Greece as to her accurate and reliable scholarship. The style is attractive; it is crisp, Herodotean, archaically simple. Theseus's adventures are told selectively and with a devilish reasonableness, but it is the boy's growth into leader that impresses, and Renault's imaginative recreation of the Cranes, Theseus's superbly coached team of bull dancers, is masterful. An ironic and Euripidean rationalism colors her versions of the Minotaur and Ariadne episodes, and they contrast neatly with the familiar, darker variations of Gide, Picasso, and Strauss. Hugh Kenner, writing in the *New York Times Book Review* (10 February 1974), found the secret to this "magic book" in "the fructive ambiguity of legend," which freed the author to respond in a strange world "to the felt identity of people's fates with slain bulls, slain horses, slain kings, in a cosmos where all life, seen

and unseen, is unified by the dark exactions of hidden gods."

The sequel, *The Bull from the Sea* (1962), brings Theseus home to Athens; his adventures continue, and among the Amazons he discovers both friend and lover in the athletic Hippolyta. In the book's pivotal episode Theseus leads the Athenians out against a horde of invading Scythians and Amazons; he goes into battle accepting that he is now the king who must die and, full of himself, he goes—consenting—to meet his death; he is deluded, Hippolyta is killed, and *she* is the king who must die. An elegiac sadness pervades the book and is personified in "Old Handy," Renault's gentle Englishing of the Centaur Cheiron. Age comes tragically to her Theseus: Athenian politics prove harder to manage than Cretan bulls, and his tall, chaste, and handsome son Hippolytus is more alien to him than any Minotaur; he dies hoping only to become a memory one day at Marathon; his world comes to an end tellingly, for nearby is the last person he thinks of before his jump—the young Achilles is waiting in the wings.

The Lion in the Gateway (1964) is a more or less nonfictional account, as its subtitle promises, of "The Heroic Battles of the Greeks and Persians at Marathon, Salamis, and Thermopylae." While packed with accurate information, the book is at times—as in the role given Pheidippides and his run to Sparta—closer to Charles Kingsley's nineteenth-century "Greek Legends Retold" than to Herodotus's inquiries. It is written (and written well) for young adults; it also tells something about the author's fondness for Herodotus and the view that "History is chaps." Later, when at work on her Alexander trilogy, she published a second nonfiction book, *The Nature of Alexander* (1975). It is a reliable and enthusiastic biography that serves as a useful guide to the geographical and chronological backgrounds of the novels; it is not only well written, but well illustrated to boot.

In both *Return to Night* and *Kind Are Her Answers* theatrical performances were used in developing appearance and reality themes; in *The Mask of Apollo* (1966)—the memoirs of an Athenian actor, Nikeratos—the ancient Greek theater is drawn up against Plato's Academy, as the touring Nico shares in Plato's and his beloved disciple Dion's efforts to effect a political revolution at Syracuse by influencing the young tyrant Dionysios II. The events cover roughly the period from Plato's first visit to Sicily, in 388 B.C., down to Niko's visit to Pella in Macedonia in 342 B.C., twelve years after Dion's murder. Like *The Last of the Wine*, to which it is an obvious sequel, *The Mask of Apollo* is as much informative history as it is imaginative novel. The vivid descriptions—theatrical performances, Olympic Games, Delphi, Plato's Academy, civil disorders at Syracuse—were singled out by reviewers for praise. The technique is firmer in the later book. Alexias and Lysis did not avoid a certain stilted pomposity both in thought and in dialogue; they were too aware that they belonged to the fifth century and the Classical Age, neither they nor their creator doing justice to Aristophanes. Nico is more convincing, more down-to-earth as, surprisingly, even Plato and Dion are.

Fire from Heaven (1969) is vintage Renault: it begins with a perceptive child getting caught up in a brawl between father and mother; the genre is Bildungsroman; the interest is homosexual. Like a true artist, Renault keeps returning to her big themes. But now she has left the Cotswolds and Cornwall and even Southern Greece. The forms are the same, but the content makes a great difference—when the mother is the murderous, mystical Olympias; the father, the domineering King Philip of Macedon; and the child, Alexander the Great. The novel is in the form of a biography of Alexander's youth from 351 to 336 B.C., when Philip was assassinated and Alexander was twenty. The historical background with the quarreling city-states, Athenian and Macedonian rivalry, the battle of Chaeronia, and trouble with Persia is unobtrusively introduced into what is more a psychological than a historical novel. The characterizations are varied and shrewdly observed, particularly the bisexual Philip and a savaged Demosthenes. Euripides's *Bacchae* puts in an expected appearance, for that performance had already been mentioned at the close of *The Mask of Apollo*. Of her young hero, an anonymous reviewer in *The Times Literary Supplement* (11 December 1970) writes: "One may fully believe that this was indeed the Alexander who 'lifted the civilized world out of one groove and set it in another.' "

The Persian Boy (1972) is Renault's finest novel since *The King Must Die*. It is also the most panoramic, describing the Asian and African conquests of Alexander during the last seven years of his life down to his death in 323 B.C. The narrator—a brilliant stroke—is Bagoas, an exquisite Persian youth, whose harrowing castration is described in the novel's powerful opening chapter. Bagoas's expertise in the ways of the Persian court is crucial to Renault's just balancing of both Greek and Persian values in this confrontation of cultures. Renault manages the ménage à trois between Alexander, Hephaistion, and Bagoas—which is critical in her view of Alexander's nature—with wit as well as sensitivity; Bagoas is never more endearing than when entertaining murderous thoughts aimed at Hephaistion. Peter Green does the book justice in the *New York Review of Books* (8 February 1979): "*The Persian Boy* seemed, as did, in a very different sense, Eliot's *Little Gidding*, to reach a resolution of inner conflicts and problems, a unity of fire and rose."

The Praise Singer (1978) is a slighter work. It tells of the travels of the poet Simonides from his island home, Keos, to the courts of Polykrates on Samos and of Peisistratos at Athens. There are lovely things here: Simonides recollecting at eighty-three his boyhood spats with his father; the art and geography of Archaic Greece; and, above all, the heroic tale of Harmodios and Aristogeiton. The dialogue is occasionally flat and even witless. The author falls into a trap that awaits all historical novelists, but which Renault is generally adept at avoiding: "the failure of the narrative to convey naturally information which, being part of everyday awareness, would not normally have been specified in a first-person narrative at all," as Paul Ableman pinpoints it in his review in *The Spectator* (24 February 1979). Still, the period dealt with (ca. 550 to 514 B.C.) is one of the most important and attractive in all of Greek history, and the main episodes are handled with skill and style.

Renault ended her Alexander trilogy powerfully; *Funeral Games* (1981) is a prosopographical tour de force (answering to the geographical expanses of *The Persian Boy*), with a preface listing forty-five "Principal Persons." Its subject is the poisonings, elephant-tramplings, and variegated butcherings that advanced the chances of those like Perdiccas, Roxane, and Olympias who tried to replace Alexander. The complex material has been martialed by Renault in chapters titled by years—"322 B.C.," down to "286 B.C.," when the principal events were being written down by the aged Ptolemy. The style is vibrant, and the characters are vividly drawn—particularly the Amazonian Eurydice, whose tragic failure as a "masculine" warrior is movingly portrayed; the hubristic Perdiccas (he of the elephants); and the ever-formidable Olympias. Peter Green writes in the *New York Review of Books* (18 March 1982): "Miss Renault's main problem has been to make these monsters and monomaniacs believable, and this, at times with disconcerting insight, she does."

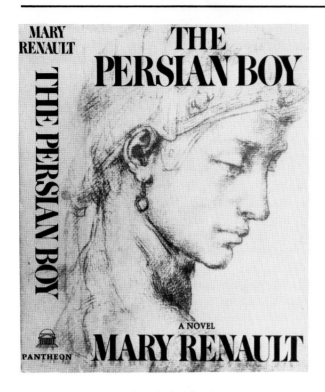 

Dust jackets for the second and third novels in Renault's Alexander the Great trilogy

After 1956 Mary Renault honed her skills at the demanding, financially rewarding, and critically underestimated genre of historical fiction. Her speculative "histories" are based on firm and detailed scholarship, and her books cover over eleven centuries of Greek history and Mediterranean geography from Sicily to Crete and the Black Sea—and with Alexander even India was reached.

References:
Landon C. Burns, Jr., "Men Are Only Men: The novels of Mary Renault," *Critique*, 6 (Winter 1963-1964): 102-121;

Bernard F. Dick, *The Hellenism of Mary Renault* (Carbondale: Southern Illinois University Press, 1972);

Peter Green, "The Masks of Mary Renault," *New York Review of Books*, 8 March 1979, pp. 11-14;

Carolyn G. Heilbrun, "Axiothea's Grief: The Disability of the Female Imagination," in *From Parnassus: Essays in Honor of Jacques Barzun*, edited by Dora B. Weiner and William R. Keylor (New York & London: Harper & Row, 1976), pp. 227-236;

Kevin Herbert, "The Theseus Theme: Some Recent Versions," *Classical Journal*, 55 (January 1960): 175-185;

Hugh Kenner, "Mary Renault and Her Various Personas," *New York Times Book Review*, 10 February 1974, p. 15;

Anne G. Ward and others, eds., *The Quest for Theseus* (New York: Praeger, 1970), pp. 252-254;

Peter Wolfe, *Mary Renault* (New York: Twayne, 1969).

A TRIBUTE ————————————
from JAMES OLIVER BROWN

I think I have read all of her books, the later ones for which she is best known, most of them in Paris before I had the honor to represent her here as her literary agent. The early ones I have read here. I am sorry never to have met Mary but we had become good friends by letter and telephone. It was always good to hear Julie Mullard's lovely voice answering the telephone and hearing her call, "Mary, it's Jim" and have Mary come on with that kind and equally lovely voice of hers. Mary was a lady with manners. I need not dwell upon her talent as that is too well known and too well accepted throughout the world for my evaluation to do anything but agree with the high opinions of those who know her writing.

A TRIBUTE

from BERNARD F. DICK

Early in 1970, when I decided to write *The Hellenism of Mary Renault*, I wrote to Miss Renault, asking the usual questions about influences, aims, methods of research, etc. I did not know it would be the beginning of a thirteen-year correspondence, nor did I anticipate the annual Christmas cards which were never the same—sometimes a Greek motif, at other times an African one. She honored me as I never was honored before. When my critical study of her work finally appeared, I was totally unprepared for her reaction: it was *she* who felt honored.

Yet it was I who profited from the relationship; I who learned from her. Each letter was an epistolary model, revealing her awesome scholarship and her knowledge of both past and present. As we began to correspond, I started imbibing her love of history to the extent that now, having moved into film criticism, I find myself writing more and more from a historical perspective—tracing the genesis of a film or documenting its accuracy.

At first I was hesitant to tell her that I had moved into film. I was trained as a classicist and it was as one that I had first written to her. But she was enthusiastic about my change of field, responding at length to each book I sent her. It was in this latter phase of our correspondence that I learned her days were not spent entirely in the library; she revealed her great love of the film *Shane*, noting that she too was working on a treatment of the Alexander novels which had attracted the attention of a filmmaker.

This year I expected the usual Christmas card which always arrived early. Instead, on 14 December, I picked up the *New York Times* to read of her death. One reaches a stage where one knows death is inevitable; one only wants it vindicated. I was grieved, but at the same time was satisfied that the obituary was detailed and that her death was cited under "International News," as was fitting.

The next day, on 15 December, I received a copy of the *Times Literary Supplement* cylindrically wrapped and postmarked Capetown, 3 December; it was the issue that contained a lengthy review of my book, *Hellman in Hollywood*. As I pulled off the wrapping, a note fell out: "See page 1273. All good wishes, Mary."

Although I did not receive the usual Christmas card, I received something that would last me through the rest of my Christmases—an acknowledgment that I mattered.

No one's life is devoid of regrets; one of mine is that I never met the woman who gave me a respect for history that, I hope, manifests itself in whatever I write.

Rebecca West
(21 December 1892-15 March 1983)

Tony Redd
The Citadel

BOOKS: *Henry James* (London: Nisbet, 1916; New York: Holt, 1916);

The Return of the Soldier (New York: Century, 1918; London: Nisbet, 1918);

The Judge (London: Hutchinson, 1922; New York: Doran, 1922);

The Strange Necessity: Essays and Reviews (London: Cape, 1928; Garden City: Doubleday, Doran, 1928);

Lions and Lambs, cartoons by David Low and text by West as Lynx (London: Cape, 1928; New York: Harcourt, Brace, 1929);

Harriet Hume: A London Fantasy (London: Hutchinson, 1929; Garden City: Doubleday, Doran, 1929);

War Nurse: The True Story of a Woman Who Lived, Loved, and Suffered on the Western Front, anonymous (New York: Cosmopolitan Book Corporation, 1930);

D. H. Lawrence (London: Secker, 1930); republished as *Elegy* (New York: Phoenix Book Shop, 1930);

Arnold Bennett Himself (New York: John Day, 1931);

Ending in Earnest: A Literary Log (Garden City: Doubleday, Doran, 1931);

St. Augustine (London: Davies, 1933; New York: Appleton, 1933);

A Letter to a Grandfather (London: Hogarth Press, 1933);

The Modern "Rakes Progress," paintings by Low and text by West (London: Hutchinson, 1934);

The Harsh Voice: Four Short Novels (London & Toronto: Cape, 1935; Garden City: Doubleday, Doran, 1935);

The Thinking Reed (New York: Viking, 1936; London: Hutchinson, 1936);

Black Lamb and Grey Falcon, 2 volumes (New York: Viking, 1941; London: Macmillan, 1942);

The Meaning of Treason (New York: Viking, 1947; London: Macmillan, 1949; enlarged edition, London: Macmillan, 1952); revised and enlarged as *The New Meaning of Treason* (New York: Viking, 1964); republished as *The Meaning of Treason, revised edition* (London: Macmillan, 1965);

A Train of Powder (New York: Viking, 1955; London: Macmillan, 1955);

The Fountain Overflows (New York: Viking, 1956; London: Macmillan, 1957);

The Court and The Castle (New Haven: Yale University Press, 1957; London: Macmillan, 1958);

The Vassall Affair (London: Sunday Telegraph, 1963);

The Birds Fall Down (London & Melbourne: Macmillan, 1966; New York: Viking, 1966);

McLuhan and the Future of Literature (London: Oxford University Press for the English Association, 1969);

Rebecca West: A Celebration (London: Macmillan, 1977; New York: Viking, 1977);

1900 (New York: Viking, 1982; London: Weidenfeld & Nicolson, 1982);

The Young Rebecca: Writings of Rebecca West, 1911-17, selected by Jane Marcus (New York: Viking, 1982; London: Virago, 1982).

When Dame Rebecca West died in London at the age of ninety on 15 March 1983, she had been delighting legions of readers with her irresistible intelligence for well over seventy years. This brilliant journalist, biographer, novelist, and critic left behind her on the Ides of March literary treasure that achieved with radiant perfection the high goal toward which she believed art, or "the strange necessity" as she once called it, should always aim: "The thing has been done, the absolute truth about

that situation has been set down, we are by that much more completely masters of reality than we were. If every such situation, every such collision of forces, were as truly described, we should be masters of all reality. . . ."

Rebecca West, whose real name was Cicily Isabel Fairfield, was born in South London on 21 December 1892. Her father was Charles Fairfield, an Anglo-Irishman who has been variously described as a journalist, a war correspondent, and a pamphleteer; her mother was Isabella Mackenzie Fairfield, a native of Edinburgh and a member of a family of distinguished musicians. Cicily Fairfield lived with her parents and her two older sisters in the house in which she was born until she was ten years old. At that time her father died, and her mother moved the family to Edinburgh.

At the age of eighteen Cicily Fairfield returned to London to make a career. Hoping to become an actress, she trained for the stage at the Royal Academy of Dramatic Art in Gower Street. She soon abandoned the prospect of an acting career, however, although not before she had appeared briefly in the role of Rebecca West in Ibsen's *Rosmersholm*. The pen name she was later to make so famous can perhaps be taken as something of a signpost to her career, for throughout her life she had an Ibsenesque scorn for the banal and pity for the underdog.

In 1911 Rebecca West began to contribute essays to the *Freewoman*; and just a year later, when she was twenty, she joined the staff of the *Clarion*, a socialist weekly. The fiery brilliance of the articles on feminism and the emancipation of women that she wrote for these two journals quickly captured the attention of the best minds in London. H. G. Wells was so impressed by her review of his novel *Marriage* (1912), which appeared in the *Clarion* in 1912, that he invited her to spend a weekend at his house, Easton Glebe. These two gifted writers soon fell deeply in love, even though Wells was twenty-six years older than West and married. Their relationship lasted for eleven years, until 1923, and seems to have been terminated with no hearts irremediably broken, as any reader of the brilliant but rather unkind novel *Heritage* (1955) by Anthony West, West's child by Wells, will confirm. Although after 1923 Rebecca saw little of the man she once described as having "the most bubbling creative mind that the sun and moon have shone upon since the days the mind of Leonardo da Vinci was showing its form," her enormous respect for his intellectual achievements endured; Wells's *Outline of History* (1920) occupied a prominent position on the top

Rebecca West, age six, being fed blackberries by her sisters Letitia and Winifred (left) and two cousins

shelf of the only bookcase in the drawing room of the elegant flat in London where she died.

After her parting from Wells, there began a new and far more glittering period in Rebecca West's life, which culminated in her marriage on 1 November 1930 to Henry Maxwell Andrews, a wealthy investment banker who shared his wife's interest in the arts. In fact, West was often fond of remarking that her husband would probably have been far happier as an art historian than he was as a banker. The Andrewses lived in great style, eventually in a Buckinghamshire mansion named Ibstone House. Henry Andrews did much to encourage his wife in her literary work, and theirs was a union of hearts and minds until the time of his death from brain cancer in 1968.

Perhaps the best way to pay tribute to the unique contribution Rebecca West made to the republic of letters will be to suggest something of the nature of her achievements in the four genres in which she was a master writer: literary criticism, biography, the novel, and journalism.

From the very beginning of her apprenticeship as a literary critic, Rebecca West took a

strong stand on behalf of the importance of intellectually oriented art, a position she never abandoned. During the early days of World War I, she wrote two essays for the *New Republic*, at that time a new publication, in which she clearly expressed the trenchant habit of mind which was to become so familiar in her reviews and essays through many years to come. First she reminded her fellow critics that it was their duty to listen to geniuses in "a disrespectful manner," and then she went on to advise them to seek other work if they were not up to the highest demands of their task: "We must weepingly leave the library if we are stupid, just as in the middle ages we left the home if we were lepers. If we can offer the mind of the world nothing else we can offer it our silence." Her first book was a brief critical biography of Henry James, a writer in whom she had a passionate interest all her life; this book published in 1916 was the third work published about James and was the first study to appear after his death.

In 1928 Rebecca West published a collection of twelve essays entitled *The Strange Necessity*. In the final, title piece in this book, she made some of the most important observations she was ever to make about the nature and significance of art and expressed her deep belief in the importance to society of good literary criticism. Art, she decided, is a branch of knowledge which, by analyzing and synthesizing experience, offers man necessary information about the true nature of reality and thereby helps to prevent him from acting out disordered fantasies of conduct that are often fatal. The critic's responsibility in judging this essential guide to life is crucial: "Criticism which applies certain standards to works of art, an atmosphere of culture which develops a general sensitivity to the quality of art, are therefore as necessary to a civilization as inspectors who tell the community whether bridges are safe or not, and a system of education which enables the community to grasp what they mean and to act upon it."

Rebecca West's *Ending in Earnest: A Literary Log*, which consisted of forty-two essays that had originally appeared as "Letters from Europe" in the *Bookman*, was published in 1931. This volume contains cultural criticism at its very best, offering an extremely episodic series of notes on some of the interesting people (Virginia Woolf, Sir Edmund Gosse, Colette) and ideas (the dangers of the New Humanism) that were uppermost in the author's mind at the time. The pièce de résistance of the collection, however, is her elegy for D. H. Lawrence, in which in unforgettable language she helped the reader master the reality of the glorious generosity of one man's spirit: "He made friends as a child might do, by shyly handing me funny little boxes he had brought from some strange place he had recently visited; and he made friends too as if he were a wise old philosopher at the end of his days, by taking notice of one's personality, showing that he recognized its quality and giving it his blessing." As any friend of West's can testify, these words, in a curious way, could stand as a near-perfect self-portrait.

In 1956 Rebecca West became the first woman ever to deliver the Terry Foundation Lectures at Yale University. In these lectures, later published as *The Court and The Castle* (1957), she drew on a lifetime's reading in an ambitious attempt to explain the preoccupation of many of the great imaginative writers of Western literature—such as Shakespeare, Kafka, and Proust—with the subjects of politics ("The Court") and religion ("The Castle"). How can any serious reader ever forget the originality of her observations on *Hamlet*, or the haunting beauty of her interpretation of Kafka's "A Penal Settlement," or the exciting wisdom in her discus-

sion of archetypes in Proust? *The Court and The Castle* becomes a part of one's intellectual equipment, a companion to one's reading to be kept in the way one keeps T. S. Eliot's *The Sacred Wood* (1920), or Edmund Wilson's *The Wound and the Bow* (1941).

Certainly the literary criticism of Rebecca West which will be remembered longest by her fellow countrymen, however, was that which appeared in the more than three hundred book reviews she wrote for the *Sunday Telegraph* between February 1961 and October 1982. Although she reviewed any book which caught her fancy, from a new anthology of Scottish love poems to Norman Mailer's *The Executioner's Song* (1979), she was at her very best when writing about biographies, memoirs, letters, and diaries because of her insatiable desire to master the reality of human character. The method of her reviews could perhaps be called "Proustian" because she retained all the color of the impressionist school of criticism without sacrificing the attempt to establish rational criteria as the basis of judgment. For sheer moral intensity, wit, the beauty of the writing, and the dazzling breadth of knowledge they display, these reviews have no equal in our time.

Although well-known for the vivid character sketches which are found in her many nonfictional works, Rebecca West wrote only one full-fledged biography, a study of the life of Saint Augustine, which was published in 1933. Aside from the beauty of its language, what is perhaps most remarkable about this small book is the detailed and penetrating psychological analysis it offers of Augustine the man. West, in effect, perceived Augustine as being a frustrated romantic writer who, because of his own intense suffering, convinced himself and far too many members of every succeeding generation that pain, never pleasure, is the only test of value.

Rebecca West published six novels during her lifetime, each of which, in some ways, seemed more distinguished than its predecessor. *The Return of the Soldier* (1918), which deals with the problems of a shell-shocked soldier sent home from France, was one of the first English novels to register the effect of some of Freud's theories. The book which followed, *The Judge* (1922), was an old-fashioned domestic tragedy in the tradition of George Eliot and Thomas Hardy, depicting the unfortunate influence that mothers often have on their children. *Harriet Hume*, which appeared in 1929, is one of West's most intriguing books. It bears the subtitle *A London Fantasy*, and it may be thought of as a kind of allegorical treatment of the central thesis of her essay "The Strange Necessity." In this wonderful book the reader discovers Arnold Condorex (his surname, meaning "king of the vultures," is significant) attempting to live without art (Harriet Hume) in his life; thus he fails to master reality and begins to live out the strangest of fantasies. *The Thinking Reed* (1936) was immediately hailed by critics as being one of the most beautiful novels of its time. Perfect in structure and with a splendid freshness of language to match (there are no more beautiful metaphors to be found anywhere), it is a kind of rewriting of Henry James's *The Portrait of a Lady* (1881) that celebrates the triumph of love and of the intellect over several potentially destructive and chaotic forces such as great wealth and loneliness.

In 1956, after twenty years of silence as a novelist, Rebecca West published her most original novel—*The Fountain Overflows*. Cast in the form of a reminiscence, it tells the story of the gifted Aubreys, a family very much like West's own, the Fairfields. The mode of narration in this book about the nature of talent and the mystery of family drew on the richest vein of the author's narrative ability. Rose, one of the Aubrey twins, tells the story as she looks back through the mists of fifty years to the delicious lost world of her Edwardian childhood. This kind of narration creates the strong impression of revealing the total truth about its subject as it blends the intense honesty of a child's reactions with the deeper perception of an experienced adult mind. *The Fountain Overflows* is the only volume that has appeared in what was supposed to have been a trilogy about the Aubrey family; however, in 1979, Dame Rebecca told me that "This Real Night," the sequel to the first Aubrey novel, was complete and resting in the hands of her publisher.

In *The Birds Fall Down* (1966), the final novel West published, she paid homage through the perfection of her technique to the three masters of fiction who had most strongly influenced her—James, Proust, and Dostoevski. Set for the most part in Paris at the turn of the century, it is the story of a wealthy Russian émigré family, the Diakonovs, and of the supporters and spies who surround them. Running to well over a hundred pages, one of the most memorable conversations in modern fiction is found in this book, as Chubinov, a revolutionary, and Count Nickolai Diakonov explain their lives to each other on a train as it moves through northern France. The key to understanding the main idea that the author was attempting to present through all the beauty of action and talk she created is found in the novel's epigraph, which she (not someone named Conway Power, as the text states) wrote:

We are all bowmen in this place.
The pattern of the birds against the sky
Our arrows overprint, and then they die.
But it is also common to our race
That when the birds fall down we weep.
Reason's a thing we dimly see in sleep.

This six-line poem is an eloquent statement of a Manichean idea that pervades the entire corpus of Dame Rebecca's work: the tragic truth that only a part of man's nature is sane and that, therefore, there is perhaps nothing rarer than a man who can be trusted not to erase progress or throw away happiness. Almost everything that ever mattered to Rebecca West (the nature of treachery, the Eastern Orthodox Church, the beauty of fin de siècle Paris) came to full ripeness in *The Birds Fall Down*, and the harvest was rich beyond belief.

Although Rebecca West achieved brilliant success as a literary critic, biographer, and novelist, it was when she combined the skills required by these professions with her ability as an historian and a master journalist that she wrote several books which made her world famous.

Black Lamb and Grey Falcon, published in 1941, clearly stands as her magnum opus. It was born out of Dame Rebecca's desire to know more about the history of the southeastern corner of Europe, where during the first third of the twentieth century it seemed that the destiny of perhaps the entire Western world was being forged. She traveled to the Balkan Peninsula in 1936 and again in 1937, with the result that she fell in love with a landscape and a people. Yugoslavia resembled the beautiful land she had often dreamed about as a child, and its people were the kind of intense and heroic seekers after truth she greatly admired. Everywhere there seemed to be Slavs with the same kind of passion to know the meaning of experience that she herself possessed. Perhaps the main truth Dame Rebecca mastered during the course of her profound meditations on the history of the Ottoman Empire, the origins of World War I, the collapse of the Austro-Hungarian Empire, the central core of fascism, and so much more is that mankind in the changing course of history seems destined to repeat two different kinds of sacrifices. There is the "Black Lamb" variety which is ugly and meaningless and which reveals the insane darkness in man's nature. But there is also the "Grey Falcon" type which convinces one anew that some men are indeed just a little lower than the angels. In Dame Rebecca's view, the heroic stand of the Yugoslavs against the Germans in World War II clearly belonged to the "Grey Fal-

Rebecca West (Arnold Weissberger)

con" category since their heroic actions were prompted by a strong preference for all that is agreeable in life, for all that gives meaning to the universe. *Black Lamb and Grey Falcon* is one of the greatest travel books, historical studies, and spiritual autobiographies written in the twentieth century.

The trials that followed World War II offered Rebecca West's talents as a journalist a fresh opportunity for pyrotechnic display. She was present at the Nuremberg Trials. Her graphic accounts appeared in the *New Yorker* and were subsequently published, together with accounts she gave of other postwar trials arising out of the relation of the individual to the state, in two memorable books, *The Meaning of Treason* (1947) and *A Train of Powder* (1955). The first of these volumes earned her the Women's Press Club Award for Journalism, which was presented to her by President Harry S. Truman, who, in making the award, called her "the world's best reporter." In 1964 she expanded her original study of quislings, introduced some sordid characters from the Cold War Era, and published the results as *The New Meaning of Treason*.

In an age when broadcasting and the style of reporting developed by such magazines as *Time* have accustomed us to the declamatory and breathless, Rebecca's descriptions of great events caught the reader's imagination by emphasizing the ordinariness of the men given outsize roles in them. She was a novelist who used her great gifts for journalism. To that fleeting work, she brought her powers of observation, her absorption with the complex motives of human conduct, and the inherent poetry of her language. And that made all the difference.

Many countries competed in showering honors upon Rebecca West. In 1937 Yugoslavia made her a member of the Order of St. Sava, and in 1957 France contributed the Legion of Honor. The United States conferred membership in the Academy of Arts and Sciences. Britain made her a Dame of the British Empire in 1959, and a Companion of Literature in 1968. This last honor was membership in an extremely select society numbering only twelve members. It is comforting to think that, for once, appreciation of genuine talent was not posthumous.

In 1977, on her eighty-fifth birthday, her publisher brought out *Rebecca West: A Celebration*, an anthology of her writings demonstrating her formidably wide range. And in 1982 Dame Rebecca published *1900*, a handsome coffee-table book, which may be taken as the wayward conversation of one time traveler's brilliant mind, as she recalls the paintings, music, literature, and political events of a single year. While reading this book, one was not really surprised to discover that Dame Rebecca still had delightfully fresh insights to offer about such figures as James, Proust, and Sargent, whom she had been discussing regularly in print for well over fifty years. And one could only feel deeply grateful to her in her investigations of such topics as the Boer War, the founding of the British Labour party, and the Dreyfus Affair, for using her peerless analytical powers once again to track through jungles of people and jungles of fact to locate those little springs, or sources, that feed the great rivers of our history.

Following the death of her husband in 1968, Dame Rebecca sold Ibstone House and moved into one of the loveliest flats in London. Located in the most fashionable part of Knightsbridge, it had a gloriously overparked look resulting from her exodus from her larger country house, where she and her husband had spent a lifetime collecting treasures. Picassos, Nashes, and Lowrys hung thickly on the walls; she owned the only nude that Constable ever painted. Sitting down in her drawing room, one found one's hand resting on the rough carved mane of a lion or the smooth arched neck of a swan. Outside her windows huge plane trees always seemed to be dancing in the wind to some faraway music which only they could hear.

But most beautiful and rare at 48 Kingston House North were the warm heart, dazzling wit, and exciting mind of its owner. So generous with her time and money was Rebecca and so interested was she in everything that was happening in the world around her that there always seemed to be a steady stream of visitors, both the very famous and the virtually unknown. And all were treated like royalty.

There were dinner parties at The Empress, The Oslo Court, or The Capital Restaurant on Basil Street. Or one might be taken for a drive in her chauffeur-driven Bentley to see the giraffes in Regent's Park Zoo, which she loved, or to take yet another look at the Keats House in Hampstead. And, of course, through it all there gleamed those delightful stories that only Dame Rebecca could tell—wild narratives about spiritualists at a Rad-

ziwill wedding or about a shopkeeper's astonishment over an "octogeranium's" buying herself maternity clothes. Once she even did a perfect imitation of Mary McCarthy's "snort" for me.

All the elegance and charm of Dame Rebecca's life-style never veiled in even the thinnest way, however, the central activity of her life—her writing. This fascinating woman who had been everywhere, read everything, and known everybody, often said that her absorption in her writing was the only thing that made old age bearable.

If future generations wish to know something of the temperament of the queen of twentieth-century English literature, as they certainly should, they could not do better than to study the expression Wyndam Lewis captured in his portrait of her in 1932; they should also ponder her description of an old woman she once met in Montenegro who was the kind of supreme master of reality Dame Rebecca believed every serious writer should seek to be: "She took her destiny not as the beasts take it, nor as the plants and trees; she not only suffered it, she examined it. As the sword swept down on her through the darkness she threw out her hand and caught the blade as it fell, not caring if she cut her fingers so long as she could question its substance, where it had been forged, and who was the wielder. . . . She desired neither peace nor gold, but simply knowledge of what her life might mean. . . . If there are but twenty people like her scattered between here and China, civilization will survive. If during the next million generations there is but one human being born in every generation who will not cease to inquire into the nature of his fate, even while it strips and bludgeons him, some day we shall read the riddle of our universe."

It was toward the splendor of that moment that Rebecca West so surely led us for over seven decades; therefore, in the circle of our respect and our affection, she can have no double.

A TRIBUTE

from G. E. HUTCHINSON

She combined a wide-ranging intellect with a generous passion for people, in whom she saw unexpected and fascinating individuality. Her judgement in conversation as in her literary criticism was often surprised and strikingly independent. At first sight she occasionally seemed inconsistent, but always reflected an attitude that needed to be heard. She delighted in beauty of every kind, natural or man-made, and had an immense capacity for finding it in unexpected places. I can imagine her in an ultimate atomic catastrophe pausing momentarily to call attention to some extraordinary visual effect. Her company was enormous fun, exuberant and occasionally outrageous.

A TRIBUTE
from FRANCIS KING

Rebecca West was an always fascinating novelist, since she was an always fascinating woman; but, except in *The Fountain Overflows*, part of a semi-autobiographical sequence never to be completed, and the short story *The Salt of the Earth*, she never achieved greatness in her fiction. That she did not do so, despite all her successes, was indicated by her failure ever to find a voice uniquely her own, so that one could say of a random paragraph—as one can say of any random paragraph by, say, Hemingway, Conrad, or Woolf—"No one else could have written that."

As a non-academic critic, however, she was supreme of her period in England. She had an amazingly retentive memory even into old age; her logic was unassailable; her style was incisive and powerful. Up to the last months of her life, she continued to work for the Sunday Telegraph, where we were colleagues. The literary editor would send her a book, asking for 800 words, and

back would come one of double that length, such as no other reviewer of his could rival in the breadth and intensity of its vision. She was a formidable woman, since she was both so unrelenting in her demolition of stupidity and cant and so reluctant to forget a slight or injury. On the Sunday Telegraph, we would call her—never, of course, to her face!—"The Dame." The nickname would probably have had different connotations on an American newspaper. On an English one, it suggested someone powerful and august, in whom one went in awe—"She Who Must Be Obeyed." Yet to those whom she liked and of whom she approved, however unimportant, no one could have been more compassionate and kinder.

A TRIBUTE
from DIANA TRILLING

Rebecca West was surely one of the major literary figures of this century, a woman of deep learning and uncommon independence and energy of mind, who made journalism into a high art. Wherever distinguished writing is appreciated, she will be remembered for her brilliant reporting of the treason trials after the Second World War and for her remarkable book about Yugoslavia, *Black Lamb and Grey Falcon*.

Tennessee Williams
(26 March 1911-25 February 1983)

Sally Johns
University of South Carolina

See also the Williams entry in *DLB 7, Twentieth-Century American Dramatists*; and *DLB Documentary Series 4, Tennessee Williams*.

Tennessee Williams's death in February 1983 freed him of the label he frequently claimed to detest: America's greatest living playwright. He saw in the words the implication that a writer's achievement is not really validated until he is dead, and he also suspected that the word *living* was used as a qualifier to indicate that he had not reached the status of Eugene O'Neill. Williams's assessment was

probably accurate on both counts. In the numerous tributes and articles about him which appeared shortly after his death, the vast majority of writers either ranked him second to O'Neill or called him the country's best playwright with the possible exception of O'Neill. (In a notable departure from this pattern, Walter Kerr simply stated, "He was the greatest American playwright. Period.") More important than debating a rank order, however, is the fact that the ending of Williams's career has brought the possibility of an evaluation of his achievement that was clouded before.

Tennessee Williams and the cast of Creve Coeur *at the 1978 Spoleto Festival in Charleston, South Carolina. On his right are Peg Murray and Shirley Knight, on his left Jan Miner and Barbara Tarbuck.*

Williams had certainly known critical and box-office failure before the years following *The Night of the Iguana* (his last major success), but in the past, failure had always been closely followed by success. It has been this period of unrelieved creative recession—eventually lengthening to over twenty years—that has been problematic for both critics and the American public. With few exceptions, his later works were called lesser reworkings of old material, full of self-indulgent excesses. Notices grew increasingly unfavorable, with certain reviewers growing increasingly venomous. (About John Simon, Williams is reported to have said, "That man is so mean he would spit in the face of the baby Jesus.") Occasionally a critic generated a brief flurry of hope that one work or another was on the level of the playwright's prizewinners, but over the years the consensus was that Williams was probably "written out." Quite possibly some of his later scripts, if they had been written by new or little-known authors, would have been received with a greater degree of acclaim; but Williams's work after

the early 1960s was measured against the benchmark he himself had set in the decade and a half before, and by those standards it was seriously flawed. That he continued to write when the results were so weakened became, as David Mamet said in an article for *Rolling Stone*, an embarrassment for a public that "readily withdraws its appreciation from any writer who does not continue to please it easily." Those who knew Williams and his work best recognized that pouring his energy into script after script—no matter what the results—was a necessary part of existence; writing was for him a way of life.

By Williams's account, communication and self-expression through written words became central to his life in early adolescence. For almost six decades he attempted to give form to the pain and isolation in his own life that he saw reflected in common human experience. For only about a quarter of this sixty-year period was he rewarded with the satisfaction that his efforts were reaching and being acclaimed by a wide audience. He had been writing for over twenty years when (at age thirty-four) he saw *The Glass Menagerie* become a phenomenal success on Broadway. The years of struggle and anonymity before recognition are common to multitudes of artists. More painful in Williams's case is that after achieving fame he had to endure over twenty years of an increasingly growing reputation as a has-been. With each premiere during this period was the expectancy that the old light would shine once more—and at the same time more than a touch of perverse anticipation that the loss of his talent would be further validated. What his death has brought is the opportunity to evaluate his career, now that it has closed, without conjecture and speculation about the future and without lament that his highest powers seem to be well in the past.

After Williams's death, most critics and theater writers—many of whom had believed for years that his career had really ended with *The Night of the Iguana*—seemed to exhibit relief that his major accomplishments could rightfully be given primary focus. His contributions to American drama are many: a poetic language unequalled by any other playwright in this country, an appreciation for the potential of the stage when the bounds of realism are loosened, significant breakthroughs in subject matter that created an easier path for the talents of other playwrights, an understanding and compassion for that combination of strength and fragility in the human spirit confronted with harshness, cruelty, isolation, and pain. Williams's weaknesses as a writer were almost his strengths carried to fatal extremes: lyrical language overblown, the off-center character or situation slipping into sensationalism. (These excessive tendencies also at times have been reflected through his most enthusiastic admirers. On a television talk show Elizabeth Ashley described speaking Williams's words onstage as "like being a medium for God.")

Anthony Rose and Julie Haydon in the first Broadway production of The Glass Menagerie *(Museum of the City of New York)*

What seems to happen, however, when an artist dies, is that the chaff is allowed to fall away. Williams's work was inconsistent, but most commentators after his death expressed the belief that his reputation—made through the giants of his career, *The Glass Menagerie* and *A Streetcar Named Desire*—will be undiminished by the flawed works of the last years of his life. As the chaff falls away—now that Williams is no longer America's greatest *living* playwright—what remains is substantial indeed.

TRIBUTES TO TENNESSEE WILLIAMS

From JACOB H. ADLER

In my view the three preeminent plays in American drama are *The Iceman Cometh, Long Day's Journey into Night*, and *A Streetcar Named Desire*. And if I say that I think the two of O'Neill's are the preeminent among the preeminent, that in no way lessens Williams's accomplishment, any more than thinking Ibsen's achievement, the greatest in earlier modern European drama, downgrades Williams's dramatic master, Chekhov. *Streetcar* has passed into our culture, as O'Neill's plays have not. Blanche DuBois has become a part of the American consciousness. She is a stunning, vivid, complex creation, the sort of character that only a genuinely great writer can produce. Another fictional Southern woman has also passed into the American consiousness: Scarlett O'Hara. But to compare Scarlett to Blanche is to compare simple addition to a complex mathematical formula.

Among the American plays which fall just below preeminence I would place *Death of a Salesman, Our Town*, perhaps two or three others which might be more arguable—and *The Glass Menagerie*. Some might want to add one or more additional Williams plays, such as *Cat on a Hot Tin Roof*, or *Summer and Smoke*, or *The Night of the Iguana*. But *Cat*, to use one example, powerful though it is, does not seem to me to survive as the utterly memorable play that *Menagerie* is. I can think of no other modern dramatist whose first successful play has such high and timeless quality—with the one exception, again, of Chekhov and his first full-length play, the great and imperishable *Seagull*.

Williams resembles Chekhov too in that he writes about a special, unusual world which turns out to be comprehensible to all humanity. When I was a Fulbright lecturer at the University of Delhi, there was a student production of *The Glass Menagerie*. They seemed to find this no more unusual than a production of Shakespeare. Obviously unfamiliar with American literature—which was what I was teaching—they already (this was 1960) considered Williams a part of world tradition.

American literature specialists—which I am not; I am a specialist in modern drama—tend to neglect, or even forget, American drama. They, and we all, need to remember that Williams is one of the truly great figures in American—and world—literature.

From CLAUDIA CASSIDY

I knew instantly that Tennessee and I were on the same wavelength that blizzardy night when *The Glass Menagerie* opened at the little Civic next door to the opera house. Tennessee of the flaring imagination, the inborn poetry, the merciless, compassionate insight into people—well, all that became public property of international delight. But I had still another, highly special reason for being pierced to the heart.

Remember Amanda in despair that her lame daughter might turn into one of those barely tolerated spinsters—"little birds without a nest, eating the crust of humility all their life"?

That is purely Southern of the period. When I was a little girl there were at least two such women in our quiet river town. One of them lived with her married sister, and all the children, including me, were sent to her for music lessons. The other lived with what I hope were kind friends. Twice a year she went to the city—that would be St. Louis or Evansville—to buy us all hats on commission. When I was in the Indian suit-Irish mail stage she brought me a wide-brimmed leghorn with flowers. A spreading adder would not have filled me with more horror. But my mother said, "You have to wear it at least once—we can't hurt Miss Myra's feelings."

Tennessee would never hurt Miss Myra's feelings. He might find her pitiful, even tragic, or hilarious—more likely all three—but he would touch her gently, if inexorably, with love.

From CHERYL CRAWFORD

I am very proud to have produced four plays by Tennessee Williams. What other author has written eight great plays?

From HELEN DEUTSCH

I had only one encounter with Tennessee Williams. I was just out of school. I had seen *The Glass Menagerie*. I don't remember whether it was at a restaurant or at a dinner party. He was talking on and on.

Suddenly he fell silent and stared at me.

"You're listening," he said.

I nodded.

"Most people don't," he said. "They just pretend to. They know all the things to do—nod, smile, make little affirmative sounds."

From WILLIAM S. GRAY

I first met Tennessee Williams in the late '40s. At that time he was very well known but not famous internationally. I was a graduate student at Tulane University in New Orleans, and I saw him whenever he was in town. He had just written *The Rose Tattoo* and had rather recently formed a close relationship with Frankie Merlo. I often wonder about the "old bunch" from those days (and the days before) that he introduced me to and with whom I became close friends. There was the mysterious Valentina (I wonder if she is still alive?), Pancho Rodriguez (who was partially the model for Stanley in *Streetcar*), Dick Orme (from whom Tennessee rented an apartment in the Quarter during part of the time he was writing *Streetcar*), Stark Young, and so many others that he doesn't mention in *Memoirs*. Those were days of wine and roses and nights of love and laughter in New Orleans. We would go to the beach a lot and read poetry to one another. He read me (and he read beautifully) Hart Crane, Charlotte Mew, D. H. Lawrence, Federico García Lorca, and others. I read to him Gerard Manley Hopkins, W. B. Yeats, Ezra Pound, T. S. Eliot, W. H. Auden, and others. Of them all, he liked Yeats and Eliot best. He kept asking me questions about Eliot, upon whom I was writing my M.A. thesis. Then, partially at his suggestion, I went to New York and enrolled in New York University. There I saw much more of him than I did in New Orleans. I shared an apartment with Mike Steen, another friend of Tennessee's, who later wrote a good book about him entitled *A Look at Tennessee Williams*. He was kind enough to ask me to write the introduction to this book. In those days, the early '50s, Tennessee and Frankie were living in an apartment above Johnny Nickleson's restaurant. It was during this period that I got to know Carson McCullers, Gore Vidal, and Truman Capote, three authors who interested Tennessee very much but for different reasons. Once we went out to Coney Island and sat in the sun. I asked him who were the writers who had influenced him the most and he thought a long time before replying. Finally he said: Chekhov, Hart Crane, D. H. Lawrence, Lorca, and Rainer Maria Rilke.

Tennessee was, I feel, essentially a lonely person. He had a tragic sense of life. And yet he had a great sense of humor. In the old days, he used to wear a little diamond ring. I think Kip may have given it to him. And when he would put his hand out, look at the ring, and say, "My diamonds are brilliant tonight," one knew the evening would be fun. He did many nice things for me, but I suppose the nicest thing he did occurred one evening in 1954. He was reading his poetry to me and I loved it. I told him that he should publish it in book form. He was hesitant about this but I insisted. Finally, he asked me if I would help him select the poems and more or less edit the book. Naturally, I was delighted to do this. After it was done, he asked me if I would mind if he dedicated the book to me. I was flattered, but I had always wondered why he had never dedicated a book to his maternal grandfather, whom he loved so much. Since his grandfather had died the year before at a great age (nearly a hundred) and also since I had liked his grandfather so very much, I suggested that the book of poems, *In The Winter of Cities*, be dedicated to him, and so it was. I am acknowledged in the front of the book. Some of these poems formed the basis for some of his short stories, which were later to form the basis for some of his plays, one-act and three-act plays. It is curious how some of Tennessee's themes that first appeared tentatively in the '40s would reappear as late as the late '70s. The poems, as many of the plays, concern the nature of the human heart, the wellsprings of our emotions, our search for compassion, sympathy, and above all, understanding. And how he loved Carson McCullers. He felt very close to her and was crushed by her death. I was with Tennessee and William Faulkner once but not much came out of that evening. Another evening I was with Tennessee and Wystan Auden. I'm afraid I did most of the talking that evening. It is strange; one hopes one's friends will relate with one another, but, alas, this is not always the case.

Tennessee liked to go to movies, and we saw many of them together, but rarely would he sit through the whole movie. This was true of plays also. He once told me that he thought everything was too long, including life. He frequently mentioned death, and on the last photograph he inscribed for me, he wrote: "For Bill, Forget me not! Love, Tennessee." When they telephoned me about his death I returned to the photograph. I will not forget him. I only hope that he met some kind strangers along the way, especially in his later life when I saw relatively little of him, though we did continue to correspond and occasionally call one another. I was (and am) teaching English here at Randolph-Macon College in Ashland, Virgina, and he was living more and more in Key West, so we seldom saw one another the last years of his life, but when we did it was always great fun. It was as if we had seen each other only yesterday. When they called and asked me to be a pallbearer at his funeral, I was deeply moved, but I was much more moved by the memory of him and his work and did not feel that I could face going out to St. Louis and the ordeal of the funeral after I had promised him that he would be buried at sea. In a certain sense, his life was always "at sea," and his death is now surrounded by mystery. But one thing is certain, and that is his genius. He is the American Chekhov and he, along with William Faulkner, certainly told not only the truth about the American South but also about the human heart.

From ESTHER M. JACKSON

Tennessee Williams: Poet in the Contemporary Theater

Tennessee Williams was a dominant figure in a period of Western theater history which saw the American drama achieve mature status, both as a popular form and a distinctive literary kind.

The period in which Williams emerged was the second in a progression which saw the rise of the American drama as a distinctive kind. The first was signalled by the opening of O'Neill's sea play, *Bound East for Cardiff*, in New York in 1916; the second by the opening of Williams's poetic work, *The Glass Menagerie*, in Chicago, in 1944; and a third by the opening of Edward Albee's urban tragedy, *The Zoo Story*, in Berlin in 1958.

Of these phases of development in the brief history of the American theater as a distinctive kind, the period between 1945 and 1958 would appear to have been most critical. For it was the period in which the American drama gained international recognition as a significant form, a genre distinct from earlier and related kinds.

Tennessee Williams was conscious of his role in this development. Indeed it was one which he

defined for himself in the beginning stages of his career. In the preface to *The Glass Menagerie*, the young artist declared that he had engaged upon the creation of a "new, plastic theatre which must take the place of the exhausted theatre of realistic conventions if the theatre is to resume vitality as a part of our culture."

Actually, efforts to create a form such as Williams described had been in progress in Western theater for much of a century. In the United States, creation of such a vital form had been a primary focus of the career of Eugene O'Neill, as well as of those of other American playwrights, including Elmer Rice, Paul Green, Maxwell Anderson, and Thornton Wilder. Even as Williams announced his artistic intent, Arthur Miller, a playwright of his own generation, was engaged in a similar effort.

The Glass Menagerie was, in effect, an expression of a development which involved a surprisingly sophisticated synthesis of forms and contents drawn from a variety of sources, including literature, the visual arts, music, dance, and the new arts of radio, television, and the cinema. It could be argued that the play represented a refinement of the idea of form shaped by O'Neill in the early decades of the century and elaborated by Rice, Green, Anderson, and Wilder.

But *The Glass Menagerie* was not to be the measure of Tennessee Williams's success in creating a "new plastic theatre," nor indeed would any single work created by the playwright exemplify the idea of form which he sought to perfect. Rather, his achievement—like that of Eugene O'Neill—can be understood only by examination of the body of his work. Through the pattern of his experimentation—from early plays such as *This Property is Condemned* to late works such as *Out Cry*, there did indeed emerge the vital American form which he envisioned.

A Streetcar Named Desire (1947), *The Rose Tattoo* (1951), *Camino Real* (1953), *Cat on a Hot Tin Roof* (1955), *Suddenly Last Summer* (1958), *Sweet Bird of Youth* (1959), *Period of Adjustment* (1960), and *Night of the Iguana* (1961) mark stages in the progression of that dynamic form.

The pivotal role of Tennessee Williams in the creation of a distinctive American form may be attributed to his ability to translate the sensibility of the world in which he lived into a poetic language.

He was able to create a "poetry of the commonplace" which could be realized on the stage. To that end, he employed an expressive language adapted from the full range of the arts—poetry, fiction, music, painting, architecture, and sculpture. To these linguistic components, he added forms and contents drawn from the new arts of radio, cinema, television, and innumerable varieties of popular entertainment.

As a writer, Williams displayed a remarkable ability to mediate between tradition and originality; that is, to adapt characters, modes of action, and ideas drawn from the history of literary genres to forms arising from the popular imagination. At the same time, he showed himself able to fashion new characters—figures drawn from contemporary American life—and to set them in recognizable environments. He was able to attribute to these original characters capacities for action, ideals, thought, and feeling associated with great heroes and heroines in more traditional forms of literature.

Because of his success in solving the problem of stage language—a problem largely unresolved in the dramaturgy of an earlier generation of American playwrights—Williams was at mid-century the dominant figure in American theater. That dominance persisted for approximately two decades; that is, from 1945 to 1965. The last of his stage successes, *The Night of the Iguana*, was produced in 1961; however, his works continued to find audiences through the medium of the cinema, a form on which he continued to draw in formulating his ideas about theater.

In the mid-1960s, the playwright appeared to suffer a loss of critical and popular favor. The decline in critical esteem which began with *The Milk Train Doesn't Stop Here Anymore* (1962-1963), continued through the late '60s, '70s, and early '80s.

Of the plays written in the period between 1965 and the playwright's death in 1983, only *The Two-Character Play* (1967; later entitled *Out Cry*, 1973) elicited continuing interest among producers, performers, and critics. No play of this later period in the playwright's career has elicited the kinds of responses from artists, audiences, or critics directed to works produced in the '40s, '50s, and early '60s.

A close look at the available texts of the plays written by Tennessee Williams during the '70s and '80s seems to suggest that the problems which they present are not in fact unlike those presented by earlier plays. A poet in the theater, Williams created scenarios which require concretization by a metteur-en-scène. As the imagery of the later plays grew more complex and the actions traced more intricate, the process of translating these scenarios into the language of theater grew more demanding for actors, directors, and designers.

But there was in this final period of Williams's career a factor of even greater significance. Today it would appear that the decline of public interest in his work followed a change in the sensibility of the age, both in American society and in the world community. New patterns—expressive of new and powerful social, political, and intellectual concerns—emerged in the arts, as in society, in the middle to late '60s. These new contents required substantial modifications of the production styles developed for earlier works. For a variety of reasons, systematic opportunities for the consideration of the nature of the production styles required for these later works appear to have been limited. The works of this final period remain, in effect, untested.

Even without a comprehensive assessment of these later works—a task which requires carefully devised production studies—the evidence of Tennessee Williams's contribution to the American theater arts is impressive. His most evident contribution to the American drama is the creation of stage speech of poetic quality, a language characterized by beauty, eloquence, and universal meaning. A second contribution is the systemization of an American mise-en-scène; that is, the organization of patterns of acting, directing, design, and theater technology in a "plastic imagery" expressive of the quality of the American imagination.

A third aspect of his contribution to the maturing form of the American drama involves his ability to reveal eternal patterns of meaning obscured beneath the patterns of modern life. To a degree equaled by few Western playwrights of his epoch, Tennessee Williams was able to transcend barriers of class, language, and culture, as well as time, place, and condition, to create a poetic form of universal appeal.

Through the comprehensive pattern of experimentation which his work represented, Tennessee Williams advanced the American drama toward maturity, both as a literary genre and a popular form of special significance in world theater.

From ELIA KAZAN

Ever since Tennessee Williams died I've been hearing nothing but how unhappy his life was, how particularly wretched his last years, with dark hints about this, that, and the other. Of course his powers declined as he came into his sixties. That's true of all mankind. Tennessee was poet enough to know that. The man lived a very good life, full of the most profound pleasures, and he lived it precisely as he chose. That is allowed to few of us. The talent he had was completely realized in plays that will not disappear from our boards, our memories, and our feelings. Who of us in the theater can say they've lived a life of work as adventurous as his and as continuous in achievement—which is certainly the deepest kind of pleasure. Imagine yourselves in his skin on the morning he wrote some of the speeches we all know so well. Or watching a performance of *The Glass Menagerie* and recognizing his family transmuted into art. In rehearsals together, what fun we had! Think of the true and grateful friends he made all over the world, wherever people read, wherever plays are mounted and films photographed. Think of the respect he's been given and deserved and the adulation—which he certainly enjoyed. Who was ever more universally admired in our time? What the hell do people who've been moaning and groaning over him expect? We should not be gathering to mourn the man, we should not be shedding public tears and making sad group noises. We should now and here do what the Indians in the East do at their great funerals of distinguished persons: celebrate his life. It was a triumph! Let us now and here celebrate his life and thank our supreme good fortune for having had him and for having had him as long as we did. I once said what I'm going to say now about another person, my first wife, Molly, and I haven't said it since. Tennessee Williams built his own monument. There's nothing left for us to do except admire the race for having produced a man like him. And perhaps whenever and wherever talent comes into our view, give it the respect and support it deserves. That's how we can best remember Thomas Lanier Williams.

From RICHARD FREEMAN LEAVITT

Tennessee Williams was gifted with an inner eye through which he saw with terrible clarity—in the most ordinary events and people—that which was spiritually significant. But the gods do not give freely. If the gift was exalting, it was also existential, and he paid for it with a lifelong sense of aloneness. But what Cavalier ever followed his heart more faithfully?

From FREDERICK NICKLAUS

Tennessee Williams, Brentano's bookstore, New York City, autumn 1957. Overseas Highway, Key West, March 1964. This was the time I knew him. The vulnerability and violence of his work, the

death of his dear friend—guilt, rage—it all comes down with the rain. We shared a glass of Scotch mixed with rainwater. Only Tennessee would have thought of that mix.

Once, when he tripped into a tree-well in Tangier, he assured me, as I helped him up, that he was made of india rubber, as his grandfather was. We walked on happily to the beach, the water.

From JAMES PURDY

Tennessee Williams's death is a deep personal loss to me. I greatly admired his use of the American language, the insight, the remarkable sympathy he had for his characters, his humor, his poetry. I also owe another debt of gratitude to him because he was one of the first American writers to be attracted to my fiction. He frequently attended productions of my plays and read the texts with care—always encouraging me to write more for the theater.

A needed light has gone off for those of us who cared deeply for him and his work.

From STEPHEN S. STANTON

Tennessee Williams was one of America's greatest Southern writers—by many he was considered, at the time of his death, the greatest American playwright. His accidental and untimely death Tennessee himself would have recognized as having the ironical ring of the absurd. "I'm not reconciled to dying before my work is finished," he said in an interview. "I have a very strong will . . . my will forces me to go on because I've got unfinished work." Whatever may be the verdict about the quality of his work since the early 1960s, Tennessee Williams had an iron tenacity of will, a courage that knew no diminution in the face of a lifetime of physical illness and, at times, acute mental depression. In one of his best known essays, "On a Streetcar Named Success," he wrote: "The monosyllable of the clock is loss, loss, loss unless you devote your heart to its opposition." And Williams did devote every day of his mature life to its opposition, thereby setting the highest possible standard for human endeavor.

From DONALD WINDHAM

I have recorded in the book of Tennessee's letters to me my liking for him, the pleasure it was for me to be with him in his salad days—from 1940 on. He was the one person I loved to whom I did not have a physical attachment. In the early years our concerns were mutual, or at least I felt that they were. His devotion to his work inspired me. Even after his success, our senses of humor, our passions, our aims as writers remained similar in my eyes. His inscriptions in the copies he gave me of his first three published plays, which I still have, suggest that he felt the same: "Battle of Angels," *To Donnie whom I met first in N.Y. and hope to know last, ever*; "The Glass Menagerie," *To Windham who first approved, with love*; "A Streetcar Named Desire," *To a fellow passenger, with love.*

–*From* Footnote to a Friendship. A memoir of Truman Capote and others, *by Donald Windham (Verona: Sandy Campbell, 1983)*

UPDATED ENTRIES

George Garrett

(11 June 1929-)

R. H. W. Dillard
Hollins College

See also the Garrett entries in *DLB 2, American Novelists Since World War II*, and *DLB 5, American Poets Since World War II*.

NEW BOOK: *The Succession: A Novel of Elizabeth and James* (Garden City: Doubleday, 1983).

A dozen years after the publication of his highly successful novel about Sir Walter Ralegh, *Death of the Fox* (1971), George Garrett has published a new novel, *The Succession: A Novel of Elizabeth and James* (1983), which both extends and fulfills the stylistic and formal advances of the earlier novel and thereby moves the historical novel itself into new and valuable territory. It is at once a recreation of the complex events surrounding the succession of James I to the throne of Queen Elizabeth and also an aesthetic meditation on the creation and revelation of meaning in the succession of moments (real, remembered, dreamed, and imagined) that make up the living nexus of time. It is a novel that refuses to give us what we have come to expect from historical fiction, which has changed very little from Scott's *Waverly* (1814) to Mailer's *Ancient Evenings* (1983), but which gives us a great deal more—a fiction of artistic subtlety and intelligence rather than of derring-do, of living fact rather than of antiquarian gesture, a fiction for grown-ups courageously written and published at a time when Stephen King's *Pet Sematary* (1983) squats at the top of the best-seller lists like an ugly emblem of our toadish literary times.

In his essay "Dreaming With Adam: Notes on Imaginary History," which appeared in *New Literary History* in 1971, Garrett defined the writing of imaginary history as the celebration of the human imagination: "Not one's own, for the subject precludes the possibility of doing what R. P. Blackmur called to *heroize* the sensibility. The subject is not art and the artist. Flaubert did that best in *Salammbo*, and who needs to imitate his triumph? The subject is the larger imagination, the possibility of imagining lives and spirits of other human beings, living or dead, without assaulting their essential and, anyway, ineffable mystery, to dream again in recapitulation the dream of Adam, knowing, as he did not until he awoke, that it is true. . . ." *Death of the Fox* made that celebration clear, both because it was centered in the life and spirit of one man, Sir Walter Ralegh, and because that man was, in addition to all of his other characteristics and identities, an artist—a poet, a literary imaginer, as well as a settler of new worlds and a political explorer. Garrett allowed himself to move into other minds and lives in that novel, but the focus was clearly on Ralegh, and the novel was in a most mysterious and meaningful way a collaboration between two poets, Ralegh and Garrett, the two of them making contact across the intervening years to create a new and singular view of time past: Ralegh looking back at his life and Elizabethan times, and Garrett looking back to Ralegh and beyond.

Death of the Fox is a fine novel, one of the finest and richest literary explorations of human identity and the complex interchange of individual consciousness and the larger realities through which it moves and lives. But Garrett was not content to rest on the success of that book, nor was he, as is now apparent, tempted to repeat its success with another book of the same nature. *The Succession* is a historical novel; it does cover much of the same historical ground as its predecessor with many of the same characters, Ralegh among them; it does have the same sort of dense, rich texture of detail, an almost palpable recreation of the things and thoughts, the manners and ways of Elizabethan England; and it is another meditative dreaming of the dream of Adam. All of that is true, but *The Succession* is nevertheless a significantly different novel, one no longer concerned with the meaning of one man's life in his times but rather with meaning itself, with time itself, with life itself.

Having decided to move beyond the concerns of *Death of the Fox*, Garrett had no choice but to move beyond its form, to develop a radical form of sufficient complexity to allow him to deal directly with "the larger imagination." The novel has no central character, although Queen Elizabeth and King James are at the center of its events; it has instead a number of almost unrelated characters—a mes-

ONE DOLLAR

POULTRY

GEORGE
GARRETT
RIDES
AGAIN

NUMBER 25

A MAGAZINE OF VOICE

Special George Garrett issue

senger bearing the news of James's birth to William Cecil, a Catholic priest disguised and on the run, a band of reivers on the Scottish border, an old courtier looking back on the days of his youth, Robert Cecil brooding over and explicating his collection of the letters of Elizabeth and James, a player who was caught up in the rebellion of Essex, a worried King James awaiting word of the death of Elizabeth, a brooding Queen Elizabeth celebrating her last Christmas, even a happy drunken plowman walking off his Christmas dinner under the reeling stars. The novel has no central time, although the death of Elizabeth and the succession of James in 1603 are at the center of its movement; it shifts in an apparently unordered succession back and forth from 1566 to 1626, not according to the memory of any one character, but according to the experiences and memories and imaginings of all these characters. The brilliance of the novel is not that it has so many characters and covers so much time, but that out of all this apparent disorder and disconnection such a coherent and orderly and meaningful whole takes shape. It does not have a modernist preoccupation with fragmentation, but rather a thoroughly postmodernist awareness of interrelatedness and interdependence. In a completely post-Einsteinian way, even though there is no readily apparent center, the center holds.

The philosophical position of the novel is that things and events, experienced directly or experienced imaginatively, are real; an alder leaf falls between two men standing "almost in the shadow of squat old St. Cuthbert's Church in Norham village": "A single leaf—waxy green on one side, dusty gray on the bottom, ribbed and shaped like the fat bowl of a lute, floating in motley shade, lighting on the chipped gravel of the footpath, resting briefly between the toes of the four boots of the two of them, then, touched by the merest sigh of a breeze, lifting all at once like a book page to tumble away." One of the men studies the leaf. We later discover that the other man is imagining the scene in which the first man studies the leaf. We know that George Garrett has imagined the two men, the scene, and the leaf. And yet, there is the leaf, more real to the reader of the novel than any leaf that falls unnoticed in the forest, as real as any leaf that falls noticed or unnoticed in any wood or on any patio or onto and into any fish pond. That Essex did not understand this (that "it was his folly to believe that the Queen had no more substance than the crown and robes she wore, that without his eyes to give her life she was diminished to the edge of nothingness") was the source of his failure, morally and politically.

But—and this is the key to it all—meaning is not inherent in any event. Meaning, rather, accrues to experience from its relationships in time (past and future and present) and in consciousness. To a Christian, the Old Testament became fully meaningful only after it was given meaning by the coming of Christ, but any action that a Christian may now take is fully meaningful only because of Christ's having lived two thousand years ago. The leaf falls; the man notices it; the other man imagines both the leaf and its observer, although the first man is a real person who does live in Norham village. The leaf and the event take on meaning as they are imagined by the character; the leaf and the event and the character take on meaning by their being part of the political events surrounding the birth of Prince James to Mary, Queen of Scots; the leaf, the event, the character, and the birth of Prince James take on meaning 37 years later upon the succession of James to the throne of England; the leaf, the event, the character, the birth of James, and the succession of James take on meaning when imagined and shaped into a novel, *The Succession*, by George Garrett some 400 years later. And, of course, this actual leaf, the ground reality of this lengthy complex of events, did not even exist until the novel was written, although king and queen and the dweller in Norham village and the imagining messenger all did exist centuries before.

The Succession does not discuss the nature of meaning and its development like a philosophical text, but its very texture and form allow us, its readers, that rare opportunity, the chance to consider the very nature of experience, to witness and participate in the actual creation of meaning and coherence and order in an apparently meaningless and incoherent and orderless world. Of course, we do it all the time, but *The Succession*, like any serious and important work of art, makes us aware of what we are doing, gives us the opportunity to understand what we are doing and even to direct it.

Aside from his talent and intelligence, both prodigious, what enabled George Garrett to write such a book is what enabled Shakespeare or Tolstoy to write their work at the level they did: a religious belief that gives them an awareness of something larger than the passing moment, that gives them awareness of the presence of the eternal in the tem-

poral, of the universal in the particular. The time and times of *The Succession* are fully imagined and realized, a world of complexity and duplicity, a world of masks and lies and players, a world in which reality and theatricality are inextricably confused, a world of sin and sinners in which the very existence of love seems in question, a world of a virgin queen without issue, a world in which the very future seems to be in serious doubt. And yet the succession occurs, the future occurs, the sinful world moves and lives on, and George Garrett ends his novel at Christmas with a happy plowman, under the stars, imagining the queen in her bed, believing himself to be as full of love and charity as he is of food and drink and gratitude. Garrett allows us to share that plowman's belief (he uses the second person to assure us that sharing) and wishes us all (and has us wish each other) "for the sake of our own Sweet Jesus, a good night." This Christian blessing is at the heart of the novel; its simplicity informs and gives ultimate meaning to all of the complexity of the novel's radical form and substance, of what William Goyen (another Christian artist) called its "magnitude and intricacy."

The Succession is George Garrett's fifth novel, his nineteenth book. He has proven himself a major American writer, and yet most of those books are out of print. That sad fact is, I suspect, just a sign of the times, of a devolution of literary values in this country, of what Richard Kostelanetz once called the end of intelligent writing in America. When the minimalist reportage of a Raymond Carver or an Ann Beattie is respected more than the subtlety and complexity and richness of a George Garrett or a Robert Coover or a William Goyen, then we are in hard times indeed, and it is very tempting to believe that the very future of literature is in serious doubt. And yet *The Succession* has been written and published even as the sinful world moves and lives on, proof in itself that intelligent writing in America is not at an end, proof in itself that meaning continues to change and to be created, proof in itself that "the larger imagination" continues to express itself and ourselves. There is occasion here for great celebration, and so should we all.

AN INTERVIEW

with GEORGE GARRETT

DLB: Why did you turn historical novelist in mid- or late career?

GARRETT: I don't think that's the only kind of

thing I'm going to be doing or would have done. I had worked on a Ralegh biography back in the fifties—nothing came of it, and everybody rejected another novel that I had written, called "Do Lord, Remember Me," except Charles Duell of Duell, Sloan and Pearce. He liked it and was going to do it, and then he merged with Meredith Press; and they asked one thing of him at the merger: he said they were not going to bother him about anything else. They asked that he would never publish this "Do Lord, Remember Me." He called up from the meeting where he was actually signing the merger and said this was the case and that if I wanted to hold him to it he wouldn't go ahead. He was an old friend, too, but he said he had gotten from them a statement that they would publish anything else sight unseen except that. So did I have any ideas whatsoever—he'd give me a contract; and I said what about Sir Walter Ralegh? I was still thinking about the biography. He said fine and hung up. Then I got a contract the next day in the mail for Sir Walter Ralegh. That's how I ended up writing historical novels.

DLB: You have said that in both *Death of the Fox* and *The Succession*, you attempted to demonstrate "Something about how history happens." How does history happen?

GARRETT: I think what I really meant to say there was something about time—something which is more evident in the second novel than in the first, although the first one is involved with memory. The second one has less organized memory than it does the kind of simultaneity. In both of them I was trying to deal in different ways with a variety of characters, some of whom really don't cause large things to happen in history but are a part of the whole picture.

DLB: Is this one of the reasons why you admire James Gould Cozzens, then? Because of his ability to show a lot of things going on at the same time?

GARRETT: Yes. I think that maybe the first time I really saw how that can work was when I read *Guard of Honor*. That was close to my own experience in the sense that I grew up in Orlando, so I knew some of the real events. And when I saw what he had done with all those different people, that certainly was an influence in the way of thinking about what you can do in a novel which I've never seen anybody do before.

DLB: O. B. Hardison has cited the influence of Faulkner on *The Succession*. Where would you say the influence manifests itself—in the narrative technique?

GARRETT: Well, maybe sometimes. . . . I hope it doesn't manifest itself in style. That's the area in which I think Faulkner has had a kind of negative influence on people. I think in a positive way his ability—remember, no two of those novels are alike, so in a sense they've always been a series of doors opening for other people coming along afterward. In a sense he's been an enormous influence in the way that he's pointed out a whole lot of different directions that you can go in. One consistent thing in his work has been his style, but if you can get around that without being hypnotized, he had all these narrative possibilities. I think that in *The Succession* maybe that's what Hardison's talking about—that each of the sections has a different narrative stance and that probably I wouldn't have thought of doing something like that if I hadn't had some sense of all the possibilities from Faulkner.

DLB: Obviously *The Succession* demands attention from the reader—those shifts in narrative stance or point of view—and inevitably it's going to cost you some readers: the readers who simply don't have the attention spans to remember from section to section. Who did what? Who said what? Did you feel then and do you still feel that it was worth abandoning these readers in order to tell the story the way you wanted to tell it from multiple angles?

GARRETT: I was hoping I wouldn't be abandoning too many readers. There aren't too many spit-backs in books, and if they started out at the beginning it might be too late to bring it back and demand their money back. On the other hand, I couldn't think of any other way to tell this particular story. If I could have, I'd have been delighted to tell it in a straightforward way.

DLB: Was *The Succession* planned or envisioned at the time of *Death of the Fox*?

GARRETT: After I finished that book I planned to do a very short novel concerning the letters (that is now just the chapter in *The Succession*), and I kept trying to do that but it just didn't really work. It evolved over a long period of time. I really had no idea at the time other than that I ought to do something about those letters that I had read and was

2X3XC487-

lightly armed horsemen. They disappear into ~~the~~ A screening
of dust. From which cloud for a long time after they hear the CONTINUE TO
sound of ~~the~~ fifes and drums.

Now more dust swirls over Newmarket Road between the wind-
mill and Cambridge as the artillery, the field guns known as
the slings, and all the baggage train of high-loaded two-wheeled
carts straggles along, strung out far behind.

--Well, says one, after they are safely down and walking
home, I pity those poor ~~rebellious~~ farmers of Norfolk.

--God help the ~~poor~~ fools. They will never have seen or
imagined anything like that.

--~~Nor~~ have I, he says. ~~(Thinking then it would be a glor-~~
~~ious thing to be a soldier.)~~   ⊃

~~(Not~~ thinking that for long....)

Only a few days into August when the news ~~reached~~ CAME TO Cambridge from dirty ~~and~~ bedraggled, white-eyed riders. How
Kett's rebels had ~~completely defeated and~~ routed Northampton's
forces. How many men, even including some of the gentlemen,
had died there. How the rebels now held Norwich. And soon THEN ENOUGH
behind the riders came a ~~ragged~~ straggle of the survivors,
most of their weapons and armor gone. Some hobbling in bloody
bandages. Those who could not walk ~~were~~ crammed in groaning
carts leaving trails of bloodstains, clot and gout, behind them.
All of them terribly thirsty, hungry enough to steal or to kill.
~~in their many.~~ Town and the colleges mustered in arms, as much or
more against these desperate scarecrows as against any possibility

Revised page from the typescript for The Succession *(the author)*

interested in. I didn't envision a book like this one at all.

DLB: How long did it take you to write it from the point when you decided this was the book you were going to write?

GARRETT: I started fooling around with it early in 1970, but it was only about 1979 that I figured out the particular scheme that I used after I had tried everything else. And I really finished it for all practical purposes by the summer of 1981, so it was a little delayed getting out.

DLB: I understand it was delayed by cutting.

GARRETT: Yes, I cut some out. It was maybe twice as long as it is.

DLB: Do you regret the cuts?

GARRETT: Some of them I do, yes. Others not so much. Essentially it was improved by cutting, I think. Whenever you do that, you lose some things that you'd like to keep in. There are a couple of chances of doing something with some of those things. The Courtier was originally all one section—and was very, very long—250 pages or so. Now it's just three little sections, I think, but I've thought sometimes of putting that all back together, in some way, somewhere down the road.

DLB: In David Slavitt's very warm, receptive review in *Philadelphia*, he calls you "the best obscure writer or the most obscure excellent writer in America." How do you feel about those designations?

GARRETT: I'm beginning to think maybe he was right as far as obscurity is concerned. I don't know about excellence. Yes, it's true, I think, in a way. I keep forgetting it's been such a long time since I had a book out that a lot of people are unaware—in the literary world—that I've done anything, so you always start from square one. And wait and see what happens.

DLB: How do you feel about the early reviews of *The Succession*?

GARRETT: Well, those that I've seen have been very generous. An interesting one to me was the one in *Newsweek* by Peter Prescott. He put his finger on a lot of things that worried me about the book. Some of them I think I solved or I hope I did, but in any

case in a sense he hit most of the vulnerable spots. It was a mixed review. But I don't know what else is to come. As of the time we're talking there haven't been any reviews in the *Times* and may not for all I know. I don't know what's going to happen, but with a couple like the one in the *Wall Street Journal* and the Richard Elman review on the radio and Slavitt's, a guy could get pretty spoiled. Those have been very extravagant, well beyond generosity.

DLB: Do you read reviews attentively? Do you feel there's been anything to be gained by the writer from reading reviews of his work?

GARRETT: I don't think there's a whole lot. I read them trying to see how maybe we're going to make out. I don't think there's anything I can do now to straighten anything out. All that you learn—something I've learned the hard way—all that you learn in doing a book is that, when you're all finished with it, you now know how you should have done it. I haven't found any reviews that pointed me in any helpful direction for the future.

DLB: They don't hurt you either?

GARRETT: No—well—yes. A siege of them, which I've had before, can hurt you with the publisher and hurt your feelings. I can imagine very well, though, problems that some writers have had in the past, where a book has been, it seems to me, misunderstood by a lot of critics. I've just seen one recently. There's a book called *Amateur's Guide to the Night*, a collection of stories from Alfred Knopf by Mary Robison. I picked the book up because it was just thin enough to go in my bag to go on the airplane last week, and I had read two or three reviews of it which made it sound like an Ann Beattie book or a Raymond Carver book. It was completely different and it was very funny. No review had mentioned that the work was funny at all. Perhaps it isn't; maybe it's just funny to me.

I sometimes think that Fitzgerald may have been hurt. . . . It makes me sad to think of him trying to fix *Tender Is the Night* in response to negative reviews about it. I like it the way it was first published, and I don't like the fixed version very much.

DLB: Somebody once said that the wise writer reads the rave reviews and throws the rest away.

GARRETT: That's a good idea. I remember Truman Capote saying that there was only one kind of review that he found extremely useful. He was asked what that was, and he said, "the flattering kind."

DLB: What next?

GARRETT: Well, immediately I've got—I'm reading proof on it right this minute while I'm talking to you this afternoon—the James Jones biography in The Album Biography Series; and I've got a book of poems coming out this spring.

DLB: Who is publishing the poems?

GARRETT: University of Arkansas Press is doing mine and John Ciardi's at the same time.

DLB: Do you think *The Succession* will lead to another historical novel?

GARRETT: I know it's going to lead to one very short one. I'm going to do a quite short, skinny one—like one of the sections in *The Succession*—which has to do with the murder of Christopher Marlowe, and then that's it—I'm done with historical fiction.

DLB: How did you get into the seventeenth century? Was that one of your interests in college?

GARRETT: In a way it was. I got into it through the poetry of the period and particularly the poetry of Ralegh. That led—beginning in the late forties—to reading as much as I could about the period. At that time it had been a long time since there'd been a full-scale biography of Ralegh. I thought I would do that. I was totally unprepared for it. Just a crazy, youthful idea. A number of them came along, but by that time I had worked on the period enough to get hooked.

DLB: When you're not writing, you're reading. Is your reading directed? Do you say to yourself: I am reading because this will help me in my writing—or do you just read higgledy-piggledy?

GARRETT: I think more and more I just read higgledy-piggledy. It will be hard to say what it's

going to be like in the future; but since a certain amount of reading had to be directed in the sense of being reading for research, my reading for pleasure was without any confusion about usefulness. Occasionally something would come along on an assignment and that again would be directed reading. So that part of the reading has always been, over the past twenty years or so, directed, and then the other part counteracted that—just reading around, taking books off the shelf, generally indulging myself. I think, though, about the research, that beyond a certain rudimentary point I didn't know what I was looking for. So in a sense I had to skim through everything, sort of letting things happen. Beyond a basic level, I had to kind of let everything go by. When you don't know what you're looking for that's kind of undirected reading too, although some of that so-called directed reading was in the sixteenth- and seventeenth-century material. So I saw a lot of things then that I would like to go back and read for pleasure sometime. Frequently I like to read a lot of poetry or nonfiction when I am writing fiction.

DLB: Does your writing of poetry and your writing of prose fiction get compartmentalized? Do you say now I'm a poet?

GARRETT: No, well, actually it's something I just noticed only in putting together these collected poems. It is clear that what happens is that they react on each other, and in part the poetry does the opposite of what I'm doing in prose. When I was writing contemporary stories the poetry tended to be formal and kind of quasilyrical. While I was writing this book the poetry tended to be kind of prosaic, anecdotal, and very contemporary.

DLB: How do you know whether something is an idea for a poem or an idea for a story?

GARRETT: Sometimes I don't at all. Sometimes the same things have shown up again in another form. The very nature of them is something too small to be a story but an anecdote that could be told in verse. As time goes on I'm beginning to see that I unconsciously reworked the material. Presumably one could do it consciously and benefit from doing it that way.

Norman Mailer

(31 January 1923-   )

Philip Bufithis
Shepherd College

See also the Mailer entries in *DLB 2, American Novelists Since World War II*; *DLB Yearbook: 1980*; *DLB Documentary Series*, volume 3; and *DLB 16, The Beats: Literary Bohemians in Postwar America*.

NEW BOOK: *Ancient Evenings* (Boston: Little, Brown, 1983; London: Macmillan, 1983).

Ancient Evenings is a fusion of vitality, frankness, sensuousness, dread, metaphysics, occultism, pretension, and cunning. A work of mythic themes, a family saga ranging back into ancient times, the novel is part of a projected cycle. Its two-to-four volumes of sequels will take place in modern times and in the future. Seldom has a book been so long and eagerly awaited. The prepublication excitement began in 1974 with the news that Mailer had received from Little, Brown a $1-million advance for the cycle.

Set in Egypt during the nineteenth and twentieth dynasties (1290-1100 B.C.), *Ancient Evenings* traces, in 709 large pages, the complex fate of one man, Menenhetet, who has been reincarnated three times. Murdered in his first life while copulating with a queen of Ramses II, Menenhetet reincarnates himself in her womb. He effects his next two reincarnations by self-inducing his death while copulating.

Menenhetet narrates the story of his four lives at a dinner party in the palace of Ramses IX. The occasion is the Night of the Pig, a time of lambent wildness when irregularities and iconoclastic talk are permitted. As thousands of caged fireflies illumine the pharaoh's pillared patio against the surrounding dark, Menenhetet imparts his autobiography to four listeners—Ramses IX, the pharaoh's Overseer of the Cosmetic Box, the Overseer's beautiful wife, and their six-year-old son, who is Menenhetet Two, the great-grandson of Menenhetet. Intensified by the social drama that frames it, Menenhetet's story extends to the threshold of the dawn, and so nearly to the end of the novel.

Menenhetet's four lives form an arc. In his first life he ascends from peasant beginnings to his apex as First Charioteer to His Majesty, Ramses II.

Norman Mailer (Renate Ponsold)

Later he becomes overseer of Ramses II's harem of queens. In his second life he is a formidable high priest whose occult practices, people say, risk profanity. In his third life he is a shrewd brothel keeper who becomes a vastly rich papyrus manufacturer. In his fourth life he is a respected nobleman—astute, corrupt, and thwarted in his ambition to be vizier to Ramses IX and eventually pharaoh himself. He dies a grave robber.

The other major narrative voice is that of the departed soul—the Ka or ghost—of Menenhetet Two, who was murdered at the age of twenty-one and now describes the dinner party from his memory of it. The desolate Ka of Menenhetet Two opens the novel with its most fascinating section, the thirty-eight-page "Book of One Man Dead." The Ka vividly describes its agonizing struggle to wrest itself free from entombment in the Great Pyramid of Khufu; quaking with fear, it recollects how two embalmers, step by horrific step, prepared its body for mummification. There is a consciousness here not met with in any other fiction. The reader is pulled into the Ka's strange cares and yearnings as it painfully orients itself to the shock of its nonmortal existence and meets the grim, awesome Ka of Menenhetet. The evocation of the Great Pyramid—its enclosed spaces and furnishings, the view from it of the immense starry night over the land—imparts a felt sense of mystery, wonder, and dread. The last scene of the novel is also striking. After 600 pages, Mailer's prose soars as the Ka of Menenhetet Two resumes its narration in the Great Pyramid and continues its talk with the Ka of Menenhetet, who guides the young Ka through the Land of the Dead. *Ancient Evenings* constitutes, then, two mountains between which lies the vast plain of Menenhetet's dinner-party narrative.

No novel resembles it. One may well ask, then, just what Mailer has done. The answer, no less true for its simplicity, is that he has written a novel about magic. Mailer is telling us—there is always that rabbinical teaching streak in him—that a life lived according to a belief in magic can be deeply vitalizing and creative, for when the gods dwell in the things of this world, energy and powerfully sustaining meaning can be found everywhere. Mailer wants us to believe that magic can make as much sense out of the world as science and its handmaiden technology. The novel's title is meant to suggest that an evening spent in Egypt three thousand years ago could well have been as fully interesting—though not the same—as an evening spent anywhere in the world today.

In an interview with the *Washington Post* (20 April 1983), Mailer informatively discussed some of the thinking that went into *Ancient Evenings*:

> "This is one of the few books I know," Mailer says, "that treats magic with respect. See, magic bears the same relation to the Egyptians that technology does to us. One of the things I wanted to shock and startle the reader with is: Look what a comprehensive world view magic gives you. When it works, it's marvelous and it fortifies their view of the universe. When it doesn't work, it's that something went wrong with the *process*. It's never the fundamental belief that's shaken." Similarly, "our belief in science is, if not tragically misplaced, certainly megalomaniacal." In fact, "it could be said by future generations, if there are any, that we're much sillier

than the Egyptians," because we use technology "to slowly but systematically deaden and debase our way of life. Each year there's more real poverty in the synapses than there was the year before." The chief (and predictable) offender: television.

"I feel as if we've all gone completely in the wrong direction. When God first conceived the world, I don't think it was His or Her notion—that much effect the women's movement has had on me!—that we would have television. I don't think all those worlds came out of the cosmos in order to have people sitting around like sheep looking at a livid luminescent screen."

But this animism he finds so appealing in the Egyptians—has he experienced it himself? "Well, let's say I find it philosophically congenial. For instance, listen to this—are you ready?" And he rips a piece out of the sandwich bag with a noisy flourish. "Now the Egyptians would doubtless have said that sound is what the god of this bag uttered when wounded. And that makes absolutely as much sense to me as some incredibly difficult and incomprehensible discussion on the collision of sine waves. I believe there are all sorts of forces in the universe, some more tangible than others, nearly all of them invisible, that sort of aid us or f— us up. One of the ways you can spot that is that you can be engaged in something that you're dead serious about. It can turn out badly or well, but you feel considerably more or less elation or despondency than you should. One knows instinctively that there were bad spirits or good ones around affecting the result."

Far better that one seek help from magic than from science, for magic, Mailer believes, speaks to the soul—to the transcendent—in man. The novel's fundamental theme forcefully addresses Western postindustrial life: man has insulated himself within rationality, shrunken himself into it, yet it can never explain what or who he is or where he has come from or where he is going.

Mailer's religious vitalism resembles that of the American transcendentalists; though, of course, he does not share their characteristic quietism. Over the past forty years, Mailer's combined works have constituted an epic satire based on his observations of what the transcendentalists were always noting—the spiritual puniness man has reduced himself to. "Man is the dwarf of himself," wrote Emerson. And so, Mailer would add, he has come to allow lifelessness—television and plastic—to surround him and stultify his nerve endings. Absorbed

Dust jacket for Mailer's long-awaited Egyptian novel, which Mary Lee Settle calls "Mailer's finest and most courageous book"

omnipotent. Like man himself, they are struggling for completion in the existential sense of making themselves. And man, far from having a bit part in the cosmic drama, is the embodiment or instrument of their endeavor to grow. They enlist man to help them and thereby impel him beyond his natural limits. Mailer refutes, then, the modern literary image of man as a sadly laughable creature caught up in a network of circumstances beyond his power to know or control. Menenhetet trembles. He falters. But he never believes that his being alive is mere happenstance. He has been launched into the cosmos by powers greater than himself, and it is his purpose to actualize those powers through the exertions of his own creative will.

Menenhetet evolves by going back—back, that is, to his primordial being. The way up is the way down. The subconscious, Mailer still believes, is the mind of primordial being. It is an energy, an intelligence, existing outside civilization and time. Menenhetet's commitment is to understand this mysterious region, to learn the face of the deep, and then to act eventfully in the world to substantiate his newfound knowledge.

Mailer intends Menenhetet's narrative to be a fiery chisel working its way into all the dull liars of American guilt and malaise. His method is to present a narrator whose senses are unsheathed, who looks at the world—smells it, feels it, hears it, tastes it—with an accelerated consciousness, who involves himself in the perilous rather than separating himself from it. "The senses," Mailer says in an interview in *Harvard Magazine* (March-April 1983), "are always an objective correction against having our minds manipulated too far in a direction that's not natural." An instinctual logic informs Menenhetet: in order to realize one's potential, the overlay of social conformity that insulates the mind and feelings must be broken through by taking risks, by pushing oneself, if necessary, to the limits of experience. Facing the dread—battling Hittites arm to arm, seducing the pharaoh's queen, invoking fearsome gods—means for Menenhetet destroying stale conceptual modes and forging new circuits of energy.

Menenhetet Two reflects that as a boy he saw "the flutter of the tiny spurwing as she nibbled at river worms embedded in the mouth of a crocodile." The spurwing symbolizes the life of ongoing renewal. The Ka of Menenhetet tells the Ka of Menenhetet Two that "one cannot gain a great deal unless one is willing to dare losing all. That is how the loveliest plunder is found." Piety is the opposite life. "Look for risk," says the Ka of

in television, he lives vicariously. And every time he uses a plastic object instead of a natural one, he chooses a bit of death over a bit of life. Plastic does not resonate. It is separate from nature. It is the waste material of oil—the excrement of oil. Mailer sounds like Menenhetet.

Mailer's outsized intention in *Ancient Evenings* is to rejuvenate the human species by showing it how life can be lived on the edge of dread and thereby intensified. Menenhetet propels himself toward physically and morally brave acts in war and in love and so builds new synapses, counteracting the perpetual forces of atrophy. He continually exchanges comfort for life and more life. When he stops doing so, he slides into convention and begins to die. There is no such thing, Mailer wants us to know, as stasis. One is either in a state of growth or death, and the gods have a stake in which it will be.

The gods in *Ancient Evenings* are most unchurchly, for they are not benign or omniscient or

Menenhetet. "We must obey it every time. There is no credit to be drawn from the virtue of one's past." To stand on the virtue of one's past is piety, which soon, Mailer believes, allies itself with corruption. After his remarkable first life, Menenhetet, in his next three lives, increasingly involves himself in fraudulent commercial enterprises. As his wealth and respect grow, he coasts, more and more, into spiritual inertia. One must change one's life or pay more for remaining the same.

There is further symbolism in this context: when the young Menenhetet Two saw the spurwing nibble worms from the crocodile's teeth, he heard boatmen on the Nile singing: "Oh, papyrus is a plant abhorred by crocodiles." Writing (the papyrus symbol) means for Mailer rejuvenation, seizing life from the teeth of death. It means poetically revealing to man how best to live in the knowledge that he is essentially supernatural, not natural. Mailer's motive in writing is at once bardic and messianic—motive, he believes, in which the gods partake. As he says in the *Harvard Magazine* interview: "If a god or devil or some demiurge is looking for a writer or has need of one, or an angel or an ogre or whatever—if there's anything up there or out there or down there that is looking for an agent to express its notion of things, then, of course, why wouldn't they visit us in our sleep? Why wouldn't we serve as a transmission belt. Just in the same sense, although this is gross, that a coach might look for a wide receiver who really has great speed of foot because he has designed some very long passes via a quarterback with a particularly powerful arm. So it might be that your own abilities would be one of the factors behind the ogre's choice of you."

Missing the metaphysics and focusing on the literal plot of *Ancient Evenings*, some reviewers have labored under two serious misapprehensions: (1) the novel takes as its subject human decadence; (2) it is historically inauthentic. When Ramses II buggers Menenhetet, who recalls at the dinner party that the pharaoh's semen flowed forth as prodigiously as the waters of the Nile, the act is not decadent. Nor is the imagery ridiculous or sensational. On the contrary, it accurately expresses how such an act was viewed by a pagan. The point is that Ramses II strengthens himself by the act. Egypt and he prosper by it. When Menenhetet eats the flesh of dead Hittite soldiers, the act is not vile. Nor are the frequent scenes of incest. The reviewers' imputations of decadence reveal their own dispositions, not the world of *Ancient Evenings*. Actually, Mailer is daring the reviewers into such a reaction to prove his point of how provincial and presumptuous the contemporary

American mind can be—how immured in its own very finite time. The novel portrays a pre-Judeo-Christian world. The two narrators are pre-Judeo-Christian. Their morality is not ours. *Ancient Evenings* is an invitation to the reader to get out of himself.

The novel's so-called noxiousness is not only Mailer's way of inveighing against American parochialism. It is his way of assailing America's ongoing obsession with sanitizing nature out of more and more areas of life. Thus *Ancient Evenings* could be the most olfactory novel ever written, profusely evoking, as it does, the odors of excrement, sweat, human and animal breath, putrefying plants and animals. Mailer is not driving readers through ancient Egypt on a sightseeing bus—he is rubbing their noses in it.

The second erroneous assumption about the novel is that it inauthentically portrays the ancient Egypt of history. Real Egyptians, the argument goes, did not believe in mental telepathy or physical reincarnation, and *Ancient Evenings* contains a considerable measure of both. If Mailer had wanted to write a factual, entirely accurate historical novel about ancient Egypt he would have or would have tried to. He has done neither because neither was his intention. He has tried, however, to evoke the spirit, the atmosphere, the feel of ancient Egypt. David B. O'Connor, curator of the Egyptian section of the University of Pennsylvania Museum, has said, in the *Pennsylvania Gazette* (May 1983), that though he found minor errors in *Ancient Evenings*, Mailer had grasped well the cultural and historical thrust of ancient Egypt.

The general critical reception of the novel has been mixed but consistently respectful. Paul Gray, in *Time* magazine (18 April 1983), called it "an artifact of evident craftsmanship and utterly invisible significance." Peter S. Prescott, in *Newsweek* (18 April 1983), concluded that "we have to push our way through this book, part of the way in four-wheel drive, but it's worth our irritation, our respect and perhaps our awe." For the most part, the magazine reviews have been unsatisfying because they focus primarily on the novel's plot and Mailer's life—both of which make for juicy copy—without saying anything about its real themes, which seriously criticize the conduct of life today from a thoroughgoing moral and metaphysical perspective.

Benjamin DeMott, in the *New York Times Book Review* (10 April 1983), said the novel is a "disaster," its characters being "ludicrous blends of Mel Brooks and the Marquis de Sade." In contrast Harold

Bloom, in the *New York Review of Books* (28 April 1983), treated the novel as a poetical, visionary text: Mailer is a "vitalistic magus" who denies the Judeo-Christian idea of death as the obliteration of human life and claims instead the antithetical Egyptian idea of personal survival through reincarnation. *Ancient Evenings*, said Bloom, is "an extravagant invention" that aspires "to join itself to an alien God."

Ambitious as the intention of this novel is, what can be said of its realization? There is certainly, one might think, enough going on in the lives of Menenhetet to keep them vivid: the Battle of Kadesh, palace and harem intrigues, the teeming common life of ancient Thebes, love affairs, gold mining, grave robbing. Yet Menenhetet's story, grandly conceived as it is, does not come sufficiently to life. The romantic and political dramas especially are almost airless. Despite even Mailer's continual use of metaphor, the richness, the radiance, and imagination that metaphor can generate are absent. And Mailer, one strongly senses, is earnestly trying to bring such qualities forth. His metaphors, though sound enough at times, are too often vague or incoherent. With his telepathic powers, Menenhetet Two has a "true glimpse" of the pictures in his mother's mind as she remembers the day when she made love to her grandfather Menenhetet in the afternoon and to her brother-husband in the evening: "At once, my mother tried to chase these pictures from her brain just so quickly as she thought them, but I had a true glimpse as clean to the sight as the white stalk of grass when the root is pulled from the ground, yes, as intimate to my ear as the sibilance of the stalk surrendering its life in earth, the first light on the white root like the knife in the flank—so sudden is the pain of the grass—so did I come into the deepest secret of my family."

Such metaphors give more heat than light. There are thousands of metaphors in this novel, but the reader would rather have one that gives that small incisive shock of illumination for every hundred that do not. Mailer has long averred that at the heart of vital articulation lies metaphor, in the same breath accusing American public language of aridity due to its lack of metaphor. The style of *Ancient Evenings* overcompensates for that language.

At bottom, the trouble with this novel is characterization. Its people are insufficiently people. They are not felt presences. Their emotions, therefore, seem empty. Graphic and frequent, for example, as the novel's sexual episodes are, they remain tepid. Make no mistake—it is not the distance of an alien 3,000-year-old culture that separates us from Mailer's characters. A man who immerses himself in the practice of magic, seduces the queen of a pharaoh, and homoerotically rapes a thief is, for all that, inextricably part of what we are. To impart that recognition is to go a long way toward transforming words into epiphany. Yet one never gets a felt experience of "how the magnitude of [Menenhetet's] desire" to be pharaoh "remained as large as his defeats" any more than one gets a convincing sense of a six-year-old boy "in his tenderness, his wisdom, his pleasure." *Ancient Evenings* excitingly raises the hope that the lives of its characters will be truly felt. As it turns out, the only life that is truly felt is Norman Mailer's.

In autumn 1983 Mailer completed the last book he owed Little, Brown under their current contract, but Scott Meredith, Mailer's agent, announced that *Tough Guys Don't Dance*, a psychological thriller, will be published instead by Random House, with whom Mailer had signed a four-book, $4-million contract that was to have become effective upon the expiration of Mailer's contract with Little, Brown. While one source at Little, Brown said that publisher had rejected *Tough Guys Don't Dance*, Roger Donald, the company's executive editor, commented only that "since Mr. Mailer's future works will not be published by Little, Brown & Company, discussions between Mr. Mailer, his agent Scott Meredith, and Little, Brown have concluded that it would be more appropriate for Mr. Mailer to change his publisher now." Meredith echoed this conclusion, calling Mailer's position with Little, Brown a "lame-duck situation" and suggesting that Random House can publish the book "with fanfare instead of a swan song."

Howard Nemerov
(1 March 1920-)

Ronald Baughman
University of South Carolina

See also the Nemerov entry in *DLB 5, American Poets Since World War II*.

NEW BOOK: *Sentences* (Chicago & London: University of Chicago Press, 1980).

Since publishing his first volume of poetry, *The Image and the Law* (1947), Howard Nemerov has been impressively productive in both quality and quantity. His major publications include fourteen books of poetry, three volumes of literary criticism, two books of short stories, three novels, one autobiography, and one play. This remarkably diverse literary canon has also earned him many awards, including an appointment as Poetry Consultant to the Library of Congress, 1963-1964; a Guggenheim Fellowship, 1968-1969; an Academy of American Poets Fellowship, 1970; election to the American Academy of Arts and Letters, 1976; and a Pulitzer Prize for *The Collected Poems of Howard Nemerov* in 1978. From 1946 to 1951, he served as associate editor for *Furioso*, a position that gave him access to a wide range of mid-century poets and poetry. He has complemented his roles as writer and editor with teaching; among the institutions where Nemerov has taught are Hamilton College, Bennington College, Brandeis University, the University of Minnesota, and Hollins College. In 1969, he was appointed Hurst Professor of Literature at Washington University in St. Louis and subsequently joined the Department of English at the same school as Professor of English, a position he still holds.

In his essay "Poetry and Meaning" from *Figures of Thought* (1978), Nemerov states that "poems ought to be approached as sacred objects. One expects not so much to learn them as to learn from them. They give a certain definition to experience, and it may be that it is to experience we should refer them, rather than to exegesis." *Sentences* (1980), Nemerov's most recent book of poetry, exemplifies what readers can learn from a gifted, wise poet's definition of experience.

In *Sentences*, Nemerov employs a three-part division justified in his poem "By Al Lebowitz's Pool": "by law / Any three things in the wide world / Triangulate: the wasp, and Betelgeuse, / And Our Lady of Liberty in the harbor; if / It's any comfort to us, and it is." The comfort gained through such triangulation is essentially that of design—or art—over the widely disparate, seemingly disordered parts of life. In this regard, the volume's organization reflects its thematic development. The first section, "Beneath," describes the nature of the sentence that most men serve as they involve themselves in demeaning activities and institutions. "Above," the second section, focuses on those who are able to connect with nature and thus somewhat elevate themselves above the ordinary. Finally, "Beyond," the volume's third section, defines true art and true artists, the poet's vehicles for connecting the world and the spirit.

In an unpublished interview Nemerov has said, "I don't view *Sentences* as any sort of radical departure [from my previous work]; maybe a touch more independence of voice, entering on old age, and a tendency of the same old age to be a touch more magisterial, for better and worse." Perhaps the writer's independent and slightly magisterial voice has caused the mixed critical response to the book, particularly to its first section.

"Beneath" attacks "the wild abyss" of ordinary life and thought, especially as it is caught in current literary posturing, in eccentric social changes, and in strident political activities. Nemerov finds appalling the dangerous elements in society: those people, for instance, who plant bombs in libraries and thus require policemen to "check out" books which, ironically, students have not checked out. A different kind of social danger is posed, in "Conversion," by the substitution of pure alcohol for OPEC oil and gasoline. Now, with "the hootch under the hood" instead of inside the driver, the young men who tend the pumps are exposed to bourbonal and sin, "affirming that we / Live not by fuel alone, but by the fumes." Furthermore, such disintegration in the social order is reflected in bogus art, especially in the literature being written by "liberated sex-maniacs," novelists "convinced they are psychiatric social-workers," and "disgraced politicians / From

Front cover for the most recent book by the writer James Dickey calls "The best poet of both wit and seriousness we have now"

the safety of minimum-security prisons." These figures become part of the chaos, feeding it and then using it as the basis for their so-called art. In the war poem "Continuous Performances," for example, both the war-makers and the protest marchers participate in and keep the war growing "Till everyone who was against the war/Was also in it, a tiny nameless part/Of the war, doing what one called 'his thing.'" Banal, self-involved, destructive, the bogus artists perpetuate their vision of "the growing war / Already sponsoring movies about itself / To let the children know what it was like." Thus degraded social or political values are linked to degraded artistic values, and as he mocks the purveyors of such values, Nemerov laments the tendency of most men to live beneath their capabilities.

Reviews of *Sentences* consistently declare section one inferior to the rest of the volume in subject matter and tone. And to a large extent such an assessment is accurate. It also, however, proves ironic: Because the poet's subject is the inferior, base features of human character and actions, his treatment matches his subject matter. The reviewers damn the writer for accomplishing the goal which he has set for himself—the portrayal of man acting beneath dignity.

Leaving "the wild abyss" of ordinary human activities, "Above," the second section of *Sentences*, focuses on modern man's relationships with nature. Because Nemerov's perspective is primarily that of the suburbanite, his nature tends to be confined to the park or the garden. Yet the natural scene is not only intrinsically beautiful but also—like its wilder counterparts in the works of such poets as Robert Frost and James Dickey—beyond human control. The first poem in section two, "In Zeno's World," functions as a thematic transition between the first and second divisions of the volume. The balance and beauty of Zeno's garden are disturbed by an archer's arrow, illustrating how man can intrude destructively in nature. In this respect, "In Zeno's World" presents that part of man's character the poet wishes to leave behind as he explores the garden. The purest perspective on the natural scene is that of the artist, either that historical figure who first named the parts of the world or the modern artist who formulates a contemporary view of the garden.

"Monet" illustrates Nemerov's vision of the proper balance between art and nature. Intending to visit a display of Monet paintings at a nearby museum, the narrator and his friends find the site crowded with people. Rather than joining the crush, they decide to spend the Sunday morning in a quiet park, the living scene of what Monet put on canvas. Nemerov offers poems which, like Monet's landscapes, reaffirm the beauty, power, and endurance of nature, the living garden. Among his subjects are the brief but hearty splendor of crocus; the intricate tangle of the Devil's Guts, a tough weed that strangles everything surrounding it yet blooms for only a day; unexpected snowstorms that paralyze the city but hide the ordinary and ugly beneath a beautiful covering. The living garden is set off against the scene in "The Dying Garden," a poem dramatizing autumn's dark beauty. Although it is troubled by man's intrusion as well as its own approaching death, the garden dies, with a quiet splendor, at the culmination of a rich harvest.

In contrast to the dying garden, Nemerov presents a comically reductive version of man's death. In "The Plain Fact" a buzzard slowly circles above an old folks' home, prompting the poet to state, "A sight can't get much more / Explicit than that, and in a poem it'd be / A recipe for getting disbelieved." Such an implausible, overt, and macabre scene might not be subtle enough for sophisticated literary circles; however, "the passing scribe" notes its implications—that man's death has seemingly slight importance. In Nemerov's examination of the garden, ordinary man's role is as the disrupter whose accomplishments are minimized by the grandeur of nature's great art. This man's death, in contrast to that of the garden, is not a matter for dignified notice but rather for almost comic dismissal. "Above" thus celebrates nature as it is perceived by the human being/artist who truly comprehends the natural world and its power.

Nemerov dramatizes his ultimate version of the artist and the creative process in *Sentences*' final section, "Beyond." The poet frequently casts prehistoric artists in almost mythical terms. In "The Makers" he praises "those first and greatest poets, / So lofty and disdainful of renown," figures very unlike many modern writers who pursue literary reputations and indulge in artistic affectations and who thus are bitterly mocked in section one. Nemerov also considers the nameless poets of antiquity great because "They were the ones that in whatever tongue / Worded the world, . . . that said the visible / And made it bring invisibles to view." These ancient makers, too, were the first to utter "above, beneath, beyond," the terms Nemerov uses in a different order to organize his book of poetry. By tracing his artistic genealogy to such origins, he defines what he prizes in his own poetic stance and process.

Nemerov vilifies the false artists and smug devotees of art throughout his volume. In "Museum," for example, he states, "The trees that mass-produce their leaves each spring / Offend the connoisseur, the sensitive / Handmaiden type who is in love with art." Such art lovers archly dismiss nature's creations as being beneath them and, in so doing, miss what is valuable in nature and art. To counter the false artist and sham art, Nemerov provides in the best poem of this volume, "By Al Lebowitz's Pool," a quiet yet powerful portrait of the true artist, the one who "words" his "world," saying "the visible" and bringing "invisibles to view."

Divided into five parts, "By Al Lebowitz's Pool" portrays the speaker at various moments in the company of friends while summer gradually slips into autumn. The poet focuses on the connections of opposites and the natural design that "the watching mind" perceives. While three beach balls float on the water's surface, the narrator observes them "triangulate," achieving "a mystery / Of pure relation that looks always right / . . . linkages / Invisible, of wind and the watching mind." The

ability to perceive design is the key to Nemerov's creative process and becomes one of the central concerns throughout the poem.

The unique display of light and shadow that occurs while the sun shines through a rainstorm aids in dramatizing the links between "the spirit and the world." The world that he lives in—the temporal existence of man mocked in section one of *Sentences*—is juxtaposed to the suburbanite's imitation of the nature portrayed in section two—the backyard swimming pool. In this location the speaker begins to see into the spirit of his life beyond, the dominating interest of the volume's third section. Occupying the midpoint of "By Al Lebowitz's Pool," part three of the poem illustrates the process of connecting the spirit and the world. As the speaker and his friend watch two teenaged girls splash in the pool, the older men tease them with a pleasant "love / Mildly distinguished from lechery, much from lust." The scene is filled with "courtship and courtesy," conveying the relaxed happiness the world occasionally provides.

The final two sections shift in mood and time from the joy of summer mornings with friends, "these times of kindness mortality allows," to the quieter moments of reflection at the end of summer. The poet returns alone to the swimming pool in the final section: "Reflections and reflexion, lovely words / I shall be sorry to let go when I let go: / . . . For things reflected are more solemn and still / Than in themselves they are, . . ." The poet reflects that moments of genuine companionship exist, yet he is also aware that "shadows of harder, more unyielding things" encroach on these moments and on the writer himself. Through the conscious act of the watching mind, however, he attempts to hold onto these periods of quiet joy, "As if I might daydream my way again / Into the world and be at one with it." As "By Al Lebowitz's Pool" illustrates, the final section of *Sentences* is artistically accomplished and philosophically serious. In "Beyond" the poet achieves authentic emotional depth, and his tone is less acerbic or distant than in the earlier two sections.

Sentences contains a wide range of poems, extending from the mocking, bitter verse of section one to the interesting but restrained appraisals of section two to the deeply moving contemplations of section three. The volume's theme—the order art gives to the randomness of life—develops with this movement from beginning to end. Nemerov's title is reminiscent of Stephen Spender's poem "Subject: Object: Sentence," in which Spender states, "A sentence is condemned to stay as stated—/ As in *life-sentence, death-sentence*, for example." As Howard Nemerov dramatizes his life and death sentences, he reveals his attempts to connect, through the power of his art, with the world below, nature above, and the spirit beyond.

Nemerov has forthcoming a new volume of poetry, *Inside the Onion*, which will be published by the University of Chicago Press in 1984. Advance notices indicate that in this book, as in his earlier works, the poet employs the events of daily life—the death of a friend, the rudeness of a postal clerk, the beautiful geometry of an onion slice—as subject matter for his incisive yet compassionate intelligence, his witty and graceful style.

Joseph Wambaugh
(22 January 1937-)

David K. Jeffrey
Northeast Louisiana University

See also the Wambaugh entry in *DLB 6, American Novelists Since World War II*, Second Series.

NEW BOOKS: *The Glitter Dome* (New York: Morrow, 1981; London: Weidenfeld & Nicolson, 1981);
The Delta Star (New York: Morrow, 1983; London: MacDonald, 1983);
Lines and Shadows (New York: Morrow, 1984).

A former detective sergeant in the Los Angeles Police Department, Joseph Wambaugh has continued to focus his attention on cops. His two recent best-sellers received favorable reviews in the popular press, where he has been compared to James M. Cain, John O'Hara, and Daumier. *The Glitter Dome* has been adapted as a made-for-TV movie and will appear on HBO in 1984. As in his five earlier works, Wambaugh portrays in these later ones both the action of police work and the psychological toll such work takes on policemen. Since his retirement from the LAPD in 1974 and beginning with *The Choirboys* (1975), Wambaugh has taken a seriocomic view of the policeman's lot, modulating the comedy, as each novel progresses, from a burlesque or farcical opening, through satire, into a bleak, black comedy which borders on the tragic. In mode and narrative structure his novels sometimes resemble Joseph Heller's *Catch-22*, a work for which Wambaugh has stated his high regard.

In *The Glitter Dome* (1981) Wambaugh vents satiric spleen at high-ranking fools in the LAPD and at Hollywood's upper levels (with whom Wambaugh has had unfortunate experiences on several occasions). The novel details the investigation into the murder of Nigel St. Claire, president of the film division of a major studio. Wambaugh focuses on the relationships of four pairs of policemen—Detective Sergeants Al Mackey and Martin Wellborn, Sergeants Simon and Schultz, patrolmen Buckmore Phipps and Gibson Hand, and narcotics officers nicknamed The Weasel and The Ferret—all of whom are involved in the St. Claire case, although two of them don't know it at first. Wambaugh devotes early chapters to the separate exploits of his four pairs, exploits which seem unrelated to the murder; in the later chapters the policemen begin to work together as their separate bits of knowledge begin to cohere. Early in the novel, Wambaugh writes ironically of "The Endless Chain" which will lead to the arrest of the murderer, the links between seemingly unrelated events which, inexperienced policemen and most readers believe, a coolly reasoning detective will discover. Later in the novel, Sergeant Wellborn (shortly before the traumas of his divorce, his religious guilt and torment, and the barely suppressed memory of a horribly mutilated child drive him to suicide) discovers that the Endless Chain may indeed exist but that its links include accident and luck. Wambaugh suggests here that any principle of causality operating in the world of policemen and criminals has very little to do with reason. The dark comedy of the novel both contributes to this sense of the world and (partially) alleviates its pain.

The Delta Star (1983) has much the same structure as *The Glitter Dome*. Opening the novel in Leery's Saloon and on the Los Angeles streets, Wambaugh introduces a bizarre array of patrol-

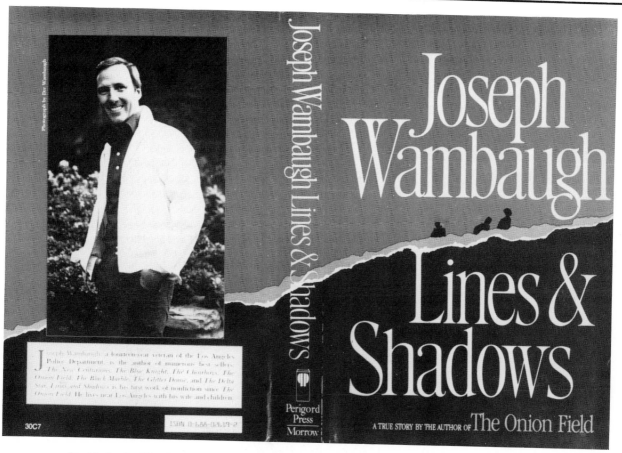

Dust jacket for Wambaugh's second nonfiction book, an account of a controversial police task force formed to combat crime along the California-Mexico border

men, including The Bad Czech, Hans and Ludwig (the largest dog in the K-9 Unit), Dilford and Dolly (the shortest woman in the LAPD), Jane Wayne a.k.a. The Bionic Bitch, and Mario Villalobos, a "counterfeit Mexican." Villalobos is a detective, and his attempt to solve the murder of Missy Moonbeam, a whore thrown from a rooftop, eventually and circuitously leads him—with Hans and The Bad Czech in tow—to Caltech's chemistry department. There he achieves a "delta to delta-star excited state" of pure creativity, prompted by exhaustion, alcohol, and drugs, in which he intuits the motive, modus operandi, and identity of the murderer. Here again Wambaugh makes clear that in the detective's arsenal, objectivity and rationality are less effective weapons than coincidence, luck, and intelligent guesswork.

Wambaugh's second nonfiction book will be published by Morrow in 1984. *Lines and Shadows* deals with a San Diego Police task force patrolling the no-man's-land at the border where Mexicans

illegally crossing into California were robbed, murdered, and raped by bandits.

The broad shape of Wambaugh's career so far seems clear. While his constant focus has been the negative psychological effect of police work on policemen, the grim earnestness of his first three books has given way to a dark comedy which intensifies his vision. The early books have concentrated on the street experiences of patrolmen, while the later novels—*The Black Marble, The Glitter Dome,* and *The Delta Star*—have included with those experiences the attempts of everyday detectives—burntout cases and borderline alcoholics, but dedicated, even driven men—to solve a mystery, which they eventually do with intuition, street sense, and doggedness. Wambaugh's characters thus resemble those of many other contemporary novelists, and Wambaugh's cop-world, dominated by coincidence and craziness, seems also like that of his contemporaries.

NEW ENTRIES

Douglas Adams

(11 March 1952-   )

Michael Adams
Louisiana State University

BOOKS: *The Hitchhiker's Guide to the Galaxy* (London: Pan, 1979; New York: Harmony, 1980);
The Restaurant at the End of the Universe (London: Pan, 1980; New York: Harmony, 1981);
Life, the Universe and Everything (New York: Harmony, 1982; London: Arthur Barker, 1982);
The Meaning of Liff, by Adams and John Lloyd (New York: Harmony, forthcoming 1984).

In the "What They're Reading on College Campuses" survey of sales at college bookstores in the 5 January 1983 *Chronicle of Higher Education*, the two top sellers were *The Restaurant at the End of the Universe* (1980) and *The Hitchhiker's Guide to the Galaxy* (1979) by Douglas Adams. Adams's blend of British wit, irreverent satire, and science fiction in these two novels and *Life, the Universe and Everything* (1982), the completion of the trilogy, has been popular not only with American college students but with a diverse audience of readers of English and ten other languages. According to the London *Times*, Adams "has attracted a cult even among those normally impervious to the mechanical charms of science fiction."

Douglas Noel Adams was born in Cambridge, the son of Christopher Douglas Adams, a management consultant, and Janet Donovan Adams, a nurse. After receiving an honors degree in English literature from Cambridge in 1974, Adams began writing scripts for radio and television comedies. He did not initially make much progress in his writing career and had to support himself with odd jobs ranging from chicken-coop cleaner to bodyguard for the royal family of Qatar. (Adams is 6' 5" and weighs 210 pounds.) The latter duties consisted of "standing up and sitting down, opening and shutting doors and running away if anyone turned up with a gun or hand grenade."

Adams got the inspiration for the works which were finally to make him successful under unusual circumstances: "I was lying drunk in a field in Innsbruck and gazing at the stars. It occurred to me that *somebody* ought to write a hitchhiker's guide to the galaxy." He took the idea for a radio series about this subject to the BBC, which paid him £1,000 for

Douglas Adams (Mary Allen)

six months' work on the pilot script. His producer then had to fight to get the program on the air, and Adams was warned to expect universal silence since no one of any consequence listened to radio. However, the 1978 series slowly developed an eager following, and paperback publisher Pan Books asked Adams to write a novelization of the series. He says that he had always thought of himself as a scriptwriter and never intended to be a novelist; but when Pan asked him to become one, "I thought that there were two ways of doing it. I could either do the normal script-novelization hack job, which involves going through the script putting 'he said' or 'she said' (and in the case of my books, 'it said' as well) at the end of each line, or I could have a go at doing it properly. I decided to see if I could do it properly." Adams did it so properly that *The Hitchhiker's Guide to the Galaxy* sold 100,000 copies in less than a month and eventually sold 2,000,000 copies in England, reaching the top of the London *Sunday Times* best-seller list. The success of the radio series and the first novel eventually led to television and further radio versions and two more novels. A similar pattern occurred in the United States, with the broadcast of the radio series on National Public Radio and the appearance of the television version on some public television stations encouraging sales of the books.

Although Adams was script editor for the BBC's long-running science fiction television series *Doctor Who* in the late 1970s, he is not a science fiction enthusiast, having read only a few novels by Isaac Asimov and Arthur C. Clarke. He finds much science fiction "so badly written as to be irritating" and is not interested in parodying the genre: "I'd rather use the devices of science fiction to send up everything else. The rest of the world . . . is a better subject to take than just science fiction."

Adams's satirizing of "everything else" has earned him comparisons with Jonathan Swift, Lewis Carroll, Kurt Vonnegut, and Monty Python. (He once collaborated on television scripts with Monty Python's Graham Chapman.) Yet Adams says that he has been more influenced by P. G. Wodehouse: "While Wodehouse didn't write about robots and spaceships, the structure of comedy—achieving surprise by setting up expectations and defeating them—is somewhat the same."

Adams defeats our expectations by turning science fiction clichés inside out. For example, he destroys the earth in the opening pages of the trilogy. "Most science fiction seems to have for the climax the great concern: is the earth going to be destroyed?," Adams observes. "Everybody knows the hero is going to save it, so I thought, why not get past that one straight off?"

His protagonists are Arthur Dent, a low-keyed Englishman; Ford Prefect, a researcher for *The Hitchhiker's Guide to the Galaxy*; Zaphod Beeblebrox, a space adventurer and Ford's "semi-cousin"; Trillian, Zaphod's girl friend; Marvin, Zaphod's constantly depressed robot; and Slartibartfast, one of those who designed Earth so that it could ask the question of life, the universe, and everything. The human characters are space-age variations on Wodehouse's Bertie Wooster and all his eccentric friends and relatives, and know-it-all-Marvin is a neurotic version of Jeeves.

In the first novel, Ford rescues Arthur just before Earth is demolished to make way for a hyperspatial express route. They end up on Zaphod's spaceship and make their way to Magrathea, once home to the custom-made planet industry. Slartibartfast tells the visitors that he helped design Earth and that it was destroyed five minutes before the completion of its purpose. The planet comes about because a giant computer, Deep Thought, arrives at the answer to life, the universe, and everything: forty-two. The Earth is then designed to come up with the question to the ultimate answer. The rest of the trilogy consists of efforts to discover this question as the characters travel backward, forward, even sideways in time.

They are occasionally helped in their quest by Ford's ostensible employer. Published in the form of a "micro sub meson electronic component"— Adams constantly parodies technological jargon—*The Hitchhiker's Guide to the Galaxy* contains all the available knowledge in the galaxy. The entry about Earth, for instance, reads "Harmless." Ford plans to update this to "Mostly harmless." Although the *Guide* may occasionally be inaccurate, "it is at least *definitively* inaccurate. In cases of major discrepancy it's always reality that's got it wrong." According to the *Guide*, there is no art anywhere in the galaxy because "the function of art is to hold a mirror up to nature, and there simply isn't a mirror big enough." One of a few annoying flaws in the trilogy is that the *Guide* plays a decreasing role as the story progresses.

One of Adams's main virtues is his gift for characterization. The adventures of Arthur and his friends are entertaining not only for all the last-second escapes from disaster but for how the characters respond to the whims of fate. Adams describes Arthur Dent as being "to a certain extent autobiographical. He moves from one astonishing event to another without fully comprehending what's going on. He's the Everyman character—an ordinary person caught up in some extraordinary events." Arthur is the kind of person who worries about "the fact that people always used to ask what he was looking so worried about." Moving from one horrendous calamity to another, he is constantly bewildered and is rarely capable of action: "Arthur had adopted his normal crisis role, which was to stand with his mouth open and let it all wash over him." Observing that "I seem to be having tremendous difficulty with my lifestyle" is as deeply philosophical as Arthur gets.

While Arthur does not know how to deal with disasters, Ford wants to avoid them altogether: "My doctor says that I have a malformed public duty gland and a natural deficiency in moral fiber and that I am therefore excused from saving Universes." Whenever a crisis begins to develop, Ford says, "I don't want to get involved, just get me out of here, and get me to a party with people I can relate to!" At the other extreme is Zaphod Beeblebrox: "adventurer, ex-hippie, good-timer, (crook? quite possibly), manic self-publicist, terribly bad at personal relationships, often thought to be completely out to lunch." Zaphod has two heads, three arms, and immeasurable self-esteem: "If there's anything more important than my ego around, I want it caught and shot now." A certified genius despite his hey-wow-I-mean-you-know inarticulateness, Zaphod charges recklessly from one escapade to another with the certainty that he will always find a way out of any difficulty. The only problem with his life is that "I can do anything I want only I just don't have the faintest idea what."

Unfortunately, Slartibartfast is primarily a device for advancing the plot, and Trillian is severely underdeveloped. Trillian is the most levelheaded one, the one who usually sees through the cant, confusion, and cowardice of the others. Marvin, in his inimitable way, judges her to be "one of the least benightedly unintelligent organic life forms it has been my profound lack of pleasure not to be able to avoid meeting." Trillian's common sense makes her rather dull.

Marvin, however, delightfully complements Arthur, Ford, and Zaphod in Adams's satire of Me-generation manifestations. His first words in the trilogy are "I think you ought to know I'm feeling very depressed," and he goes on to find at least fifty other ways of expressing his despondency. "Life, don't talk to me about life" sums up the philosophy of the Paranoid Android, as Zaphod calls him. Marvin becomes separated from the rest as they travel about in time, and he spends 576,000,003,579 years waiting for them while parking spaceships in the lot outside the Restaurant at the End of the Universe: "The first ten million years were the worst, and the second ten million years, they were the worst too. The third ten million I didn't enjoy at all. After that I went into a bit of a decline." The reader can always count on Marvin to see the worst in everything: "The dew has fallen with a particularly sickening thud this morning." Anyone annoyed by excessively cute robots like those in the *Star Wars* films cannot help loving Marvin.

Adams's main interest in presenting these

Dust jacket for the third volume in Adams's satiric science-fiction trilogy

characters and their misadventures is satirical. Among the targets of his satire are bureaucracies, bad poets, literary critics, scientific theories, nightclub entertainers, religion, philosophy, labor unions, economists, tax laws, clichés—"have a nice diurnal anomaly"—structural linguists, rock'n'roll, sentimentality, cricket commentators, and Paul McCartney's wealth. The strongest satire comes with the attack on war, imperialism, and xenophobia in *Life, the Universe and Everything*. Life on Krikkit is idyllic because its inhabitants are unaware of the rest of the universe until a spaceship penetrates the dust cloud surrounding the planet and crashes. The Krikkiters set out to conquer the universe through "the destruction of everything that wasn't Krikkit."

The most amusing satire comes in *The Restaurant at the End of the Universe* when Arthur and Ford suddenly find themselves thrown several million years back in time and onto a spaceship on its way to colonize the primitive planet Earth. The ark carries fifteen million hairdressers, television producers, insurance salesmen, personnel officers, security guards, public relations executives, management consultants, telephone sanitizers, and the like. These useless citizens have been tricked into leaving their native planet so that the remaining two-thirds of the population can live "full, rich and happy lives," and they do until all die from a disease originating with a dirty telephone. The settlers run into all sorts of difficulties on Earth. They cannot invent the wheel because they are unable to decide what color it should be, and fire also presents a problem, as a marketing analyst explains: "When you've been in marketing as long as I have you'll know that before any new product can be developed it has to be properly researched. We've got to find out what people want from fire, how they relate to it, what sort of image it has for them."

Adams tries to make fun of almost every possible concern of humans from their quest for knowledge and power to their obsession with prolonging life. In *Life, the Universe and Everything*, Wowbagger the Infinitely Prolonged finds immortality so boring that he decides to insult everyone in the universe in alphabetical order: "He imagined for a moment his itinerary connecting all the dots in the sky like a child's numbered dots puzzle. He hoped that from some vantage point in the Universe it might be seen to spell a very, very rude word."

Finally, there is the inspired silliness of Adams's style: Ford once speaks to Arthur "as slowly and distinctly and patiently as if he were somebody from the telephone company accounts department"; a torture chamber called the Cathedral of Hate is "the product of a mind that was not merely twisted, but actually sprained," and it contains "gargoyles that would have put Francis Bacon off his lunch"; Zaphod "inched his way up the corridor as if he would rather be yarding his way down it." Despite his similarities to Wodehouse, Vonnegut, Monty Python, and others, Adams is an original humorist.

Adams has enjoyed mostly positive responses from book reviewers on both sides of the Atlantic. Writing about *The Hitchhiker's Guide to the Galaxy* in the *Los Angeles Times Book Review*, David N. Samuelson suggested, "If you've had it with people imputing philosophical depth to 'Star Wars' and the like, and just want to get off on silliness for its own sake, this may be the book for you." But Adams is not merely an entertainer, as Tom Hutchinson notes in reviewing *Life, the Universe and Everything* in the London *Times*: "There is a serious undertow to all this . . . a Vonnegut-appreciation of the universe's futility which allows Mr. Adams to slip in some moments of sly terror so that the smile freezes on our face like ancient winter."

References:

Douglas Crichton, "Douglas Adams Explains *Life, the Universe and Everything*—Mice Included—in a Sci-Fi Trilogy," *People*, 19 (10 January 1983): 33-34;

Jennifer Crichton, "Douglas Adams's Hitchhiker Trilogy," *Publishers Weekly*, 223 (14 January 1983): 47-50;

Linda Langway, "Turn Left at the Nebula," *Newsweek*, 100 (15 November 1982): 119;

Philip Oakes, "Cultists Find a Guiding Light," [London] *Sunday Times*, 2 December 1979, p. 39.

Sandy Asher
(16 October 1942-   )

Judith S. Baughman

BOOKS: *A Song of Sixpence*, as Sandra Fenichel Asher (Elgin, Ill.: Performance Publishing, 1976);

The Great American Peanut Book, as Sandra Fenichel Asher (New York: Tempo, 1977);

Dover's Domain, as Sandra Fenichel Asher (Denver: Pioneer Drama Service, 1980);

Summer Begins (New York: Elsevier/Nelson, 1980);

Daughters of the Law (New York & Toronto: Beaufort, 1980); republished as *Friends and Sisters* (London: Gollancz, 1982);

The Mermaid's Tale, as Sandra Fenichel Asher (Elgin, Ill.: Performance Publishing, 1981);

Just Like Jenny (New York: Delacorte, 1982; London: Gollancz, 1982);

Things Are Seldom What They Seem (New York: Delacorte, 1983; London: Gollancz, 1983);

Missing Pieces (New York: Delacorte, 1984).

PLAYS: *Come Join the Circus*, Springfield, Missouri, Springfield Little Theater, December 1973;

Afterthoughts in Eden, Los Angeles, Los Angeles Feminist Theatre, February 1975;

How I Nearly Changed the World, but Didn't, Springfield, Missouri, National Organization for Women Herstory Fair, November 1977;

Food Is Love, Springfield, Missouri, Drury College, January 1979;

The Insulting Princess, Interlochen, Michigan, Interlochen Arts Academy, May 1979;

Sunday, Sunday, Lafayette, Indiana, Purdue University, March 1981;

The Grand Canyon, Alexandria, Virginia, Little Theatre of Alexandria, December 1983.

PERIODICAL PUBLICATIONS: *The Ballad of Two Who Flew*, as Sandra Fenichel Asher, *Plays*, 35 (March 1976): 71-76;

Witling and the Stone Princess, as Sandra Fenichel Asher, *Plays*, 38 (January 1979): 41-49;

The Golden Cow of Chelm, as Sandra Fenichel Asher, *Plays* (October 1980): 57-62.

In a speech delivered at several university conferences on children's literature, Sandy Asher declares, "The biggest difference, it seems to me, be-

Sandy Asher

tween writing for adults and writing for young teenagers is that when you write for young teenagers, there's a very good chance some of your readers will take you seriously." This at first glance facetious statement suggests the extraordinary demands placed upon writers of young adult fiction. Mature readers rarely turn to novels to shape their value systems or personalities: twelve-to-sixteen-years-olds, on the other hand, use every source, including the books they read, to fulfill their quests for information, ideas, and values. In a statement that surely reflects the concerns of all good writers for teenagers, Asher says, "Knowing how vital a part I may play in some young person's life, I feel a heavy responsibility to be careful about what I say and how

I say it. I'm not talking about censorship of my words and ideas, but of thoughtfulness: What do I really think about things and what do I want to tell the next generation?"

Asher's dual concerns with "what I say" (subject matter/theme) and "how I say it" (technique) are clearly manifested in her five young adult novels published to date. The books treat serious problems facing most teenagers—strains in parent-child or sibling relationships; confusions about sexuality; uncertainties about one's own place in the home, the school, or the community at large; emerging perceptions of change and loss. Yet the dominant tone of each novel is comic, and its focus is not upon the problem addressed, the issue to be resolved, but instead upon the young person who is confronting it. The typical Asher protagonist is a bright, energetic, well-intentioned, fallible young girl. She is a "nice kid" whose insights and actions are both believable and interesting. Surrounded by a richly developed supporting cast of parents, teachers, and teenaged friends and adversaries, she normally discovers, to echo one of Asher's titles, that "things are seldom what they seem," that problems and people are rarely as difficult or as simple as they first appear. In so doing the young protagonist takes her first halting steps toward maturity, and in honestly and sensitively recording her journey, Asher produces first-rate literature.

The daughter of Dr. Benjamin Fenichel and Fanny Weiner Fenichel, Sandy Asher was born and raised in Philadelphia. From 1960 to 1962 she attended the University of Pennsylvania and then transferred to Indiana University where she became a scriptwriter for WFIU-Radio's "Indiana School of the Sky." A 1964 Phi Beta Kappa graduate of Indiana with a B.A. degree in English and a minor in theater, she worked for nearly a year as an advertising copywriter for Ball Associates in Philadelphia. On 31 January 1965 she married Harvey Asher, a Ph.D. candidate in Russian history at Indiana, and during 1966-1967 she served as drama critic for *The Spectator*, an off-campus alternative newspaper. The Ashers' son, Benjamin, was born in 1966, and the following year the family moved to Springfield, Missouri, where Harvey Asher became a professor of history at Drury College and where the Ashers' daughter, Emily, was born in 1968. During 1973 Sandy Asher did graduate work in child development at the University of Connecticut; she earned certification in elementary education from Drury College the following year.

Asher has described the period between the appearance of her first article in a Philadelphia newspaper and the publication of her first young adult novel as a twenty-year apprenticeship. Bolstered by her "favorite fairy tales . . . about how such and such a novel was rejected 107 times before it was sold for 1.5 million dollars, or even about how such and such a poem was rejected 1.5 million times before it was sold for 107 cents," Asher wrote and had published many short stories, poems, articles, and plays during the 1960s and 1970s. Two of her poems for adults received awards, in 1970 and 1975, from *Envoi* and *Bitterroot* magazines, and one of her plays, *Afterthoughts in Eden,* which has been produced by several professional and university theater groups, won honorable mention in a 1974 contest sponsored by the Unitarian Universalist Religious Arts Guild. Although by the mid-1970s Asher's interest had begun to shift toward children's literature, she also wrote an engaging volume of facts and fables, *The Great American Peanut Book* (1977), the publication of which came during the first year of Jimmy Carter's presidency. In 1978 Asher was awarded a National Endowment for the Arts Fellowship in playwriting, and since the mid-1970s, six of her plays for children have been published. Two other juvenile and five adult plays have been produced, including *The Grand Canyon,* which in 1983 won the fifth annual one-act play contest sponsored by the Little Theatre of Alexandria, Virginia. Since 1978 Asher has taught creative writing at Drury College, an experience which she credits with giving her a fuller understanding of her craft. And when, as she says, she discovered in a children's literature class the exciting potentialities of young adult fiction, her direction was at last clear: "The craft and the vision finally came together and I was on my way. After twenty years of wandering. Well, my ancestors wandered forty in the desert, so I figure I got off easy."

Asher's first young adult novel, *Summer Begins* (1980), introduces a theme which is treated in at least four of her five books to date—the necessity of adolescents to separate themselves from their parents in order to establish their own identities. The novel's protagonist and narrator, thirteen-year-old Summer Smith, has serious problems in this regard. Because her father is a well-known literary critic and her mother a celebrated former Olympic swimmer and diver, Summer feels unable to compete with them, particularly with her mother. Viewing herself as "nothing special," she steadfastly avoids drawing attention to herself, even to the extent of suppressing any possible opinions: "I made a special point never to have opinions. I found that kept me out of trouble about 99.9 percent of the time. I've never liked trouble. . . . I have no enemies. I would die if I had enemies. I couldn't stand it." Called upon to write an editorial for the eighth-grade newspaper, Summer chooses what she believes is a perfectly innocuous subject— consideration for non-Christians in the university school Christmas program; her essay, ironically, causes an uproar in her family, school, and community. In facing up to the controversy, she begins to assert herself and thus to initiate meaningful communication with her parents and friends.

The transformation of the protagonist from an intentional nonentity to a young woman who can say "I was Summer Smith and I knew it and I was glad" is skillfully handled. In the early sections of her narrative when she still casts herself as a merely accidental heroine, Summer's account is punctuated by all sorts of verbal hesitations: "I guess" seems her favorite phrase; her reluctant judgments are expressed in the most uncertain terms; she constantly corrects her own grammar. Later, as she begins to assert her own identity, her statements become more complete and emphatic and her observations more sage: When her parents erroneously think they have prevailed on a certain point, for example, Summer reports, "They each said, 'See? You never know unless you try,' two or three times, and I tried my best to look as if I'd learned a truly valuable lesson that I would carry with me into adulthood."

Both the structure of the novel and the development of the supporting characters are admirable. The crisis provoked by Summer's editorial is complemented by a second crisis involving her relationship with a popular senior, Rod Whitman. As they come to know one another, Summer discovers that she is, in fact, the stronger of the two, yet Rod and his problems are treated quite fully and sympathetically. Furthermore, Summer's apparently rather overbearing and insensitive mother proves to be a woman who fears that her life is over, that she can no longer compete with other women, especially with her own daughter. Thus she emerges as an understandable figure with legitimate concerns of her own. A remarkable first novel, *Summer Begins* was reprinted in 1982 as a Bantam paperback.

Unlike the rest of her young adult fiction thus far, Asher's second novel, *Daughters of the Law* (1980), employs a third-person point of view and is set in a time other than the 1980s. The book's action occurs in 1973-1974 and focuses upon an oddly matched pair of seventh graders: Denise Riley, who is a funny, bumptious would-be crusader against all

of the world's evils, and Ruthie Morgenthau, who is a frail, repressed victim of her family's history as concentration-camp survivors. Haunted by her partial knowledge of her parents' experiences in the camps, Ruthie is torn between the models provided by her recently widowed seamstress mother, Hannah, and her outspoken councilwoman aunt, Sarah. Whereas Sarah wants her niece to function as a vigorous symbol of Jewish survival and triumph, Hannah seems, in her despair-ridden silence, to forbid affirmation. Ruthie thus withdraws into her escapist drawings and into her relationship with Denise, whose world she fantasizes as perfectly ordered, happy, loving. Denise, on the other hand, rebels against the smug conformity of her classmates and teachers and the apparent unwillingness of her parents to do anything about earthquake victims in Bucharest or other sufferers from evil. The two girls, through their deepening friendship, ultimately come to see themselves and their worlds with greater clarity and understanding.

Daughters of the Law treats several themes that Asher has defined as central to her novels. Once again mother-daughter relationships are examined as Denise tries her mother's almost infinite patience and understanding and as Ruthie bears and even protects her mother's haunted, fragile reserve. In each case painful secrets must be shared by mother and daughter to effect real communication. Furthermore, the novel introduces the idea that nobody can solve, once and for all, really serious problems—that the best he or she can do is just keep trying. Thus Ruthie must learn that she cannot make amends for the horrors her parents have endured, and Denise must perceive that the world is not such a black-and-white place as she had once thought: "It was all much too confusing. The bad guys weren't all that bad; the heroine was less than perfect; friends could be distant sometimes and enemies could be kind. She had a lot of thinking to do." Finally the novel focuses upon a motif that is also crucial to all the subsequent novels, a motif that Asher labels "one of the best-kept secrets in the world"—the importance of nurturing relationships between women or between girls. As she points out, it is rare that the media portray caring, trusting, utterly dependable female friendships which can vie with, say, Butch Cassidy and the Sundance Kid, or Hawkeye Pierce and B. J. Hunnicutt. Yet such solid relationships between girls and between women do exist and endure great hardships, as *Daughters of the Law* and the later works reveal. In its themes and characterization, this book, which has been reprinted in Dell and Fontana paperbacks, is a fine accomplishment.

Asher's third novel, *Just Like Jenny* (1982), is perhaps her closest examination of a relationship between young girls, a relationship which is both founded on and threatened by the central figures' dedication to dancing. From the day of her first dance class, Stephanie Nordland, the thirteen-year-old protagonist-narrator, has idolized and wanted to be "just like" Jenny Gianino, her lovely, talented fifteen-year-old friend. During the seven years they have attended the Oldham Dance Academy, the girls have shared the dream of becoming professional dancers, of joining those whom the stern Mr. Oldham labels "the gifted, gutsy few." Yet when both she and Jenny are invited to audition for Workshop, Oldham's prestigious semiprofessional dance group, Stephie, caught up in adolescent uncertainties, refuses the opportunity. The remainder of her novel dramatizes the young protagonist's confused efforts to define more clearly both the nature of her friendship with Jenny and her own identity and goals.

That Stephie allows her image of Jenny's perfection to blur her conception of herself is revealed through her relationships with several of the book's supporting characters. Although her mother constantly challenges Stephie's dependence upon the older girl, the protagonist suspects that Mrs. Norland's trust and encouragement result simply from her newly awakened feminism: "Before that, she knew there was nothing *she* couldn't do if she tried. It was the rest of womankind, including me, she only recently became sure of." Furthermore, because Mr. Oldham's invitation to audition for Workshop is preceded by much severe criticism, Stephie fears that he has asked her only to insure that Jenny will try out. Similarly, the narrator's friendships with two eighth graders in her school are measured against what she believes Jenny would do or think: Stephie, who likes but unintentionally embarrasses Matt Greenspan, reflects, "Jenny has so many boyfriends.... The word is probably out all over West Hartford that a guy will never get his feelings hurt while being nice to Jenny Gianino"; Stephie's relationship with the Barbra Streisand-idolizing Barbara Crane—"the only girl I know who wishes her nose were bigger,"—is disturbed by a chilling question: "Was I to Jenny what Barbara was to me—half of a one-way best friendship?" Only when the older girl fails to live up to her perfect image and then confesses her own need for Stephie does the protagonist begin to understand how much more difficult—and rewarding—it is "to love someone real," either Jenny or herself.

Besides tracing the development of an enduring friendship between young girls, *Just Like Jenny* examines the motivation which underlies commitments to difficult but worthwhile goals. Asher has said that although the novel appears to be about dancing, it is actually about her own writing career, about her discovery that "accepted or rejected, I am still one of the luckiest people in the world, because I get to do something I love doing every single day of my life, and very few people have that privilege." This sentiment is, in turn, transmitted to Stephie by several of the adult figures in the book: Mr. Oldham, whose own dancing career has been ended by an accident but whose school allows him still to engage in the art he loves; Mrs. Deveraux, a successful junior-high music teacher who regrets not having pursued a career as a singer and actress; Mrs. Nordland, whose praise for others and whose own life are testimonies to "people who truly *love* their work." This novel thus interweaves at least two significant themes—the nature of real friendship and the motivation underlying commitment to hard but fulfilling goals.

As Asher has noted, her fourth book for teens, *Things Are Seldom What They Seem* (1983), is catalogued by the Library of Congress under "Child molesting—Fiction," yet she abhors the common practice of categorizing a young adult novel by one of the topics it explores: "This book is about death. This book is about learning disabilities.... This book is about spiders. Is that any way to describe *Charlotte's Web?*" To label, Asher suggests, is to reduce, to give the "problem" treated precedence over all other elements essential to good fiction. And, in fact, the real focus of *Things Are Seldom What They Seem* is not upon the child molester, who appears in only two brief scenes, but instead upon the interactions of several young people who come in contact with him. In examining a whole range of adolescent relationships—girl friend/girl friend, girl friend/boyfriend, sister/sister—the novel reveals teenagers contending with deceptions and partial perceptions which initially obscure their views of themselves and their world.

The book's protagonist-narrator is Debbie Palermo, a funny, bright ninth grader who regards herself as an oddball and who fears that high school will turn into a continuation of the "two years of boredom highlighted by severe attacks of loneliness" which had been junior high: "It was okay to be smart in elementary school. In junior high smart went out. Pretty and popular came in. Due to circumstances beyond my control, I stayed smart." Debbie's fears seem to be confirmed by her older sister's transformation, under the tutelage of the charismatic drama coach Mr. Carraway, from the "perfectly normal, reasonably obnoxious" Maggie of old to the imperious, uncommunicative Margaret of the present. Furthermore, when Debbie's closest friend, Karen Jackson, also is mesmerized by Carraway and spends most of her time in play rehearsals, Debbie feels doubly isolated. Luckily, however, she finds Murray Gordon, a fellow oddball who is extremely intelligent, very funny, and four inches shorter than Debbie. As the two exchange quips and share insights, they begin to feel more comfortable about themselves and their positions in the high school. Yet when Debbie discovers that both Karen and Margaret have been sexually victimized by Mr. Carraway, a secret that she promises not to tell Murray, her fledgling romance and newfound self-confidence are threatened. How these complexly developed fourteen- and fifteen-year-olds deal with their discovery that things are seldom what they seem, that deceptions or misperceptions do undermine relationships, is the central focus of their story.

This theme finds expression through all of the major character involvements in the novel. When Murray first kisses Debbie and then fails to mention his action for several days, she believes that he may have found the experience—and her—repugnant. Yet as Murray explains, he is simply concerned by the "unwritten law" that boy-girl relationships must inevitably escalate: "They have to see how far they can get. . . . And the next thing you know, one of them gets scared and the other gets angry. Or one of them gets bored and the other one gets hurt. Or they both get scared or angry or bored or hurt. And they break up." As Debbie and Murray deal with their misunderstanding, they decide that they won't, at this point in their lives, "mess with a good thing," the relationship they already have. (Asher has remarked that because today's teenagers are under so much pressure to have sex, they now need to be gently reassured that *no* is as acceptable an option as *yes*.) In another context Debbie has to disabuse Murray of his apparent notion that boyfriends outrank girl friends, that she should share with him Karen's confidences in order to preserve his trust. Debbie understands, in fact, that her friend has endured considerable pain in quitting the school play without publicly revealing her reasons; the protagonist, therefore, must preserve Karen's secret until she can muster the very real courage required to expose it fully. Again, Debbie must both protect Margaret, whose imperious behavior is really a mask for her sense of degradation

at having been victimized by Carraway, and at the same time encourage her to reveal the truth so that she can resume fulfilling relationships with Debbie, their parents, and her own boyfriend. Throughout this novel the central figures convincingly discover and come to terms with the destructive effects of deception and misperception. As a chronicle of their struggles, the book is complex and compelling.

Asher's most recent young adult novel, *Missing Pieces* (1984), primarily focuses upon the necessity—and the very real difficulties—of maintaining communication between parents and children. High school sophomore Heather Connelly, the book's central figure and narrator, suffers terrible losses between Thanksgiving 1981 and Thanksgiving 1982: Her father suddenly dies; her mother seems disturbingly composed and distant; her beloved uncle lies senile in a nursing home; her newly married older brother has moved too far away to offer much comfort; and her boyfriend, Nicky Simpson, threatens their recently begun relationship through his unpredictable mood shifts. She discovers that Nicky has also experienced both the loss of a parent, his mother, and the acquisition of a despised stepmother; and Heather is quite aware that her best friend, Cara Dale, has been virtually fatherless since her parents' divorce shortly after her birth. This trio of young people therefore must try to fill the holes in their lives. As Heather says, "It's like putting a jigsaw puzzle together, only you know there's a piece missing and you'll never be able to replace it, but you still have to make the picture come out right. I can't figure out how to do that." What Heather discovers is that she and her friends—like the central characters in *Daughters of the Law*—must constantly keep trying to break down those barriers which both they and their parents unwittingly have erected.

Through Heather, Cara, and Nicky, *Missing Pieces* portrays a wide range of parent-child involvements. At first glance the relationship between Cara and Liz Dale seems almost ideal: a dynamic advertising account executive, Liz appreciates her daughter's own irrepressible nature and communicates freely with her. When, for example, Cara complains that during her infrequent visits with her father they have nothing to say to one another, Liz replies, "Funny . . . he and I never had much to say to each other either. That's probably why we ended up with you!" As close as the Dales' relationship is, however, Cara frequently longs for a greater degree of privacy and independence. In a speech which, Asher believes, defines a problem besetting many mothers and daughters, Cara declares, "I used to

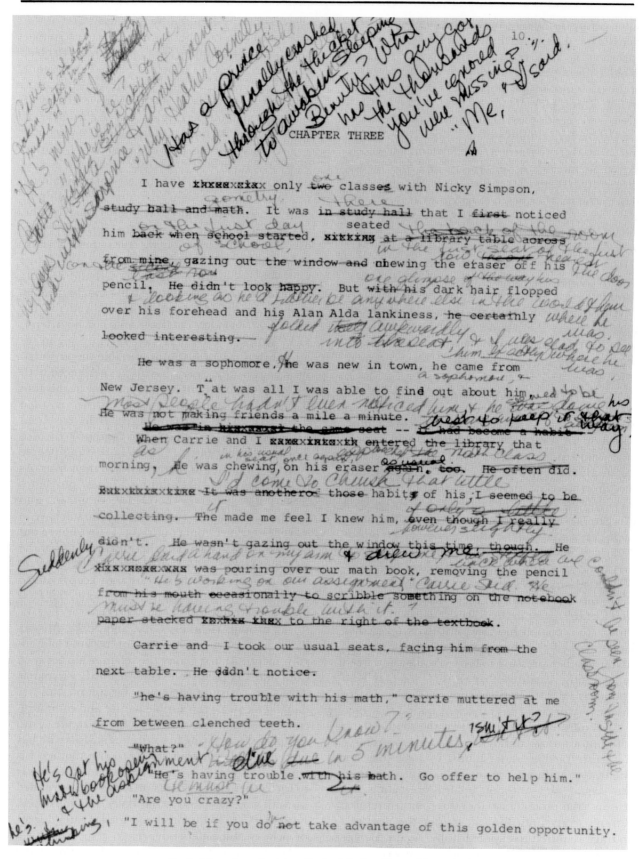

CHAPTER THREE

I have xxxxxxxxx only two classes with Nicky Simpson,
study hall and math. It was in study hall that I first noticed
him back when school started, xxxxxxx at a library table across
from mine, gazing out the window and chewing the eraser off his
pencil. He didn't look happy. But with his dark hair flopped
over his forehead and his Alan Alda lankiness, he certainly
looked interesting.

He was a sophomore, he was new in town, he came from
New Jersey. That was all I was able to find out about him.
He was not making friends a mile a minute.
He was in xxxxxxx the same seat -- it had become a habit.
When Carrie and I xxxxxxxxxxxx entered the library that
morning, he was chewing on his eraser again. too. He often did.
Ruxxxxxxxxxxx It was another of those habits of his; I seemed to be
collecting. The made me feel I knew him, even though I really
didn't. He wasn't gazing out the window this time, though. He
xxxxxxxxxxxxxx was pouring over our math book, removing the pencil
from his mouth occasionally to scribble something on the notebook
paper stacked xxxxxx xxxx to the right of the textbook.

Carrie and I took our usual seats, facing him from the
next table. He didn't notice.

"he's having trouble with his math," Carrie muttered at me
from between clenched teeth.

"What?"

"He's having trouble with his math. Go offer to help him."

"Are you crazy?"

"I will be if you do not take advantage of this golden opportunity.

Revised page from the typescript for Missing Pieces *(the author)*

want to be just like her [Liz], but lately it kind of scares me. . . . There's already one Liz Dale. Who needs two? The more I think about it, the crazier it gets. To grow up, I have to become *more* like her, but to be *me*, I have to become *less* like her. How do I do that? How does anybody do that?"

Whereas Cara feels somewhat smothered by her mother's candor and example, Nicky suffers from a sense of parental abandonment. Deserted at the age of eight by his natural mother, he feels that his intimacy with his father is now being seriously threatened by a harried, demanding stepmother with two young children of her own. Regarding himself as abandoned by both parents, Nicky decides to search for his mother, who, he believes, may now welcome and value him.

Heather, who is neither overwhelmed by affection nor stricken by a sense of desertion, feels that an uneasiness, a reserve, has developed between her mother and herself. Mrs. Connelly, following her husband's death, has thrown herself into a myriad of activities, and when she is with her daughter she seems to "wrap herself ever more tightly in a blanket of solitude": "She was there in the house with me . . . and yet she wasn't there at all, at least not so that I could really reach her." Heather, like her two friends, perceives serious barriers between herself and her parent.

The adult-child connections that are ultimately achieved—or at least begun—depend heavily upon the youngsters' loving support of one another. Near the novel's conclusion Cara asks Heather, "Is there something wrong with me? Is there something missing?" Heather assures her— and promises to do so again and again—that she's "not a second-rate Liz Dale": "You're you and you're fine. No. You're *terrific*." Furthermore, Heather's confidence in her friend finds abundant support in at least two scenes where Cara's independent nature is displayed: her account of her epic wrestling match with an honors student who is also a "part-time sex maniac" and her dressing down of a condescending shoe salesman. Nicky, too, draws upon his trust of Heather to perceive clearly that he deserves part of the blame for the disintegration of relationships in his home. In confronting his culpability and his delusions, he is able to start reaching out to his father and stepmother. And Heather, supported by Cara's and Nicky's love, also begins

the process of establishing genuine communication with her mother. Each of them, Heather insists, must struggle to become real parts of one another, to share their lives, to occupy that middle ground between being "a burden and . . . a missing piece." Thus, in this novel, Asher intelligently and sensitively treats complex difficulties in parent-child relationships and the sustaining nature of the best adolescent friendships.

During the late fall of 1983 Delacorte/Dell accepted for publication Asher's first novel for eight-to-ten-year-olds. Titled *Teddy Teabury's Fabulous Fact* and featuring the author's only male protagonist to date, the book chronicles a young boy's efforts to put his hometown back on the map after a highway bypass threatens the village's existence. The novel was inspired by youngsters from Otterville, Missouri, who asked Asher, at a children's literature festival, to write a story featuring a huge family of gerbils. Over the next couple of years she experimented with a picture book on the subject and fielded queries from her impatient young fans. The project finally evolved into a short comic novel set in the fictional village of Thistledown, "about twenty-five miles from Otterville." The book, appropriately, will be dedicated to the children of Otterville, Missouri.

Asher's novels have received generally favorable reviews in such journals or newspapers as *Publishers Weekly, Bulletin of the Center for Children's Books, School Library Journal*, the *Horn Book Magazine, Voice of Youth Advocates,* and the *Times Literary Supplement*. That these notices tend to be little more than useful but brief descriptions of each book's subject matter and probable audience suggests, however, the absence of serious critical attention for most young adult fiction. As Asher has said, "I am often asked, 'Why do you write for children?' Or, more commonly, 'How come you write for children?' (asked as if to say, 'How come you write for Martians?' or 'How come you write for chimpanzees?') with the very clear implication that children are not quite human somehow, certainly not as human as adults, and that therefore their books are not quite real books." Yet in her creation of fully realized characters confronting believable and compelling problems, Sandy Asher proves that young adult fiction can achieve the same high standards as the best of adult literature.

David Bottoms

(11 September 1949-)

Rick Lott
Florida State University

BOOKS: *Shooting Rats at the Bibb County Dump* (New York: Morrow, 1980);
In a U-Haul North of Damascus (New York: Morrow, 1983).

OTHER: *The Morrow Book of Younger American Poets*, edited by Bottoms and Dave Smith (New York: Morrow, 1984).

David Bottoms is already considered one of the most promising poets of his generation on the basis of his two published volumes. About *Shooting Rats at the Bibb County Dump* (1980), his first book, Robert Penn Warren said, "David Bottoms is a strong poet and much of his strength emerges from the fact that he is temperamentally a realist." James Dickey, one of many who greeted Bottoms's second book with praise, wrote, "Bottoms has come into American poetry quickly; his place is already high, and will be higher."

Bottoms was born and reared in Canton, Georgia, the only child of David H. Bottoms, a funeral director, and Louise Bottoms, a registered nurse. He received a B.A. from Mercer University in 1971. In 1972 he married Margaret Lynn Bensel, whom he met while in college. After spending a year selling guitars in a music store in Macon, Georgia, he attended West Georgia College, where he received an M.A. with a thesis on the poetry and critical theory of Henry Timrod in 1973. Bottoms taught high school and worked part-time in the Georgia Poets-In-The-Schools program before continuing his education in 1979 at Florida State University, where he was awarded two university fellowships, and he received a Ph.D. with a concentration in creative writing in 1982. He has since served as assistant professor of English and creative writing at Georgia State University and as poetry editor of *Atlanta*.

Although Bottoms makes abundant use of Southern locales and culture in *Shooting Rats at the Bibb County Dump*, winner of the 1979 Walt Whitman Award sponsored by the Academy of American Poets, he transcends regionalism. As David M. Cicotello writes in *Prairie Schooner*: "Readers will

David Bottoms

discover that while Bottoms draws upon the landscapes, characters, scenes, and smooth dialectical cadences of the South, he simultaneously delights his audience with a rich and transcendent level of meaning."

David Bottoms's South is not the South of his literary forebears such as John Crowe Ransom, Allen Tate, and Donald Davidson. The traditions that the twelve Southerners tried to shore up with the agrarian manifesto *I'll Take My Stand* (1932) are in shambles, and as a Southerner, Bottoms deals in his writing with the breakdown. The South he writes about is that of Faulkner's Snopeses, the "white trash" heirs of the Old South. Although some of the poems in *Shooting Rats at the Bibb County Dump* are set in the country, Bottoms writes in narrative free verse mainly about hardscrabble lives in small Southern towns, with poems set in bars, motels, and pawnshops and featuring truckers, waitresses, vandals, faith healers—people described by G. E. Murray in the *Chicago Sun-Times* as "characters light years away from the American Dream, characters whose hopes have broken down like so many old farm tractors."

The central hope of these people, as for the nation of immigrants at large, is escape. In Bottoms's poems people often dream of breaking out of their inadequate or wretched lives. In "Coasting Toward Midnight at the Southeastern Fair," the speaker attempts a temporary breakout via the escapism offered by a fair, only to find himself trapped once more: "Stomach in my throat / I dive on rails and rise like an astronaut, / orbit this track like mercury sliding / around a crystal ball." Even the performers at the fair are dissatisfied and desire to flee the emptiness of their lives: "Hercules feels the weight of his profession, / Mother Dora sees no future / in her business." Although these characters yearn "to break our orbits . . . to take our lives in our own hands / and hurl them out among the stars," the only stars available to them are the artificial stars of mundane reality: "Below me a galaxy of green and blue neon / explodes from the midway to Industrial Boulevard, / and red taillights comet one after another / down the interstate toward Atlanta." "A Trucker Drives Through His Lost Youth" presents an aging trucker who seeks to escape into reminiscence. Driving the interstate at night, he tries to recapture the excitement of his youth by recalling the days when he hauled moonshine in a stripped-down Ford to the nightclubs of Atlanta. The shadow of a bridge (a neat transition: memory is the insubstantial bridge to the past) falls upon the trucker's face, and he looks into the rear-view mirror and sees the change the years have wrought in him. In his memory, the trucker "will search again for the spirit / behind the eyes in his rear-view mirror," and in his imagination "his foot will floor the stripped-out Ford / till eighteen wheels roll, roll, roll / him backwards as far as his mind will haul."

The poem most expressive of the wreckage of traditions in the modern South is "Wrestling Angels," in which scavengers come to a cemetery to steal ornamental ironwork and an occasional "urn or bronze star" from the graves to sell to scrap-metal dealers. Not content to pillage the past, the mean-

spirited vandals wreck monuments to their predecessors: "But if there is time / we shatter the hourglasses, / slaughter lambs asleep on children's graves, / break the blades off stone scythes, / the marble strings on stone lyres." The last four lines brilliantly meld the breakdown of traditions with a subsequent loss of spirituality: "Only the angels are here to stop us, and they have grown / too weak to wrestle. / We break their arms and leave them wingless / leaning over graves like old men lamenting their age."

As the title *Shooting Rats at the Bibb County Dump* suggests, refuse is a motif in several of the poems. Bottoms uses the dump as a symbol of spiritual debilitation, as Fitzgerald uses the ash heap in *The Great Gatsby*. The rubbish heap represents simultaneously the breakdown of tradition and the spiritual sterility of modern man. In the title poem, several drunks go to the county dump to shoot rats frozen in the car's headlights:

Shot in the gut or rump, they writhe and try
                                       to burrow
into garbage, hide in old truck tires,
rusty oil drums, cardboard boxes scattered
                                  across the mounds,
or else drag themselves on forelegs across our
                                      beams of light
toward the darkness at the edge of the dump.

It's the light they believe kills.
We drink and load again, let them crawl
for all they're worth into the darkness we're
                                       headed for.

The ambiguous concluding line suggests that man and animal are joined in the equality of death and, at the same time, that the drunks' brutal actions indicate a spiritual desolation that is animal in nature. The juncture of man and animal here foreshadows a theme developed in a later section, that of man's repressed animal nature.

Bottoms considers himself essentially a religious poet because his poetry often searches for some underlying meaning in things. According to Bottoms, "I don't know if there is any undercurrent of meaning or anything like that, but as I get older I find myself at least more willing to accept the possibility of it. I even find myself hoping for it. Also, the word religion comes from the Latin word *religare*, which means to tie or bind. I like what William Irwin Thompson says about that. He says that to tie or bind the individual to the universal is to commit a religious act. That is essentially what good poetry does." Although Bottoms may be a religious poet in a broad sense, he has revolted against the Protestant Christian heritage of the South, and despite his frequent allusions to hymns and to the Bible, he characteristically repudiates organized religion in his poetry. In "The Lame" a boy with a clubfoot attends a rural religious service—a faith healing at a river. Ingeniously using the traditional Christian symbol of the fish, Bottoms has the boy step into the water, where he "dreams he feels fish gnaw the swollen ankle, / carry off in their bellies chunks of his deformity." Through the key word *dream*, Bottoms is saying that the hope of spiritual redemption, as well as physical restoration, is an illusion. As the boy emerges from the river, his relatives watch anxiously for the "promise," but they are destined to disappointment: "When the twisted foot breaks light, flops across sand / like a dying fish, mama closes the blanket, daddy the book. / All the whole and newly healed leave the river lame." The phrase "like a dying fish" is emblematic of both the inefficacy of religion and of the boy's dying faith.

Bottoms yields to nihilism in "All Systems Tower and Collapse." The speaker lies alone in a dark motel room, drinking and reflecting on the emptiness of his life. Although his mood is one of despair and spiritual desolation, he ignores the promise offered by the ubiquitous Gideon Bible, saying that its "premise is all wrong," as is that of any philosophy, for "Here's the natural gospel of it all: / all systems tower and collapse, and we / babble in darkness, seeking foundations / for other reconstructions, knowing all / along that what works always is nothing."

The poet Coleman Barks once told Bottoms, referring to a term coined by James Dickey, that the "boss image" of Bottoms's poems is the moral void. While this assessment is perhaps simplistic, Bottoms's poems sometimes do embrace a core of amorality, particularly poems such as "The Farmers," in which two men take a bound and gagged woman into a hayloft, strap her to the floor, and rape her. As the farmers take turns, the woman forces her mind away from them, concentrating on the sounds of barnyard animals. This barnyard imagery suggests man's bestiality, but the poem conveys no sense of moral outrage; the tone is detached and objective, and the ending seems to imply that the farmers' crimes will have no consequences: "One unties a leg, / the other a wrist. You open your eyes, struggle / with the other rope, watch them walk / down the steps, back to the fields and the reaping."

The six poems in the third section of *Shooting Rats at the Bibb County Dump*, "All the Animal Inside Us," deal with the relationship of man to animal,

particularly man's perception of his repressed animal nature. Bottoms handles this theme wittily in "Crawling Out at Parties," a poem that grew out of his reading Carl Sagan's discussion of the evolution of the human brain in *The Dragons of Eden*. Sagan writes that the brain is composed of three parts, each added by evolution. The oldest is the R-Complex, or reptilian brain, largely responsible for aggressive behavior, territoriality, ritual, and the establishment of social hierarchies. Alcohol suppresses the neocortex, allowing the R-Complex, with its ancient reptilian impulses, to function more strongly. The speaker of "Crawling Out at Parties" observes this phenomenon with wry humor: "My old reptile loves the Scotch, / the way it drugs the cells that keep him caged / in the ancient swamps of the brain. / He likes crawling out at parties / among the tight-skirted girls." The other poems in this section focus on the R-Complex's desire for dominance. It is tempting to speculate that Bottoms longs for a return to a past so far back that its values are not threatened by disintegration. The speaker (all voices seem to belong to the same persona) has a reluctant desire to abandon civilization, reverse eons of evolution, and return to a primeval, animalistic relationship with nature. For example, in "Hunting On Sweetwater Creek," a hunter led into the woods by "an old reptile at the top of [his] spine" becomes lost and, as darkness falls, experiences an ominous epiphany: "I listen and wait, afraid / there is something to be said for being lost / and finding again a creature that crawls in the gut, / arcs the spine, curls hands inward toward claws."

The last two sections, "How Death Isolates" and "No Ticket for the Body to Travel On," are about death. The three poems in the former section deal with the irrevocability of death, while those in the latter section deal directly and personally with the death of Bottoms's grandparents. These poems are concerned essentially with the poet's inability to believe in an afterlife, and the reader senses that the poet regrets his lack of faith. In "Speaking to the Darkness"—an obviously autobiographical poem, for the speaker's description of himself looking in a mirror is precisely a description of Bottoms—the speaker dreams of Luke's finding a living body in Christ's tomb and of Christ's raising Lazarus from the dead. The poem, however, ends with the poet saying, "Grandfather, I am holding nothing in my clenched hands. / Speaking into darkness is the closest I can come to prayer."

Although they retain the strong sense of place that is one of Bottoms's strengths, the thirty-one poems in his second volume, *In a U-Haul North of*

Damascus (1983), are not as intensely Southern in their landscapes and imagery as those of his first collection, perhaps because Bottoms lived in Florida while writing most of *In a U-Haul North of Damascus*, his doctoral dissertation; and though Florida is in the South, it is not of it. While many of these poems develop themes raised in the first book, a large portion of them tend to be more introspective and domestic, less apt to employ narrative masks. They are the poems of one who has reached early middle age and is beginning to concern himself with the responsibility and the disillusionment of maturity.

Typical of these poems is "Sign for My Father Who Stressed the Bunt," a poem about Bottoms's realizing the value of his father's insistence on basics in baseball, particularly the bunt, and the wider application to one's life of the ability to sacrifice. "Under the Boathouse" explores the value of the quotidian and the saving grace of love. The speaker dives off a dock and is trapped on the lake bottom by a fishhook snagged in his left hand. Just before his wife, who has an armful of groceries, frees him by undoing the fishing line tied to the dock, he sees her "shadow like an angel / quivering in a deadman's float," and he sees a "shower of plastic knives and forks / spilling past . . . in the lightened water, a can / of barbequed beans, a bottle of A.1., napkins drifting down like white leaves, / heavenly litter from the world [he] struggled toward." That these ordinary domestic items acquire significance suggests an insight into the value of the quotidian, gained through the speaker's nearness to death. The reader is prepared for this enlightenment by the lines "what gave first / was something in my head, a burst / of colors like the blind see," which immediately precede the speaker's vision of his wife's redemptive shadow.

"Hiking Toward Laughing Gull Point" probes the loss of dreams that provide channels for the hopes and energies of young adulthood. The speaker watches Laughing Gull Point, symbol of his dreams, recede miragelike as he walks along the beach toward it. A motif of dishonest real estate deals reinforces the theme of disillusionment, and the speaker identifies with a gull that catches a bait in midair only to be hooked and jerked into the sea:

> I think how the point
> keeps drifting farther away
> like some water-mirage
> or a piece of land in a speculator's dream.
> How each summer I search for my dream
> vacation, only to find myself feeling more
> like some gull

climbing toward the edge of an island,
a hook, the end of the line.

Although bleak, Bottoms's world view is not entirely negative. Relief from desperation and loss is available, but transient, as the speaker of "Rest at the Mercy House" discovers when he and other tourists—"survivors of wrecked or uncharted lives"—tour a House of Refuge for shipwrecks: "Here nothing is molested, all blest. / For travelers like us, a tour of the house, a vision, / a momentary rest." The adulterous lovers of "In the Wilderness Motel" find momentary release from desperation only at the expense of guilt and anxiety. The ruined motel they choose for a trysting place becomes a metaphor for their lives, and their love affords only temporary solace:

> Somewhere
> in all these wrecked rooms, there is a darkness
> we can slide
> into, a shredded mattress that will ease us
> into love
> and sleep.
> And when we wake
> in the caked layers of leaf-rot, blown-dirt. . . .
> We can celebrate
> the comfort, the company of ruin.

Many of these poems continue Bottoms's concern with subjects explored in *Shooting Rats at the Bibb County Dump*. "The Boy Shepherd's Simile," for example, deals with the negation of Christianity. The speaker, likely a reminiscing Bottoms, is one of a group of children engaged in a live Nativity scene on an icy December night. The closest the speaker can come to believing in Christ is to believe that Mary Sosebee's Christmas doll, which represents the Christ child, is *like* a child. The poem takes an ironical turn: "For this [the doll] we shivered in adoration. / We bore the cold." Bottoms puns meaningfully, as he frequently does, in the last line; "bore" can be read both as *withstood* and as the past tense of *bear*, meaning to produce or yield. Hence, the boy's pretense that the doll is Christ begets the "cold" knowledge that Christ is a pretense.

"Recording the Spirit Voices" is about Bottoms's ambivalence toward religion: Although he cannot believe, he longs to. A psychic investigator hunts for proof of the supernatural by placing his tape recorder "on the grave of a young woman killed in a fire." As he waits crouched under a stone angel, he is divided in his hopes, wishing for success, yet "afraid to hear a woman scream from a burning house, / to record some evidence her tombstone

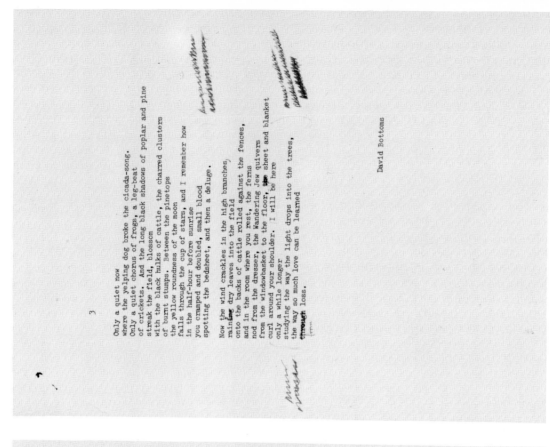

3

Only a quiet now
where the yelping dog broke the cicada-song.
Only a quiet chorus of frogs, a leg-beat
of crickets. And the long black shadows of poplar and pine
streak the field, blossom
with the black hulks of cattle, the charred clusters
of burnt stumps. Between the pinetops
the yellow roundness of the moon
falls through the cup of stars, and I remember how
in the half-hour before sunrise
you cramped and doubled, small blood
spotting the bedsheet, and then a deluge.

Now the wind crackles in the high branches,
raining dry leaves into the field
onto the backs of cattle rolled against the fences,
and in the room where you rest, the ferns
nod from the dresser, the Wandering Jew quivers
from the windowbasket to the floor, the sheet and blanket
curl around your shoulder. I will be here
only a while longer
studying the way the light drops into the trees,
the way so much love can be learned
through loss.

David Bottoms

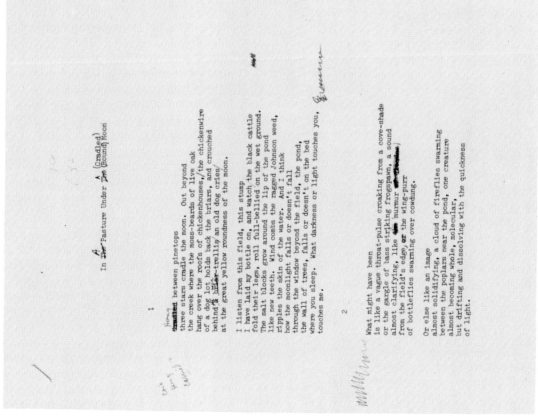

In The Pasture Under The (Round) Moon
                     (Cradled)

1

Cradled between pinetops
three stars cradle the moon. Out beyond
the creek where the moss-beards of live oak
hang over the roofs of chickenhouses,/the chickenwire
of a dog lot holds back the briars, and crouched
behind a briar-trellis/ an old dog cries
at the great yellow roundness of the moon.

I listen from this field, this stump
I have laid my bottle on, and watch the black cattle
fold their legs, roll full-bellied on the wet ground.
The salt blocks grow around the lip of the pond
like new teeth. Wind combs the ragged Johnson weed,
ripples the skin of the water. And I think
how the moonlight falls or doesn't fall
through the window beyond the field, the pond,
the wall of trees, falls or doesn't on the bed
where you sleep. What darkness or light touches you,
touches me.

2

What might have been
is like a vague throat-pulse croaking from a cove-shade
or the gargle of bass striking frogspawn, a sound
almost clarifying, like the murmur of
from the field's edge or the wing-purr
of bottleflies swarming over cowdung.

Or else like an image
almost solidifying, a cloud of fireflies swarming
between the poplars near the pond, one creature
almost becoming whole, molecular,
but drifting and dissolving with the quickness
of light.

Revised typescript (the author)

lied, / bury the truth these angels stand on: *born* and *died*."

A large number of these poems sustain Bottoms's preoccupations with death and with the animal nature of man. Most are about hunting and fishing, but Bottoms neither attacks the killing of animals for sport nor apologizes for it; he uses it to explore fundamentals of human nature. In these ancient rituals, man engages directly in the universal cycle of life and death. For example, "Gigging on Allatoona" is a vivid, though one-dimensional, account of men preparing at dusk to gig frogs. The metaphor that makes this poem more than just a straightforward description of frog-gigging comes in the last two ambiguous lines and connects the insignificant death of the frog with the truth of man's impending death: "the small twitch of legs kicking air at the end of the gig, the wake / rolling away from the boat far out across the black water."

"Kinship" is dedicated to James Dickey, who Bottoms says taught him to hunt snakes with a blowgun. This dedication reflects the double entendre of the title, which refers to Bottoms's awareness of his place in a Southern poetic tradition as well as to the poem's theme that man shares with water moccasins an animal nature that makes him dangerous: "All of this to revive a venomous kinship / when the plane of air is slashed by the dart / and the last of the chambered breath / exits the blowgun with something like a hiss."

Bottoms deals in a few poems with the preoccupation with history that has long obsessed Southern writers. "Fog on Kennesaw" is typical in that it is double-exposed, the past superimposed on the present. The characters, identified only as "we," camp illegally for the night on Kennesaw Mountain at a site once occupied by Confederate troops during a Civil War battle. The double-exposure is accomplished through comparison: the campers lean their "pick and shovels against the trees / like the rifles of Joe Johnson's army." Because the environs remain the same, rifle balls are still embedded in trees, the campers experience history as a ghostly presence: "But tonight / we have found something seeping up through the leaf-cover, / the pine straw, something drifting across old earthworks, / maneuvering on Kennesaw."

Critical response to Bottoms's two books has been almost unanimously favorable. Critics generally agreed that *Shooting Rats at the Bibb County Dump* eminently deserved the Walt Whitman Award. David M. Cicotello declared in *Prairie Schooner*: "An exceptional volume, *Shooting Rats at the Bibb County Dump* marks a propitious beginning. . . . It is a vol-

ume that will repeatedly instruct and delight the reader." Anthony Harrington, reviewing *In a U-Haul North of Damascus* in the *Atlanta Journal*, rates Bottoms a high place in American poetry: "Roethke once reckoned that, in any one generation, only from five to fifteen people had 'a real talent for writing poetry.' A real talent is alive, well, and at work in Atlanta. He's David Bottoms and his new book, *In a U-Haul North of Damascus*, assures him a place in the Roethkean number." Bottoms's award-winning first book marked him as a young poet of great promise. The maturing artistry evident in his second volume bodes well for his future.

References:

David M. Cicotello, "Loss and Ritual in the South," *Prairie Schooner*, 55 (Spring/Summer 1981): 311-313;

Kelly Claspill, "David Bottoms' *Shooting Rats at the Bibb County Dump*," *Quarterly West*, 16 (Spring/Summer 1983): 182-187.

AN INTERVIEW
with DAVID BOTTOMS

DLB: You have a Ph.D. in creative writing. Do you think the poetry workshops you participated in ultimately benefited or harmed your development as a poet?

BOTTOMS: Actually, I had written *Shooting Rats* and won the Whitman Award before I had ever taken a poetry workshop. So when I entered the program at Florida State University my first book was already scheduled for publication. Still, I do think the workshops I took at FSU were beneficial. Anything that directs your attention toward poetry is beneficial. Also, it was helpful to be around a community of poets. You actually get the feeling that poetry is an important thing. The only way I can imagine a workshop harming a poet's development would be a situation where a very young poet becomes discouraged because of overly harsh criticism. Part of the function of a good workshop, I think, is to offer some support as well as solid criticism.

DLB: Does your job as a teacher interfere with your writing poetry?

BOTTOMS: Of course. I would much rather spend all of my time reading and writing for my own pleasure. Teaching gets in the way. We may as well be honest about that. Of course, there are rewards in teaching. As professions go, teaching offers a great many benefits for a writer. Nothing is more important than time. Teaching gives you more free time than any other job. Still, sometimes I can't help wanting more.

DLB: Do you read much poetry? Criticism?

BOTTOMS: I read a great deal of poetry. And the poetry I always seem to like best has a strong narrative content. I don't read a lot of criticism. Occasionally, when I'm teaching certain poets. But certainly not for pleasure.

DLB: What are your writing work habits like? Do you have a regimen, or do you work only when you feel like it?

BOTTOMS: I don't have any writing habits. All of my poems start from situations and I don't even approach the typewriter until I have a fairly clear idea of what the situation of the poem will be. Any other method is too frustrating. Writing anything at all is painful enough. To labor without a clue about the finished product is something I can't do.

DLB: So, like Yeats, who often could squeeze out only a few lines in a day's work, you find writing arduous?

BOTTOMS: It is extremely difficult, even when it's going pretty well. Every poem seems to get harder. Now I find myself working on one poem for months. This wasn't always the case.

DLB:When did you first have an inkling that you wanted to be a poet?

BOTTOMS: Early on. I don't remember exactly when. But very early. Sometime in my teens.

DLB: What sort of literary apprenticeship did you serve? Did success come easily?

BOTTOMS: I published my first poem in 1972, I think. I was in graduate school working on an M.A. in English. I published for six years in magazines before my first book was accepted for publication. A little less than half the poems I'd published in magazines were collected in that book.

DLB: Your poetry tends to be strongly narrative and

realistic. How do you account for these qualities?

BOTTOMS: I'm sure it has something to do with being from the South, from hearing stories all my life. That's about all I can say about that.

DLB: You have played professionally in bluegrass and country-western bands. Has being a musician affected your poetry?

BOTTOMS: I don't think it has had much positive effect. But I don't know. Maybe one positive effect is material—people I've met, places I've been, et cetera. But as far as the relationship between country music and poetry—there isn't any that I can see. Also, I wouldn't say that I've ever played professionally in country bands. I was closer to a semipro. I could never make my living doing it.

DLB: Many of your poems are replete with local color. Do you use local color deliberately for a particular effect? How would you defend yourself against a charge of regionalism?

BOTTOMS: Local color is simply detail of place. All good poetry has detail of place. It has something to do with what Coleridge called a reader's "willing suspension of disbelief." This is to say that a reader is naturally skeptical. The burden of interest then is not on the reader, but on the poet. The poet must be convincing enough to make the reader willingly suspend any disbelief. Detail of place is one way to do this. All good poems, I think, are regional. But they are also more than regional. There must be something there to transcend the place and send the poem into another level.

DLB: What is your attraction to fishing as subject matter for poems? Do you just like writing about fishing because you enjoy fishing, or is there some thematic or philosophical reason for using fishing so frequently?

BOTTOMS: I've thought about this and I'm still not sure. I suspect that fishing has for me some kind of religious significance, or some sort of magic. It has to do with mystery. With dredging something up out of the unknown. You could probably make all sorts of stuff out of that. I only know that I have recurring dreams about fishing, and I feel like they are tied to the need to discover whatever is submerged or hidden, if anything is. That's why I call it religious, I guess. Also, I have always fished. All my life.

DLB: Have you ever thought about living someplace other than the South, and if so, have you ever thought about how such a move might affect your writing?

BOTTOMS: I think I'd like to live for a while out West. I've read several times in Texas and Wyoming and always to a very good response. I think the people out there are a lot like people in the South, or at least like the people who used to be in the South. By this I mean that they are very independent. In the West the emphasis is still on the individual, not on the group. There is still that old notion of self-reliance. And I like that. You still see some of that in the South, mostly in the mountains. Certainly not in the cities anymore.

DLB: Do you think that writers tend to live vicariously in their work, to create for themselves experiences they have missed or declined, and to develop in fictive characters facets of their personality they repress? If so, how does this tendency apply to you?

BOTTOMS: I'm not sure about this. I suspect that it's true for most writers, to one degree or another. Though it is probably different for fiction writers. Most of my poems have some degree of autobiography. They are about things I've done or about things I've seen done. This is not to say I won't lie about something if it makes the poem better. Who said that a poem is a lie to tell a greater truth?

DLB: What was your response to winning the Walt Whitman Award?

BOTTOMS: I was excited, of course. Most anyone would be. But I think I was more excited because Warren was the judge. Or let's say doubly excited. Actually, I only submitted the manuscript because I'd heard he was judging that year. So his decision meant a great deal to me. Most prizes, and the Whitman is no different, are very unevenly awarded. One year you get a very good book, the next you get an awful one. This is especially true when the judge or panel of judges changes every year. The Whitman series, I think, is extremely uneven. But then so is the Yale. So, a large part of my excitement centered around Warren's choosing my book. I'd never met him. He didn't know me from Adam, and he chose my book over thirteen-hundred others. That was very gratifying.

DLB: You have written short stories and published some. Do you think you will continue to write fiction as well as poetry?

BOTTOMS: No, I'm not much interested in short fiction. Warren says that stories kill poems. There's something to that. If I get the stuff of a good story, I might be able to get a good poem out of it. I'd rather have the poem.

DLB: What do you see as the direction of your work in the future? Are the poems you are writing now different from those in your two books?

BOTTOMS: They seem to be getting quieter. Better, too, I hope.

Jerome Charyn
(13 May 1937-   )

Michael Woolf
Tottenham College

BOOKS: *Once Upon a Droshky* (New York: McGraw-Hill, 1964);

On the Darkening Green (New York: McGraw-Hill, 1965);

The Man Who Grew Younger and Other Stories (New York: Harper & Row, 1967);

Going to Jerusalem (New York: Viking, 1967; London: Cape, 1968);

American Scrapbook (New York: Viking, 1969);

Eisenhower, My Eisenhower (New York: Holt, Rinehart & Winston, 1971);

The Tar Baby (New York: Holt, Rinehart & Winston, 1973);

Blue Eyes (New York: Simon & Schuster, 1975);

Marilyn the Wild (New York: Arbor House, 1976);

The Education of Patrick Silver (New York: Arbor House, 1976);

The Franklin Scare (New York: Arbor House, 1977);

Secret Isaac (New York: Arbor House, 1978);

The Seventh Babe (New York: Arbor House, 1979);

The Catfish Man: A Conjured Life (New York: Arbor House, 1980);

Darlin' Bill: A Love Story of the Wild West (New York: Arbor House, 1980);

Panna Maria (New York: Arbor House, 1982);

Pinocchio's Nose (New York: Arbor House, 1983);

Four Novels (Marilyn the Wild, Blue Eyes, The Education of Patrick Silver, Secret Isaac) (London: Zomba Books, 1984).

OTHER: *The Single Voice*, edited by Charyn (New York: Collier-Macmillan, 1969);

The Troubled Vision, edited by Charyn (New York: Collier-Macmillan, 1970).

Jerome Charyn (Deborah Flomenhaft)

Jerome Charyn is the author of sixteen novels and a collection of short stories. In addition to this output, he has encouraged new fiction as an editor and as a teacher of creative writing and contemporary literature. It is as a novelist that he has made his most notable contribution. He has synthesized experimental styles with a profoundly moral perspective, and he has developed a subversive comic voice with which to confront and reveal "the terror, the loneliness, and the perversity of human experi-ence." Charyn's critical assertions sustain his view that "the contemporary writer has been left with little else than a sense of dislocation, a splintered reality, and the shards and bones of language." In common with many postmodernist theorists of fiction, he asserts that "the personae of our best writers drift through their fictive landscapes half-asleep, locked within the muted, disordered tones of the catatonic, in a dream-riddled violent world." Charyn modifies these theories, however, in the body of his work with a concrete sense of location, a complex moral uneasiness, a rich responsiveness to detail, and an original, disturbing comic tone. The energies of experimental fiction, comic narration, and Jewish moral consciousness are merged into a unique body of contemporary fiction.

The sources of Charyn's creative energy, and the methods by which those sources are transformed, are revealed in this description of his childhood:

> I was born in the hour of the ostrich, 4 am, when even the dark is confused as it awaits that first, false dawn. I haven't given up the ostrich hour, living with my head in the ground.
>
> I came from a family of ostriches. My mum and dad were part of some atavistic migration out of Sweden, Russia, Portugal, or wherever ostriches tend to cling. They stumbled upon this continent and never quite recovered from their journey. And I'm their offspring, an ostrich with dark hair.
>
> How could I have discovered English in the ordinary way when my father grumbled no language at all? It wasn't Russian or Swedish of the lower depths. It was a primitive cry of want. I woke to that cry and went to sleep with it. It was the sound I started to gurgle in my ostrich crib.

Charyn's childhood forms a base out of which a personal mythology is evolved. His achievement is to have translated that mythology into a substantial body of major fiction.

He was born the son of Sam Charyn (a furrier) and Fannie Paley Charyn in the Bronx on 13 May 1937. He attended the High School of Music and Art in New York and graduated from Columbia University in 1959. Since then, he has retained contact with the academic world through posts in which teaching responsibilities have sometimes been combined with writing fellowships. At the age of twenty-seven he was assistant professor and visiting writer at Stanford University, where he became involved in the experimental "Voice Project" with John Hawkes. He has held visiting professorships at Rice, City University of New York, Columbia, and the University of Texas at Austin. He is currently teaching at Princeton. Charyn has won the following awards: National Endowment for the Arts Award, 1979, for *The Catfish Man*; Rosenthal Award of the American Academy and Institute of Arts and Letters, 1981, for *Darlin' Bill*; Guggenheim Fellowship, 1982-1983, for work on *Pinocchio's Nose*. His interest in fiction is also expressed in his role as a founding editor of the *Dutton Review*, executive editor of *Fiction*, and editor of *The Single Voice* and *The Troubled Vision*, two influential anthologies of contemporary fiction.

The experience of a Jewish childhood in New York has richly influenced Charyn's fiction. The city itself is a frequent protagonist in his work, as well as a fertile source of fictional detail. Charyn has melded his background with a complex literary awareness: "As far as the actual writing is concerned, both my strengths and background are very limited—a few blocks in the East Bronx were my complete universe. It was a provincial world, but I tried to shove as much sophistication as I could into that particular province."

At the heart of Charyn's fiction is a deep mistrust of the contemporary world, frequently expressed in alienation from mechanized, antihumanistic institutions. At the same time, particularly in his later work, Charyn celebrates man's heroic capacity for survival in the face of that reality. A typical Charyn protagonist, moving from passivity to active defiance, engages in a frequently doomed but heroic revolt asserting finally the fragile persistence of moral and spiritual values in an inhospitable world. A Jewish consciousness is frequently expressed in the association of the doomed hero with the ethnic stranger, although Charyn's version of ethnic dislocation is by no means limited to the Jews. Throughout his work he combines a concrete particularity with nonrealist procedures to create a range of fictional worlds that reverberate against the reader's perception of contemporary reality. A central issue in these novels is the nature of conflict—the dispossessed confront the pervasive power of the antihumanistic institution. The moral conflict established is frequently balanced against a view of war as a contagion that breeds surrealistic and chauvinistic distortions. There is also a transaction throughout between theories of literature and the process of fiction-making. Charyn's work is recognizably within both the mainstream of contemporary American fiction and the fertile tradition of Jewish storytelling. A complex synthesis of extravagant fabulation, deep moral disquiet, and rich comedy characterize this work.

After the publication of the short story "On Second Avenue" in *Commentary*, July 1963, Charyn's first novel, *Once Upon a Droshky* (1964), appeared. The first chapter was a rewriting of the story, and it signaled the novelist's careful concern with the rhetoric of his fiction. The additions and modifications invigorate the writing and are indicative of a mature literary sensibility in the work of the twenty-six-year-old writer. The novel exhibits a sense of nostalgia for a disappearing Yiddish-American world. The cafeteria and the Yiddish Theatre of the Lower East Side of New York represent aspects of a rich culture besieged by contemporary pressures. The title evokes the language of the fairy tale to suggest the mythical and magical status of that culture. As often in Jewish writing, the novel coheres around the conflict between father and son; more unusually, the situation evolves through the perspective of the father, Yankel Rabinowitz, who tells the story in an English heavily modified by Yiddish speech patterns. The son is an agent of a legalistic, inhumane America. He represents the momentum of a future against which the forces of the father have little potency. Charyn draws heavily upon the region of his childhood for both the details of place and the language of the narration. The Yiddish-English permits a sustained comic tone while revealing an extravagantly magnified reality and a precise moral perspective.

On the Darkening Green (1965) adopted a more conventional narrative voice but sustained a sense, as the title suggests, of bleak momentum. The narrator, Nick, is one of a series of Charyn's heroic innocents; and, like *Going to Jerusalem* (1967), the novel is essentially an ironic Bildungsroman in which the process of education ends not in enlightenment but in failure and fragmentation. Charyn operates an interplay between the historical reality of prewar and wartime New York and the absurd, quasisurreal institution of "Uncle Nate's Home for Wayward Boys"—a microcosmic version of totalitarian order dominated by the grotesque figure of Uncle Nate. While parodying Jewish chauvinism through that character, Charyn embodies a more affirmative version of Judaism in the rabbi, who sustains a dualistic view in which social responsibility and spiritual possibility are synthesized. The rabbi's assertion that "the devils are in charge of the world" leads toward a conspiracy theory of reality, in which the values of Uncle Nate are supreme, and toward a moral obligation to engage in an act of finally impotent revolt. While exploiting the events of recent history, the novel forms around tensions that are traditional in Yiddish literature: the struggle between the righteous and the demonic. The righteous, in contrast to the mechanized and simplistically dehumanized world of Uncle Nate, exhibit a complex combination of worldly corruption, spiritual affirmation, and profound human sympathy for the oppressed. The narrator of *On the Darkening Green* is a less fully realized figure than Yankel in *Once Upon a Droshky*, but the novel goes further in guiding the reader toward a generalized moral awareness. It is a less coherent unity, but a step nearer the combination of bitter humor and moral outrage that is expressed in

the later novels. In *On the Darkening Green*, the whimsical elements of *Once Upon a Droshky* are abandoned.

Going to Jerusalem, a novella, appeared in 1967 and exhibited a number of influences; in *Partisan Review* (Winter 1968), Maureen Howard identified "Nabokovian devices" and a "Pynchon-like ingenuity. . . ." It is an ambitious attempt to experiment with narrative form and owes something to Charyn's work with Hawkes. It makes the assertion that in a world gone mad the moral man is reduced to clown or lunatic. The model for contemporary experience is the psychic cripple moving through a fantastic and perverse world. The central character, Ivan Farkus, is taken on a journey across an America infected with madness. Under orders from his father, he pursues an ex-Nazi chess champion with a six-year-old prodigy who finally defeats the champion. The obsession behind the pursuit derives from Admiral Farkus, who corrupts and mythologizes the tournament into an extension of World War II. Charyn creates a complex and, at times, bewildering analysis of contemporary America—a fable for our times that begins and ends in madness. The structure of the novel is episodic; the journey supplies the narrative movement and underlies the harsh irony of the title. There is no "Jerusalem." The process of "going to" ends in a lunatic asylum—the exact microcosm of the world created. Most of the novel is told in the present tense, and the effect is to enforce a sense of a character denied perspective, selection, or retrospection. Ivan, in a perverse world, is adrift in time and space. *Going to Jerusalem* is a very ambitious book. It attempts, for example, to create the paradoxical vision of the Nazi as victim. However, the cohesiveness of the novel is problematic. It finally relies on the chess metaphor, which, set against the episodic structure, is a fragile device. The overall impression is of a succession of moments that do not cohere enough to carry the profound meaning that Charyn clearly intends.

The collection *The Man Who Grew Younger and Other Stories* also appeared in 1967 and is more akin in tone to Charyn's first two novels. Indeed, one of the stories, "Faigele the Idiotke," had appeared in *Commentary* in March 1963 and was, like "Sing, Shaindele, Sing," rewritten for book publication. In both cases the book version is a more effective and economical performance, and there is evidence of Charyn's growing power of stylistic selectivity. He creates a succession of characters who construct alternative mental landscapes within concrete and detailed environments. The protagonists are touched, in varying degrees, by a persistent refusal to locate meaning exclusively within the world of social fact. In this sense, they mirror the procedure of the novelist and in microcosmic form reveal the assumptions of the fiction of which they are a part. The motif of war is recurrent, and in the best story, "1944," the perception of the child narrator reverberates against the harsh realities of wartime poverty and loss. The story moves with great skill between that version of the world and a child's alternative vision where God is the most heroic of all heroes. The figures of Faigele and Imberman are versions of figures recurrent in Jewish-American literature. They are ambiguous holy fools who undermine the literal perceptions of the respective narrators. These protagonists move the narrators toward a recognition of the spiritual potential ostensibly denied in the contemporary environment.

Charyn's anger at racism and totalitarianism found a concrete historical occasion in *American Scrapbook* (1969). Based upon the treatment of Japanese internees during World War II, the novel seeks to undermine stereotypes of hero and villain by presenting the Japanese as victims in American camps. His specific political anger is directed at the absurdity of a national policy that defines the "enemy" on the basis of ethnicity. The Japanese, like the other ethnic strangers in Charyn's fiction, illustrate the tensions of the ethnically isolated American who is not permitted to feel fully American but has only vestigial remnants of his original culture as an alternative. They are displaced persons in both a geographical and a cultural sense. The novel is comprised of a series of first-person narratives that Samuel Bellman called in the *Saturday Review* "stream of consciousness reports in the Faulknerian mode. . . ." The interaction of these voices serves to dramatize the predicament. It is an uneven book, but it is rescued by its political and moral intensity and its profound sense of sympathy with the suffering of the weak and the powerless. The metaphor of the camp, a potent one for a Jewish novelist, serves to generalize the meaning of the specific events recorded.

The concrete historical basis is abandoned in *Eisenhower, My Eisenhower* (1971), though essentially similar issues are raised. The Azazian gypsy Toby Malothioon marks Charyn's attempt to fuse conditions of persecution and alienation in one character. The Azazians are essentially comic figures with tails and a belief in an anarchic god, Karooku. Charyn's achievement is to make these figures both credible and representative victims. He creates a fictive system with its own logic, history, and structure while

revealing a perspective upon cultural predicaments rooted in the grosser absurdities of modern America. Toby's narrative is fragmented, impressionistic, and chronologically distorted, reflecting the consciousness in an activist mode—the seeker in an engagement with a bewildering reality. The image is of a world reduced. The Azazians are cut off from their sources of magic and power, and like the Jews of *Once Upon a Droshky* or the Japanese of *American Scrapbook*, they are left with only vestiges of their culture. Toby's transformation into reluctant revolutionary also recalls Charyn's first two novels. In 1971, Charyn returned to the themes of the earlier books, but with the procedures of nonrealism paradoxically offering an incisive analysis into the real predicament of the ethnic stranger in a hostile society.

The Tar Baby (1973) reflects two aspects of Charyn's developing career. His interest in experimental narrative forms is shown in the manipulation of modes of expression that seek to represent the perceived fragmentation of contemporary experience. His work in the universities also offered a rich vein of satirical material which supplies much of the comic momentum in the novel. The novel parodies the form of a literary periodical and is comprised of a series of articles. Ostensibly, it is an attempt to record the life of Anatole Waxman-Weissman. However, the various contributions primarily reveal the jealousies, vanities, and affectations of the contributors. Anatole remains shadowy, a complex eccentric and the creator of a fictional Wittgenstein in a much-revised memoir. The contributors inhabit a version of a California small town that is a quasisurrealistic construct and a source of vivid absurdity. It is also a place destructive of the ethnic outsider and the eccentric intelligence. Anatole is a victim of a society and an institution profoundly hostile to the creative imagination. Charyn integrates into the fiction a critical commentary on itself that serves both to emphasize the process by which fictions are made and to cast doubts upon the veracity of any single "voice." This procedure reveals the influence of Vladimir Nabokov and a growing interest in formal issues, though it is never allowed to become arid or purely theoretical. *The Tar Baby* paradoxically achieves a sense of Anatole's suffering and isolation while the rhetoric of the fiction suggests the impossibility of creating character within the constraints of contemporary fiction. Albert Guerard has described the novel as "an experiment in complex impressionistic and involutional form, striking and original in the extremes to which it juxtaposes comic stereotype and real suffering" (*TriQuarterly,* Spring 1974).

In *Blue Eyes* (1975), *Marilyn the Wild* (1976), and *The Education of Patrick Silver* (1976), Charyn focuses his creative energy upon the urban detective story. The novels represent an attempt to mold the traditional shape of the detective story into an American epic, a radical reinvention and extension of the possibilities inherent in the form. Harvey Charyn, the novelist's brother, is a homicide detective, and with his help Charyn delved into the criminal environment of the Bronx. The material that emerged was transformed and structured into a sequence of shapes that are startlingly fresh within the context of the genre.

Blue Eyes is built around the figure of Manfred Coen, a detective-wanderer, obsessed by death, in a city populated by grotesques. His mentor, Isaac Sidel, is engaged in a feud with the Guzmanns, a group of Marrano pickpockets, and it is this feud that leads to Coen's death. *Marilyn the Wild* presents an earlier period in Coen's life in which Sidel's daughter emerges as another ambiguous "blue-eyed angel." In a complex panorama of characters and events, the novel focuses on Marilyn's ambivalent relationship with Coen and her father. In *The Education of Patrick Silver* and in *Secret Isaac* (1978), Charyn exploits the same fictive environment but shifts the emphasis to the grief and guilt of Isaac, who emerges as a combination of detective-wanderer in the underworld of the city and suffering father in search of the dead son. The ghost of Coen hovers over the head of Isaac and around the action of both novels. Charyn cites the influence of Ross Macdonald, but he goes further than Macdonald in creating a collection of fiction that is effective both within the genre and within an expanded idea of what the genre can achieve. The wider context of the work is revealed in Charyn's description of the central relationship: "Isaac was the sinister chief, and Coen was his blue-eyed angel, a kind of Billy Budd." The work is formed around, and brings together, seemingly disparate sources: the underworld of criminal activity and the literary antecedents that Charyn employs to bring a radically original perspective upon that material.

Charyn's urban landscape in these novels is characterized by violence and by fierce ethnic loyalties expressed in a form of tribal warfare. He exploits the narrative pace offered by the detective genre to transcend the form and create a sense of a world dislocated from the norm, populated by a vast range of grotesques and corrupted angels. This world permits a process in which figures like Blue Eyes and Marilyn the Wild assume quasimythical status rather than complex psychological density. The traditional emphasis of the detective story on plot rather than character gives Charyn a formal shape through which to evolve a view of the urban landscape not solely dependent on the creation of character. These are the first novels in which Charyn abandoned first-person narrative. The third-person voice creates a sense of distance, and the reader is presented with a world in which dislocation and distortion are clearly characteristic not only of a single perception but of society itself.

The Franklin Scare (1977) marked Charyn's return to the historical landscape of the war. In this uneven novel Charyn integrates the historical figures of the Roosevelts with the figure of the sailor Oliver Beebe, protected and befriended by the president. The novel covers the year of Franklin D. Roosevelt's death, and the action is set against a background of conspiracy and intrigue. The motif of baseball in the novel reflects Charyn's use of sport as a metaphor of alternative experience. As in *Blue Eyes* and later in *The Seventh Babe* (1979), sport is used to establish a version of conflict in a simple, archetypal form which is set in contrast to the bewildering complexities of a wider world also characterized by conflict. *The Franklin Scare* reflects Charyn's responsiveness to forms of contemporary experimentation, marking his attempt to produce a novel in which historical fact is merged with fiction. This type of novel emerged as a quasigenre in the 1970s, but it is not an area in which Charyn is comfortable. His most effective fiction comes out of the freer areas of fabulation where, paradoxically, he goes beyond the surface of real event to render the underlying texture of experience with great insight and clarity. This novel lacks the incisiveness of much of his work.

The same cannot be said of *Secret Isaac*, the fourth book of the detective tetralogy. Isaac is now police commissioner of New York but, as his status increases, he is haunted more and more by the figure of the dead Coen. The novel again raises the spectre of a world insane: "Psychosis is everywhere . . . in your armpit . . . under your shoe. You can smell it in the sweat of this room . . . we're all baby killers, repressed or not . . . how do you measure a man's rage? Either we behave like robots, or we kill. Why do you expect your Police Force to be any less crazy than you?" That sense of a world deranged, and the disturbing questions raised in that world, coexists in the novel with references to Joyce's *Ulysses.* The novel moves into a Dublin that exists both as a real city and as a literary antecedent. Charyn establishes a transaction between Joyce's Dublin and New York's underworld imagined in the shape of a surrealistic nightmare. The novel records "the history of Isaac after his fall from grace." In what is almost a city of the dead, Sidel emerges as a Bloom-type figure in search of Coen, the dead son. In a process of transformation "he becomes Coen and barks his own song of innocence and experience." *Secret Isaac* concludes the sequence of detective novels. Together they form a complex epic that moves with great skill between literary sources and criminal reality, the whole offering a fertile vision of a world where both are richly integrated. With these novels, Charyn explodes the boundaries of the genre.

The Seventh Babe (1979) traces the transformation of Babe Ragland into a mythic hero and, as in Philip Roth's *The Great American Novel* and Robert Coover's *The Universal Baseball Association*, the motifs of victory, defeat, and conflict are used to generate a form of epic. Baseball supplies Charyn with a world in which magic remains a potent element, and it is an apt environment in which he can forge the magical transformations characteristic of his fiction and of his treatment of character as a fluid element within the fictional systems created. Additionally, the movement of Babe Ragland from team to team permits a panoramic sweep across the American landscape; but, as is often true in Charyn's work, the geographical journey is as much a journey into self as into space. The humor that Charyn has called "undermining" is richly in evidence, but it is a humor mixed with pathos. At the end of the novel Babe Ragland exists as a forgotten hero—an image of heroic potential reduced in the harsh world of the present. Thus the figure of Babe Ragland is used to express the dehumanizing pressures emanating from a version of contemporary reality that is deeply hostile to an expanded self. William Plummer noted in the *New York Times Book Review* that, as in the detective novels, "Charyn explodes the genre and the reader's expectations."

The Seventh Babe signaled a growing if belated recognition of Charyn's work in the literary press and in the wider cultural environment. Work on *The Catfish Man: A Conjured Life* (1980) was supported by a National Endowment for the Arts Award. It is the first Charyn novel in which the first-person narrator assumes the role of author. It is essentially a Kunstlerroman in which the author-protagonist echoes some of the material of Charyn's earlier work, particularly *Going to Jerusalem* and "1944." As in the later novel *Pinocchio's Nose* (1983), however, this is no act of mere literary retrospection; neither

is it a traditional "portrait of the artist as a young man." The Bronx is both the setting and the source from which the novelist-protagonist gains power. The "catfish" is employed as a central image of the persistent capacity for both mired corruption and transcendent wonder within the urban landscape. It is, in short, a crystallized symbol of Charyn's view of reality. Within that world Charyn invents a protagonist who is himself an inventor. Thus the life "conjured" is both that of the novel and that of the novelist. The elements of autobiography are transformed by an immense inventiveness that creates a dense fictional world in which magical transformations coexist with a concrete location. Charyn seduces the reader into a suspension of disbelief in which the magical catfish is as credible as the walls of an apartment building. The novel is also introspective in that it contains a record of its own construction: the first sentence is the sentence that the protagonist achieves in the conclusion of the book. This device raises the theoretical issues of fiction-making within the novel and permits an insight into the processes of creation by which "all the changing colours the past can fling at you" become transformed and unified within the single vision. By the end of the novel, the protagonist emerges as "Catfish Jerome," who takes on the resonance of that symbol in a joyful celebration that affirms the fragile persistence of love, wonder, and creativity. The novel unifies the themes of Charyn's work and reflects a mature, inclusive imagination where the self becomes a protagonist in the dramatic reinvention of landscape and memory. It is a major work that affirms Charyn's status among the most significant living American authors.

In the same fertile period *Darlin' Bill: A Love Story of the Wild West* (1980) appeared and received the Rosenthal Award. The genre of cowboy fiction gave Charyn a narrative shape in which to examine the mythology of the West and to humanize that form through the perspective of the narrator, Sally Ovenshine. Western motifs offer material for a comic but incisive perspective on a landscape characterized by violence. The mechanics of this fiction recall the detective tetralogy, in which the reader's expectations of the genre are partly realized, partly reshaped and expanded. Charyn exploits traditional American myths to make original deviations from the norm. The reader's sense of surprise is precisely triggered by that manipulation of expectation. Thus the entirely traditional conclusion, "The horse perked up his ears and pulled us out of Deadwood," frames a fiction in which Wild Bill Hickok is reduced to a half-blind tramp. Charyn

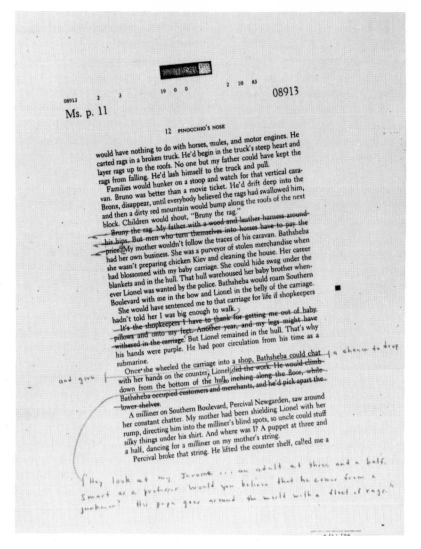

Revised proof (the author)

establishes a transaction between legend and actuality in which what persists is the human capacity to survive and love. He delves beneath the mythology to create a world of rich emotional ambiguity.

The theme of survival is also examined in *Panna Maria* (1982), an ambitious attempt to trace the development of immigrant society through the turbulent first three decades of this century. Various ethnic groups are seen in political conflict that frequently degenerates into tribal warfare. The novel coheres around the building of Panna Maria, an apartment block that houses a brothel and is the center of a Polish immigrant group. The protagonist, Stefan Wilde, is mythologized into the figure of "tzarevitch," who assumes a magical status in the eyes of the other characters. There is a tension, however, between the figure as an heroic "magus" and the figure as a poverty-stricken, alienated immigrant. The novel traces a bewildering succession of events and transformations. Finally, the accumulation of detail tends to swamp the reader's perception of the fiction. There are fine moments when, for example, a surrealistic perspective on World War I reveals the conflict as a kind of commercial transaction. Indeed, commerce is the binding material of the society created; it governs not only war but politics, law, and love. Charyn has created a panoramic view of immigrant society; but the historical scale—the accumulation of characters and the dense nature of the plotting—tends to work against an effective focus on Stefan Wilde. The heart of the novel is encapsulated in Stefan's "triumphant survival": "A whole city conspired against the tzarevitch, and he'd won back his life." In that sense, Stefan is an archetypal immigrant protagonist. However, his story is somewhat undermined by a narrative complexity that finally weakens the effectiveness of the novel.

Charyn's most recent novel, *Pinocchio's Nose* is, among other things, a playful act of fictional retrospection in which some of the earlier subject matter is reexamined and the author is himself transformed into a narrator-protagonist whose identity becomes a comic issue. "Jerome Copernicus Charyn" moves between that fragile identity and the role of Pinocchio—the wooden boy. He is suffering from *"Mythopsychosis*, the terrifying need to mythologize one's existence at the expense of all other things. The sufferer of mythopsychosis seeks narratives everywhere, inside and outside of himself. He cannot take a move and not narratize it." Through this device Charyn raises the essentially serious issue of narrative invention within a comic framework. The transformation of the narrator is both a self-referential device—a means of examining the making of the fiction within the fiction itself—and a reflection of the degree to which identity is seen as fragile and mutable, subject to irrational and often menacing changes. In an essentially picaresque form, Charyn traces the survival and growth of the fluid narrator as he surveys both the world of myth and the world of his own earlier fiction. The motif of the revolt of the dispossessed recurs, and aspects of *Going to Jerusalem, The Tar Baby*, and "The Man Who Grew Younger" are revisited.

The growing recognition of Charyn's achievements also has an international dimension. In England, the detective novels have been published in a single volume; and he is currently working on an illustrated novel for the French magazine *A Suivre*. Jerome Charyn is one of a handful of living American novelists who combine prolific creativity with stylistic originality and imaginative zest. The recent air of qualified affirmation might indicate the direction in which his work is likely to develop. However, part of this novelist's claim to our attention is precisely his unpredictability. He has taken hold of a wide range of American myths, locations, and dreams and reshaped these within his rich imagination. Jerome Charyn has created a body of work characterized by a unique voice and a troubled, but fertile, vision.

References:

Albert Guerard, "Notes on the Rhetoric of Anti-Realist Fiction," *TriQuarterly*, 30 (Spring 1974): 36-49;

Beatrice Levin, "Once Upon a Droshky," *Chicago Jewish Forum*, 23 (Summer 1965): 320-321.

Kelly Cherry
(21 December 1940-   )

Mark Harris
Jackson Community College

BOOKS: *Sick and Full of Burning* (New York: Viking, 1974);

Lovers and Agnostics (Charlotte, N.C.: Red Clay Books, 1975);

Relativity: A Point of View (Baton Rouge: Louisiana State University Press, 1977);

Augusta Played (Boston: Houghton Mifflin, 1979);

Conversion (New Paltz, N.Y.: Treacle Press, 1979);

Songs for a Soviet Composer (St. Louis, Mo.: Singing Wind Press, 1980);

In the Wink of an Eye (New York: Harcourt Brace Jovanovich, 1983);

The Lost Traveller's Dream (New York: Harcourt Brace Jovanovich, 1984).

SELECTED PERIODICAL PUBLICATIONS:
Fiction:

"Tycho Brahe's Gold and Silver Nose," *Red Clay Reader 4* (1967): 30-37;

"Covenant," *Commentary*, 51 (May 1971): 49-60;

"Where the Winged Horses Take Off Into the Wild Blue Yonder From," *Story Quarterly*, no. 4 (1976): 117-129;

"Creation," *Story Quarterly*, nos. 5-6 (1977): 41-72.

Kelly Cherry (Norman Lenburg)

Poetry:

"Heartwood: a Diary," *Southern Review*, 14 (July 1978): 500-501;

"The Family," *Southern Poetry Review*, 19 (Spring 1979): 41-45;

"Letter to a Censor," *Georgia Review*, 33 (Winter 1979): 784-785;

"Hunting: a Story," *Midwest Quarterly*, 22 (Winter 1981): 126-131;

"Questions and Answers," *Anglican Theological Review*, 64 (January 1982): 42-46;

"A Scientific Expedition in Siberia, 1913," *Southern Review*, 18 (January 1982): 161-165.

Kelly Cherry was born in Baton Rouge, Louisiana, where her father taught music theory at Louisiana State University. In 1944 her parents, J. Milton and Mary Spooner Cherry, moved to Ithaca, New York, to further their musical careers; both were violinists and specialized in Beethoven's later string quartets. Her parents' dedication impressed Cherry. She remembers her mother staying up night after night typing menus for a restaurant near their home to earn enough money for food. Perhaps knowing that her parents "believed in starving for art" influenced Cherry's choice of

career; she also has a sister who is a musician and a brother who is a writer.

Cherry received her B.A. from Mary Washington College in 1961. From 1961 to 1963 she did graduate work toward a Ph.D. in philosophy at the University of Virginia, where she was awarded a Du Pont Fellowship. She completed an M.F.A. at the University of North Carolina, Greensboro, in 1967. She was married to Jonathan Silver in 1966; they were divorced in 1969. She currently is a full professor at the University of Wisconsin, Madison campus, where she teaches poetry, fiction, and essay writing as well as one of the few novel writing courses in the country.

Cherry writes that what concerns her most as a writer is "structure, aesthetic, moral and epistemological." She works in a variety of forms because each has its best uses. In a sense her career embraces three separate careers, for she has published some fifteen short stories (including a *Best American Short Stories* award winner in 1972) in addition to three novels and two collections of verse. Certain "motifs"—she prefers that word to "theme"—recur in all three forms. These include birds, music, money, redemption, time, and "words as a way of establishing the existence of a world beyond the self." For Cherry, "Fiction is the root civilizing act. It is how the world is made inhabited; it is how we move beyond solipsism; it is a way to other minds." Any author who simplifies issues or characters to serve a particular end is false to what Cherry sees as the main aim of fiction: "creating a world, or worlds, that will sustain within an aesthetic framework the contradictions that in real life threaten to divide us."

By her own account Cherry for many years considered herself a poet, although, "like most poets," she did write a few short stories. Her M.F.A. thesis, which launched her career, was a collection of poetry titled "Benjamin John and other Poems." Many of the poems in this volume are lyric poems. One, "A Lyric Cycle," consisting of eleven poems, was set to music by the Soviet composer Imant Kalnin. The most memorable poem in the cycle is an unrhymed piece of five lines entitled "Roses." The airiness of the first two lines collapses in the third, and the thudding, juggernaut rhythm of the final line composes an unusual portrait of roses.

> As I was a child,
> You pampered me with roses.
> In this airless room,
> I shuffle their petals, and inhale
> Their thick, dull, deadly, pink perfume.

But the strongest poem in this first volume of verse is the title piece. Consisting of twenty-nine separately titled units, the poem traces the life of an economist, Benjamin John. In the first unit, "The Lightfoot Boys," the protagonist is a young man "Sneaking slugs into Stanley's jukebox" and remembering back to his childhood in Ithaca, New York. The final unit is called "A By-Line: On his Cancer." It ends with a confession: Benjamin John admits to a growing fondness for "this oddest of my maladies that *stays* with me." The poem was published in its entirety in the *Carolina Quarterly* and excerpts appeared in *Coraddi*, the *Greensboro Reader* (an anthology), and the *Greensboro Review*. It is a splendid achievement for a young poet, offering remarkable insight into the life of an academic Walter Mitty. The verse itself is memorable for its unpretentiousness. Lyricism, while present, never overwhelms the images or the message they convey. Even the choppiness of the short units is suggestive of the theme. The poem is the inventory of a life, and such a catalogue is by definition selective and somewhat abrupt.

Perhaps the interest in narrative poetry Cherry revealed in "Benjamin John" led her to experiment further with the short story. She began writing short stories while working on her M.F.A. and continued to write stories using material and techniques she later incorporated into novels. Her first published story, "Don't Forget to Call, Darling. The Play Begins at Eight," appeared in a collection of stories called *The Girl In The Black Raincoat* (1966), edited by George Garrett. (Cherry was "the girl in the black raincoat.") This very brief story anticipates Cherry's later short fiction in being self-consciously experimental. The narrative unfolds solely through the dialogue of the two characters, in the way that certain Hemingway stories do. The frame of the tale—the narrator's comments on the setting and characters—disappears after the opening page, and the reader simply observes two characters interacting.

Other of Cherry's short stories, while perhaps not so experimental in terms of technique, also reveal her use of the short story to test ideas and characters. "Where the Winged Horses Take Off Into the Wild Blue Yonder From," for example, attempts a lyrical approach to the narrative. The narrator/protagonist, torn between her pianist ex-husband and a composer named Peteris who lives in Latvia with his wife and children, finds a resolution to her problems in the realization that she too is capable of music and that "sound is pure structure." Similarly, the earlier "Tycho Brahe's Gold and

Silver Nose" offers superb portraits of each of the Chabasinskis, a Polish emigré family living in Virginia. The theme of this story is intergenerational conflict, and if Cherry fails to develop the significance of the title, the story is memorable for its sharp insights and finely drawn characters. Reading her short fiction, the reader has a sense of watching Cherry work out themes and ideas for her novels. Even when the stories themselves are not altogether successful, they provide interesting glimpses of Cherry's creative process.

"Covenant," perhaps her most successful short story, was first published in *Commentary* in 1971 and was included in *The Best American Short Stories, 1972*. The story is more overtly autobiographical than her poetry and anticipates her use of personal material in her novels. Consequently, it possesses an immediacy and intensity absent in some of her earlier work. The story focuses on the relationship of the protagonist (who narrates the story in the first person) with Felix Seligman, a Jewish moviemaker who is her ex-husband's best friend. Their relationship begins auspiciously enough. When she first meets Felix on her wedding day, she instantly desires him. After the wedding, they grow closer from having Ezra, her husband, in common: He bullies and uses both of them. Their friendship deepens through shared pain. Felix's marriage begins to break up. The narrator finds life with Ezra difficult. Still, despite the fact that Felix is divorced and, eventually, the narrator is too, years pass before they actually consummate their relationship.

Even after they are lovers Felix continues to think of her as "Ezra's wife," and the course of the story is the narrator's growing awareness that certain bonds are like God's covenant with Israel: They cannot be altered by human action. It is a large theme for a short story, but Cherry handles it deftly. Cherry's penchant for large questions, so apparent in her novels, makes its first appearance in this short story.

The success of "Covenant" helped Cherry acquire an agent, and while she continued to publish her poetry in small journals such as *Bitterroot, Crazy Horse, Southern Poetry Review*, and *Sou'wester*, and in better-known publications such as *Esquire* and the *Georgia Review*, she explored new terrain as well. In the summer of 1971, while working as a live-in tutor for a handicapped girl, Cherry began working on the novel that became *Sick and Full of Burning* (1974). Like many first novels, the result was strongly autobiographical. Her real-life employer was "rich, lonely, and dangerously addicted to barbituates." The daughter was "into Jim Morrison and The Doors." Cherry herself was "trying to work out an identity" as she faced her thirtieth birthday, "newly unmarried and just beginning to have my consciousness raised." Mary "Tennessee" Settleworth, the fictional Kelly Cherry, began as a writer but became in later drafts a medical student who "enrolled at Mount Sinai with a view of becoming a gynecologist" after her lover walked out on her.

The novel's intricate plotting reflects Cherry's turmoil during this period. The many subplots combine to produce a caricature of contemporary ideological fashion. The protagonist, for example, belongs to a woman's group which meets to discuss "feminist" issues. Eventually, however, she is asked to stop attending. She simply refuses to take herself as seriously as the others do. Worse, she admits openly and often to her desire to be married. The editors of *Ms.* magazine found this element of the book so distressing that they declined to print a review of the book on the grounds that the novel's ending was "insufficiently feminist."

Cherry's irreverent wit, apparent in her affinity for taboo topics, also finds expression in *Sick and Full of Burning*. Female sexual frustration is one of Cherry's favorite topics, suggesting both the perversion of instinct and a parody of male libido. Like many of Cherry's other heroines, Tennessee Settleworth is unable to enjoy more than a casual friendship with the men she meets. Adrien, the chief object of her affections, is another in the line of sexually inaccessible males that runs through Cherry's work. He is direct kin to Peteris in "Where the Winged Horses Take Off Into the Wild Blue Yonder From." The best friend of the protagonist's lover, he in fact introduced Tennessee to the man who walked out on her and precipitated her enrollment in medical school. Now, however, she is alone, and Adrien lives in New Hope, Pennsylvania. From there he sends vaguely provocative letters inviting Tennessee to come to live with him. When he visits her in New York, however, he refuses to make love to her. Another of Tennessee's male friends, Peter, is very willing to make love to her, but unable. Since his divorce, he is impotent. The essential pessimism of the novel finds a certain anodyne in the protagonist's humorous attempts to relieve her sexual frustration first by seducing Adrien and later by mechanical means.

Cherry wrote *Sick and Full of Burning* with the idea that it should "begin by being a comedy with an undertone of the tragic, and end with these elements reversed, the sense of the tragic foremost."

Indeed, the novel does describe a spiral toward the tragic. Tennessee's relationships with men, at first so comic, come to represent the essential inability of one person to help another. Her relationship with her employer, at first a godsend providing a place to stay and cash to help meet the costs of medical school, becomes a living entombment, representing in Cherry's words "the question of martyrdom." Should Tennessee live her own life or devote herself to her two very real invalids? To what extent is she responsible for the drug addiction of her employer, Lulu Carlisle? For the daughter's future? A novel which poses such questions is more than comic. Cherry begins writing a novel "with a question that can be answered both yes and no— whether the question is made apparent to the reader or not." In her first novel, the reader's growing awareness of both the importance and the difficulty of "the question of martyrdom" makes Tennessee's story memorable.

Reviews of *Sick and Full of Burning* were enthusiastic and favorable. *Kirkus Reviews* noted that it was "just about perfect." Phoebe Adams in *Atlantic Monthly* termed the book "mischievously funny." *Publishers Weekly* found in the novel "what critics find so lacking in much feminist literature— humor, satire, genuine pathos." Negative criticism, with one exception, was slight. The "Notes on Current Books" section in the *Virginia Quarterly Review* asserts that the title, which Cherry says was chosen by her brother from a poem by Robert Lowell, "accurately describes the plight of its heroine," but that the novel "fails to illuminate the tragedy behind the narrative."

In 1975 Cherry collected many of her poems that had appeared in magazines between 1967 and 1974 in *Lovers and Agnostics*, which won favorable reviews in newspapers and small magazines but escaped larger notice. *Relativity: A Point of View* (1977), a collection of new poems, earned her much wider recognition. Paul Ramsey wrote in the *Sewanee Review* that Cherry might "well become a truly important poet"; an unsigned review in *Choice* noted that she "might be a poet to watch." The poems collected in this second volume demonstrate Cherry's mastery of fixed forms as well as free verse. "A Riddle," for example, is written in the classic riddle form, developing its subject without revealing it. At the end of the poem, Cherry prints the answer to the riddle and the sequence of word associations which led her to make the poem. "Sequence Sonnet" employs the traditional sonnet form, popular with poets in every age, to present one relationship as an analogue for civilization:

In our passage from love to the last, wild,
                                                    selfish grief
Which knows nothing, I will conduct
This gentle man through the garden
                                        of courtship.
Civilization is a sweet though short trip.

Several of the poems in *Relativity* reveal Cherry's agile wit. "Translation: After Petronius Arbiter" (subtitled "To His Uncoy Mistress") offers outrageous double entendres and reveals Cherry at her ribald best. Its parenthetical ending echoes, rather incongruously, Gerard Manley Hopkins: "(And in such sexual evolution, through our night's eternity, overturning nature, will I please you, and you, please God, please me!)" At times Cherry's wit unfolds in very few lines. "Baby Friedman," for example, flashes on the reader like sunshine:

grow fat on your father's grin
& someday let your mother know you're glad
she said yes and let him in

Cherry's lyricism and wit are not always devoted to gaiety, however. "Curie," a tribute to the discoverer of radium, praises Madame Curie's analytical ability but ends on this arch note: "A modest miracle, but one / admirable in woman." Similarly, in "My Marriage" the bitterness of the narrator's view of her marriage is made more pointed by the understatement of the final lines: "Divorce keeps it real and intact, / like a fossil." Some of her shorter poems employ brevity to increase the impact of individual images. "Snapshot, 1945" captures in four lines the awfulness of the ex-soldier who, growing old, looks back on the war he fought in his youth as the happiest time of his life:

The Butterfly Boy, Private First Class,
                                        flies, flits
From bar to bar, glancing on the flowers
Of Tokyo; and when he's old he sits
By his small fire, robbing dreams from the
                                        crushed hours.

Negative critical responses to *Relativity* concentrated on these shorter poems. One reviewer found them frequently "skimpy, underdeveloped" in comparison to Cherry's longer poems. Her ability to sustain a narrative by clustering and repeating images does indeed lend itself to longer forms, and "A Bird's-Eye View of Einstein," the longest poem in the collection, is an example of Cherry at her poetic best.

The poem depicts the spiritual desiccation of the twentieth century from a woman's point of view. It consists of three sections in free verse. After an introduction of sixteen lines which establishes the connection between the bird of the title and the narrator of the poem, the first section, "Concerning the First Relation: Bridegroom," describes a married couple making love. It compares their conjugal relation to the Eucharist. Adultery, in contrast, is compared to starvation. The wasteland imagery is heavy and explicit throughout, but the section is redeemed from mere derivation by passages unmistakably Cherry's own.

Section two, "Concerning the Middle Term: Ghost," is an exploration of death, or more simply of the transformation of matter from one state to another, something the poet sees as a kind of betrayal. Beginning with the personal, the poet moves outward to consider the world. The section concludes with an image of eternity:

I see disaster brooding
Over the past. Her wide and nervous wings
Eclipse the echoing moon, but soon the sun
Startles her into flight. Not until night
Does she return, bringing burning and old
Mad grief for the fatherless and unborn.

The final section of the poem, "Part Three: Infinity," fuses intense, physical images with abstractions. Parts are almost certain to remind the reader of Wallace Stevens:

Here is the room
Where the music is made.
                                        Here is the room
Where violins are played, and light is made
Of light, and sound falls to the ground
                                        like fruit
Shaken from a full tree.

Other parts are reminiscent of Sylvia Plath:

I lap lightstruck nails
Under my tongue, and spit them out one by
One. My hammer drives holes into the hands
That never touched me but only ideal
And melody, . . .

The final fifty lines, with the repeated imperative

"Cry woe," achieve an emotional intensity that is rare in Cherry's verse. The reader feels viscerally the narrator's isolation and despair: "When I whisper no one / Replies, and nothing blinks or sighs or moves. . . . / Disaster / Picks the brainpan clean." The last lines artfully employ the flexibility of the blank-verse line. In so doing they fix— fossilize, to use Cherry's own image—the tone and theme of the poem:

> Now is the hour
> Of closure.
>   Now is the hour of reprise.
>   Now is
> The hour of recapitulation.
>   Time
> Sings in the tree.

Cherry's poetry since *Relativity* suggests that she has continued to develop away from the shorter lyric and toward a "pure" narrative. "The Family," published in the *Southern Poetry Review* in 1979, uses a series of dramatic monologues to relate a family's response to the death of the father in a hunting accident. "Hunting," another recent narrative poem, also employs simple images for complex effects. Cherry's narrative line here is tighter and more evocative than the looser line of "Benjamin John," and the poetry consequently much more powerful. The themes which frequent her fiction during this period—the futility of passion, the anatomy of human relationships, the search for identity—make these poems some of her best.

Cherry's second novel, *Augusta Played*, appeared in 1979. Despite the switch from first- to third-person narration, the novel retains strong autobiographical elements. The protagonist of this novel, Augusta Gold, whom Cherry describes as "Tuesday Weld by Vermeer," may have been in part modeled on Elaine Shaffer, a renowned American flutist who died in 1973 and to whom Cherry dedicated a poem in *Lovers and Agnostics*. Augusta's marriage to Norman Gold demonstrates Cherry's fine eye for human behavior, especially that between the sexes. At bottom, however, the Golds' marriage is simply another in the long line of thwarted intimacies Cherry depicts in her work.

The novel begins as Norman, a "cultural musicologist," rebounds in Augusta's direction when his affair with Bunny Van Den Nieuwenhutzen ends. After a brief courtship—less than a month—the two are married against the wishes of both their families. (Norman is in fact disinherited.) *Augusta Played* is in some respects William Dean

Howells's *A Modern Instance* reset in twentieth-century New York City. Augusta and Norman, like Bartley and Marcia Hubbard, never succeed at bringing out the good in each other. Instead, they bring out the petty: he is domineering, arrogant; she is submissive but furtive. Both are suspicious. He is prone to violence. On their wedding night when a bellhop surprises them in flagrante delicto, Norman punches the embarrassed fifteen-year-old in the jaw. Once he tears a mole on Augusta's back while they are making love; at the climax of the novel he knocks two people unconscious before being knocked out himself.

Like *Sick and Full of Burning*, *Augusta Played* contains multiple subplots. Augusta's former lover, a composer named Richard Hacking, still lives in town with his wife and children. He wants to resume their affair. Norman blackmails his father to subsidize Augusta's musical career and his education after he discovers his father's long-standing affair with a hooker cum exotic dancer named "Birdie" Mickle. Augusta assumes that Norman is having an affair when he sneaks off to have lunch with his father and collect his weekly hush money. Norman assumes that Augusta has resumed her affair with Hacking when one of his books is returned to him by Hacking's wife, Elaine, who, in addition, mistakenly tells Augusta that Norman is having an affair with Birdie Mickle.

Augusta Played relies on improbable events and a series of misapprehensions much as the eighteenth-century comedy of manners did. To criticize the novel on the basis of its absurd plot, as Nora Johnson did in the *New York Times Book Review*, is to miss the point of the book entirely. The mixture of realistic detail and improbable coincidence allows Cherry to explore a commonplace in our time—the breakdown of a marriage—in a refreshing and interesting manner. Without the baroque plotting, the novel is simply one more chronicle of a marriage that did not work. With it, the dynamics of the marriage, and of the society around it, are clearer. And, although the reasons for the breakup are never directly apparent (even to Norman and Augusta), the reader shares the couple's sentiment that the breakup is somehow for the best. Thus, in the epilogue when Norman and Augusta meet for lunch four years after their divorce, their ritualistic quarrel dampens neither their spirit nor the reader's. In fact, the book ends on an optimistic note. Augusta cheerfully pursues her music; Norman eyes passing women on the way to the Columbia library, feeling "terrific."

In *Augusta Played* Cherry's use of third- rather

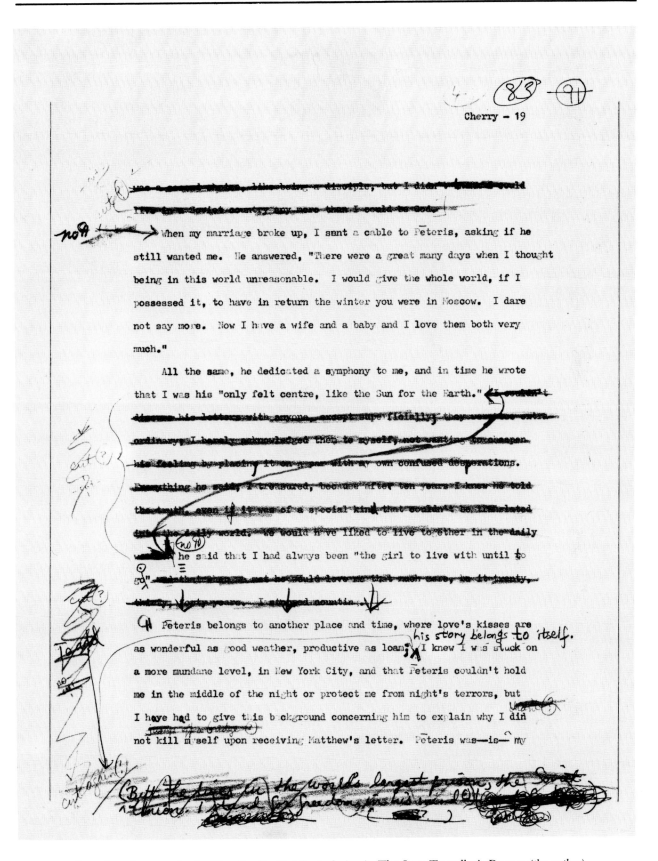

When my marriage broke up, I sent a cable to Peteris, asking if he still wanted me. He answered, "There were a great many days when I thought being in this world unreasonable. I would give the whole world, if I possessed it, to have in return the winter you were in Moscow. I dare not say more. Now I have a wife and a baby and I love them both very much."

All the same, he dedicated a symphony to me, and in time he wrote that I was his "only felt centre, like the Sun for the Earth."

he said that I had always been "the girl to live with until to go."

Peteris belongs to another place and time, where love's kisses are as wonderful as good weather, productive as loam. *his story belongs to itself.* I knew I was stuck on a more mundane level, in New York City, and that Peteris couldn't hold me in the middle of the night or protect me from night's terrors, but I have had to give this background concerning him to explain why I did not kill myself upon receiving Matthew's letter. Peteris was—is— my

Page from the typescript for "Creation," edited for inclusion in The Lost Traveller's Dream *(the author)*

207

than first-person narration allows her to escape the limitations of one character's perspective and obtain a wider view of the world. This process of going beyond the individual, which Cherry relates to Keats's "negative capability," for her is "intimately linked with the act of *significant* creation." Using third-person narration provides Cherry easy access to other characters' viewpoints, making not only the reader's experience of the world but the fictional world itself larger. *Augusta Played* begins and ends from Norman's point of view. For Cherry this act of expansion is a form of redemption: "To become negatively capable is to escape the self *as it exists in time*."

Augusta Played received a great deal of critical attention. With the exception of Nora Johnson's review, this attention was favorable. Robert Taylor, writing in the *Boston Globe*, found behind the comic plot "the sad music of morality." Many reviewers noted the compassion with which Cherry treated even the minor characters, from the crotchety Sidney Gold to the fading Birdie Mickle to a gay English dwarf named Cyril. While the novel certainly asks much of its readers, particularly the intricate plot and the numerous awkward hundred-word sentences, it offers a good deal too: warmth, insight, and joy in the simple triumph of survival.

Cherry's third novel is more closely allied with *Augusta Played* than with *Sick and Full of Burning*. Titled *In the Wink of an Eye* (1983), the novel mixes techniques adapted from other novelists. The affinity for eighteenth-century novels which one reviewer detected in Cherry's second novel is equally evident here; the chapter headings might have been taken from *Tom Jones*, and the plot is as complicated as the score of a fugue. In contrast, the characters could have stepped from a Thomas Pynchon novel.

The plot of the novel, however, marks the work as Cherry's own. In South America two revolutionaries, Miguel and Ramon, take over Bolivia. Then, with the aid of an exiled German named Herman App, they take over all of the continent and Central America as well. Meanwhile, in New York a struggling sculptress whom we know as Jane smokes cheap cigars and refuses to pay the government sixteen dollars in back taxes. A disgruntled sewer worker in Oklahoma, fed up with low wages and high taxes, plants pipe bombs on all the major aqueducts in the country. Unless his demands for lower taxes are met, he will detonate the bombs simultaneously and turn the United States into a desert. No short description can hope to create the effect of Cherry's elaborate plot with its dozens of

characters and numerous subplots. Each individual part is captivating. But the relationships between the parts, which are linked by an "omniscient narrator" named God, occasionally remain unfocused.

The book, like much of Cherry's work, contains an element of parody. If often it is not clear who or what is being parodied, it is because everyone and everybody, including the author, are being parodied. The dedication suggests that the book is a sincere (if idealistic) exploration of revolutionary causes: "Dedicated to Oppressed Peoples Everywhere In Hope." But an epigrammatic quote from Che Guevera undermines the sincerity of the dedication and makes it seem ironic: "*It is ridiculous to sabotage a soft drink factory. . . .*" As always, Cherry provides interesting insights into the lives and minds of her characters. In *In the Wink of an Eye* it is apparent, however, that the characters are not as important as the message Cherry wishes to convey. At times the characters seem to grow thin and pale, so that their function in the story becomes mechanical. Consequently, the reader has difficulty fixing his feelings for the characters, and his experience of the novel is less immediate.

While Cherry continues to write poems and short stories, recently she is best known to readers as a novelist. All of her work shares a concern with large issues, the tougher questions of life. She has written that her novels are attempting a sequence of these questions, what she hopes is a logical sequence. *In the Wink of an Eye* suggests that this sequence is leading Cherry toward ever larger questions and a wider scope. The theme of the novel is "the problems of the distribution of wealth," a subject Cherry believes is best treated as comedy. The perspective here is even wider than that in *Augusta Played*, which in turn had a wider scope than *Sick and Full of Burning*. Both *Augusta Played* and *In the Wink of an Eye* stress the wealth, as it were, of the imagination.

It is clear that Kelly Cherry takes the life of letters seriously. In addition to her fiction and poetry, she has written reviews on authors as various as Elizabeth Bowen and Howard Nemerov. She also teaches, gives readings, serves on panels, and holds tutorials in addition to meeting the daily page quota she sets for herself. Her sense of the comic often prevents her work from mere solemnity—an easy liability when one deals in large issues, as Cherry often does. If her cleverness sometimes works against her by overwhelming her characters and her themes (not every reader appreciates or enjoys her type of wit), she manages to capture, in very readable stories, the indecisiveness and mute desperation of life in the twentieth century. It is, she feels, "a moral thing to do."

AN INTERVIEW ——————————————

with KELLY CHERRY

DLB: Is Augusta Gold in *Augusta Played* a tribute to (or portrait of) Elaine Shaffer?

CHERRY: Augusta Gold is based on three people: I drew on my ex-sister-in-law Joanne as a model for her looks; I drew on my sister Ann as a model for her career; I drew on myself as a model for her marriage. I say "drew on" because each of these models served only as a starting point.

My sister, Ann Cherry, is a solo concert flutist, living in London. She was the last of William Kincaid's protégées; she was sixteen or seventeen when she studied with him in Manhattan and Maine. However, Elaine Shaffer—who was a good deal older than my sister and was at that time already a performing professional—does figure in here: Shaffer had preceded Ann as a Kincaid protégée, and in my poem "In Memory of Elaine Shaffer," Elaine becomes a "sister" in art.

DLB: How much do your characters owe to people you have known? That is, do you draw a character based on someone you have known (or a composite), or do you work to make your characters solely products of your imagination?

CHERRY:The answer to this question varies widely with the particular case. For example, in *Augusta Played*, Norman's father, Sidney, was based in the beginning on someone I knew of who had disowned his son. I never met the man, but I borrowed the cigar, the profession, and a few other details from him. Then something strange happened. I fell in love with Sidney. He became a wonderfully likable and funny creature, not at all resembling the man he had begun as. Then something stranger happened. Sidney, being the Sidney he had become, turned out to be involved with a stripper named Birdie Mickle. Now, I never knew a Birdie Mickle. Who created Birdie Mickle? Did I create her, or did Sidney?

I don't always start with a model. Sometimes the character appears sui generis. I begin my novels by thinking of a question—this allows me to avoid any propagandizing, something that I think is fatally sentimental and all too common—and the question implies a questioner. This is how Miguel turned up in *In the Wink of an Eye*.

I like to write about men and women; I like to write about men and women from a woman's point of view and from a man's point of view; I like to write about old people, young people; I like to write about professionals and revolutionaries; I like to write about people all over the world. But only some of these characters are based on people I have known, and only some of them are solely products of my imagination. Some of them are products of *their* imaginations.

DLB: Is one of the genres a preferred form for you? Why?

CHERRY: This is a tricky question. In general, I try to avoid answering it, because if I say I prefer one form to the others, I seem to be saying that I am less serious about the others. I am serious about all the forms. Nevertheless, the poetry touches me most deeply, and it is also, for me, the most fun.

Why? Because it goes to the heart of the matter—my heart.

As for what "the matter" is—somewhere I said that "it's in poetry that thought and time most musically counterpoint each other, and I like a world in which the elements sing." I still do. Always did; always will.

But music is structure, and I care about all kinds of structure. I have a special fondness for long works, whether fictional, poetic, or nonfictional, because the extended developmental passage offers the opportunity for the most intricate, most daring structuring.

DLB: Could you comment on the advantages and disadvantages of working on several texts simultaneously?

CHERRY: Sooner or later, a writer is probably going to have periods when he has nothing or little to write in a particular form. Such periods—I warn my students—are likely to drive the writer to drink, drugs, adultery, or translation.

Alfred Coppel

(9 November 1921-   )

Patricia L. Skarda
Smith College

BOOKS: *Hero Driver* (New York: Crown, 1954);

Night of Fire and Snow (New York: Simon & Schuster, 1957);

Dark December (Greenwich, Conn: Fawcett, 1960; London: Herbert Jenkins, 1966);

A Certainty of Love (New York: Harcourt, Brace & World, 1966; London: Heinemann, 1967);

The Gate of Hell (New York: Harcourt, Brace & World, 1967);

Order of Battle (New York: Harcourt, Brace & World, 1968; London: Hutchinson, 1969);

The Clash of Distant Thunder, as A. C. Marin (New York: Harcourt, Brace & World, 1968; London: Heinemann, 1969);

The Rebel of Rhada, as Robert Gilman (New York: Harcourt, Brace & World, 1968; London: Gollancz, 1970);

The Navigator of Rhada, as Robert Gilman (New York: Harcourt, Brace & World, 1968; London: Gollancz, 1971);

A Little Time for Laughter (New York: Harcourt, Brace & World, 1969);

Rise with the Wind, as A. C. Marin (New York: Harcourt, Brace & World, 1969; London: Heinemann, 1970);

The Starkhan of Rhada, as Robert Gilman (New York: Harcourt, Brace & World, 1970);

A Storm of Spears, as A. C. Marin (New York: Harcourt Brace Jovanovich, 1971; London: Hale, 1973);

Between the Thunder and the Sun (New York: Harcourt Brace Jovanovich, 1971);

The Landlocked Man (New York: Harcourt Brace Jovanovich, 1972; London: Macmillan, 1975);

Thirty-Four East (New York: Harcourt Brace Jovanovich, 1974; London: Macmillan, 1974);

The Dragon (New York: Harcourt Brace Jovanovich, 1977; London: Macmillan, 1977);

The Hastings Conspiracy (New York: Holt, Rinehart & Winston, 1980; London: Macmillan, 1980);

The Apocalypse Brigade (New York: Holt, Rinehart & Winston, 1981; London: Macmillan, 1982);

The Burning Mountain (New York: Harcourt Brace Jovanovich, 1983).

Alfred Coppel (Vano Photography)

Twenty novels in twenty-nine years suggests that Alfred Coppel has a working formula for his fiction, but that is far from the case. His novels range in scope from the small world of sports-car racing in *Hero Driver* (1954) to the vast panorama of the invasion of Japan in *The Burning Mountain* (1983). In the stretch of novels from the simple first—narrated through the single consciousness of a daring young car racer—to the complex last—structured by multiple perspectives of American and Japanese military men—Coppel tells of spies and traitors, lovers and families, the powerful and the powerless. He writes family novels as ably as thrillers, cracks conspiracies as prophetically as he anticipates international conflicts, and describes Mongolia as easily as Northern California, where he makes his home. His is a fertile intelligence and a disciplined one, as the many facts and factions in his recent novels prove. He provides tight contexts and taut tensions in a rarely mismatched partnership of setting and character. His visual effects make most of his novels good candidates for films, and his dialogue far surpasses the clichés of most popular fiction in his several genres. Why then has he never had a blockbusting best-seller?

His most recent book, *The Burning Mountain*, should have claimed the attention of historians and psychologists as well as readers eager for a well-written story. With the failure of the atomic bomb test in New Mexico on 16 July 1945, America and Great Britain have no choice but to invade Japan. Operation Coronet follows with an hour-by-hour account of Allied attacks and Japanese counterattacks on Honshu. The action focuses on men and machines in a panoramic view of alternate history made real and rich by the cultural conflict between West and East. Through the minds and hearts of dozens of warriors on either side, Coppel deftly illustrates the human pasts that make the world's future. His fictional invasion, stunning in accurate details and vivid descriptions, compassionately and objectively narrows attention to a handful of men struggling for life or meeting death.

As an example of the mix of allegiances and histories, Coppel returns again and again to the private battles and human loyalties within and between one American and one Japanese soldier. First Lieutenant Harry Seaver, who grew up in Japan, fights his love for Japanese Samurai culture, while Kantaro Maeda, who grew up with Seaver, fights his love for Western progress and human rights. Divorced from their commands by sympathy for the enemy, Seaver and Kantaro close in and finally meet one another in a close combat neither wins. Despite the Japanese concept of *on* (the debt of family and heritage) and *gimu* (the mandatory repayment of that debt), and despite patriotism and commitment to American democracy, Kantaro and Seaver are brothers, not enemies. Both meet death but not without love in a remarkable conclusion that shocks an American Nisei and sends loyal Japanese servants to a suicidal seppuku jump. No one in particular wins a war, Coppel implies, and no war resolves the eternal conflict between cultures or violates the ultimate similarity between men. *The Burning Mountain* weighs loss and gain in the bloody passion of individuals rather than nations. The tenuous equilibrium of justice mocks metaphysical differences in light of T. S. Eliot's eerie prophecy, Coppel's epigraph:

> Time present and time past
> Are both present in time future,
> And time future is contained in time past.

Coppel's brilliant control of action and reverie sweeps past personal misfortunes to military victory with ease and perfect pacing:

> As he struck the highest masts and yard of the hospital ship, his last vision was of fire, his last feeling a desperate desire to live.
> Speechless with horror and outrage, Major Connel watched the Kamikaze bury itself in USS *Solace* just behind the bridge. The bomb the Jap carried exploded somewhere deep within the ship, which was instantly wreathed in plumes of steam and fire.
> Connel could hardly believe what he had seen. It was an incredible act, an act of barbaric savagery. He could not contain himself as he banked low over the white ship, now dead in the water and burning. He screamed, raging at the dead Jap.

MacArthur and Truman are as true to themselves as the kamikaze and shinyo pilots are to the emperor. Their conversations reveal as much about their relationship as about the war:

> "How are we going to deal with these people if we continue to kill civilians in such numbers?"
> "Civilians, yes. Not noncombatants, Mr. President."
> Truman regarded the general shrewdly. "Yes, we have been hearing about that, General. I understand that there was a massacre of civilians at some place called . . . Ishioka."
> MacArthur's eyes hardened. "A forward position of the 231st Infantry Regiment was overrun by more than 1,000 members of the civilian Volunteer Defense Force. They were severely mauled, but they held their ground and repulsed the enemy."
> "In other words, they had the choice of dying at the hands of a mob or perpetrating a massacre. And, not too surprisingly, they chose the second alternative," Truman said, almost gently.

"That is true, Mr. President," MacArthur said coldly.

Strategic conversations include statistics with personalities so that the war of nations and ideologies becomes one between people. Reviewers applauded the thoroughness of Coppel's research and the distinctiveness of his perspective, yet the book never reached the best-seller list.

From the comfort of his home in Portola Valley, California, Alfred Coppel observes international conflicts with detachment and dismay. He regularly reads four newspapers a day to collect an informed vision of international news. Then he releases his imagination in fictions that comment on hidden scenarios eerily consistent with world events. Coppel predicted the division of the Sinai in *Thirty-Four East* (1974), the first of several novels that brought him national acclaim. By suggesting a demilitarized zone through the Sinai Desert, Coppel anticipated history, as he did in announcing laser weapons in *The Dragon* (1977), nuclear Armageddon in *Dark December* (1960), and computerized war games in *The Hastings Conspiracy* (1980).

Thirty-Four East builds on terrorism and character types made familiar in current news. Enver Lesh, professional anarchist, joins Leila Jamil, lesbian Arab guerrilla leader, in kidnapping the American vice-president on his way to signing a peace accord with the Soviet Union that would bring peace to the United Arab Republic and Israel. While the Soviet deputy premier pursues his ideological narrow-mindedness through to its ridiculous conclusions, the American president dies an untimely death in a plane crash caused by a pilot's aneurysm but suspected to be a result of Soviet sabotage. In the Sinai at two rounded hills that "resembled the breasts of a reclining woman," American and Soviet representatives meet one another face to face in hopeful conversation laced with promises of military confrontation for errors committed by subordinates on both sides of the global power structure. Eventually, an American general defies orders to attack the ancient Monastery of St. Katherine, gains the confidence of the Soviets on the scene, and heroically burrows his way through the catacombs to release the vice-president, now the president, from the terrorists' madness. In the War Room in Washington, an incompetent Speaker of the House delegates almost all of his authority to a hawkish chairman of the Joint Chiefs of Staff; nuclear war is narrowly averted. For half of the novel, time stands still as Coppel unravels the

psychological kinks of the principals and a host of supernumeraries. Against the powerful portraits of men, Coppel sketches strong figures of women: Israeli Captain Deborah Zadok, victimized by her beauty, and secretary Elizabeth Adams, victor over her own jealousy and neurotic passion.

In a review in the *Wall Street Journal*, Benjamin Stein blames the vice-president for making the improbable possible by his dovish principles: "More dangerous than the war hawks, more dangerous even than a few terrorists, are those who will not see, and who threaten the safety of all mankind by pretending that danger does not exist." Coppel exposes self-righteous idealism in *Thirty-Four East*, but he also reveals many of the essential ingredients of heroism and romantic love. He values more than philosophical postures; he values people—both men and women.

Perhaps Coppel's realism and admitted empathy cloud his characterizations. None of his heroes are supermen; all are flawed by their own humanness. In *Thirty-Four East*, the vice-president refuses military escort into the Sinai to prove his dovish principles; a peace-keeping general regards himself as "a failed husband and, though he regretted it bitterly, a failed father"; an air force colonel threatens the peace mission by acting on his longing for battle. The antagonists have their weaknesses too. In *The Dragon*, a Soviet minister of defense monomaniacally tests his political theories with nuclear attack on China; a Chinese military scientist tests his laser weapon by shooting down a manned satellite of the Soviet Union; and the Soviet first secretary "allowed himself to grow old and ill without, apparently, watching his bright, bloody-minded genius in the Ministry of Defense closely enough." Tough-minded preservers of peace are few in Coppel's fiction, but even they tire, hunger, drink too much, and indulge in illicit sex or at least passionate love. In short, protagonists and antagonists alike are human, and many are tragically flawed.

As Coppel matures as a writer, so do his heroes. The improbable foolishness of sports-car racer Scott Warren gives way to grander allegiances and greater stakes. Regardless of whether his characters are ambitious, foolhardy youths or bitter, flamboyant generals, the chameleonlike Coppel enters each character himself, reacting the way he did or would in a race or combat, bar or bed, meeting or crisis. Something of Coppel occurs in almost all his fiction, but he has never yet written a novel based explicitly on himself or his family.

Coppel claims Spanish, French, German,

3

1. <u>Washington, D. C.</u>

14pt Avenir Garde Bold u&l.c.
indent 3EM - 1/4 below to text -
opening line indents 3EM

The waters of the Potomac felt like warm velvet as the
girl swam slowly around the anchored sloop in the summer twilight. The heat of the day had raised a thin mist from the river:
it haloed the lights that were coming on along the shore of Cobb
Island and almost obscured the glow of Colonial Beach on the
western shore. The wind, never strong at this time of year,
had died completely, leaving the surface of the river dark and
smooth as a mirror.

As she swam, Candace Moran could see the tiny anchor light
on the <u>Pandora's</u> spar reflecting a thin, yellow path on the water.
The finger of light seemed to follow her as she moved gracefully
through the water. She noted that Cole had the cabin lamps on
now. She guessed that he was still hunched over the chart table,
working on those papers that had demanded all of his attention
since they had dropped anchor a thousand yards from the shore
of Cobb Island.

It had not been one of their more notable afternoons, the
girl thought sulkily. She had been Cole Norris's mistress for
almost a year, and she understood that a man of his age—and
one with so much on his mind—could not always behave like a
young lover. But recently Cole's moods had become impenetrable,
and Candy was apprehensive about the future.

Their assignations aboard the <u>Pandora</u>, Cole's small sloop,
were a reasonably well-kept secret in the Central Intelligence
Agency. This was remarkable in Washington, where gossip and
loose talk were common coin. But if the Director of Central

23 lines of text on opening page

Page from the setting copy for The Hastings Conspiracy *(the author)*

213

Jewish, and Italian blood. The ethnic mix gives him cause to include national backgrounds often and accurately in his fiction. During the Civil War his family moved to Mexico. His father, one of nine brothers, moved to Oakland to run the U.S. end of a business that varied from crushing copra for coconut oil to silk manufacture. Coppel did not speak English until he went to school, and he still remembers his Mexican nanny fondly; his novels often include a touch of the Spanish language of his youth. He went to Stanford as a journalism major, but dropped out to join the air corps in 1942. He was stationed at Edwards Air Force Base, Hamilton Field in San Francisco. In 1943 he married Elizabeth Schorr; she is still his wife and always the first reader of his fiction. After the war, Coppel raced cars and boats, worked for a public relations firm, and finally turned to the work of writing full-time. His father's success gave him the financial cushion to begin the only career he ever wanted — that of a writer of fiction. Along the way, he has fathered two children. His son is a systems analyst, and his daughter is a buyer for a clothing store.

Coppel's own experiences loving and parenting, racing or fishing, flying or working in public relations provide him with only some of the resources for his novels. More Alfa Romeos are in his thrillers than were ever in his garage, and Stanford degrees and journalism are more common to his characters than to Coppel. Through his heroes, Coppel often completes his degree and fulfills his major; journalism is often a useful pose for his characters.

In *The Apocalypse Brigade* (1981), Michael Rivas, a journalist of Mexican descent, avenges the death of his Anglo brother as a sympathetic observer of the principal personalities of a group of international vigilantes. As observer, Rivas is present and thinking, but distanced and objective; he is a quiet, perceptive figure like Alfred Coppel himself. Neither Rivas nor Coppel condemns the perpetrators of the final disaster suggested by the foreboding title; instead, both understand them. By reserving judgment, Rivas and Coppel avoid moral outrage, anger, and empty melodramatic heroics. Love is Rivas's reward, as it often is in Coppel's fiction.

Romantic love counters the holocaust following the paralysis of oil fields by radioactive ruthenium spray. Rivas stands above political doves as a daring spokesman, witnessing a disaster made possible by influence and power and political incompetence. Opposite Rivas is General Col-

lingwood, who imposes his love of military glory on a world hungry for heroes. In joy and pride he launches an attack to rock the world. Never does he wince at the deaths he orders; never does he doubt that the Christian moral of returning good for evil is destroying the West; never does he question his leadership of international bandits set on ending Third World domination by oil production. With military might and the backing of an enormously wealthy paranoid personality, posing as a philanthropist of the impoverished, General Collingwood clears the way for apocalypse with his well-trained brigade.

Apocalypse Brigade resolves Third World domination of the West by using the terrifying forces of military technology, a possibility more real now than when Coppel wrote his compelling tale. Long before the consciousness-raising about Third World domination and nuclear arms, however, Coppel wrote of the aftermath of nuclear war. In *Dark December*, the wooded Pacific Northwest is pockmarked with craters and stripped of foliation by Soviet attack. One lone missile officer from Alaska makes his way home to Northern California through desolate country doubly ravaged by biological warfare and radioactive contamination. In the nuclear desert Major Gavin encounters and opposes a fanatic officer, Major Collingwood, who anticipates the figure in *Apocalypse Brigade* by waging a private war for his own glory and power. The climactic scene occurs on a damaged drawbridge where Gavin, his newfound love, and adopted son leap to safety, and where the insane Major Collingwood leaps and falls into the water below. Now he has the choice between life and death, a choice he gave none of his subordinates or victims. Major Collingwood kills for pleasure, just as the Germans killed Jews. Like Rivas, Major Gavin had repeatedly refrained from killing, and, in the final climactic scene, Gavin extends his hand to offer the drowning Collingwood life. Collingwood, however, refuses to drop his pistol, "his final gesture of defiance in the face of defeat," and pulls the trigger. The gun misfires; Collingwood drowns in the tide of his own murderous hatred. Even nuclear holocaust cannot eradicate irrational jealousy, pride, or hate, Coppel implies. He ends his tale with an epilogue on the reunion of Major Gavin with his daughter, for no war, however devastating, can eradicate either love or family. The unstated morals are dramatized in action that describes mental and physical landscapes in a haunting and credible fiction.

In a suspense story duplicated now in Latin American news, *Rise with the Wind* (1969, published under the pseudonym A. C. Marin), Coppel tells the story of German-born William Clay, who masquerades as a journalist on a U.S. intelligence mission in Puerto Cruz in an unnamed "People's Republic." He is looking for George Arnold Cade, a Canadian war hero who escaped Germany with Helmuth Christl, a Nazi war criminal. Coppel settles comfortably into his Latin American setting, with flashbacks to Germany in 1943-1946. Clay gets his man despite his employers' duplicity and his own errors, because his job becomes his personal passion. Under the alias Robert Bourne, he becomes involved in a new revolution that prophetically resembles the Coard coup in Grenada. The similarity between wars heightens as the conflicts between people and groups, nations and nationalities, erupt in bloodshed and death. Clay's mission in Puerto Cruz redeems him from an earlier failure, but he draws no satisfaction from his labors and no praise from his colleagues or superiors. Clay's journalistic pose, however, allows Coppel the satisfaction of free comment on the perversity of the human heart in all men at all times—Latinos, Germans, Jews, Canadians, or Americans, during the war and after.

Coppel's own wartime activities could not possibly have been as varied as those in his novels, but *Order of Battle* (1968) describes psychological effects Coppel knew intimately and recalls passionately. The novel focuses on pilots and World War II generally, and on three men and their women in 1944 specifically. In the fiction, a fighter squadron at Bourneham, England, prepares for the invasion of Normandy while Mark Devereaux, Harry Ward, Ray Porta, and their respective women reflect on life beyond the war. The protagonist Devereaux, another oblique figure for Coppel, tells the primary tale of love and asks the principal questions about himself and Anne Charing, the English widow who loves him first and Harry later. The tensions of love thematically offset those of war with battles in bed and bar equaling those in the air and on the ground. Letters from Devereaux's forsaken wife punctuate the present with the past; song fragments and poetry anticipate the fictional future. Devereaux precipitates his own crises by forcing Anne to love him despite his marriage entanglements. Then in a bombing run on a railroad, Devereaux's P-38 suffers a "metallic *bang* on the underside of the nacelle" that damages the landing gear. Forced to make a belly landing, he earns a long gash on the forehead that puts him out of action long enough for Harry to encounter Anne Charing. Later Harry leaves the field after breaking both his legs in a dramatic jump from a burning airplane. Ray Porta kills himself and

a ground-gripping lieutenant in a daredevil joy ride. Sadder and wiser for the loss of his friends, Devereaux volunteers for duty as a forward observer with the infantry on the west bank of the Moselle. He learns that "in war one learns to test his courage. . . . In love one learns faith. . . . In war you test. In love you learn not to." Courageously he risks his life and sacrifices others by ordering napalm bombs to stop an attack of German tanks. He alone survives, with serious burns on his hands and legs. Then he risks a leap of faith for love. He leaves the hospital and the war with Anne Charing. "When you commit something you have to be prepared for losses"; it's the unstated rule—the order of battle.

Order of Battle didactically resolves Mark Devereaux's tensions as D-Day resolves the war. The closure is neat, definitive, positive, charming. Happy endings fraught with tragedy often bring Coppel's fictions to conclusion, but most of them contain more surprise. In *Between the Thunder and the Sun* (1971), a commercial pilot learns that age can bring wisdom and dignity rather than ignorance and ignominy. Captain Aymar successfully lands an aircraft crippled by a hijacker's violence and a hurricane's fury. Dozens of passengers confront the facts about themselves and their relationships to other people and other ideologies, while Aymar battles "grimly against the bucking and twisting of the controls," fate, and chance. The microcosm within the plane psychologically duplicates the natural forces without, and tragedy surrounds the whole. The hijacker, Raoul Rivas Belmonte, recalls his past just before he is "spinning and cartwheeling through space" toward the "storm-driven sea":

> The memories and thoughts that were the essence of his personality—the remembrance of a sunlit childhood on his father's *finca*, the deep love he once had known for his wife and his daughter, the terrors of revolution and massacre, the horrors of the Bay of Pigs, the hatred of Ernesto Fuentes, and the triumphant dark joy of the opportunity for vengeance—all that made him the man he had been, were bloodily erased by the spikes of metal penetrating his brain.

Even the antagonist is excused for his violence and merits as great a measure of sympathy as Captain Aymar. Despite the tragedy of the deaths and the comedy of the self-realizations, Coppel ends the novel with renewed love in Aymar's call to his estranged wife: " 'Kate, oh, Kate, my darling, let me tell you—' He had never said such a thing before, and it felt wonderful."

What Coppel admires in the fiction he reviews regularly in *The San Francisco Chronicle* and elsewhere, he achieves in his own—clear motivations, genuine sentiments, soft love, hard violence, and controlled suspense directed by an ever-narrowing perspective on a final scene. Coppel's admiration for cars and planes and functional machines is transferred to his fiction in his strong control of narrative structures. Vignettes and flashbacks enrich present and past as he drives relentlessly toward the future and quick closure. He concentrates intently on particularities of places, persons, occupations, and the subunits of society that define each character. No characters lack contexts larger than themselves. Spies work for agencies more flawed than they; radicals represent countercultures less interesting than their members; families explain fathers and brothers better than the individuals can themselves. Sociological units and national subunits define the perimeters of action and emotion without blatant caricature or simple stereotyping. Everyone comes from somewhere and someone, and the source or identity must be acknowledged, whether by rebellion or acceptance, as the individual chooses. The choices are not infinite, but finite, and no reader can question their verisimilitude. Families and factions prescribe behavior and attitudes for protagonists and antagonists alike. Coppel does not deal in moral dimensions; he toys with backgrounds, jobs, and interrelationships.

In his first suspense thriller, *The Clash of Distant Thunder* (1968, published as A. C. Marin), Coppel builds characters by backgrounds. Dr. John Wells, a U.S. intelligence officer, returns to Paris, where he worked for the OSS and where his wartime friend Paul de Lattre now works for the French Foreign Ministry. Wells's helpmate, Aviv Bergner, whose father is with the fictional Israeli Embassy in Dublin, is a member of Sherut Bita Chon, the Israeli secret service. Her Irish background allows her to translate a comment (from an Irish prostitute posing as an English schoolteacher in France) about "the crooked knives." Other characters represent minor groups, such as the "Croix de Feu" in the 1930s, Americans of the 1950s, an underground escape organization for former members of the Nazi SS, the Bannführer SS, the Gestapo, Neo-Nazis, the Palestine Liberation Army, and the Egyptian intelligence service. Double identities proliferate. As various allegiances compete with one another, Wells confuses Aviv with a wartime lover, Martine Goss, Paul de Lattre's cousin who was killed in a concentration camp. Even a nervous Jewish-American woman sitting near Wells on the plane to Paris reappears late in the narrative as a doctor and officer of the Sherut Bita Chon and a friend of Aviv Bergner. National loyalties make it possible to get an Italian-Swiss mechanic to repair an Alfa-Romeo while a German-Swiss porter looks on. The catalogue of units and subunits, sympathies, and loyalties casts suspicion on everyone, including Wells. His mission to find a defector is almost forgotten in the swirl of factions. Ultimately he succeeds, alone and unaided, discreet and valiant to the end. But, like Coppel's other heroes, he alternately doubts and believes, forgets and remembers, despairs and presumes. His job and his identity as a human being are carefully distinguished but equally important.

In the late 1960s and early 1970s, Coppel found fictional material nearer home. In *A Storm of Spears* (1971, Coppel's third thriller as A. C. Marin), Frank Charles, an English teaching assistant at Stanford in the late 1960s, risks his job and his life to rebuff the counterculture that once attracted him. With the burdens of a crippled wife and his own Vietnam veteran's cynicism, he rebels against all he knows is right by indulging in sex with a misguided undergraduate whose friends are dangerous. For his sins, he suffers blackmail and forced involvement in stealing a government plan for racial counterinsurgency. The plan turns out to be a Chinese plant, but Frank Charles is fooled long enough to break a number of laws and strain all the friendships he thought secure. Most of the friends are not worth mourning, however, and Frank Charles ends up wiser and more conventional in his morality.

Conventional morality controls *The Landlocked Man* (1972), a touching love story about a fifty-year-old man, Robert Martin, art and creative director of an advertising agency, and Christiane Margaret Petersen, twenty-three, a young radical turned lover. Martin tells his own story, like several of Coppel's early heroes, and, in the doing, he ruefully enumerates his faults. He meets Christy in a demonstration for lettuce workers outside his own art show. Their escape from demonstrations and business results in ideal, selfless love in a refuge on Twelve Mile Creek above the Santa Clara Valley. There they love shamelessly, read avidly, and paint admirably. Martin, like the landlocked trout imprisoned in a shallow pool where he came to spawn, locks Christy in his love and his pool of experience. Chest pains, a warning of his own mortality, remind him of his age and responsibility to his own daughter and to Christy. Gracefully, he lets Christy go to make her own mistakes. Christy's charm, he discovers, is unique to her age, interests, and libido. But she changes: "Lovers remake one another. They can't help it, it's in the nature of love to be both generous and demanding. She could not make me young, so she was making herself old."

Coppel admits to conceiving the whole of *The Landlocked Man* while fishing alone, and references to fishing begin, end, and punctuate the novel. But the generation gap closes in love—however temporarily. Coppel speaks through Martin: "The world is dividing up into people who brood on history and those who have no sense of history at all. But that doesn't mean they can't love one another across the barricades." So love they do until time and mortality force them apart.

Love and alienation and struggle, Coppel says, are not reserved for demonstrators of the Vietnam years. World War II produced the same sense of displacement. In *A Little Time for Laughter* (1969) Coppel traces the lives of six 1940 high school graduates in the San Francisco Bay area through military and personal battles to 1969. The novel shapes itself by changing points of view. First there's Lucas, a parentless hero with a premature sense of responsibility: "Responsibility," he learns on his graduation night, is "willingness to do what others expect of you—what you expect of yourself." Then there's Julius, a latent homosexual, advantaged by class and money, disadvantaged by a domineering mother's expectations. And the third man is Mitchell, football player turned alcoholic, whose fears of battle are the inverse of his sexual braggadocio. The women haunt the men: Megan Green, dead before life begins; Daisy Tibbets, lover and mother of almost more than she can manage; Reeder Morgan, a manipulative bitch who marries Mitchell to defy her father; Ruth Darian, who dies with Julius in a bizarre effort to be with him forever; Leah Bergner, a German-Jewish refugee who becomes Lucas's wife—for a time. In and out of these lives, Coppel sews personal and generational challenges—met and avoided—in vignettes as real as the people who stage them.

In his science fiction on Rhada, Coppel (pseudonymously Robert Gilman) writes of a primitive future and fragmentary past, remembered in bits of poetry. Spaceships guided by incantations of navigator-priests link the feudal present to the Golden Age, by bringing Kier, star king of Rhada, to single combat with king Tallan to reestablish a twelve-year-old king. Blind mind readers, called Vulks, comment on the human propensity for self-destruction and mistrust of knowledge,

while allusions to Chairman Mao, John Brown, John Donne, and, no doubt, Alfred Coppel himself repeat the truths of previous cultures torn by the same strife. As Kier puts it in *The Rebel of Rhada* (1968, as Robert Gilman), "We must stop warring on one another or we will surely vanish from the universe."

Whether writing of romantic or familial love, international or national conspiracies, alternate or real histories, or science fiction, Coppel redresses wrongs by a glance at all that is right. He reduces poseurs to people more familiar than readers of best-sellers might wish, but his soldiers and politicians, agents and professionals, are lovers and friends with pasts and futures more real than their situations might suggest. Coppel's insights and imaginative fictions touch both hearts and minds provocatively and poignantly. Perhaps his next attempt will reward him with the best-selling laurels he seeks.

References:

Gay Andrews Dillin, "Settings from Avalon to WWI and II," *Christian Science Monitor*, 23 March 1983;

Ed Hutshing, "Japan Invaded: In WWII, What If. . . ?," *San Diego Union*, 20 February 1983;

Berton Roueche, "Cold Warriors," *New Yorker*, 24 November 1980;

Benjamin Stein, "On the Way to Doomsday," *Wall Street Journal*, 19 July 1974;

Dan Tooker and Roger Hofheins, *Fiction! Interviews with Northern California Novelists* (New York: Harcourt Brace Jovanovich, 1972), pp. 71-85.

INTERVIEW
with ALFRED COPPEL

DLB: Do you keep a journal?

COPPEL: I've always had the notion that writers *should* keep journals. When I was a very small boy, I kept a diary, but discovered that there were always too many pages that said, "Today nothing happened." So I gave it up. Now when I travel I keep a journal of impressions. I find it helpful in recapturing scenes and feelings I have had in a particular time and place. Some of my books, such as *A Certainty of Love* and *The Landlocked Man*, derive specifically from these kinds of journal entries. Others do not.

DLB: You obviously do a great deal of research. Do you do it before you write or while you're writing?

COPPEL: Both, though I think my work may give the impression that there is more research involved than is actually the case. In a sense I'm doing research all the time. Ever since I learned to read the language, I have been a voracious reader. Everything I read seems to get packed away and can be recalled on demand. I love poetry, and most of my epigraphs come from that source. I write poetry myself, none of which is published or ever will be. But one of the epigraphs in *The Gate of Hell* is mine. Anything you see attributed to a poet named Chameau was written by Coppel. Epigraphs focus the mind. I admire poets extravagantly. They speak so clearly and succinctly. I draw on a Yeats or an Auden as a gesture of respect and admiration. How marvelous to set down truth in a couplet!

DLB: Do you model your characters on actual people?

COPPEL: Loosely. I have known Seavers and Tanakas, Gilmans and Martins and Christys, but I avoid the roman à clef. I don't take cheap shots in fiction. There are characters in my books who have the same characteristics of people I know or have known, yet never do people see themselves lampooned in my books. I pick up some information from socializing. I think I have a sharp ear for conversation and dialogue. That is essential to fiction. If my characters are developing properly, I can almost hear them talking. I prefer to believe they speak their own lines—not lines I have heard at some social event.

DLB: Are you a critic of conversation on television and film?

COPPEL: I'm afraid so. I think television talk is grim and the level of film dialogue isn't much higher. But that's to be expected in an age when one gets one's information from talking heads in an electric box. People should read more. They might learn to use language better.

DLB: Your dialogues and descriptions read easily, naturally. Do you find it easy to achieve facility or is it work?

COPPEL: There are times when any writing is simply hard work, but there are other times when the act of writing is a delight. Pain or pleasure—it all depends on how the work is going. It can be hell or a real high. I have rather self-indulgent work habits. If the writing is going poorly, then I just break away and do something else. Though I consider myself a pro, I have all the faults and virtues of the upper-middle class, so I have other things I can turn to. I've given up on sailboat racing because it takes far too much time. I had to divest myself of a beautiful sloop. But I enjoy golf and fishing and just staring out the window. Of course, while I'm doing any of these things, somewhere in the subconscious, the writing is still going on. When the writing is going well, I work from morning to night, scarcely conscious that I am flogging myself—until I try to straighten up in my chair. Writing becomes progressively compulsive as a novel develops.

DLB: Can you describe a typical working day when you aren't in the white heat of finishing a book or a scene that is writing itself?

COPPEL: I start work about eight o'clock in the morning, work through until about noon, take a break for maybe an hour or so, then work another two or three hours. Then, depending on time, circumstance, weather, I do something else until the next day. However, when the work is galloping, then it becomes very hard to break away. Social life suffers, but my friends have known me long enough now to leave me alone when I'm in that state. I love my work. It's the only thing I ever really wanted to do—write. I have done some nonfiction, some criticism, but my profession—my obsession—has always been the writing of fiction.

DLB: Do you have any unfinished manuscripts or books that never became books?

COPPEL: Once in a rare while I will develop an opening scene that is so marvelous that I'm at a loss how to follow it up with a full book. That kind of manuscript is put away. I tell myself that one day I'll go back to it and see if there's something there I can use. But I have *never* used any of these false starts. One of the attributes of a fiction writer is the instinct that tells him when he's gone wrong, and it is time to reload and start again. Anyone can write himself into a corner. The trick is to be willing to turn out of blind alleys, no matter how painful it may be to abandon a stack of manuscript.

DLB: You've said, in another place, that the first few

pages are the most difficult. Is that still true for you?

COPPEL: Yes, for me they are, and I have some odd quirks that make matters worse. For example, I can cast about—literally for days—just finding names for my characters, names I can live with for the months or even years it may take to write a book. The beginning is absolutely critical for any novel. This is true whether it is a suspense novel or a novel of sensitivity. The reader must be engaged. It's not an easy thing to accomplish. But once done, there is a sense of satisfaction and a powerful urge to go on. I pack a great deal of information in at the beginning, but I think it's essential for a reader to have all that is needed to make sense of the story that is beginning to develop as soon as possible.

DLB: How do you begin? Do you outline or work from a prose synopsis or from notes?

COPPEL: I tend to make notes on anything handy so there tends to be a snowstorm of paper bits, most of which gets lost immediately and never is seen again. But making the notes is important to me. I don't outline. I'm not that disciplined or systematic. My approach to writing is largely emotional rather than intellectual. I attempt to get the feeling of the book going as quickly as possible. Then, if I've succeeded, the book will eventually take command of its own destiny—and mine, of course.

DLB: Do you always conceive of the whole, or at least the ending, before you write?

COPPEL: Yes, that's essential. I don't know every detail, but I have to know where the book is going. I must have the ending before I have the beginning. The last scene of any novel should be implicit in the first. One must know where the people are going. It's this quality of certainty that gives a novel movement. Too many novels tend to drift about like *New Yorker* short stories. I'm too old-fashioned for that sort of thing. When I read a story, I want it to have a beginning, middle, and end. That's the way I want to write, too.

DLB: You seem to understand people intimately. Have you studied psychology or sociology?

COPPEL: Like most of us nowadays, I've been dipped in psychoanalysis. But I can't escape the feeling that Freud is a bummer. Will Rogers knew ten times what Sigmund knew about people.

DLB: Wordsworth said of his poetry that "the feeling therein developed gives importance to the action and situation and not the action and situation to the feeling." Are you more concerned with action and situation or with feeling?

COPPEL: I have recently been writing large-scale thrillers heavily dependent on action, but if you read them carefully you'll see that the force of the novels derives from the feelings and emotions of the characters. The action is part of the ambience, not gratuitous. I think this may be the one thing which distinguishes my thrillers from others of the genre. Of course, one is forever at the mercy of the trite critic who will write about "cardboard characters." One can only consider the source and hope that the next reviewer will read more than the dust jacket copy.

DLB: I notice in your earlier fiction that you use all the characters you introduce, but, in the later novels with broader scope, you seem to be willing to allow a great many characters to remain supernumeraries. Is that conscious?

COPPEL: It just happens that way. In a panoramic story that has the scope of *Thirty-Four East* you have a lot of spear-carriers; whereas tighter novels, such as *The Landlocked Man* or *A Certainty of Love*, are more spare. *A Certainty of Love* is the story of a man and woman in love, very little else. The events of the outer world are only peripheral. The novel depends entirely for its pace on the interior life of the protagonists. *Thirty-Four East* and *The Dragon* are broader books about events in the world as well as love stories. The large novel is more like real life than the small novel, in that people drift in and out and quite often vanish. Life goes on. *The Burning Mountain*, however, is about an event of such magnitude that it cannot be encompassed on a small scale. Dozens of characters are needed to tell the story, and though they can't all be presented in detail, they still must have dimensions. It must be done succinctly, or you can end up with a 2000-page novel. *The Burning Mountain* and all such books are, of necessity, a compromise between a novel of action and a novel of character.

DLB: Have you ever written for films?

COPPEL: In college I wrote a number of plays. One was produced. I might once have turned to drama, but no longer. And screenwriting was never for me.

Compared to the novel, a film script is sketchy, shallow, and too slavishly devoted to the visual. To say movies are an art form is stretching the definition of art. It is rather like calling the six o'clock news journalism.

DLB: How would you describe your imagination? Visual?

COPPEL: I don't know. Empathic, perhaps, or is that a cop-out? I've just trashed films—yet I do write from visual images. I was asked the question at a Stanford seminar by the chairman of the department of English. I told him I wrote from images. I was astonished when he said he never visualized; he simply intellectualized. I am still unsure of what he meant. I just don't see how that can be. Perhaps he was more interested in the expression of an idea than in the dramatization of it.

DLB: Have you any comments on your own style or that of others?

COPPEL: Style is instinctive in a writer; you either have it or you don't. However much style you have, you're going to have to be satisfied with it. One of the greatest wrongs that an editor can perpetrate on a writer is to try to make him into a so-called stylist. I've known writers go into shock, into a block, because an editor has tried to make them into something they are not. A writer's prose style is unique and "personal"—not to be messed about.

DLB: What classical or popular literature do you read regularly?

COPPEL: I've never really lost my taste for science fiction. I love it, but that's clearly an escape. I tend not to read my contemporaries, not because they are bad but because I find them distracting when I'm working. I have certain favorites that may seem a bit tedious for the 1980s. I enjoy Thackeray, who tends to bore most people. Reading John O'Hara is always a pleasure. The early Hemingway books are well worth reading and rereading, and I tend to reread Faulkner quite often. I don't know whether this is because I really like Faulkner or because it is such a challenge to try to extract his meaning. Many years ago, Anthony West wrote *The Vintage*, a book I reread often. It tells of a trip through a modern hell, not a subject I dwell on—but West's treatment is enigmatic and compelling. I really enjoy Jessamyn West. I love the way she uses the language—so

American. I live up on a hilltop in the coast range behind Stanford, and I have all the instincts of a recluse. So I have to read four newspapers every day to see what's happening in the world.

DLB: How would you describe the many subgenres in which you've written? Thrillers, science fiction, a three-generational novel?

COPPEL: I have one family novel—*A Little Time for Laughter*. I want to do another, one based on my own family history. I don't know how such a book can be placed in any genre. I may know when it is completed. I wrote *A Certainty of Love, The Gate of Hell,* and *The Landlocked Man* because I was making a statement or two about our times. I did the thrillers to make a different sort of statement to a larger audience. The pseudonyms allowed Harcourt, Brace and World to list two or more of my books in the same year. I have been fortunate in having editors who have given me my head. Julian Muller at Harcourt is a marvelous editor. Now I work with William Abrahams at Holt, Rinehart and Winston. Another of the best. Thanks to these two men I haven't had to limit myself to one genre—even though to have done so might have made me a big money-maker for the publisher involved.

DLB: A number of your books have been translated into foreign languages. Which is the most popular abroad?

COPPEL: *Thirty-Four East* had the widest circulation abroad. It was translated into Afrikaans, Turkish, Hebrew, and all Western European languages. Almost all of my books have been published rather widely in Europe. I've had only one published in Japan; that was *Dark December*, and that was years ago. The Japanese response to *The Burning Mountain*, needless to say, has not been overwhelming.

DLB: Your fiction often uses small factions or sociological subcultures to characterize your principal characters. Why do you rely on these associations?

COPPEL: I think our society is constructed of these subunits. We are not a cohesive or homogenous people. These subunits have strong characteristics that are useful to the writer. One must not stereotype, of course, but externals are indications of what lies within. If someone were characterizing me, he could look at the way I live, at my possessions, read a few of my books, and he would know a great deal about me. I'm finally outgrowing my adolescent love of wheels, for example, though in the garage right now is a Morgan Roadster. Still, I'm getting to an age when a Volvo might be more suitable.

DLB: Do you find it easier to characterize men or women?

COPPEL: I don't really believe there is a distinction. In a peculiar sort of way I believed in female equality long before it became fashionable. Men and women are not all that different as human beings, and, consequently, I think that some of my women are pretty good. I have loved—and respected—all of my heroines. Wallace Stegner read *The Land-locked Man* and disliked Christy because she used rough language. But he was wrong. She had a perfect right to speak as she did. She was a child of the 1960s. I didn't approve, but how could I write her differently? I thought she was absolutely charming and well-rounded. Deborah in *Thirty-Four East* is a brave, gallant woman and a competent soldier. Elisabeth in *A Certainty of Love* is as real to me as any flesh-and-blood woman—and as haunting. I think my books are bought by women for their men. Then they read them and are surprised that they like them. Women are, I think, more interesting than men. There is a depth of feeling and emotion in the feminine character that men try to deny themselves. If there is a difference—other than biology—in men and women, this is it: Women are more human.

DLB: As you look back over your long and successful career, do you have any regrets? Do you regret, for example, never having finished your degree? Do you regret having written in one mode rather than in another?

COPPEL: I used to be rather sorry that I didn't go back to Stanford and finish my course, but, actually, it would have served no purpose in my life. I was a journalism major, yet I would have never gone to work for a newspaper. I consider myself fortunate that I made no attempt to become a journalist. I would have been a poor one and I might never have written fiction. I do regret that I'm not a better writer. And I am sorry that I don't write huge best-sellers. But hope springs eternal.

DLB: Is there any work in progress or on what you

call your "writer's curriculum vitae" that extends into the future that you'd like to talk about?

COPPEL: This family book that I'm beginning is a more massive project than I've ever attempted before. It's projected as a two-volume novel, or a novel with a sequel because it deals with a family from 1857 to today. I'm working up quite an enthusiasm for the project. It's not yet white hot; it's sort of on preheat right now. The working title is "The Marburg Chronicle." It may or may not end up being called that. If it does break up into two books, each book will have its own title.

DLB: You've been so often prophetic in your fiction about the situation in the world. Was that intentional or coincidental?

COPPEL: It seems to me that my "prophecies" were easy. Anyone with an inquiring mind and a sharp eye could have made them. I find it astonishing, as I look at the world today, that so many stupid things are being done and no one can "foresee" what they will lead to. I "foresaw" Reagan's "Star Wars" proposals in *The Dragon*. Yet anyone who read the technical journals of the last ten years could guess that lasers were tomorrow's weapons. Where's the trick in that? How do you write a million-copy best-seller? Now if I had the answer to that—!

DLB: Do you see any large areas you would like to write about now?

COPPEL: I'm beginning to get a bit tired of politics. To say over and over again that international and national policy is in the hands of a group of blithering idiots is bound to start boring people sooner or later. Reiterated truth becomes cliché. I think I will stay away from politics for a while. Perhaps after my family novel I'll come back to the world situation with a fresh viewpoint.

DLB: Have you had any mentors? Do you now serve as a mentor to young writers?

COPPEL: I was helped a great deal by a writer named Darwin Teilhet. Teilhet was a damned good writer. He never really attained the success he should have had. But he was a professional. When I was a young writer, he took the trouble to read my material, make suggestions, even helped me get an agent. I shall always be grateful to him. *Thirty-Four East* is dedicated to him and his wife. I don't have any disciples myself, although from time to time, people do come and talk to me. I guess I'm not much of a teacher. Academics rarely make it as professional writers. Not because they lack the ability. I think it's the tenured life. A writer has to be hungry. There are some few exceptions. Wallace Stegner, for example. He's a man who has been successful as an academic and has done some real writing. But I don't think that a person can maintain a teaching schedule and devote enough time to his own writing to be a novelist. As a professional writer, you have to be available for your work on short notice or no notice at all. If you have classes to teach, the class is going to be a distraction. And if you have

a steady salary, you'll never be really hungry. I think all artists *need* to be a little bit hungry. An occasional bite from the wolf at the door makes you aware of the fact that what it is that you do is write books.

DLB: Have you any advice for young writers?

COPPEL: Don't talk about writing—write! Don't "be a writer"—write! What else is there? Well, one thing more—don't bury your writing in the bottom drawer. Seek the challenge of the marketplace. It is a cruel and often unfair test, but it is the test you have. Face it.

Gordon Eklund
(24 July 1945-)

Mark Lidman
University of Mississippi

BOOKS: *The Eclipse of Dawn* (New York: Ace, 1971);
A Trace of Dreams (New York: Ace, 1972);
Beyond the Resurrection (Garden City: Doubleday, 1973);
All Times Possible (New York: DAW, 1974);
The Inheritors of Earth, by Eklund and Poul Anderson (Radnor, Pa.: Chilton, 1974);
Serving in Time (Don Mills, Ontario: Harlequin, 1975);
Falling Toward Forever (Don Mills, Ontario: Harlequin, 1975);
The Grayspace Beast (Garden City: Doubleday, 1976);
If the Stars Are Gods, by Eklund and Gregory Benford (New York: Putnam's, 1977; London: Sphere, 1979);
The Starless World (New York: Bantam, 1978);
Devil World (New York: Bantam, 1979);
Find the Changeling, by Eklund and Benford (New York: Dell, 1980);
The Garden of Winter (New York: Berkley, 1980);
Lord Tedric: Space Pirates #2 (New York: Ace, 1980).

OTHER: *The Shrine of Sebastian*, in *Chains of the Sea*, edited by Robert Silverberg (Nashville: Nelson, 1973);
"Free City Blues," in *Universe 3*, edited by Terry Carr (New York: Random House, 1973);

"Underbelly," in *Best Science Fiction Stories of the Year*, edited by Lester del Rey (New York: Ace, 1973);
"The Beasts in the Jungle," in *Fantasy and Science Fiction* (November 1973);
"Moby, Too," in *The 1974 Annual World's Best Science Fiction*, edited by Donald A. Wollheim (New York: DAW, 1974);
"What Did You Do Last Year?," by Eklund and Gregory Benford, in *Universe 6*, edited by Carr (New York: Popular Library, 1976);
"Vermeer's Window," in *Universe 8*, edited by Carr (New York: Popular Library, 1978).

A member of the new generation of science-fiction writers, Gordon Eklund was born to Alfred and DeLois Eklund in Seattle in 1945. "I wrote my first story when I was nine and submitted my first one to a magazine when I was twelve," he says. "None of this activity was particularly successful, so I gave it up for a dozen or so years." Eklund served in the air force from 1963 to 1967 and returned to writing while stationed at Travis Air Force Base in California. He began writing more seriously soon after his discharge. His first published story, "Dear Aunt Annie," which concerns a robot advice-to-the-lovelorn columnist on a newspaper of the future, appeared in *Fantastic* in 1970 and received a

Gordon Eklund

Nebula Award nomination in 1971.

Although Eklund attended Contra Costa College in San Pablo, California, from 1973 to 1975 and took courses in elementary physics, his science background is not as strong as that of most of his peers. However, his solid literary background, the product of study and reading, is evident in his novels and stories.

After leaving the air force, Eklund settled in the San Francisco area and worked as a postal clerk, a letter carrier, a teletype operator, and at various other odd jobs before devoting his full attention to writing science fiction. In 1969 he married Dianna Mylarski; they have a son, Jeremy Clark. During the 1970s Eklund developed a reputation in his field. While his material remained essentially traditional, much of his prose contained a kind of carefree wit that often marks recent science-fiction writing. Eklund lived in the San Francisco Bay area in the 1970s; now separated from his wife, he makes·his home in Tacoma, Washington.

Eklund has not received much critical praise since early in his career, and much of that attention took the form of hope that his potential would be

realized. Critical comments in recent years have stressed the competence of his past work with attendant hope for quality in future endeavors.

Much of Eklund's work deals with life in America in the future. His first novel, *The Eclipse of Dawn* (1971), concerns the presidential election of 1988 in an America half ravaged by atomic war. In this election, leadership ability is no longer a criterion for selecting a president; instead, the outcome is determined by media hype and unrealistic campaign promises.

Sen. Robert Colonby challenges the incumbent President Coombs and makes an unrealistic campaign promise based on the information of a young telepath, Susan Jacobi. She has assured Colonby that if he is elected, the country will be rebuilt with the aid of the Octaurians, protean immortal beings now living on Jupiter, who will impart all their knowledge of how aging, death, and disease can be prevented.

But extraterrestrial assistance is no guarantee of victory, and in the middle of the novel, Colonby delivers an important speech from the ruins of Washington. An attempt on his life fails—the assassin's gun contains only blanks. The whole event is the brainchild of one of Colonby's chief campaign strategists. A cross-country whistle-stop train tour in the mold of Harry Truman's successful 1948 maneuver is tremendously successful, and Colonby, with a blend of politics and evangelism, overtakes the president in the public-opinion polls just before election day. Colonby brutally murders Susan Jacobi, and her brother tells the president; but, because Coombs wants to be defeated, he does nothing, and Colonby wins in a landslide. When it is learned that the Octaurians are a hoax, the people realize they must seek help from within themselves, not from extraterrestrial sources:

> While I stood at the window, watching the dawn and listening but not believing, I waited. While I waited, I thought, believing in myself now, the one thing I had never believed in before. I knew that the voices came from me not from the sky, and I believed in myself and not in the sky.

Another early Eklund novel which deals pessimistically with the American political landscape is his alternate-history novel, *All Times Possible* (1974). This novel treats the familiar science-fiction theme of the alternate world—an image of Earth as it might be, had history been changed. Generally, alternate-world novels suggest that ours, if not the best of all possible worlds, is the only correct one, but Eklund's novel asserts that other worlds may be "correct" as well. Its hero, Tommy Bloome, leads a leftist revolution in the mid-twentieth century and creates an America vastly different from the one we know. But existing history is not changed. Bloome finds he is living in only one of a number of histories, on a parallel time line, and in each history he must confront his nemesis. He learns that all times are the same; only historical details differ. *All Times Possible* has been admired for its characterization and its "nice evocation of the Steinbeckian *Grapes of Wrath* leftist revolutionary mood," but like *The Eclipse of Dawn*, it occasionally displays carelessness in style.

According to Gregory Benford, a friend and sometime collaborator, Eklund's "most deeply felt" work was his early novel *Beyond the Resurrection* (1973). Set in New Morning School, a private school on Puget Sound early in the twenty-first century, the novel revolves around three major characters: Gregory Tallsman, a middle-aged cinema teacher; Corlin McGee, a twenty-three-year-old therapist; and the school's eighty-two-year-old director, a former Hollywood columnist who is dying of cancer, Joyce Larkin. A young student, Melissa Brackett, sneaks off one night to make love with August, a mysterious twelve-year-old. Melissa is returned, but August remains at large. The government, fearing August is a spy, wants to capture him. Milinqua, the area supervisor, promises to arrest Larkin for compliance and to shut down the school if August is not found by noon of the following day. A group of students, who want everyone associated with the school absolved of all blame, kidnap Milinqua in retaliation.

It is difficult to know exactly what to make of August. Rutgers, Milinqua's assistant, fears that August is an enemy agent—a deliberate biological mutation who makes zombies out of those he contacts. But those August "transforms" become "enlightened gods" with deeper insight and fuller self-awareness. Larkin explains that August is a laboratory creation who has been placed in New Morning School so that his creators can watch him mature and develop in a controlled environment. Near the end of the novel, Milinqua shoots and kills August, but not until Milinqua himself has been transformed by this "Christ of the scientific age." The supervisor knows that scientists will eventually kill what they have created, and killing August now has saved the boy's disciples from suspicion and guilt through association. Set in a future complete with automated cars and mindless professional soldiers,

Beyond the Resurrection looks at the frightening aspects of genetic engineering and the moral issues involved, with the center of attention an outsider alienated from the mainstream of humanity.

While *Beyond the Resurrection* may be Eklund's most "deeply felt" work, his most praised is the Nebula Award-winning novelette *If the Stars Are Gods* (1977), written with Gregory Benford. Bradley Reynolds, an astronomer and former hero of a successful Mars expedition, is sent as an emissary to an alien starship which has recently landed at the United States moonbase. He meets two giraffelike aliens, Jonathon and Richard, who distrust machines in spite (or because) of their advanced technology. These aliens seek advice and guidance from the stars in a form of star-worship and have come seeking a benevolent star to save their world. They feel that their star is angry with them, but human scientists see this "anger" as extreme temperatures resulting from the eccentric orbit of the aliens' planet. Since Reynolds does not believe that men can actually communicate with stars, he tries to show Jonathon and Richard that humans explore space for other reasons, namely to aggrandize the achievements of an entire race through the accomplishments of individuals.

Now Reynolds tries to answer Jonathon's question. If anyone could, it should be him. "We wish to go to the stars because we are a dissatisfied people. Because we do not live a very long time, as individuals, we feel we must place an important part of our lives into the human race as a whole. In a sense, we surrender a portion of our individual person in return for a sense of greater immortality. What is an accomplishment for man as a race is also an accomplishment for each individual man."

But with the help of an old alien named Vergnan, Reynolds is able to communicate with the Sun for what he calls the "second moment of real completion" in his rather distinguished life. The meaning of the communication, however, remains unclear. At the end, after determining that the Sun produces more blackness than benevolence, the aliens leave.

The climax of the novelette is Reynolds's communion with the Sun. At the Sun's core, he senses a cold, valueless nothingness, which parallels the aliens' judgment that our sun is less benevolent than they had hoped. The extent of contact he makes with the aliens is unresolved, even in his own mind, for though he feels their blinking indicates when they are lying, at the end Reynolds sees that the aliens do not always telegraph what he takes to be prevarications. Because we view the aliens

No ~~more~~ fool *or lunatic* could have *Formulated the* ~~planned the expeditions~~. *She had made.*

He asked ~~her~~ if she would be interested in going to work for him *as a confidential secretary*

She ~~thought~~ *Considered* for a brief moment, then nodded.

He asked if she would mind explaining for his own curiosity ~~the meaning of the attacks on Beverly Hills.~~ *who + what she was.*

She said she had been born the daughter of a very wealthy ~~man~~ *real estate broker* slain by the Dardex but had upon attaining the age of eighteen turned the bulk of her fortune over to charity.

She had then gone to live among the poorest, most miserable people she could find ~~The expeditions to Beverly Hills--not to mention her home--were evidence of his.~~

~~Ek~~ She said it was *her belief it was* wrong for some ~~people~~ to be rich while others were *not* ~~poor~~. She said she believed all people were equal.

~~Blue admitted that he was a very wealthy man himself.~~

~~She asked if he was also a good man.~~

Blue thought for a moment then told her that he honestly believed that ~~he was~~ *was so himself*.

She ~~went~~ *agreed* to work for him.

Lacy Bach: selfless, compassionate, caring, *+ Kind* ~~considerate.~~

Thus Nadia, the ~~efficient~~ *devoted*, Crystal, the sane, ~~and~~ Lacy, the caring, *(,)* *Formed*

Together they ~~made~~ *Formed* a team: a whole *even* greater than the sum of its brilliant parts.

And they served Desmond Blue.

Revised typescript page (the author)

through his eyes, we, like Reynolds, can never be sure whether the aliens are speaking the truth. What we do notice, however, is the alienness of the creatures and the emergent alienness of Reynolds himself. He keeps telling them that he is not typical of his race, that he hates the Earth, and at the end of the story he even wants to accompany the aliens to their next star. More and more, Reynolds begins to identify with what he thinks is the alien viewpoint. The aliens believe in something foreign to Western minds, but any spiritual belief transcends the material quests of the other humans. At the end we see that Reynolds is a less than perfect interpreter as he misjudges the aliens at several junctures. His experiences, which had previously taken him to outer space, now lead to introspection.

Several of Eklund's stories are less concerned with the future than those discussed previously. In "The Beasts in the Jungle" (1973), Eklund tells an adventure reminiscent of H. G. Wells's *The Island of Dr. Moreau* set not in the future, but in 1933. The story is pure adventure, containing a film crew, a mad scientist, and, of course, his collection of hybrid "beasts." In "Underbelly" (1973), Eklund deals with physical immortality. Gabriel Solar is employed at a government installation in a postrevolutionary Latin country and takes the same immortality injections the laboratory rats receive. As a result of the injections, Gabriel is able to stay underwater for fifteen minutes while trying to rescue a drowning boy, and when he is bitten by a scorpion, his finger does not bleed. His wife, convinced he is a witch, kills herself, but Gabriel's attempts to follow suit are thwarted. He cannot die. The characterizations of Solar and the clean, well-lighted cantina where he goes to cut his throat evoke Hemingway. Even the style at times seems imitative.

> He could not remember anything right now. Raising the mug to his lips, he drained most of the beer, then placed what was left at the center of the table. He fixed his hands one on each side of the mug.
> Then he began to pray.
> He prayed first to the Son and then to the Father. Then he prayed to both. He said, *Our Father Who Art In Heaven* . . . and so on. He told the Father that his fear was not that of any man who had lived before. Even the Son had been allowed to die so that he might live again. He said that he knew that suicide was a sin of mortal consequence, but that the choice of accomplishing this act was no longer his to make.
> He asked simply for death. For release.

For death to fulfill Christ's promise that he might live again. Hadn't Dr. Goddard said that installation's work was the most important in the entire history of the human race? And wasn't he, Gabriel, still a man?

Eklund takes a less pessimistic view of the future in his 1973 novella *The Shrine of Sebastian*, published in *Chains of the Sea* (1973), which deals with robot religion and mythology. The new pope, Don Julian, accompanies robot Andrew to the Shrine of Sebastian in order to bury the late Pope Donna Maria. Upon reaching the shrine, Don Julian learns that both he and Donna Maria are androids, artificial beings made from organic material; all humans had left Earth years before in spaceships. This novella contains a good bit of humor and irony, and its futuristic setting enables its author to comment wryly on what might lie in store for us.

Another Eklund narrative with a surprise ending is *The Grayspace Beast* (1976), a tale-within-a-tale told by a narrator whose identity remains a mystery until the end of the novel. Commander Kail Kaypack leads a crew of misfits to find and destroy the beast. The audience of children often interrupts the narrative, complaining about what seems to them to be an excessive amount of background material. Instead of using this technique as an instrument for revealing character, Eklund lets the device set up the reader for a surprise ending. The interruptions seem far too frequent, though occasionally the children make perceptive comments:

> "Your story's still going no place," said a girl, one of my best students. She spoke with sorrow. "Nothing's happened yet at all."
> "Well, something soon will," I promised. "This is the end of the first segment. The second is more direct and action filled."
> "The beast gobbles up Kaypack?" said a boy.
> "Oh, we haven't come to the beast yet," I said. And quickly before their moans and groans could drown me out, I began to cough like a braying mule.

Eklund's finest achievement of the late 1970s is the story "Vermeer's Window" (1978), in which a frustrated, unnamed artist in twenty-first-century Europe undergoes an operation which transforms him into the seventeenth-century artist Jan Vermeer. While the artist remains in his own time, he finds himself recreating Vermeer's masterpieces quite involuntarily and at times he confuses his own identity with that of Vermeer. Even details of his present life parallel the Dutch painter's. As the paintings automatically flow from his brush, he finds no beauty outside his studio. He learns too late that the audience and not the artist determines genius and that his works are doomed to failure in twenty-first-century Amsterdam. As he lives out his life, finishing his last painting—as did Vermeer—at age thirty-eight, he realizes that though his works were Vermeer, he was not.

"Vermeer's Window" is Eklund's most recent work of high quality, for in the past few years writing seems to have become increasingly difficult for him. The personal involvement with his work so noticeable in *Beyond the Resurrection, All Times Possible*, and *If the Stars Are Gods* has not been evident

lately. Eklund has been actively writing in the last few years, however. He has contributed *The Starless World* (1978) to the Star Trek novels series and has completed some of the late E. E. "Doc" Smith's unfinished manuscripts. A new novel has been completed. His other recent ventures seem to be commercial rather than artistic efforts, and it is hoped that Eklund can recover the enthusiasm and involvement with his work that made him one of science fiction's most promising figures in the 1970s.

Reference:

David N. Samuelson, "From Aliens to Alienation: Gregory Benford's Variations on a Theme," *Foundations* (1977-1978): 5-19.

Betsy Fancher
(Betsy Hopkins Lochridge)

(17 October 1928-   )

Orin Anderson

BOOKS: *Blue River*, as Betsy Hopkins Lochridge (New York: Macmillan, 1956; London: Macmillan, 1956);

Voices from the South: Black Students Talk about Their Experiences in Desegregated Schools (Atlanta: Southern Regional Council, 1970);

The Lost Legacy of Georgia's Golden Isles (Garden City: Doubleday, 1971);

Savannah. A Renaissance of the Heart (Garden City: Doubleday, 1976).

SELECTED PERIODICAL PUBLICATIONS: "We're Cheating Our Children," *Saturday Evening Post* (29 September 1962): 10ff.;

"The Voice of the Phoenix," *Gentlemen's Quarterly* (April 1967): 100ff.;

"The Warm Springs of F.D.R.," *Saturday Review*, 52 (8 March 1969): 42ff.;

"Georgia Sea Island that Slumbers like a Time Capsule," *Holiday*, 47 (May 1970): 56-59ff.

Betsy Fancher is an Atlanta journalist and human rights advocate who, as Betsy Hopkins Lochridge, published an exceptional volume of sixteen finely crafted stories in 1956. Harry Hansen interviewed her in the *Chicago Tribune*, and Sterling

North, writing in the *New York World Telegram,* said that Betsy Hopkins Lochridge "immediately steps into the class of Katherine Ann Porter and Shirley Ann Grau as one of the most distinguished short story writers ever to come out of the Southland. . . ." *Blue River* is a remarkable work, and all the more so because it remains the only published fiction by Betsy Hopkins Lochridge, now retired journalist Betsy Fancher.

Betsy Hopkins was born in Atlanta, Georgia, 17 October 1928, the first daughter of Elizabeth Hawkins and John L. Hopkins, grandson of the John L. Hopkins who wrote the Georgia Code of Law. Just after Betsy's birth, John Hopkins, a third-generation lawyer, decided to move out from under his father's shadow and took his young family west. After three years in Dallas, Texas, and two more daughters the family moved to Tennessee. They had barely settled in Memphis when the full force of the Great Depression struck the South. John Hopkins lost everything, began to drink heavily, and attempted suicide, driving his wife away. She took the children with her back to Atlanta, to the house of her sister Helen Clarke.

From the age of four, Betsy Hopkins grew up in that large Tudor-style manse in the company of

Betsy Fancher, circa 1956 (Erich Hartman)

her mother and sisters, grandmother Hawkins, widowed aunt, and cousin Helen. The Hopkins women were "poor relations," and although they lived well enough in Aunt Helen's household, they were always aware of their poverty.

To help alleviate the family's financial strain, at the age of twelve Betsy Hopkins went to work as a page in the Ida Williams Library in Atlanta. By the time she left employment at the repository at fifteen, she had become assistant librarian. The following summer, she took a job writing society news for the *Atlanta Constitution*, and in the fall she enrolled in Wesleyan College, Macon, Georgia, where she paid for her board and tuition by working as a reporter for the *Macon Telegraph*.

Hopkins graduated from Wesleyan in June of 1949 with an A.B. in English and the school's Creative Writing Award for a volume of poetry she submitted as her thesis. Dr. George Gignilliat, her thesis advisor, encouraged her to submit the volume for publication, and although the poetry was not accepted, she established contact with Macmillan's

southeastern representative, Norman S. Berg, who became her friend and advisor. It was through Berg, who in 1971 reprinted *Blue River* for his own Selanraa Press, that her short fiction came to the attention of Macmillan.

After graduating from Wesleyan, she returned to the *Atlanta Constitution*, this time as a daily columnist, and on 18 March 1950 she married her childhood sweetheart, Marshall Lochridge. The period of the Lochridge marriage seems to have been filled with unfortunate circumstances. Two months after the wedding, Betsy Lochridge was struck down at the corner of Courtland and Cain Streets in Atlanta by a cement truck, sustaining a back injury which still plagues her. Before she had fully recovered from the worst effects of the accident, her husband was transferred to the Korean War zone. As Betsy Hopkins Lochridge, she continued to work for the *Constitution* and gave what spare time she had to writing a novel, "The Profit and the Loss," based on the accounts of the Korean War in Marshall Lochridge's letters home. The novel remains unpublished.

Upon his return from the Korean War and subsequent release from the U.S. Navy, Marshall Lochridge entered a training program for Westinghouse Corporation, which took him and his wife across the northeastern United States. Away from Atlanta and the *Constitution*, Betsy Lochridge and her husband gradually grew apart, and by the mid-1950s the marriage had ended. Encouraged by Norman Berg, she turned to a series of short stories about the fictional Southern community Blue River. The book was published by Macmillan in 1956 and enjoyed widespread critical success. (*Blue River* won the Georgia Writers Association's fiction award in 1956 and was published in Italy by Opere nuove in 1957, as well as in braille the same year.) For Betsy Hopkins Lochridge, her book's publication marked the end of a segment of her life.

Disappointed by the $400 earnings from her book, she abandoned fiction writing and returned to work at the *Atlanta Constitution* as book editor.

On her birthday in 1959, 17 October, Betsy Hopkins Lochridge married James K. Fancher, Jr., a widowed law student with three small girls. Betsy Fancher took care of the children and worked once again at the *Atlanta Constitution*, at *South Today* as associate editor (covering civil rights stories throughout the South), and at *Atlanta* magazine as senior editor. At the same time, she produced *The Lost Legacy of Georgia's Golden Isles* (1971) and *Savannah* (1976), the first of which won the Georgia Writers Association's nonfiction award.

Fancher left *South Today* as the result of another serious accident: a steel shed collapsed on top of a taxi in which she was sitting in Columbia, South Carolina, in 1973, reinjuring her back and aggravating her degenerative spine condition. She retired from full-time staff work on *Atlanta* magazine in December 1982, but remains a contributing editor. She also continues her human rights work, particularly through her involvement as a volunteer worker for the Emaus House Chaplaincy of the Episcopal Church, in the Summerville ghetto of Atlanta. Emaus House is the focal point for a fictionalized biography by Fancher, "Cross of Flowers," which is in progress. Although she still free-lances articles for magazines, she lives "quietly in the family home" with her husband and has no plans to return to writing short fiction. *Blue River*, that "slender, lyrical, comprehensive near masterpiece," as the *New York World-Telegram* called it, in all probability will continue to be the lone example of Fancher's work in the genre.

The first story in *Blue River* is "The Town," Fancher's taut history of her fictional community: its settling and prosperity, the introduction of slaves, the Civil War, Reconstruction, the First World War, the Depression, and finally its fading from thriving community to small, drowsy village that takes its name from a river whose water is usually blood-colored with red earth, or yellow and sluggish under the summer sun, blue "only in the rare days after the haze of autumn, the time and season of its discovery by the Reverend Matthew Glenn." Blue River is a Southern town founded by a Yankee whose own life was plagued by ambiguity: "The minister had come from New England to convert the Indians to the Baptist faith. An angel of the Lord had appeared to him in a vision and dispatched him on this mission. Through years of humdrum toil he had been sustained by a dream of martyrdom, and the angel's words had set his soul afire. Putting himself in the hands of God, he set out in a covered wagon with his wife and four sons. After a summer of unspeakable hardships he reached the valley of the Blue River, which he believed to be the place ordained for him. That winter he died without ever having seen an Indian."

Such gentle irony is pervasive in *Blue River*, capturing the essence of "Southern-ness," in particular what might be called the combination of a static and vivid quality of life, a sense of wistfulness for the past, and of latent violence under a polite surface. These ingredients lend themselves admirably to Fancher's handling of the short story, reinforced by her perception of the inherent linking factors of the South: the preeminent role of women, the legacy of slavery, the casual familiarity with religion, the saturation of history, and the bond of place.

"The Town" is followed by tales variously entitled with eight women's and six men's names (the sixteenth story is "Death"); yet in all but two of the sixteen ("The Town" and "Will Davis") women hold central positions.

It is Fancher's insight into the history and lives of Blue River's black people that elevates the book to masterpiece or "near masterpiece." The first of the *Blue River* stories is "Foots," about the black gardener demeaned beyond right or reason. As told by the narrator, Jane (never obtrusively present), Foots's relationship with his employer, "Miz Sarah" (the Grandmother), is amiable and fond, but rigidly set in a master-and-servant mold which seems a legacy of the days of slavery, for the Grandmother blames him for her failings, and he feels that she could not exist if he were not there to shoulder both his burdens and hers. (In "Death," Foots considers his life at an end when the Grandmother dies, that he has to join her, because "dere's Miz Sarah up dere wid nobody to help her 'long and nobody to fuss at when de notion strikes.") In "Foots," the two are awaiting the delivery of some camellia plants on a cold November morning. They talk fondly of setting them out in the face of neighborhood jealousy and the teeth of the cold weather. Foots gently reminds the Grandmother about the money to pay for them, and when she can't find the sum when the delivery truck arrives, she blames Foots and makes him go into the pantry and take off his torn clothes piece by piece while she searches them. At the end of the humiliating act, Foots remembers where he has seen the Grandmother place the money (in an old purse). The Grandmother is stricken by the event, but says nothing, only sighs. The narrator goes to help her, "for the hall was very dark and the cold was setting in."

The flavor of the collection is reminiscent of Katherine Ann Porter's "Miranda" stories (with the theme of initiation being more subdued), bringing to mind as well works of Eudora Welty, Shirley Ann Grau, and Flannery O'Connor. Welty, particularly, is recalled in "Ida Sims" and "Callie Daniel." Ida Sims fails to escape the parochialism of Blue River, to "walk free as a man walks." After being socially ostracized for going to the woods with the Blue River boys, she leaves to "study composition" in New York. She joins with a young artist named Collins, but soon becomes aware that unmarried life with him does not give her the freedom she seeks, as

Come let us linger in the garden, the lonely little walled garden of Emaus House — Emaus, the village where the disciples met Christ after the Resurrection. How sweet it is in the early morning to sit with you in the garden on Easter watching the doves dip and soar around the bath at the feet of the Statue of St Francis, here where crab apple blossoms shield us from the Reeking Tenements, the empty bellied babies gnawed by rats and the cries of abandoned mothers and sad and sodden men and the

and in the dawn, for just this hour the children who hunger are asleep, the abandoned mothers weep silently on wet pillows, the sad and sodden ragged men have sunk into oblivion. The sirens that all night answered the desperate calls of violence are stilled and death, the futile death which has never known life, is overcome by the promise of Spring.

Oh Father, where did it all begin, this long and agonizing journey which has brought me here, here among the smoldering Roses and the violets in the little walled garden of Emaus House with you beside me, tall and still, your gentle brown eyes blessing me, welcoming me home, forgiving everything as if there were nothing to forgive, I also

First page of the manuscript for "Cross of Flowers," a novel in progress (the author)

he forces her into the traditional female role. Her return to Blue River brings little understanding from her neighbors and coworkers there, and the confused sexuality of the male-dominated world brings bitter resignation with a crushing finality.

There is "no place," either, for the golden-skinned girl of Fancher's "Callie Daniel," whose startling beauty "caused men to forget that she was the daughter of a washerwoman and lived in the Hollow." As in "Ida Sims," Fancher's female protagonist is at the mercy of arbitrary sexual mores, but with the added handicap that Callie Daniel is black. "When she was fourteen, she became involved in a love affair with the young son of the family for whom she worked as a housemaid. As they lay together in the woods beyond the Hollow, he promised to marry her and take her away to some island where they could live as they pleased. When she became pregnant, however, he had her dismissed from her job and threatened to kill her if she ever spoke of what had passed between them." This is the first in a series of betrayals of Callie as she tries to find room in either the white world or the black, growing to an "old and grotesque" woman as "fatigue dulled her mind." Finally, a trip to New York to see her son, whom she had put through college and who was taken "as a white man," ends in unspoken disaster. Fancher does not recount the scene; she merely has Callie Daniel reappear on the streets of Blue River three weeks after she went off in pride to "live with her son," telling Miss Fanny, her old employer, "Dere's trouble in de land, ma'am, trouble in de land."

Like her fellow Georgian and friend Flannery O'Connor, Fancher has an exquisite ear for the cadences of common everyday speech and a substance of story, ideas of character and personality which produce a marked subtlety of effect. Fancher and O'Connor met in 1956 after the publication of *Blue River*. They took to each other immediately and became such fast friends that O'Connor delegated Fancher to accept awards and speak in her name on the luncheon-and-dinner circuit. At first, O'Connor didn't like *Blue River*, but she soon wrote to Fancher from Milledgeville that her first impression was awry: "I was wrong about *Blue River*—It needed more reading."

"Will Davis" is one of the stories that caught O'Connor's eye. The title character has "a remarkable mind" which proves a curse, foretold by the narrator's grandmother: "What's the use of it? . . . It'll never get him a better job or a decent place to live. No, he'll only grow discontent with what he has." The schoolmaster gives Will Davis an education and aspirations beyond the limitations of Blue River, and the Episcopal minister's evasion of the truth regarding a black boy's opportunities sends Will "up Nawth," where he finds that being Southern and black there has as many restrictions as being black in the South. He returns to Blue River and vents his anguished frustration on the rector and his church, hitting the minister and smashing the church's stained-glass windows: "You ain' nevah been to hell; You an' yo' little prissy white God. Christ, what do you know?" The anger and outrage is too much for Blue River. Townsmen chase Will Davis down and hang him, and the schoolmaster proclaims the boy's fate "to be the will of God."

Despite the evocative nature of Fancher's stories, her style is all her own. The town is hers, and its characters. There is an essence of "Southernness" about her work, a Southern idea that the past (glory, propriety, goodness) is slipping away, and the characters seem familiar: the various Reverend Glenns, lineal descendants of Blue River's founder, and the Lewis girls in their eighties. The element which takes *Blue River* into the company of Porter, Grau, Welty, and O'Connor is Fancher's finely distanced control and her affliction, as Ralph M. called it, "with the burdensome ability to see both sides of many causes."

From *Blue River*, Fancher's life moved on to direct action in the modern field of human rights. It is as though a line begun in Fancher's childhood is completed in the book, the South captured before it fades in cramped furnished rooms of the Northeast, or among the Southern Babbitts of New Atlanta. Fancher says that as she wrote *Blue River*, she felt as though she were writing above her head, that the words "just appeared" in many instances, and that the work was one like nothing she had done before and "probably would not do again." Over a quarter of a century later, although the promising critical predictions which met *Blue River*'s publication have yet to be realized, it does seem that, for a moment, however brief, the Southern short story had found a natural exponent.

References:

"Bright New Talent Deep in Georgia," *New York World Telegram* (26 September 1956);

"Visit with a Gentle Lady: Betsy Fancher," *Georgia Review* (April 1971): 10, 38.

AN INTERVIEW

with BETSY FANCHER

DLB: Given that journalism is your first love and that "Foots" was derived from a real incident in your childhood, where does the rest of *Blue River* originate?

FANCHER: *Blue River* grew out of its people. I've always been fascinated with people: my daily column for the *Constitution* was called "These Interesting People," and my job was to get out on the city streets, to find and interview Atlanta's characters—the sidewalk evangelists, the winos, the bag ladies. I had a store of characters flooding through my imagination. After I had finished writing "Foots," I conceived of the town as the only possible unifying medium for them. Later, my introduction to *Winesburg, Ohio* and *Tilbury Town* confirmed the decision to bring my characters together in the town of Blue River.

The characters are primarily derivations or composites of people I had known in Georgia before my first marriage. I was very homesick when I wrote *Blue River*. The story which became the first chapter, "The Town," I wrote in Mrs. Gussie Hankle's boardinghouse in Pittsburgh, Pennsylvania. I was determined to escape my new environment—the alien North, the furnished rooms, the unsettled wandering. And, I did.

DLB: If written out of homesickness, *Blue River* is strangely removed from the usual emotionalism associated with such a condition. Since you're not given to endless practice of the short story genre, the distance and control exhibited in the book seem to be unusual accomplishments.

FANCHER: Any distance or control in *Blue River* was hard won. I compiled lengthy genealogies on all the characters in the book. I wrote, rewrote, and polished exhaustively. "Will Davis," an eight-page story, took two months to write. When I had finished the book, Norman Berg suggested that I rewrite it in the third person. I did, but the book didn't work. I rewrote it again in the first person, submitted it directly to Macmillan, and they accepted it immediately.

DLB: You've mentioned Norman Berg: was *Blue River* written for yourself, or with an eye toward publication?

FANCHER: *Blue River* began out of homesickness

—it took me back to Atlanta. It was an experiment in writing. Before, as well as after, I wrote poetry or worked in journalism. Or rather, it was begun as an experiment, but by the time I had finished the first four chapters I had begun to think of it as a publishable book. I had no knowledge or interest in markets, however. Norman Berg read and critiqued my work, but I was writing from an inner imperative.

DLB: Why have you done no other short fiction, considering the critical success of your one collection?

FANCHER: *Blue River* stands alone because becoming an instant mother with my second marriage made fact more interesting to me than fiction. I was deeply embroiled in life; I had no room of my own, and I had to make a living, so I embraced journalism. Editing, writing daily columns, bringing up three daughters, and being a wife leave little time for short fiction. I've said before that I'm not a closet short story writer.

DLB: You've spent most of your life so far in journalism. What is it about journalism that has captured you?

FANCHER: I believe journalism to be an art form as precise and exacting as poetry. It is *the* art form of our fast-paced, modern lives. My own career in journalism has been rich and challenging. I was at my typewriter during the entire course of the civil rights struggle in the South. There wasn't time for fiction when fact was so exciting, even dangerous: driving Dr. Donald Gatch (spokesman for the hungry on the South Carolina coast) to Atlanta to escape the FBI; departing Mobile, Alabama, just ahead of the police who were arresting all media personnel as "agitators"; and barely escaping arrest in Beaufort, South Carolina, for "trespassing" in an all-white school. I lived for ten years on the edge of danger, and I loved it. It's all over, now. My friends in the movement are selling real estate; the Southern Regional Council is operating on a skeletal staff; and I am writing my memoirs. Perhaps now is the time to return to the short story.

DLB: If you are not a closet short story writer, are you a private novelist? What does the future hold?

FANCHER: "The Profit and the Loss," the novel I wrote before I worked on *Blue River*, has some good passages. I am told that it's a "beautifully written but terribly flawed" novel. From time to time I dust it off and send it around, but apparently it is not publishable. "Cross of Flowers" is fictionalized autobiography, my "memoirs." I'm only fifty pages into it, and I plan to devote the winter to it. After

that, who knows? . . . I still maintain connections to journalism. But, now I have a room of my own; my girls are all grown and settled; and the well, which had run dry, is filling up again.

John Graves
(6 August 1920-   )

Timothy Dow Adams
West Virginia University

BOOKS: *Home Place: A Background Sketch in Support of a Proposed Restoration of Pioneer Buildings in Fort Worth, Texas* (Fort Worth, 1958);

Goodbye to a River: A Narrative, illustrated by Russell Waterhouse (New York: Knopf, 1960; London: Macmillan, 1961);

The Nation's River (Washington, D.C.: United States Government Printing Office, 1968);

The Water Hustlers, with Robert H. Boyle and T. H. Watkins (San Francisco: Sierra Club, 1971);

The Last Running: A Story (Austin: Encino Press, 1974);

Hard Scrabble: Observations on a Patch of Land (New York: Knopf, 1974);

From a Limestone Ledge: Some Essays and Other Ruminations About Country Life in Texas, illustrated by Glenn Wolff (New York: Knopf, 1980);

Blue and Some Other Dogs (Austin: Encino Press, 1982).

OTHER: Introduction to *Texas Heartland: A Hill Country Year*, with photographs by Jim Bones, Jr. (College Station: Texas A & M University Press, 1975);

Introduction to *Landscapes of Texas: Photographs from Texas Highways Magazine* (College Station: Texas A & M University Press, 1980).

Born in Fort Worth, Texas, John Graves has outgrown his strong regional identification and emerged as an important American writer in the naturalist mode. To the list of recent writers such as Edward Hoagland, Annie Dillard, Noel Perrin, John McPhee, and Wendell Berry, who have inherited that particularly American combination of autobiography-natural history-philosophy handed down from Thoreau and William Bartram through Louis Bromfield, Joseph Wood Krutch, and John

Muir, the name of John Graves should be added.

Following a childhood spent in parts of Fort Worth that still bordered on rural in the 1920s and 1930s, Graves went to Rice University, where he studied under George Williams, who also taught such Texas writers as Larry McMurtry and William Goyen. After graduating, Graves joined the Marines in 1942 and spent the next three war years in various foreign outposts, including Saipan, where he sustained an injury that eventually caused him to lose the sight in one eye. He returned to America following the war and attended Columbia University, where he received an M.A. in English in 1948 before going to teach at the University of Texas at Austin, from 1948 to 1950. The tedious life of a beginning English instructor, the breakup of his first marriage in 1952, the false security brought on by the *New Yorker*'s acceptance of his first story, and the lure of the exotic countries he had seen during the war all combined to attract Graves into nearly a decade of wandering. He lived in Majorca and Tenerife, briefly in New Mexico and New York City, and then in Spain, often writing travel pieces for *Holiday* magazine. He described himself during this period as "not a real traveler but a moseyer and sojourner who had bogged down in a number of different places for a while. . . ."

In the late 1950s John Graves returned—because of a family illness—for what he thought would be a brief stay in Texas; except for a short interval, he has lived in Texas ever since, slowly producing a series of books and articles focused on his immediate surroundings, amplified and refracted through the international perspective he developed during those years of wandering.

During his travels, Graves had written articles and stories for such popular magazines as *Atlantic*, *Esquire*, and *American Heritage*. While living tem-

John Graves (Shay Bennett)

porarily in his boyhood home and teaching part-time at Texas Christian University, he agreed to chronicle his one-man canoe trip down the Brazos River for *Sports Illustrated.* Graves's account of his trip grew beyond sport and became too poetical, too philosophical, and too important for just a magazine assignment. Although a shorter version eventually appeared in *Holiday,* the trip that began 11 November 1957 and ended some one hundred and seventy-five miles downriver on 2 December that same year became the source and the subject of Graves's first published book, *Goodbye to a River* (1960).

Goodbye to a River is a difficult book to classify. Although Graves echoes such famous literary river-writers as Thoreau and Twain, his book has a particular flavor all its own. A 1971 Sierra Club/ Ballantine paperback edition carries the code Nature-084 on its back cover, but Graves subtitled the book "A Narrative" and prefaced it with a note to the reader which advises that the narrative contains fictionalizing beyond the usual change of a name or two. The author claims that "some of the characters, even the one I call myself, are compos-ites." The book takes both rhythm and shape from the Brazos River itself—it flows along in one direc-

tion telling the story of Graves's journey, giving such practical advice and knowledge as the varia-tions different woods can make of a campfire-cooked meal: "Cedar's oil eats up its wood in no time and stinks food too, but the tinge of it in the air after supper is worth smelling if you want to cut a stick or so of it just for that." Then the story flows backward against the current as Graves recounts the local history of various bends and hills along the river's course. The stories are of Comanches and cowboys, historical feuds, famous Texans, typical home-steaders, and local eccentrics, told with brevity and sound historical background, supported by a four-page bibliography at the book's end. *Goodbye to a River* is part autobiography, part history, part philosophy, and part woodlore, loosely tied to the erratic but steady flow of John Graves's canoe down twists of the river through both yellow-blue and rain-ruined November days and on into December snow and freezing northers.

The narrative includes anecdotes, chance meetings, journal entries, historical documents, and Graves's renderings of bird sounds and local dialect. Flushed bobwhites whistle "Where-you? where-you?" while barred owls break the silence with "Who, who, whoo, whoo, whah, whah, hah, HAH, HAH, WHO ALL!" Equally accurate and simple are his renditions of the speech of local people: "Looked at her. . . . Liked her. Guess she liked me. Still both do," says a man Graves met on the river-bank near Mineral Wells. Further on down the river, in the Somervell County cedar country, a local man says of a rattlesnake, "Hin bi' me. Hin bi' oo. Le'm be." Graves's writing style is highly polished and literate, reflecting the wide variety of influences alluded to in chapter headings and in the body of the book itself, writers such as Thoreau, Yeats, Shakespeare, Thorstein Veblen, George Herbert, and the author of *Sir Gawain and the Green Knight.* And yet, for all of his literary ancestors, Graves's style is peculiarly his own, his syntax characterized by rhythmic stops and starts, like a boat caught momentarily on an obstruction in the current, now catching and spinning backward, now speeding downstream. Graves imparts this rhythm to his sentences by a constant use of ellipses, fragments, dashes, and parentheses. His style is reminiscent of Whitman ("You're no more bored with the same-ness of your days and your diet and your tasks than a chickadee is bored . . . you know the sovereign pulse of being") and yet sometimes suggestive of Milton ("Gray sky, gray pale green of the willows not yet turned by frost . . . ingrained gray of great sand-stone boulders tumbled along the shore. Gray blow of the gray wind, counterthrust of the gray current").

Reviews of *Goodbye to a River* were virtually all highly praising. Paul Horgan wrote in the *New York Herald Tribune Book Review* that "even the smallest details in his ruminative passage down the river come to us in larger terms than we might expect, for he has artistry of word and heart to give meanings as well as facts and impressions." Although an anonymous British critic in the *Times Literary Supplement* found it "humorless, absurdly self-conscious, and sometimes embarrassingly studded with the home-spun philosophy," *Goodbye to a River* is a strongly affecting book whose individual rhythms and thoughtful diversions into such subjects as ecology, hunting, pets, and loneliness call for rereading. Sometimes the author's personal quirks—an antifemale streak, a loner instinct, and an apparent disregard for conservation movements—cause annoyance, but the overall effect is so positive, the style so winning, that *Goodbye to a River* is clearly John Graves's best book.

In 1958 Graves married Jane Cole; they have two daughters, Helen and Sally. By 1962 the experience with early Texas buildings that Graves had gained from his work on *Home Place: A Background Sketch in Support of a Proposed Restoration of Pioneer Buildings in Fort Worth, Texas* (1958) proved valuable as he began hand-construction of his own home place on land just outside Glen Rose, Texas. Although he still lived in Fort Worth, Graves was increasingly attracted to the idea of living in Glen Rose, a plan that he realized in 1970, after three years of working for Stuart Udall, then secretary of the interior, in Washington. Graves's work for Udall led to *The Nation's River* (1968), a government study of our national waterways, and *The Water Hustlers* (1971), a Sierra Club book published as a three-part study of water bureaucracy in Texas, California, and New York. Graves's portion of *The Water Hustlers*, "Texas: 'You Ain't Seen Nothing Yet,' " is a serious study of the disadvantages of the 1968 Texas Water Plan. While covering historical, geographical, ecological, and economic aspects of the plan, Graves still manages to maintain his compelling writing style. Against the plan's statistics and government language stands his authentic personal voice: "40 percent of marine life gone in a few brief years, for God's sweet sake; we came out of the sea."

Living in Glen Rose, Graves continued to write while devoting himself to the restoration and management of his 400 acres of limestone hills and cedarland, which he calls Hard and Soft Scrabble. In 1974 Encino Press, publishers of collector's edi-

tions of Texana, brought out *The Last Running*, a short story which had originally appeared in *Atlantic* in 1959. *The Last Running* is a fictionalized version of the story of the final ritualistic buffalo hunt which Graves told as nonfiction in *Goodbye to a River*.

Graves also had his second major book, *Hard Scrabble*, published in 1974. It is an account of his life on the land where he has laboriously and thoughtfully been making inroads on the self-consuming task of restoring the property to working condition for farming while indulging in what he calls "such archaic irrelevances as stonemasonry, the observation of armadillos, vegetable gardening, species of underbrush, and the treatment of retained afterbirth in ruminants. . . ."

Like his first book, *Hard Scrabble* is highly personal and erratically structured. Edward Hoagland wrote in the *New York Times Book Review* that it was "a kind of homemade book—clumsy once in a while in the way it's put together or rhetorically empurpled—imperfect like a handmade thing, a prize." That homemade quality comes partly from the author's purpose; he warns at the start that his book is not an expert's look at nature on a large scale; nor is it "an account of a triumphant return to the land, a rustic success story." Rather, the book represents Graves's working through his own questions about his need for such a strong relationship to the land, what he calls "The Ownership Syndrome," his need to spend so much time on such a small plot of earth when his previous years have been characterized by constant travel. His answer comes only after he has led us through a journey as nonlinear as the one he took down the Brazos River almost twenty years earlier.

Like *Goodbye to a River*, *Hard Scrabble* is highly fictionalized. After an introductory chapter, Graves gives an account of the history of the county, then of the property, and finally of his own relationship with his land. He orients the reader through geographical descriptions, maps, and graphs, then suddenly jumps into a highly fictionalized chapter, "Ghosts," set in the form of a local man's biography of his father. Graves provides lyrical descriptions coupled with harsh factual accounts ranging over an enormous variety of subjects related to life on Hard Scrabble. He touches on vegetation, animals, machines, hand tools, migrant workers, agricultural economics, building a limestone cabin, and the building of fences, all interspersed with ruminations on water, weather, hunting, age, and ecology. The book's eclectic quality can be surmised from its wide variety of epigrams: quotations from Thomas Traherne, Nathaniel Hawthorne, Wallace Stevens,

Ecclesiastes, and Chaucer.

In between the more straightforward chapters, which often have internal digressions, the author has inserted two chapters—"An Irrelevance" and "Another Irrelevance"—that deal with his past experiences with people who lived for the land, memories that occur to Graves while seated "slanchwise on the tractor and looking back as the tandem disk slices mellow trashy earth in autumn. . . ." Other chapters which pull against the narrative flow include a fictionalized sketch of two illegal aliens from Mexico; a one-page interlude which features Graves's daughter's drawing of an idyllic farm scene, a rustic nursery rhyme, and the label "a sop for those who would have preferred a happy homestead sort of book . . ."; and "His Chapter," a long fictional story with an unnamed protagonist, called "O. F." for Old Fart, whose meaning of life is defined by rough ranching and hard scrabbling that eventually give way to a rough-hewn pantheism. In an interview with Patrick Bennett, Graves called his last chapter pure fiction, a story that "grew out of the air at that point."

In another section of *Hard Scrabble* the author defines an "old fart," a category of human which clearly includes John Graves: "While he knows men must use the earth, he knows too that it matters for its own sake and that it must stay alive, and therefore according to such understanding as he may have he tries to keep his dealings with it right and gentle, and only thereafter reflects on fiscal gain. . . . He is not always right in his judgments and may be capable of unecological murderous rage against rattlesnakes and coyotes and such. But after his own individual fashion he cares about the earth and earthy things and how they work."

The writing style in *Hard Scrabble* is as individual as that of the author's previous books, even on such topics as rattlesnakes, which "are much more productive of narrative than of hurt," or the taste of old and insufficiently parboiled armadillo, about which he notes, "a chewed hunk of it gets bigger and bigger and bigger in the mouth." Once again his ear for the nuances of country speech is strong: "Men may speak not as themselves but as their holdings, creating flash images that can disconcert, as when a large beefy type avers, 'I got broomweed sprouting all over me this year.'"

By the end of the book, Graves has demonstrated that hard labor on the land has not diminished his love of nature as it really is; nor has the equally hard scrabble of reworking sentences, cultivating ideas, and building paragraphs prevented

him from accomplishing those tasks with equal strength and a love of graceful writing for its own sake. For some readers the disjointed structure of *Hard Scrabble*, the agricultural details, and the author's occasional crotchetiness on some topics might be irritating at times, more jarring in the relative civilization of the author's farm than similar eccentricities were out on the river in his first book. But for scope and detail, for the harsh juxtaposition of nature at its worst with a sweet afternoon rain in early autumn, *Hard Scrabble* is nearly equal to *Goodbye to a River* in its power to make the reader stop reading and consider moving to the countryside. Positive reviews in such publications as the *New York Times Book Review, New Yorker, Atlantic,* and *Sewanee Review* alerted even readers with no particular interest in nature writing to Graves's work.

In the next few years Graves continued to write short pieces related to his previous work, such as introductions for *Texas Heartland,* a collection of photographs taken by Jim Bones, Jr., and *Landscapes of Texas*, collected photographs from *Texas Highways* magazine. Concentrating almost solely on nonfiction, he began to publish a series of essays in *Texas Monthly* magazine, the best of which were collected in *From a Limestone Ledge* (1980). Many are sequels to subjects first brought up in *Hard Scrabble.* The author refers to his essays in the introduction as "footnotes . . . expansions or variations on themes found there." The essays are divided into three broad categories. In the first, "Coping," Graves considers such topics as home winemaking, meat, trash as treasure, native eccentric builders, and a brief dissertation on fences, which proves that, unlike Robert Frost's New England, where the only rustling is of autumn leaves, in Texas good barbed-wire fences make good neighbors.

The second main section, "Creatures," takes up cows, goats, bees, chickens, and dogs. The chapter on dogs, called "Blue and Some Other Dogs," has been reprinted by Encino Press in a separate edition. The last part of *From a Limestone Ledge,* called "Ponderings, People, and other Oddments," is a catch-all category which covers what Graves calls the "noticingness of rural life," such things as weather, treasure hunters, country auctions, and a mini-anthology—"Tobacco Without Smoke"—part one of which details snuff dippers, part two tracing chewers.

Even though these pieces were written for a popular magazine, they are more than mere journalism—they are as highly crafted and as thoughtful as Graves's best work. Although generally less anecdotal and less fictional, the essays still

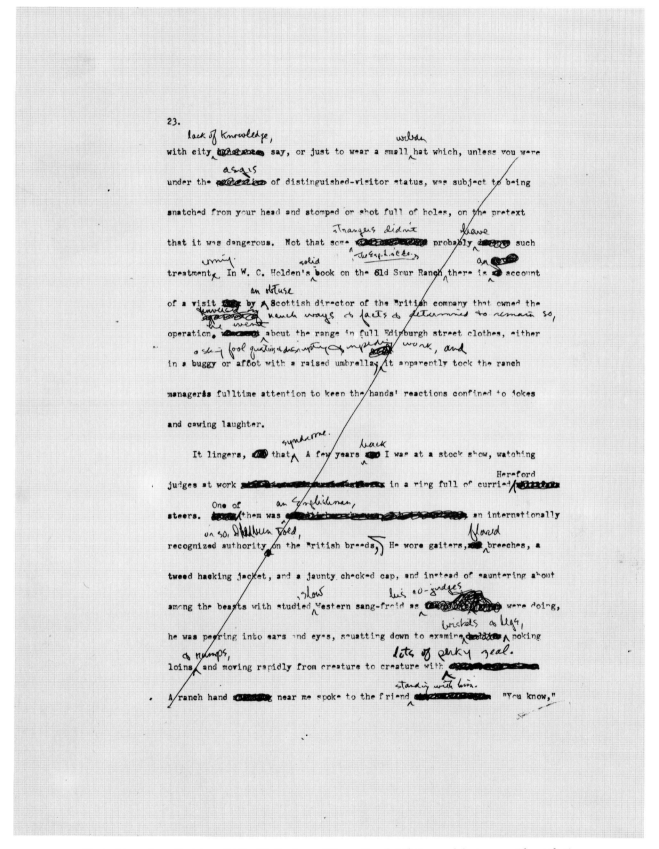

23.

with city *lack of knowledge,* say, or just to wear a small hat which, unless you were *urban*

under the *aegis* of distinguished-visitor status, was subject to being

snatched from your head and stomped or shot full of holes, on the pretext

that it was dangerous. Not that some *strangers didn't* probably *have* such *The Explorers,*

treatment. In W. C. Holden's book on the Old Spur Ranch there is *an solid* account

of a visit *an obtuse* by a Scottish director of the British company that owned the *he went*

operation, about the range in full Edinburgh street clothes, either *a sky fool questions & annoying & impeding work, and*

in a buggy or afoot with a raised umbrella. It apparently took the ranch

manager's fulltime attention to keep the hands' reactions confined to jokes

and cawing laughter.

It lingers, *syndrome.* that. A few years *back* I was at a stock show, watching

judges at work in a ring full of curried *Hereford* steers. One of *an Englishman,* them was an internationally *on so, I'llbeen told,*

recognized authority on the British breeds. He wore gaiters, *flared* breeches, a

tweed hacking jacket, and a jaunty checked cap, and instead of sauntering about *slow his co-judges*

among the beasts with studied Western sang-froid as were doing, *briskets & legs,*

he was peering into ears and eyes, squatting down to examine poking *& rumps,* *lots of perky zeal.*

loins, and moving rapidly from creature to creature with *standing with him.*

A ranch hand near me spoke to the friend "You know,"

Revised page from the typescript for "Reflections of Texas Ranch Life," a work in progress (the author)

show evidence of the author's ear for speech, as when he imitates the sound of a country auctioneer: " 'Urba durba dibba rubba hurty-fie,' said the auctioneer. . . . 'Hurty-fie hurty-fie hurty-fie, who say fitty? Fitty, fitty, fitty, fitty, durba dubba ibba dibby who say forty-fie?' " *From a Limestone Ledge* was as widely reviewed as Graves's other work and was nominated for an American Book Award in the nonfiction category. An early assessment by Lee Milazzo, called "Rewards of a 'Paleo-Rustic,' " argues that "these pieces could be, should be, studied as models of the essay form." Spencer Brown, writing in the *New Yorker,* praises the book's "quasi-musical structure" and calls it "a meditative lyric of prose." *From a Limestone Ledge* is illustrated by Glenn Wolff with drawings that combine the rustic with humor and sophisticated design—unlike Russell Waterhouse's illustrations for *Goodbye to a River* or John Groth's drawings for *The Last Running,* both of which are sometimes too stylized and too romantic for Graves's prose.

Although he had fiction published early in his career and received a Guggenheim award for an unfinished novel, John Graves is now concentrating solely on his particular brand of nonfiction in a fictional form—nature writing which is characterized by the informal style reflected by the subtitles of his three major books: narrative, observations, and ruminations. While *Goodbye to a River* is ostensibly about a leavetaking from the river the Spanish named the Arms of God—the dam-threatened Brazos—*Hard Scrabble* is about being damned in another sense, a farewell not to the arms of God, but of man, for looming behind Graves's property are the towers of a nuclear power plant with the ironic name of Comanche Peak. And yet, even with the major symbols of his books—river and land—under constant threat, John Graves has managed to instill in his readers his own ability to remain faithful to the land and the water in these endangered times. Without polemics or escapism, he has been able to reinforce the theme that runs through all of his writing—there are still people for whom the land and the water matter very much.

Reference:

Patrick Bennett, "A Hard Scrabble World," interview with John Graves, in his *Talking with Texas Writers: Twelve Interviews* (College Station: Texas A & M University Press, 1981), pp. 63-88.

Marianne Hauser
(11 December 1910-   )

Alice S. Morris

SELECTED BOOKS: *Monique* (Zurich: Ringier, 1934);
Shadow Play in India (Vienna: Zinnen, 1937);
Dark Dominion (New York: Random House, 1947);
The Living Shall Praise Thee (London: Gollancz, 1957); republished as *The Choir Invisible* (New York: McDowell Obolensky, 1958);
Prince Ishmael (New York: Stein & Day, 1963; London: Joseph, 1964);
A Lesson in Music (Austin: University of Texas Press, 1964);
The Talking Room (New York: Fiction Collective, 1976).

OTHER: "ASHES: a fragment from a novel in the making," in *Statements II, New Fiction* (New York: Fiction Collective, 1977), pp. 141-144;
"Marianne Hauser Introduces Lee Vassel," in *Writers Introduce Writers*, edited by E. B. Richie and F. B. Claire (New York: Groundwater Press, 1980), p. 75.

PERIODICAL PUBLICATIONS:
Fiction:
"The Colonel's Daughter," *The Tiger's Eye*, 3 (March 1948): 21-34;
"The Sun and the Colonel's Button," *Botteghe Oscure*, 12 (Fall 1953): 255-272;
"The Seersucker Suit," *The Carleton Miscellany*, 9 (Fall 1968): 2-14.

Marianne Hauser (Aina Balgalvis)

Nonfiction:

"Marrakesh: Descent into Spring," *Harper's Bazaar*, 3054 (May 1966): 188-203;

"Mimoun of the Mellah," *Harper's Bazaar*, 3061 (December 1966): 114-182.

Marianne Hauser was born and raised in Strasbourg, Alsace, within range of the city's great bell-haunted cathedral. At seventeen, already a fluent writer in French and German, she was commissioned by a Swiss publication to travel in China, India, and Egypt — and, when she was twenty-six, to the United States, where she "fell in love with the language."

Her two earliest novels, published in Zurich and Vienna, have not been translated into English. On the evidence of *Dark Dominion* (1947), her first American novel, however, one might think English her mother tongue. Her use of it is impeccable and spontaneous; ingeniously her prose depicts the vertiginous relationships between a nondreaming New York dream-analyst; his wife, whom he wins

when he analyzes her dreams; the wife's obsessively devoted brother; and her overtly matter-of-fact lover who is covertly consulting the analyst. The individual fantasies by which this quartet insulate themselves against reality are explored with compassion and comic gusto.

The role of fantasy, both as insulation and as a means of instilling life with excitement, is a theme central to Marianne Hauser's fiction — one aspect of what she sees as the individual's desperate, often humorous struggle to wrest some acceptable meaning from existence and "build a Heaven in Hell's despair." In his review of *Dark Dominion* for the *Chicago Tribune* Paul Engel wrote: "I cannot believe that the year will produce a richer, more original novel by any writer, new or old."

A small midwestern town in America's "Bible belt" is the setting of *The Choir Invisible* (1958), for which the author received a Rockefeller grant. "The fantasy of Main Street," she notes, "exceeds that of the Cathedral of Strasbourg in all its Gothic elaboration." Floyd Walker, a young bank clerk and choirmaster, told that he has leukemia and three months to live, resolves to live his remaining time to the hilt. His dramatic shift of gears, as well as his mortal predicament, makes him the cynosure of the town of Ophelia. He quits his wife and children to run off with a local beautician; becomes the confidant of a lady reincarnationist who claims to have dined with a pharaoh; is taken up by a worldly family named Wisdom, in whose far-flung domicile the local intelligentsia gather for luminous evenings by the fire; and embarks on escapades with his wondrous, all-accepting Aunt Ada. Ironically, Floyd winds up where he started: still alive, and restored to his family.

An exalted sense of joy pervades this novel where the end of the road seems forever to lead into a new, astonishing beginning, and the satire reveals how the same event can be both beautiful and foolish, poignant and absurd. The author's view is always positive. Her wit echoes with humility, her irony with wonder. On the dust jacket of *The Choir Invisible* Mari Sandoz says that the author "lets the reader see through her talented and ironic European eye, and writes the story with the wit and poetic horseplay of her adopted America."

Prince Ishmael (1963), which was nominated for the Pulitzer prize, unfolds in early nineteenth-century Nuremberg, where Caspar Hauser (no relation, but a figure the author has lifted out of German legend) appears at the city gates, a "tottering spook" of sixteen, clotted with mud and forced to shield his eyes from the light. He can neither speak nor walk properly, knows neither who he is nor whence he came. His origin remains a taunting mystery. Is he a princeling ripped from his cradle and reared in a cave? Is he a charlatan, a con man, a pauper? The old schoolmaster who stays with Caspar when he is thrust into jail—who teaches him the alphabet, mathematics, and the names of the Muses from the constellations visible at night between the prison bars—believes Caspar to be an angel.

As these tantalizing conjectures proliferate, Caspar becomes the darling of Nuremberg's hoi polloi and its elite. He is feted at balls, courted by earls and countesses; then, to his astonishment and dismay, he is jettisoned, sent packing, to a humble job in the small town of Ansbach. As abruptly as they originally flocked to him, his idolaters, unable to solve his enigma, have fallen away. The only person left to him is the police inspector who has tailed him relentlessly—his shadow, his double, Caspar surmises, perhaps his only true father. In the novel's closing passage, Caspar lies dying, struck down in the snow by an unknown assailant, and the inspector, donning his quarry's discarded rose-embroidered vest, becomes indeed Caspar's mirror image:

> "He thinks I don't hear him because I am asleep, because I'm dead. They all think that of me, that I hear nothing when my ears are so clever, I can hear the harebells ring under the snow. . . ." His figure, distant, minute in the glass, begins to shake. But perhaps only the glass shakes. For his hand seems steady enough as he picks up the scissors and holds them poised, a little above his chest, while he feels for the beat of his heart with the left hand, standing there with the hand on his heart almost . . . like an ancient knight or saint. The briefest interval of remorse or wonder. Already he is thrusting out his right arm savagely, ready to plunge the scissors through my spoiled garden into his heart to prove to the world—what? What? My own heart stops. I raise my head and cry, "No!"—the first word I have said to him through all these frozen hours, this longest night. Just one word, *no*, but no means yes, stay, live, you are my shadow. You're all I ever had, maybe. . . . Already our eyes have met in the mirror. He drops the scissors. And like two conspirators we smile.
>
> Are we smiling still? I can't say. My head is back on the wet pillow. Now I can rest in peace, and my mind is an hourglass filling with snow. "Good night, son. Until tomor-

row." He has thrown his dark cape over his shoulders. Is he wearing my vest under the cape, my wounded rose on his heart? That too I cannot tell. I have forgotten. His shadow cape flies out the door into this frozen night where the street lamp, a lighted hedgehog or crown, bristles among the uncountable stars.

In his review of *Prince Ishmael* in the *New York Times* Gene Baro wrote that "Hauser succeeds in fusing the fantastic and the ordinary. If her theme is informed with wit, her purpose is serious." On the dust jacket of the British edition, novelist Mary Renault described *Prince Ishmael* as "a strange, lyrical and haunting book, written with great vividness and beauty."

In 1964 *A Lesson in Music*, a group of Hauser's short stories, was published. Anaïs Nin commented: "When people will tire of noise, crassness and vulgarity, they will hear the truly contemporary complexities of Marianne Hauser's superimpositions. A new generation trained to imagery by the film may appreciate her offbeat characters and skill in portraying the uncommon."

The Talking Room (1976), Marianne Hauser's most recent novel, for which she received a grant from the National Endowment for the Arts, is told through the voice of B, a thirteen-year-old, overweight, sex-smitten, pregnant girl who listens from her upstairs bedroom to all that transpires below in the "talking room." She has been begotten—via test tube? adoption? sexual intercourse?—to bestow an aura of propriety to the lesbian ménage of her mother, J ("wild, lost, beautiful") and Aunt V, a successful real estate operator. Their household in New York's West Village proposes comedy as well as chaos. The narration alternates between the outrageous and the bawdy yet branches out into passages of pathos and surpassing tenderness that absolve the protagonists' transgressions.

The story ends with J's homecoming after one of her periodic and protracted prowls through sleazy bars and flea-bitten hotels—outings that have Aunt V distractedly combing the waterfront and B, from loneliness, indulging her gluttony. At last, B sees J in her doorway:

> Hi, kid, mom whispered as she crept into my room out of the rain which had fallen through so many nights, had perhaps started that night when she had last disappeared, or so it seems to me now. Her rain-glazed face was swimming out of the door frame, toward my bed. And there was on her breath that

2

staging for her sake ~~or~~ and mine a perfect last act. ~~She always did have a theatrical bent, just like myself.~~

~~But~~ And now my ashes were gone. That was what appalled her and brought the tears to ~~the~~ her eyes. She had bungled the epilog he of my demise.

Every other detail had, thanks to her methodical ~~procedure~~ nature, come off without embarrassment to anyone. No queers or winos living it up in the kitchen. No party crashers falling off balconies. Nor had I chosen to rise from the ~~ashes~~ dead ~~visibly, a phoenix in the guise of a man,~~ to mortify her with one of my notorious, ~~absurd~~ impromptu scenes - a blow she may indeed have feared, despite her ~~sensible~~ stern dismissal of superstn~~i~~ous ~~nonsense such as ghosts and similar nuissances.~~

However, ~~the~~ ~~faintxremainsxmy~~ my lost ashes. ~~were gone~~ There was a phenomenon ~~reality~~ ~~That~~ ~~that~~ she ~~m~~ couldn't dismiss. ~~and was it~~ Had Mimi perhaps ~~Mimi who~~ her taken them to keep as a memento mori, ~~in honor of her departed dad?~~ But Mimi, her mother reminded her in ~~/~~ a disgruntled tone, hadn't even seen fit to attend my last rites ~~but had flown back to she forgot what~~ a breach of etiquette sure to raise eyebrows, ~~obscure college.~~ the old lady reminded her ~~It most assuredly wasn't Bryn Mawr or~~ impatiently ~~However, Gwen's mom added, shrugging, she never had been consulted~~ n't

Ah, well. She waved a hand. She had no intention to ~~on the matter. Let bygones be bygones. She had no intention to~~ stet ~~change her will and cut her only~~ randchild out of it. ~~cut poor little Mimi out of her will.~~

-It's not your will I'm worried about. It's his ashes!

Gwen was tearing at her hair. How could she, a rational woman, cope with the mystery, unless of course, she put the blame on me? Each object in the house had a fixed place, and what seemed to be missing was only hiding. Yes, I'm convinced she would have liked to point a finger at me. But I was dead and consequently must be blameless. For Gwen did not believe in

Revised page from the typescript for "The Memoirs of the Late Mr. Ashley," a recently completed novel (the author)

mysterious odor I well remember from other nights when she'd surface after her trip through oblivion: an odor no longer of gin but of something more highly distilled, rarefied, and almost otherworldly like a liquid reserved for angels.

Rain dripped from her poncho onto my face, my eyes as she was standing over me, trying to smile. Hi, kid. Hi, Mom. My face was wet with rain.

"The beauty and magic of *The Talking Room*," Larry McCaffery writes in *Contemporary Literature* (Winter 1978), "is difficult to analyze. The key would seem to be in the book's extraordinary prose patterns, which create in their complex, interrelated images a sustained vision of loneliness, the desire for love, and the necessity for escape, and always a haunting, dreamlike lyricism."

Since coming to the United States in 1937, Marianne Hauser has lived in Greenwich Village and, with her former husband, musician and composer Frederick Kirchberger, in the South and Midwest. She has spent time in the Pacific Northwest and Alaska with her son, Michael, a filmmaker; has traveled from Spain to North Africa, and from Yucatán through Guatemala to Peru. In the spring of 1980 she visited Brazil. Her spontaneous travels are reflected in her books, especially her story collection, *A Lesson in Music*.

For the past fifteen years her permanent address has been Manhattan; she has taught at Queens College (1966-1978) and New York University (1979). At present she lectures, studies Tai Chi, and, under an NEA grant, is completing a new novel: "The Memoirs of the Late Mr. Ashley." The narrator, an actor manqué, is dead and cremated, his ashes lost. But his voice—mischievous, arch, and inescapable—is fiercely alive, directing his own doom (or salvation?); his tragicomic figure emerges as the prototype of today's antihero.

As a private individual, Marianne Hauser is by nature adventurous, intrepid, intelligent, and witty. She is adamant and active in her stand against war and discrimination. Irreverent, even mocking, toward accepted norms, she finds pretense a subject for ridicule. The only thing she holds sacred is the human being—hapless, abused, absurd, and beautiful.

References:

"Anais Nin on Marianne Hauser," in *Rediscoveries*, edited by David Madden (New York: Crown, 1971), pp. 115-120;

John Tytell, "666 Words on Marianne Hauser," in *A Critical Ninth Assembling*, edited by Richard Kostelanetz (Brooklyn: Assembling Press, 1979).

Papers:

A collection of Marianne Hauser's manuscripts is at the University of Florida Library, Special Collections.

William Herrick
(10 January 1915-   )

Max L. Autrey
Drake University

BOOKS: *The Itinerant* (New York: McGraw-Hill, 1967; London: Weidenfeld & Nicolson, 1967);

Strayhorn (New York: McGraw-Hill, 1968; London: Weidenfeld & Nicolson, 1968);

Hermanos! (New York: Simon & Schuster, 1969; London: Weidenfeld & Nicolson, 1969);

The Last to Die (New York: Simon & Schuster, 1971);

Golcz (Frenchtown, N.J.: Columbia, 1976);

Shadows and Wolves (New York: New Directions, 1980);

Love and Terror (New York: New Directions, 1981);

. . . Kill Memory . . . (New York: New Directions, 1984).

Although he did not begin writing until 1956 and did not produce his first novel until 1967, William Herrick had long been stockpiling personal

William Herrick (Dick Duhan, courtesy of New Directions Publishing Corp.)

experiences that furnish subject matter for his fiction. The son of Nathan and Mary Saperstein Horvitz, he was born in Trenton, New Jersey, on 10 January 1915. The family moved to New York City when he was young, and he received his education in the public schools there. On 31 August 1948, he married Jeannette Esther Wellin, a family therapist; they have three children—Jonathan, Michael, and Lisa. The Herricks have lived mostly in the New York City area, presently residing in Old Chatham, New York.

As a young man during the Depression, Herrick worked on an anarchist farm commune in Michigan, hoboed around the country, organized black sharecroppers in the South, and worked for the furriers' union in New York. Later in that decade, he fought for the Republic in the Spanish civil war and was wounded on the Madrid front. From 1943 to 1969, he served as an official court reporter for the U.S. District Court, taking some time off to work as a writer on some of Orson Welles's projects.

Having had time to reflect on these personal experiences, Herrick makes direct, extensive, and repeated use of the autobiographical in plotting his narratives and sketching in the backgrounds of his characters. For example, his first novel, *The Itinerant* (1967), is an absorbing record of an adventurous young man's experiences during the 1930s and 1940s.

The Itinerant records the life story of Samuel Ezekiel (Zeke) Gurevich, the son of a poor Jewish family in New York City. Zeke emerges bawling and brawling from the womb and continues to so express himself throughout his early life. A self-styled maverick, he is deeply involved in life—loving, laughing, sharing, and being constantly on the move. His early life is filled with a variety of people, and he encounters numerous philosophies, religious beliefs, and political views.

As both child and man, Zeke is obsessed by whatever he loves or hates, and his life is a constant quest. For example, searching for his roots, Zeke periodically returns to the slums of New York City and eventually journeys to Europe to trace his family origin in Russia, France, and Lithuania. Even more important is his constant search for love. A child-rake, he tries to make love to his sister, Rebecca; permits the attention of a homosexual; and has his first major love affair with the beautiful, one-handed Miriam, his first cousin. At the age of thirteen he meets Rachel Farrell, an eighteen-year-old Irish girl, and is immediately possessed by love for her. This love is to endure throughout her lifetime, even though each of them marries twice. In love with loving, Zeke also lives for three months with a skinny peroxide blonde in the Mojave desert, has a brief and stormy marriage with a fellow union worker, and finally marries Pacifici, with whom he rears a family.

A maturing boy during the Depression, Zeke is precocious, wild, and rebellious, participating in various protests and searching for an ideal existence and a better world. This quest leads him to the Newday Co-operative Farm in Michigan, a utopian refuge, primarily for anarchists, from the Depression of the 1930s. Later, he devotes his life to searching for ways to relieve oppression in the world. He organizes black sharecroppers in Georgia, serves for two years with a maverick battalion fighting the fascists in the Spanish civil war, and later participates in World War II, first in the Canadian army and then in the U.S. infantry.

Central to his movements and activities is Zeke's search for self, which leads to much experimenting with and sampling of different beliefs and ways of life. Self-discovery necessitates understanding and acceptance of self. Eventually maturing, Zeke recognizes that guilt and death are inescapable. Further, he realizes that life holds no guarantees or even promises, but that it can yield much, although only briefly, if lived with honor.

As a first novel, *The Itinerant* is an uneven but promising work, which demonstrates considerable skill in characterization. In Zeke, it offers a sensitive portrait of a complex character—one who, in many ways, is representative of his time. The novel presents essentially a self-centered world, but one that is rapidly expanding. Complementing this broadening vision is the host of interesting personalities Zeke encounters; particularly noteworthy is the sensitive handling of the blacks in Georgia.

The narrative is highly episodic. The only continuing plot line is the periodic relationship between Zeke and Rachel; the only continuing movement is the general one leading to self-knowledge and mastery. In general this novel lacks the subtleties of Herrick's later works.

The Itinerant was not well received by critics. Granville Hicks, writing for *Saturday Review*, referred to it as "a strange novel, full of energy, written in a rough-and-ready style, wandering as restlessly as the itinerant himself." He further noted, however, that "Herrick has written a first novel that is full of flaws but does bring to life the Thirties and Forties."

Herrick had his second novel published the following year. Although he would soon return to subject matter relating to his personal experiences, in *Strayhorn* (1968) he offered evidence of his versatility as a writer by changing the theme, focus, and tone. This short novel records a crucial period in the life of David Strayhorn, whose existence has been chaotic following the violent deaths of his wife and daughter. Feeling totally deserted and driven by despair, he quits his job and seeks degradation. His efforts to escape by this means, and also through sex and madness, soon fail, and Strayhorn is beset by overwhelming inertia and fear. His life is marked by alternating violence and ennui. Strayhorn then enters into an unlikely relationship with an obese, mute singer, Madeleine Dearing, Opera Star. Both Strayhorn and Madeleine have sought escape—he in degradation and she in overeating. Both need someone to relate to physically, emotionally, and intellectually. Their on-again off-again romance leads to self-discovery for each character; and, becoming one, they find freedom in each other.

Strayhorn could be read as a psychological case study. Herrick skillfully handles contrary and conflicting emotions, offering penetrating insight into the paradoxes of love and hate, cruelty and kindness, and reveals the dimensions of human potential. Characterization and action are buttressed by parallels drawn from opera, myth, and legend.

The central relationship, which takes place in the present, is described by means of Strayhorn's direct narration; the reasons for his dilemma, rooted in the past, are presented through numerous flashbacks. These flashbacks are used to examine his relationships with his father (who does not love him), his schizophrenic mother, a dwarf (who is estranged from others by his physical appearance), a prostitute with whom he had a childhood encounter, and a lonely old miner. These scenes from the past—along with dream sequences, visions, and fantasies—are effectively inserted in Strayhorn's narration and gradually fill in the total picture.

Variations in style reflect the mental states being projected. Characters' language ranges from colloquial to formal expression, and from fragmentary utterances to poetic prose. The mood is essentially ambiguous: the narrative is often tongue-in-cheek; but, at times, the work represents a sincere treatment of penetrating human conditions and emotions. Similarly, the tone ranges from light and flippant to serious. The constant mixing of humor and pathos usually works, with one heightening the other.

Suffering a fate similar to that of Herrick's earlier novel, *Strayhorn* was unfavorably reviewed. Martin Levin called it "a work of modern primitivism," noting that "Otherwise, we would have to conclude that the author is simply inept and forgetful. How else to explain this medley of drama, fantasies and overheated imaginings?"

Producing his third novel in three years, Herrick returned to an event in which he had participated and which he had handled briefly in *The Itinerant*. Set in 1936 and 1937, during the Spanish civil war, *Hermanos!* (1969) records the conflict between Franco's forces, the Nationalists, supported by fascists inside and outside Spain, and the Loyalist forces of the legally elected Spanish republic, fighting to prevent fascism from taking over in Spain as it has in Italy and Germany. A third party is headed by Daniel Nuñez, a peasant who leads his guerrilla band against both of the major forces.

The novel focuses on Jake Starr, a twenty-five-year-old, swashbuckling American revolutionary who is the protégé of Carl Vlanoc, Stalin's representative in the Western hemisphere. Starr is a divided man: a dedicated, disciplined comrade, he is also an individual with a great need to succeed, to be a hero; under his controlled facade are the traits of a romantic. On his way to fight for the Loyalist cause in Spain, he stops in Paris, where he meets and falls in love with fellow party worker Sarah Ruskin.

The fighting in the novel occurs primarily in Madrid, the symbol of Free Spain, where Loyalist Spanish troops and their Interbrigade allies try to save the city from Nationalist forces. Among the volunteers serving in the American battalion of the Interbrigade are Joe Garms, a street fighter and army deserter who demonstrates outstanding courage on the battlefield, and Greg Ballard, a black who feels a great need to fight against the racial hatred of Hitler. The American volunteers suffer severe losses and seem to face certain defeat. Then, melodramatically, Jake Starr appears in the midst of the fighting and rallies the troops. Consequently, he is viewed as the savior of Madrid and becomes a legend in Free Spain.

Jake is next assigned by Vlanoc to hunt down and execute fifth columnists, a brutalizing experience. Learning how complex and dirty a revolution can be, Jake becomes hardened. The revolution calls for cold-blooded action; emotion, morality, and abstract thought are set aside. Reacting accordingly, Jake executes a man who has accused the American and his fellow party members of perverting socialism, committing acts of atrocity, being conscienceless, and not helping the cause of freedom. In doing so, however, Jake realizes that he has become a cold-blooded killer and feels guilt and shame. The tormented romantic hero has run the gamut of emotions: having reached a high with his love for Sarah and exultation as hero, he now reaches a low of despair and loneliness.

When the Loyalists go on the offensive to raise the siege of Madrid, the encounter is presented essentially from the American soldiers' viewpoint. Many are slaughtered; several others become disillusioned with the party. Sent to Barcelona, Jake helps Sarah and Ballard, who have denounced the party, to escape from Spain. In aiding them, he has betrayed the party; he is considered a traitor and ordered killed.

In *Hermanos!* Herrick balances actual combat and the related political manipulations. The perspective shifts from the filth and death of the battlefields in Spain, to the cunning and conniving of the party leaders in Paris. The novel is a perceptive study of war, concentrating on the personalities of those involved. War is seen as a force that strips its participants of the protective veneer of tradition and civilization, forcing the individual to struggle not only against the enemy but also within himself.

Although not highly original, Herrick's direct treatment of the war is effective and demonstrates his firm grasp of military conditions, as well as his understanding of the complexities of human relationships. He offers a study of courage, comradeship, and justice and shows at the same time how war can corrupt the human spirit.

Comparing *Hermanos!* to Ernest Hemingway's *For Whom the Bell Tolls* (1940), A. M. Rotondaro conceded Herrick's novel "comes out in second place," but in some respects, he added, it surpasses the Hemingway novel. Among the strengths Rotondaro noted were its world view, centralizing the hero, control, and its narrative of "man's quest for self and world discovery." Writing for the *Library Journal*, R. D. Harlan applauded Herrick's handling of the terrifying battle scenes, and Martin Levin, who had severely criticized *Strayhorn*, called *Hermanos!* a compelling novel whose "greatest distinction is its author's ability to articulate the Byzantine conflicts among the Loyalists with the flesh-and-blood participants who illustrate the name of the game."

In his fourth novel, Herrick also handled civil war but chose a smaller canvas. *The Last to Die* (1971) is the personal narrative of Ramón Cordes, who for twenty years has been a wandering professional revolutionary who "strums his lute and blood spouts from men's eyes." He has a predilection for conflict, with the knowledge, experience, instincts, and discipline to make him highly effective as a soldier; however, he is sometimes accused of being a romantic and has proven to have a fatal attraction to lost causes.

In the novel's frame narrative Ramón has been taken prisoner in the mountains of South America. During his confinement, while awaiting probable execution, he produces a written account of the activities leading to his arrest. In doing so, he assesses his life and arrives at an understanding of himself.

Ramón's account deals primarily with his recent activities as the leader of a small band of revolutionaries that attacks a silver mine. Deceived by a superior, they fail at their mission and all but Ramón are killed. Pursued by an army patrol, Ramón flees alone toward the border, facing difficult personal questions and demonstrating great feeling for his comrades and for Marguerite, whom he loves, while considering the politics of revolutionary actions.

When his thoughts turn to the more distant past, Ramón remembers his youth and some of his earlier combat experiences. He realizes he has found life "in the great confraternity which is an intensely fought battle." The various strands of the narrative converge at the end, with Ramon's incarceration. At the end of the novel he is given a pistol with which to shoot himself.

Although it is a short novel, *The Last to Die* is a penetrating study. As Ramón gains self-knowledge, the reader gains insights into the human condition. As the narrative offers a forceful study of a man of violence and his violent end, it also examines the nature of heroes and heroism.

The pace leading up to the assault on the mine is masterfully handled. Even though the reader has known the outcome from the beginning of the novel, suspense is maintained. Here, Herrick reveals his talent for presenting action scenes as well as depicting periods of stasis. The reader shares Ramón's experience.

The diction of Ramón's confession is simple and colloquial; the rhythm is natural and free-flowing. The imagery includes frequent and apt uses of highly poetic analogies often based on Greek mythology. Also giving distinction to Herrick's style is the underlying tone of subdued savagery.

Five years after the publication of *The Last to Die*, Herrick made a radical shift in both form and content when he produced his next novel. *Golcz* (1976) begins by emphasizing the complexities of an adult personality, especially the contrasting natures that coexist within the individual. Then it moves to an example of such a fragmented personality in the presentation of the title character. In this study of the two sides of one man, Bonaventure Golcz is the rational and civilized man while his doppleganger, Buzzard Golcz, is the physical and animalistic. Referring to him as his "curse," Bon laments Buzz's domination. Virtually a demonic force, Buzz thwarts Bon's decency and self-respect, ridicules him, creates obstacles to his plans, causes him to act according to his will, and humiliates him.

The narrative is a triangular love story. Bon becomes emotionally involved with a virgin aerialist, Clotile Gray, who is called the Silver Comet. Buzz eventually intrudes on the sexual relationship between Bon and Clo, bringing a new dimension to it. Clo finds that, although she needs Bon, she desires Buzz, adoring his bestiality. Consequently, she too develops a split personality. Becoming discontented and feeling a need to be free, Clotile goes to a woman's growth center, the Freedom Institute in Nebraska, where she receives supportive therapy and finds redemption through self-love. When Bon, aided by his liberated cousin Laura Golcz, goes to Nebraska to retrieve his Clo, he finds he is no match for the Amazons armed with their vibrators.

A victim of the female revolution, Bon dedicates his life to that revolution.

In the last episode, Clo is arrested for smuggling the *Communist Manifesto* into Russia, but she is released long enough to present her new aerial act at Moscow. Before CIAKGBMAO agents and the Central Committee, she performs her death-defying act, while below her, Buzz puts bears through a complementary act; he loses control and beast faces beast. At this point, the bestial Buzz disappears and the civilized Bon takes over, using his intelligence to overcome the bears. After he and Clo escape, Bon feels he has lost something in the arena. Clo tells him that what he misses is his childhood; further, she says she has lost the best lover she ever had. Clo and Bon, now unified personalities, drive over the Alps, making love along the way.

Essentially a "pop art" work dealing with significant timely subjects, *Golcz* is concerned with contemporary value systems and the shaping forces in society. Based on certain underlying assumptions and implications, the novel deals with such matters as cultural myths, the nature of man, and the accepted ways of viewing things. More specifically, it is concerned with psychology, sex, women's liberation, human evolution, and maturation of the individual. Through the character of Golcz, Herrick shows good and evil, right and wrong—the socially acceptable and unacceptable all springing from the same source. Viewed as an "animal with genius," man is struggling to subdue and overcome his natural bestiality.

The form complements the subject matter. In addition to the exaggerated opposing sides of Golcz's personality, the novel also exaggerates actions and speech and makes hyperbolic statements. For example, actions such as lovemaking are frequently presented as ritualistic, part of a choreographed dance of life. The result is facetious and irreverent. Yet the style is often poetic, marked by indirection, condensation, metaphor, and striking imagery. As *Publishers Weekly* noted, "This tale is written in a kind of shorthand that moves from the ribald vernacular to lyrical heights." Further, the writing is frequently punctuated by exclamations and sound effects. Despite a dependence on such gimmicks, the total effect is refreshing and entertaining.

Herrick again dramatically shifted his narrative approach in the superb short novel *Shadows and Wolves* (1980), where his literary expression is marked by stark simplicity, a high seriousness of tone, and an artistry that seems so natural that it may easily be underestimated.

Shadows and Wolves is set in Sevilla, Spain, forty years after the civil war and nine months after the death of Franco. Young revolutionists are becoming increasingly active, advocating liberty and justice and anticipating the time that they will govern. One of the leading rebels is Rodolfo Alfara, who has recently returned from a ten-year self-exile in England. The epitome of the angry young man, Rodolfo not only shares the objectives of his fellow terrorists, but he also intends to avenge the brutal murder of the socialist poet Federico García Lorca. The person suspected of the killing is General Luis Alfara Fernandez, Rodolfo's father. An old-time *falangista*, General Alfara is diametrically opposed to his son; a member of the ruling class, he opposes progress and sees depravity manifested in the violent actions of the young liberals. As the Alfara family is split, so is Spain divided by factions.

Paradoxically, the lives of these two opposing forces are entwined. Both men are stubborn and willful and cannot overcome the affinity of blood; both have committed acts of atrocity; both live lonely lives; and both seek out the same courtesan. Even their goals are similar; each has sworn to avenge a murder for which he feels the other was responsible. Also, both father and son almost worship at the statue of the great Spanish painter Murillo, whose works express the beauty of hope, the gentleness of yearning, and the despair and tragedy of life and death.

Throughout the novel Rodolfo stalks the general, seeking confirmation of his father's guilt. The climax comes late in the narrative with a direct confrontation between father and son. Despite its political basis, the problem is resolved on a human level; the conflicting emotions of love and hate soon give way to feelings of grief and sorrow. The worlds of both father and son are ending, and a new Spain is emerging.

In *Shadows and Wolves* Herrick offers an interesting handling of the hunt motif, of a cat-and-mouse game, skillfully shifting between the two primary viewpoints and between past and present. The result is an emotion-charged narrative that effectively sustains suspense; described with restraint and control, the action seems to be slowly building, moving toward an explosive conclusion. The style is marked by simplicity and directness, which effectively convey powerful emotions.

As one comes to anticipate in a Herrick novel, the strength of *Shadows and Wolves* is found in characterization. In its psychological probing of character, the novel concentrates on the duality of the two central characters and the paradox of their being both diametrically opposed and inextricably entwined. Caught in such microcosmic treatment is the total atmosphere of Spain during a crucial period. As Page Edwards explained in his review for *Library Journal*, "Though the mechanics leading to the confrontation between father and son are operatic and, at times, tedious, the symbolic meeting of old and new Spain is well done. Herrick is especially good at evoking the mood of Civil-War Spain and the aura of Lorca himself."

Herrick offers another timely study in *Love and Terror* (1981). Here the subject of the revolutionary is given significant redirection, which results in an outstanding literary study of international terrorism. As the novel begins, the Israelis have recently made a raid on a terrorist hideout— killing all the revolutionists and rescuing the Israeli hostages. The narrative is then presented in retrospect through the journals kept by two of the terrorists, Viktor X and Steven Wenders, and through interviews with older terrorists recorded by an unidentified American writer.

In its inclusive view of the subject, *Love and Terror* presents two generations of terrorists. Among the leaders of the young activists are Viktor X and Gabriele Rainer. Viktor is the embodiment of the revolutionary working class seeking to right the injustice of capitalism; however, he has self-doubts and finds it difficult to "liquidate his human feelings." His female counterpart, Gabriele, comes from an affluent family but is dedicated to supporting the working class; she is suffering from guilt over her background and seeking punishment for it. As the title indicates, the novel is a study of the close relationship between love and terrorism. Although deeply in love, Viktor and Gabriele struggle to set aside their personal feelings. The violence of their lives dictates the nature of their relationship. After they commit a violent terrorist act, Viktor and Gabriele return to their flat to make violent love. They eventually realize their killings in the name of the revolutionary cause are possibly the expression of a desire to kill each other in the name of love. In contrast to the young ones who are dedicated to the cause, the three old terrorists, "the old ones," are tired of violence, chaos, killings, and treachery. Clara Z., Avram ben Itzchak, and David Grad have come to an understanding which enables them to put things in their proper perspective, and they feel responsible for the young terrorists because they also had once held their great dream as more important than human life and, therefore, "helped to destroy the moral character of the great quest for a freer world, a more equitable world." One genera-

272.

was out of Hamburg. Gottfried thought of bribing ~~A~~ (the)

driver of a staff car, but it was too much of a risk.

Bribery was a capital offense for which a man could be

stood at the wall.

     "We were people of proven courage and great patience,"

~~Dora~~ (Clara) Z. now said, "otherwise we should not have been given

(that) ~~this~~ mission and survived to that point. But now that we

had decided to make a run for it, our courage began to

fade and with it our patience. Our mission was at an

end, we had no purpose but to run, so run we must.

Perhaps our antennae had relayed a message. You under-

stand, the sort of life Gottfried had led for so many

years, and I, though ~~of~~ (for a) shorter ~~duration~~ (time), makes every

hair on one's body an antenna. We had a multitude and

each was relaying a message. Danger! Run! We had

simply misread the type of danger. But run was pre-

cisely on point.

     "When the courage begins to break and the patience

~~to become~~ (becomes) short, there's a short circuit in the wiring,

and the ensuing fire makes poached eggs of the brain.

I should simply have picked up Karl, walked to the quay,

lifted my skirt above my knees and stepped on (to) the barge

heading down the Elbe. Women did that every day. Any-

thing to get away from the inferno. Having given up my

favors, received one in return, I and Karl could have

Revised page from the typescript for Love and Terror *(the author)*

248

tion of terrorists has made a questionable bequest to another.

The central action involves the carrying out of Plan Israel by the German and Arab terrorists. They hijack a flight from Tel Aviv to Paris and hold the Israeli passengers—including the three old terrorists—hostage, demanding the release of imprisoned comrades. The revolutionary spiral is now out of control, and the result is a bloody confrontation and death at the hands of Israeli commandos.

Serving virtually as a textbook on terrorism, *Love and Terror* is a realistic treatment of a current world problem, placing emphasis on the tragedy inherent in the loss of human potential that results from total dedication to destructive actions. In offering a detailed study of terrorists, the novel humanizes but does not excuse or damn them; instead, it presents an objective, dispassionate treatment. The terrorist view is complete, detailed, and intimate; the authenticity of the material is furthered by Herrick's explanation in a prefatory note that, although the characters and events in the novel are drawn from his imagination, his imagination has been informed by extensive reading of radical journals.

In his narrative Herrick skillfully interweaves two methods of presentation. The journal entries serve as interior monologues, revealing the thought processes, emotions, hopes and fears of the characters. In contrast, information obtained from interviews is essentially factual. The result is a novel that critics acclaimed for its intensity of feeling, its chilling impact, and its powerful exploration of the inextricability of love and terror.

. . . *Kill Memory* . . . (1984), Herrick's most recent novel, completes his terrorist trilogy. Set in Paris, the novel focuses on one day in the life of an old-time Stalinist, seventy-one-year-old Elizabeth. While she occasionally meets old comrades, such as Clara Z., most of the book is devoted to her memories of earlier party activities. Alan Cheuse of the *New York Times Book Review* called Herrick's spare, vivid narrative "a contemplative conclusion to a terrorist trilogy that offers both the intensity of thrillers and the depth of mainstream fiction."

Having published eight significant narratives since 1967, William Herrick has firmly established himself as an important contemporary American novelist. He writes on a consistently high level, demonstrating a knowledge and mastery of his craft, a superior imagination, an integrity of statement, and keen insight into character, conditions, and philosophies. Instead of delineating heroic actions, Herrick emphasizes the conditions, motivations, and states of mind that lead to such actions and the impact of confrontation on the individual. Restricting his focus, Herrick writes scenes that are crucial and revealing. The results are a noteworthy handling of characterization, a penetrating and often painful analysis of the nature of man, and an incisive exploration of the dimensions of contemporary society. In his intellectually and emotionally charged short novels, Herrick concentrates on the more elevated qualities of human life—honor, justice, courage, comradeship, and virtue. He presents these qualities from multiple viewpoints and explores them in a writing style that ranges from simple and straightforward to complex and eloquent.

Maureen Howard

(28 June 1930-   )

David M. Taylor
Livingston University

BOOKS: *Not a Word About Nightingales* (London: Secker & Warburg, 1960; New York: Atheneum, 1962);

Bridgeport Bus (New York: Harcourt, Brace & World, 1965);

Before My Time (Boston: Little, Brown, 1974);

Facts of Life (Boston: Little, Brown, 1978);

Grace Abounding (Boston: Little, Brown, 1982).

OTHER: *Seven American Women Writers of the Twentieth Century: An Introduction*, edited, with an introduction, by Howard (Minneapolis: University of Minnesota Press, 1977).

PERIODICAL PUBLICATIONS:

Fiction:

"Bridgeport Bus," *Hudson Review*, 13 (Winter 1960-1961): 517-527;

"Bed and Breakfast," *Yale Review*, 50 (March 1961): 390-404;

"Sherry," *Hudson Review*, 17 (Autumn 1964): 372-411;

"Three Pigs of Krishna Nura," *Partisan Review*, 38 (Winter 1971-1972): 423-436;

"Three Cheers for Mr. Spears," *Ms.*, 3 (October 1974): 60-65;

"Facts of Life," *Hudson Review*, 31 (Summer 1978): 249-268;

"Plagiarism," *New Yorker* (30 November 1981): 50.

Nonfiction:

"Recent Novels: A Backward Glance," *Yale Review*, 65 (Spring 1976): 404-413;

"Charting Life With a Daughter," *New York Times*, 1 June 1977, pp. C1, C14;

"Writers' Writers: Maureen Howard," *New York Times Book Review*, 4 December 1977, p. 74;

"Nobel Laureate: Isaac the Fool," *New Republic* (21 October 1978): 15-17;

"A Variety of Variations," *New York Times Book Review*, 8 June 1980, pp. 3, 44-45;

"The Making of a Writer: 'Before I Go I Have Something to Say,'" *New York Times Book Review*, 25 April 1982, pp. 7, 16;

"Why a Writer?," *Writer*, 95 (November 1982): 5-6;

" 'Buon Natale, Roma': A Holiday Visit to Italy Re-

kindles the Spirit," *New York Times*, 19 December 1982, pp. 9, 23;

"Forbidden Fruits," *Vogue*, 173 (March 1983): 384, 386, 428.

Maureen Howard exercises her considerable literary talent in a variety of forms, with an exceptional reverence toward her craft and a studied, disciplined style. The author of four novels and an autobiography, she is also a critic, essayist, editor, and teacher. The scope of her interests is evidenced in a sampling of fairly recent publications: an evaluation of the status of the novel in the *Yale Review*, a speculation of Isaac Singer's response to the Nobel Prize in the *New Republic*, a distinction between the pornographic and the erotic in *Vogue*, a poem for her writing students in the *New Yorker*, a travel piece about Christmas in Italy, a parody of Judith Krantz, and a piquant narrative on life with her daughter in the *New York Times*. Although she writes in the *New York Times Book Review* that she is "not a trained academician," Howard has taught literature and writing at the University of California at Santa Barbara, New York's New School for Social Research, Amherst College, Brooklyn College, and Columbia University. She describes teaching as "arduous and wonderful, not always at the same time" and expresses a grievance familiar to teachers of creative writing, what she calls a "popular nonsubject": "Imaginative power, like good looks or a rich uncle, is not distributed democratically." Her limited recourse involves going "back to craft, to discipline."

But the teaching, the essays, and the criticism are respites (she calls them "distractions") from her principal interest of writing fiction. Howard tells Sybil S. Steinberg in an interview for *Publishers Weekly*, "When I write a novel, when I'm writing something I really care about, I don't do anything else—I don't teach, I don't allow myself any distractions. . . . I work with great intensity, and I can't dilute it with other activities." She describes herself as a "slow writer," a characteristic reflected in the painstaking detail of her fiction and the polished precision of her prose. The care which she lavishes

Loretta Howard

received fellowships from the Guggenheim Foundation and from Radcliffe Institute. Howard currently resides with her third husband, a stockbroker, in Manhattan. She has a daughter, Loretta, from her first marriage.

Such biographical statistics lie unobtrusively in Howard's powerful, cathartic autobiography, *Facts of Life* (1978), which won a National Book Critics Circle prize for general nonfiction. The overall tone of the work is one of bitterness, and the work itself is exorcistic, the author's purging of the familial, social, religious, cultural, and economic spirits that have programmed and manipulated much of her life. Howard defines the facts of life as Culture, Money, and Sex and divides the work accordingly. She writes at some length about how she and her brother, George, growing up in Bridgeport, "a vaudeville joke of a town," were bandied between their mother's somewhat dilettantish insistence on "culture" and their glib father's anti-intellectual pose. Loretta Kearns, the daughter of a handsome, rags-to-riches Irishman who amassed a fortune through land speculation and an asphalt plant, was "a lady, soft-spoken, refined," but unfortunately "fey, fragmented." Conjugating Latin verbs and quoting disjointed bits from the classics, she fed her children a diet of artistic scraps, "broken off bits of art . . . a touch here and there," exemplified in the "Lehmbruck nude clipped out of *Art News* tacked in the pantry" and the "green pop-eyed Sienese Madonna folded in the Fannie Farmer cookbook." Loretta's desire to save her children from the cultural barrenness of their neighborhood led to ballet, piano, modern dance, elocution, and etiquette lessons for Maureen as well as to excursions to Bridgeport's limited offerings of art. Howard writes, "It would never have occurred to my mother that the finer things might be complicated for us, less than sheer delight," and she attributes her adult ambiguity toward art to her mother's influence: "I'm split, split right down the middle, all sensibility one day, raging at the vulgarities that are packaged as art, the self promotion everywhere, the inflated reputations. . . . Then again, everything is acceptable to me. . . . I am often sick of art." Counterweighing her mother's aspirations was her father's droll dismissal of the refined. William Kearns is described by Howard as "perverse and crude," a man who "once lathered up . . . could go on with great disdain about 'educated' people." Seminary trained and multitalented with an innate facility for languages, William served twenty years as detective of Fairfield County and was an enigma to his daughter until she understood that "the truth is that

on her writing accounts perhaps for her prudent handling of the product. "I never write hundreds of pages and then discard enormous amounts," she tells Steinberg. "I'm a Depression kid; you never threw out anything; you always made do, and you always did it with special care." The literary frugality is also evident in the fact that Howard's work often appears in much the same form in different publications.

Maureen Howard was born in Bridgeport, Connecticut, where her Irish Catholic family enjoyed a position of prominence within their working-class North End neighborhood. She took her B.A. from Smith College in 1952, following which she worked for two years in publishing and advertising. Her own teaching and that of her first two husbands, Daniel F. Howard and David J. Gordon, both college professors, have kept her close to academic settings, but she has traveled often and has lived in Italy and England. In 1967-1968, she

he loved roles, did a superb job of playing the seminarian, the cub reporter, the law student, the businessman, but like many inventive actors he tired of long runs." Howard poignantly relates her love-hate relationship with her father, labeling him "a terrible man . . . who easily drove his daughter to distraction" but concluding that "I learned more from his cruelty than from my mother's care."

Howard recounts with some hostility how her parents, ostensibly disinherited by her maternal grandfather when Loretta married the rakish, unpromising William, developed a "diseased attitude toward money" that required the family to live in sham poverty and sent her to work at sixteen in the public library. She bitterly questions why her grandfather's six-thousand-dollar diamond ring lay at "the bottom of a cracked sugar bowl in our pantry for years while my brother worked his ass off in a bursar's job at Yale and I went to Smith with humiliating clothes stitched up on my mother's sewing machine." It is also with bitterness that Howard recounts her prolonged ignorance of sex, blaming her mother for not having adequately informed her. She recalls her haunted childhood perceptions of sex, shaped by her stringent training at the Academy of Our Lady of Mercy and by the aberrant sexual behavior of the adults around her. Having herself been married twice at the time of the writing, she metaphorically describes "the amazing feats of modern marriage" as "the death-defying escapades of a man and woman on the high trapeze without a net."

Howard also explores the forces, such as the expected role of the young professor's wife and the demands of the American publishing industry, that have attempted to orchestrate her adult life. *Facts of Life* is her personal manifesto of apostasy, her declaration of freedom to exercise her own will—to the extent that she believes one can affect one's life through the exercise of will. As Alfred Kazin writes in the *New Republic*, the autobiography is "a ruthlessly personal story told, like all good self-histories, to deliver the author from evil, to liberate her from some pressing burdens." The liberation, however, does not produce the expected joy, a phenomenon that Kazin attributes to the fact that Howard "is a dogged snipper of the human heart who, despite life with other breeds, retains a narrowly focused Catholic suspicion of enthusiasm, especially her own."

Critics have often commented on the novelistic form of *Facts of Life*. Kazin notes the work's "sheer novelistic skill," and Katha Pollitt writes in *Saturday Review* that if the autobiography "has a flaw

it is that it is not a novel," for "Howard's people have the vitality of fiction characters, and her efforts to use them to explain her own life sometimes diminishes them." Frances Taliaferro describes the work in *Harper's* as "a writer's notebook, a rich source of portraits any one of which might turn into a novel." Many of the incidents and situations do appear in Howard's fiction. The pretentious and shallow academic partying sketched in *Facts of Life* is captured in detail in her first novel, *Not a Word About Nightingales* (1960), and the climax of that novel is drawn from the seven-year-old Maureen Howard's theatrical suicide attempt (performed with a harmless grapefruit knife and occasioned by the disgrace she wreaked upon her family by breaking her fast in preparation for her First Holy Communion). Howard's second novel, *Bridgeport Bus* (1965), also relies heavily on autobiographical detail, particularly in the descriptions of the city itself.

In *Facts of Life*, Howard speaks deprecatingly of *Not a Word About Nightingales*, calling it "a mannered academic novel, actually a parody of that genre and so at a further remove from life." The novel did not gain Howard a large readership, but critics have treated it more kindly than the author. *Not a Word About Nightingales* is the story of the temporary upset of order in the lives of the Sedgely family occasioned by the father's desire to change his life. Fifty-year-old Albert Sedgely, a relatively successful scholar and full professor at a reputable New England college, decides while on sabbatical in Europe with his wife of almost twenty years that his life, although not unpleasant, has been "trivial and anticlimactic" and that his memories are "dreary beyond reason." While visiting Perugia, he makes a conscious and what he then believes to be a rational decision to live there, allows his wife, Anne, to return home, abandons his study of Pope's versification in the *Dunciad*, and begins to assimilate the trappings of his new life of "feeling"—yellow suede shoes with pointed toes, a gaudy striped suit, an enormous tapered moustache, a dark tan, a Rubenesque Italian mistress, and a congenial reputation among the locals. Eighteen months later, Albert's daughter, Rosemary, is dispatched to Perugia by the distraught Anne to jolt her father back to his senses and bring him home, but her father's waning joy in his new life—his growing realization that his life is not the success he thought it to be, "that no true emotion would *ever* come to his already dying, now tediously repeated, passion" for his mistress—is paralleled by Rosemary's growing enchantment with Italian life. The discovery of her father's affair and her fear of her own awakening

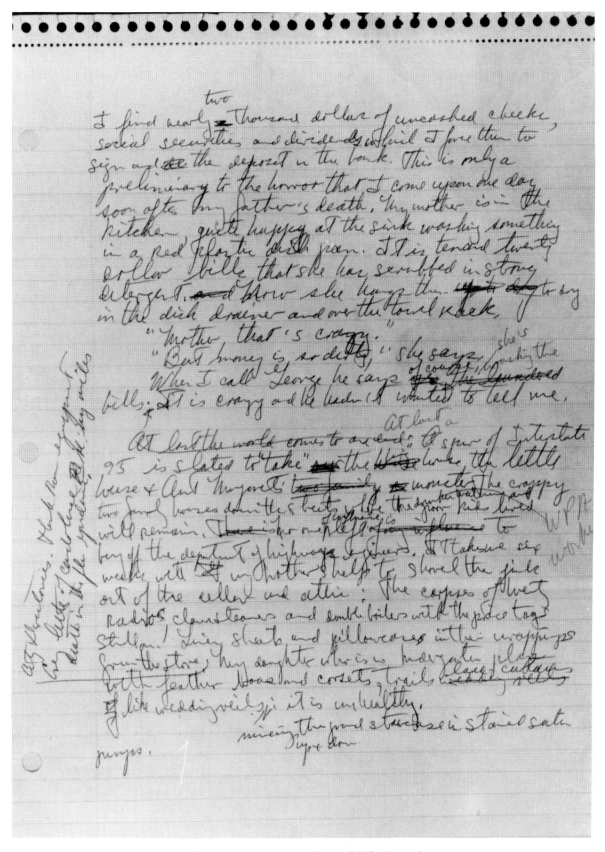

Page from the manuscript for Facts of Life *(the author)*

sexuality after a comical encounter with a young Italian turn the eighteen-year-old Rosemary's delight into revulsion, and her staged suicide attempt conveniently allows her and her father to return home. Ironically, Anne suffers the most from the rapprochement, sacrificing her newly found love for Will Aldrich, the sage, much respected dean of a men's college, in order to return the Sedgely household to the status quo. The reestablishment of order is a matter of complacent acceptance instead of joy for Albert and Anne, an enactment of Will's assessment of life: "We go from pose to pose, not hearing, not listening—our voices are drowned out." Only Rosemary is happy in her recovered safety, finding the Sedgely house "exactly the way she wanted it . . . quiet and so divinely normal."

Doris Grumbach writes in the *New York Times Book Review* that Howard's intent in *Not a Word About Nightingales* is to tell "about the deadly continuity of the marital condition," a condition from which "there is no permanent exit, only acceptance and repetition of marriage's inexorable routine." But the subplot involving Carol Perkins suggests that Howard is making a larger statement about the limited results of willful attempts at change and the necessary stoic acceptance of order. A mousy, middle-aged philosophy scholar, Carol decides at the birth of her first child that life has escaped her. She turns from her scholarly journals to the world of young motherhood, typified by Elaine Green, a beautiful but brainless professor's wife, whom Howard draws convincingly down to the lisp. But Carol's immersion into the world of hair rinses and bottle warmers is short-lived, and she returns, albeit with sadness and questionable conviction, to her scholarly regimen. Howard writes of her first novel in *Facts of Life*: "If there is any strength there (I will never look back to see) it can only be in what I wanted that book to reflect: a sense of order as I knew it in the late fifties and early sixties with all the forms that I accepted and even enjoyed: that was the enormous joke about life—that our passion must be contained if we were not to be fools."

Howard's subsequent novels reflect the changed philosophy documented in *Facts of Life*. Her characters have limited control of their fates, but the exercise of will to effect change is championed rather than discouraged. It appears that the author believes that things will generally turn out badly, but the attempt at change is worthwhile. Howard says in the 1982 *Publishers Weekly* interview that men must face the unbelievable challenges of the modern world "with grace and integrity" and "must carry on in an absurd world as balanced,

mature individuals." She adds, "I want my characters to echo the excitement of real lives—lives that appear placid and ordinary on the surface but are really heroic efforts of will." The change in philosophy is accompanied by a change in technique. The later novels are more loosely structured, more tangential than *Not a Word About Nightingales*, with a versatile handling of point of view and an eschewing of tidy denouement. Howard says in *Publishers Weekly*, "I like spare books. I like density, not volume. The large, realistic, telling-it-all novel is not of interest to me. I like to leave something to the imagination." Her current concept of the novel makes it something of a prolonged allusion to life, dependent for consummation upon the reader's participation. "The most exciting thing in the world for me is the idea of audience," she says, "the knowledge that someone has had to do some work on the other side—to understand what you've implied, to imagine something in a new way." Not all critics have agreed with Howard's belittling estimate of her first novel nor with her redirection toward "spare" books. Anatole Broyard, writing in the *New York Times Book Review*, expresses a preference for Howard's first novel over her most recent, *Grace Abounding* (1982). Countering Howard's comment on her preference for novels "that leave something to the imagination," Broyard writes, "I didn't find 'Not a Word About Nightingales' spare. On the contrary, it was pleasingly full of life and fine details. And while I didn't have to fit the pieces together, it certainly left something to my imagination." The difficulty with *Grace Abounding*, Broyard explains, is that "I was so engrossed in trying to fit the pieces together that I'm afraid I wasn't able to feel or think about the characters, much less identify them," adding that Howard's "spareness seems like an unnecessary anxiety about sophistication, a fear of talking too much or too effusively." Martin Levin expresses similar sentiments in his comments on *Bridgeport Bus* in the *New York Times Book Review*, calling *Not a Word About Nightingales* "a beautifully orchestrated little tour de force" and saying that *Bridgeport Bus*, although "still a sunburst with more than the average quota of sparkle and depth," is "written in a different key" and "lacks the tidy proportions of her first."

Bridgeport Bus is an expansion of the short story of that title, which was published first in the *Hudson Review* and later included in *Prize Stories 1962: The O. Henry Awards*. The protagonist of the novel is the gaunt, unattractive Mary Agnes Keely, a thirty-five-year-old virgin possessed of a wry wit, a tendency toward self-deprecation, and a talent for writing. She has worked for seventeen years at the Standard Zipper Factory in Bridgeport and resides with her widowed mother, with whom she plays a "cannibalistic" game—each chewing away at the other through their nonstop bickering. Ag lives vicariously through literature. "I feel pain where I have never been touched, dissipation in my early-to-bed soul," she says upon her reading of the modern French poets. A final confrontation with her mother sends Ag off to New York, where her romantic illusions about embracing life dissipate in the face of reality. She secures a job as a copywriter for Wunda-Clutch, the invention that is to render the zipper obsolete, and enters into an affair with Stanley Sarnicki, an advertising-agency artist. Her circumstances deteriorate rapidly after she is impregnated by a member of a group of bohemian artists she has adopted, and the novel ends with Ag, alone, unhealthy, and grotesquely fat, in labor with her child in the Good Shepherd Home for wayward girls. But she is in mental labor as well and births an epiphanic declaration about her life: "I will say to my child, your mother burst forth upon the whole dry world and knew . . . she had triumphed, that it was no great sin to be, at last, alone."

The portrait of Ag is enriched by that of her roommate, Lydia Savaard. Lydia's storybook marriage has crumbled around her husband's violent insanity, and as Ag reaches forth, almost gluttonously, to embrace the world, Lydia wants "nothing for herself except to go back to the beginning, stand in the first Garden and say, 'I don't care for apples, thank you.' " Also serving as foil for Ag is Francis, her conformist FBI-agent brother. Whereas Ag concludes "that permanence and knowledge may not be the perfectly grand keystones of Western Civilization we have always believed; we hold on sentimentally when we should push forward disastrously," Francis, like a "larva moth," follows "the expected road without any hitches" and becomes "nothing more, nothing less than his training and his character dictated." Another prominent character is Ag's showgirl cousin, Sherry, the prototypical promiscuous yet innocent starlet driven to suicide by the rapacious forces of show business. Several critics have remarked that Sherry's story violates the structure of the novel. Daniel Stern writes in *Saturday Review* that "Sherry's persistent presence is never fully integrated into the tale, and the resulting imbalance is a serious flaw in what is otherwise so fine a book," and Martin Levin comments in the *New York Times Book Review* that Ag's "mundane reminiscences of her cousin" cause the

novel to lose "a fluency it never quite regains." The novel, however, is by its very nature loosely structured, with point of view shifting between third-person omniscient and the first person of Ag's journal entries, sketches, and drama. This structure allows Howard to explore characters and subplots that add resonance to the primary story of Ag. Sherry, like Lydia and Francis, serves through contrast to heighten the reader's perception of Ag's condition and achievement. The loose structure also allows Howard to engage in artistically handled special effects. The episode in which Ag accompanies Stanley to Brooklyn to meet his mother and sister is interspersed with lines from Spenser's "Prothalamion," but the shallow pretentiousness of the Sarnickis' lives makes it clear that the Thames of Ag's wedding song is that of Eliot's *The Waste Land*, a corrupted version of the original. Similarly, a chapter in which Ag's circumstances continue to deteriorate is sprinkled with lines from children's rhymes—the nonsense verse of Ag's condition.

Bridgeport Bus is a declaration of independence for its female protagonist, but Howard is wary of the feminist label. She tells Steinberg in *Publishers Weekly*, "I wrote 'Bridgeport Bus' . . . , which I think is one of the most heartfelt feminist novels, long before that genre appeared. But the kind of blatant statement which seems to be what some women have to hang novels on, is nothing I'd be interested in." In her introductory essay to *Seven American Women Writers of the Twentieth Century: An Introduction* (1977), a collection of biocriticism which she edited, Howard de-emphasizes the sex of the writers, explaining that "the particular problem of being a woman is no more or less difficult for a real artist than problems of place or diction—or for that matter the problem of being an American or an accurate reflection of one's time." She adds that although "the dimension of female concern and response is there" in the works of Carson McCullers, Eudora Welty, and the other writers who are included, "a laundry list of feminist grievances is as harmful to any serious study of women's literature as the critical contrivance of politely rushing to open doors for the ladies."

Howard's third novel, *Before My Time* (1974), is as loosely structured as *Bridgeport Bus*, and critics have often likened the work to a collection of related short stories. Two portions of the novel did appear earlier as stories in *Ms.* and *Partisan Review*. The nucleus of the various segments is the relationship between Laura Quinn, a forty-year-old Cambridge journalist and housewife, and her second cousin, seventeen-year-old Jim Cogan, who is sent from the

Bronx to stay with the Quinns while he awaits arraignment on charges of drug possession and conspiracy to blow up the main branch of the New York Public Library, both charges a result of his half-hearted affiliation with the Krishna Nuru religious sect. Like Eliot's Gerontion, Laura believes that her time has passed without her having experienced the great moment: "I've drunk too little and now the good wine's gone to vinegar. Something was supposed to happen that was not prose." Her writing, which "has been a kind of thin flowing-out from herself, a false abundance," has not penetrated to the personal and thus has not satisfied, and she has spent her life in competition with the spirit of her charismatic brother, Robert, now dead twenty years. Jim Cogan is for Laura a reincarnation of Robert, and she loves and envies him, envies particularly his youth. *"I want to be as he is now*, to crouch at the starting line and I'm furious that it can't be," Laura says. "I have grown thin and old . . . in my spirit." She decides to save the self-assured, recalcitrant Jim, to discourage his plans to run away by making him acknowledge the interconnections between his life and the lives of others and making him understand that his story, "so special, wild, wonderful to him," is "absolutely ordinary." But in the process of leading Jim to discovery, Laura arrives at her own discovery that she can defeat the "good girl" that she despises in herself. In the closing pages of the novel, Laura entreats Jim to live out her reckless fantasies by running away, but Jim, ironically, tells her, "It isn't reasonable" and returns to New York to face the charges. The new Laura is reconciled with her estranged husband, realizing that her time has not passed, that it is yet to come.

The stories of numerous other characters appear in *Before My Time*, many of which are only obliquely related to the core story of Laura and Jim, but each of which is satisfying in itself. Howard's detailed portraits of the Cogans of New York are particularly well executed. Jim Cogan's mother, Millicent, is a middle-aged woman who copes with the death of her private dreams through her afternoon tippling, her embellished memories of her earlier career as secretary to the president of a publishing firm, and her hopes for her children. His father, Jack, is a chronic gambler and a failed salesman who finds peace through an odd friendship with an aged Jewish tycoon who has been put out to pasture by his sons. The Cogan twins, Cormac and Siobhan, described early in the novel as "two bodies with one mind," make a futile attempt to halt time as maturity forces their separate identities.

Howard's most recent novel, *Grace Abounding*, also accommodates a host of characters. A nominee for the 1983 PEN/Faulkner Award for Fiction, *Grace Abounding* features a female protagonist not unlike Laura Quinn. Maud Dowd is a forty-three-year-old widow living an excruciatingly lonely and static existence in her Shrewsbury, Connecticut, farmhouse with her teenage daughter, Elizabeth. Maud's feeble battle against ennui involves her persistent sexual fantasies; a voyeur's interest in the lives of her spinster neighbors, the Le Doux sisters; and a mania of collecting curios and their histories, as if "each useless thing brought into the house . . . could be invested with some history to approximate intimacy and warmth." Maud's dying mother's dying nurse describes Maud as "that pathetic creature with her neutered widow's ways, her life a series of distractions." The turnabout in Maud's life occurs when in one season her mother dies, she has "an idle and disastrous affair with a coward," and she discovers her daughter's marvelous singing talent. Mother and daughter move to New York so that Elizabeth can receive vocal training, and Maud marries, takes a doctorate in psychology, and begins a career as a therapist, primarily for children. Life does not, however, become painless for Maud—it never does for Howard's characters—but the exertion of will, the active participation in life, effects a substantial amelioration of her previous condition. Elizabeth's life follows much the same pattern as Maud's. She abandons her singing career for marriage, leading her mother to lament that "her daughter's art was sacrificed to a crass man with a corporate image." But Elizabeth's chance encounter with Mattie Le Doux revitalizes her drive to perfect her talent. One of the most colorful characters in Howard's fiction, Mattie is an earthy, garish spinster as renowned in Shrewsbury for her sexual promiscuity as her sister, Jane, is for the poetry published under her name, but written by Mattie. When Mattie, racing to complete her voluminous history in verse in the face of her approaching death, reveals the truth about the authorship of the poetry, she tells Elizabeth what most Howard protagonists strive to say on the eves of their deaths: "I had it all, perfection of the life and of the work."

Sybil Steinberg notes that "there is every indication that 'Grace Abounding' may be the breakthrough book" for Howard, the work that gains her a much deserved wider readership. But Steinberg adds that "Howard affects unconcern one way or the other," saying, in character with one who has proved herself to be an earnest and studious practitioner: "I will continue to write as I do in any case. I'm not going to say: 'This line of goods isn't selling, let's try another.' "

References:

Leslie Bennetts, "Creative Women of the 20's Who Helped Pave the Way," *New York Times*, 10 April 1978, p. A20;

Anatole Broyard, "On Maureen Howard," *New York Times Book Review*, 21 November 1982, p. 51;

Walter Clemons, "Lantern Show: *Before My Time*," *Newsweek* (20 January 1975): 74-76;

Haskel Frankel, "Seductive Sabbatical," *Saturday Review* (10 March 1962): 26;

Paul Gray, "Lost Generation: *Before My Time*," *Time* (27 January 1975): 78;

Doris Grumbach, *"Before My Time," New York Times Book Review*, 19 January 1975, p. 5;

Diane Johnson, "Dining Out in Her Own House," *New York Times Book Review*, 12 November 1978, pp. 13, 24;

Alfred Kazin, *"Facts of Life," New Republic* (9 September 1978): 37-38;

Martin Levin, "A Reader's Report," *New York Times Book Review*, 29 August 1965, p. 28;

Katha Pollitt, "Midlife Writing," *Saturday Review* (28 October 1978): 43-44;

Elaine Reuben, "Recent, Notable Fiction: *Before My Time*," *New Republic* (8 February 1975): 25-26;

Roger Sale, "The Realms of Gold," *Hudson Review*, 28 (Winter 1975-1976): 616-628;

Sale, "Staying News," *Sewanee Review*, 83 (Winter 1975): 212-224;

Sybil S. Steinberg, "Maureen Howard," *Publishers Weekly* (15 October 1982): 6-7;

Daniel Stern, "No Sin to Be Alone," *Saturday Review* (25 September 1965): 42;

Frances Taliaferro, *"Facts of Life," Harper's*, 257 (November 1978): 91-92.

John Jakes

(31 March 1932-   )

Martin H. Greenberg and Walter Herrscher
University of Wisconsin at Green Bay

BOOKS: *The Texans Ride North* (Philadelphia: Winston, 1952);

A Night for Treason (New York: Bouregy & Curl, 1956);

Wear a Fast Gun (New York: Arbor House, 1956; London: Ward, Lock, 1957);

The Devil Has Four Faces (New York: Mystery House, 1958);

This'll Slay You, as Alan Payne (New York: Ace, 1958);

The Seventh Man, as Jay Scotland (New York: Bouregy, 1958);

The Impostor (New York: Bouregy, 1959);

I, Barbarian, as Jay Scotland (New York: Avon, 1959); revised as John Jakes (New York: Pinnacle, 1976);

Johnny Havoc (New York: Belmont, 1960);

Strike the Black Flag, as Jay Scotland (New York: Ace, 1961);

Johnny Havoc Meets Zelda (New York: Belmont, 1962);

Sir Scoundrel, as Jay Scotland (New York: Ace, 1962); revised as *King's Crusader*, by John Jakes (New York: Pinnacle, 1977);

The Veils of Salome, as Jay Scotland (New York: Avon, 1962);

Johnny Havoc and the Doll Who Had "It" (New York: Belmont, 1963);

G.I. Girls (Derby, Conn.: Monarch, 1963);

Arena, as Jay Scotland (New York: Ace, 1963);

Traitor's Legion, as Jay Scotland (New York: Ace, 1963); revised as *The Man from Cannae*, by John Jakes (New York: Pinnacle, 1977);

Ghostwind, as Rachel Ann Payne (New York: Paperback Library, 1966);

Tiros: Weather Eye in Space (New York: Messner, 1966);

When the Star Kings Die (New York: Ace, 1967);

Famous Firsts in Sports (New York: Putnam's, 1967);

Brak the Barbarian (New York: Avon, 1968; London: Tandem, 1970);

Making It Big (New York: Belmont, 1968);

Great War Correspondents (New York: Putnam's, 1968);

Great Women Reporters (New York: Putnam's, 1969);

The Asylum World (New York: Paperback Library, 1969; London: New English Library, 1978);

Mohawk, The Life of Joseph Brant (New York: Crowell-Collier, 1969);

The Hybrid (New York: Paperback Library, 1969);

The Last Magicians (New York: New American Library, 1969);

The Planet Wizard (New York: Ace, 1969);

Tonight We Steal the Stars (New York: Ace, 1969);

Secrets of Stardeep (Philadelphia: Westminster, 1969);

Brak the Barbarian Versus the Sorceress (New York: Paperback Library, 1969; London: Tandem, 1970);

Brak Versus the Mark of the Demons (New York: Paperback Library, 1969; London: Tandem, 1970);

Six-Gun Planet (New York: Paperback Library, 1970; London: New English Library, 1978);

Black in Time (New York: Paperback Library, 1970);

Mask of Chaos (New York: Ace, 1970);

Master of the Dark Gate (New York: Lance, 1970);

Monte Cristo 99 (New York: Curtis, 1970);

Mention My Name in Atlantis (New York: DAW, 1972);

Violence (Elgin, Ill.: Performance Publishing, 1972);

Wind in the Willows, music by Claire Strauch (Elgin, Ill.: Performance Publishing, 1972);

Witch of the Dark Gate (New York: Lancer, 1972);

Conquest of the Planet of the Apes (New York: Award, 1972);

A Spell of Evil (Chicago: Dramatic Publishing, 1972);

Stranger with Roses (Chicago: Dramatic Publishing, 1972);

Time Gate (Philadelphia: Westminster, 1972);

Gaslight Girl, music by Strauch (Chicago: Dramatic Publishing, 1973);

Pardon Me, Is this Planet Taken?, music by Gilbert M. Martin (Chicago: Dramatic Publishing, 1973);

On Wheels (New York: Paperback Library, 1973);

Doctor, Doctor!, music by Martin (New York: McAfee Music, 1973);

Shepherd Song, music by Martin (New York: McAfee Music, 1974);

Wear a Fast Gun (New York: Arcadia House, 1974; London: Ward, Lock, 1975);

The Bastard, 2 volumes (New York: Pyramid, 1974); republished as *Fortune's Whirlwind* (London: Corgi, 1975) and *To an Unknown Shore* (London: Corgi, 1975);

John Jakes (Jeff Amberg, The Island Packet*)*

The Rebels (New York: Pyramid, 1975; London: Corgi, 1979);

The Seekers (New York: Pyramid, 1975; London: Corgi, 1979);

The Furies (New York: Pyramid, 1976; London: Corgi, 1979);

The Titans (New York: Pyramid, 1976; London: Corgi, 1979);

The Warriors (New York: Pyramid, 1977; London: Corgi, 1979);

The Best of John Jakes, edited by Martin H. Greenberg and Joseph D. Olander (New York: DAW, 1977);

The Lawless (Garden City: Doubleday, 1978; London: Corgi, 1979);

Brak: When the Idols Walked (New York: Tower, 1978);

The Bastard Photostory (New York: Jove, 1980);

The Americans (New York: Jove, 1980);

Fortunes of Brak (New York: Dell, 1980);

North and South (New York: Harcourt Brace Jovanovich, 1982; London: Collins, 1982).

PERIODICAL PUBLICATIONS: "The Historical Family Saga," *Writer,* 92 (November 1979): 9-12ff.;

"Three Essentials for a Successful Writing Career,"
    Writer, 94 (July 1981): 9-12ff.

John Jakes was a well-established commercial writer in several genres when he was thrust into national prominence with the publication of *The Bastard* (1974), the first of his "Bicentennial Series" of novels timed to coincide with the celebration of the two-hundredth anniversary of the signing of the Declaration of Independence. The series ultimately totaled eight books and became a landmark in American publishing—all eight were best-sellers on the major listings; volumes four through eight were number one on the lists, and the last three went straight to the first position on publication. In addition, the process by which the books appeared played a major role in changing American paperback publishing.

John Jakes was born and raised in Chicago, the son of John Adrian and Bertha (Retz) Jakes. His father became general manager at the Railway Express Company. After a year at Northwestern University Jakes transferred to DePauw University in Greencastle, Indiana, which had a noted creative writing program, from which he graduated with an A.B. in 1953. He was already writing for submission while an undergraduate, selling short stories and completing *The Texans Ride North* (1952), a historical novel for young adults that was published by Winston. While at DePauw he met and married Rachel Ann Payne.

He entered graduate school at Ohio State University the following year, completing an M.A. in American literature. A natural storyteller, he had little trouble breaking into the genre markets in the twilight of the pulp era, selling to such magazines as *Amazing Stories* and *The Magazine of Fantasy and Science Fiction,* whose editor, Anthony Boucher, had purchased his first story. For the next sixteen years he worked in the creative departments of several regional and national advertising agencies, after an initial job as copywriter. In 1960 he moved to the Rumrill Company in Rochester, New York, working as a copywriter until 1961, when he attempted to write full-time, an effort that lasted until 1965. While he sold steadily during this period, his income was not sufficient to support himself, his wife, and four children. In 1965 Jakes joined Kircher Helton and Collett in Dayton, Ohio, as a copywriter, leaving that firm in 1968 to join Oppenheim Herminghausen and Clarke, also in Dayton, as copy chief and then vice-president. In 1970 he became creative director of Dancer Fitzgerald Sample in the same city.

Jakes was writing during his spare time and selling almost everything he had written. In the sixteen years between 1954 and 1970 he sold some thirty-eight books and 200 short stories to an array of magazines, ranging from *Galaxy Science Fiction* to *Mike Shayne's Mystery Magazine*. His short fiction included two dozen Westerns; some sixty mystery, suspense, and spy stories; and about seventy-five science fiction and fantasy stories. In addition, between 1970 and 1974 Jakes wrote four plays and the librettos and lyrics for six musicals, which are performed by stock and amateur groups throughout the United States. This prodigious output, produced while Jakes was holding demanding full-time jobs, is, not unexpectedly, uneven. Of the thirty-eight books one is a Western, eight are mystery/suspense, seven are historical adventures, four are nonfiction for young adults, and the remaining eighteen are science fiction or fantasy. Most of the novels are characterized by attention to detail, careful plotting, epic sweep, and—where required— strong historical research.

Of his early novels and stories, the best are in the historical and the science-fiction/fantasy fields. Jakes was much more than simply a pedestrian science fiction writer. He did some outstanding work in this demanding popular genre, and his collection, *The Best of John Jakes* (1977), contains excellent work, most notably the novella *Here Is Thy Sting*, which focuses on the meaning of death, and "The Sellers of the Dream," a moving and devastating attack on our consumer society.

Within the science fiction field Jakes is best known for his tales of "Brak the Barbarian," entertaining spoofs of the "Sword and Sorcery" subgenre. Unfortunately the Brak material has tended to obscure his more important work, which leans in the direction of social satire. Of his more than twenty science fiction/fantasy novels and collections, at least three deserve special mention: *Six-Gun Planet* (1970), *Black in Time* (1970), and the brilliant *On Wheels* (1973).

Six-Gun Planet reflects Jakes's interest in the historical and mythical American West. Patterned on the formula Western, it describes a society on another planet, complete with gunfighters, Indians, and horses—some of whom are robots. The planet called Missouri turns out to be an attempt to create a replica of what some people believe to be an ideal past, one uncorrupted by modern technology and modern concerns. The planet is, of course, a product of the most modern technology available, and the novel can be read as a humorous but grim warning. *Six-Gun Planet* is superior social satire, rich in accurate Western detail with several memorable scenes, especially the climactic gunfight, which parodies the conventions of the Western without disrespect for them.

Black in Time is noteworthy for its choice of subject matter, which is the history of blacks in the United States and Africa. It features Harold Quigley, a young black professor who travels back in time studying the history of his people. He becomes involved in a struggle to prevent others from changing history in an effort to perpetuate slavery, while at the same time fighting against the militants of BURN (Brothers United for Revolution Now), who intend to murder Mohammad and thus prevent the destruction of the black empires that once flourished in West Africa. Although the book was very much a product of its time and is now rather dated, it nevertheless contains considerable dramatic tension and accurate history. It was also one of the first American science-fiction novels to treat this subject matter.

On Wheels is Jakes's finest effort in the science-fiction field, a superior novel depicting a richly detailed future American society based on this country's infatuation with the automobile. It tells of a time when overpopulation has forced large numbers of people to live on the interstate highway system, constantly moving and organized in clans with names like the Cloverleafs, the Holidays, the Johnsons, and others taken from the environment in which they live. Jakes carefully develops this culture, which never permits its members to go below forty miles per hour and whose central myth is the Firebird, seen only in the final moments before death. This almost totally neglected novel is a minor masterpiece of social speculation.

Many of Jakes's early historical novels were published under the pseudonym "Jay Scotland," and they proved to be very important to the development of his career. All are solidly researched, well-plotted commercial novels with believable characters. Their existence made possible Jakes's authorship of the Bicentennial Series (The Kent Family Chronicles), since he was recruited on the basis of a recommendation by fellow fiction writer Don Moffitt, who had been impressed by them. The series was conceived by book-packager Lyle Kenyon Engel, who sold the idea to Pyramid Books, one of the smaller and less prestigious paperback houses. The success of the series was overwhelming; there

are currently some forty-five million copies of the eight books in print.

The Kent Family Chronicles is notable for its historical scope. In these eight novels, Jakes covers American history from the Revolution to the beginning of the twentieth century by creating the robust Kent clan, whose adventurous lives form the basis for the various narrative threads in the novels. A vivid, sometimes lurid, depiction of the American past, these multigenerational novels feature strong action, appealing characters, and large dollops of romance and sex—all of which have contributed to their phenomenal success.

Jakes attributes the appeal of this series partly to its timing. Because we live in an uncertain age, he says, "We are anxious to be reassured that although we have gone through bad times before, we have survived. The past helps us more readily understand and cope with the present" ("The Historical Family Saga," *The Writer* [November 1979]). He thinks that in the Kents he has created the "kind of people we would like to see more of in America today. They are by no means perfect, but the best of them are courageous, idealistic and patriotic without being blind to the country's mistakes and flaws" (Robert Hawkins, "Foreword" to *The Kent Family Chronicles Encyclopedia* [New York: Bantam Books, 1979]).

In *The Bastard* (1974), the first book in the Kent Family Chronicles, Jakes tells the saga of Phillipe Charboneau, the illegitimate French son of an English duke. In London, where he has been summoned by his gravely ill father, Charboneau sets out to learn the printing trade. He meets Benjamin Franklin, whose ideas stimulate his interest in America. One of his first acts upon arriving in Boston is to change his name to Philip Kent. Later he becomes involved in the Boston Tea Party and in the first battles of the Revolutionary War near Lexington and Concord. Through the life of Philip Kent, Jakes develops well-known subjects from the American experience: the promise of liberty in the New World in contrast to European oppression; the struggle of immigrants who survived through pluck and hard work; the impulse to shed the European identity and become the new American man; and, finally, the restrictive English policies that helped bring about the Revolutionary War.

The Rebels (1975) continues the adventures of Philip Kent, mostly during the Revolution, up to the time of the surrender of Cornwallis at Yorktown in 1781. A prominent character is Judson Fletcher, son of a Southern tobacco plantation owner, who gets involved in political activity in Philadelphia and, as a member of Congress, associates with such men as Benjamin Franklin, John Adams, Thomas Paine, and Thomas Jefferson. Kent is with George Washington at Valley Forge; he also renews his acquaintance with the Marquis de Lafayette, whom he had first met in France. This novel, like all the rest in this series, demonstrates Jakes's facility in combining history and fiction. The fictional characters provide the romance and adventure, the main ingredients in any historical novel aimed at the mass market, while the historical figures and events satisfy the reader's need for authenticity and knowledge of the past. The American Revolution emerges from this account as a magnificent accomplishment, even though the human beings associated with it are flawed.

The Seekers (1975) concerns itself with the growth of the young republic during the period from 1794-1814. Philip Kent is now a successful and conservative Boston publisher. His son, Abraham, who had served with the army in the Northwest Territory, rejects his father's desire that he join the family's business and decides to go to the frontier by heading west across the Alleghenies. The frontier venture is unsuccessful and tragic, and Abraham returns to Boston to find that his father has died. The publishing business has now passed into the hands of Gilbert Kent, Abraham's half brother, who takes in Abraham's small son, Jared. Jared later joins the navy, serving aboard the frigate *Constitution*, which engages in battle with the British *Guerrier*. Gilbert's daughter Amanda and Jared journey together down the Ohio River and set off along the Cumberland Trail, where they spend two weeks with a family named Lincoln. Later Amanda is kidnapped and sold to white traders heading for Sioux Country.

The Furies (1976) continues the saga of Amanda Kent. Freed from her Indian captors, she marries a struggling farmer in Texas and is present at the fall of the Alamo. She becomes the companion of a Mexican officer who is later killed at the Battle of San Jacinto and who is the father of their son Louis. Amanda travels to the California gold fields, where she prospers in her business dealings. Later she returns to the East, meets Frederick Douglass, and becomes involved in the slavery issue. She also buys the family firm, Kent and Son. Shot by thugs, she dies at the conclusion of the novel.

Both *The Seekers* and *The Furies*, besides depicting the beginnings of the westward movement and national expansion with all its restlessness and violence, demonstrate Jakes's characteristic long and careful research into American history. He is particularly good in his depictions of the harshness of frontier life and in the courage and determination of the pioneers as the country expanded westward.

The Titans (1976) deals with a more compressed period than previous novels in the series. The action takes place in the years 1860-1862, and it chronicles events and attitudes of the period and some of the early military battles of the Civil War. The principal member of the Kent family depicted here is Jephtha (Jared's son), who had been a minister until he was defrocked for his antislavery views. Jephtha becomes a reporter in Washington, D.C., in which capacity he interviews President Lincoln and becomes involved with Edward Lamont, a Southern sympathizer married to Jephtha's ex-wife, who has custody of their three sons. One of Jephtha's sons, Gideon, joins the First Virginia Cavalry and sees action at Manassas.

Besides painting a vivid picture of the strong emotions, the plots, and the counterplots that were part of the prelude to the Civil War as the nation divided over slavery and secession, this novel provides social history and background. Like the rest of Jakes's novels, *The Titans* is grounded in authentic detail that colorfully brings to life a tumultuous and decisive period in American history.

Jakes's account of the Civil War and the period after it continues with the sixth novel, *The Warriors* (1977), which covers the years 1864-1868. The title refers to the sons of Jephtha Kent. Jeremiah Kent, after serving in the Confederate army, finds himself on a Georgia plantation, where he witnesses the bloody and fiery depredations of marauding Yankee troops. Afterwards he moves into the Western wilderness. Gideon Kent, captured at Yellow Tavern, lands in a Union prison; later, in New York, he becomes a spokesman for exploited workers. Matthew Kent expatriates himself to Paris to paint. The novel also includes the story of Michael Boyle, the son of a poor Irish immigrant family, who becomes closely associated with the Kents. He heads West, where he engages in violent adventures with Indians and whites. *The Warriors* presents a harsh account of the social changes that characterized the period after the Civil War. Jakes does not gloss over the horrors of the conflict, the grim aspects of the struggles of the budding labor movement, or the violence of the westward expansion.

The same somberness characterizes *The Lawless* (1978), the seventh volume in the Kent family saga. Covering the years 1869-1877, it chronicles the further adventures of Jephtha and his sons. Matthew, who has exiled himself to paint in France, is befriended by Manet, Cézanne, and Whistler. At the urging of his brother Gideon, he returns to paint the American frontier. Although the novel clearly shows why Matthew (and others like him) chose to flee to France in dismay over American materialism and corruption, it also demonstrates that American political freedom is preferable to the intrigues and instability of Europe. Jeremiah Kent, now on the Western frontier, lives by his guns. Later, he goes to Chicago, where he dies in a shooting precipitated by his brother Gideon's involvement in the labor movement. Gideon, a newspaperman with a strong social conscience, believes in the right of workers to organize and in his own right to expose the machinations of acquisitive monopolists. Equally fervent in the fight for women's rights is Julia Sedgwick, who becomes Gideon's unconventional paramour. Like the rest of the novels in this series, *The Lawless* highlights dramatic and notable events in American history such as the Chicago fire, The Philadelphia Centennial Exhibition of 1876, and the building of the Brooklyn Bridge.

In 1978 Jakes moved to Hilton Head Island, South Carolina, where he wrote the eighth and last book in the series. *The Americans* (1980) focuses on the family of Gideon Kent, a Boston publisher in the 1880s. His daughter Margaret, following her bent for the theater first displayed in *The Lawless*, is now a respected actress and happily married. The best-drawn character is Will, Gideon's youngest son, who like his father has a responsible social conscience and has to make a choice between his desire to be rich and his principles. After living on Theodore Roosevelt's ranch, Will graduates from Harvard Medical School and practices medicine in New York slums. A third major character is Carter Kent, son of Louis Kent and Julia Sedgwick (Gideon's longtime friend), who heads West and becomes active in California Democratic politics and is familiar with the social circle of William Randolph Hearst. One of the main themes of the book concerns the duties of citizenship.

Leaving the Kent family behind but still employing the same narrative devices he used so well in the Bicentennial Series, Jakes published *North and South* (1982), the first volume in a projected trilogy dealing with events before, during, and after the Civil War. He focuses on two families in the period 1842-1861: the Mains own a Carolina rice plantation; and the Hazards own a prosperous ironworks in Pennsylvania. Orry Main and George Hazard first meet at West Point. The novel, painted on a broad canvas involving many characters and shifting scenes, dramatizes the tensions and the painfully divided loyalties preceding the Civil War, including aspects of the Mexican war, in which both Orry and George serve.

Reviewers' reactions to Jakes's work was predictable. In general, they applauded the accuracy of the historical framework for Jakes's fiction. They saw his novels as entertaining accounts by a writer "with a special talent for popularizing history," satisfying the desire of Americans in the bicentennial years "to know where they came from." Reservations were expressed about accounts that were "seemingly straight out of reference works" or narratives that suffered from "clumsy interjections of historical bits and pieces." One reviewer dismissed the novels as "footnotes to Yankee pop culture." Another called them a "grand exercise in literary historical kitsch." Jakes's style was praised as readable and readily accessible. "The style is in no way demanding," said one reviewer; another called the prose "plain but practical"; and another called it "pure pulp but readable enough."

Jakes's historical novels cannot be judged by usual literary standards. They are unabashedly fiction for the mass market, and it cannot be expected that they display the virtues of interpretive fiction. The characterizations, although usually vivid and striking, are not complex. His novels depend for their success primarily on plot. The action is fast and well-paced, with a good deal of violent conflict, suspense, and many startling coincidences that help to link narrative threads. They provide readers with many hours of absorbing and informative reading, but they do not impart a sense of artistic unity in which character and plot are inextricably part of a total meaning. Nor do Jakes's plots, although they have many different characters and settings, essentially differ from each other. Jakes's formula places members of a fictional family group in significant historical settings—sometimes including real historical characters—generating travel, excitement, and danger. Eventually most of the conflicts are resolved or the stage is set for their continuation in the next novel of the series.

Jakes's novels do not provide that main quality we expect from interpretive fiction: a sharper and deeper awareness of life, often in memorable prose. But Jakes has not claimed to be this kind of writer. In an afterword to *North and South* he says that his primary purpose is to entertain; and if a writer is to be judged solely on the success of his intentions,

-91b-1-

Further evidence--he found Mallory still at work in the Department's second floor offices. Everyone else had gone except another of the Secretary's three aides, the dapper Mr. Tidball, who was carefully locking his desk as Cooper walked in.

"Good evening," said Tidball, squaring a pile of papers so it aligned with the corners of the desk. Tidball was a drone with no original ideas but remarkable organizational skills. He complemented the other two members of the triumvirate--Commodore Forrest, a blustery, white-haired old blue-water sailor who understood seamen and their ways, and Cooper, who served as an extension of Mallory's inventive nature; both men were always more prone to say "Let us try" than "We can't." Tonight, however, Cooper wearily brought back the latter answer.

"He's been awaiting your return," Tidball said with a crisp nod at the inner office. Tidball left and Cooper went in to find the Secretary examining engineering drawings in a pool of light cast by a lamp with a green glass shade. The wick flickered as the scented oil burned; the gas mantles were shut down and the rest of the cluttered office lay dark.

"Hallo, Cooper," said Mallory.

He had ~~with~~ a tilted nose, plump cheeks, and bright blue eyes that usually danced with curiosity and excitement. Tonight tiredness seemed to dull his glance, though he still reminded Cooper of an English country squire. "What luck?"

Cooper sneezed. "None. ~~As I suspected,~~ the design for the cradle and cannister are good enough, but the problem is the one we both saw when we first looked at the plans. A torpedo made of driftwood will do just that--draft. Without guidance, it could blow a

He was a roly-poly man of fifty, born in Trinidad and reared mostly in Key West, by an Irish mother and a Connecticut Yankee father.

Revised page from the first-draft typescript for Love and War, *the sequel to* North and South *(the author)*

then John Jakes is without doubt one of the most successful and important writers in the history of commercial fiction.

References:

Robert Hawkins, *The Kent Family Chronicles Encyclopedia* (New York: Bantam Books, 1979);

Herbert Mitgang, "Behind the Best Sellers," *New York Times Book Review*, 83, 30 April 1978, p. 74;

Ray Walters, "Paperback Talk," *New York Times Book Review*, 84, 7 October 1979, pp. 41-42.

Papers:

The University of Wyoming Library has a large collection of Jakes's manuscripts and books as part of their Archives of Contemporary Writers.

AN INTERVIEW

with JOHN JAKES

DLB: You were very successful in business while moonlighting as a writer. It must have been a strain or you must have had to neglect your family. Why did you keep pushing to make it as a writer?

JAKES: Well, two reasons. First of all, I think I had that basic drive that all writers have: the demand that they write. Secondly, I had a financial motive: We had four children. I was in the advertising business and doing well, but not as well as I would have if I had worked in New York or Chicago, where the salary scales were much higher than they were in Rochester, or Dayton. Consequently, when Rachel and I worked up a little chart of our four kids going to college, I saw that I needed a hell of a lot of money during a relatively short time—so that really was the practical spur. Virtually everything that I made from my writing went into a sinking fund for their college education.

DLB: Tuition, not fame, was the spur?

JAKES: That is right. I think perhaps like every writer I hoped one of these days it might pay off with a little of the fame, too; but it was really to make up the salary difference. I didn't want to go to work in New York in the advertising business, and that was the best compromise.

DLB: The publishing community refers to your work, or much of it at least, as "genre books" or "category books." How do you feel about those designations?

JAKES: I think that was certainly true of much of the earlier stuff that I wrote. I don't know how historical novels fit, really. They always seem to kind of escape that pejorative of genre fiction or genre material. I think historicals are a genre in themselves, but they seem to have a little more respectability. I do know that when I was doing mostly paperbacks in science fiction, I did feel categorized, and in a literary ghetto. I no longer feel that way, but I also think those literary ghettos are breaking down. In the last five years we've seen Frank Herbert and Asimov and science fiction writers who never would have been on the hardcover best-seller list, even ten years ago, popping onto the list. So I think that category stigma has kind of broken down. It was unfortunate while it lasted, but it was understandable.

DLB: Speaking of categories, you've written in all the standard categories—mystery, spy, science fiction, history, if that's a category. Were you shopping around?

JAKES: Yes.

DLB: Sort of testing the various categories?

JAKES: I was doing that. I was accepting commissions that my then agent, Scott Meredith, offered various writers in his stable. One of many problems that I've always had is that I like too many things. I like too many kinds of material. I enjoyed writing private-eye novels when I wrote them. I very much enjoyed science-fiction novels and really gave a couple of them everything I had, with no discernible results. So I felt when I was in my late thirties that I had spread myself too thin and that I really had no audience because I liked to do too many things; and unfortunately I think if you do too many things you never achieve any success with any one of them.

DLB: Is it accurate to say that your breakthrough came when you took an assignment from a packaging house?

JAKES: Yes—when I took Lyle Engel up on that offer that happened to be a lucky combination of a good project at a time when the paperback market was just beginning to boom. I was at a very low ebb in my writing career. I was thinking I probably should give it up, but I was challenged by the opportunity of that series. All I was given by Engel was a one-sentence, back-of-the-envelope concept.

DLB: Can you remember what it was?

JAKES: Well, it was basically an American family through two hundred years of American history, period. Everything else I built from the ground up. Lyle has put some things in print to imply that he contributed much more than he ever did. He may work that way with other writers, but he didn't with me. Everything from the name of the family to the names of the books is my doing, and I gave it everything I had. Never imagining, of course, that what did happen would happen; but that certainly was the breakthrough, and despite the many, many differences I've had with Engel and certain things I don't like about his style of operation, I will always be grateful to him for the opportunity. I cannot deny that he gave me that and it was a very handsome one.

DLB: Nobody in publishing, not even the writers, knows why, how, when, where, lightning strikes. What's your guess—why did lightning strike you when it did?

JAKES: I think there were several reasons why it did. I've thought a lot about this over the last ten years because I've been asked the question a lot in connection with the Kent books. I think there were several things. Number 1: To start with the simplest—I try to tell good stories. Number 2: I think we were just coming into a period when the family saga was on the brink of a rebirth. God knows, the Kent books have spawned you know how many imitators. But certainly I would never claim that that was an original idea. You look at Zola and other family-cycle things—*The Forsyte Saga*—but those had been kind of forgotten for a while, and I think the Kents came in right at a time when there was a hunger for that. I had a sociology professor up North tell me a few years ago that he thought people liked to read family sagas because so many real families were deteriorating. So they liked to read about strong families succeeding. Now, I don't know if that's true or not but there might well be a grain of truth in it. So that's the second reason. The third, I think, is that I came into doing those books with a very strong feeling about this country. I sat through the Viet Nam-Johnson-Nixon-Watergate years—the terrible years, as we all did. I felt when I began researching American history, which I had

not looked into deeply for a long time, that there was a great deal good about this country that we had forgotten. I set out to try to state some of those positive things. I never wanted to do a Pollyanna work by any means, and if I ever did that I would throw up my hands in horror. I don't think I did. I didn't try to gloss over the slavery question or the stealing of Indian lands, but nevertheless there's a good deal about this country and what it stands for that we had kind of lost sight of in that really crappy time that we went through. I think this played through strongly in the books. My mail told me that it did, and again that was a matter of sounding the right bell note—because I really believed it was the note to sound—but also of sounding it at exactly the right time by sheer accident. So those three things are the best factors or reasons I've been able to come up with.

DLB: If God were to come to you this afternoon and say He was going to give you the choice of being any author who ever lived, who would you pick?

JAKES: That's a toughy—do I get more than one choice?

DLB: Yes—or you can answer it in terms of, if He said, I'll make you the author of any book that's ever been written, what book would you pick?

JAKES: I know who I would want to be, if I had a choice, and it's a very obvious one and that's William Shakespeare. I love the theater, and as far as we can tell, he was such a thoroughgoing professional and he happened to have had the dust of genius laid on him on top of everything else. I read avidly about his life—what little is known—and what I admire about him is his tremendous professionalism, which just happened to be overlaid with that genius. I suppose that's a fairly obvious one, but if I had only one choice, I suspect that would be it.

DLB: Speaking of the theater, you have a kind of secret life. You've done a lot more in the theater than most of your readers suspect. What about that secret life? Is that for kicks?

JAKES: Yes, that's really for fun. I began to write little plays for community theaters about ten years ago—lucky enough to have some of them produced and put into catalogues. I have acted from time to time—that's just for fun. I have done some directing. I have now just started a collaboration for the first time in ten years on a new musical with the composer who scored the Broadway musical *Tintypes*—happens to be a fellow raised here in South Carolina who now lives in New York. I think theater work has some very practical benefits for novel writing. One, it gives you a much better ear for dialogue because if you're familiar with how actors say lines you have a better and sharper ear for novelistic dialogue. Secondly: it gives you an objectivity about your work that you don't always get when you're simply sitting off writing a book. If you're standing in the back of a theater watching something you've done being performed and the audience is hating it, there is *no* excuse in the world that you can formulate other than that the material must be no damn good. You can't say the salesman didn't get out and sell it or the cover was wrong or anything like that. I do the playwriting for fun, and I would like to take it all the way to New York one of these days. I really do enjoy it and I also think it sharpens the novelistic side of the blade, too.

DLB: How about movies and telly?

JAKES: I don't have any desire to do that. I'm happy to see someone like David Wolper—a man of his quality—pick up *North and South* and the sequel and start to develop them, but I wouldn't want any permanent part of that society out there. The few screenwriters I've ever met, while they are just loaded with bucks, all seem to want one thing—their name on a novel. So I don't think so. I've done

a couple of film jobs. I did one a couple of years ago that I was very proud of that never got off the ground. It was a 150-page treatment for a twelve-hour miniseries version of *The Magnificent Ambersons*. I did it for RKO—they were going to revitalize their production outfit. I got a lot of money for it, and I had great fun doing it. But they changed management and shelved the project. Still, I had a good time doing it. That's the kind of work I'd like to do in that area, but nothing permanent.

DLB: Why *The Magnificent Ambersons*? Did you pick it or did they pick it?

JAKES: They picked it because they owned the film rights, but I quite fell in love with it once I read the novel and screened a print of the Welles picture.

DLB: Are you going to stick to historical novels or are you going back to some of your former affairs?

JAKES: I don't know. I've got to finish the trilogy for Harcourt Brace Jovanovich, and what I will do after that I can't say. I want to take a sabbatical. I am working on this musical with my collaborator. I suppose one of these days I might try some other things. I would like to delve into the contemporary short story just to see if I could do it again—noncategory—just to try it. But I don't know. That's a long way down the road.

Donald Justice

(12 August 1925-   )

Cathrael Kazin
University of Iowa

BOOKS: *The Summer Anniversaries* (Middletown, Conn.: Wesleyan University Press, 1960);
Night Light (Middletown, Conn.: Wesleyan University Press, 1967);
From a Notebook (Iowa City: Seamark Press, 1972);
Departures (New York: Atheneum, 1973);
Selected Poems (New York: Atheneum, 1979; London: Anvil Press, 1980).

OTHER: *The Collected Poems of Weldon Kees*, edited

by Justice (Iowa City: Stone Wall Press, 1960; Lincoln: University of Nebraska Press, 1975);
Midland, edited by Justice, Paul Engle, and Henri Coulette (New York: Random House, 1961);
Contemporary French Poetry, edited by Justice and Alexander Aspel (Ann Arbor: University of Michigan Press, 1965).

PERIODICAL PUBLICATIONS: "Songs from *The Telephone Booth in the Woods*" and "Songs from

M.A. degree in English from the University of North Carolina, where his thesis was "The Agrarian 'Myth,'" a study of the prose and poetry of John Crowe Ransom, Allen Tate, and Robert Penn Warren. In 1947 he also married Jean Ross; they have one son, Nathaniel. From 1948 to 1949 he studied at Stanford University with Yvor Winters.

Since 1982 Justice has been a professor of English at the University of Florida. Although he eventually taught at several other universities (including Syracuse, Hamline, and the University of California) before returning to Florida to teach, the University of Iowa remains the school with which he has been most closely associated. In 1954 he received a Ph.D. from the Writers Workshop, where his teachers included John Berryman, Robert Lowell, and Karl Shapiro; he taught there himself from 1956 to 1966 and from 1971 to 1980.

Justice has long been what is sometimes known as a poet's poet. The precision of his language, his fascination with poetic technique, and the meticulous and supple quality of his diction have all had a particular appeal for other practitioners—or at least those in a position to appreciate craft. Justice seems in turn to appreciate his primary audience: "I don't mind thinking that it's mostly poets who read what I write.... It's better, surely, because they know a bit more about what I'm actually doing." At the University of Iowa Writers Workshop, Justice's rigorous attention to language and his emphasis on control influenced poet-students.

But his work has also been read and admired outside of poetry workshops, as many forms of recognition testify. His first book, *The Summer Anniversaries*, was the Lamont Poetry Selection for 1959; *Departures* (1973) was nominated for the 1973 National Book Award. His short stories have been included in the O. Henry Prize stories annual collections. He has received awards from the Rockefeller and Guggenheim foundations, as well as from the National Endowment for the Arts. With the 1979 publication of *Selected Poems*, however—and the consequent Pulitzer Prize—Justice has come to be recognized not only as one of America's most elegant and distinctive contemporary poets but also as one of its most significant.

Although Justice has often been celebrated for his brilliant use of forms, his last volume displays a more profound and varied body of work than might previously have been realized. "At times, his most recent book, *Selected Poems*, reads almost like an anthology of the possibilities of contemporary poetry," wrote Dana Gioia. "There are sestinas, villanelles, and ballads rubbing pages with aleatory

LaVerne H. Clark

"Don Juan in Hell," *Antaeus*, 20 (Winter 1976): 112-115;
"Meters and Memory," *Antaeus*, 30/31 (Spring 1978): 314-320;
"Piano Lessons: Notes on a Provincial Culture," *Antaeus*, 45/46 (Spring/Summer 1982): 145-155.

Donald Justice was born 12 August 1925 in Miami, Florida. In the jacket notes to his first volume, *The Summer Anniversaries* (1960), he saw fit to mention that his family was originally from south Georgia—but "definitely not of the plantation aristocracy, which was always two-thirds myth anyhow." His father, Vasco, was a carpenter. His mother was Mary Ethel Cook.

Justice has since called the Miami of his youth a "sleepy, middle-sized Southern city," and he had a Southern childhood, never leaving the South or seeing snow until his late teens. After attending Miami schools, he received the B.A. degree from the University of Miami in 1945. In 1947 he took an

poems [those derived from chance methods], surreal odes, and Williamsesque free verse." Justice's work has recently taken on still another dimension: He is quoted exhaustively in John Irving's novel *The Hotel New Hampshire*. The role of poetic guru is a surprising one for Justice, whose early work was often characterized as "modest," "unassuming," and "understated."

This is "a poetry of small scale dooms and dim light," Charles Molesworth wrote in the *New York Times Book Review* about *The Summer Anniversaries*. Muted though its tone may be, the first volume takes on large themes: It deals with the despairs of ordinary life, with erosion and decay, and also with madness, as in the subtle but frightening "Counting the Mad" and "On a Painting by Patient B of the Independence State Hospital for the Insane." Several of the poems draw on Justice's childhood in the South, particularly the then not-yet-developed Miami of the Depression. He returns to both the time and the terrain in the previously uncollected work of *Selected Poems*.

His treatment of childhood, while evocative, avoids sentimentality and self-pity. The poems reflect disease (a close friend died, at nine, of rheumatic fever; Justice came down with osteomyelitis soon after), the experience of being what Justice terms "near poor," and the indifference, sometimes cruelty, of adults. "The Poet at Seven" and "On the Death of Friends in Childhood" drily present the world as essentially menacing; "To a Ten Months Child" sympathizes with the infant for hesitating to be born. "The Poet at Seven" is fundamentally alone, "lick[ing] his wounds in secret." The poet's attitude toward his young self is distanced—he does, after all, speak of himself in the third person—but there is a haunting undercurrent to the boy's desire for "someone dear to come / And whip him down the street, but gently, home."

"From the beginning of his poetic career, Donald Justice has focused obsessively on a central theme: loss," Thomas Swiss has observed. His poems go beyond simple lamentation, however: He is as interested in the processes of memory and recovery as he is in the specific memories themselves. In "On the Death of Friends in Childhood," the friends who died live in the poem's statement of their absence:

> We shall not ever meet them bearded
> in heaven,
> Nor sunning themselves among the bald
> of hell;

If anywhere, in the deserted schoolyard
at twilight,
Forming a ring, perhaps, or joining hands
In games whose very names we have
forgotten.
Come, memory, let us seek them there
in the shadows.

Justice's poems present, therefore, an attractive paradox: in the guise of lamenting a loss, they perform acts of preservation: "So far as I can psychologize it, one of the motives for writing is surely to recover and hold what would otherwise be lost totally—memory or experience."

His is also a poetry of irony, slyness, and self-consciousness. What distinguishes it from the Formalist poetry of the 1950s it superficially resembles (Justice does, however, admire Ransom greatly) is the complex relation he establishes between form and subject. For him the two are not simply paired, or compatible: "It is a false notion, I am sure, to propose that poetry comes only from subject, is never more than an extension of content." In other words, the memory may spring as much from the meter he employs as the meter may derive from the memory. This conviction gives Justice's poems their abstract, even impersonal, quality: Their impetus may be the working out of a poetic, rather than emotional, problem. For Justice, "poetry [is] at its best, is fulfilling its nature most entirely, when it has a great mastery of form, or technique, and shows considerable, though perhaps a hidden or disguised interest in its own formal or technical character."

The Summer Anniversaries contains a number of ornate and potentially unwieldy forms, especially sestinas and an idiosyncratic brand of the villanelle. It is difficult to write a sestina which does not sound silly; the form is, by definition, limited and repetitive. In "Sestina: Here in Katmandu" (which Justice has himself characterized as having "a small place in the history of the form"), Justice makes no attempt to disguise the repetitions involved. In fact, repetition is the theme of the poem, as well as its method. The acts of climbing the mountain and looking back at it are brilliantly echoed in the ascending/descending movement of the form:

> It is terrible to come down
> To the valley
> Where, amidst many flowers,
> One thinks of snow,
>
> As formerly, amidst snow,

Climbing the mountain,
One thought of flowers. . . .

In this and other poems he appears to be delivering the nascent life of the forms, seeming to allow them to determine the direction of the poems. His attitude toward his own poems presents a contradiction: He is at once distanced and controlling—or perhaps able to control because distanced: "I have in my poems conscientiously effaced my self, I think, if not my personality."

In his second book, *Night Light* (1967), he continues to deal with the themes of memory and erosion; again, he implicitly proposes poetry as a stay against mutability. But these poems are closer to middle age than childhood: The tone is muted, domesticated—or perhaps even quietly despairing. "Men at Forty," which ends with a moribund allusion to "mortgaged houses," shows the adult subsuming the remembered child.

Men at forty
Learn to close softly
The doors to rooms they will not be
Coming back to.

. . . .

And deep in mirrors
They rediscover
The face of the boy as he practises tying
His father's tie there in secret

And the face of that father,
Still warm with the mystery of lather.
They are more fathers than sons
                                                themselves now.
Something is filling them, something

That is like the twilight sound
Of the crickets, immense,
Filling the woods at the foot of the slope
Behind their mortgaged houses.

The central image of the poem is one of Justice's most pervasive: the mirror. In various guises, the image dominates the collection—as well as much of *Selected Poems*. His very attitude toward memory is a form of mirroring, as is his frequent use of literary allusions, other texts. But his mirrors are always distorting images—not perfect representations of "reality." The mirroring is a form of earnest game-playing. Justice is a serious gambler and chess player, and he engages in versions of both activities in his poetry: "Probably more than other poets I know, I play games in my poems (as I do in

my life), and one of the unwritten rules of the game, for me, as I like it played, is that you can risk this much personality or that much confession if the voice is promised to be that of someone else to begin with." Justice's mirrors are, in fact, forms of self-effacement rather than self-reflection. He often presents the mirror as having an identity of its own; the mirror in "Things" is characterized simply as: "My former friend, my traitor. / My too easily broken. / My still to be escaped from." This sparse stanza captures the tenuous relation between thing and image, self and presentation. The flat mirror, put down, takes the face with it; held up, it is a "still," a freezing photograph—or a yet-enclosing prison.

"The Thin Man" is another poem which explores the paradoxical luxury of self-effacement:

I indulge myself
In rich refusals.
Nothing suffices.

I hone myself to
This edge. Asleep, I
Am a horizon.

This small poem displays the wonderful fullness Justice achieves with his slim poetics. Over and over, the master of control engages in "rich refusals." The refusal is both a form of hunger—nothing would ever be enough—and a form of satiety: Nothing *is* enough.

The "skinny lines" of this and other poems, as Justice calls them, may derive in part from his reading of the early William Carlos Williams, a poet whose influence is more easily seen in *Night Light* than in the other books. The technique, style, and locale all seem to allude to Williams. The volume contains free verse and also a number of distinctly American poems, "American Sketches" (dedicated to Williams) and "Bus Stop" among them.

The volume also reflects new continental influences—Justice had been preparing an anthology of contemporary French poetry and discovered the work of Eugene Guillevic. One of his techniques has been "conscientiously to mistranslate," as he puts it, to use the sounds and suggestions of foreign poetry to open up new possibilities for his own. This results in a number of almost surrealistic poems, as in "Hands," "The Man Closing Up," and "The Missing Person."

If even the title of *Night Light* evokes the most muted of illuminations—or a child's fearfulness—*Departures* clearly announces a taking off. There is a faintly Chinese quality to many of these poems: They are often small, precisely worded, haunting, and mysterious. There are more and more fragments, more poems made up of short, obliquely connected stanzas. The technique of "mistranslation" is here augmented by other attempts to introduce controlled randomness into the poetry, most notably with the "all too notorious cards" of his chance methods. Ever the gambler, Justice put a large number of words culled from other poems onto note cards, coded them according to parts of speech, shuffled the decks, and then "dealt" himself poems. He was, he has said, attempting to simulate the effects of a small computer without actually using one.

One of the most appealing, if elusive, of the chance poems is "Twenty Questions." The game as it is traditionally played leads from total mystery to clarification, as the possibilities for what "it" is get narrowed down. Instead, Justice starts with an ordinary question, which simply by inversion becomes surreal. "Is it raining out?" gives way to "Is it raining in?" and then to "Are you a public fountain?" Justice has said that for him "the surreal image is most powerful when it is rooted in the real." He exposes the richness of ordinary language through the strangeness of the context; "Are you by chance a body of water?," the seventh question, reminds us that we are all "bodies of water"—and "by chance," along with so much about us. The poem and others in the collection emphasize Justice's fascination with language and its power, the ease with which it creates worlds, delineates conditions. "An Elegy is Preparing Itself" takes still further the eerie power of poetic language. Depicting the coffin, the shroud, the headstone even before they are created—or necessary—the poem creates the elegy to accompany them:

> There are pines that are tall enough
> Already. In the distance,
> The whining of saws; and needles,
> Silently slipping through the chosen cloth.
> The stone, then as now, unfelt,
> perfectly weightless. And certain words,
> That will come together to mourn,
> Waiting, in their dark clothes, apart.

"Variations on a Text by Vallejo" takes the poet's own elegy one step further, imagining the day, the place, the very setting: "I will die in Miami in the sun. . . ." Finally, in the third stanza, the fantasy reaches its logical end: "Donald Justice is dead."

The future which poetry may realize is closely allied to the past which it recreates. "Sonatina in Yellow," one of Justice's best poems, brings together two of his most insistent themes: the importance and instability of memory, and poetry as preservation. But although the past is preserved in an album, attempts to arrest decay, whether photographic or verbal, themselves erode:

> The pages of the album,
> As they are turned, turn yellow; a word,
> Once spoken, obsolete,
> No longer what was meant. Say it.
> The meanings come, or come back later,
> Unobtrusive, taking their places.

The "yellow" of the title is decay; it is also "Forgotten sunlight still / Blinding the eyes of the faces in the album."

Like many of Justice's poems, "Sonatina in Yellow" is, obviously, musical. His first art was, in fact, music rather than poetry: He studied piano as a child and taught himself how to compose. A number of his works attempt to combine music with poetry, as in "Two Blues"; he has also written librettos. "Sonatina in Yellow" (there is an accompanying "Sonatina in Green") attempts to use music as structure rather than as sound. As Justice told interviewers:

> The sonatina is a modest classical form which involves an A part and a B part. It involves saying A again and saying B again in a key different from the one it was said in the first time around.
>
> The only thing I had to find was an A thing to say and a B thing to say, and—which was trickier—a way to change the key of B. . . . I tried to find a change of key, a modulation, which would be linguistic or grammatical rather than musical.

Justice confided to his interviewers that he has written a prose commentary to go with the poem. It is another demonstration of the intensity of his desire for control: "You'd like not only to write the poems but to write the commentary, you know; don't leave that up to the others, who're likely to get it wrong anyhow."

In "Childhood," one of the previously uncollected works in *Selected Poems*, Justice does offer a marginal gloss, one which is mainly, if quirkily, factual. Perhaps the commentary reflects most of all his sense that the world of Depression-era Miami is now gone forever. Like so many of Justice's poems, it is a reflection which itself contains mirrors: his own "wrinkled" face in the lily pond which he prods "with the slow teasings of a stick"; his "ghostly image skimming across nude mannequins" in the department store window. The artificial—but magical—store he enters seems to contain an endless series of mirrors:

> O counters of spectacles—where the bored
>   child first
> Scans new perspectives squinting through
>   strange lenses;
> And the mirrors, tilting, offer back toy sails
> Stiffening breezeless towards green shores
>   of baize . . .

This poem, the last in *Selected Poems*, presents Justice at his most typical—and masterful. It acknowledges frankly that his is an artificial world, his a poetics of self-control, craft, invention. If we incline toward the poem hoping to see the poet's self, we are offered, instead, a mirror. But it is a mirror in which nearly anything may appear, where toy boats sail triumphantly in fabric "bays."

Interviews:
"The Effacement of Self," *Ohio Review*, 16 (Spring 1975): 40-63;
"An Interview with Donald Justice," *Iowa Review*, 11, 2-3 (Spring-Summer 1980): 1-21;
"An Interview with Donald Justice," *Missouri Review*, 4 (Fall 1980): 41-67.

References:
Thomas Swiss, "The Principle of Apprenticeship: Donald Justice's Poetry," *Modern Poetry Studies*, 10 (Spring 1980): 44-58;
Vernon Young, "Two Hedgehogs and a Fox," *Parnassus*, 8 (Fall-Winter 1979): 227-237.

Papers:
The university library of the University of Delaware has a collection of Justice's notebooks, preliminary drafts, galleys, page proofs, and correspondence.

Steve Katz
(14 May 1935-   )

Sinda J. Gregory and Larry McCaffery
San Diego State University

SELECTED BOOKS: *The Lestriad* (Lecce, Italy: Edizioni Milella, 1962);
The Weight of Antony (Ithaca, N.Y.: Eibe, 1964);
The Exagggerations of Peter Prince (New York: Holt, Rinehart & Winston, 1968);
Creamy and Delicious (New York: Random House, 1970);
Posh, as Stephanie Gatos (New York: Grove, 1971);
Saw (New York: Knopf, 1972);
Cheyenne River Wild Track (Ithaca, N.Y.: Ithaca House, 1973);
Moving Parts (New York: Fiction Collective, 1977).

OTHER: "A Story of Infidelity," in *Stories from Epoch*, edited by Baxter Hathaway (Ithaca: Cornell University Press, 1966);
"Two Poems," in *Modern Occasions*, edited by Philip Rahv (New York: Farrar, Straus & Giroux, 1966; London: Weidenfeld & Nicolson, 1967);
"Three Satisfying Stories," in *Experiments in Prose*, edited by Eugene Wildman (Chicago: Swallow Press, 1969);
"Wonder Woman," in *Innovative Fiction*, edited by Jerome Klinkowitz (New York: Dell, 1972);
"Death of the Band," in *Statements*, edited by Jonathan Baumbach (New York: Fiction Collective, 1975);
"Parcel of Wrists," in *New Directions Annual 30*, edited by James Laughlin (New York: New Directions, 1976);
"Two Seaside Yarns," in *Statements II*, edited by Baumbach (New York: Fiction Collective, 1977).

PERIODICAL PUBLICATIONS: "Made of Wax," *Seems: Prose and Poetry*, 2 (Summer 1975): 34-46;
"Two Seaside Yarns," *Seems: Prose and Poetry*, 2 (Summer 1975): 91-93.

Steve Katz

"The potential for mystery is everywhere, and infinite," writes Steve Katz in "43," one of four fictions collected in his latest book, *Moving Parts* (1977), "and the world of events cannot be circumscribed by a predetermined order no matter how complex and involuted a system of psychology, physics, religion, or occultation is applied." Beginning with his first novel, *The Exagggerations of Peter Prince* (1968), Katz has consistently focused on this infinite potential for mystery and on the way in which our imagination can free us from stale, prepackaged systems of organizing experience. As Judith Karfiol comments in an unpublished dissertation, "New American Fiction and the Aesthetics of Camus and Robbe-Grillet," the most perceptive and extended treatment of Katz's work: "Katz's particular artistry rests with the force of his speculative powers to invent codes for and contexts of experience that are unlike any we know, transforming familiar ideas and a familiar world into strange, often funny, and highly implausible ones. . . . Hav-

ing no intention of representing the world as it is habitually perceived, the fiction explores the creation of experience, and asserts the power of the imagination to dominate our understanding of reality." Katz's fiction startles and amazes as it displaces and disrupts words, ideas, and images from their usual meanings and contexts; it transforms these elements into newborn, new-formed creations that challenge and amuse us with new games and visions.

Born in the Bronx to Alexander Katz, who sold fireproof doors, and Sally Goldstein Katz, Steve Katz grew up in the Washington Heights area of Manhattan. His fiction has always evoked, in its peculiar fashion, the shape of American experience; and the experience of growing up in Manhattan during the 1940s and 1950s naturally had a sustaining effect on all of Katz's work. Katz has commented: "The most significant things about my childhood were the view of the George Washington Bridge out my bedroom window; the New York Bullets Social and Athletic Club; the movies at Loew's 175th St. (now a Rev. Ike Church); the New York Yankees, bleacher seats or general admission; the Museum of Modern Art; once a week, Birdland, when I got old enough to lie about my age; and the Palladium, when I was brave enough to learn to mambo from Killer Joe and Rosita." Katz is quick to insist that other writers have had relatively little impact on his writing. In an interview published in *Anything Can Happen,* Katz has emphasized that it was the nonliterary aspects of his youth which had lasting importance: "The fantastic side of my work has as much to do with seeing Rousseau's *Sleeping Gypsy* once a week when I was a kid, and Hieronymus Bosch, and being around the Ensor, the Matisse, Picasso, Mondrian, Tanguy, Malevich, Soutine . . . as with the later influence of writers. And listening to Charles Ives and Bela Bartok informed my work. Ives was using American popular culture at the turn of the century. And Joe Louis, when I was real young. I often wanted to write a story that lands like the right hand he used to flatten Tami Mauriello. Or to make art with as much continuous energy communicated in a fight between Rocky Graziano and Tony Zale. Those events I witnessed in my childhood, so perfect in form and expression, such icons, informed my work, not for the sake of nostalgia or trivia, but in helping determine the actual shape of my work."

Yet when Katz enrolled at Cornell University in 1952 as a preveterinary student, he began to read extensively—Kafka, Faulkner, Gogol, Lermontov, Pound, and William Carlos Williams. He was also writing, beginning his first novel, "The Steps of the Sun," in 1955. He describes the novel, never published, as "relatively straight, with a lot of Faulknerian grotesqueries." Indeed, Katz suggests that experimentalism per se has never much concerned him: "Although the conventions of character development and psychological verity in fiction were depleted very early for me, innovation doesn't interest me as much as exploring, discovering, maybe inventing the forms appropriate to my understanding of the world; so I don't generally think about straight or innovative forms when I'm composing my books, but I find that different modes of experience require different formal approaches." Katz's interest in alternative formal approaches was ideally suited for the Cornell of the 1950s. During this period, with the figure of Vladimir Nabokov looming over the campus literary scene, the school was home for a number of writers who were to shape the direction of postmodern American fiction during the 1960s—Ronald Sukenick, Richard Farina, Thomas Pynchon, Harold Schimmel (all of whom Katz met and talked with), and William Gass.

After graduating with honors from Cornell in 1956, Katz entered the University of Oregon at Eugene, where he began work on an M.A. in English. By the time he had received his degree in 1959 (his thesis was on Coleridge's criticism—imagination and fancy), Katz and his wife, Patricia "Jingle" Bell, whom he had married in 1956, had three sons, whom he was supporting by doing various odd jobs: he was a shipping clerk in a department store; a waiter; a mucker in the quicksilver mines near McDermit, Nevada; and a smokechaser and lookout for the forest service in the Idaho Clearwater Forest. In 1959 he moved himself and his family to Italy, "mainly to see Massacio's Tribute Money in the Brancacci Chapel of Santa Maria del Carmine," he said. Katz lived in Italy for three years, until the fall of 1962—in the towns of Lecce in the south and Verona in the north; during this period he supported himself mainly as an itinerant lecturer at various overseas branches of the University of Maryland. He also spent considerable time in Tuscany and Umbria on pilgrimages to see the works of Piero della Francesca, Giotto, Simone Martini, Signorelli, Baldovinetti, Duccio, and Fra Angelico. Katz has acknowledged that his love of Italian Renaissance painting and his lifelong interest in contemporary art have had an important impact on his fiction: "It's always amazed me how few writers study the visual arts very carefully. They tend to be very conservative in their appreciation of other arts in general. I get a lot of my ideas and energy from watching what's happening in the recent visual arts. The 60s, for example, were a very exciting time. Carl Andre, Bob Morris, Charles Ross, Robert Smithson, Richard Serre, Mike Heizer—they've all been very important to me, probably more than other contemporary writers. There's also an aspect of my work I see coming from my love of Italian Renaissance painting—I admire the magic clarity of the space around all their figures."

During this time of study and travel in Italy, Katz also wrote fiction and poems, including his first published work, *The Lestriad* (self-published in 1962). More than his previous writings at Cornell, this fiction anticipated the voice and form that are particular to Katz. He says of this early work: "I learned from writing it the potential plasticity of narrative form, and the stateliness of augmented repetition." A book of poems completed in Italy, *The Weight of Antony,* was not published until 1964 after Katz returned to Cornell to teach. These poems, published by a friend and colleague, Stephen Gottlieb, were "readable" according to Katz, but were more an outlet for his anger and discontent than successful poetry.

In 1962 Katz returned to the United States to teach at Cornell, first as an instructor and later as an assistant professor of English. From 1962 until 1964 he completed another relatively traditional novel, "Kulik in Puglia," which Katz has described as being "a love song of sorts to Southern Italy, particularly the Salento, where I had lived for a while. It is a straight-forward, lyrical story, with characters, a modest plot, conflict and interaction, empathy requested." Although several trade publishers expressed interest, "Kulik" was never published. It was at this point, in 1965, that Katz began his first major work, *The Exagggerations of Peter Prince,* a novel into which he poured material that had been accumulating for almost a decade. It may seem ironic that *Peter Prince,* which defies all traditional rules of storytelling, was accepted for publication while the more conventional, less controversial "Kulik" withered on the vine; but the year of *Prince*'s publication, 1968, was a year in which postmodern experimentation, especially as found in highly self-conscious, metafictional works such as Katz's novel, was establishing itself as a significant form in contemporary American fiction. *Peter Prince* appeared at the same time as other experimental works in a similar vein—John Barth's *Lost in the Funhouse,* Ronald Sukenick's *Up,* William Gass's *Willie Masters' Lonesome Wife,* and Donald Barthelme's *Snow White.*

But in many of its formal features *Peter Prince* was even more extreme and openly disdainful of traditional narrative approaches than these other works. *Peter Prince* was greeted with bewilderment, misrepresentation, and apathy when it first appeared, and even today most critics have been unable or unwilling to deal with the novel on its own terms. Indeed, with the possible exception of Gass's *Willie Masters' Lonesome Wife*, probably no other book published during the 1960s flaunts narrative experimentation so outrageously and demands from its readers so different a conception of a book's visual, narrative, and spatial organization. Katz creates in *Prince* a series of improvisations upon topics associated with the name "Peter Prince," which denotes at various times a character, a town, a ship, and a character in another character's fiction. Karfiol has summarized Katz's method: "There is no apparent motivation behind the arrangement of the narrative portions of the book; these appear to be associative or merely additive in nature. The narratives are often interrupted by unrelated topics and are seldom concluded; problems and tensions that are created are never resolved, but forgotten or lost as they generate others. Some scenes are constructed with alternative or multiple forms; some are questioned or flatly denied their 'truth' by other portions of the text; some are literally crossed out with a large 'X' that covers the page. All form parts of a text in which chaos and contingency are assumed in the organization and substance." Meanwhile, Steve Katz is also busy reflecting upon his own performance in passages such as: "Enough! Katz, you're making this all up. It doesn't make a bit of sense. It's not a promising beginning. Why can't you follow instruction? You can't write whatever you want. . . . Where's the story? How are you going to catch us up in it and write a novel so the reader won't be able to put it down, he's so involved?" In short, Katz creates the impression that the fictional sequence of his text is absolutely provisional. As Karfiol explains, "Katz's capricious imagination throws out the possibilities, improvising on the name, the situation, and the physical form he has created."

Karfiol's comparison between Katz's approach to form and that of jazz musicians was first articulated by Jerome Klinkowitz in *The Life of Fiction*: "Of all his colleagues, Katz is the closest to being a jazz musician with language, using his gift for sound and circumstance to create dazzling improvisations upon the most unlikely subjects. . . . Katz reminds us that the conventions of life are merely that, arbitrary assumptions never meant as an absolute end in themselves. As a writer, he uses those conventions not as a representational base, but simply as the

bone structure for his improvisations." Katz has directly acknowledged the impact which jazz has had on his conception of form in *Anything Can Happen*: "Jazz was my childhood and it had a deep influence on all my work; but it wasn't a love for the 'freedom' of improvisation that drew me to it, but rather that jazz was the first art in which I began to perceive what *form* was, and that thrilling tension between the freedom of blowing and the imperatives of order. And I began to realize that art has a formal influence on the emotions, and is permitted through form to enrich the intellect. It's instantaneous at the moment that the form is perceived. I got that from jazz, and it opened the way for me to understand form in all the other arts."

In *Peter Prince* Katz fully exploits this tension between "the freedom of blowing and the imperatives of order." As *Prince*'s events and images develop, often separated spatially from each other through various typographical devices, Katz not only shows off his narrative versatility but, more subtly, reinforces his epistemological skepticism. While the reader observes characters and events shifting in and out of contexts, he soon loses all sense of duration and logical causality; or, as Peter Prince says at one point, "Sometimes it's so hard to tell what has really happened. It's impossible to know. That's why I want to develop multiple possibilities simultaneously." Thus, like Robert Coover, Alain Robbe-Grillet, and other contemporary writers who develop simultaneous narrative alternatives, Katz uses this technique to reinforce his own pluralist view that reality cannot be reduced to a single vision presented by a single persona.

As might be expected critical reaction to the novel was mixed. It was dismissed by some reviewers as experimental quackery—Robert Cassill described it as "a filibuster without apparent object"; Sara Blackburn called it "a doggedly vacant novel . . . intent on attracting negative reviews"—and yet the same audacious departures from conventional narrative techniques were cited by other reviewers as daring and fun. Robert Baker, in the *Library Journal*, called it "a fine example of contemporaneity of form." But these extremes in critical opinions were less important in the novel's reception than the publisher's handling of the book. In fact, Katz's first novel suffered from the kind of bad luck that would plague the publication of his first three books. Initially, confident that *Peter Prince* was an important new type of work, Holt, Rinehart and Winston agreed to a large promotional campaign; but at the last minute the publishers withdrew most of the promotional funding. Consequently, despite the book's costly production, it received almost no promotion. When the book failed Katz was, he says, "left stranded and feeling lonely because I had trusted this function of collective greed to handle my work. That made me realize that I had to reorganize my own thinking about what I was doing as a writer. If that kind of success—becoming famous, making a lot of money—comes my way, that would be fine; but it is highly unlikely in this system."

After receiving the first reports that Holt had agreed to publish *Peter Prince,* Katz felt energized to begin a new book, a collection of short pieces entitled *Creamy and Delicious.* These "mythologies," as Katz calls them, were all written during the summer of 1967 while Katz was working part-time in a Nevada quicksilver mine under a peculiar, self-imposed condition: "The limits of it were to write a story every day and to spend only two hours actually writing the stories. . . . But except for tampering with a few of the loose ends, I never revised any of the mythologies beyond those first drafts." Such an approach is highly unusual in a work of fiction since the element of composition is being added to the artistic process. This sort of arbitrary restriction, of course, had precedents in the visual arts, which Katz was well aware of, as when Jackson Pollock set time limits for some of his drip and canvas paintings.

Presented in a defiantly unfinished form, the stories in *Creamy and Delicious* aim at exploiting the transformational possibilities of myth and using the elements of contemporary popular culture to create myths which speak directly to the contemporary sensibility. As Larry McCaffery has written, Katz is attempting "to disrupt any sense of myth's universality, fixated order, and immobilizing power by introducing new and actively disruptive elements into the systems." In each of these tales Katz begins by selecting a name that is mythic in the sense that it suggests familiar story lines and clusters of other narrative elements. But in addition to the classical mythic names—Faust, Achilles, Hermes, Goliath, Apollo—Katz devotes equal time to the characters of contemporary culture: Nancy and Sluggo, Wonder Woman, Plastic Man, Gandhi, and Nasser. Once the stories begin, however, Katz divorces the names from their conventional associations—as when Nancy and Sluggo are revealed to be a gay cowboy and a "terrible gulch-riding bandit," respectively—and creates purely imaginative adventures. The Faust mythology, for example, begins: "Don't believe any of those stories you had to read in college about Faust, the big scientist who wanted to know all the shit of the world, so he turned on the devil. Don't believe all that. It's a big put-on, and

maybe some of it is almost true, but none of it is really true, and if you fall for it you deserve to be pasted on the wall like a wall-paper pattern." The remainder of the story has little or nothing to do with the original Faust legend; instead it tells of Faust, a farmer with an eye for the ladies, his amorous adventures with one notorious Lulu, and a later encounter with a woman named Margaret. The Katzian Faust story, then, plays with our expectations, which have been aroused by Katz's use of the coded signal "Faust," as a completely new story line is pursued. Since all received versions of the past have been fundamentally falsified in the act of their transmission, Katz implies, the contemporary writer should feel free to invent whatever variations his imagination can concoct.

The publication of *Creamy and Delicious,* like that of *Peter Prince,* went virtually unnoticed by reviewers, critics, and readers. With little prospect of earning a living from his writing, in the fall of 1969 Katz reluctantly returned to teaching, this time as a lecturer in fiction at the University of Iowa Writers Workshop; in 1970 he returned to his native New York City as a writer-in-residence at Brooklyn College; and in 1971 he began a stint that lasted until 1975 as an adjunct assistant professor of English at Queens College. Katz did take time off in 1971 to work as a scriptwriter on the movie *Grassland* (released in some places as *Hex*). Though the movie, featuring Keith Carradine and Gary Busey, failed commercially, the on-location filming at an Indian reservation in South Dakota inspired Katz's modern epic poem entitled *Cheyenne River Wild Track* (1973). As he explains the poem's gestation: "I suddenly found myself directing traffic at an incredible intersection of the many vectors of American culture—the redneck, Henry Crow-Dog, the Sioux holy man, hippies, money, drugs, motorcycles, movie industry dream machine, artists compromised and not, animal trainers, South Dakota land/spacescape, the wind, the Missouri River, the rip-off—all these elements and more were plunged together right in front of my eyes into the incredible pressure-cooker of a movie-making experience. I felt obliged to testify to my experience there and *Cheyenne River Wild Track* were the 'pages' I produced." During this same period Katz published his next novel, *Saw* (1972), and also wrote most of what would become *Moving Parts.*

Perhaps even more than in his previous books, in *Saw* Katz allows his imagination freedom to create scenes, characters, and events restricted not by the validity of their human "truths" or the accuracy of their psychology but generated by spontaneous and private rules of transformation. These rules serve to organize and direct certain structural aspects of the novel. For example, the book is divided into five parts with the title of each section being simply a number seemingly chosen at random—17, 5, 11, 3, 7. The numbers, however, add up to forty-three, the prime number chosen arbitrarily by Katz several years earlier to be used in all fictional circumstances in which a number is required. Likewise, Katz reveals in a later story ("43" in *Moving Parts*) that he chose the title *Saw* as follows: after ascribing a number to each letter of the alphabet, one to twenty-six, he then eliminated all those letters corresponding to integers that are not primary. With those that remained, he examined the ones which would, when combined, add up to forty-three. Among the letters appropriate to this scheme were *a, s,* and *w* (corresponding to one, nineteen, twenty-three). "Was" was a possibility, but Katz eventually chose "Saw" since it evokes perception, construction, and deconstruction, all essential to the creation of fiction. Although such a strategy seems far removed from the usual way that titles denote theme, suggest content, or initiate the emotion behind the work, it is still a conscious, extrapolative decision that creates the resonances that Katz, like all writers, seeks in his fiction.

The story line of *Saw* is wholly dreamlike and discontinuous, although certain characters and motifs recur in each of the novel's five sections. A brief summary of the book's first section should give a sense of how the book unfolds. It opens with a young girl named Eileen going to Van Cortland Park in New York City with a puppy, which her friend, a hawk, carries off and eats. The hawk returns with bits of puppy gristle clinging to its hooked beak and says, "Thanks a million. It sure is swell of you to keep on bringing me these tender pups. They make me feel so good. A hawk in New York is like a fish out of water these days. No eats here. Everything frozen or in cans." While talking with the hawk and noticing the jets rising in great poisonous profusion from Kennedy, La Guardia, and Newark, Eileen spies a big sphere rolling her way "full of a milky irridescence that looks like life." The sphere makes her smile, and soon they are carrying on a conversation that probably sounds familiar, despite the peculiar context. (Thus, after exchanging laments about their sense of loneliness and alienation, the sphere tells Eileen, "My father was a pyramid and my mother was rhomboid. The last thing they expected to have was a sphere, and they had no idea how to cope with me. As soon as I could roll off on my own I put distance between

us.") After they spend the afternoon together and make love, the Sphere announces that he is, in fact, "The Astronaut" who will henceforth be the main character in the novel; Eileen is told she can either leave the story or agree to become a secondary personage in the book. Eileen agrees to stay on if the Astronaut will help her blow up the *New York Times*; the section concludes, "Forty-three minutes later the *New York Times* is a heap of rubble."

Despite the fantastic quality of such scenes, *Saw* is a strangely cohesive book which makes its own kind of sense. This is due partly to Katz's ability to create scenes of such hallucinatory vividness that the life of the page cannot be denied. But as with Donald Barthelme's equally peculiar fiction from this period, *Saw* successfully evokes for the reader an undeniable sense of the alienation, need for communication, rebellious energy, and the paradoxical qualities of beauty and ugliness that were very much a part of the real New York City in the early 1970s. Remarkably, then, *Saw* is very much a relevant novel about the times, a book whose self-enclosed, metaphorical existence nevertheless suggests ways of thinking about the world even as it resolutely refuses the pretension of being real. Unfortunately, another publishing problem insured that *Saw* would never be treated seriously by reviewers or the public: not enough glue was placed into the binding of the book; thus as readers paged through the novel, it rapidly fell apart.

In part out of a sense of frustration and disappointment with the way his fiction had been promoted and misrepresented by the publishing industry, Katz decided to publish his next book, *Moving Parts,* with the recently formed Fiction Collective, a nonprofit writers cooperative in which the writers themselves make all decisions regarding the editing and promotion of their books. Katz was one of the writers involved in the formation of the Collective in 1973, along with Sukenick, Jonathan Baumbach, and Peter Spielberg. Free to control the book's textual arrangement and visual design exactly as he wished, Katz created in *Moving Parts* his most accessible and aesthetically successful book to date. It is also the most self-reflexive of Katz's works in the way that it focuses attention on how the author is affected by various imaginative systems that have made their way into his personal and aesthetic worlds. Thus the four individual sections of the novel are united, as Karfiol notes, by Katz's "attempts to fix experience in logical or meaningful structures, which fail, thus abandoning Katz to confrontations with his real and fictional experiences, confrontations in which nothing can be resolved."

In "Female Skin," the first section, Katz tries to exorcise a woman who has, metaphorically, gotten under his skin. This woman, Wendy Appel, is the character in the fiction; but she is also a character in Katz's life, and her photograph is included along with a signed and dated document giving Katz permission to use her name and details from their relationship. Thus, from the beginning, *Moving Parts* is probing the borders that separate and unite fiction and reality: first Katz creates a story in which he literally climbs into Wendy's skin, and then he reports the reactions of various real people to this story. With the assistance of journal entries, photographs, and assorted other imaginatively recreated experiences, readers observe how Katz's story begins to affect his real life and relationships with others.

"Parcel of Wrists," the next section, opens with a passage typical of Katz's eerie ability to create a meticulously realized scene that is wildly improbable: "In this morning's mail I received a parcel postmarked from Irondale, Tennessee. It was wrapped in heavy, glazed brown paper, like thick butcher paper. The box was of even dimensions, two feet high, two feet deep, three feet long, and it was packed from top to bottom with human wrists. The wrists were clean and odorless. They had been prepared so neatly, without a trace of torn flesh, that it occurred to me they might never have been attached to hand or forearm." The story goes on to describe Katz's efforts to track down the origin of these wrists. Arriving in Tennessee, he discovers that there is no such city as "Irondale," though an Iron City does exist. After having adventures in a local commune outside the town and in an Indian burial ground, Katz finally returns to his home in New York City to discover that the wrists he has left behind in forty-three flower pots have sprouted into big plants whose buds eventually bear different parts of human anatomy (lips, legs, and so forth). In the next story, "Trip," written three years after "Parcel of Wrists," Katz decides to explore the fictional territory invented for the previous story by taking an actual trip to the area of Tennessee described in "Parcel of Wrists" to see if there is any correspondence between the world and his imagination. Naturally, Katz soon discovers that although the reality of his trip is infused with the fiction that generated it, the real world has a way of correcting fantasy. Thus the bus station in Nashville, invented by Katz in the earlier story, is not at all as he had imagined it—a situation which leaves him feeling disappointed: "Nothing here out of Parcel of Wrists. Reality is too fucked up to coincide. Experi-

ence accumulates and discrepancies pile up like useless by-products." At other times, however, unnerving overlaps between fiction and reality, again reinforced by actual photographs of Katz in Tennessee, create in Katz a spooky sense that his identity has become suspended and his experiment is turning him into a provisional entity. When the people of Iron City wave greetings to Katz, he feels that "It is more like being home than being home. Everyone is friendly, waving at my body, communicating with my accompanying ghost. I haunt this place out of my own fiction, living in one world and in another at once, but alive now in neither. Admitting no history in one, having none in the other."

Katz's actual experiences in Tennessee led him to conclude that notions such as "Truth" and "Reality" are outmoded concepts which fail to acknowledge that they are contingent upon the perspective of the teller. If truth exists in fiction at all, Katz suggests, "it's not constructed in language, but generated as resonances by the art of telling." In the last section of *Moving Parts*, "43," Katz returns to this idea as he explains how he came to use the number forty-three in his fiction and how the number has subsequently created unexpected reverberations in his life. In 1964, after reading an article in *Scientific American* about prime numbers, Katz decided to use forty-three whenever he needed a number in his fiction. A bit later, he "began to collect bits of information about the number that happened to cross my life, or appeared in newspapers and books." Gradually, however, the number began to haunt his life curiously, especially after friends sent him accounts of their own encounters with the number. The result was that this pure abstraction soon began to affect Katz's daily life in a direct and forceful manner; it began "to come first, before sex, before food, before the drive for popularity." The story concludes with Charles Ross, an artist-friend of Katz's, explaining that he has discovered that forty-three plays an important role in certain astronomical calculations he has been making. Knowing that Ross will now always note the number and associate it with him, Katz concludes the story by saying with satisfaction, "He could no longer forget, I realized. My number was embedded now in his great astronomical art project. The difference is 43 degrees, 43 degrees. 43."

Since 1978 Katz has been an associate professor of English at the University of Colorado. He has been at work on several projects, including a full-length stage play, "Bunkers"; a collection of found poetry, "Journalism," composed out of conversa-

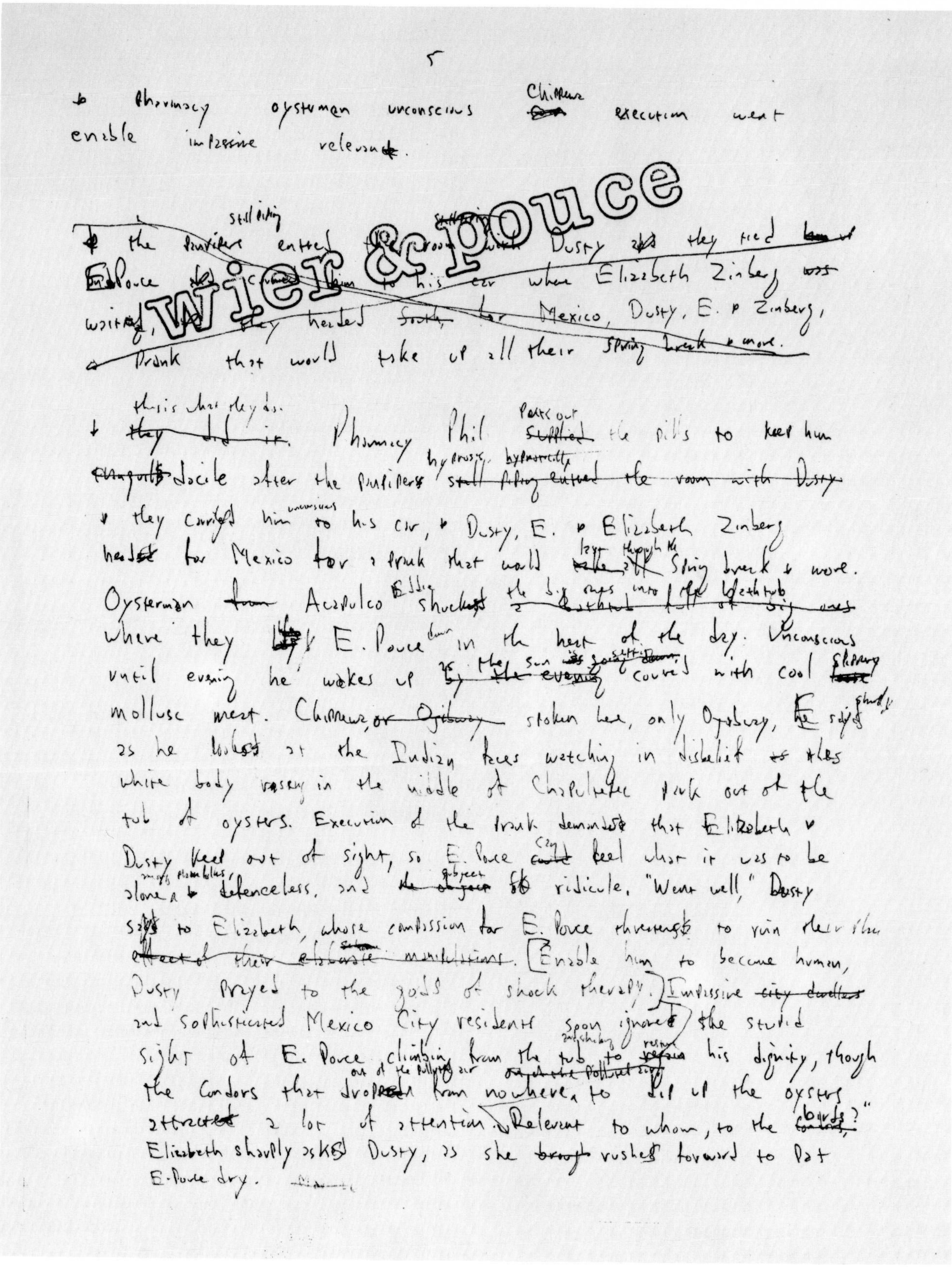

Page from the manuscript for a work in progress (the author)

tions overheard in prisons; a novel, "Weir and Pouce"; and a collection of stories.

Katz's fiction, as challenging, amusing, and innovative as it is, has gone virtually unnoticed by critics thus far. Jerome Klinkowitz was the first critic to treat Katz's work seriously (in *Literary Disruptions* and *The Life of Fiction*), and there have been passing references to Katz by several other postmodern critics. The final comments in Judith Karfiol's unpublished dissertation, the most perceptive study of Katz's work, offer a fine summary of why his fiction, with its absurd surface features, its verbal play and exuberance, and its metafictional ironies and dislocations, deserves to be considered seriously: "Assuming the existential imperatives of freedom and invention, Katz creates imaginative worlds that reflect the disorder and unreasonableness of man's experience by setting his characters, and himself, adrift in a fictional universe where anything is possible and where all points of reference or epistemological codes are arbitrary and provisional. . . . Katz's imaginative dislocations lead us intentionally further from the actual, until we recognize the independent artifact that is fiction, and notice its self-consciousness." Despite its relative anonymity among critics and the public, Katz's work has undeniably influenced other experimental writers and artists, like Raymond Federman and Ronald Sukenick. It also illustrates the direction fiction has been taking since the postmodern outburst of the 1960s when the mimetic tradition in literature was challenged by the claim that art is primarily invention, not duplication.

References:

Judith Karfiol, "New American Fiction and the Aesthetics of Camus and Robbe-Grillet," Ph.D. dissertation, University of Southern California, 1978, pp. 83-147;

Jerome Klinkowitz, *The Life of Fiction* (Urbana: University of Illinois Press, 1977), pp. 104-115;

Klinkowitz, *Literary Disruptions* (Urbana: University of Illinois Press, 1975), pp. 18-20;

Larry McCaffery, "The Fiction Collective," *Contemporary Literature,* 19 (Winter 1978): 114-115;

McCaffery, "The Fiction Collective: An Innovative Alternative," *Chicago Review,* 30 (Autumn 1978): 107-126;

McCaffery, "Form, Formula, and Fantasy: Generative Approaches in Contemporary Fiction," in *Bridges to Fantasy,* edited by Eric Rabkin, Robert Scholes, and George Slusser (Carbondale: Southern Illinois University Press, 1982), pp. 21-37;

McCaffery, "An Interview with Steve Katz," in *Anything Can Happen: Interviews with Contemporary American Novelists,* edited by Tom LeClair and Larry McCaffery (Urbana: University of Illinois Press, 1983), pp. 219-234.

John Keeble
(24 November 1944-   )

J. D. Brown
University of Oregon

BOOKS: *Crab Canon* (New York: Grossman, 1971);
Mine, by Keeble and Ransom Jeffery (New York: Grossman/Viking, 1974);
Yellowfish (New York: Harper & Row, 1980).

OTHER: "The Transmission," *American Review: The Magazine of New Writing,* 25 (1976): 36-61.

John Keeble's *Yellowfish* (1980), a novel which is ostensibly a suspense story, elicited many admiring reviews. Raymond Carver deemed it "without qualification or hedging, a great work of imaginative literature, smack in the mainstream." Mary Lee Settle called it "a bright vision of the morals of necessity, beautifully told." Most reviewers praised the novel's style and regional content. "The people, places, and traditions of the Northwest are precisely delineated in language at once sinuous and sensual," William Hjortsberg remarked. Two prominent Northwest writers seconded this notion, James Welch calling *Yellowfish* "a complex, almost Faulknerian portrait of the Pacific Northwest," and Carolyn Kizer heralding it as "the first major novel to be situated in the Northwest," or at least that

John Keeble (James D. Burns)

uncelebrated, arid sector east of the Cascades. While there were some less enthusiastic reviews, it is clear that with this novel John Keeble has joined the ranks of the best current novelists in the Northwest, among them Ken Kesey and James Welch.

To label Keeble as a regionalist, however, is too restrictive. Not only were his first two books set ouside the Northwest, but as Keeble himself told Fred Newberry in an interview: "One doesn't want one's art to be region bound." Preferring to speak of place, not region, Keeble insists that the writer should not be "concerned with region, really. One is concerned with place as reality, not as an idea. One is concerned with certain kinds of weeds and with the way the land lays in a certain place. But that's actual. Whereas regionalism is a literary idea, and I don't think writers can write according to literary ideas." It is a detailed measurement of the physical place, if not the abstract region, which is crucial in Keeble's fiction, shaping his characters and defining their metaphysical journeys.

Certainly the places John Keeble has lived figure prominently in his work. The son of a minister,

Raymond Charles William Keeble, and his wife, Olivia Wallace Keeble, he was born in Winnipeg and spent his early years in Saskatchewan on the arid prairie of that Canadian province. He attended high school south of San Diego in a small navy town. While an undergraduate at the University of the Redlands, on 4 September 1964 he married Claire Shelden. Both Canada and California are prominent places in Keeble's first novel, *Crab Canon* (1971). After graduating magna cum laude from the University of the Redlands in 1966, Keeble attended the University of Iowa Writers' Workshop and received his M.F.A. in 1969. The state of Iowa became the setting for his second novel, *Mine* (1974), a collaborative effort with Ransom Jeffery. Keeble was writer in residence at Grinnell College (1971-1972) and Brown University (1972-1973). He then moved west, and after settling in eastern Washington near Spokane, he was hired to teach at Eastern Washington State University in Cheney, Washington. With his wife and their three children, Keeble now lives on a ranch near Medical Lake, Washington, in a house built of logs that he and his wife cut. This area provides the setting for Keeble's third novel, *Yellowfish*.

Crab Canon is a display of the raw ability and apocalyptic excesses which Keeble would hone into *Yellowfish*. Extravagant in style, complex in structure, dense in character and detail, *Crab Canon* is a modern-Gothic Western. Its language is Faulknerian, and many of its passages are surrealistic. A superb, mostly realistic opening section, "Steppit Burroughs: Duodenary Virgo, Tongue-and-Groove," introduces the twelve characters who chapter-by-chapter narrate the novel. Their stories shift freely through time (the 1930s to the 1960s) and place (primarily San Diego, Saskatchewan, and Lagoon, Wyoming), but they are all part of a world that is both nightmarish and metaphysical. Plot is incidental. One of the narrators, David Roschenstein, seeks to discover his true father, and his quest requires him to untangle the violent, fantastic interrelationships delineated by the eleven other character-narrators. Samuel Gloucester, a major character who is not one of the twelve narrators, becomes the satanical (or divine) father figure. A gigantic, mechanical crab arching over the surreal landscape apparently represents the torturous search for the demonic father. The darkness, the Gothic curse at the heart of the story, submerges successive narrators in an allegorical landscape. This submergence slows the pace of the novel, making turgid what should be compelling. The dazzling, evocative prose becomes exhausting, and the explosive surrealism deafening. The urgent, underlying human story is blunted by such excesses. While *Crab Canon* reminds the reader of the grotesque fictions of Flannery O'Connor or John Hawkes, its psychological and magical effects become too shrill. Unrestrained, the prose grows tiresome. It is a version of Faulkner's *As I Lay Dying* (1930) written for the psychedelic generation, with the works of William Burroughs and Thomas Pynchon goading the author on.

Keeble recalls that he "worked very hard" on James Joyce and William Faulkner. Both authors influenced—too strongly—the composition of *Crab Canon*. Joyce's architectonics and Faulkner's expansive, philosophical lyricism are too evident. Over the next ten years, he learned to bring to his writing a commanding simplicity rather than a dazzling, smothering excess. Yet *Crab Canon* is a notable start, an intricate novel of distinct, robust characters, rendered in an intriguing, if too insistent, style. Portions of *Crab Canon* appeared from 1968 to 1970, during the author's early twenties, in *Confluence #1*, *Confluence #3*, and *Works in Progress*; he was only twenty-six when the novel was published.

In analyzing the differences between *Crab Canon* and his later work, Keeble characterized his first novel as "apocalyptic and parodist," and he suggested that "the change in writing from *Crab Canon* to *Yellowfish* is a change from seeking a kind of other-worldly magic to finding a this-worldly magic." Places in *Crab Canon* are, he says, "inventions of the mind," but in *Yellowfish* "the landscape is accepted as something which is actually there, and which is fully as mysterious as the impossible landscape of *Crab Canon*."

By the time *Crab Canon* appeared, Keeble had begun to collaborate with Ransom Jeffery on an Iowa novel, *Mine*. Keeble and Jeffery had both attended the Iowa Writers' Workshop, and they and their families lived together during part of 1972 while the two men composed early drafts of *Mine*. After Keeble took a position at Brown University later in 1972, they finished the novel by telephone and mail.

The motive for their collaboration was initially mercenary: "When my friend Ransom Jeffery and I sat down to write our collaborative novel *Mine*, we were both in a creative doldrum," Keeble recalls. "We sat down and said, all right, we're going to write a potboiler." Shades of the conventional thriller remain in *Mine*, but the form quickly becomes more an experiment in narration than a bid for the best-seller list. Part of its experimental nature comes

from the collaboration itself: Jeffery and Keeble alternately wrote the twelve chapters, with Jeffery's written from the first-person view of one character, Rag, and Keeble's from the first-person view of another, Saint James. Action and character become increasingly fantastic and allegorical as the novel progresses. *Mine*, nevertheless, is more straightforward and less surrealistic than *Crab Canon*. Judging by the style and approach in Jeffery's chapters, one can speculate that the collaboration acted to restrain some of the excesses exhibited in Keeble's previous novel. Events in *Mine* are more solidly anchored in the literal world.

The novel concerns a shipment of marijuana brought to Iowa City by a free-spirited young woman, Annie. Saint James, the distributor of the goods, misses his meeting with Annie, but Rag happens by and takes Annie home. She has previously been the lover of both men. Annie stashes the marijuana in Rag's barn, and when Rag wakes up later Annie and the shipment have disappeared. Saint James comes looking for Rag, Annie, and the shipment, at the same time trying to avoid two local hoodlums, Cully and Cream. At first, *Mine* keeps within the boundaries of the suspense genre, but since it is essentially a Gothic romance, its events quickly assume fantastic shapes and its characters grotesque dimensions. Demonic forces entrap the characters in a snare of improbable coincidences.

Human relationships in the novel are labyrinthine. Saint James is beset by a multitude of demons, including Leon Hogue, who has a hook at the end of his artificial arm. The night Hogue's mother lay dying, he "raped" Saint James's mother (a willing victim) in the same house and made everyone aware of his actions. Soon after Hogue's mother died, Saint James's mother married Hogue's father, who had kept her as his mistress. Thus, Saint James is now stepbrother to a man who raped his mother. Fearful of Hogue, repulsed by his mother's behavior, Saint James married a woman named Maude, whom he divorced before the birth of their son, Dandy. Maude then married Leon Hogue, making him stepfather to Saint James's son. It is his son whom Saint James seeks to make his own again—the "mine" of the title.

Each of the major characters in *Mine* is obsessed with making "mine" what is, and yet is not, truly theirs. Their inability to possess fully anyone (or anything) beyond themselves erupts in violence. The crucial act is the shooting of Saint James's son, Dandy. All the characters are indirectly responsible and must come to terms with both their guilt and the destructive nature of their desires to possess others.

This theme of possession unifies the novel. In the Gothic context of events, what one can possess, if one can possess anything at all, becomes a central moral issue.

Keeble made significant advances in *Mine*. While still overwriting in a Faulknerian manner and relying on the type of flashy, overwrought flourishes which load down *Crab Canon*, he began to turn toward a hard, direct, realistic style to support and animate his metaphysical leaps. Many of the elements developed in *Yellowfish*—the geographical detail, the natural metaphors, local history, the romance of machinery and travel—were already in place in *Mine*.

Such growth was obvious in the short story, "The Transmission," which appeared in *American Review* in 1976, a few years after Keeble moved west. The language is as spare as the setting (rural eastern Washington). There is hardly a sentence of abstract contemplation or a passage of feverish surrealism. The first-person narrator helps his neighbors, Louis and Rose Crofoot, to move a truck transmission so that it can be taken to town for repair. The couple is in the midst of a violent quarrel over money; the narrator is trying to put the pieces of his life back together. Rose leaves her husband that night and sleeps with the narrator, who is confronted by the husband in the morning. The broken transmission comes to symbolize the broken relationships in the story—and the narrator's stoic, faltering attempts to patch them back together. Without lyrical or metaphysical effusion, Keeble defines an ambiguous, severe, compelling moral landscape. The writing seems almost too restrained, reflecting perhaps the influences of two contemporary writers Keeble admires enormously, Tillie Olsen and James Welch. In *Yellowfish* Keeble is able to reintroduce some of the metaphysical and lyrical elements of *Crab Canon* while retaining the understated, realistic power of "The Transmission."

Yellowfish is the narrative of a journey on the roads from Vancouver, British Columbia, to San Francisco, California. The geography of the region is exhaustively rendered, and the plot makes for what a book-jacket blurb would call "an action-packed thriller." But the novel is far more than a suspense story set in the wide open spaces of the West.

The hero, Wesley Erks, who lives with his wife, Ruby, and their son on a ranch in eastern Washington, supplements his income from his farm and machine shop by running illegal Asian immigrants ("yellowfish") across the Canadian-U.S. border, a scheme devised by the shadowy (and aptly named) Lucas Tenebrel. On a mission to deliver four Chinese illegals to San Francisco, he becomes uneasy almost immediately. He is being followed; one of his passengers has been wounded and refuses medical care; and his most important passenger, Ginarn Taam, is mixed up with the Triad, a criminal syndicate which controls gambling operations in Nevada.

Neither Erks nor the reader knows who is pursuing Erks, how the threatening Triad is involved, or what Taam's purpose is. Erks eventually makes his delivery, only to see Taam gunned down in the streets. Erks returns to his ranch, still confused about the nature of his travels, but determined to sever his connections with the smuggling operation.

What keeps the reader moving over the surface of this journey are the repeated sections where Erks is thwarted or threatened (although he is determined to continue and survive his ordeal) and the sense of dislocation and mystery which pervades the novel. This sense of dislocation and uncertainty is established in a prelude where Erks makes a typical delivery and feels himself "growing larger, more conspicuous. Uncertain as to what was expected of him, as to whether or not he should speak, or for that matter what he was even doing here—the entire proceeding, words, bodies, conduct, and transaction, was a cipher to which he had not a clue except that Lucas had said money would be paid him here—he hung on to his valise as if it were his anchor." Erks is a practical, self-reliant man, and ambiguities trouble him. The reader is told he has "an eye for land and weather and crops . . . or at a distance for seeing doves on a wire, or the hump of a coyote's back behind a rock, an eye used to sighting down a fence line and the barrel of a shotgun," and he is, at the same time, self-aware, contemplative. He knows his eye for detail, however splendid, lacks depth and the ability to supply a third dimension which will bring meaning to his observation. The goal of Erks's inward journey is established early in the novel when he comes upon a solitary figure in deep contemplation: Erks "appreciated the distance, himself from the man, the man from himself, and himself—Erks, the traveler—from himself, the two men like two points in space triangulated by magic. Erks imagined that the man was on the brink of resolving his difficulty, that the subject of his interior dialogue drew near its conclusion." Erks, about to undertake a dangerous, mysterious outward journey, is forced to measure himself—his conduct, the nature of his activities—and find some way to triangulate, to add depth and meaning to his observations. This quest for meaning continues throughout the novel until Erks's own interior dialogue (and his outward journey) conclude.

The complex rhetoric of the novel—realistic, yet meditative and abstract—has evoked praise from some and objections from others. A critic for the *New Yorker* (28 April 1980) commented that "the reader who can abide the neo-rococo vocabulary will enjoy a thoroughly entertaining tale." In *Newsweek* (11 February 1980) Walter Clemons praised Keeble's ambition and his "strenuous effort to write fiction of grander-than-usual dimensions," but he felt that "the story has a very hard time getting itself told." Clemons found that "Keeble's pondered, deliberate prose is essentially undramatic and apt under stress to lapse into bathos." The reviewer for *Time* (4 February 1980), R. Z. Sheppard, was more sympathetic, citing the "intensely perceived set pieces" of the novel, although he admitted that "Keeble's prose can get a bit steamy, especially when he intends to foreshadow ominous events. But once on the road, the author restores the tired abstractions of great Western space and silence with fresh feelings of motion and flight."

The least sympathetic view was contained in Edmund White's devastating review for the *New York Times Book Review* (10 February 1980). White praised Keeble's portrayal of women, the landscape, the action, and a "tense, very American sensuality," but, he added, "all of these strengths are subverted by the clumsy prose, the gooey thickening that has been added to the clear broth of the tale." The reader, said White, was burdened "with pages of pretentious twaddle." Characterizing much of the writing as "illiterate" or "vacuous," White added that "the language gropes its way through several different tones, all lamentable." Concluded White: "Our country is perhaps unfortunate that so many of its standard authors are eccentric; one thinks of Melville, Faulkner, Pynchon. These are writers (in every other way dissimilar) who depend on the power of rhetoric to animate and unify their books. They do not fashion a careful *progression d'effect*; their style is not chaste; their plots are not coherent. Instead, their strange, teetering, homemade novels are fueled by genius alone. They are dangerous models for a writer who has not yet found his own voice."

Nevertheless, in *Yellowfish* Keeble has found his own voice, a strong one which draws from the American literature associated with writers in and of the West. It draws together the same expansive, contradictory syllables and cadences which power other novels of this region, from Joaquin Miller's to

Ken Kesey's. Keeble's voice is a major one in that tradition. At one point in *Yellowfish*, Erks observes that the early explorer Simon Fraser "took on the language of the West and in so doing seemed akin to the excessive, often brutal, and yet exact language of other Westerners to come: Joaquin Miller, Norris, London, Jeffers, Ginsberg, Kerouac, Spicer, and Bukowski." Keeble uses this language, which is carefully sculpted and controlled in *Yellowfish*.

Moreover, the novel itself is not loosely constructed. Its structure is tightly wound and deeply layered. Erks's meditations on Western explorers, particularly Simon Fraser, provide one layer of this deeper vision. Erks's travels parallel those of the past, making the novel a new version of the westward movement in America. This historical overlay is effective. For example, when Erks crosses the border in desperate flight to avoid (possible) pursuers, his run across the night border is linked to Simon Fraser's shooting the rapids in the early 1800s. The overlay is effective, too, in characterizing Erks: Simon Fraser is "one of Erks's own kind, an itinerant, an adventurer," struggling to find the correct route and deal honorably with others who are "like the river, like the land, forever swelling out of control." Above all, Erks believes that Fraser made sense of his journey by discovering a "moral pivot." In *Yellowfish* Erks must find his own "moral pivot," act upon it, and so define the meaning of an otherwise obscure, aimless movement through the landscape.

Within this wild, historically etched landscape is the physical action of the novel—the adventure, the long chase scenes—and these are paced and drawn with authority too, so much so that at the end of one shattering escape from pursuers, as Erks rests his battered car and steps across the dark road, Bigfoot makes a credible and genuinely terrifying appearance. Keeble evokes the Sasquatch legend convincingly—concretely but symbolically. Keeble later called this episode "the one point in the novel where there is an explicit magical emanation of landscape." Finally, there are the characters, some tangential, some essential. Erks himself is believable, perhaps because he is a moral man dealing outside the law. While his activity is questionable, he is often conventional and old-fashioned in his conduct. Erks is more than a stick figure narrator or stand-in for John Keeble. He is complex, both good and bad (and sometimes indifferent), a severe judge of himself. Equally convincing, although perhaps more comic and streamlined, are the low-life characters of *Yellowfish*. One is the self-serving, incompetent, opportunistic man from the East, Sand-

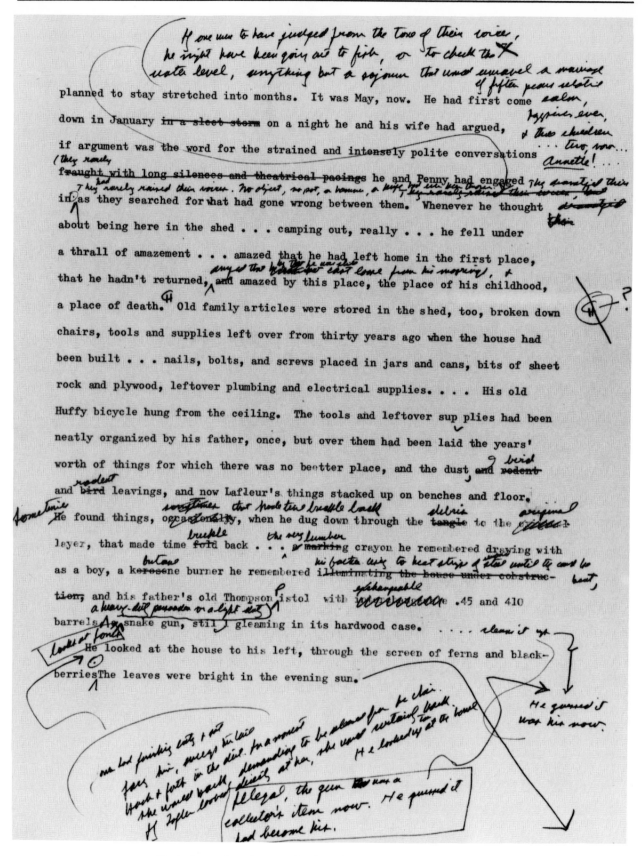

Revised page from the typescript for a forthcoming novel (the author)

man (dispatched by Ruby Erks in one of the novel's finest episodes). Others include the rural Idaho brothers, Bud and Zack—angry, violent creatures who are competent with machinery and self-reliant but are unable to keep from brutalizing those around them. "All of his people live and breathe on the page," observes Carolyn Kizer. "The men are wonderfully drawn, and the women!—the women are superb" (*Northwest Review*, no. 1, 1982). Indeed, the women are strong, complex beings. Ruby Erks is particularly competent, wise, vital—fully herself and able to express herself, not a woman mastered by a man or by crushing circumstances. Even more memorable is Lily Tenebrel, wife of Erks's shadowy employer. Lily, who accompanies Erks on the last half of his journey, is the strongest being in the novel. She is the first to reach a crucial "moral pivot," and she has the strength to change—to cut herself loose from the oppressive evil associated with her husband—what Erks must do at the end of the novel.

Yellowfish is a novel of measurements. Erks is measuring himself (his conduct) against history, against nature, against death, against others, against the dark pattern of events. Measuring becomes his primary activity because everything powerful seems inaccessible (from the landscape to the backroom manipulations of the Triad). Erks's need to measure is heightened by the novel's structure of uncertainty. Each situation is shaped so that not enough is revealed to render certain judgment. The crucial third point necessary for triangulation usually eludes Erks. He is lost, but he is aware he is lost; and, after his journey ends with the death of his cargo, Taam, he returns home, determined to cut his ties with his employer. His choice is a moral decision, a rerouting of his "spiritual traffic" which echoes the earlier decision of Lily Tenebrel. In the closing passage, Erks again receives an intimation of the third point in his moral and spiritual triangulations—the cries of coyotes "interwoven and dense and ornate as a gospel choir . . . without text . . . utterly abstract and yet powerfully concrete." The final paragraph locates Erks in the complex and not fully knowable universe he has journeyed through.

Asked to tie together many of the events, images, and meanings of the novel, Keeble has reluctantly said of Erks: "He's alive. His wife's there and his child, and he's learned something from Taam. He has all that, which is pretty damn good, but the closing image of the book is those coyotes singing. He can't place them, or locate the sound, or grasp it quite, and when they stop he's scared. So there's something out there still that he can't master, and mustn't try to master, asserting itself over him . . . the coyotes, those mysterious, conniving, and very indigenous creatures. They belong there and so does Erks. I really shouldn't have tried to answer this question, but I guess the book asserts that: place, belonging to it, and some glimmering of eternity—as opposed to immortality in the way we've been using that word—is the mortality and even horror of belonging."

Keeble is describing a measurement here, making a triangulation of place and of belonging by means of the metaphysical power linking man and nature together. This triangulation is achieved at death—but intimations of the link unify the discontinuous elements of life (and the many layers of *Yellowfish*). The novel is in this sense existential, its existentialism as naturalistic as it is romantic.

Shortly after *Yellowfish* was published, Keeble told a local reporter that the Northwest was a region without a distinct literary tradition. "Having no tradition," he said, "can be an advantage or a disadvantage. The advantage is that the artist can rove about, collecting a menagerie of characters and historical sources, to compile a work of fiction." In measuring this largely unsettled, unsurveyed region, John Keeble has opened a promising route for literary exploration. He is presently at work on his fourth novel, one "in the category of" *Yellowfish*, which concerns the construction in eastern Oregon of a city modeled after the mythological city of Quivira.

Interview:

Frederick Newberry, "Dialogue with John Keeble," in *Dialogues With Northwest Writers*, edited by John Witte (Eugene, Oreg.: Northwest Review Books, 1982), pp. 7-25.

Jonathan Penner

(29 May 1940-   )

Christopher McIlroy
University of Arizona

BOOKS: *Going Blind* (New York: Simon & Schuster, 1977; Edinburgh: Paul Harris, 1979);
The Intelligent Traveler's Guide to Chiribosco (Baltimore: Galileo Press, 1983);
Private Parties (Pittsburgh: University of Pittsburgh Press, 1983).

OTHER: "Monkey Business," in *Under 30: Fiction, Poetry and Criticism of the New American Writers* (Bloomington & London: Indiana University Press, 1969); republished in *The Best of TriQuarterly*, edited by Jonathan Brent (New York: Washington Square Press, 1982).

SELECTED PERIODICAL PUBLICATIONS:
Fiction:
"The West-Chop Season," *TriQuarterly*, 5 (Winter 1965-1966): 41-53;
"Monkey Business," *TriQuarterly*, 10 (Fall 1967): 128-148;
"Ending It All," *Cimarron Review*, 10 (January 1970): 5-14;
"Foxy-Loxy," *Louisville Review*, 2 (Spring 1977);
"Title," *Uncle*, 1 (Fall 1981);
"Highway Robbery," *Black Warrior Review*, 9 (Spring 1983);
"Honey," *Formations*, forthcoming;
"All True Rites and Lawful Ceremonies," *Missouri Review*, forthcoming.
Nonfiction:
"The Novelists: Richard Yates," *New Republic*, 179 (4 November 1978).

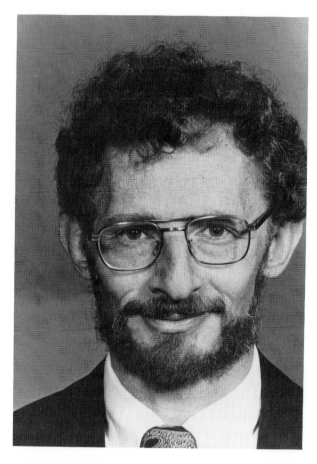

Jonathan Penner (Ross Catanza, The Pittsburgh Press)

With compassion and insight, Jonathan Penner's fiction honors the underdog. An exacting craftsman, Penner has published two full-length books, a comic novella, and numerous literary essays. Critical acclaim for *Going Blind*, runner-up for the 1977 Hemingway First Novel Award, established his reputation. Winning the 1982 Drue Heinz Literature Prize for *Private Parties*, a short-story collection, has consolidated it. Penner bluntly identifies many of his protagonists as "losers," and in the literal sense, they are. Losses haunt them. Yet in struggling for self-respect and meaning in their lives, they achieve a dignity that is finally their triumph. Critics praise Penner's simplicity and directness, gained in part from mastery of form. The precision and inventiveness of his prose make him an admired stylist.

Born in 1940 to Sidney Lincoln Penner, a doctor, and Leonore Koskoff Penner, a piano teacher, Penner grew up in the moderately well-to-do East Coast milieu that provides the setting for many of his stories. The family lived in Stratford, Connecticut, sixty-five miles from New York City on the shores of Long Island Sound. After his mother died in 1957, Penner battled through seven years of undergraduate work before receiving his B.A. from the University of Bridgeport in 1964. Though a reluctant student, Penner was discovering a talent for writing. His first short story was humorous, foretelling the wit and insinuating drollness that enliven even his most disturbing stories. Penner studied fiction writing at Bridgeport and at Harvard Summer School, where his teachers included Bernard Malamud and John Updike. Despite his poor academic record, a group of Penner's short stories gained him admission to the University of Iowa Writers Workshop, where he earned his M.F.A. in 1966.

Penner's chief influence at Iowa was Richard Yates. In a 1977 *New Republic* essay, Penner wrote, "Yates's creative instincts owe much to tradition, little to fashion. In an age embarrassed by storytelling, half-persuaded by chic critics that fiction should repel innocent belief, he tells stories we believe. In a time when experiment with language is more highly valued than skill with it, he experiments no more than a fish does with swimming. . . . He dares, even, to be clear." The virtues Penner appreciates in Yates have come to distinguish his own fiction.

While a student, Penner made his first short story sale, to *TriQuarterly*, in 1965. "The West-Chop Season" echoes John Cheever in title and territory, the beachside playgrounds and deceptively decorous passions of the upper-middle class. Already the central character is distinctively Penner's however—a schlemiel whose foolishly dramatic invitation to adultery is rebuffed: "Are you *crazy*? . . . Why does everybody have to be *crazy* today? Fred, you horse's ass, get up!" Encouraged by an agent's and a publisher's interest in "The West-Chop Season," Penner returned to Connecticut to write. In 1967, *TriQuarterly* published "Monkey Business," one of several stories Penner has written from a child's or adolescent's point of view. For such characters, the adult world typically holds a frightening, oppressive magic. "Monkey Business" was anthologized in *Under 30: Fiction, Poetry and Criticism of the New American Writers* (1969) and *The Best of TriQuarterly* (1982).

On 21 April 1968, Penner married Lucille Recht, now the author of three published cookbooks. Teaching at Housatonic Community College and the University of Bridgeport until 1970, he then returned to Iowa for his Ph.D., which he completed in 1975. *Going Blind* (1977) was his doctoral dissertation.

Going Blind is a polished, psychologically complex exploration of love and loss, self-destruction

and self-renewal, paced as tautly as a thriller. It required five years' writing and a half-dozen major drafts. To ensure authenticity, Penner, who had no personal experience with blindness or the blind, interviewed blind people and ophthalmologists, read extensively on the subject, and toured medical facilities. Walking the novel's New York setting, he would close his eyes to record a nonvisual map of the locale. Blind readers who have corresponded with Penner since the novel's publication assume initially that the author is blind, as well. One closed his tape-recorded letter "from one out-of-sightnik to another."

Though chilling and immediate as a nightmare, *Going Blind* tells Penner's most affirmative story. Paul Held is a mediocre academic, teaching English literature and fiddling with "one forever unfinished book." In contrast to his brilliant friend, August Blum—dedicated teacher, respected scholar, politically committed—Held's lone attribute seems to be physical vigor; August is dying, eaten away by an agonizing cancer. Held and August's wife, Ruth, fall in love. In a careless auto accident Held loses the sight of his right eye. Though warned that he risks, through sympathetic ophthalmia, blindness in the good eye, Held stubbornly refuses surgery to remove the dead organ. In terrifying detail, Penner conveys Held's dimming vision. The healthy eye aches and tears. Objects blur. A subway breakdown traps Held in a dark tunnel; then the train suddenly accelerates, "hurtling us through the black. . . . Brilliant signal lights swept by my window, but before I could fix my eye upon them they fled with the speed of panic."

Held will not concede that his old life has been blotted out. He fears that Ruth, exhausted by August's long death, will not marry another invalid and that blindness will doom his work in progress and chances for tenure. Desperately, he first denies his fading sight to himself, then stakes love and career on concealing it from others. The book's title becomes metaphorical for Held's plunge into deceit.

Held's audacious, misguided attempt is only partly successful. Ruth tearfully confronts him and, as he had expected, leaves him. Blunders give him away to a few students and colleagues. Finally, when Held is mugged and a young black acquaintance is beaten to death, a news article reports both as blind, and Held is exposed. But in practicing deception, Held has unconsciously prepared himself for reality. Learning the special skills of the blind, he is becoming self-sufficient. He scores a breakthrough in his research. The department grants him tenure. Ruth, reassured by his determination, comes back to him. In the novel's final scene, Held, totally blind, is traveling alone to confer with a colleague—in Iceland.

Penner's fiction places his characters in peril, most often, as with Held, from their own self-destructive impulses. They are torn between equally strong drives to resist and to succumb, and this conflict gives Penner's stories poignancy and force. In rescuing himself, Held is more nearly a traditional hero than any of Penner's other creations. Ironically, his handicap makes him more vital and whole. Blind, he comes to perceive clearly the necessity of accepting himself and facing others honestly. The implication, both uplifting and somber, is that perhaps human beings rise to their possibilities only through the most shattering ordeals.

While the book's resolution is optimistic, loss is a pervasive theme. Visiting August in the hospital, Held laments, "Death was nothing, a word to fascinate children. It was his no longer living that was an outrage, not his having nothing but his losing everything—his clothes and shoes, his long education, his genitals and tongue and skin." Held's real and anticipated losses—his best friend, sight, love, work, ultimately his identity—are devastating.

Despite its stern outlook, *Going Blind* rewards the reader with acuity of characterization and elegant writing. Genuine tenderness warms Held's relationships with women. Penner draws even minor characters vividly, and his portrayal of the principal figures is tough but just. He understands their failings too well to condemn them. At its best the novel's language is clean and penetrating, given to imagery of striking power. Held describes the closing in of blindness: "At night my ceiling fixtures hid in a cloud, like the sun trapped in smoke from immense catastrophe." Rarely, Penner's facility for language exceeds control, and a passage is overly literary, as when tears become "a tributary salvo to the last of a friend."

Accepted by the first publishing house to which it was submitted, *Going Blind* gained Penner immediate recognition. "An excellent first novel" that "expands in one's head," said *Newsweek*. The *New Yorker* praised "a truly virtuoso performance." Doris Grumbach called it "sparingly, economically and beautifully written . . . the academic novel at its best . . . a convincing piece of evidence for the arrival of an impressive new fictional talent." *Going Blind* won the Great Lakes Colleges Association First Novel Award and helped earn the first of Penner's two NEA fellowships and a Guggenheim grant. After a year as a postdoctoral fellow at the

University of Edinburgh, 1977-1978, Penner began to teach at the University of Arizona in Tucson, where he lives with his wife and two sons.

Success has brought Penner the tangible benefit of increased writing time, and teaching is a satisfying, complementary profession. Recent stories have appeared in such magazines as *Antaeus*, the *Yale Review*, and *Harper's*, and a novel is in progress. Through book reviews and literary essays, Penner espouses a consistent philosophy of writing that values character and craftsmanship while deploring obscurity and affectation. Teaching is "so closely related to writing that it's difficult to distinguish between the two," Penner believes. "The same kind of thought goes into both—what works and what doesn't. A good class has the coordination of a dance."

Private Parties, the 1983 Drue Heinz Literature Prizewinner, is one of two books Penner had published in 1983. *The Intelligent Traveler's Guide to Chiribosco*, a slight but entertaining comic novella, won the Galileo Press Short Novel Prize. Humorously, the novella takes up a persistent theme in Penner's work—compulsion as a sign of emotional sickness. Alan Archer, exquisitely unpleasant, loathed by all acquaintances, is a foot fetishist. He constantly interrupts his "travelogue" with rapt, perverse musings and extravagant denunciations of his audience.

Private Parties is a collection of fourteen stories written over the past decade and a half. More obviously than *Going Blind*, *Private Parties* explores Penner's fascination with the loser. In "Temblor," Barry Greenberg is a brilliant inventor of board games more complex than chess; husband and father of brainy, loving women; and a failing real estate agent. He is also a 300-pound mass of compulsions. He gambles at casinos, plays the horses and dogs, and overeats. He is hypersensitive. A new day, the sight of a palm tree, fill him with joy. Trucks—"their huge wheels and hot smell"—he finds sensuous. He imagines his daughter a victim of rapists. Greenberg is sensitive beyond endurance. Leading a double life, he burglarizes wealthy San Diego homes and fences the goods across the Mexican border. Careening toward exposure throughout the story, he welcomes disaster as a long-awaited calm.

This sense of relief is shared by David Kaplan at the end of "Investments." Spurred by his domineering stockbroker, Kaplan shops for a psychiatrist to ease his anxieties about the stock market, where the broker is ruining him. An absurd chain of misfortunes strips Kaplan of everything,

THINGS TO BE THROWN AWAY

This is the shell of a horseshoe crab. It came from
near here, some May or June--the season they hit our beaches,
coupling in the shallow water, spawning in mud, often getting
stranded by the withdrawing tide. My father and mother brought
Howard and me to see them.

Most that we found high on the beach were still alive,
helpless on their backs. My father and Howard lifted the
great horny things by their tails: the ten legs wiggling
wildly in air, the abdominal gills flapping and rippling
in such desperate thirst that I ran to my mother. She lifted
me by my armpits. Leave them, I yelled, but they carried
them down to the water, holding them away from their bodies
at rigid arm's length. You're heartless, Adam, shouted my
father. They swung them in with smacking plops, Howard jumping

First page of the typescript for one of the short stories collected in Private Parties *(the author)*

leaving him a modern, comic Job. "He was as grateful as a gambler in love with a crooked game, who is cleaned out at last, and can go home and sleep."

Most pathetic is Martin Levy of "Sailing Home" (published in *Harper's* as "The Sensational Madeline Lee"). Affable, bland, Levy is the played-out end of a line of vigorous furriers. Meeting Madeline, a beautiful singer on board the Queen Elizabeth II, rouses him to the first passion of his life, but instinct seems to tell him he lacks the substance for love. He lets the opportunity slip by, defeated finally by a defect in the fly of his tuxedo. At home, he looms forlornly in the display window of Samuel Levy furs, hoping Madeline will some day appear through the glass.

The protagonists of *Private Parties* lose their battles, but claim the reader's affection and respect. The title character of "Uncle Hersh" is oppressed by his dynamic, egotistical brother. Congressman Bert Dvorsky rents his servant's cottage to the Hersh Dvorsky family and borrows Hersh's barbecue grill for publicity photos. Hersh takes refuge in ridiculous tantrums and expertise in the trivial—he knows all the best freeway routes. A ranting argument over whether or not to wipe the Congressman's windshield contributes to Hersh's death when he rips off his shirt, in midwinter, to do the job. A tragicomic figure, Hersh engages the reader's sympathies with his conscientiousness—while the Congressman is suspected of tax fraud—and his consuming need for his life to matter.

A similar pattern appears in "Harry and Maury." When a stroke fells Harry Sugarman, his wife is shocked. Steady, temperate Harry would seem much less vulnerable to illness than his explosive brother Maury, who overeats, scorns exercise, and cheats on his wife. But now it is Harry who lies home, struggling to remember the word *pill*. Harry's life with Maury has been a series of financial humiliations, and he is deeply hurt that his brother did not visit during his weeks of convalescence at the hospital. Yet the love between the brothers is so strong that when Maury finally steps into the room Harry must forgive him.

Young Steven Karpilow, bullied by a crude friend, Carl, from the poor side of town, accidentally condemns his pet snake to a gruesome death in "Amarillo." Touchingly, he buries the animal deep in the ground, as if to protect it from the horrors of poverty, cruelty, and death he has discovered.

Shared disgrace on the basketball court unites the Bienstocks, the fat, maladroit father and son of "At Center." Bonded also by love, they are lucky. In *Private Parties* love is elusive. Philly, the narrator of

"Emotion Recollected in Tranquillity," rescues his lifelong love, Diane, from a parade of brutal louts, then discovers he cannot abide her any more than they can. Still, he will not leave her, and when an anti-Semitic former gang leader—Philly and Diane are Jewish—arrives to reclaim her, Philly mourns. Michael runs the household in "A Way of Life" while his mother types the numbers from one to a million sequentially—her ticket to the Arthur Godfrey show, she believes—and his father endlessly practices the same seven-note phrase on the piano. Revolted by his father's weakness for prostitutes, Michael grows up with a distaste for sex. Years later, when he realizes his mother connives in her husband's vice, the family door is literally slammed in Michael's face.

Responsibility is a key concern in all Penner's work, yet with a curious application. When his protagonists transgress, they, like Paul Held, suffer the consequences. In "Shrinkage," Ward enlists his friend Danny in a theft scheme to help finance their trip to Europe. Danny goes to jail, while Ward, younger and better connected, gets off. In the sour meaninglessness of his European tour alone, Ward tastes a loss of innocence. The narrator of "Men Are of Three Kinds" has his tycoon grandfather declared *non compos mentis*; only at the story's conclusion does he miss the emotional closeness his treachery denies him. Meanwhile, Congressman Dvorsky, Maury, Carl, and their like brazenly aggrandize themselves at others' expense, winning even the love of those they misuse. Truly, the writer seems to say, at some level the world is "a crooked game."

Penner excels at the basics of fiction, creating characters who affect the reader and whose dialogue snaps with the life of real speech. His openings are irresistible hooks. The stories are pithy, swift-moving, sometimes with surprising sentence patterns that create an eccentric rhythm. Underlying this surface, their progressions are logical and inevitable, formally contained. Commenting on *Private Parties*, Richard Yates said, "Everything works: the phrasing is precise and swift, the characters come instantly alive, vivid scenes and uncommon situations carry you along in their own momentum until each story achieves the forceful, resonant conclusion it has earned for itself." Penner's gift for description illuminates Martin Levy's first sight of Madeline Lee: "She never gestured, just moved her head from side to side, looking at everyone, and she did it all with her eyes and her voice. A girl that young and slim. There wasn't a sound in the room while she sang—you could just see the cigarette smoke curling up from the tables, and tiny suns reflecting off a percussion set—and under the floor you could feel the ship's big screws vibrate through the water, spinning at the ends of their shafts."

Penner's commitment to the mainstream of fiction does not preclude technical innovation, however. Bold leaps in time carry "Emotion Recollected in Tranquillity," "A Way of Life," and "Things To Be Thrown Away" to their resolutions, and give "Frankenstein Meets the Ant People" an aching sweetness. Penner takes his greatest risks with forms that seem impossibly rigid. "Uncle Hersh" moves on a four-part cycle of the seasons. "Men Are of Three Kinds" adopts as its organizing principle a medieval notion—the man of action, man of reason, man of feeling. In both stories, form is deftly, unobtrusively absorbed into story. In "Things To Be Thrown Away" the balance between form and story is more tense. Recent stories such as "Men Are of Three Kinds" and "A Way of Life" experiment with evocative endings that expand rather than close.

The newer stories also mark an important departure in attitude. No longer are their protagonists utterly destroyed. Throughout "Frankenstein Meets the Ant People," Perry bitterly fights his widowed father's remarriage to a woman Perry loathes. But even for Perry, the wedding party's "joyous clamor" of automobile horns sounds a note of hope. Against the overwhelming certainty of loss Penner's characters pit defiance, resignation, acceptance. Perhaps the greatest victory is hope.

AN INTERVIEW
with JONATHAN PENNER

DLB: *Going Blind* is a rarity in your fiction—the main character succeeds in his aims, though at great cost.

PENNER: That's right. It's a novel of, if not triumph, at least survival. I do think there's a note of affirmation that comes out of the ashes, and that's cheering.

DLB: The characters in *Private Parties* may suffer defeat valiantly, or nobly, or in some sympathetic way, but they are almost invariably overcome.

PENNER: I tend to write stories about losers. I think the short story lends itself to sad notes in a lot

of ways. Maybe you can earn joy in a novel—it's long enough. Contemporary fiction writers may be wary, as well, of seeming like Pollyannas, sentimental, goody-goody, too cheery. We're afraid it's going to seem superficial if we tell happily-ever-after stories.

There's a cynicism, maybe, in the writing of many of us, a bleak notion of what the world is really like. I think there's a personal element in it also. In many ways I see myself as a loser, and I write about that aspect of myself. I don't know why; maybe it's an act of exorcism that you get rid of that part of your nature by objectifying it, putting it down on paper. I think that as I get older, I write less in that vein. I'm ready to take a more complex view of life.

The paradigm of my loser story is "Sailing Home," because the character is soft and weak. At the end he's standing in the store window with the rest of the pelts—he's just a skin. He's a man who's really a loser. That kind of story often has emotional force for me.

DLB: Self-destructiveness is a strong element in many of the stories.

PENNER: The loser story has to be a story of self-destruction because plot has to come out of character. If it all happens to you from the outside, then there's no fiction. You can't just have someone walking down a street, and a safe falls on his head and kills him. That's comic, because it's sheer irrelevance. The events of a story have to grow out of character. What the characters' natures are determines their choices, and those choices determine the plot. And the plot, in turn, has to matter to the characters. This is the relationship between plot and character that I think more and more about every year.

DLB: How did you begin as a writer?

PENNER: In high school I wrote a few poems, and I continued to write poems in college. I wrote my first story in my abortive freshman year at Columbia, for the humor magazine *Jester*. They couldn't publish it because it was scatological, but they admired it, and that was very encouraging.

In the summers of my sophomore and junior years I took creative writing at Harvard Summer School, the first summer with Malamud, the second with Updike. They were the first writers I had ever known. I measured myself against the other aspiring young writers in class, because for a long time writing was something I'd wanted to do, without knowing if it was a realistic hope or just a crazy dream. I came away from those summers feeling that a writing career would take a lot of work, but it wasn't ridiculous to try for.

DLB: What writers have influenced you, or do you particularly admire?

PENNER: I hear Richard Yates, Updike, and Nabokov in my work. I didn't pattern myself after them, but they sensitized me to certain things—character and emotional effects with Yates, the handling of chronology in plot construction with Updike. With Nabokov, language.

DLB: I see elements of Bellow occasionally in tone and characterization. The stockbroker Steve in "Investments" reminds me of a Bellow character in his deviousness—someone you absolutely cannot trust.

PENNER: Steve is a mysterious guy. He sits there with his shining bald head, unwrapping a candy bar. You can't even get him on the phone. I think of the enigmatic Dr. Tamkin in Bellow's *Seize the Day*—brilliant and phony. The complex emotional relationship between son and father in *Seize the Day* taught me more than any psychology textbook about family relationships.

Malamud I've profited from through dialogue. My own faint impressions of Yiddish locution come partly from his.

One other writer is Graham Greene. *The Heart of the Matter* is a writer's book.

DLB: As a reader and a writer, what do you value most in fiction?

PENNER: I don't have a checklist. To begin with, you have to write about a character who's in some way sympathetic to the reader. He can be flawed in all kinds of ways, but if the reader's feeling for him is unalloyed distaste, then you have a problem, unless you can make it clear to the reader that you're aware he's a hateful character.

The story has to—right away I come up against one of the hardest things to talk about—the story has to matter. It has to have some meaning, some moral significance, or emotional significance. It doesn't matter how great a disaster you might show in a story—a continent might sink into the ocean—and the reader won't care at all unless it matters to the character in some special way, not just—oh, my God, the continent is sinking beneath the ocean—but: I'm never going to see so-and-so

again, or I'll never be able to put on this outfit that I like, and park my car by the Dairy Queen on Saturday night, and watch the girls go by.

Usually a story has to appear to be heading somewhere else. It's as though there were a cover story for the real story. Then the reader has to discover what the story is about. There's a subtext, as it were, and the reader realizes this at the end. He says, "Ah, now I understand why it was put together this way. I understand the relationship of the parts to the whole; I understand the ordering of it."

DLB: Do you find form in itself particularly pleasing?

PENNER: I have a weakness for form, I must admit. I like a story that has some closure. Lately my sense of that is a little freer, more abstract. My recent stories aren't always wrapped up as neatly as they once were, and that freedom can be dangerous. On the other hand, the ends can be tied up *too* neatly, and then you have something like genre fiction. There has to be a compromise between the closure that we expect in fiction and the open-endedness that we find in life. But the material does need to be shaped. We already have life in all its wonderful meaninglessness. The job of fiction is to find meaning.

DLB: Do you ever write a story on the basis of an idea?

PENNER: Sometimes, but as I write the story that usually fades. Whatever gets you interested is okay, but after a while life takes over. It's like the weeds and vines growing up around the shell of this wrecked idea, and after a while all you see is the jungle, which is life.

DLB: What do you appreciate in language itself?

PENNER: Interesting ways of talking about things. Not always to use the first phrase that comes to mind. Not, on the other hand, to choose a wildly contorted, obviously strained way of expressing something. Finding that graceful yet fresh-seeming way of saying what you mean.

DLB: For you, the telling image or metaphor seems important in conveying meaning.

PENNER: I use a lot of metaphors. I think they can bring the reader into the situation with tremendous immediacy. An image I'm particularly fond of is in the story "Things To Be Thrown Away." The narrator remembers his father jogging around the block with his stopwatch while he and his brother played. When he was done, the father would flop on the step, sweating, "smelling hot and acrid as some process of heavy industry." The image brings the reader there and makes the nostrils dilate a little.

DLB: What do you object to in fiction?

PENNER: Fiction that I can't understand I don't like. I'm not willing to take the attitude that it's my own stupidity and the author's brilliance that is keeping me from understanding it. Bad writing is harder to understand than good writing. Sheer difficulty won't turn me off—if the author clearly is in control, and something is happening, and there are riches in the writing, then I can enjoy it. But a lot of writers will offer you difficulty in place of other virtues, because they think that obscurity means profundity. I have little patience with them.

DLB: Are you a fast or a slow writer?

PENNER: Unfortunately, slow. The closest I came to writing a story in an hour was "Amarillo." I was bemoaning slowness with a friend, and we made a compact that we would write a story in an afternoon. I wrote two skeletal answers to the question: what

happens to all the dead birds in the world? My first hunch of how to explain that was complicated and mystical. I liked it better, but everyone disagreed with me, and the second version became the fully developed story.

DLB: You mentioned the need for a moral significance in your writing. There is definitely a moral stance to your work. Are you aware of predominant moral concerns?

PENNER: If I have to stop and think about it, that means the answer is no. I have a moral sense—I think everybody does—and it finds its way in. Maybe if there's an overriding moral position in my work it's to say that people matter and life matters. In some fiction you sense nihilism, that the author thinks that the world is meaningless, that the triumph or destruction of a person is meaningless, and that the attitude one takes towards human beings and their behavior is one of detached amusement or irony. I take people seriously. I take their problems seriously. I'm concerned about the characters. I like the characters. I feel sorry for the characters. Asking the reader to care whether someone succeeds or fails is a moral stance, because it's based on the premise that there *are* certain values that we all care about.

Samuel Pisar
(18 March 1929-)

Nancy D. Hargrove
Mississippi State University

BOOKS: *Coexistence and Commerce: Guidelines for Transactions between East and West* (New York: McGraw-Hill, 1970; London: Allen Lane, 1971);
Of Blood and Hope (New York: Little, Brown, 1980; London: Cassell, 1980).

In his book *Of Blood and Hope*, Samuel Pisar presents his readers with three distinct but inseparable subjects. On one level the book is an account of his experiences in the Nazi concentration camps of World War II and of the ways in which those experiences informed and influenced the entirety of

his life; thus it falls into the category of "Holocaust literature" with its appalling revelations of the brutality and evil of which humanity is capable. On another level, *Of Blood and Hope* is an autobiography of a man who, against tremendous odds, achieved great success on an international scale, and in this sense it is an inspiring and hopeful work suggesting humanity's ability to endure and to prevail. Finally, it is a treatise on international politics and economics, with special emphasis on the need for coexistence between capitalist and communist countries, especially the United States and the U.S.S.R. It both suggests ways in which coexistence

Samuel Pisar (Kathleen Blumenfeld)

can be attained and warns of the horrifying dangers of "a global Auschwitz" if this goal is not reached. This diversity in subject matter explains the diversity of reactions to the book. Thus Dorothy Rabinowitz, who appears to view it mainly as a political document expressing an "enlightened liberal opinion" with which she does not agree, ends her review in the *New York Times Book Review* (29 June 1980) with a caustic comment: "The real lesson of Mr. Pisar's book—far from having anything to do with the lessons of the Holocaust—is that cant can never be made to seem other than it is, even clothed in the authority of the Holocaust." On the other hand, George Theiner, who seems to have read it basically as an autobiographical record of achievement, closes his article in the *London Times Literary Supplement* (25 April 1980) with words of praise: "This story of one man's moral and spiritual redemption makes inspiring reading." Because the three subjects are closely linked, it is imperative to consider them all.

A great deal of biographical information about Pisar is transmitted in the book, although the exact chronology and particular dates are not always clear. Pisar was born on 18 March 1929 in Bialystok, Poland, to a prosperous Jewish family,

and his early childhood was uneventful, even after the Soviet occupation in August 1939. However, with the German takeover in the summer of 1941, his life changed drastically. Forced to leave their home, the family lived for some months in the Jewish ghetto, during which time his father was executed by the SS. When the ghetto was razed and its inhabitants sent to concentration camps, the thirteen-year-old boy was separated from his mother and sister. Dressed by his mother in long pants to look like a man rather than an "expendable" child, he began a four-year journey through concentration camps—Maidanek, Blizin, Auschwitz ("the crown jewel of the star-studded Nazi archipelago of concentration camps"), Kaufering, Dachau. There he endured deprivation and suffering of nightmarish proportions: disgusting food, inadequate clothing, freezing weather, sickness and disease, beatings, lack of sleep. On numerous occasions, either luck or shrewdness saved him from death. The most memorable of these took place at Auschwitz: While waiting to enter the death chamber, young Pisar spotted a pail and brush and literally scrubbed his way out of the building and back to life. The only positive aspect of his years in these camps was his close friendship with two other prisoners, Ben and Niko. In 1945 after escaping during a transfer from one camp to another, he was saved by American forces; the sixteen-year-old boy was pulled by a black G.I. into a tank marked with the American white star, a scene indelibly impressed on the adult Pisar's memory and referred to many times in the book.

The next period of his life could have had disastrous results, but again Pisar was almost miraculously saved—this time from a life of crime. Immediately after the war he became a small-time gangster and black-marketeer in Landsberg, Germany, was eventually arrested and imprisoned, and seemed set on a downward course. However, an aunt tracked him down and convinced him to come live with her family in Paris. At this point a renewal or rebirth began for Pisar. At the age of seventeen he went from Paris to Australia to live with an uncle and to rebuild his life in a positive direction. He graduated from high school at nineteen and had begun undergraduate studies at the University of Melbourne when tuberculosis forced him to spend a year as a semi-invalid. However, this apparent disaster opened up a new world to him because he had time to read many of the great works of literature. Returning to the university, he received a law degree in 1953 and in 1954 went to the United States to attend Harvard Law School on scholarship. Both the United States and democracy were much admired by Pisar: "The longed-for America of my childhood stood up pretty well under the firsthand scrutiny of the fascinated adult.... [With] all its imperfections [democracy] seems to be the only system capable of dealing with complex human issues, in a continually decent and intelligent way." This love of and appreciation for America, both as his physical and intellectual savior and as a land of freedom and democratic values, continued throughout Pisar's life. In 1955 he married Norma Weingarten, in 1956 received his doctorate in law from Harvard, and then accepted a job with UNESCO in Paris. Thus the second stage of his life, rebirth through education, came to a close.

The years from 1956 to the present were filled with successes and accomplishments in varied arenas, political, professional, financial, social, and literary. In 1960 Pisar left Paris for Washington, D.C., where he spent two years as a member of President Kennedy's task force on foreign economic policy, as a consultant to the State Department, and as an adviser to the Joint Economic Committee of Congress. In these positions he expressed his ideas on establishing economic ties between the United States and the U.S.S.R., ideas which were somewhat controversial. In 1961 he was made a citizen of the United States by a special act of Congress. He returned to Paris in 1962 to open an international law firm, and soon his clients included huge corporations as well as movie stars such as Richard Burton and Elizabeth Taylor. From 1965 to 1967 he also studied for and received a second doctorate of law, this one from the University of Paris, and he began to write "a massive, technically detailed and documented work" in which he would explain his theories concerning economic relations between East and West and would show that those theories were not "utopian, but practical, achievable—even essential." As Pisar himself notes in *Of Blood and Hope*:

> I packed everything I could into [the book]: my conviction that the conventional methods of diplomacy could never drain the poison from Soviet-American relations; that only the growth of living commercial and human tissue between the two societies could accomplish this aim; that only by engaging the Soviets economically could we begin to ease open their society; that only through this patient process could we persuade the Russian rulers to relax their grip and permit the Eastern countries to restore their natural ties with the West; that only the bold initiative on the

part of the United States as the strongest and most vital power on earth, could get this indispensable project under way.

Coexistence and Commerce was published in 1970 and received many positive reviews. J. J. Servan-Shreiber in the *New York Times Book Review* said, "The publication of Samuel Pisar's monumental book . . . is a major event," and David Schoenbrun in *The Saturday Review* commented, "For the general public it offers authoritative, specific, and compelling answers to the question we all ask: Can East and West learn to live together peacefully and constructively."

In 1971 Pisar and his wife were divorced, and he married Judith Frehm. During the 1970s he participated in many international conferences, particularly the Dartmouth Conferences, at which Russians and Americans exchanged views in a private capacity. His acquaintances and colleagues included Henry Kissinger, Valery Giscard d'Estaing, Jacqueline Onassis, and Moshe Dayan, and his travels took him to Moscow, Stockholm, Rio de Janeiro, and ultimately even to Auschwitz. In the late 1970s, disturbed by the precarious and potentially explosive situation of the world, he decided to write *Of Blood and Hope* as a warning of possible future catastrophe; as he says in the book,

> . . . I felt impelled to . . . contribute what I could to the cause of justice and peace, lest the horrors I witnessed revisit our world in some new, unpredictable form. . . . [When] I see mankind heading once again toward some hideous collective folly, I feel that I must either lapse into total silence or broadcast to the world my urgent sense of the horrors that threaten to destroy our own and our children's future.

His ultimate goal was, by warning of it, to avoid that catastrophe: ". . . I found myself drawing on [my] past for insights into why my world had once collapsed, into how my children's world could be preserved." Thus the book is about the future as much as about the past. "It is our children that I have in mind as I write this book, a book that is not about the past, but about the future, a future that belongs to them." The book, which contains numerous photographs of Pisar and the people in his life, was a best-seller in France and Germany, and it received generally favorable reviews when it was published in 1980 in the United States.

The themes of Pisar's work are multiple. As a memoir of the Holocaust, it conveys man's savage

55

          All that is on the surface. Within me, I bear little

resemblance, I feel, to the conventional man of affairs. Having

survived what I survived has simplified, for me, everything that

often seems to encumber my colleagues and acquaintances with

complications and worries. It has also endowed me with ×××××××××

direction and purpose. I hope it does not seem pretentious when I
                                   who escaped
say that to be one of the few among the millions who perished

leaves you with a sense of obligation ×××××××××××× that takes over

your life. Very soon after my ordeal, I began to feel that in
                                             on the hazard
pushing me away from her into the adult world, ×××××××××× that the

this would give me a better chance of surviving, my mother gave me

a second birth, and that it was my duty to make the most of this

gift   a link of
×××××××××××××××××××× and to act as a living tissue between her
×××××××
and it those of our family who h were scattered in other parts of

the world. And as the years passed, and I fulfilled that obligation,
                                 contribute
I found myself increasingly impelled to do what little I could do to

the ××× cause of peace, lest the horror I witnessed revisit the world

Page from the typescript for Of Blood and Hope *(the author)*

capacity for evil and cruelty; as Pisar notes in an interview in *Publishers Weekly*, "The next Holocaust will be the definitive one, a global gas chamber. Our capacity for evil is as great as our capacity for genius. Everything is possible." Yet it also suggests man's ability to endure, to survive suffering and extreme hardship, and it affirms the value of human solidarity, of the sustaining and strengthening power of friendship, through the account of his alliance with Ben and Niko. As the autobiography of one man's rise to success on an international scale, it presents the theme of triumph despite incredible odds, the title of the Prologue, "Fire from the Ashes," clearly evoking the idea of resurrection. Finally, as a political/historical treatise, the book has a double theme. First, according to Pisar, coexistence between East and West is necessary for the survival of our world and can be attained by means of actual contact through commerce and personal relationships: "For my part, I continue to believe that in the Western world's historic contest with communism, our most effective weapon is not our costly and far-flung military establishment but our superior capacity for economic progress, and the human rights that must go with it." Juxtaposed to this positive theme is the negative one which warns that the countries of the world, beset by problems and rushing madly forward in the arms race, are hovering on the brink of global disaster: "[Sometimes], at moments of dark premonition, I see in the images of political helplessness, hysterical mobs, religious fanaticism, refugee boats, and mushroom clouds the vision of a global Auschwitz." This final theme, frightening and unsettling, seems to dominate the other themes.

The book's structure, in its broad outlines, is chronological, as indicated by the chapter titles. However, within this chronological framework, there are numerous shifts between present and past. For example, the book opens with a scene set in 1975 when Pisar accompanied Giscard d'Estaing to Auschwitz, moves to the present time of the writing of the manuscript of *Of Blood and Hope*, and then with Part I shifts back to Pisar's childhood in Poland in 1938. These shifts from present to past give the book a kind of double vision, reinforcing the important ideas of the influence of the past on the present and of the possible repetition of history; yet they are often confusing (the dates of many time periods being ambiguous), and sometimes the relationship between two periods is not clearly established.

Concerning the style of the book, Pisar himself says that he sought a straightforward, sincere, and restrained style:

> I wanted to shed the elegant style of the orator at some important international convention, I wanted to drop the learned jargon of the expert expounding on legal, economic, or political subjects of his competence, embroidered with the science and knowledge of the world's finest thinkers.
>
> If my warning was to be heard, I had to find my own voice, not the voice of Melbourne and Harvard and the Sorbonne, not the voice of Washington and London and Paris. . . .

To a great extent, he succeeded in attaining that style, striking a fine balance of forcefulness and restraint, elegance and simplicity. However, there are some instances in which the style becomes overly sentimental, dramatic, or pompous, dangers innate to autobiography. Although for the most part his vocabulary is direct and entirely accessible to the general reader, it is also effectively varied: sometimes urbane and sophisticated, occasionally crude or colloquial when demanded by the content. His dominant metaphor, which runs from beginning to end, is that of Auschwitz and the gas chamber expanded to terrifying proportions in the modern world. Closely associated with this metaphor are others suggesting violence and destruction — storms, typhoons, cataclysms, bleeding wounds.

Clearly Samuel Pisar's book is multifaceted and complex both in its content and in its intentions. It is in many ways horrifying and depressing in its depiction of the future as well as the past:

> I wanted to write the present book because of a mounting presentiment that we live at a time when military, political, and economic forces of unimaginable destructiveness are building up around the world. . . . I also felt I had some special insights to offer on the dangers that people prefer not to think about, insights based on the premises of past tragedy and the tragedies that may lie ahead.

Yet Pisar himself, both in the book and in interviews, emphasizes its positive elements. As an account of his past, *Of Blood and Hope* is, he says in an interview in *Publishers Weekly*, a "book of triumph and not a horror story[,]. . . a kind of confessional poem, a Homeric vision of things. I wanted to convey how in just 40 years I saw the world destroyed, then redeemed." As a warning of future dangers, it will, he hopes, be a means of averting global disaster: "[We] can prevent future tragedies and doomsday itself. I hope my book inspires people to think in these terms."

Interview:

Genevieve Stuttaford, "Samuel Pisar," *Publishers*

Weekly, 217 (23 May 1980): 10-11.

Reference:

"Sam and Judith Pisar Meld the Disparate Worlds of Cage and Kissinger in their Marriage," *People*, 14 (25 August 1980): 97-101.

David Plante
(4 March 1940-   )

John R. Kaiser
Pennsylvania State University

BOOKS: *The Ghost of Henry James* (London: Macdonald & Co., 1970; Boston: Gambit, 1970);

Slides (London: Macdonald & Co., 1971; Boston: Gambit, 1971);

Relatives (London: Cape, 1972; New York: Avon, 1974);

The Darkness of the Body (London: Cape, 1974; Harmondsworth: Penguin, 1977; Paris: Gallimard, 1977, as *Le Nuit des Corps*);

Figures in Bright Air (London: Gollancz, 1976);

The Family (London: Gollancz, 1978; New York: Farrar, Straus & Giroux, 1978);

The Country (London: Gollancz, 1981; New York: Atheneum, 1981);

The Woods (London: Gollancz, 1982; New York: Atheneum, 1982);

Difficult Women (London: Gollancz, 1982; New York: Atheneum, 1983).

OTHER: Andreas Embiricos, *Two stories: Argo, or the Voyage of a Balloon*, translated by David Plante and Nikos Stangos (London: A. Ross, 1967);

"The Fountain Tree" and "The Crack," in *Penguin Modern Stories 1*, edited by Judith Burnley (Harmondsworth: Penguin, 1969);

Preface in *Beyond the Words: Eleven Writers in Search of a New Fiction*, edited by Giles Gordon (London: Hutchinson, 1975);

"Work," in *Prize Stories 1983. The O. Henry Awards*, edited by William Abrahams (Garden City: Doubleday, 1983).

PERIODICAL PUBLICATIONS:
Fiction:
"The Buried City," *Transatlantic Review*, 24 (Spring 1967): 78-85;

"The Tangled Centre," *Modern Occasions*, 1 (Spring 1971): 356-360;

"This Strange Country," *New Yorker*, 55 (7 January 1980): 32-40;

"Mr. Bonito," *New Yorker*, 56 (7 July 1980): 30-34;

"Work," *New Yorker*, 57 (21 September 1981): 41-48;

"The Accident," *New Yorker*, 58 (9 August 1982): 28-38.

Nonfiction:
"The State of Fiction. A Symposium," *New Review*, 5 (Summer 1978): 59-60;

"Jean Rhys: A Remembrance," *Paris Review*, 21 (1979): 238-284.

David Plante's reputation as a promising novelist was established with the publication of his first four works of fiction, which appeared in Great Britain between 1970 and 1974. Like his contemporaries, Plante was caught up in a new wave of experimental writing, and his novels were—and continue to be—experimental in design although realistic in detail. No one could define Plante's fiction as "the novel which raises no questions," Michel Butor's phrase for the traditional novel. Plante's settings, plots, and chronology are usually vague; his characters often lack surnames and seem to dwell in a timeless state, an eternal present. Plante

David Plante (Fay Godwin)

seems to be interested most in the subtleties of human relationships, and he makes special demands on his readers to follow him as he explains that mysterious zone which lies between what is apprehended and what is understood.

David Robert Plante was born in Providence, Rhode Island, the sixth in a family of seven sons. His parents, Anaclet Joseph Adolph and Albina Bisson Plante, were of French-Canadian descent, including a part-Indian heritage from his father's side. Plante received both his primary and secondary schooling in Catholic institutions in Providence; he attended a French parish school, Our Lady of Lourdes, then La Salle Academy, run by the Christian Brothers. From 1957 to 1959, and then again from 1960 to 1961, Plante went to Boston College. During the year from 1959 until 1960 he took courses at the University of Louvain in Belgium. After graduating in 1961 with a B.A. in French, Plante first went to Rome where he taught English as a foreign language at the English School; then from 1962 until 1964 he worked as a researcher and guide-book writer for *Hart's Guide to New York,* and from 1965 until 1966 he taught French at St. John's

Preparatory School in Danvers, Massachusetts.

It was during the time with *Hart's* that Plante began to practice his skills as a writer, but it wasn't until after 1966 when he went to London—intending a brief visit—that he had his first short story, "The Buried City" (1967), published in *Transatlantic Review.* Staying on in London, where he still resides, unmarried, Plante next published "A Visit," a translation of a short story by the Greek writer Costas Taktsis, in *London Magazine* (July 1967). In the same year he saw the publication of the book *Two stories: Argo, or The Voyage of a Balloon* by the Greek writer Andreas Embiricos, which he had translated with Nikos Stangos. Next came two short stories—"The Fountain Tree" and "The Crack"—published in *Penguin Modern Stories 1* (1969), the first of his short stories to appear in book form.

Plante's first novel, *The Ghost of Henry James* (1970), tells of the drifting lives of four brothers and a sister of New England lineage. They are Henry, Claud, Charles, Julian, and Charlotte. Each of the five, in his own way, is afraid of the rugged, sensual world outside the family. As the five characters drift about internationally in such places as Boston, New York, London, and cities in Italy, each one becomes involved with someone who poses a psychological threat to the intimate safety of the family as a group: Henry by an attractive underworld figure, Claud by an adoring mistress, Charles by an elusive male lover, Julian by an elderly man who attempts to help him develop intellectually, and Charlotte by a dynamic social-political activist. Each of the family members fails to cope successfully with these outside forces, and after the death of Henry, there is a complete withdrawal into the family circle, the ultimate refuge from real life.

The Ghost of Henry James is written in sixty-seven chapters—vignettes, actually—made up of the fragmentary dialogue of the characters as they gropingly relate to one another and the outside world in their moves from country to country and from city to city. As in Plante's later work, patches of realism alternate with fantasy.

The title invites the reader to look for Henry James in this novel, and to be sure, there are clear echoes. Plante's characters wander through America and Europe much as James's Americans did in their search for their lost European roots; however, Plante's characters are ghosts of James's characters, and the world in which they live and move is contemporary but has a quality of Jamesian genteel isolation. Moreover, a Jamesian reticence gives a nostalgic quality to Plante's novel—the reticence of the characters to betray their true emotions as well as the author's reticence to reveal every detail about his characters and the physical world they live in.

As a first novel, Plante's *The Ghost of Henry James* was generally very well received by both American and English critics, one calling it "a splendidly intelligent and ambitious first novel."

In his second novel, *Slides* (1971), Plante again uses an American author as his inspiration or touchstone; in this case it is Nathaniel Hawthorne. The epigraph to *Slides*, a comment on Hawthorne's work by Henry James, reads: "His tales all go on more or less 'in the vague.' " This quite aptly describes Plante's own book.

As in *The Ghost of Henry James*, the characters are again five in number, young, American, and unsettled in their lives. They are Bob and Julia, who are lovers; Ralph, who keeps to himself—a loner; Clair, who is chaste and secretly devoted to Ralph; and Jim, who is promiscuous and vaguely lusts after Ralph. The five characters are always in claustrophobic contact with one another, and even though there are no apparent family connections, their relationships have the flavor of incest. Each of the characters inhabits a particular solitude. Not one has the fortitude to stand alone, and they simply, vaguely, live while surviving on each other's doubts and enthusiasms. Their fragmented lives only achieve a unity when the five are in the Mithraic shrine under San Clemente in Rome; here they join a long line of American pilgrims who, in search of themselves, discover the past.

The word *slides* of Plante's title probably refers to the sixty-seven short chapters in which the story is told; in each chapter the author focuses on a particular mood, incident, or impression which is held or examined but is ultimately left unresolved to be changed for another. As with Plante's first novel, there are very few facts known about his characters. They have no family names, no jobs, no ambitions, no aims; furthermore, the reader really does not know what they look or sound like, how or when they met each other, or why they developed their close relationship. Given Plante's technique of telling so little about his five characters, it is up to the reader to respond to what are signals rather than information. The tone of *Slides* is, incidentally, much more sensual than that of *The Ghost of Henry James*, with vivid descriptions of places and evocations of the moods and lusts of Plante's characters.

In his third novel, *Relatives* (1972), Plante introduces us to Val and Ann Chambers, a brother and sister who have embroiled themselves in an intense, albeit presumably platonic relationship after the mysterious disappearance of Val's wife. To shoot further excitement into their incestuous affair, Ann picks up Russel, a stranger, in a train station. Ann makes Russel her lover, although she seems originally to have intended him for Val, who also is attracted to him. Their sexual feelings for Russel somehow involve their feelings for each other, and through Russel they begin to glimpse the infinite possibilities of their mutual love. The affair between Ann and Russel lasts for a time, then slowly dies. The three characters separate, but come together at the end of the novel. Not for long, however, since Russel realizes that the brother-sister relationship of his friends is too strong for him to have any major role.

In *Relatives* Plante's themes are those common to his other novels: fragile relationships, fidelity, worldliness, and the emptiness Plante's characters experience because they exist only in the private world of their emotions, cut off from the real world.

The novelist's techniques and development of characters in this work are typical of Plante's manner. The novel is presented in a chronological series of brief scenes in a variety of settings. The tone of *Relatives* is one of lyrical fantasy with occasional realistic touches. The characters lack real, objective individuality since they tend to convey fairly similar sense-impressions in contact with one another and the outside world—bespeaking author involvement, each character being merely a facet of the author's own personality. Plante's interest, rather than to create objective characters, is to evoke the subtle, even symbiotic relationships between them.

In his fourth novel, *The Darkness of the Body* (1974), Plante's Val of *Relatives* becomes Valerian Chambers. During the course of a cruise from one unidentified country to another, Valerian meets a married couple, Jonathan and Marion Rack. The attraction that quickly builds among the three of them is at first ambiguous. Valerian, apparently bisexual, at first is drawn toward Jonathan but soon turns his attention exclusively to Marion. Marion is not well, and we do not know if the problem is psychological or physical or a combination of the two. Marion constantly rebuffs Valerian, but finally realizes that she is fighting against a force that will eventually overwhelm her as Valerian persists. Jonathan, seeing that Valerian is in love with Marion, quietly leaves. Thus the way is cleared for Marion and Valerian to surrender themselves to the claims of a passion and love that neither fully understands.

In this novel, as in others, Plante seems to be saying that every relationship is a mystery. People are drawn to one another for inexplicable reasons and are caught up by a force to which they know they must inevitably yield. It is this state of knowing but not understanding, this singular sphere between the worlds of the intellect and the emotions, which interests Plante. In focusing upon the delicate patterns of human relationships Plante leaves people and places in a blur and does not allow the plot, the settings, or the chronology to obscure his field of vision. What seems to interest Plante is the inner topography, so to speak, of his characters—in this case, their emotional responses to passionate love and personal magnetism. Readers of this novel, and others by Plante, will often have to renounce even some of the basics of the traditional novel such as credibility in exchange for the pleasure of exploring with Plante the intricacies of a whole group of human emotions. To fill in the background, to give flesh and blood to the personae, readers are left to their own devices.

Plante's fifth novel, *Figures in Bright Air* (1976), is perhaps his most avant-garde in that it lacks even the intermittent verisimilitude of his previous four books. Basically it is the story of a love relationship between the narrator and another, the boy Ewan, and of the relationship each has with his parents. The troubled narrator strays from the "country" of his estranged parents into an alien territory, where there are isolated beaches, black ice, waves, glowing embers, gigantic rocks, and gaping crevasses. Here he meets Ewan, whom he pursues and loses, and Ewan's parents, whose marriage eventually shatters and dissolves. At the end of the novel, Ewan drowns but is resurrected as a figure in bright air: "He is in this air, and will step, bodily, from it. The air glows with his presence."

Written in a stream-of-consciousness technique reminiscent of the French New Novel, Plante's book is perhaps his most obvious effort to revitalize or somehow completely change the course of the traditional twentieth-century novel. Plante's use of elemental imagery to describe his characters, their emotions, and the setting in which they exist is his way of reducing, as it were, the traditional aspects of the novel to nothingness as his setting and characters are continually made to fade and disappear before our eyes. The landscapes in the novel tend to resolve into geometrical shapes. Described in long swirls of prose, Plante's characters are also often seen as squares, triangles, and circles: "her sadness, round, circumscribing his square, the circles and squares revolving on one another and, fi-

nally, separating from them, rising up around their heads in greater and greater arcs and angles, expanding out into air." The boy, Ewan—the love object—symbolically emerges as the narrator's lover-soulmate-alter-ego as Plante attempts to combine the emotional world of a Jean Genet with the literary techniques of a Robbe-Grillet. But if this novel by Plante was originally intended to be a harbinger of important change in twentieth-century fiction, it has somehow failed, for it has not altered significantly the course of Plante's later work or the novel of today.

Leaving the realm of Eros for that of nostalgia, Plante's sixth novel, *The Family* (1978), introduces us to the Francoeurs, a working-class French-Canadian family living in Rhode Island. There is Daniel, twelve years old, the sixth of seven sons, who is the narrator; the father, Jim Francoeur, who is stubborn, unable to cope with change, and, when he will not cooperate with the union, loses his job; the mother, Reena, completely subservient to her husband and who loves all the men in her family but cannot cope with the pressures of life and has a nervous breakdown; and finally, the other six sons, who with Daniel struggle to keep the family together while maintaining a life for themselves outside it.

Following an established tradition of American writing in portraying familial and domestic life, Plante is especially successful in being neither melodramatic nor sentimental. It is perhaps Plante's first full-fledged novel in the sense that he has gone to basic storytelling and has produced a novel quite unlike his previous work up to this point in his career. The story elements—plot, action, characterization, and setting—are forthright and recognizable. The novel is, in effect, an affirmation of the institution of the family. Religion, or perhaps grace, is the pervading force in this story—grace as expressed in humble prayer. Plante subtly expresses Catholicism here by means of thought and action and not exclusively in terms of ritual. As the novel opens, Daniel is uneasy about his family, but he knows that life must be lived in faith, and the novel closes with a prayer for his troubled home, thus making the resolution of the novel totally one of the spirit. By Plante's own admission, *The Family* is one of his autobiographical novels.

With *The Family*, Plante has produced a very realistic, accessible book which is a credible likeness of his model. As background for the Francoeur family and the complex weave of their relationships and attitudes, Plante has created superb depictions of the physical environment with a painterly care

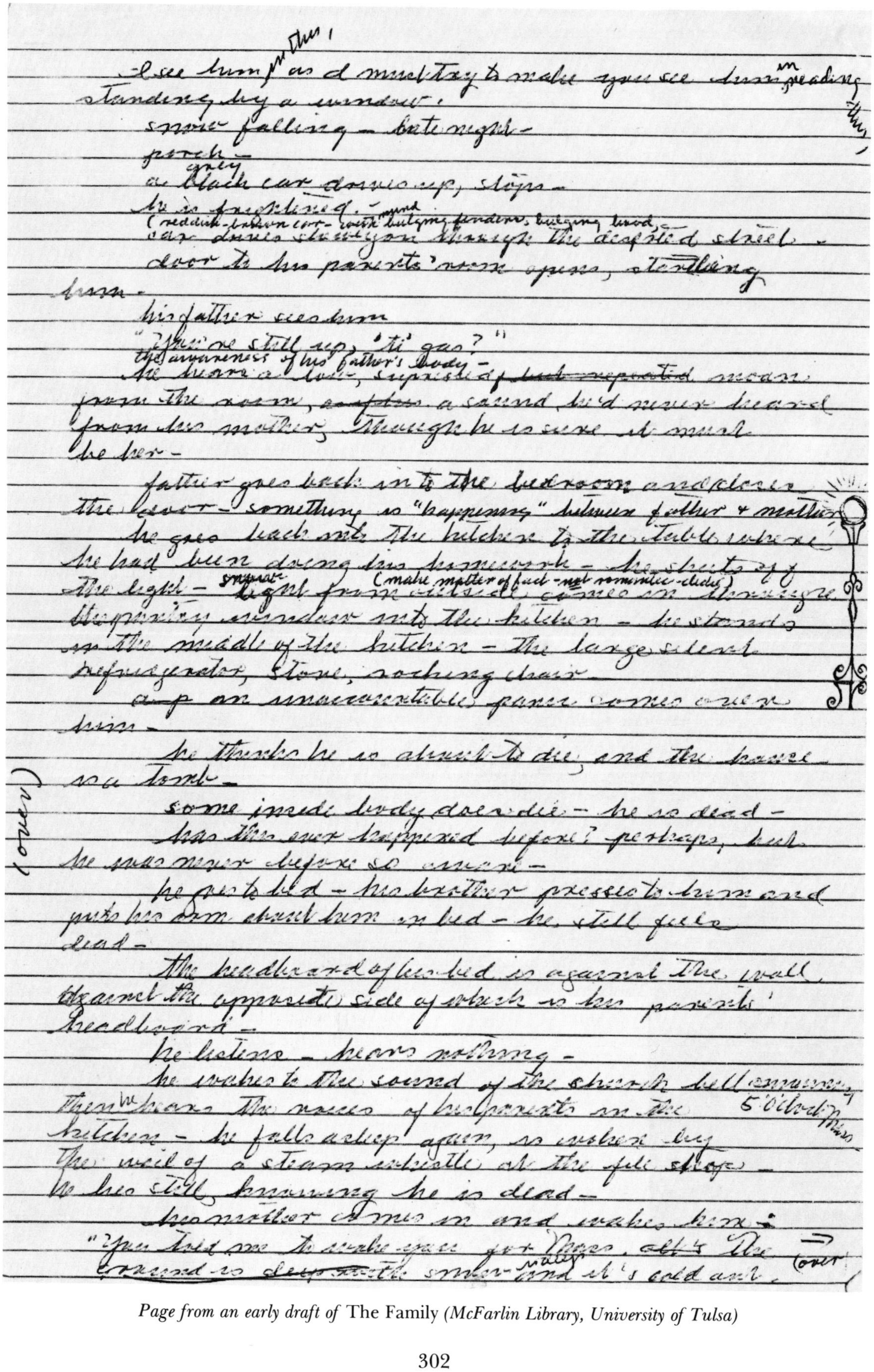

I see him, mother, as I must try to make you see him, in reading standing by a window.
snow falling - late night -
porch -
a black (grey) car drives up, stops -
he is frightened. - and
(reddish-brown car - with bulging fenders, bulging hood) -
car drives slowly through the deserted street -
door to his parents' room opens, startling him -
his father sees him
"You're still up, 'ti gars?"
the awareness of his father's body -
he hears a low, suppressed [illegible] moan from the room, a sound he'd never heard from his mother, though he is sure it must be her -
father goes back into the bedroom and closes the door - something is "happening" between father + mother
he goes back into the kitchen to the table where he had been doing his homework - he shuts off the light - snow light from outside comes in through the pantry window into the kitchen - he stands in the middle of the kitchen - the large silent refrigerator, stove, rocking chair -
[illegible] an unaccountable panic comes over him -
he thinks he is about to die, and the panic is a tomb -
some inside body does die - he is dead -
has this ever happened before? perhaps, but he was never before so aware -
he goes to bed - his brother presses to him and puts his arm about him in bed - he still feels dead -
the headboard of his bed is against the wall against the opposite side of which is his parents' headboard -
he listens - hears nothing -
he wakes to the sound of the church bell ringing, then he hears the voices of his parents in the kitchen - he falls asleep again, is woken by the wail of a steam whistle at the [illegible] shop -
he lies still, knowing he is dead -
his mother comes in and wakes him:
"You told me to wake you for Mass, although the ground is deep with snow and it's cold and [illegible]"
(make matter of fact - not romantic - cliché)
5 o'clock Mass
(over)

Page from an early draft of The Family (McFarlin Library, University of Tulsa)

for lights, shadows, and colors.

Continuing the saga of the Francoeur family in his seventh novel, *The Country* (1981), Plante delineates the reactions of the narrator, Daniel, to his parents, his six brothers, and his brothers' families as he returns to their home in Providence, Rhode Island. In part one, Daniel returns twice from London to visit his aging parents; in a flashback in part two, we have Daniel, his parents, and his six brothers visiting the house in the country on a lake that they have bought for their parents; and in part three Daniel again returns from London for the funeral of his father.

Plante's style is restrained and the action is minimal. Each word reports something heard, seen, or touched or the very ordinary conversations and behavior of the Francoeur family. The book lacks a strong plot line but possesses instead a certain unity of theme as it shows the brothers growing up together, moving away, and coming together again as they witness the death of one parent and the physical and psychological deterioration of the other. It is clearly a portrait of a family that is undergoing a tragic transition from one generation to another. It is also the story of a young man who gains a greater sense of himself as he comes to appreciate his heritage.

An interesting feature of this novel is the dramatization of Plante's authorial relationship to his characters. In part two of the novel, although Daniel is writing in the first person, he is virtually an absent narrator; he describes scenes where he was not present and emphasizes his nonparticipation in the scenes. In contrast to this, parts one and three show how the creative act is brought about by the awakening of interest in things which had been disregarded but within reach all the time. One example of this is Daniel's interest in his family's tribal ancestry; knowing that he has both French-Canadian and Indian blood in his lineage, Daniel becomes virtually obsessed with this fact and actively sets out to discover where his family came from, what language they spoke, and what his family really feels and thinks now. As one critic has noted: "the novel's fastidious realism flowers into a complex analysis of the creative sensibility."

Plante's eighth novel, *The Woods* (1982), is the third in a triptych with *The Family* and *The Country* concerning the Francoeur family but with the emphasis on Daniel. The settings are again Providence, Rhode Island, Boston, and the country roundabout; the time is the 1950s. The construction of the novel is also a triptych: in part one, "The Reflection," Daniel Francoeur is eighteen as he finishes his first year at a Boston college; in part two, "The Woods," Daniel spends the summer months at his parents' country house; and in part three, "The War," he returns to college.

In this very short novel, Daniel faces many concerns typical of those in the 1950s—a college career, making a living, obligatory military service, and the prospects of marriage and children. But it is basically the interior landscape of a young man's consciousness that Plante explores as Daniel passes through that shadowy zone between youth and adulthood, transfixed by a physical awareness of himself and others.

As in most of Plante's work, his prose here is marked by an extensive use of figurative language and imagery. Visualizing a body in space, Daniel has "a vivid sense of that body, more vivid than his sense of his own body, but he knew that to try to see it was like trying to see the soul." At the same time, Daniel is preoccupied with "the space, large and empty" which surrounds, or rather envelopes, those about him. In a description of his roommate at college "it seemed to Daniel that behind Charlie's body was a space, a large deep space, and looking at Charlie's body, he was looking at that stunning space." Receiving Communion at an early Mass, the body of Christ becomes this indescribable space—"the immense Body, standing, its arms out, above them a great space which included everything, everything. . . ."

And, as in his other novels, the action is sparse. In *The Woods*, Plante portrays in Daniel a person who wants his body, his world to be inviolate; but in all his relationships—be they with Charlie, his college roommate; with Lillian, the older woman at the lakeside cottage with whom he has a brief affair; or with Albert, his Marine Corps major brother whose views of the world are realistic but sympathetic—Daniel finds that the world cannot be as he would have it. Back at college, in the third section of the novel, Daniel files for the military draft as a conscientious objector, but it is Albert's letter which makes Daniel realize that he must face the real, adult world: "You hate war. You are right to hate it. But we hate what we most long for, and your hatred against what we long for will not change the world. You want a different world, but the fact is that you must live and die in this. . . . I know that we destroy ourselves more in peace than in war, and in war you are allowed to hate. I bear a world I hate. And you will." One critic aptly noted that "the range of emotion and experience in Plante's art is narrow; the depth of insight within that limit, often profound."

Difficult Women (1982), Plante's first work of

nonfiction, recounts his impressions of Jean Rhys, Sonia Orwell, and Germaine Greer, whom he had encountered in the literary circles of London and elsewhere. Plante's book consists of both a personal memoir and character sketches. He felt personally drawn to these women and questions himself continually as to why. He was not blind to their shortcomings; indeed, he saw them as "difficult" women.

Plante had come to know Jean Rhys only in her unhappy old age. His interest in Rhys was that she was a writer. As a young writer himself, he felt honored to be on an intimate footing with a famous elder. The fear of being a "false" friend to Rhys and of using her worried Plante. But if there was exploitation, it was mutual, for Rhys accepted Plante's services in helping her get her thoughts on paper, and she apparently showed no interest at all in his work. It is a fact that Plante acted as Rhys's amanuensis, and his part is acknowledged in the preface to *Smile Please*, Rhys's unfinished biography published shortly after her death.

Sonia Orwell, who had introduced Plante to Jean Rhys, was the widow of George Orwell, whom she had married only a few months before his death. Like so many widows who become heirs to their husbands' literary estates, Sonia Orwell made a profession of her position by surrounding herself with literary and intellectual people, by playing hostess, mentor, and troubleshooter to creative people of all sorts. In Plante's sketch she appears to be a loud and restless woman, pitiable because she, like Jean Rhys, was so fundamentally miserable: "I saw Sonia as an unspeakably unhappy woman. I was in love with the unhappiness in her."

Germaine Greer, with whom Plante was a fellow teacher at the University of Tulsa in Oklahoma, is the subject of the third sketch. Like Sonia Orwell, Greer generally comes across as a loud, abrasive, but generous woman for whom Plante has a great deal of admiration. The anecdotes Plante relates concerning her life—her ability to care about unwanted children and generously help those in need, to build a house, fix a car, cook brilliantly, hold forth on such subjects as female circumcision in Africa, and claim that sex is ninety percent in the mind—show her to be a warm and funny friend whose energy and erudition have made her a public figure. In this section on Greer, even more than in the other two, Plante ruminates on his own complicated motives for devoting himself to these "difficult" friends and thus adds to his picture of three women a self-portrait.

Since David Plante published his first novel in 1970 his work has remained and probably will continue to be experimental in design but conventional in detail. This combination characterizes the bulk of his work. The tendencies that are present in a mix in most of his work find an extreme and almost exclusive expression in two works: *Difficult Women* is written entirely in the tradition of the conventional memoir, whereas the novel *Figures in Bright Air* represents a complete break from realism into a world of fantasy and imagery. Taken as a whole, Plante's work is most reminiscent of the French New Novelists who were noticed first in the mid-1950s. His theories and techniques resemble theirs closely: the opposition to the conventional or realistic novel, the presentation of characters from the outside with the author standing between his characters and the reader, a disregard for chronology, the importance given to objects and space, and an unorthodox treatment of dialogue. Like Michel Butor, Plante pays almost photographic attention to detail and, especially in *Figures in Bright Air*, writes long, complicated sentences which extend to whole paragraphs. Like Marguerite Duras, the characters in Plante's novels are always seeking something, the meaning of life, fulfillment, or happiness; and both authors' novels are at times full of conversation. With Robbe-Grillet Plante shares an affinity for unorthodox narrative structures as well as a disregard in general for chronology, and like Claude Simon Plante's style is rich in sensual imagery. James Joyce, Gertrude Stein, Henry James, and the Surrealist painters come also to mind when reading Plante. These echoes have not, however, diminished the critical success he has achieved on both sides of the Atlantic. Speaking of *The Darkness of the Body*, the Scottish poet Robert Nye claimed that Plante's prose was "as elegant as anyone's now writing in English." While many critics noted that Plante's techniques in his earlier novels were influenced by such writers as James, Hawthorne, and Stein, they generally thought that Plante found "his own voice in the low-key and largely autobiographical saga" of *The Family*, *The Country*, and *The Woods*. To the general reader perhaps a word of caution is in order. What one critic said about *Relatives* might be applied to his work as a whole: "Just as it takes a specialised frame of mind to write a book like this, it takes a specialised reader to respond."

Interview:
John F. Baker, "David Plante," *Publishers Weekly*, 222 (24 December 1982): 12-13.

Reference:
Ronald Hayman, *The Novel Today 1967-1975* (London: Longman, 1976), p. 10.

Papers:
David Plante's papers are at the University of Tulsa, Oklahoma.

Michael Shaara
(23 June 1929-   )

Walter W. Ross

BOOKS: *The Broken Place* (New York: New American Library, 1968);
The Killer Angels (New York: David McKay, 1974);
The Herald (New York: McGraw-Hill, 1981);
Soldier Boy (New York: Pocket Books, 1982).

Michael Shaara, the author of three novels, a screenplay, and over seventy-five short stories, writes in a variety of genres including science fiction, history, and medical journalism. He is a slow, careful writer who is more interested in the sheer enjoyment of telling a story well than in writing for a mass audience or making money. In the introduction to *Soldier Boy* (1982), a collection of his short stories, he recalled: "I've written for a long time and it has always been fun to do, because every time I'm ready to write the story, the story is out there waiting to be told, to be *seen*, and there are ahead such moments as those with Chamberlain on the hill at Little Round Top, or with McClain going into the ring with Dover Brown, or with Nielson killing Maas, or in the mind of a robot seeing the maker coming, and all those worlds are real, and when I read I can sometimes go back, and writing to me has always meant just that: going for awhile into another, real world."

Like John O'Hara and Ernest Hemingway, two of his favorite writers, Shaara had his share of unusual experiences as a young man. He worked as a merchant seaman and walked a beat as a policeman in St. Petersburg, Florida. In the late 1940s he served in the army as a paratrooper in the 82nd Airborne Division, where he rose to the rank of sergeant. Shaara has always loved boxing, and his four uncles were all professional boxers. In an interview in fall 1982 with Michael Kernan of the *Washington Post* Shaara said: "When I was twelve my father had me jab the laundry bag and taught me the short right hand." Later he went on to win

Michael Shaara (© Jerry Bauer)

seventeen out of eighteen of his boxing matches.

Shaara was born in Jersey City, New Jersey, to Michael Joseph, Sr., an Italian immigrant, and Alleene Maxwell Shaara. His father worked on behalf of newly emerging unions, and at one time he was a campaign manager for Republican Congressman Peter Rodino. Shaara's mother came from the South, proudly proclaiming she could trace her ancestry back to Thomas Jefferson and "Light-Horse Harry" Lee. The Northern and Southern elements in his parentage brought Shaara in touch with two societies. "You see, I've lived half and half, two different worlds. Both worlds are gone today. The loss of the South is like a fantasy that disappeared," he said in a 1974 interview.

From an early age Shaara showed great promise in many areas. In high school he won more awards than any other student in the history of the school. During his senior year he was editor of the yearbook, president of his class, and president of the school choir. He was also a star athlete. He earned letters in basketball and track, but was best known as a baseball pitcher. In his interview with Michael Kernan he said: "My father would hold the glove on his left knee and I'd throw the curve at it till I could hit it every time. Then he'd go to the right knee. . . ." After high school Shaara enrolled at Rutgers University, where he completed his B.A. degree in 1951. He went on to do graduate work at Columbia University and the University of Vermont.

Shaara established his reputation as a short-story writer mainly on science-fiction themes. His first published short story, "All the Way Back," was accepted by the editors of *Astounding Science Fiction* for $209.70 in 1951. Shaara recalls that he wrote the story for a creative writing course that he was taking as an undergraduate at Rutgers. He put the story together

> while sitting all night in a small kitchen, my feet propped up on the door of the refrigerator, writing on a notebook in my lap. Wrote with true excitement, wandering around in the new world. I gave it to the professor, an elderly chap named Twiss, and three weeks later he gave it back to me, looking down on me with sad distaste, and he said, "Please don't write this sort of thing. Write *literature*."

Shaara has been writing short stories ever since. His most recent book, *Soldier Boy*, contains some of his best writing from the 1950s. Originally these stories appeared in magazines and periodicals ranging from *Dude* to the *Mississippi Review*. Most of the stories in this collection are science fiction or fantasy. "Grenville's Planet," an adventure about two men who lose their lives while mapping the terrain of a distant planet, stands out as the most memorable of the science-fiction selections. But it is "Come To My Party" that displays Shaara's writing skill at its best. This was his first story based on personal experience. It is an account of a boxer who loses a prizefight only because his opponent backs

off and refuses to slug it out with him. In the afterword to *Soldier Boy* Shaara wrote: "I did fight a guy once who boxed, but couldn't hit, and I nailed him in the fifth round of a six-round fight, and he went down but got up, and I never caught him again, and for the rest of my life have known that he won on the rules, but he would never have won in natural life, in a fight in a bar. . . ."

In 1961, deciding to combine short-story writing with teaching, Shaara accepted an offer to teach creative writing and literature at Florida State University in Tallahassee. While he was at Florida State he earned what he has always regarded as his highest recognition. In 1967 the student body voted him the outstanding teacher of the year and presented him with the Coyle Moore Award. Years later Shaara said: "I worked at teaching very hard. There were students with talent and no desire; desire and no talent; and a little of each. It's a challenge to find what you can do for each of them."

During the time that he was at Florida State Shaara completed his first novel, *The Broken Place* (1968). The title was taken from Hemingway's *A Farewell To Arms*: "The world breaks everyone and afterward many are strong at the broken places. But those that will not break it kills."

On the surface the novel seems to be little more than a conventional story about a recently discharged Korean War veteran who returns home to renew acquaintances with old friends, fall in love with an innocent college girl, and take up again his interest in prizefighting. A closer reading, however, brings the realization that *The Broken Place* is a penetrating study of Tom McClain, the central figure, who is unable to come to terms with his new life.

Beneath an often carefree front, McClain is driven by an uncontrollable rage, the source of which Shaara only hints at during the course of the novel. This rage surfaces positively in McClain's effort to make sense of what is happening to him and negatively whenever his killer instinct emerges, as it usually does when he is engaged in finishing off his opponent during a boxing match.

At the beginning of the novel McClain has almost been given up for dead during a skirmish in the Korean War. After months of recuperation in a hospital, he is finally well enough to return to civilian life—physically, but not psychologically. Soon he is back on the college campus where he had been a pre-med student. Little more than a week or two later he realizes that he will not be able to fall into the daily routine of academic life. His mental distress keeps him from making plans for the future, from planning a career, and despite his growing love affair with Lise Hoffman, he knows that he cannot stay and settle down.

When McClain had been a soldier, his closest buddy, Tony Wilson, had spoken of a wish to see Singapore after the war was over. McClain now decides they should go, and the two friends make a journey to the Orient that becomes part of McClain's quest to find meaning in life. Their travels take them through the Holy Land, where they visit the Wailing Wall and the Via Dolorosa, and where they search for the place Jesus is said to have walked and preached his gospel. But the long, arduous, sometimes fascinating journey brings no cure to McClain's troubled mind. And, toward the end, just short of Singapore, Wilson succumbs to fever and dies on a desolate road in the Himalayas.

Again McClain comes home, this time to take up the only thing he believes he does well: prizefighting. The critics agree, and rightly so, that the fight scenes are the best part of *The Broken Place*.

As it turns out, McClain's last fight promises a new beginning for his life. In previous fights he could count on some inner demon to take over and drive him to finish off his opponent. But not this time. McClain is dealt a powerful blow to the chin that knocks him to the floor unconscious. His left eye is badly injured; the doctor's diagnosis is a concussion. It is clear that McClain will never enter the ring again. The significance of this defeat is that he welcomes it as a breakthrough. He now seems ready to make something of his life.

Shaara's first novel received no more than qualified praise from the critics. Most agreed that the author failed to furnish an adequate explanation of the cause of McClain's mental distress. There are hints along the way: the horrors of war, alienation from his father, the breakdown of his Christian faith. In the end, however, the reader can only guess at the cause. Despite this flaw, there is much that is good about the book. Shaara writes sparely, with often a phrase or a sentence conveying more than a page of another writer's work. Above all he demonstrates that he has the gift of the storyteller, a skill that is increasingly evident in his subsequent work.

Shaara's second novel, *The Killer Angels* (1974), brought the author the Pulitzer Prize for fiction in 1975 as well as high praise from critics. Thomas LeClair wrote in the *New York Times* of Shaara's account of the Battle of Gettysburg: "Admirably avoided are the panoramic view and the muck and blood view, which tell us too much and too little. Always there is the filter of intelligent personality and the attendant minutia that give the immense

motions of intellect and men their reality." In recounting the events of this battle Shaara does not champion the Blue over the Gray. The story is told from both the Northern and Southern points of view in alternating chapters throughout the novel, with such figures as Robert E. Lee and James Longstreet serving as the consciences through which the Confederate view is fitted, while John Buford and Chamberlain serve in a similar capacity for the North.

In the foreword to the book Shaara tells why he chose to write about Gettysburg: "Stephen Crane once said that he wrote *The Red Badge of Courage* because reading the cold history was not enough; he wanted to know what it was like to *be* there, what the weather was like, what men's faces looked like. In order to live it he had to write it. This book was written for much the same reason." Such scenes as the parched terrain in Pennsylvania, the look of Cemetery Ridge where the Union forces dug in after the first day of fighting, Chamberlain's long and exhausting march from the Potomac, and the mass slaughter of Pickett's brigade at Little Round Top are memorably recreated.

One of the most intriguing aspects of the novel is Shaara's skill in showing the large role chance played in determining the outcome of the battle. The Confederate side might have won if Stonewall Jackson had not been killed at Chancellorsville two months earlier or if General Richard Ewell had continued his offensive drive to gain control of Cemetery Ridge instead of stopping on the first day. Jeb Stuart was supposed to keep Lee informed about the location of the Northern army, but this "joy rider," as Longstreet dubbed him, failed to send any messages and did not show up at Gettysburg until the battle was well underway. At times Lee felt that the decision-making of the generals might be of less importance than the vagaries of the weather.

Shaara's descriptions of the leading characters in the tragedy are vivid. Although Lee is only fifty-seven, he is old; Longstreet notices when he shakes Lee's hand that it is smaller than it had been and that some of the firmness is gone. Lee is suffering from heart disease, an ailment that will take his life in 1870. There is Joshua Chamberlain, the stalwart Northern colonel who recalls with amazement that a year ago he was a college professor at Bowdoin, where he would return in 1865, eventually to become its president. There are unforgettable descriptions of George Pickett, fearless, flamboyant, a graduate of West Point at the bottom of his class, and General Ewell, who "had the look of a great-beaked, hopping bird. He was bald and scrawny; his voice piped and squeaked like cracking eggshells."

Military strategy and tactics told in nontechnical language are an integral part of the story. Despite the warm affection between Lee and Longstreet, the two differed sharply on how to fight the enemy. Longstreet was the champion of defensive warfare, even opposing the decision to deploy troops across the Potomac into Northern territory. Lee, on the other hand, was a proponent of the Napoleonic tactic of taking an aggressive stance by attacking the enemy at the first opportunity. To do otherwise Lee regarded as unbecoming for a commanding officer. One of the most poignant episodes of the novel pertains to Lee's unshakable conviction that a concentrated assault must be initiated against the entrenched Northern forces on Cemetery Ridge.

In writing this historical novel Shaara devoted careful attention to geography, not just by studying the maps of the time, but by returning over and over again to the site in order to survey the land on foot and from the air in his own plane. Although he deliberately avoided studying controversial historical interpretations of the battle, he read the diaries, letters, and other documents of the leaders in the hope of presenting their views as accurately as possible. Above all, Shaara managed to capture the temper of those July days, the spirit of the battle as it was played out in what Winston Churchill called, referring to the war as a whole, " . . . the noblest and least avoidable of all the great mass conflicts of which till then there was a record."

The Herald (1981), Shaara's third book, is short and compact, resembling a long story more than a novel. The title is a descriptive name associated with the man who seems at first to be the arch-villain of the story. A. M. Shepherd, who makes only a brief appearance, is a brilliant geneticist and former professor at Berkeley, where, because of his radical views, he enjoyed a following. Deeply influenced by the writings of Friedrich Nietzsche, particularly the concept of the Superman, Shepherd hoped to find some way to bring about a utopia on earth: a Nietzschean master race, devoid of weak and diseased human beings. Under the leadership of the chosen ones, the world would no longer be plagued by such evils as war, disease, and injustice. To achieve this goal Shepherd had invented a deadly radiation machine which had the power to kill off undesirable individuals without harming the exceptional ones. The mad scientist was the herald of a brave new world.

The novel opens with the central character,

Nick Tesla, an army veteran, flying his plane into Jefferson City, a small city in southern Georgia. As Tesla approaches the landing strip he senses something is wrong. He is unable to make radio contact with the control tower, and as his plane descends he notes that there are no movements below. After landing, Tesla finds out why his suspicions were aroused. Wherever he goes—in the terminal, the restroom, the restaurant—he finds corpses sprawled out on the floors. Driving into town later, he encounters a live human here and there, but from what he can tell, the city's population has largely perished.

By now Tesla guesses that some kind of radiation has engulfed the city, and without delay he flees the contaminated area. On the periphery of the radiation zone, some thirty miles from the downtown section, he finds a large contingent of army tanks, weaponry, and armed personnel. He decides to join forces with the army in conducting an investigation into the cause of the catastrophe. In a few days, Tesla, now equipped with a high-powered pistol, several days' supply of food, and a walkie-talkie, returns to Jefferson City to track down the source of the radiation.

But instead of continuing in an earnest effort to search out and destroy the deadly radiation machine, Tesla gradually comes to appreciate Shepherd's invention. In the heart of the city he finds a survivor, a young, terror-stricken woman who has been incarcerated over the past five days in the jailhouse. Tesla nurses Ruth back to health and soon they find themselves falling in love. Ironically, the city becomes a kind of macabre paradise. Most of the city's dead are not visible and because of the killing agent no smell comes from the corpses. The lovers revel in the pristine silence, the lack of restraint, the opportunity to do as they please. Despite all that has happened, Jefferson City promises a better life than the outside world.

Time is running out, however. Remote-controlled tanks begin to roll into the city and open fire. Shepherd is fatally wounded, but before dying he reveals the location of an even deadlier machine that at the touch of the button has the capacity to send out radiation all over the world. When Ruth is brutally shot down and killed, Tesla activates the larger machine. Soon the winds begin to carry the radiation in all directions. As the military and civilian populations try to flee from the path of destruction, the reader is left to wonder if the few survivors will be able to build a better world.

Since the publication of *The Herald*, Shaara has been to Hollywood, where he has written the

-229-

Nick sat in a moment of thundering silence. He remembered
that moment in the desert, looking up at the night sky, the white
stars, waiting for the message that never came. After a while he
said:

-One thing. Want to make clear. Why me? Why you and me . . . and . . .
~~thisxgirlyxthisxxxxxxxlovelyxthing?xxWhy?x~~ why us?

-Adaptation.-

-You mean . . . hell, what do you mean? ~~Whexaiss?xWhere?xHow~~ Why?-
~~manyfS~~Shepherd talked slowly. His voice was calm and colder now, his
mind was backing away. He said:

-The human body adapts to change. It learns. Just how it does
that, and why so many fail . . . - he shrugged. -But when something
dangerous comes into view, the human being fights back, or adapts.
                                    but
~~Ixthinkxthat~~ When it began . . . radiation has always been there.
It may be that there are only a very few in certain places, near
exposure to massive radiation just in the last century. That may be.
But it may also be that a small ~~Eush~~ tribe of Bushmen lived over a
strong uranium deposit in South Africa and has adapted long ago, or
even one somewhere else, some other tribe, with only radium perhaps.
No way yet to tell. ~~Butxwaliixknewxxx. .xpmatiyxsaonx Tharexare
menxanxearthxwith AllxIxknewxirw~~ Why us? Why you and me? Ah. We
are . . . a genetic fluke. Or perhaps Darwin was right and we are
. . . the fittest. Accident. Or plan. I think of that . . . all the
time now. I think all night long. Hail Mary, full of grace. God
is with thee.-

Nick chilled, looked at Ruth. God be with thee. He looked at
the white sky. Have you sent the message?

Shepherd was looking past Nick up the hill. Ruth said something,
Nick didn't hear. He focused on: the tool box. Radio in there. Ah.

Page from the typescript for The Herald *(the author)*

screenplay for *The Killer Angels*. Recently Shaara traveled to Ireland in search of sites that might be used in shooting the movie. In addition to his work on the West Coast, Shaara has plans to write a novel about Shakespeare. In his 1982 interview with Kernan he noted why he was particularly interested in the great playwright. "He was a first son, so was I; his father was political but no good with money, so was mine; his father lived to be 76, mine lived to be 78; his mother was an Arden, mine was a Jefferson; he had a younger brother named Richard, so did I; he stayed married to the same woman 30 years but got involved with a Dark Lady, so did I; he lost his son, so did I; he wrote all kinds of different things, and so do I." The book was due out in 1982, but

Shaara says it will not be ready for some time, perhaps several years.

Shaara has been writing short stories and novels for over thirty years now, but his reputation rests mainly on his novel *The Killer Angels*, published almost ten years ago. It remains to be seen whether he will be remembered for it and a handful of short stories, or if in the years ahead he can add any other works of real substance.

Interviews:
Cindy Miller, "Shaara: A Writer's Battles," *Tallahassee Democrat*, 15 September 1974, pp. 410-411;
Michael Kernan, "The Ordeal of Michael Shaara," *Washington Post*, 29 September 1982, B1, 15.

Katherine Drayton Mayrant Simons

(21 January 1890-31 March 1969)

Mary C. Anderson
University of South Carolina

SELECTED BOOKS: *Shadow Songs,* as Kadra Maysi (Charleston, S.C.: J. J. Furlong Press, 1912);
The Patteran, as Kadra Maysi (Columbia, S.C.: State Company, 1925);
Roads of Romance and Historic Spots Near Summerville, as Kadra Maysi (Charleston, S.C.: Southern Printing and Publishing Company, 1925);
Stories of Charleston Harbor, as Kadra Maysi (Columbia, S.C.: State Company, 1930);
A Sword from Galway, as Drayton Mayrant (New York & London: Appleton-Century-Crofts, 1948);
The Running Thread, as Drayton Mayrant (New York: Appleton-Century-Crofts, 1949; London: Quality Press, 1950);
First the Blade, as Drayton Mayrant (New York: Appleton-Century-Crofts, 1950);
White Horse Leaping, as Drayton Mayrant (Columbia: University of South Carolina Press, 1951);
Courage Is Not Given, as Drayton Mayrant (New York: Appleton-Century-Crofts, 1952);
The Red Doe, as Drayton Mayrant (New York: Appleton-Century-Crofts, 1953);
Always a River, as Drayton Mayrant (New York: Appleton-Century-Crofts, 1956);

Lamp in Jerusalem, as Drayton Mayrant (New York: Appleton-Century-Crofts, 1957);
The Land Beyond the Tempest, as Drayton Mayrant (New York: Coward-McCann, 1960).

PLAYS: *Golden Slipper,* by Simons and J. Whilden Blackwell, Troy, Ala., Troy State Teachers College, 8 March 1950;
Bewley's Bewitched, Charleston, S.C., Dock Street Theatre, 24 January 1952;
Held in Splendor, by Simons and Patricia Colbert Robinson, Charleston, S.C., Dock Street Theatre, 16 April 1953.

During her lifetime, Katherine Drayton Mayrant Simons, a native of South Carolina, became known in Europe and America as a poet and novelist. While her poetry spanned a period of over six decades, all eight of her novels appeared within twelve years, 1948-1960. However, she worked on her first novel for years, beginning research on it in 1936, laying it aside during World War II, and rewriting it after the war for publication. All of her novels were based on historical events and legends which interested her throughout her life.

Katherine Simons (South Caroliniana Library, University of South Carolina)

The daughter of Katherine Drayton Mayrant and Sedgewick Lewis Simons, she was born in Charleston, South Carolina, and grew up a few miles inland, in Summerville. She attended Brownfield School in Summerville and the Sass School in Charleston. At Converse College in Spartanburg, South Carolina, from which she earned a Bachelor of Letters degree in 1909, Simons began seriously writing poetry. Following her graduation, she became a teacher in the Summerville Graded School, and in 1912 her first volume of poetry, *Shadow Songs*, was published. During World War I she assisted her mother in work for wounded French soldiers through the Red Cross, work for which she was decorated by the French government. In the 1920s Simons became an associate editor of the *Summerville Journal* and the founding editor of a second newspaper, the *Summerville Forester*; she also wrote the poems published as *The Patteran* (1925) and the sketches collected in the two slender volumes *Roads of Romance and Historic Spots Near Summerville* (1925) and *Stories of Charleston Harbor* (1930). For a short time in the early 1930s, Simons was a free-lance war correspondent in Spain. She also began, during this period, to supplement her income by writing short stories—mostly mysteries and local color tales—for popular magazines.

From the early 1920s until the first years of the 1940s Simons used the pseudonym Kadra Maysi, an abbreviated form of her four names. However, be-

cause some readers of the *New York Times* objected to the publication of works by an apparently Japanese writer during World War II, she was asked to use a different pen name. Appalled by the biased reaction but wishing to have her writings accepted, Simons selected her two middle names as her future literary signature. All eight of her novels, as well as her last two volumes of poetry, were published under the pen name of Drayton Mayrant. Having experimented with dramatic forms in the 1940s, she began writing plays about 1950. All of her plays were produced, but although Row-Peterson bought one, none were published. During her adult years, Simons traveled widely, involved herself in the cultural life of Charleston, and gave much of her time to regional literary, historical, and patriotic organizations; she served, for example, as the only woman president of the Poetry Society of South Carolina, which numbered among its members DuBose Heyward and Hervey Allen and which included among its speakers Sacheverell Sitwell, Seumas MacManus, Robert Penn Warren, and Donald Davidson. In 1952 Simons received an honorary degree from Converse College. The most prestigious of her many literary awards was the William Gilmore Simms Prize conferred the week before she died. Her last novel appeared in 1960, but she continued to write and receive praise for her poetry until her death.

Katherine Simons's first book of poetry, *Shadow Songs*, completed before her twenty-second birthday, contained thirty-six poems of varying themes and styles. Although they showed the influences of such well-known writers as Sidney Lanier, Henry Wadsworth Longfellow, and Bret Harte, most of the poems were sensitively written and a few were remarkably mature. The volume attracted favorable attention throughout the country.

Thirteen years later, *The Patteran*, Simons's second book of poetry, was published. Most of the seventy-four poems collected in this volume had appeared earlier in the *New York Times*, *Contemporary Verse*, *Edison Monthly*, *Southern Women's Magazine*, and other such periodicals. Included also were seven reprints from her first volume. *The Patteran*, though out of print for over fifty-five years, remains a remarkable collection of fine poems, well worth serious study. In this volume Simons established a strongly individual style marked by evocative imagery and musical rhythms. *The Patteran* is overall the richest of her books of poetry in the wide selection of forms and themes.

Simons's first novel, *A Sword from Galway* (1948), sold well, was selected for distribution by a book club, and received generally good reviews. The novel drew its plot from the legend of an Irish knight who sailed with Columbus, a story which Simons first heard during the 1930s in the ancient Saint Nicholas' Church of Galway as she stood by the tomb of Rice de Culvey. Years of research and the writing of a first draft followed. Putting the manuscript aside during World War II, she revised it in the late 1940s and submitted it to Appleton-Century-Crofts, who accepted it and remained her publisher for all but her final novel.

Dominating the book is Rice de Culvey, a swashbuckling adventurer of heroic mold, accompanied by his Irish wolfhound Crum Dubh. Parted from his Irish love because of a family feud, the Galway knight becomes the protector of Dona Carla Sagrando de Viga, a Spanish grandee's daughter. After sailing the Atlantic in one of the ships of Cristóbal Colón, de Culvey endures the hardships of beautiful but savage Haiti before returning once again to Europe in 1494.

Reviewers admired the accuracy of the historical background, the colorful portraits of the people and places, and the well-knit plot. French translation rights were sold to Les Editions Hachette of Paris in December of 1948.

The next year, Simons's second book of fiction, *The Running Thread* (1949), was published, receiving mixed reviews. Its author had earlier developed the story as a three-act play for a local DuBose Heyward contest, but upon its rejection, she reworked the script and used it as an outline for the novel. The title, too, came from an earlier work by Simons, the poem "Weavers," which dealt with the ancient concept of life as a tapestry that could be ruined by the careless pulling of a thread. The theme of the novel concerned the impact of the actions of an individual upon the lives of others.

Focusing upon teenaged Dinah Corley, whose courage and intelligence sustain her, the book's plot parallels a true story from South Carolina history. Dinah Corley, sent from her native Aran Islands to prevent her marriage to a British soldier, John Croft, lands in Charleston in 1858 and finds protection with a wealthy family. The events in Charleston and Columbia prior to and during the Civil War, including those concerning General William Tecumseh Sherman, were taken from historical accounts, Simons's paternal grandmother's recollections, and family documents.

Richard Match in a *New York Times* review panned the novel for lacking raw power and not mentioning Abraham Lincoln's name. A New York *Herald-Tribune* critic praised it for its vitality and "happy use of fresh material," and a reviewer in the

Lowell *Sun-Telegram* called it one of the sleepers of 1949, "worth anyone's reading at any time." In general, *The Running Thread* was praised for its portrait of Charleston society, its finely detailed action, and its colorful historical background. The reading public was impressed with the novel; in less than two months a third printing was ordered. *The Running Thread* was a book club selection; it appeared in an English edition from the Quality Press of London; and an American magazine bought condensation rights.

Simons's third novel, *First the Blade* (1950), was completely different in locale and characters. Based on the thirty-eight words in the New Testament concerning Pontius Pilate and his wife, the story was composed through selection from conflicting extant legends and through meticulous research into the customs and the settings in the Roman Empire during the reign of Tiberius. Simons first became interested in the period when she studied Guerber's *Tales of Ancient Rome* as a young girl at the Sass school. *Tales of Ancient Rome*, Macaulay's *Lays*, and the Bible were her original sources for the book.

The title, *First the Blade*, in keeping with its biblical theme of the growing Christian faith of Pilate's wife, Claudia Procula, came from the parable of the Sower in the Gospel of Mark. Reviewers saw in this novel a story true to the historical and biblical records. Charles Lee of the *New York Times* called it "a warmly imaginative biographical novel." Bradford Smith of the *Saturday Review of Literature* praised the Roman background material but thought that the book seemed too carefully planned. Most reviewers considered the characterizations well done in this novel that contrasted pagan corruption with Christian ideals.

In 1951 *White Horse Leaping*, Simons's third and last volume of poetry, was published. Most of the fifty-five poems, collected from the best she had written in the twenty-six years since *The Patteran*, had appeared earlier in nationally known periodicals. Although not divided into sections, the poems were placed in the book according to subject matter. The best of these works included "Photograph from a Rocket," an Italian sonnet which showed a subtle maturity in her concept of the planet Earth; "Hag-Hollerin' Time," an explanation of "the twilight wind"; "The Doe," a description of a mother's love; "Mother of the Thief," a biblical poem; "In Ships," a tribute to modern and past heroes; and "Nineteen Fifty-One," a startlingly strong antiwar cry.

Reviewers praised her graphic images and her ease in telling stories in ballad form with a lilting meter. Originality and depth of feeling marked this collection of well-wrought poems.

Finely drawn portraits of early French settlers in South Carolina are found in *Courage Is Not Given* (1952), Simons's fourth novel. Three-fourths Huguenot herself, she showed a clear understanding of the qualities ascribed to the French Protestants who fled from their homeland to escape torture and death. Moreover, almost every incident in the novel—including the plight of the peasants in the Cévennes, a young girl's escape from Bordeaux in a wine barrel, the life of the silk weavers in the London slums, the capture of indentured servants by pirates, the detailed descriptions of indigo culture, and even the scenes from the French Santee church—can be documented by historical records. The title, which is taken from the letters of soldier-poet Théodore Agrippa d'Aubigne, provides the first clue to the book's theme—that God does not give courage permanently to anyone but instead lends it to those in need. The heroine of this skillfully told story is Feuille Joany, a fourteen-year-old girl who is forced to leave her beloved vineyards and undergo much suffering before finding a haven on a South Carolina indigo and rice plantation.

Courage Is Not Given was a Doubleday Book Club selection, and the critics were enthusiastic, praising the novel's simplicity and restraint and its authentic descriptions of eighteenth-century life in rural France, industrial London, and Colonial South Carolina. In this novel the writer successfully blended history, adventure, characters, and theme.

Simons's fifth novel, *The Red Doe* (1953), is a Revolutionary War story with a South Carolina setting. The novel shows the war from the point of view of the Partisans who after Charleston has surrendered continue to strike at the British and then disappear into the swamps. Besides the excellent portrayal of Gen. Francis Marion, the Swamp Fox, the book contains interesting and accurate vignettes of other well-known figures, both American and British. The novel's hero is Lexington Mourne, one of Marion's scouts, who is drawn to the twin sisters of his friend Toff Lane. His adversary in battle and in love is Major Evelyn Fay, the owner of the Red Doe, a blooded mare brought from England. When Fay's men capture Mourne, he escapes on the horse, as did Andrew Hunter, the historical model for this character. The Red Doe strain can, in fact, still be found in many of South Carolina's thoroughbred horses.

Reviewers liked the novel with its carefully drawn eighteenth-century characters. Several critics pointed out that the important part played by the horse suited the action, the times, and the type of warfare. Others admired the vivid descriptions of the countryside and the authentic details of historical events. This novel was a People's Book Club selection.

Always a River (1956), Simons's sixth novel, returns to her favorite historical period, the Colonial era. The title refers to the three Puritan settlements of the story: Dorchester on the Frome in England, Dorchester on the Neponset in Massachusetts, and Dorchester on the Ashley in South Carolina. Contrasting the stern ways of the Puritans in the North with the more tolerant outlook of the Huguenots in the South, the novel shows the possibility of cooperation between two dissimilar groups who have come to the New World seeking religious freedom. The protagonist is Ampersand Purbeck, educated at Harvard and sent south to teach in the new colony. His first love is Gentleness Goodman, a New Englander who is unjustly accused of witchcraft. His second love is Nicole Lenoir, whom Sandy regards as frivolous until he realizes that she uses laughter to counter tragedies of her childhood in France.

Reviewers of *Always a River* again noted Simons's historical accuracy. Charlotte Capers in the *New York Times* pointed out the excellence of the Americana scattered throughout: witchcraft in New England, sericulture in South Carolina, and two historic settlements of the Independent Church. Janie Lowe Paschall in the St. Louis *Post Dispatch* praised the poetic style and the "finely drawn picture of the people and conditions of the times." Other reviewers cited the naturalness of the dialogue, the development of the theme, and the dramatic action. The Family Book Club made the novel its May 1956 selection, and *Always a River* was well received in both the North and the South.

Urged by her publishers to write another biblical story, Simons acceded, and in 1957 *Lamp in Jerusalem*, her seventh novel, was published. The book's title and its central conflict between the worshipers of Baal and the believers in the God of Israel came from the Old Testament. Set in Judea in 800 B.C., the novel deals with the life of Zibia, the maiden from Beersheba who married the son of King Joram, Prince Ahaziah. Zibia's son Joash became king of Judea.

Critics praised *Lamp in Jerusalem* for telling an engaging story and for accurately recreating Jewish history, customs, dress, and settings. In spite of good reviews, the book was not a financial success and was the only Simons novel which was not a book club selection.

The Land Beyond the Tempest (1960), her eighth and last novel, was Simons's labor of love, combining her varied interests in the theater, the early

Colonial period, and poetic description. The main sources for her last major work were William Strachey's account of the ill-fated seventeenth-century voyage of *The Sea Venture* carrying supplies to Jamestown; the life of William Shakespeare; Shakespeare's play *The Tempest*; and Simons's own travels. Set in England and the New World, the novel vividly presents life in Cornwall, London, Bermuda, and Jamestown. Quotations from *The Tempest* are liberally used, and Shakespeare himself appears in the London segment. Other writers such as Inglis Fletcher, Gwen Bristow, and Elizabeth Boatwright Coker were quick to praise *The Land Beyond the Tempest*. Reviewers from across the country agreed that the accuracy of the Cornish dialect, the eerie atmosphere established in the Bermuda section, the detailed descriptions of clothes and food of the period, and the rapidly paced story were especially effective.

Katherine Drayton Mayrant Simons's books are now out of print. During her lifetime, however, she won many awards for her poetry and considerable popularity for her fiction. Her historical documentation, vivid descriptions, and fast-paced plots in her novels merit her rediscovery by readers and critics, and her poetry includes a score of pieces technically and thematically worthy of survival.

References:

J. C. Hungerpiller, *South Carolina Literature* (Columbia, S.C.: R. L. Bryan Company, 1931);

Katherine M. Jones and Mary Verner Schlaefer, *South Carolina in the Short Story* (Columbia: University of South Carolina Press, 1952).

Papers:

The bulk of the Katherine Drayton Mayrant Simons papers are in the Caroliniana Library at the University of South Carolina.

Lee Smith
(1 November 1944-   )

Katherine Kearns
University of North Carolina

BOOKS: *The Last Day the Dogbushes Bloomed* (New York: Harper & Row, 1968; Germany: Hoffman & Campe, 1972);

Something in the Wind (New York: Harper & Row, 1971);

Fancy Strut (New York: Harper & Row, 1973);

Black Mountain Breakdown (New York: Putnam's, 1981);

Cakewalk (New York: Putnam's, 1981);

Oral History (New York: Putnam's, 1983).

Lee Smith has always known that she wanted to be a writer, but it took twenty years for her to realize that she had become one: "For years, when someone asked me what I did, I would say, 'I work on a newspaper,' or 'I teach seventh grade in Nashville' . . . or 'I'm the mother of two boys.' But at some point, after about 32, I started to say, just all of a sudden, 'I'm a writer.' And it wasn't that I was writing any more. It just seems that at some point it comes time to take yourself seriously."

Others have been taking her work seriously for considerably longer. Her latest novel, *Oral History* (1983), was acclaimed in the *New York Times Book Review*, the *Washington Post*, and the *Village Voice*. Her first novel, *The Last Day the Dogbushes Bloomed* (1968), written while she was still in college, won one of twelve fellowships given nationally by the Book-of-the-Month Club. Her fiction has appeared in popular and literary magazines, and her short stories have won a number of awards, including, for "Mrs. Darcy Meets the Blue-Eyed Stranger at the Beach" and "Between the Lines," two O. Henry Awards.

Smith's changing attitude toward herself as a writer is the clue to her fiction, which has explored all the ways that women search for identity. Her characters are plagued by passivity, a flaw she has "fought against all her life" in herself. She says, "Those of us who grew up in the South were always trying to fit ourselves to an image that was already there for us, and some of us got really good at fitting the image that our parents expected of us and then whatever man we married expected of us." Up until

Lee Smith (Susan Woodley Raines)

her last novel, *Oral History*, Smith peopled her fiction with women fighting to find something essential about themselves; for every one woman, like Florrie in "Cakewalk," who succeeded, there were many others whose compromises with their nominal identities left them at best partially fulfilled.

Her characters try on identities, but find anything made by someone else to be ill-fitting. Geneva, in "Heat Lightning," puts on clothes that have been left by a friend, "a wild thing" who has run off and left her husband for another man. In red short shorts and a white ruffled halter, she becomes, in spirit if not in act, a wild thing, too, for the afternoon at the carnival. For Geneva it is enough to realize that, dressed as she is, she could run away with a carnival man and wash out her clothes "on every rock in every river in the world." Those who are lucky in Smith's fiction can make temporary escapes into fantasy and return to accept the muted pleasures of home and family. Others, starting from nothing, return to nothing.

The most damaged of Smith's characters are capable only of reflecting others' needs. Although they change their personae chameleonlike with the circumstances, the fragmented parts never coalesce. Crystal, who paralyzes herself into cata-

tonia at the end of *Black Mountain Breakdown* (1981), is the extreme example of Smith's spiritually paralyzed women. Unable finally to fulfill any more expectations, she retreats into absolute immobility, crystallizing, giving pleasure to those who sit by her bedside by affording limitless opportunity for transference. "Crystal scared me to death," says Smith, "but once I did her I think I faced the worst and got through with it. There's nothing much beyond catatonia." Having created her most profound fear, she has finally purged herself of it. She is pleased to be nearly forty years old and to have outlived the worst dangers of self-destructiveness. She feels liberated, aware of new possibilities in herself and her fiction.

Smith was born to Virginia and Ernest Lee Smith (a businessman) in Grundy, a small coalmining town in the Appalachian mountains of western Virginia. She was a voracious and indiscriminate reader, and she started writing when she was very young, knowing always that she wanted not just to write, but to be "a writer." Her last two years of high school were spent at St. Catherine's, a private preparatory school in Richmond, Virginia. She found those years difficult ("I just didn't quite fit in with the girls from the west end of Richmond," she says). She had gone reluctantly, at her father's suggestion, because she realized that Grundy High School might not be adequate preparation for her career as a writer.

From St. Catherine's, she entered Hollins College, near Roanoke, Virginia, which had an MFA program in writing and a reputation for producing good writers. She majored in English and took creative writing classes every semester for four years. She learned what made fiction good: "I had been writing for a long time, lots and lots of awful stories—love stories with O. Henry surprise endings, heavily ironic surprise endings. Romances that involved dark mysterious strangers and registered nurses and things that I didn't have any knowledge of. They were almost always set in foreign countries where I had never been." Two professors, Louis D. Rubin and Richard Dillard, were instrumental in teaching her how to write. In her senior year she submitted an early version of *The Last Day the Dogbushes Bloomed* and a collection of her stories to the Book-of-the-Month Club Writing Fellowship Contest and won one of twelve $3,000 scholarships given nationally. She was graduated with a B.A. in 1967.

She was married in 1967 and moved, with her husband, poet James E. Seay, to Tuscaloosa, Alabama, where they lived for three years. There she was a feature writer, film critic, and editor of the Sunday magazine for the *Tuscaloosa News* from 1968 to 1969. Her newspaper career both helped and hindered her writing of fiction: "I would either fictionalize the news or I would write a story and tell all the main events in the first paragraph," she says. Despite its limitations in terms of her writing, journalism afforded her the opportunity to step outside the academic community at the University of Alabama, where her husband was teaching, to meet and talk with all kinds of people. The reporter's license to ask questions legitimized her writer's fascination for detail.

In 1968 Smith covered the Tuscaloosa Sesquicentennial, from which much of the material in *Fancy Strut* (1973) comes directly. *Fancy Strut* includes one of Smith's alter egos, society reporter Miss Iona, the arbiter of taste in Speed, Alabama, by virtue of her elaborately fictionalized accounts of dinners, weddings, and funerals. Miss Iona dresses up the truth until it becomes fiction, because storytelling is more agreeable than unadorned reality. Like Miss Iona, Smith has "an unutterable boredom with true stories, autobiographical and otherwise. The fun of it is making stuff up." Storytelling, for her, is not reductionist, as reporting necessarily is, but expansive. Life, like fiction, "takes long writing."

On 23 December 1969 Smith's first son, Josh, was born, and in 1971 the family moved to Nashville, Tennessee. Their second son, Page, was born 22 May 1971. Smith was writing *Something in the Wind* during her pregnancy and finished the novel "in a race" six weeks before his birth. From 1971 to 1973 she taught the seventh grade at Harpett Hall School in Nashville. In 1974 she moved with her family to Chapel Hill, North Carolina, where she now lives.

Smith sees her children as a major factor in her writing because they are of primary importance in her life. They have taught her the possibilities of pain, as well as joy, and on a practical level they have brought a whole other world into her academically oriented life. They provide her access to institutions, teachers, other parents she would otherwise never know. They are a fixed reference point outside herself, and living contradictions to her skepticism: "I think that if you don't believe in God, don't believe in heaven, don't believe in anything beyond what's right here, then children become vital, on a philosophical level as well as in your daily life."

Smith has never had enough time to write, she says, and that claim is substantiated by the long list of positions she has held. From 1975 through 1977 she taught full-time at the Carolina Friends School. She worked for a few months at Creative Printers in Chapel Hill, until she discovered that she was allergic to printer's ink (an irony that still delights her). From 1977 through 1981 she taught creative writing at the University of North Carolina. Her writing habits grew from working around other jobs. She does not, for example, keep a journal, although she always urges her writing students to do so. When she has time to write anything she writes fiction. In the long periods when she is not actively writing she is "gathering things inside and processing them.... These hiatuses are very important to me, important to the whole way I go about writing fiction," she says.

She sometimes spends months mulling over an idea—she calls this process "prewriting"—developing characters in her head, inventing their lives. When she finally begins to write, the characters have taken on such distinct form that they "dictate" their stories. She does very little revision. Smith acknowledges that plot is her most difficult technical problem. She fears that the colloquialisms that come so naturally from her characters' mouths may sometimes be too glib, and she worries that her surfaces are too slick, her situations without depth. She characterizes herself as nonanalytical, particularly about her own fiction, and claims to have no philosophical beliefs to shore up her storytelling. Yet her fiction is growing in length; where once she considered herself primarily a short-story writer, she now thinks of herself as a novelist. The short story, a form which she never tires of, has gotten too small to contain her perceptions of life as process rather than epiphany. "The long haul" interests Smith now, an interest which she feels may be a function of age. She very much believes that the short story is a young writer's form, the novel form a necessary tribute to life over time. Her first three novels each emerged from one or more short stories, and only with *Oral History* did she decide first that she was going to write a novel.

The Last Day the Dogbushes Bloomed developed from a short story about Eugene, a disturbed city child who becomes an intruder among innocent children, and his imaginary friend, Little Arthur. The novel is told by nine-year-old Susan Tobey, whose family is falling to bits around her. Her mother is in love with another man; her father, angry, hurt, bewildered; her older sister, disillusioned and rebellious. The novel reflects Smith's interest in language, for Susan's innocence does not allow her to perceive these truths directly. She cannot know consciously how to accommodate her changing world, and it is only in her language, the way she tells her story, that she communicates her own increasing bewilderment.

Susan distances herself instinctively from her family by seeing them as fairy-tale royalty, herself as a commoner. Her mother is the queen, but Susan knows, without being able to explain why, that her father is not the king. She is at first disturbed by the man who makes her mother, one of Smith's beautiful, laughing, butterflylike women, so happy; but she reconciles herself by making him a baron, and "Barons and Princesses and Queens have other rules from the rest of people." Her sister, Betty, is the princess, and the maid, Elsie, the queen's handmaiden.

Although Susan doesn't know it, she is the court historian, the one who watches and records. She is not like her mother and sister. "Is Susan gay?," asks Betty, and her mother laughingly answers, "Oh, maybe she's not. . . . Perhaps Susan isn't gay. . . . I don't know. She may even be somber. I declare I don't know where she got it. Certainly not from me!" Susan's mother and sister are like birds, always moving, fluttering, and they "glittered and glittered, they were always laughing," in the early part of the novel. Susan does not glitter, but absorbs, watching and naming. When she can think of nothing to say, she tells her sister, "I'm a real good speller." She's been learning a word a day, spelling and definition: "Yesterday I learned hyacinth. H-Y-A-C-I-N-T-H, hyacinth. It's a flower. Sara Dell has some in her yard." She creates fantasy worlds under the dogbushes (which she has named for the collie she found under them once) and in the "wading house" under the willow tree.

She fights to keep her world beautiful by translating, for as long as she can, the real into fairy tale, but the facade crumbles. Her mother leaves; Frank, the eternal, dependable, wordless gardener, dies; and Betty becomes engaged and leaves home. In the end only Susan and her father are left. Susan's imaginative powers have been countered by reality on one side and by Eugene's demonic preoccupation with the pornographic and the violent on the other. He has brought into Susan's garden the figure of Little Arthur, 462 years old, in a long black coat, a red hat, and black boots, armed with a gun. In the end, when Eugene has been sent away, Susan inherits Little Arthur. She has lost her innocence literally through a rape and figuratively as she uproots an old woman's rose garden. Susan moves

from looking outward, fictionalizing her surroundings, to the autonomy of a single imaginary playmate, who is in reality a fearsome part of herself.

The Last Day the Dogbushes Bloomed was not widely reviewed, although it was noted in such periodicals as *Kirkus Reviews, Publishers Weekly,* and *Bookworld.* James J. Kilpatrick, Smith's friend and former employer, generated interest for the novel by writing a nationally syndicated column about it. The *Washington Star* saw this first novel as "clean, original, flawlessly honest," and predicted that Smith was "headed for the bright circle of shining stars" that included writers like Ellen Glasgow, Eudora Welty, and Harper Lee.

Martin Levin, in a short review in the *New York Times Book Review*, focused on Smith's youth, but his tone was favorable. In 1969 Ballantine published the novel in paperback, and in 1972 Hoffman and Campe published a German translation. Despite these multiple editions, *The Last Day the Dogbushes Bloomed* was not a financial success; the paperback edition did not sell out its first printing.

It is tempting to see Brooke Kincaid, the protagonist of Smith's second novel, *Something in the Wind* (1971), as an extension of Susan Tobey's character, for she too is the recorder of events and an artist inventing characters. Brooke Kincaid inherits Susan's fragmented self. Her best friend, Charles, has died in an automobile accident, and without him to help her she does not know how to function: "Charles had made my mind and if he was really dead like everybody kept saying, then I didn't know what would go on in my head," she says. She carries *Ripley's Believe It Or Not* as a talisman, and listens, without success, for a message in the clackety-clack of the train wheels as she rides to Charles's funeral.

She looks into herself and sees nothing. Although she knows that there is a Brooke and a "Brooke Proper," she is not able to distinguish the "real" from the artificial self. She proceeds by "life plans," rigidly designed to meet the expectations of others: She is first a mirror of the proper Southern girl; when that mirror cracks and she "psyches out," she turns to the more flexible, but no less artificial, bohemian world. She tries on identities, viewing herself in the third person and reporting on herself dispassionately. Like Susan, she is interested in language, playing word games and doing crossword puzzles; but the language she uses to describe herself comes out, she often senses, as if it is spoken in somebody else's voice.

Like other of Smith's characters, she seeks genuine feeling in sexual encounters, but until she meets Bentley T. Hooks she describes intercourse as if it were an endurance test. With Houston, she thinks about the gear shift in her back, about the frost on the car windows, about the Tastee Freez sign, whose orange-flaming arc looks almost like a new moon. Foreplay is "like taking isometric exercises," and she likens the final moment of sex to a sneeze. She finds in Bentley a combination of mystery, danger, and passion; and she discovers, through his potential for violence and his intensity, a form of self-reliance that approximates real identity.

Something in the Wind is, in Smith's estimation, "an uneasy" combination of two earlier short stories. Brooke's is an initiation story, and Bentley's character comes from a ghost story based on newspaper accounts of a young, unmarried couple's experiences with psychic disturbances. Smith, who does not herself believe any longer in the supernatural, creates characters who generate these phenomena in an effort to approximate some genuine link with mystery. Her characters often go through intensely religious phases, but they are never true believers, and without belief they are driven to fabricate the supernatural. Once able to spark her own mystical visions, Smith misses the "fire and glory" that marked that phase of her life. Her characters' self-induced visions are often their only brush with genuine feeling.

Something in the Wind did not receive much critical attention, although it, like her first book, was reviewed favorably in such periodicals as *Booklist*, *Kirkus Reviews*, *Publishers Weekly*, and the *Virginia Quarterly Review*, and was briefly mentioned in the *New York Times Book Review*. The book was not widely publicized by Harper and Row and was not financially successful.

Fancy Strut, Smith's third novel, is now out of print. A comic novel without the dark undertones of her first two books, *Fancy Strut* tells the story of Speed, Alabama, in its sesquicentennial glory. The novel covers the weeks leading up to the grand pageant, "The Song of Speed," an extravaganza packaged by the White Company and directed by Buck Fire, an out-of-work and never very successful actor. Smith peopled the novel with broad caricatures: Manly Neighbors, the upright, handsome, slightly boring newspaper editor; Monica, Manly's wife, who is afraid of her housekeeper and shops a lot; Miss Iona, the relict of the past, living in faded grandeur and slipping into senility; Sandy DuBois, the town bitch, wealthy and promiscuous; Buck

Fire, who wears turquoise jumpsuits and gold chains and sleeps with housewives in every town.

Fancy Strut is filled with surprises, however, for, as in the best comic fiction, its characters refuse to behave predictably within their stereotypes. The pleasure in reading *Fancy Strut* is twofold: the place, the circumstances, the people are all perfectly familiar and therefore comfortably comical; but the characters become just real enough in the course of the novel to elicit the reader's identification with them as human beings. Monica Neighbors, for example, has a "past." She is now a respectably married woman, but the summer before she graduated she went to Europe and slept with several Italians and a Swede, finding it "lovely, a lark." "Europeans didn't count; sleeping with a European was the next thing to sleeping with no one at all," she explains. Monica's confession epitomizes Smith's comic technique in *Fancy Strut*, as it embodies, in one breathless sentence, inchoate need wrapped in suburban trappings.

Monica, once she marries Manly, settles into a "life plan" of Junior League respectability. Like so many of Smith's women, however, she cannot completely reconcile herself to an ordered life run flawlessly by her "treasure" of a maid, Suella, and her upstanding, cleanly handsome husband. She fantasizes about an affair that "would plumb the depths of degradation," love consummated in a sleazy, smoke-filled motel room. Speed is filled with people who have these same secret desires. The novel remains comic because none of them, including Monica, has the capacity for degradation of heroic proportions. Monica imagines degradation to have something to do with making love all afternoon, "on the bed, on the floor, in the closet, in the bathtub, atop the color TV." Bob Pitt imagines it to be running off with his wife's cousin, Sandy DuBois, but the farthest his imagination takes him with her is to Florida.

Fancy Strut came out the same week that Harper and Row released Eric Segal's *Love Story*. Buried by the massive publicity accorded to Segal's novel, *Fancy Strut* was not widely reviewed, but the responses were generally favorable. Martin Levin, in the *New York Times Book Review*, called it "a display of comic fireworks that are a pure delight." It is, he said, "that rarity, a genuinely funny book that is satiric without being mean." Levin's interest in *Fancy Strut* was shared by others who had reviewed *The Last Day the Dogbushes Bloomed* and *Something in the Wind* and found them flawed. The *Virginia Quarterly Review*, which judged *Something in the Wind* only a qualified success, found *Fancy Strut* a deft, well-paced comedy. More importantly, the reviewer signaled his faith in Smith's potential to "develop material matching her innate capacities and engaging narrative skill."

Black Mountain Breakdown is the only one of Smith's novels that sets out to be an exemplum. Taken from her earlier "Paralysis, A True Story," *Black Mountain Breakdown* single-mindedly explores the dangers of passivity. Crystal Renee Spangler, a delicately beautiful girl who searches for some confirmation of herself, ages from a twelve-year-old child catching lightning bugs by the river to a thirty-two-year-old woman lying catatonic, but more beautiful than ever, in her childhood bedroom. She has experimented with all the standard initiation devices, and none has opened the way into her innermost self. At the end, the reader is left to puzzle one of Smith's most essential paradoxes: Is Crystal motionless because she has failed to find anything beyond her passivity, or is she motionless because there is nothing there to find?

Crystal does not fit in the world Smith creates around her. Annie Gottlieb, in the *New York Times Book Review*, found Crystal to be "not a failure, but simply a stranger," passing through life at a different angle. She inherits her separation from Grant Spangler, her dying father, a man who waits in the darkened parlor for the alcohol, cigarettes, and emphysema to finish him off. He never leaves the room; Crystal comes to him, terrified and delighted by the poems he reads to her and, later, moved by the long mountain stories he tells. When Grant Spangler dies Crystal loses her only ally, for there is no one else, anywhere in the world, that she can love. Her northern lover, Jerold, tells Crystal that she is "doomed," a judgment compromised by his apparent unreliability ("Jerold was into doom," Crystal thinks), but nonetheless true. She is doomed because she is an outsider, a watcher, a nonparticipant.

Crystal wants to be told stories, to be moved the way her father moved her with the poems read in a darkened room:

> Grant grins at her, a surprisingly incongruous mischievous grin in his sick wrecked face. He raises his voice and continues over Crystal's pleas.
>
> > " 'Now don't you go 'til I come,' he said, 'And don't you make any noise.' "
>
> "Oh, oh," Crystal says, but it's hard to tell by the tone of her voice whether she's delighted

or upset—intense emotion all unfocused—and her usually dreaming face is wholly alive.

She instinctively gravitates toward storytellers: Mack Stiltner, a true storyteller; and Jerold, a fraudulent one. She asks for stories from her aunts. She finally begs Odell, her stepfather, to tell her the old stories, and he answers, "I don't know no stories, now. . . . Grant was the one with the stories." "Tell me something true, then," Crystal pleads. In the end she obsessively reads the everyday life of a woman long dead. Emma Turlington Field's diary, which she sees as "something to establish the past, continuity," provides a tenuous link, and at the very last, when she cannot tell her husband Roger Lee, "I feel like a person in a play," she takes up Emma's diary to awaken memories of her own past. When Roger Lee burns the diary, Crystal has nothing left to tie her to reality.

Crystal lacks the means for survival that Susan Tobey, Brooke Kincaid, and even a comic figure like Monica possess. Each of the others becomes her own storyteller: Susan and Brooke play with words, create fictions, and when one identity slips they invent a new one for themselves. Monica has a rich fantasy life, adorned with the specifics of time, place, and circumstance. Crystal, who reads *Madame Bovary* and *Miss Lonelyhearts* and writes a poem comparing life to a candle flame, cannot reinvent her life, but must have a procession of others to do it for her. She cannot even retreat into irony, the way her brother Jules has; he is an intellectual who is doomed always to see both sides of every question, and that ambivalence is his identity. Crystal is empty, in a way none of Smith's other characters have been, for she is neither a doer nor an artist who can translate what has been done into fictive worlds.

Smith's point of view in *Black Mountain Breakdown* counterbalances Crystal's movement toward catatonia at the same time it reinforces Crystal's own incapacity as storyteller. Unlike the first-person narratives of the first two novels, or the third-person narration of *Fancy Strut*, *Black Mountain Breakdown* is told by an omniscient narrator. But while Crystal cannot tell her own story, the narrator tells it in the present tense, as it happens, as if there is no finality to Crystal's choice to paralyze herself. Agnes, who sits with her and talks, imagines that one day she "might jump right off that bed . . . and go off and get her Ph.D. or do something else crazy." As in all of Smith's novels, the comic, if it does not actually prevail, mitigates the tragic. Smith argues that she meant for the ending to be a balance between the comic and the tragic, a sort of cautionary tale with the moral "If you don't find an interest that is your own self you'll go catatonic."

Black Mountain Breakdown, Smith's first novel published by Putnam's, received a great deal of serious critical attention. Those who, like the reviewer for the *Virginia Quarterly Review*, had been waiting for Smith to find material to match her capacities and narrative skill saw in *Black Mountain Breakdown* evidence of new maturity and confidence. Christopher Lehmann-Haupt, in his *New York Times* review, attributed the success of the novel to the narrator's voice, likening it to a country music ballad or Southern Appalachian breakdown, and finding in it many moods and a generous quality "that reveals unhesitantly every banal and tawdry detail about her . . . characters without for a moment patronizing them." Annie Gottlieb, in the *New York Times Book Review*, commented on the immediacy of Crystal's character: "We experience her life as she does, and it surprises us at every turn; we feel we are in the presence of someone 'fully alive . . . more than real.' " *Black Mountain Breakdown* was published by Ballantine paperbacks in 1982, but its success has been more critical than financial.

Smith's fiction is ultimately a comment on the nature of "art" itself. A genuine artist, in Smith's world, is a woman like Florrie in Smith's book of short stories, *Cakewalk* (1981). Florrie, of the book's title story, bakes wonderful cakes for people, always from scratch. Each cake is unique: a green sheet-cake golf course with tiny water hazards made of mirrors and a small silver golf ball, a typewriter cake stacked in ascending layers with Necco Wafer keys and a sheet of paper in the platen iced with a message in black typewriter script. The cakes are to be eaten. Smith eliminates the step that solidifies art, defining it only by virtue of its permanence; she does not see it as some immutable projection of the ego. The importance of the cakes for Florrie is in the baking, and in the pleasure, artistic and culinary, that they give to others.

Florrie's cakes are oral history. Like stories told aloud or songs that are sung, they are evanescent. She makes an autumn leaf cake: "It looks like a real leaf exactly." The icing runs from red to flame to orange to yellow to gold until "it's hard to tell where one color leaves off and turns into another, the way they flow together in the icing, and the icing itself seems to crinkle up, like a real leaf does, at all the edges of the cake." Her sister, Stella, asks whom she made the cake for, and Florrie says, "Why nobody. . . . Just nobody at all. . . . But you can have it if you want it. . . . Go on, take it, you and Claude can have it for dinner." The secret of Florrie's happi-

ness, the reason Stella's husband, Claude, has been her lover for twenty years, the reason their mother, icy Miss Bett, chooses to live with her and leaves her the family home, the reason children and grandchildren and her ex-daughter-in-law come back to live with and near her, lies in her artistry. She has the capacity to create and to give; she is, in Smith's eyes, the consummate artist.

Many of the stories in *Cakewalk* document Smith's interest in the reciprocal function of art as something that pleases the giver by pleasing others. Those who are successful fill their own lives. "Mrs. Darcy Meets the Blue-Eyed Stranger at the Beach" shows Mrs. Darcy, a plump, ordinary-looking woman with grown daughters, transforming herself into a healer because of a vision she has on the beach. Smith would deny the objective existence of the stranger, but she would not deny the validity of Mrs. Darcy's self-motivated vision. Because it changes her, it allows her to change others. And because she is not prideful—"It's not me at all," she says, "I'm just an agent . . . an intermediary"—her strange power is not frightening, but sustaining.

Mrs. Darcy accepts her gift and uses it, but those who balk, like Georgia Rose in the story of that name, are damned. Georgia Rose can see into the future, and she sees mostly pain, death, infidelity, and broken promises. She does not realize the implication of her visions—that one lives one's life *knowing* that there will be pain and broken promises. She is only alone in her foresight, not in what she sees, but the visions subvert her life completely. She cannot love or marry, because she fears disaster to herself.

Self-importance is, to Smith, the easiest way to a failed existence. Georgia Rose seems almost tragic; characters like Paul in "Saint Paul" or the grandmother in "Artists" are laughable. "Saint" Paul is a self-styled intellectual who loves from afar. When the object of his fantasies comes and wraps her arms around him he pushes her away, saying, "It wasn't you, it wasn't ever really you, it was the *idea* of you. . . ." Like Richard Burlage in *Oral History*, Paul finds some fulfillment in masturbatory fantasy, but he is not capable of genuine consummation. "Artists" looks at an old woman who has forfeited all connection with the present for the sake of a dubious notion of refinement based on self-improvement courses from the LaGrande University of Correspondence. She sits alone painting cardinals and woodpeckers while her husband dies, attended by his mistress of the last twenty-five years, and she dies alone, senile, with the TV tuned to stock-car racing. "What are you watching," her granddaughter asks, in one of her last visits. "Art . . . I'm watching art, Jennifer," she says.

Many of the characters in *Cakewalk* fall between the extremes of fulfillment, as embodied in Florrie, and failure. Mrs. Joline B. Newhouse, of "Between the Lines," is one for whom art, self-defined, does not quite suffice. She writes fortnightly columns for the *Greenville Herald* detailing the social activities of the twenty families of Salt Lick. She thinks she knows how art works: "I like to keep an ace or two up my sleeve. I like to write between the lines." She knows how to dress up the truth: She writes of Mrs. Alma Goodnight's pleasant recuperation in the nice modern hospital, not mentioning that Alma is hospitalized "because her husband hit her up the side with a rake and left a straight line of bloody little holes going from her waist to her armpit after she yelled at him, which Lord knows she did all the time, once too often."

For Smith, "art" is nurtured by life, and vice versa, and Mrs. Newhouse's life has been marked by a momentary and entirely memorable passion. She made love, twice, with a visiting evangelist when she was a young married woman: "It was just something I did out of loving pure and simple," she says, "did because I wanted to do it." Although she calls it her "great sin," she does not regret having done it; she would do it again, and she "would not trade it for anything." Married to a good man, whose own burden is an ongoing love for his gypsy cousin, she accommodates herself to life and lives it with generosity and humor.

Others of Smith's characters look for some moment of passion to color their lives and are not so fortunate as Mrs. Newhouse. Helen, in "All the Days of Our Lives," runs off for only two days to Daytona Beach with an insurance claims adjustor, and her husband divorces her. She is left with three children and nostalgia for Howard, who used to have the sheets changed three times a week and lock himself in the bathroom for hours. Martha, of "Dear Phil Donahue," out of some fundamental sympathy and identification, hides a nineteen-year-old psychotic boy in her garage. Her husband, appalled, takes their children and leaves. She does not call what she does madness: "It isn't madness; it's simply something different. Something different starts here. This is when I start being different from what I do." What she does is feed her husband, feed the babies, sleep with her husband, go out to a party, get a permanent; but what she feels is a link with the slobbering, wordless, foul-smelling stranger curled in the fetal position in her garage.

Cakewalk shows the discrepancies between what people do and what they feel, what they appear to be and what they are, what they *think* they are and what they are. The characters who approach integration with their surroundings are those who can change the givens artistically and offer them freely to others. Sometimes foolish, they are never mean—the worst thing Joline Newhouse can do is whisper to a dying man that she made up Mr. and Mrs. Cardinal in her column. Women who can find nothing else look, as Crystal, Monica, and Brooke did, for fulfillment in sex; and while sex is never simply enough, it sometimes sparks identity. Geneva knows, in "Heat Lightning," that "it's not supposed to be that way," that life has to be more than stringing beans and tending house for a good, but boring, husband. She needs only to realize that she *could* go off with the gypsy man at the carnival to regain some sense of herself. Life is art, Smith seems to be saying in *Cakewalk*, if you're artist enough to make it be that way.

Cakewalk was financially unrewarding, but it was widely and enthusiastically reviewed. Katha Pollitt in the *New York Times Book Review* found the stories, if not ambitious, "lively and compassionate," and she praised Smith's "sharp ear for the rapid pithy speech of her neighbors" and her "amused eye for the sheer oddity of small-town popular culture." The collection was briefly noted in the *New Yorker* and reviewed in the *Village Voice Literary Supplement*, the *Wall Street Journal*, and other national periodicals. The *Wall Street Journal* called *Cakewalk* "impressive and entertaining . . . its tales shrewdly observant of segments of North Carolina life," and the *San Diego Union* put Smith in the tradition of Flannery O'Connor, Eudora Welty, Carson McCullers, Harper Lee, and Katherine Ann Porter. *Cakewalk* was published in paperback by Ballantine Books in 1983.

Oral History, Smith's fifth and latest novel, has been highly praised by critics, some of whom have likened it to Faulkner's work. Such a comparison makes Smith laugh, and she deprecates her own part in its complexity and richness. She claims for the material an intrinsic value and lists the "true" stories with which the book is filled—such as the witch's curse passed down from generation to generation or the story of the witch pretending to be a real girl, but riding her lover at night. Smith says she read an account of a hog killing and was so impressed that she decided to have one in her book; a friend's husband sang the dirty songs Little Luther sings at the butchering. Another friend, acknowledged in the author's note, gave her the line about "a phone call from hell." The author's note also lists

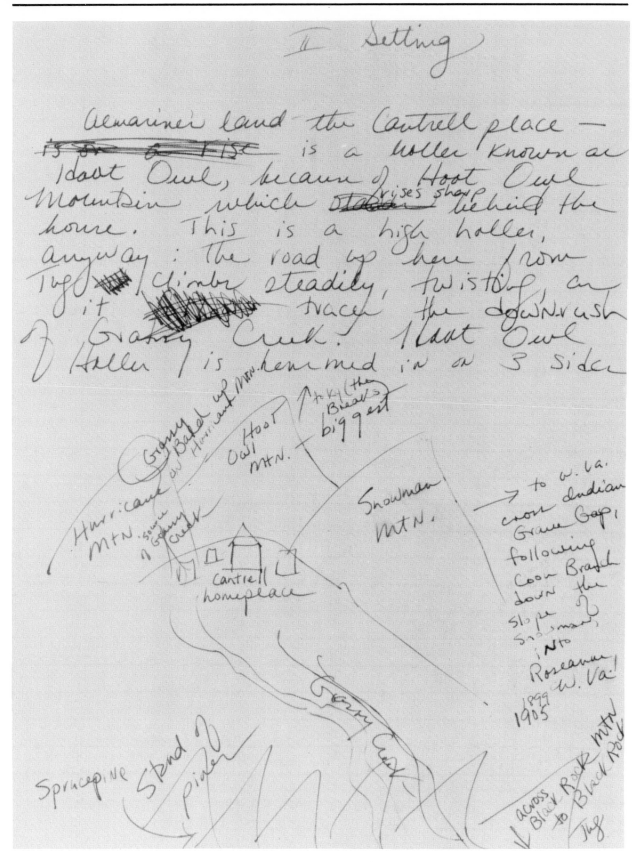

Notes for Oral History *(the author)*

a number of sources on Appalachia. But whatever went before the writing has been translated by Smith's voice into the paradox of a novel called *Oral History*. She makes the story sound as if it is being told aloud, the old legends and the newly invented ones merging into storyteller's magic.

Oral History begins in the present, where the materialism of the New South is countered only by ancient Ora Mae Cantrell's forbidding presence and Little Luther Wade's astonishing songs from the past. The family has left the cabin in Hoot Owl Holler because it is haunted. Almarine Wade is putting carpet in his van. His wife Debra, dressed in a "Foxy Lady" T-shirt, climbs in to help and they make love—an act that in retrospect becomes clearly parodic. The children are racing in to watch "Magnum" on television. The outsider, Jennifer, a college student come back to discover her roots and to tape the ghosts in the old Hoot Owl Holler cabin, is mooning over these people who are "the salt of the earth."

Smith strips off this veneer quickly and moves back in time to the original Almarine, born in 1876. He is twenty-two, and the inheritor of all the land he can see from his mountain cabin door. He sets out to find himself a wife and instead, led by a magical redbird, finds Red Emmy, the witch. Naked to the waist, her skin white, her hair a cascade of deep red, her eyes black as night, her mouth red as a cut, her nipples red as blood, she is the archetypal temptress. Almarine wins her and is consumed by her passion until he is wasted down to skin and bones. Finally, on the insistence of the medicine woman, Granny Elder, he makes Red Emmy leave. Soon afterward he takes a young girl as wife; deeply in love with her and happy in his land and his children, he flourishes. But Red Emmy has cursed the Cantrell family, or so it is said, and his wife Pricey Jane and his son Eli die.

Oral History traces the Cantrell family through some hundred years of births, marriages, and deaths, and through all the metamorphoses of Red Emmy's curse. Each of the five long sections begins with a genealogical chart which shows the complex interweaving of unions based on inheritance and proximity. The novel is told from several points of view: The framing sections are omniscient, and within the body of the novel the narrative is mostly in first person, with Granny Younger, Rose Hibbits, Richard Burlage, Mrs. Ludie Davenport, Little Luther Wade, Jink Cantrell, Ora Mae, and Sally telling their own versions of the story. The narrative slips unobtrusively into omniscience in "Pricey Jane," "Almarine," "At the Burying-Ground," and

"At the Smith Hotel." The characters upon whom the curse falls, Almarine and Pricey Jane, Dory, Pearl, and Billie, never speak for themselves, thus reinforcing the mystery of their deaths.

This novel is filled with universal types, personalities that Smith has explored in earlier fiction. Richard Burlage, who has by far the longest section, is a Richmond man who would rather talk than act. Keeping a journal and taking photographs remove him from the action and allow him to participate voyeuristically rather than directly. He is an intellectual, and even his reporting of events has the pompous, inflated sound of self-importance. Justine Poole is the generous, sexually accommodating woman for whom sex is something to do to keep the door closed against "death or fate or sudden sorrow." Rose Hibbits is crazy, her delusions springing from a life of sexual frustration beginning when she stood in the first spring rain to make herself beautiful.

There are survivors, like Little Luther Wade, able to turn his anger over Dory's love for Richard Burlage into a song and then to win her in marriage. There are those like Ora Mae who simply endure, like stones against which others break themselves. And there are those who are destined not to survive, "cursed" like Dory and Pearl. And there are those who reach genuine fulfillment, like Sally, who is in love with a good man and happy with her life.

There are, finally, the ones for whom the past is meaningless. They exist as if every minute were the present: Almarine Wade, after Ora Mae and Little Luther are dead, Billie has been shot, and Pearl has died of complications of childbirth, turns Hoot Owl Holler into "a wildly successful theme park and recreation area." The only remnant of the past is the old cabin, surrounded by a chain-link fence, and fronted by an observation deck, where people sit and watch "when the dark comes and the wind and the laughter start . . . when that rocking chair starts rocking and rocks like crazy the whole night long." Smith does not allow Almarine Wade to defeat the curse of Hoot Owl Holler, and thus she promises that the oral history will continue even beyond the slickly veneered present.

Oral History derives complexity and beauty from its layering of the past as told by many voices. It answers the accusation that a writing teacher once made, an accusation that Smith feared for a long time: "You write very well, but you have nothing to say." The secret of Smith's fiction lies in her ability to listen, not to talk. The beauty of it is that she has no preachments to make, no narrow arguments to set forth. She is, finally, a storyteller, passing down the oral history of the past and present mountain South, making it new at the same time she preserves it on paper. The mountains might otherwise succumb to strip-mining, poverty, ignorance, fear, and the novelties of the present, but they are held timeless in *Oral History*.

The critical enthusiasm for *Oral History* was virtually unqualified. The critics saw Smith's fifth novel as a fulfillment of their great expectations for her as a novelist. Rod Steier's final comment in the *Hartford Courant* was typical: "With *Oral History* Smith should finally break out of the 'good Southern writer' category. She is a great writer." Christopher Lehmann-Haupt, in the *New York Times*, said, "The rural folk that it treats may long ago have been turned into clichés by imitators of William Faulkner, Flannery O'Connor and Eudora Welty, but in *Oral History* Lee Smith brings them back to life again." Smith is proud of *Oral History*; it is, she feels, the best work she has done. Sales have been better than for any other of her books; *Oral History* has not

only paid off the deficit accrued by *Cakewalk* but has been her first book to produce a royalty check.

Smith is currently taking a semester's leave from her full-time faculty position at North Carolina State University to work on her new novel. In December 1983 she began researching the project by working at a local beauty shop, where she takes copious notes on permanents, the cost of beauty shop chairs, and the mysteries of hair coloring. She has also tried her hand at shampooing, but that is as far as she wishes to take her participation in the beautician's art. Lee Smith is confident now, as her readers and the critics have been for some time, that she is first and foremost a writer.

References:

Anne Goodwyn Jones, "The World of Lee Smith," *Southern Quarterly*, 5 (Fall 1983);
Lucinda MacKethan, "Artists and Beauticians: Balance in Lee Smith's Fiction," *Southern Literary Journal* (Fall 1982): 3-14.

Steve Tesich
(29 September 1943-   )

Dorn Hetzel
Pennsylvania State University

BOOKS: *The Carpenters* (New York: Dramatists Play Service, 1971);
Baba Goya (New York: French, 1974);
Passing Game (New York: French, 1978);
Summer Crossing (New York: Random House, 1982);
Division Street & Other Plays (New York: Performing Arts, 1982).

PLAYS: *The Carpenters*, New York, St. Clement's Church, 10 December 1970;
Lake of the Woods, New York, American Place Theatre, 8 December 1971;
Baba Goya, New York, American Place Theatre, 9 May 1973; reopened under the title *Nourish the Beast*, New York, American Place Theatre, October 1973;
Gorky, New York, American Place Theatre, 16 November 1975;
Passing Game, New York, American Place Theatre, 1 December 1977;

Touching Bottom—includes *The Road, A Life,* and *Baptismal*, New York, American Place Theatre, 17 December 1978;
Division Street, Los Angeles, Mark Taper Forum, 22 May 1980; New York, Ambassador Theatre, 8 October 1980.

SCREENPLAYS: *Breaking Away*, 20th Century-Fox, 1979;
Eyewitness, 20th Century-Fox, 1981;
Four Friends, Filmways, 1981;
The World According to Garp, Warner Bros., 1982.

Although he is a playwright with six off-Broadway productions to his credit, Steve Tesich is best known for his work in films—most notably for the screenplay of *Breaking Away*, which won him an Academy Award in 1980 for best original screenplay.

Tesich (whose baptismal name is Stoyan) was

Steve Tesich (© Jan Lucas)

in favor of bicycle racing, anchoring the winning team in the university's annual "Little 500" race—the race featured in the climax of *Breaking Away*.

Tesich graduated Phi Beta Kappa and went on to attend Columbia University, earning a Master's degree in 1967 in Russian literature. During his time at Columbia, he gained firsthand experience of the student protests against the war in Vietnam, experience he would later concern himself with in his work—both in his original screenplay *Four Friends* and in his Broadway play *Division Street*.

Tesich continued his studies in Russian literature, entering the Ph.D. program at Columbia, but found himself more and more intrigued with writing. He began taking classes in playwriting with Jack Gelber and in the short story with Harvey Swados and Grace Paley. He dropped out of the Ph.D. program and took a job in Brooklyn with the Department of Welfare in order to earn a living while writing. Tesich had the good luck to find a co-worker, Rebecca Claire, who was sympathetic to his desire to become an author. She did his work as well as her own, leaving him free to go home and write. According to Tesich it was a perfect match: "I was deciding to be a writer and Becky always wanted to be the woman who supported one of those." Together they moved west to Colorado and were married in 1972 at the Denver City Hall.

The 1970s proved to be a prolific decade for Tesich. He made his mark as a promising young playwright with six plays produced off-Broadway, all but the first at the American Place Theatre. *The Carpenters* opened in December 1970 at St. Clement's Church. The play centers around an American family caught in the midst of disintegration and introduces a theme frequently appearing in Tesich's later work—the breakdown of communication between father and son. In *The Carpenters*, the son, a political radical and college dropout, brings home a bomb with which he intends to kill his father. The plan is discovered by the father, who turns to the other members of the family for support, only to find them in agreement with the son's violent intent.

The play met with lukewarm reviews from the major critics. Tesich was acknowledged as a potential talent, but the general reaction was typified by Walter Kerr in the *New York Times*: "The present piece is oppressed by obvious and top-heavy symbolism. We know that the household is decaying because the toaster, the washer, and the sump-pump are all simultaneously on the blink. . . . The

born in 1943 in the small town of Titovo, Yugoslavia, where he was raised by his mother. His father, a lieutenant in the Yugoslav army, fled his country to join the government in exile while his son was still an infant. One of Tesich's favorite pastimes as a child was to entertain the old men of the village by inventing fanciful stories about going to America, for which the villagers nicknamed him "Truman." The stories, however, proved to be prophetic when the boy's father, after an absence of fourteen years, sent word for his family to join him in America. In 1957 Tesich, along with his mother and older sister, immigrated to East Chicago, Indiana, where his father was employed as a steelworker. The long anticipated reunion lasted only three years; Tesich's father died in 1960. Of that period in his life, Tesich recalls, "Our getting together never really worked for him. Too much time had passed . . . I did get to know my father, but only from a distance. He was a very unhappy man who just wasn't living the kind of life he wanted to live."

After a year spent learning English, Tesich attended high school in East Chicago and won a wrestling scholarship to Indiana University in Bloomington. Once in college, he gave up wrestling

building itself may soon topple over because it is weighted in a single direction, daddy's; that sort of thing."

Tesich's second play, *Lake of the Woods*, drew similar critical response when it opened in December 1971 at the American Place Theatre. The piece concerns the existential adventures of a metropolitan advertising executive named Winnie, who, along with his family, has gone for a vacation to a touted summer resort called Lake of the Woods. Once there, he finds a dried-up hole in the ground instead of a lake, and a barren wasteland instead of green woods. Winnie proceeds to endure a miserable night of uncertainties, arguments, and soul searching (not to mention pillage by a wandering band of rock musicians), ironically to emerge from the disastrous experience with a new spirit of optimism. Clive Barnes noted the obviousness of the play's theme, representing America in a state of dissolution, and complained it was "a play where symbolism falls like snow."

These early plays differed from the ones that would follow, as Tesich explains: "I used to begin with a conflict. I don't do that anymore. I am absolutely 100 percent convinced that if you invent real characters, give them a real point of view, set them off against each other and follow the little things they do, the drama *will* be there."

The emphasis shifted in his writing from heavily metaphoric conflict to a more gentle drama of character when *Baba Goya* opened at the American Place Theatre in May 1973. The play met with favorable critical reviews and established Tesich's reputation as a skillful creator of offbeat yet affable characters. The work centers around the members of a Brooklyn household run by Baba Goya, a wisecracking earth mother known for advertising in the newspapers whenever she is in need of a new husband. The rest of the family includes Goya's current husband, Mario, who is convinced he is dying from an unnamed disease; her daughter, Sylvia, who has returned home after a divorce to sob out her liberal guilt (she voted for Nixon in the last election); an adopted son, Bruno, now a policeman depressed over having to arrest what he labels "orphaney" looking criminals; and the Old Man who once answered one of Goya's ads for a husband, but, because of his age, was cast, much to his displeasure, in the role of grandfather.

Both Edith Oliver in the *New Yorker* and Harold Clurman in the *Nation* compared *Baba Goya* to Kaufman and Hart's *You Can't Take It With You*. Clurman went on to say: "It's no use: there's no way of or point in summarizing the plot of this play; you

may seek for symbols in it if you like, but it makes only the sense of a delighted and intermittently delightful senselessness. The comment is in the play's refusal to take anything in our screwed-up society seriously, except the fondness we may have for one another." (The play reopened at the American Place in October 1973 under the title *Nourish the Beast*.)

Tesich put to use his knowledge of Russian literature in a dramatic biography of the Soviet revolutionary/playwright *Gorky*, which opened at the American Place in November 1975. The play was notable for the device of splitting the main character into three separate personas and having them confront each other on stage. Alex, the young boy, provides a romantic view of the early life; Maxim is the fiery idealist and revolutionary; and Gorky is the disillusioned old man on the verge of death. The narrative of the play is aided by accompanying music, mainly Russian folk songs, for which Tesich served as lyricist.

Clive Barnes and Walter Kerr, both writing for the *New York Times*, split over the play. Barnes's review was favorable; he declared that the long-promising Steve Tesich had finally "arrived," and called the device of splitting the main character "a wonderfully dramatic concept." Kerr disagreed: "The device doesn't give us three Gorkys for the price of one; it gives us one-third of a Gorky all over the place. . . . In short, we have a writer at hand who has written out no one character in full and who has permitted irrelevant music to take up the slack."

Tesich's *Passing Game*, produced at the American Place in 1977, is the story of two actors with careers on the decline, who recognize all too well their professional compromises and failures. Both are haunted by wives who insist on holding to lovingly idealized views of their potentials, continuing to offer support and encouragement even as their husbands' chances for success grow slimmer and slimmer. The men, unable to live up to such adoration, bring their wives to a wooded resort that has been the site of several psychopathic killings, in hopes that the women will be the murderer's next victims. The rationale behind this plotting is offered by one of the men, who explains that, with his wife dead, "there will be nobody to remind me of my potential."

T. E. Kalem for *Time* magazine commented: "Playwright Tesich partially redeems this shaky premise by reminding us that failure is not a private affair in the U.S. It is a public humiliation. By shutting their wives' eyes, the two men hope to shut the world's eyes." But, for the most part, *Passing Game* was received as too melodramatic and implausibly plotted to be convincing. It was directed by Peter Yates, who later directed *Breaking Away*.

In 1978 the American Place Theatre staged an evening of three of Tesich's one-act plays, collectively entitled *Touching Bottom*. All three plays—*The Road*, *A Life*, and *Baptismal*—were written in the tradition of the absurdist style of Samuel Beckett. Mel Gussow, reviewing in the *New York Times*, noted the similarity to Beckett and went on to observe: "Though the work may seem grounded in cliches, it is lifted by Mr. Tesich's ebullient gift for language and for characterization. . . ."

During this same period of time in the 1970s, Tesich wrote a half-dozen screenplays, none of which made it into production. One of these, "The Eagle of Naptown," a story about bicycle racing, was written for Hollywood producer Ray Stark. Another of these early scripts was "The Cutters," a story about quarry workers and their families. This script had been written under the sponsorship of Peter Yates, who had a deal with Paramount to develop several possible story ideas for film projects; but there was no financial backing for the finished screenplay, and "The Cutters," too, went unproduced. It was Yates who eventually suggested to Tesich that he merge the two scripts. Tesich thought it was an unlikely combination at first, but decided to give it a try. The result was *Breaking Away*.

Breaking Away is set in Bloomington, Indiana, home of Indiana University. The story revolves around four boys, "townies," caught in the gap between adolescence and adulthood, between their pasts as sons of "cutters" (quarry workers) and their as yet undecided futures.

One of the boys, Dave, turns out to be a first-class bicycle racer, whose heroes, the Italian National Racing Team, he attempts to emulate by embracing everything Italian (their language, their opera, their "ini" foods)—much to the chagrin of his very American, used-car salesman father.

Tension rises in the film's story as a long-standing class rivalry between the townies, or "cutters," and the more privileged college boys erupts into a brawl in a campus cafeteria. The resolution of this tension provides the film with its climax—a bicycle race, the "Little 500," pitting the two groups against one another. In an all-out effort, Dave leads his team to victory and in doing so wins for himself the confidence to escape his past and begin a new life—as a college student.

Much of *Breaking Away* is drawn from Tesich's own past—he uses his own alma mater as his set-

ting; he shares with Dave a fascination for bicycle racing and a victory in the "Little 500" race. Tesich's own history as an immigrant allows him to identify with the feeling of alienation the cutters experience being nonstudents in a college town. The following monologue is spoken by Mike, the angriest of the four, as they all sit on a hillside overlooking the campus football stadium (where the college team is warming up):

> You know, I used to think I was a really great quarterback in high school . . . still think so, too. Can't even bring myself to light a cigarette cause I keep thinking I gotta stay in shape. . . . You know what really gets me though? I mean, here I am, I gotta live in this stinkin' town and I gotta read in the newspapers about some hot-shot kid, new star on the college team. Every year it's gonna be a new one. Every year it's not gonna be me. I'm just gonna be Mike, twenty year old Mike . . . thirty year old Mike . . . old mean old man Mike. These college kids out here, they're never gonna get old or out of shape—cause new ones come along every year. They're gonna keep calling us "cutters." To them it's just a dirty word. To me it's just something else I never got a chance to be.

The pursuit of understanding between father and son, a main concern throughout Tesich's writing, as well as in *Breaking Away*, is the source of much of the film's humor and poignancy. Tesich, who never really got to know his own father, instills in the character of Dave a profound need to have his father be proud of him. Tesich portrays the father in the film as a man who loves his son, but is unable to communicate his feelings without embarrassment. One of the film's most effective scenes is a talk between father and son as they walk along at night, past the buildings Dave's father helped cut from the quarry. The father, in his taciturn way, hints at his disappointment with his own life, and at his expectations for his son's:

FATHER: I cut the stone for this building.

DAVE: You did?

FATHER: Yup. I was one fine stone cutter. Mike's dad, Moocher's, Cyril's, all of us. Well, Cyril's dad—never mind. Thing of it was, I loved it. I was young and slim and strong. I was damn proud of my work. And the buildings went up. When they were finished the damndest thing happened. It was like the buildings was too good for us. Nobody told us that—just, just felt uncomfortable, that's all. Even now I'd like to be able to stroll through the campus and look at the limestone, but I just feel out of place.... You guys still go swimming in the quarries?

DAVE: Sure.

FATHER: So the only thing you got to show for my twenty years of work is the holes we left behind.

DAVE: I don't mind.

FATHER: I do.

The film received unanimous critical acclaim. Richard Schickel in *Time* called it a "loose, warm, funny movie. . . . The kids' style of hanging out— their scrapes, gags and their frustrations—is observed with a tart affection and a truthfulness that are very refreshing." Janet Maslin in the *New York Times* called it a "classic sleeper . . . wonderful . . . a movie so fresh and funny it didn't even need a big budget or a pedigree." In addition to winning an Academy Award for original screenplay, *Breaking Away* won the New York Film Critics Circle Award for best screenplay and the National Society of Film Critics Award for the best film in 1979.

As well as providing him with his first real critical and popular success, Tesich found writing for film to be a breakthrough experience creatively. "I could portray reality as reality, and say things that meant a lot to me, without adding a layer of heightened theatricality in order for it to have meaning." Still, Tesich admits it was a difficult adjustment for him to make as a writer, shifting from theater to film, and learning to attune himself to the visual language of small realizations; realizations shown instead of spoken. "In the theatre you look to language for some eternal truth. Films are much more lifelike. In real life, people don't have enormous scenes. They will hint at things, look out the window and see something that means more to them than, say, the friend they haven't seen in five years."

Nevertheless, Tesich returned to the theater in 1980 with a new play, *Division Street*, which opened to rave reviews at the Mark Taper Forum in Los Angeles. The play, essentially a farce, centers around a middle-aged man named Chris, once a well-known radical/activist in the politically con-scious 1960s. With the movement dead, Chris has settled in Chicago as an ordinary businessman, content to leave the turmoil of the past behind. However, his life is soon thrown into chaos. A photographer on the street happens to snap a shot of Chris falling ill after eating in a cheap Serbian restaurant. The photograph, reprinted in papers throughout the country, is mistakenly interpreted as Chris launching a new tirade against American society. Suddenly Chris finds his apartment becoming a rallying point for his former allies from the 1960s in search of a cause (plus an odd assortment of other Tesich-style eccentrics who add to the confusion).

The play made the transition to the Ambassador Theatre on Broadway in October 1980. However, the reviews were considerably less enthusiastic than those in Los Angeles. Writing in the *New York Times*, Frank Rich said: "If the promise of fun and trenchant satire is everywhere at the Ambassador, *Division Street* ultimately proves more frantic than funny, more well meaning than well crafted. By the end, we're still waiting for Mr. Tesich's farce to boil over into hilarity and for his characters to come to honest terms with their teargas-scented past." The play closed after twenty-two performances.

In 1981 Tesich had two other original screenplays produced, *Eyewitness*, again teamed with Peter Yates as director, and *Four Friends*, directed by Arthur Penn. Both films were based in part on autobiographical material.

During a summer vacation from college, Tesich had worked as a night janitor in a Chicago office building, a job he gave to his main character, Daryl Deever, in *Eyewitness*, although he changed the setting to Manhattan. Daryl, a rather ordinary, unambitious young man, suffers from an infatuation with a pretty television reporter named Tony Sokolow. (Tesich admitted to having once had a similar infatuation with CBS newswoman Lesley Stahl.) When a Vietnamese businessman is murdered in the building, Daryl gets his once-in-a-lifetime chance to meet Tony, who has been sent to cover the story. In hope of getting closer to her, Daryl hints to Tony that he might have information about the killing, and in so doing, puts them both in danger.

Richard Corliss in *Time* acknowledged that Tesich "has the Saroyan sense to devise a solid foundation on which his eccentrics and lowlifes dance to their own ricochet rhythms. But when it comes to complicating and resolving a plot, Tesich falls back on the conventions of melodrama." For the critics and the public alike, it was a respectable but disappointing successor to *Breaking Away*.

Four Friends, the most autobiographical of all of Tesich's works to date, is about three young men and a young woman coming of age in the 1960s. The primary focus of the film is on a character named Danilo Prozor, a twelve-year-old Yugoslavian immigrant who, along with his mother, has come to the United States to be reunited with his father. The family settles in East Chicago, Indiana, where Danny's father is employed in a steel foundry. Danilo begins trying to sort out his immigrant-fantasy vision of America from its reality, a task which is to occupy him throughout the time span of the film—the next fifteen years of Danilo's life. His divided heritage creates a clash between the traditional values of his parents, especially those of his blue-collar father, and those of the newly arising 1960s antiestablishment counterculture.

The film received sharply mixed reviews. Vincent Canby in the *New York Times* called it "the best film yet made about the 60's. . . . It has the quality of a legend, a fable remembered." However, writing in the *New Yorker*, Pauline Kael disagreed, saying that "*Four Friends* views the American sixties as a sturdy burgher from central Europe might: these kids don't appreciate their freedom; they have a lot of growing up to do." Kael found the film's patriotism and optimism "hard to take," declaring: "There's a flag waving underlayer to this picture's love affair with America the melting pot; Tesich is the screenwriter as national cheerleader."

In 1982, Tesich's adaptation of John Irving's best-selling novel, *The World According to Garp*, reached the screen. The film was directed by George Roy Hill and starred Robin Williams in the title role. The story follows the adventures of T. S. Garp from his conception out of wedlock, through his unorthodox upbringing at the hands of his exceedingly liberated mother, to his demise at the age of thirty-three from the bullet of a childhood playmate turned radical feminist. The film itself garnered mixed reviews from the critics, but most commended Tesich on a faithful and imaginative job of adapting Irving's loosely structured mélange of black humor and eccentric characters.

Tesich turned out the first draft of the screenplay in only two and a half months, far ahead of schedule and a remarkably short time for so complex, anecdotal, and lengthy a novel as *Garp*. It is a story Tesich might well have found easy to identify with, concerning as it does a fatherless main character who becomes a wrestler in school and grows up to be a writer whose natural optimism is tempered by anxiety in a world of great beauty continually visited by sudden and irrational violence.

Though initially reluctant to take on the assignment, Tesich changed his mind because of the chance to work with a director he admired and, more profoundly, because of the unexpected similarities he found between Irving's philosophies of life and many of his own deepest beliefs. As Tesich summed it up, "*Garp* says to me that life can be an adventure. That you must have a life before you die. That you must dream and strive to make your dream a reality. That anything is possible here. The only thing holding you back from your dreams is fear or laziness."

Also in 1982, Tesich published his first novel, *Summer Crossing*, which combines themes and story elements familiar to audiences of both *Four Friends* and *Breaking Away*. The setting is East Chicago, Indiana, where the book's protagonist, high-school senior Daniel Price, is facing graduation and an

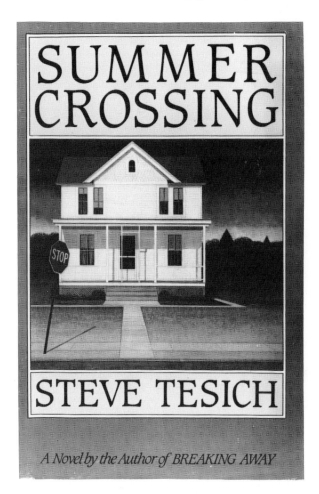

Dust jacket for Tesich's first novel, the story of a working-class teenager

329

undetermined future. His bickering parents are both working-class: his father labors in a factory; his mother cleans houses. Daniel clearly dreads the thought of becoming like his parents—a phenomenon he already sees happening in some of his classmates. He dreams of escaping this factory town and its air of stagnation and failure, but is trapped by the complications of love (an enigmatic young woman named Rachel) and of death (his father dying of cancer).

Writing in the *New York Times Book Review*, Dan Wakefield commented that Tesich "gives us a deeply moving story with a cast of unexpectedly intriguing characters. . . . The story plunges us to depths of feeling that go way beyond the light and breezy implications of the book's title. This is a painful passage, told with integrity as well as talent."

This world to which Tesich continues to return in his work is filled to overflowing with an extraordinary richness of themes: the combat of family life; the struggles of outsiders—the foreign, the orphaned, the displaced; the violent shifts of fortune and falls from grace. And yet all of it suf-

fused with the light of a childlike hopefulness and trust. This world, of course, is the world of America, a shining, immigrant's America. An America that Tesich himself has called, and seems to deeply believe is, in his own words, that most treasured of unmapped landscapes: "the frontier of possibility."

References:
Robert Berkvist, "From 'Breaking Away' to 'Division Street'—In Love With America," *New York Times*, 5 October 1980, Sec. II, p. 1;

Donald Chase, "Tesich and Yates," *Horizon* (December 1980): 26-32;

Barney Cohen, "Steve Tesich Turns Memories into Movies," *New York Times Magazine*, 17 January 1982, p. 42;

Bernard Drew, "Yates and Tesich Shift Gears," *American Film* (March 1981): 49-55;

Lawrence O'Toole, "Broadway to Hollywood," *Film Comment* (November/December 1981): 22-25;

Jean Vallely, "Breaking Away," *Rolling Stone*, 17 April 1980, pp. 31-32.

Lella Warren
(22 March 1899-3 March 1982)

Nancy G. Anderson
Auburn University at Montgomery

BOOKS: *A Touch of Earth* (New York: Simon & Schuster, 1926);

Foundation Stone (New York & London: Knopf, 1940; London: Collins, 1941);

Whetstone Walls (New York: Appleton-Century-Crofts, 1952).

PERIODICAL PUBLICATIONS:
Fiction:
"The Wrong Twin," *Cosmopolitan*, 82 (February 1927): 78-81, 130;

"Kiss in the Dark," *Cosmopolitan*, 82 (April 1927): 78-81, 156, 158-159;

"Bad," *McClure's*, 59 (September 1927): 44-47, 91-92;

"The Little Girl Next Door," *Good Housekeeping*, 87 (October 1928): 46-49, 264, 266-267, 269, 271-272;

"Rich Girl, Poor Girl," *College Humor*, 16 [17] (April 1929): 34-37, 125-129;

"The Other's Porridge," *Story*, 10 (February 1937): 9-28.
Nonfiction:
"Every Town's a Small Town," *McClure's* (December 1926): 30-31, 94;

"George Washington University," *College Humor*, 13 (March 1928): 50-51, 128-129;

"Before the Flight," *Collier's*, 88 (18 July 1931): 18-19, 42-44.

The publishing career of Lella Warren began in 1926 with the publication of her first novel, *A Touch of Earth*, and continued through the 1952 release of her third novel, *Whetstone Walls*, and the printing of several autobiographical essays in 1952 and early 1953. But her writing career was much

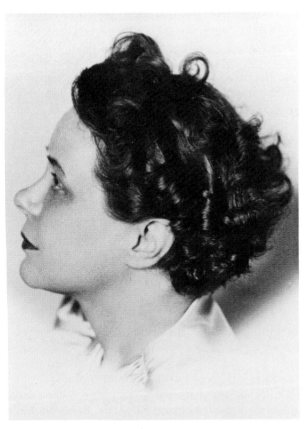

Lella Warren

longer: It began with stories and descriptions in notebooks when she was eight years old and continued until her death, which stopped her work on the sequel to *Whetstone Walls*. Despite this long literary career and its summit of a best-selling novel in 1940-1941, Lella Warren died unknown to, or forgotten by, the reading public.

She was born in Clayton, Alabama, the birthplace of her father, Benjamin Smart Warren, a doctor with the United States Public Health Service; he and his wife were descendants of pioneers in the settling of Alabama—the Warrens, the Underwoods, and the Lawsons. Dr. Warren's assignments took him and his family all over the world to U.S. Marine hospitals and quarantine stations before they settled in Washington, D.C., but he continued to emphasize loyalty to family and sense of place by returning with his family to Alabama for extended vacations.

Lella Warren was educated in Alabama—

actually in one of the "plank" schools that appear in her novels—and at various military installations; she ultimately graduated from Western High School in Washington. There she attracted the attention of Miss Margaret Bell Merrill, her high school writing teacher and a published author, who sent one of Warren's stories to William Dean Howells and William Rose Benét for advice; Benét responded: "The girl who wrote 'Red Brick' will inevitably be a writer." She attended Goucher College before transferring to George Washington University to complete her degree. In undergraduate and graduate courses Warren studied with Dr. Robert Bolwell, her creative writing professor at George Washington University, who also encouraged her to pursue her writing.

A Touch of Earth, in the tradition of initiation novels, is the story of Jean Ingle Cheney Kent, known as "Jick," the daughter of an army doctor. "Autobiographical in tone and feeling though not in event," the novel covers Jick's childhood, education, marriage to army officer Jim Travers, conflicts between her traditional marriage and her aspirations to be a writer, and her physical and temperamental attraction to newspaper correspondent Caulder Seables. The critical reception was mixed; many reviews criticized the naive, childlike style of the first portion of the novel and praised the second part. This latter portion of the novel is devoted to Jick's struggle with the conflicts that develop in her life:

> Suffering was part of life, part even of beauty. Pain and Life and Beauty. Beauty that resolved itself into poetry, the poetry of life. *Life blew three notes on a silver horn—* Something that had always been fluttering, stirring within her, first weakly then strongly, was twisting, turning, throbbing now—working in travail, demanding to be born! *Life blew three notes-----*

The novel sold well and attracted the attention of Ray Long, editor of *Cosmopolitan*, who took an option on Warren's short works for publication in *Cosmopolitan* or other Hearst publications.

To support herself during the Depression, Warren wrote short stories and nonfiction articles for magazines, was a free-lance journalist for three Washington papers (the *Post,* the *Star*, and the *Times-Herald*), and held various governmental and public-relations jobs. The stories generally use traditional initiation plots and themes of children becoming young adults and then young adults becoming involved in love triangles. Though a specific place, or setting, is not evident in these works, family ties and frequently social status are important. The nonfiction articles include works about cities where she had lived, George Washington University (*College Humor,* March 1928), and the preflight preparations of Charles Lindbergh (*Collier's,* 18 July 1931).

Warren felt that she was wasting her talents on these short works. In retrospect, she concluded that "a few of the things I wrote had some merit and showed some advance, but most of it soon became tripe." This dissatisfaction with her achievements in these short works and challenges from her family, especially her father, motivated Warren to turn to work on a novel that her father had urged her to write: a novel about the "true South" as they both knew it.

Though she had begun preparation of this novel as early as 1928, Warren began serious, concentrated research and writing in the mid-1930s. She worked from history texts, local Alabama newspapers, wills and deeds, court records, maps, diaries and letters provided by relatives and friends, and oral tradition in her family. Her research notebooks reveal extensive and meticulous work for the background of the novel about a family that settled Alabama. She corresponded with Dr. Lewy Dorman, a noted Alabama historian, for nearly five years, and these letters confirm her concern for accuracy of historical detail.

Foundation Stone (1940), a novel opening in South Carolina in 1823 and concluding in post-Civil War Alabama, is the result of this research. The will of William Whetstone, based on a will in the Warren family, brings his foster daughter's child from New York to South Carolina to receive her inheritance. Thus Gerda van Ifort meets Whetstone's oldest son, Yarbrough, sixteen years her senior. After a brief courtship, their marriage, and the birth of twins a year later, Yarbrough and Gerda face the reality of worn-out land on a once prosperous cotton plantation. The solution is a move to the new state of Alabama, where cotton grows "like wildfire." They create a home in the wilderness and build the town of Turberville in Turber County, based on Warren's native Clayton and Barbour County. The struggles of a pioneering family in southeast Alabama reflect Warren's research without distracting from the story and characters. The Whetstones and their friends fight nature, the Indians, and—on occasion—each other. Yarbrough's death does not weaken the family, for its strength has always been Gerda. The plot follows the second-generation Whetstones, but Gerda, based generally on Warren's great-grandmother Lucinda Ifort Warren, remains the foundation stone of the clan. The title and epigraph of the novel are from the description of Elspeth Mackay in Stephen Vincent Benét's *John Brown's Body,* a work that Warren considered her bible. This quotation sounds the themes of family and land inherent in this saga:

"But she held her word and she kept
                              her troth,
Cleared the forest and tamed the wild
And gave the breast to the new-born child
While the painted Death went whooping by
—To die at least as she wished to die
In the fief built out of her blood and bone
With her heart for the Hall's
                              foundation-stone."

The family survives the Civil War and promises to prosper again because of the strength of their heritage.

This 754-page novel had a most inauspicious origin: 50 pages of manuscript plus an outline for 800 more pages presented to Knopf for an advance. Warren laughingly recalled later that of these original pages only 5 survived in the published novel and they were quotations of wills and other documents that could not be rewritten. She told of instances when she burned hundreds of pages, retaining only 35. In interviews Warren said that editors for Knopf finally saw a manuscript, and one reader, Carl van Doren, urged the publishers to get the rights immediately, for *Foundation Stone* would be "an American epic." Despite this prediction, Knopf apparently did not anticipate its success since, according to *Publishers Weekly,* the publishers planned the standard publicity campaign and a first printing of 7,250. However, success was immediate and extensive: three printings ordered before release on 9 September 1940 (the second printing of 5,500 was ordered by 12 August); six printings totaling 30,750 copies by 13 October 1940; and at least fourteen separate printings. An advertisement in the *New York Times* on 17 October 1940 states that the seventh printing of the novel is "on press" and the book is selling at the rate of 1,000 copies a day. "Currents in the Trade" in the 19 October 1940 *Publishers Weekly* states that *Foundation Stone* was "in its fortieth thousand," with a record order for Knopf of 3,000 copies in one day. *Foundation Stone* was tenth on the *New York Herald Tribune* best-seller list by 5 October 1940. The novel remained on these lists through the fall and winter of 1940-1941, reaching as high as second on lists with Thomas Wolfe's *You Can't Go Home Again*, Ernest Hemingway's *For Whom the Bell Tolls*, and Thomas Mann's *The Beloved Returns*. Even before the release of the novel, the British edition was announced, and it was released in January 1941. (This edition sold 13,468.) The novel was translated into Danish and Portuguese and transcribed into braille; the January 1941 issue of *Omnibook* also contained a condensed version of *Foundation Stone*. At one point, editors at Knopf told Warren that *Foundation Stone* was "the best selling American novel in the world."

The major reviewers praised the careful weaving together of narrative, numerous characters, and authentic historical and geographical backgrounds. Edith H. Walton in the *New York Times Book Review* observed that rarely does a Southern novel combine all three themes of wilderness, plantation life, and the Civil War, but *Foundation Stone* does in "a book of scope and stature...." Several passages were cited in various reviews as examples of particularly fine writing: Yarbrough's first view of Alabama, Yarbrough's death, and the description of the Whetstone family burying ground. The description of this site is drawn from Warren's memories of her own family's burial ground in Clayton. Gerda's retreat to this setting at the end of the section "The Land Yields" creates a tranquil tone before the exuberant opening of the next section, "The Cotton Snobs":

> The next day, near its close, she went where she had not gone for a long time, up to the family burying-ground. She turned her eyes in a circle. This was a fine place, where she could see far and wide. There was nothing meek about their dead. They were all dressed up in their Sunday best, with rings on their fingers and stick-pins in their shirt bosoms. There were no willows for them either, but the prickle and scarlet of holly, until she felt more like wishing "Christmas gift!" to company than saying prayers for the dead. And here in their midst she felt like Sister God indeed, standing on a piece of high ground!

The comparisons with *Gone with the Wind* were inevitable, and Margaret Mitchell's novel was favored in many reviews, especially in the South, though *Foundation Stone* was admired for a broader scope. Critics compared Warren favorably with John Galsworthy and Sigred Undset for family

sagas and Thomas Wolfe for treatment of time. Some reviewers criticized the novel for its length and for having too many characters, several agreeing that it could be two, or even three, novels. Warren was named one of the women of the year—along with Margaret Mitchell, Marjorie Kinnan Rawlings, and Mary Martin—by the Women's National Press Club and was awarded the George Washington University Alumni Award for Notable Achievement in Literature for *Foundation Stone*.

After months of autograph tours and a lecture circuit, Warren began work on *Whetstone Walls*, the sequel to *Foundation Stone*. Much of the research on Alabama history and the development of Tulane Medical School had been part of the work for *Foundation Stone*, but Warren spent another ten years working on this sequel that turns to the third generation of Whetstones as they move toward the twentieth century and settings outside Turber County. The central characters are Rob Whetstone (grandson of Gerda and Yarbrough) and Clymens Rutherford, a talented pianist whose education is encouraged by Rob's aunt Lucinda. Gerda is dead when this novel opens, but her strength and responsibilities are gradually assumed by the enigmatic Lucinda. The Whetstone homeplace, Rock Wall Place or Whetstone Stand, remains the bond for the family, but various members move to Washington and New Orleans. The story ends with Rob's completion of medical school, his vow to practice in foreign lands, and his proposal to Clymens; these events certainly promise a sequel.

The success of *Whetstone Walls* was limited, at least by comparison with that of *Foundation Stone*, but the book sold well. A telegram from editors with Appleton-Century-Crofts, dated 7 November 1952, announced that the third printing had been ordered; there was a fourth printing in December. Reviews in the large newspapers were favorable or mixed: Coleman Rosenberger, of the *New York Herald Tribune Book Review*, said *Whetstone Walls* was "fashioned slowly and painstakingly and affectionately." Mary McGrory of the *Washington Star* criticized it for "a lack of suspense and a theme" but praised the book because Warren "gives life to her characters." The short reviews nationwide were generally favorable, and *Whetstone Walls* was a bestseller in such diverse places as Indianapolis, Little Rock, and Los Angeles.

Family loyalty and a sense of place pervade these last two novels of Lella Warren. As she said in the Appleton-Century-Crofts press release for *Whetstone Walls*, "The over-all theme of any of my Whetstone books is clan feeling and family solidar-

38. 39

"Do tell," muttered Ratt, but under his breath so's not
to be sassy to a young Miss. He followed ree-ectfully while ~~J~~hey *enough*
went up to sit at a table, where tallow candles sputtered when the
moths flew too close. *Everyone seemed in a jangle. Mister Guy spilled gravy,* ~~Miz Lisbeth tried to pass the damson pre-~~
grocey got the hiccups, and Gerda's appetite was completely gone. ~~serves around twice, but they stopped a t Gran's place who finished~~
~~them off.~~ *Gran rudely ignored the others and* ~~He~~ talked Low Dutch to Marta who was at supper tonight,
because there was only ~~part of~~ the family and no second table.
presently Ven crooked a finger to ~~the~~ *his* hovering Cudge. "~~Get~~ *Fetch* her," he nodded
towards Marta, "some ale from somewhere." She put her hand on
her hip, and gazed over it at him.

"Nev' mind," grinned Ven, "nev' mind _that_, for me. I don't
hanker for women."

Marta was blowing red in the face, when she spied Miz Lizbeth,
reprovingly who said, "Please to pass me the salt." Marta sent it up from
where she sat ~~to~~ below it.
[observing her coyness] Gerda stared at Marta with something like hatred for her
feckleness ~~feebleness.~~ What about her Hans? Did she not recall him? And
the surge there had been between them, resembling this ocean tide
of her~~s~~ *now* toward Yarbrough?.Or was ~~she~~ *Marta* plump for any man's picking?
Miz Lisbeth ~~continued,~~ *spoke again* "This ~~May haw~~ *eldeberry* jelly... bitter. ~~Wormy~~
~~fruit.~~ What's that Lucey? You~~r~~ say use geranium leaf to take
away the rankle taste. My, pee-_yukey_, no ma'am! Well, I didn't
mean to put you into such a swivvey...touchy tonight, ain't you
Lucey? And Willy looks jumpy too." Gerda wondered if the old
suddenly lady was gently masking malice, and she felt some apprehension
Miz Lisbeth's about ~~her~~ reception of Yarbrough's choice.

~~The twilight lay down over the day outside.~~

Typist note
no paragraph
break between
choice & next
page.

Revised page from the typescript for Foundation Stone *(© 1983 Jerry Morgan Medley, Auburn University at Montgomery)*

ity." Although one criticism of the books was that there are too many characters and coincidences, Warren brings people together with these family ties and friendships, with a Dickensian technique. Though Rob may leave Turber County to go to Tulane, the bonds of family follow him so that meetings are usually results of connections, not coincidences. For all of Warren's attention to historical details, the people were her major concerns, their looks, dialects, dress, personalities, eccentricities. Included in the notebooks of historical research are pages cataloguing details about her characters and dates of events in their lives to maintain accuracy and credibility in fictional as well as historical material.

A characteristic of all her fiction, novels and short stories, is the open-ended conclusion, or "upward surge," as she described it. The ending of each work seems to promise another story, and, in the case of the novels, she had originally planned at least a trilogy.

At the time of her death, Lella Warren had recently finished revising an "interlude" novel about some minor characters from the Whetstone saga. The major work-in-progress was the sequel to *Whetstone Walls*, a work following Rob as he practiced medicine with the U.S. Marine Hospital Service and became instrumental in the founding of the U.S. Public Health Service, obviously heavily based on the life of Warren's father. There are numerous other unpublished works among Warren's manuscripts, including at least one other completed novel, portions of several sequels to the story of the Whetstones, poems, autobiographical sketches, and short stories. The qualities that remain constant in these diverse works are descriptive ability, depth of characterization, the theme of family loyalty, and, as characters move far from home, the sense of place.

Though Lella Warren died in relative obscurity, with her novels noted only in the brief *Washington Post* obituary, her works have a place in American literature. In a review of the literary scene of 1940 for *Publishers Weekly*, Harry Hansen observed, "Entertainment has a big place in writing," and then he rated *Foundation Stone* among the novels of 1940 deserving recognition in the entertainment category. But *Foundation Stone* and Warren's other major works are more than entertaining novels; they are good literature with an authentic and effective historical background.

Interviews:

"Lella Warren," *New York Herald Tribune Book Review*, 12 October 1952, pp. 14, 52;

"Lella Warren," *Alabama Librarian*, 4 (January 1953): 5-6.

References:

Nancy G. Anderson, "Lella Warren novel traces state history," *Montgomery Advertiser/Alabama Journal*, 25 April 1982, F8;

Angele De T. Gingras, "District Novelist Mows Down Magnolias & Modifies Legends of the Old South in Her Family Sagas," *Washington Times-Herald*, 24 July 1952;

Robert Van Gelder, "The Extraordinary Career of Lella Warren," *New York Times Book Review*, 8 December 1940, p. 2.

Papers:

Lella Warren's manuscripts are at Auburn University at Montgomery for cataloguing prior to final deposit at Auburn University at Montgomery and the Alabama Archives.

Literary Awards and Honors Announced in 1983

ALFRED HARCOURT AWARD IN BIOGRAPHY AND MEMOIRS

Elizabeth Young-Bruehl, for *Hannah Arendt: For Love of the World* (Yale University Press).

AMERICAN ACADEMY AND INSTITUTE OF ARTS AND LETTERS

AWARDS IN LITERATURE
Alfred Corn, Stephen Dixon, Robert Mezey, Mary Oliver, David Plante, George Starbuck, Leo Steinberg, Edmund White.

AWARD OF MERIT MEDAL FOR THE SHORT STORY
Elizabeth Spencer.

GOLD MEDAL FOR FICTION
Bernard Malamud.

HAROLD D. VURSELL MEMORIAL AWARD
Jonathan D. Spence.

MILDRED AND HAROLD STRAUSS LIVINGS
Raymond Carver and Cynthia Ozick.

RICHARD AND HINDA ROSENTHAL FOUNDATION AWARD
A. G. Mojtabai, for *Autumn* (Houghton Mifflin).

ROME FELLOWSHIP IN LITERATURE
Gjertrud Schnackenberg.

RUSSELL LOINES AWARD IN POETRY
Geoffrey Hill.

SUE KAUFMAN PRIZE FOR FIRST FICTION
Susanna Moore, for *My Old Sweetheart* (Houghton Mifflin).

WITTER BYNNER PRIZE FOR POETRY
Douglas Crase.

AMERICAN BOOK AWARDS

BIOGRAPHY
HARDCOVER: Judith Thurman, for *Isak Dinesen: The Life of a Storyteller* (St. Martin's).
PAPERBACK: James R. Mellow, for *Nathaniel Hawthorne in His Times* (Houghton Mifflin).

CHILDREN'S FICTION
HARDCOVER: Jean Fritz, for *Homesick: My Own Story* (Putnam's).
PAPERBACK: Paula Fox, for *A Place Apart* (Signet), and Joyce Carol Thomas, for *Marked by Fire* (Avon).

CHILDREN'S NONFICTION
James Cross Giblin, for *Chimney Sweeps* (Crowell).

FICTION
HARDCOVER: Alice Walker, for *The Color Purple* (Harcourt Brace Jovanovich).
PAPERBACK: Eudora Welty, for *The Collected Stories of Eudora Welty* (Harcourt Brace Jovanovich).

FIRST NOVEL
Gloria Naylor, for *The Women of Brewster Place* (Viking).

GENERAL NONFICTION
HARDCOVER: Fox Butterfield, for *China: Alive in the Bitter Sea* (Times Books).
PAPERBACK: James Fallows, for *National Defense* (Vintage Books).

HISTORY
HARDCOVER: Alan Brinkley, for *Voices of Protest: Huey Long, Father Coughlin and the Great Depression* (Knopf).
PAPERBACK: Frank E. Manuel and Fritzie P. Manuel, for *Utopian Thought in the Western World* (Harvard University Press).

ORIGINAL PAPERBACK
Lisa Goldstein, for *The Red Magician* (Pocket Books).

POETRY
Galway Kinnell, for *Selected Poems* (Houghton Mifflin), and Charles Wright, for *Country Music* (Wesleyan University Press).

SCIENCE
HARDCOVER: Abraham Pais, for *"Subtle Is the Lord . . ." The Science and Life of Albert Einstein* (Oxford University Press).
PAPERBACK: Philip J. Davis and Reuben Hersh, for *The Mathematical Experience* (Houghton Mifflin).

TRANSLATION
Richard Howard, for Baudelaire's *Fleurs du Mal* (Godine).

BANCROFT PRIZES
John P. Demos, for *Entertaining Satan: Witchcraft and the Culture of Early New England* (Oxford University Press), and Nick Salvatore, for *Eugene V. Debs: Citizen and Socialist* (University of Illinois Press).

BOLLINGEN PRIZE IN POETRY
Anthony E. Hecht and John Hollander.

BOOKER MCCONNELL PRIZE FOR FICTION
J. M. Coetzee, for *Life and Times of Michael K.* (Viking).

CALDECOTT MEDAL
Marcia Brown, for *Dicey's Song* (Atheneum).

CAREY-THOMAS PUBLISHING AWARD
Penguin Books, for the Penguin Contemporary American Fiction Series and the Penguin Originals Series.

COMMON WEALTH AWARD FOR LITERATURE
Christopher Isherwood.

CONGRESSIONAL GOLD MEDAL
Louis L'Amour.

DELMORE SCHWARTZ MEMORIAL POETRY AWARD
Sherod Santos.

DRUE HEINZ LITERATURE PRIZE
Jonathan Penner, for *Private Parties* (University of Pittsburgh Press).

EDGAR ALLAN POE AWARDS
GRAND MASTER AWARD
Margaret Millar.

NOVEL
Rick Boyer, for *Billingsgate Shoal* (Houghton Mifflin).

FIRST NOVEL
Thomas Perry, for *The Butcher's Boy* (Scribners).

FACT CRIME
Richard Hammet, for *The Vatican Connection* (Holt, Rinehart & Winston).

CRITICAL/BIOGRAPHICAL/AUTOBIO-GRAPHICAL
Roy Hoopes, for *Cain: The Biography of James M. Cain* (Holt, Rinehart & Winston).

ORIGINAL SOFTCOVER NOVEL
Teri White, for *Triangle* (Ace).

JUVENILE
Robbie Branscum, for *The Murder of Hound Dog Bates* (Viking).

SHORT STORY
Frederick Forsyth, for "There Are No Snakes in Ireland," in *No Comebacks* (Viking).

EDITORS' BOOK AWARD
Frank Stiffel, for *The Tale of the Ring: A Kaddish* (Pushcart Press).

ELLEN KNOWLES HARCOURT AWARD IN BIOGRAPHY AND MEMOIRS
Sharon N. White, for *Mabel Loomis Todd: Gender, Language, and Power in Victorian America* (Columbia University Press).

ELLERY QUEEN AWARD
Emma Lathan (Mary Jane Lastis and Martha Henissart).

ELMER HOLMES BOBST AWARDS
CRITICISM
Kenneth Burke.

DRAMA
Arthur Miller.

FICTION
Bernard Malamud.

NONFICTION
Russell Baker.

POETRY
Denise Levertov.

PUBLISHING.
Alfred A. Knopf.

ERNEST HEMINGWAY FOUNDATION
AWARD

Bobbie Ann Mason, for *Shiloh and Other Short Stories* (Harper & Row).

HUGO AWARDS

NOVEL
Isaac Asimov, for *Foundation's Edge* (Doubleday).

NOVELLA
Joanna Russ, for *Souls*.

SHORT STORY
Spider Robinson, for "Melancholy Elephant."

NONFICTION BOOK
James Gunn, for *Isaac Asimov: The Foundation of Science Fiction* (Oxford University Press).

PROFESSIONAL EDITOR
Edward L. Ferman, for *Fantasy and Science Fiction*.

IRMA SIMONTON BLACK AWARD

Charlotte Graeber, for *Mustard* (Macmillan).

JANET HEIDINGER KAFKA PRIZE
FOR FICTION

Mary Lee Settle, for *The Killing Ground* (Farrar, Straus & Giroux).

JERUSALEM PRIZE
V. S. Naipaul.

JOHN W. CAMPBELL AWARD

Paul O. Williams, for the Pelbar Cycle Series (Del Rey Books).

LAURA INGALLS WILDER AWARD
Maurice Sendak.

LOS ANGELES TIMES AWARDS

ROBERT KIRSCH AWARD
M. F. K. Fisher.

HISTORY
Fernand Braudel, for *The Wheels of Commerce: Civilization and Capitalism, 15th-18th Century* (Harper & Row).

FICTION
Thomas Keneally, for *Schindler's List* (Simon & Schuster).

BIOGRAPHY
Seymour M. Hersh, for *The Price of Power: Kissinger in The Nixon White House* (Summit Books).

POETRY
James Merrill, for *The Changing Light at Sandover* (Atheneum).

CURRENT INTEREST
Walker Percy, for *Lost in the Cosmos: The Last Self-Help Book* (Farrar, Straus & Giroux).

MAXWELL PERKINS EDITOR'S AWARD
Barry Gifford.

NATIONAL BOOK CRITICS CIRCLE AWARDS

FICTION
Stanley Elkin, for *George Mills* (Dutton).

GENERAL NONFICTION
Robert A. Caro, for *The Path To Power* (Knopf).

POETRY
Katha Pollitt, for *Antarctica Traveller* (Knopf).

CRITICISM
Gore Vidal, for *The Second American Revolution and Other Essays 1976-82* (Random House).

IVAN SANDROF AWARD
Leslie Marchand, for *Byron's Letters and Journals* (Harvard University Press).

NATIONAL JEWISH BOOK AWARDS

JEWISH FICTION
Robert Greenfield, for *Temple* (Summit Books).

HOLOCAUST
Irving Abella and Harold Troper, for *None Is*

Too Many: Canada and the Jews of Europe 1933-1948 (Lester & Orpen Dennys).

ISRAEL

J. Robert Moskin, for *Among Lions* (Arbor House).

JEWISH THOUGHT

Bernard Septimus, for *Hispano-Jewish Culture in Transition: The Career and Controversies of Ramah* (Harvard University Press).

HISTORY

Yosef Hayim Yerushalmi, for *Zakhor: Jewish History and Jewish Memory* (University of Washington Press).

SCHOLARSHIP

Jeremy Cohen, for *Friars and Jews* (Cornell University Press).

CHILDREN'S LITERATURE

Barbara Cohen, for *King of the Seventh Grade* (Lothrop, Lee & Shepard).

VISUAL ARTS

Andrew S. Ackerman and Susan L. Braunstein, for *Israel in Antiquity: From David to Herod* (Jewish Museum).

YIDDISH LITERATURE

Chaim Spilberg and Yaacov Zipper, for *Canadian Jewish Anthology* (National Committee on Yiddish of the Canadian Jewish Congress).

NEBULA AWARDS

NOVEL

Michael Bishop, for *No Enemy But Time* (Timescape).

NOVELLA

John Kessel, for *Another Orphan*, in *Fantasy and Science Fiction*, September 1982.

NOVELETTE

Connie Willis, for *Fire Watch*, in Isaac Asimov's *Science Fiction Magazine*, February 1982.

SHORT STORY

Connie Willis, for "A Letter from the Clearys," in Isaac Asimov's *Science Fiction Magazine*, July 1982.

NELSON ALGREN AWARD

B. H. Friedman, for "Duplex," in *Chicago Magazine* (October 1983).

NEWBERY MEDAL

Cynthia Voigt, for *Shadow* (Scribners).

NOBEL PRIZE FOR LITERATURE

William Golding.

O. HENRY AWARD

Raymond Carver, for "A Small, Good Thing," published in *Cathedral* (Knopf).

PEN/FAULKNER AWARD

Toby Olson, for *Seaview* (New Directions).

PEN/LOS ANGELES CENTER PRIZES

LIFETIME OF WORK

Christopher Isherwood.

FIRST BOOK OF FICTION

Henry Bean, for *False Match* (Poseidon).

THOMAS THOMPSON NONFICTION BOOK AWARD

Tom Reiterman, for *Raven: The Untold Story of the Reverend Jim Jones and His People* (Dutton).

POETRY AWARD

Thom Dunn, for *Passages of Joy* (Farrar, Straus & Giroux).

WRITING FOR YOUNG PEOPLE

Zilpha Keatley Snider, for *The Birds of Summer* (Atheneum), and Clare Bell, for *Ratha's Creature* (Atheneum).

PUBLISHER OF THE YEAR

Ward Ritchie.

PULITZER PRIZES

FICTION

Alice Walker, for *The Color Purple* (Harcourt Brace Jovanovich).

BIOGRAPHY

Russell Baker, for *Growing Up* (Congdon & Weed).

GENERAL NONFICTION

Susan Shoehan, for *Is There No Place on Earth For Me?* (Houghton Mifflin).

HISTORY
Rhys L. Isaac, *The Transformation of Virginia, 1740-1790* (University of North Carolina Press).

POETRY
Galway Kinnell, for *Selected Poems* (Houghton Mifflin).

DRAMA
Marsha Norman, for *'night Mother*.

RIBALOW PRIZE
Chaim Grade, for *Rabbis and Wives* (Knopf).

ROBERT F. KENNEDY BOOK AWARD
Stephen B. Oates, for *Let the Trumpet Sound: The Life of Martin Luther King, Jr.* (Harper & Row).

SHELLEY MEMORIAL AWARD
Leo Connellan.

WHITBREAD AWARD
William Trevor, for *Fools of Fortune* (Viking).

W. H. SMITH LITERARY AWARD
George Clare, for *Last Waltz in Vienna: The Rise and Destruction of a Family 1842-1942* (London: Macmillan; New York: Holt, Rinehart & Winston).

Checklist: Contributions to Literary History and Biography, 1983

This checklist is a selection of new books on various aspects and periods of literary and cultural history; biographies, memoirs, and correspondence of literary people and their associates; and primary bibliographies. Not included are volumes in general reference series, literary criticism, and bibliographies of criticism.

Allard, Marie-Françoise. *The Other Man: Conversations with Graham Greene.* Translated by Guido Waldman. New York: Simon & Schuster, 1983.

Appel, Alfred, Jr. *Signs of Life.* New York: Knopf, 1983.

Archibald, Douglas. *Yeats.* Syracuse, N.Y.: Syracuse University Press, 1983.

Barzun, Jacques. *A Stroll with William James.* New York: Harper & Row, 1983.

Beningfield, Gordon, and Anthea Zeman. *Hardy Country.* London: Allen Lane, 1983.

Benson, Jackson J. *The True Adventures of John Steinbeck, Writer.* New York: Viking, 1983.

Berry, Faith. *Langston Hughes: Before and Beyond Harlem.* Westport, Conn.: Lawrence Hill, 1983.

Bjornvig, Thorkeld. *The Pact: My Friendship with Isak Dinesen.* Translated by Ingvar Schousboe and William Jay Smith. Baton Rouge: Louisiana State University Press, 1983.

Bogarde, Dirk. *An Orderly Man.* New York: Knopf, 1983.

Bowen, Elizabeth, and Anthony Burgess, Lord David Cecil, Graham Greene, and Kate O'Brien. *The Heritage of British Literature.* London: Thames & Hudson, 1983.

Bradford, Sarah. *Disraeli.* Briarcliff Manor, N.Y.: Stein & Day, 1983.

Brazeau, Peter. *Parts of a World, Wallace Stevens Remembered.* New York: Random House, 1983.

Bresler, Fenton. *The Mystery of Georges Simenon: A Biography.* New York: Beaufort Books, 1983.

Brock, Michael and Eleanor. *H. H. Asquith: Letters to Venetia Stanley.* Oxford: Oxford University Press, 1983.

Broun, Heywood Hale. *Whose Little Boy Are You? A Memoir of the Broun Family.* New York: St. Martin's, 1983.

Bruccoli, Matthew J. *James Gould Cozzens: A Life Apart.* New York & San Diego: Harcourt Brace Jovanovich, 1983.

Buñuel, Luis. *My Last Sigh: The Autobiography of Luis Buñuel.* Translated by Abigail Israel. New York: Knopf, 1983.

Callan, Edward. *Auden: A Carnival of Intellect.* Oxford: Oxford University Press, 1983.

Cook, Bruce. *Brecht in Exile.* New York: Holt, Rinehart & Winston, 1983.

Ciment, Michel. *Kubrick.* New York: Holt, Rinehart & Winston, 1983.

Connolly, Joseph. *P. G. Wodehouse: An Illustrated Biography.* New York: Beaufort Books, 1983.

Cranston, Maurice. *Jean-Jacques: The Early Life and Work of Jean-Jacques Rousseau 1712-1754.* New York: Norton, 1983.

Dale, Alzina Stone. *The Outline of Sanity: A Biography of G. K. Chesterton.* Grand Rapids, Mich.: Eerdmans, 1983.

Davies, James A. *John Forster, A Literary Life.* New York: Barnes & Noble, 1983.

Donnelly, Honoria Murphy, with Richard N. Billings. *Sarah and Gerald: Villa America and After.* New York: Times Books, 1983.

Dornfield, A. A. *Behind the Front Page: The Story of the City News Bureau of Chicago.* Chicago: Academy Chicago, 1983.

Duke, David G. *Distant Obligations: Modern American Writers and Foreign Causes.* New York: Oxford University Press, 1983.

Edel, Leon. *Letters of Henry James, Vol. IV: 1895-1916.* Cambridge, Mass.: Harvard University Press, 1983.

Edwards, Anne. *Road to Tara: The Life of Margaret Mitchell.* New York: Ticknor & Fields, 1983.

Eisenstein, Sergei M. *Immoral Memories: An Autobiography.* Translated by Herbert Marshall. Boston: Houghton Mifflin, 1983.

Elledge, Scott. *E. B. White.* New York: Norton, 1983.

Field, Andrew. *Djuna: The Life and Times of Djuna Barnes.* New York: Putnam's, 1983.

Fifield, William. *In Search of Genius.* New York: Morrow, 1983.

Fink, Augusta. *I-Mary: A Biography of Mary Austin.* Tucson: University of Arizona Press, 1983.

Fitch, Noel Riley. *Sylvia Beach and the Lost Generation.* New York: Norton, 1983.

Fitz-Simon, Christopher. *The Irish Theatre.* London & New York: Thames & Hudson, 1983.

Frank, Joseph. *Dostoevsky: The Years of Ordeal 1850-1859.* Princeton, N.J.: Princeton University Press, 1983.

Freedland, Michael. *The Warner Brothers.* New York: St. Martin's, 1983.

Gardner, John. *On Becoming a Novelist.* New York: Harper & Row, 1983.

Glendinning, Victoria. *Vita: The Life of Vita Sackville-West.* New York: Knopf, 1983.

Goldman, William. *Adventures in the Screen Trade: A Personal View of Hollywood and Screenwriting.* New York: Warner, 1983.

Graves, Richard Perceval. *The Brothers Powys.* New York: Scribners, 1983.

Green, Martin. *Tolstoy and Gandhi, Men of Peace.* New York: Basic Books, 1983.

Griffin, Bryan F. *Panic Among the Philistines*. Chicago: Regnery Gateway, 1983.

Hadfield, Mary Alice. *Charles Williams: An Exploration of His Life and Works*. New York: Oxford University Press, 1983.

Harlan, Louis R. *Booker T. Washington: The Wizard of Tuskegee, 1905-1915*. New York: Oxford University Press, 1983.

Harrison, Gilbert A. *The Enthusiast*. New York: Ticknor & Fields, 1983.

Hayman, Ronald. *Brecht: A Biography*. New York: Oxford University Press, 1983.

Hayward, Max, ed. *Writers in Russia 1917-1978*. New York & San Diego: Harcourt Brace Jovanovich, 1983.

Higgins, D. S. *Rider Haggard: The Great Storyteller*. New York: Stein & Day, 1983.

Hobson, Laura Z. *Laura Z.: A Life*. New York: Arbor House, 1983.

Hoffer, Eric. *Truth Imagined*. New York: Harper & Row, 1983.

Houseman, John. *Final Dress*. New York: Simon & Schuster, 1983.

Hyde, Mary, ed. *Bernard Shaw and Alfred Douglas: A Correspondence*. New York: Ticknor & Fields, 1983.

Johnson, Diane. *Dashiell Hammett, A Life*. New York: Random House, 1983.

Johnson, Joyce, *Minor Characters*. Boston: Houghton Mifflin, 1983.

Kaplan, Fred. *Thomas Carlyle, A Biography*. Ithaca, N. Y.: Cornell University Press, 1983.

Karl, Frederick R., and Laurence Davies, eds. *The Collected Letters of Joseph Conrad: Volume 1, 1861-1897*. Cambridge & New York: Cambridge University Press, 1983.

Katz, Jane. *Artists in Exile: American Odyssey*. New York: Stein & Day, 1983.

Kelly, Tom. *The Imperial Post: The Meyers, the Grahams and the Paper That Rules Washington*. New York: Morrow, 1983.

Kenner, Hugh. *A Colder Eye: The Modern Irish Writers*. New York: Knopf, 1983.

Kert, Bernice. *The Hemingway Women*. New York: Norton, 1983.

Kolb, Philip, ed. *Marcel Proust: Selected Letters (1880-1903)*. Translated by Ralph Manheim. Garden City: Doubleday, 1983.

Koszarski, Richard. *The Man You Loved To Hate: Erich von Stroheim and Hollywood*. New York: Oxford University Press, 1983.

Lacouture, Jean. *Leon Blum*. Translated by George Holloch. New York: Holmes & Meier, 1983.

Lago, Mary, and P. N. Furbank, eds. *Forster: Vol. I: 1879-1920*. Cambridge, Mass.: Harvard University Press, 1983.

Lanchester, Elsa. *Elsa Lanchester Herself*. New York: St. Martin's, 1983.

LeClair, Tom, and Larry McCaffery. *Anything Can Happen: Interviews with Contemporary American Novelists.* Champaign: University of Illinois Press, 1983.

Levenson, J. C., et al. *The Letters of Henry Adams. Volume One: 1858-1868. Volume Two: 1868-1885. Volume Three: 1886-1892.* Cambridge, Mass.: Harvard University Press, 1983.

Levy, Alan. *W. H. Auden: In the Autumn of the Age of Anxiety.* Sag Harbor, N.Y.: Permanent Press, 1983.

Logue, Calvin M. *Southern Encounters: Southerners of Note in Ralph McGill's South.* Macon, Ga.: Mercer University Press, 1983.

Lorca, Federico García. *Selected Letters.* Edited and translated by David Gershator. New York: New Directions, 1983.

Lorenz, Clarissa M. *Lorelei Two: My Life with Conrad Aiken.* Athens: University of Georgia Press, 1983.

Love, David, ed. *Turgenev's Letters.* Translated by David Love. Ann Arbor, Mich.: Ardis, 1983.

May, Antoinette. *Witness to War: Marguerite Higgins.* New York: Beaufort Books, 1983.

McBride, Joseph, ed. *Filmmakers on Filmmaking: The American Film Institute Seminars on Motion Pictures and Television* (2 volumes). Los Angeles: Tarcher, 1983.

McConkey, James. *Court of Memory.* New York: Dutton, 1983.

Meeker, Richard H. *Newspaperman: S. I. Newhouse and the Business of News.* New York: Ticknor & Fields, 1983.

Morris, Wright. *Solo. An American Dreamer in Europe: 1933-34.* New York: Harper & Row, 1983.

Nagel, Paul C. *Descent from Glory: Four Generations of the John Adams Family.* New York: Oxford University Press, 1983.

Najder, Zdzislaw. *Joseph Conrad: A Chronicle.* New Brunswick, N.J.: Rutgers University Press, 1983.

Nicosia, Gerald. *Memory Babe: A Critical Biography.* New York: Grove Press, 1983.

Nin, Anaïs. *The Early Diary of Anaïs Nin: Volume Three, 1923-1927.* New York & San Diego: Harcourt Brace Jovanovich, 1983.

Nolan, William F. *Hammett: A Life at the Edge.* New York: Congdon & Weed, 1983.

Oates, Joyce Carol, comp. *First Person Singular: Writers on Their Craft.* Ontario: Ontario Review Press, 1983.

Olivier, Laurence. *Confessions of an Actor.* New York: Simon & Schuster, 1983.

Osborne, Charles. *The Life and Crimes of Agatha Christie.* New York: Holt, Rinehart & Winston, 1983.

Paul, William. *Ernst Lubitsch's American Comedy.* New York: Columbia University Press, 1983.

Phillips, William. *A Partisan View: Five Decades of the Literary Life.* New York: Stein & Day, 1983.

Powell, Anthony. *The Strangers All Are Gone: The Memoirs of Anthony Powell, Vol. IV.* New York: Holt, Rinehart & Winston, 1983.

Powell, Violet. *The Constant Novelist: A Study of Margaret Kennedy 1896-1967*. London: Heinemann, 1983.

Prokosch, Frederic. *Voices: A Memoir*. New York: Farrar, Straus & Giroux, 1983.

Pullen, John J. *Comic Relief: The Life and Laughter of Artemus Ward, 1834-1867*. Hamden, Conn.: Archon, 1983.

Quennell, Peter. *Customs and Characters: Contemporary Portraits*. Boston: Little, Brown, 1983.

Redgrave, Michael. *In My Mind's Eye: An Autobiography*. New York: Viking, 1983.

Robinson, Phyllis C. *Willa: The Life of Willa Cather*. Garden City: Doubleday, 1983.

Rose, Phyllis. *Parallel Lives: Five Victorian Marriages*. New York: Knopf, 1983.

Ross, Lillian. *Takes: Stories from the Talk of the Town*. New York: Congdon & Weed, 1983.

Round, Richard. *A Passion for Films: Henri Langlois and the Cinémathèque Française*. New York: Viking, 1983.

Royster, Vermont. *My Own, My Country's Time: A Journalist's Journey*. Chapel Hill: Algonquin Books, 1983.

Rudisill, Marie, with James C. Simmons. *Truman Capote: The Story of His Bizarre and Exotic Boyhood by an Aunt Who Helped Raise Him*. New York: Morrow, 1983.

Salisbury, Harrison E. *A Journey for Our Times*. New York: Harper & Row, 1983.

Sandburg, Carl. *Ever the Winds of Change*. Introduction by Margaret Sandburg and George Hendrick. Champaign: University of Illinois Press, 1983.

Schulberg, Budd. *Writers in America: The Four Seasons of Success*. New York: Stein & Day, 1983.

Selznick, Irene Mayer. *A Private View*. New York: Knopf, 1983.

Seymour-Smith, Martin. *Robert Graves: His Life and Work*. New York: Holt, Rinehart & Winston, 1983.

Shivers, Alfred S. *The Life of Maxwell Anderson*. New York: Stein & Day, 1983.

Snow, Philip. *Stranger and Brother: A Portrait of C. P. Snow*. New York: Scribners, 1983.

Spalding, Frances. *Vanessa Bell*. New York: Ticknor & Fields, 1983.

Spoto, Donald. *The Dark Side of Genius: The Life of Alfred Hitchcock*. Boston: Little, Brown, 1983.

Stirling, Nora. *Pearl Buck: A Woman in Conflict*. Piscataway, N.J.: New Century, 1983.

Strachey, Julia, and Frances Partridge. *Julia: A Portrait of Julia Strachey*. Boston: Little, Brown, 1983.

Straight, Michael. *After Long Silence*. New York: Norton, 1983.

Stutman, Suzanne, ed. *My Other Loneliness: Letters of Thomas Wolfe and Aline Bernstein*. Chapel Hill: University of North Carolina Press, 1983.

Taylor, John Russell. *Strangers in Paradise: The Hollywood Emigrés 1933-1950*. New York: Holt, Rinehart & Winston, 1983.

Tehan, Arline Boucher. *Henry Adams in Love: The Pursuit of Elizabeth Sherman Cameron.* New York: Universe Books, 1983.

Thomas, Donald. *Robert Browning: A Life Within Life.* New York: Viking, 1983.

Todd, Michael, Jr., and Susan McCarthy Todd. *A Valuable Property: The Life Story of Michael Todd.* New York: Arbor House, 1983.

Tolstoy, Nikolai. *The Tolstoys: Twenty-four Generations of Russian History, 1353-1983.* New York: Morrow, 1983.

Tomalin, Ruth. *W. H. Hudson: A Biography.* London: Faber & Faber, 1983.

Torrey, E. Fuller. *The Roots of Treason: Ezra Pound and the Secret of St. Elizabeths.* New York: McGraw-Hill, 1983.

Van der Post, Laurens. *Yet Being Something Other.* New York: Morrow, 1983.

Waley, Alison. *A Half of Two Lives: A Personal Memoir.* New York: McGraw-Hill, 1983.

Wasson, Ben. *Count No'Count: Flashbacks to Faulkner.* Jackson: University Press of Mississippi, 1983.

Webb, Beatrice. *The Diary of Beatrice Webb, Volume One, 1873-1892.* Edited by Norman and Jeanne MacKenzie. Cambridge, Mass.: Harvard University Press, 1983.

Weintraub, Stanley, ed. *The Playwright and the Pirate: Bernard Shaw and Frank Harris—A Correspondence.* University Park: Pennsylvania State University Press, 1983.

Williams, Dakin, and Shepherd Mead. *Tennessee Williams: An Intimate Biography.* New York: Arbor House, 1983.

Wilson, A. N. *The Life of John Milton.* Oxford: Oxford University Press, 1983.

Wilson, Edmund. *The Forties: From Notebooks and Diaries of the Period.* New York: Farrar, Straus & Giroux, 1983.

Wilson, Edmund. *The Portable Edmund Wilson.* Edited by Lewis M. Dabney. New York: Viking, 1983.

Necrology

Desmond Bagley—13 April 1983
Lesley Ballantine—9 July 1983
Ted Berrigan—4 July 1983
Geoffrey Bocca—7 July 1983
Jenny Bradley—3 June 1983
Winifred Bryher—28 January 1983
Henrietta Buckmaster—26 April 1983
Luis Buñuel—30 July 1983
Douglas Bush—2 March 1983
Robert Carson—19 January 1983
Turner Catledge—17 April 1983
Henry Chapin—4 September 1983
Kenneth Clark—21 May 1983
Christine Sadler Coe—25 June 1983
Reginald Denham—4 February 1983
Owen Dodson—21 June 1983
Alexander Donat—16 June 1983
James W. Drought—2 June 1983
John Fante—8 May 1983
Constantine FitzGibbon—23 March 1983
Joe Flaherty—26 October 1983
Ira Gershwin—17 August 1983
William Goyen—30 August 1983
David Greenhood—26 March 1983
Paul Griffith—23 April 1983
Lee Head—13 August 1983
Eric Hoffer—21 May 1983
Allen Kanfer—6 July 1983
I. J. Kapstein—6 August 1983
Ezra Jack Keats—6 May 1983

Arthur Koestler—3 May 1983
Wheaton J. Lane—29 November 1983
Jonathan Latimer—23 June 1983
Catherine Marshall LeSourd—18 March 1983
Richard Llewellyn—30 November 1983
Nora Lofts—10 September 1983
Dwight Macdonald—19 December 1983
John Macrea, Jr.—7 October 1983
John Masters—6 May 1983
John K. M. McCaffery—3 October 1983
Vincent McHugh—23 January 1983
Robert Mead—4 June 1983
Kenneth Millar—11 July 1983
Marion Monroe—25 June 1983
Alan Moorehead—29 September 1983
Robert Payne—18 February 1983
Zelda F. Popkin—25 May 1983
Mary Renault—13 December 1983
Kyrill S. Schabert—7 April 1983
Elizabeth Seifert—17 June 1983
Christina Stead—31 March 1983
Louis Vaczek—30 September 1983
Theodore Ward—11 May 1983
Joe Wechsberg—10 April 1983
Louise Weiss—26 May 1983
Rebecca West—15 March 1983
Leonard Wibberly—22 November 1983
Lawrence Williams—3 January 1983
Tennessee Williams—25 February 1983

Contributors

Michael Adams ....*Louisiana State University*
Timothy Dow Adams ....*West Virginia University*
Orin Anderson ....*Myrtle Beach, South Carolina*
Mary C. Anderson ....*University of South Carolina*
Nancy G. Anderson ....*Auburn University at Montgomery*
Max L. Autrey ....*Drake University*
Judith S. Baughman ....*Columbia, South Carolina*
Ronald Baughman ....*University of South Carolina*
Brigid Brophy ....*London, England*
J. D. Brown ....*University of Oregon*
Mary Bruccoli ....*Mount Holyoke College*
Matthew J. Bruccoli ....*University of South Carolina*
Philip Bufithis ....*Shepherd College*
John Y. Cole ....*Center for the Book*
Joseph Cotter ....*Pennsylvania State University*
Thomas E. Dasher ....*Valdosta State College*
R. H. W. Dillard ....*Hollins College*
Mark Dolan ....*University of South Carolina*
George Garrett ....*University of Michigan*
George Gibian ....*Cornell University*
William B. Goodman ....*Boston, Massachusetts*
Martin H. Greenberg ....*University of Wisconsin at Green Bay*
Sinda J. Gregory ....*San Diego State University*
Nancy D. Hargrove ....*Mississippi State University*
Mark Harris ....*Jackson Community College*
Walter Herrscher ....*University of Wisconsin at Green Bay*
Dorn Hetzel ....*Pennsylvania State University*
Sally Johns ....*University of South Carolina*
David K. Jeffrey ....*Northeast Louisiana University*
John R. Kaiser ....*Pennsylvania State University*
Cathrael Kazin ....*University of Iowa*
Katherine Kearns ....*University of North Carolina*
Kimball King ....*University of North Carolina at Chapel Hill*
Howard Kissel ....*New York, New York*
Mark Lidman ....*University of Mississippi*
Rick Lott ....*Florida State University*
Larry McCaffery ....*San Diego State University*
Christopher McIlroy ....*University of Arizona*
Alice S. Morris ....*New York, New York*
Michael Mullen ....*Indian Hills Community College*
Ira B. Nadel ....*University of British Columbia*
Sidney A. Pearson, Jr. ....*Radford University*
Tony Redd ....*The Citadel*
Jean W. Ross ....*Columbia, South Carolina*
Walter W. Ross ....*Columbia, South Carolina*
Aram Saroyan..*Bolinas, California*
Patricia L. Skarda ....*Smith College*
Lola L. Szladits..*Berg Collection, New York Public Library*
David M. Taylor...*Livingston University*
Lewis Turco ....*State University of New York at Oswego*
Michael Woolf..*Tottenham College*

Yearbook Index: 1980-1983

351

The Scorpion God

THREE
SHORT NOVELS BY
William Golding

PRIVATE PARTIES

JONATHAN PENNER

THE MOONS OF JUPITER
S T O R I E S
ALICE MUNRO

Augusta Played
by Kelly Cher